A country
nourished on self-doubt

A country

nourished on self-doubt

DOCUMENTS IN POST-CONFEDERATION CANADIAN HISTORY *3rd edition*

EDITED BY THOMAS THORNER WITH THOR FROHN-NIELSEN

UTP

UNIVERSITY OF TORONTO PRESS

LIBRARY AND ARCHIVES CANADA CATALOGUING IN PUBLICATION

A country nourished on self-doubt : documents in post-confederation Canadian history / edited by Thomas Thorner with Thor Frohn-Nielson.—3rd ed.

Includes bibliographical references.

First published 1998 under title: "A country nourished on self-doubt" : documents in Canadian history, 1867-1980.

ISBN 978-1-4426-0019-5

1. Canada—History—1867- —Sources. I. Thorner, Thomas II. Frohn-Nielsen, Thor, 1955-

FC18.C68 2010   971   C2010-900483-3

We welcome comments and suggestions regarding any aspect of our publications—please feel free to contact us at news@utphighereducation.com or visit our Internet site at www.utphighereducation.com.

North America
5201 Dufferin Street
North York, Ontario, Canada, M3H 5T8

UK, Ireland, and continental Europe
NBN International
Estover Road, Plymouth, PL6 7PY, UK
tel: 44 (0) 1752 202301

2250 Military Road
Tonawanda, New York, USA, 14150

FAX ORDER LINE: 44 (0) 1752 202333
enquiries@nbninternational.com

ORDERS PHONE: 1-800-565-9523
ORDERS FAX: 1-800-221-9985
ORDERS E-MAIL: utpbooks@utpress.utoronto.ca

The University of Toronto Press acknowledges the financial support for its publishing activities of the Government of Canada through the Book Publishing Industry Development Program (BPIDP).

This book is printed on paper containing 100% post-consumer fibre.

Book design by Black Eye Design.

Printed in Canada.

FSC Recycled
Supporting responsible use of forest resources
www.fsc.org Cert no. SGS-COC-003153
© 1996 Forest Stewardship Council

Contents

Contents

Contents

(Preface to the Second Edition)

Many publishers annually incorporate relatively minor changes to produce yet another edition of their textbooks. This usually prevents students from selling their old editions and from purchasing cheaper used books for courses. In this case well over half of the material is entirely new. The idea of a revised edition originated with a number of specific problems. First, one of the most compelling documents in the original collection turned out to have been fabricated. Without any hint of its fictional nature, Gerald Keegan's diary can still be found in one of the best anthologies concerning the Irish in Canada. Yet its authenticity sparked a major controversy in Ireland during the early 1990s. The "diary" turns out to have been written as a short story by a Scottish immigrant 50 years after the events it describes and was not the account of a genuine Irish famine victim. The Keegan material also leaves the impression that the main motives for migration centred upon dispossession, nationalism, and Anglo-phobia, a version sharply contradicted by the De Vere account which now forms part of this new edition. Second, students wanted to hear more from the perspective of Native peoples. Therefore a new opening chapter comparing cultural perspectives as well as an entire chapter devoted to Native dissent was added to the volume dealing with pre-Confederation documents. Third, some critics thought that a single chapter on the early Maritime colonies was grossly inadequate. In its place are four new chapters. With the volume covering the period after 1867, many readers sought more material on classic Canadian issues and coverage beyond 1982 (which still remains the termination date for our post-Confederation history at Kwantlen University College). Another common suggestion was to include study questions, which previously had been available only in the study guides provided to instructors.

The first edition also failed to provide sufficient acknowledgement to the library staff at Kwantlen—in particular Margaret Giacomello and Jean McKendry—as well as Karen Archer, Jacinta Sterling, Kathie Holloway, Ann McBurnie, Judy Isaac, and Nancy Smith—who always managed to keep the interlibrary loan material, upon which so much of this book was based, flowing.

Finally, this project would never have been possible without the steady support of Michael Harrison, Vice-President and Editor of Broadview Press.

YET ANOTHER EDITION

(Preface to the Third Edition)

C ritics of the second edition told us that many of the chapters were too long, included too many points of view and focused too much on economics. They also wanted more information about the context in which each document was written and biographical details of each author. The result is a trimmer third edition that includes new chapters on the disappearance of the Beothuck, the War of 1812, and the Loyalists in *A Few Acres of Snow* and new chapters on Victorian Canada's attitudes to sex, treaties in the far north, drugs, and the counterculture of the 1960s in *A Country Nourished on Self-Doubt*. These revisions would not have been possible without a research grant from Kwantlen Polytechnic University.

GENERAL INTRODUCTION

(First Edition)

a country nourished on self-doubt
where from the reverse image of detractors
an opposite nation is talked into existence
that doesn't resemble any other one
a cross-breed plant that survives the winter
—Al Purdy, "A Walk on Wellington Street," 1968

Ours is a history of self-doubt. From the moment of Confederation Canada has often been threatened by disintegration. Part of this problem stems from the fact that neither cultural symbols, a shared heritage, nor even a common language united Canadians when the nation emerged in 1867. Because much of the nation's growth in the years that followed could be attributed to immigrants who often retained their hyphenated ethnic status and never felt totally at home here, ambiguity about the significance of Canada or what it meant to be a Canadian was hardly surprising. The sheer problem of communication over vast distances and distinct regional economies also promoted disunity. By the 1880s Canada had already lost much of its lustre. Political tensions and economic depression caused many to doubt whether the nation could or should continue to exist. In Quebec separatist emotions had grown more pronounced, and the Nova Scotia legislature had endorsed a resolution favouring secession. Young Canadians by the thousands expressed their discontent with their feet when they left for better opportunities south of the border. After Macdonald's "national policy" had failed to generate prosperity or unite the country, the country's leading intellectual, Goldwin Smith, asked: What justifies Canada's existence? He concluded that Canada could not be considered a nation because it had failed to mould competing cultures and regions into a single community. In his mind Canada was nothing but an artificial entity totally at odds with the natural geographical and economic factors operating in North America.

The twentieth century, however, saw some Canadians beginning to celebrate the cultural diversity that Smith found so abhorrent. Particularly in contrast to the American "melting pot," they put forth the idea of the cultural mosaic as the very foundation of Canada's strength and identity. But as articulated by W.D. Scott [Chapter 4 in this edition], most Canadians remained doubtful whether building a nation with the discontented and dispossessed of the world was sound practice. Canada's immigration policies of the period between the two world wars could hardly be characterized as promoting cultural diversity and tolerance. Instead, many immigrants found the pressure to conform just as pronounced as it was in the United States.

But the gravest doubts about Canada in the mid-twentieth century focused upon foreign relations, not domestic affairs. While it had taken several decades of the new century for Canada to finally cut most of the vestiges of British control, World War II saw a nervous Canada give up much of its military independence in return for American protection. The school texts of the period proudly proclaimed our growth from colony to nation, but based upon American economic and cultural domination, critics increasingly characterized Canada's status as having shifted from a British colony to an American satellite. In 1965 the philosopher George Grant went so far as to announce Canada's death as a sovereign nation.

More recently the challenges to Canadian sovereignty came from within as demonstrated by the FLQ crisis and the rise of the Parti Québécois. When the separatists came to power as the government of Quebec in 1976 and remained a viable political entity throughout the 1980s and 1990s, many wondered if Canada would indeed survive.

Yet Purdy's poem alludes to positive aspects: a "nourishing" self-doubt, a nation that "doesn't resemble any others," and a "cross-breed plant" that survives the winter. While Canadians have remained profoundly uncertain of who they are and their place in the world, other nations have regarded this modesty as comfortably non-threatening, especially in comparison to the crass boosterism of the Americans, and as such viewed Canada as an ideal candidate for international peacekeeping assignments. It is also a rather strange quirk of history that Canada's inhibited national consciousness is now taken by many outsiders as a sign of our maturity in an increasingly post-national world.

Many collections of Canadian readings on the market today reprint articles from academic journals as models of scholarship. Although such articles may certainly be of great value, they naturally tend to be written with a scholarly audience in mind. Coupled with standard survey texts, the near-total reliance upon secondary sources has had wide-ranging consequences. A student registering for a course on the Victorian novel would, no doubt, expect to read Victorian novels, not simply digest what secondary sources had to say about them. Even if the raw materials were as dense, drab, and dull as the popular perception of Canadian history makes them out to be, bypassing them would be disturbing. But primary sources are far from dull. What historians usually find most enjoyable about the craft is research—the labyrinthine quest in primary sources for answers about the past. What follows is a volume that attempts to bring together compelling excerpts of divergent eyewitness accounts of specific topics in post-Confederation Canadian history. The fascination of primary sources lies in their personal perspective and the immediacy of experience they convey. However lacking in objective insight they may be, they were written by people at or close to the source of the events they describe. In the same way, readers of this book are encouraged to analyze the arguments and information in the sources for themselves.

This is still very much a book aimed at those largely unfamiliar with the subject. In order to make available the greatest possible amount of original material that is interesting and important, some less pertinent passages have been deleted. Exercising even a minimal shaping hand will sacrifice some dimensions of the past, but even if the occasional reader feels uncomfortable that the integrity of some documents has been violated, one hopes that in the interest of engaging a wider readership and lifting the veil of boredom from Canadian history, the end will have justified the means.

Editors of document collections such as this must also be sensitive to the criticism that reproducing historical documents such as these perpetuates negative images, particularly about ethnic groups, and as such constitutes hate literature. Without a doubt many documents written by ethnocentric Anglo Canadians form part of a literature written to justify assimilation and domination. But it hardly follows that reprinting these inaccuracies constitutes disseminating hate literature. Instead these documents may provide a means of exposing those falsehoods, of demonstrating the basis of intolerance, and of understanding that prejudice is commonplace. In some respects these documents may be used to confront the current complacency or smugness of Canadians who assume that, especially compared to the United States, ours has been a kinder, gentler history and therefore lacks a foundation for bigotry and racism.

USING PRIMARY HISTORICAL SOURCES

When first approaching history texts, students are usually overwhelmed by the amount of new information and find it difficult enough to distinguish key points or determine the author's main thesis. They have no reason to doubt authors' veracity and assume that any published account must contain a measure of truth since it would otherwise not be an assigned text. As their understanding of history increases, they will find that historians divide source materials into two categories. Textbooks, written by contemporary authors who never experienced the historical events themselves, are referred to as secondary sources, while any accounts or material that was recorded when an event in the past occurred are known as primary sources. In other words eye witnesses are distinguished from those who may have studied the event but did not observe or participate directly in its occurrence. Considerable debate exists between the utility of secondary sources as opposed to primary sources. Secondary sources are often able to take a broader, more objective perspective. Much like the expert witness in court, secondary sources evaluate many of the first-hand accounts and offer an overall assessment, usually by a distinguished professional historian. However, most textbooks also project a sense of completeness and authority that suggests a lack of controversy. Even when standard historical textbooks deal with debatable points, they imply that there is one "right" answer and one linear narrative. As in life, historical events were never simple or viewed from the same perspective. One could even suggest that the fatal flaw in most secondary historical writing comes from the disadvantage of hindsight. Later writers knew the outcomes that were unknown to the participants. Textbooks are also written in tune with the cultural norms of their age. Much of what was said in the past is now excluded as "hate literature" since it is no longer politically correct and would offend many groups within our society. Our society also equates objectivity with a lack of emotion. Few textbooks probe the human characteristics that link us directly to people in the past.

Courts, as well as historians, invariably prefer eye witnesses to experts. Primary documents contain a sense of intimacy with the past that simply does not exist in most secondary accounts. The difficulty for students is that historians read primary sources as pieces of conflicting testimony, not as overviews or more stories of the past. Just as one would cross-examine a witness, primary documents call for series of litmus tests in order to assess their credibility. At the outset one needs to consider the type or kind of document itself. Diaries, journals, letters, official reports, speeches, census returns, newspaper editorials—all have their own strengths and limitations. Do diaries contain mostly fantasies or our deepest personal thoughts? Surprisingly in the nineteenth century when many Canadians still maintained diaries they simply recorded the weather. Would someone have been more likely to tell the truth in a letter to their mother or in an official report to their employer? Some argue that the best types of documents are the least intentional, in other words those that someone scribbles without giving a second thought to who might eventually read it or respond to it. Others argue that publicly available or published documents are more credible since they would be subject to wider scrutiny and confirmation.

Next, it is useful to consider the place where the primary source was created. Was it composed in close proximity to the events it describes? If so, that suggests that the author had an appropriate vantage point from which to observe the events in question. One also needs to address the issue of time. Did the author write the document immediately after or during the event in question? Alternatively, did years go by before anything was recorded? Generally speaking, the longer the interval between observation and recording, the more likely that some details have been forgotten or adjusted to coincide with subsequent developments. Many memoirs or autobiographies suffer from this problem. While place and time may be relatively easy to determine, the prevailing cultural milieu in which a document was produced is far more problematic. Nowhere is this more obvious than in the area of language. A seventeenth-century French Canadian did not use the term "sauvage" in the same sense that we use the term "savage," nor did the Hudson's Bay Company mean what we understand when its officials commented upon having a "gay time" at New Year's.

Much less daunting is the basic question: what was the purpose of this document? Why did someone bother to create it? Did they need to convince someone of something, set the record straight, or justify an action? If there was a clear intent, it may indicate obvious bias. Next one looks at the audience for whom the document was intended. Different recipients may have conditioned the formalities of language, the way the events are described, and even the contents of the document. For example, in the highly competitive travel literature market, the publisher of James Cook's voyages inserted references to cannibalism among Natives of the West Coast simply due to the expectations of his European readers. He also turned what was a rather tedious ship's log into an adventure story.

However, nothing may be more important than the authors themselves. One needs to know how familiar they were with the subject being described and their ability to articulate their observations. Knowing that the average Canadian soldier in World War I had a grade six education has led to a number of comments about the limitations of their wartime journals. The position or occupation of authors may have also had an impact on their observations. Consider the document by the lawyer Charles Fitzpatrick, whose job it was to provide Louis Riel with the best defence possible. Lawyers are notorious for putting their clients' actions in the best light and arranging the facts to help their clients. To make matters still more complicated, one finds that age, gender, ethnicity, and class may have had a direct bearing on the contents of a primary document. Sociologists suggest that people tend to dwell disproportionally upon events that occurred in late adolescence or early adulthood. Would women have experienced the Great Depression differently than men?

Evidence suggests that the pressure to maintain their role as breadwinner drove far more men to suicide in the 1930s than women. The document by HDP in Volume 2 also indicates that working-class women saw suffrage differently than their middle-class neighbours.

Next, one moves to the document itself. Does it provide facts or opinions? Does it rely on logic or emotional appeal? Does it exaggerate, distort, or omit vital information? Does it include details or generalizations? Does it contain contradictions? Does it demonstrate narrow-mindedness? Afterwards, and still much like adversarial legal proceedings, the historian considers corroborative evidence from other primary sources. Do they verify or contradict the account in question? With older documents, particularly from the Middle Ages, one confronts the question of authenticity. How do we know a particular document was not forged, plagiarized, or ghost written? Questions of accurate translation or transcription usually surround ancient documents, but a close look at the works of noted Canadian author Thomas Chandler Haliburton indicates how nineteenth-century Canadian authors shamelessly plagiarized from their British counterparts. In the end, we even need to ask questions about ourselves. Are modern biases and preconceptions distorting our view of historical documents? In other words, do we only accept what makes sense to us and fits our culture? Does our desire to explain the present distort our view of the past? Will different readers in our society get different impressions from this document? Do these documents have any relevance today? Why are they worth reading or saving?

Since history has often been referred to as a "soft "or "inexact" science, historians are deeply concerned with developing critical tests to justify not merely their interpretations but also their methods of arriving at them. Most students do not ordinarily question the historian's authority to explain what happened in the past and why. Yet, confronted with examples of divergent perspectives, they will realize the difficulty of creating history. Through primary sources students confront three essential facts. First, every document is created in a context—a particular place, a particular time, a particular culture, a particular situation—and must be examined with that context in mind. No document can be understood on its own, in a vacuum. Second, one must accept the fact that there is always more than one version of what actually happened. Third, students bring to the sources their own biases, created by their own personal situations and the social environments in which they live. In the end students need to realize that any history reflects an author's interpretations of past events. Therefore, it is subjective in nature. Finally, it may be worth adding that the ability to understand and make appropriate use of many sources of information is not restricted to historical research: it requires constant cultivation in our society where a sophisticated mass media assumes that their advertising and political images can manipulate passive recipients.

CHAPTER I

"A Fate Worse Than Death"

SEXUAL ADVICE IN VICTORIAN CANADA

INTRODUCTION

The Victorians were infamous for their prudery. Bodily functions became taboo under Victoria's censorious gaze, particularly in the second half of the nineteenth century. Vocabulary evolved into obscurity so no one need mention "the unmentionable." Urination became "passing water," done in the wc (Water Closet). Sex, euphemistically referred to as "marital relations," apparently disappeared from people's lives, and many a naïve young woman fled her wedding bed in shock when she 1) saw her husband in his altogether and 2) understood what came next. Needless to say, pre-marital sex was forbidden—though men were excused episodic losses of control, indulgently referred to as "sowing their wild oats." Adultery, too, was unacceptable, though again less so for men. Artificial means of birth control were unavailable and illegal, and sex was something married people did for procreation. Masturbation came in for particularly virulent attack because it wasted the limited "vital life force" and was self-indulgent, and therefore antisocial. Homosexuality among men was illegal, a perversion punishable by hard prison labour, as Oscar Wilde discovered. It supposedly did not exist at all among women, and therefore lesbianism did not even feature in law, literature, or science.

In these circumstances, the idea of sex as leisure and pleasure was unsurprisingly frowned upon—if even admitted to. Women, in particular, were expected to service their husbands as a way of maintaining family harmony, furthering the race, and encouraging national peace. This was not about pleasure. Sex became a socio-political act that was not discussed and that women did because they had to. The popular advice for them was to "lie back and think of England."

There was, however, a hypocritical side to Victorian moral self-righteousness. There were never more prostitutes than during the Victorian period. Sexually transmitted diseases wreaked havoc. The middle-class birth rate was in decline (without any evidence of diminished sexual activity), and the back pages of women's magazines bulged with advertisements for "medicines" to deal with "women's problems": abortifacients for pregnant women who did not want to be. A husband could not, in law, rape his wife. There was disquiet among social observers, politicians, religious leaders, and the Victorian "chattering classes" about the apparent contradiction between a puritanical public sexual ideal and everyday reality. The medical profession, in particular, tried to reconcile social contradictions by offering a scientific spin to morality, thereby giving objective scientific credibility to normative values. This was essentially a Sisyphean task, as attested by the enormous volume of published scientific material on sexuality in the second half of the nineteenth century.

Issues of female sexuality were particularly troublesome, as illustrated by the proliferation of medical treatises specifically on it, compared to the very few dealing with men. The reason for this was that society perceived of women and men as being so very different that their responses and needs were commensurately different too. Equally, there is no doubt that Canada was a thoroughly patriarchal society in which women were subordinate to men. Thus, it is possible that much of the discussion of female sexuality, the vast majority of which was written by male doctors, is really about control and emancipation. Sexual passion, after all, implied abandonment to the senses. If women had passions, did that not imply that they might abandon the private sphere prescribed for them and become aggressive sexual huntresses? This spectre was deeply worrisome to the men traditionally charged with sole jurisdiction over the "public sphere." It also went against the idea that a woman was purer and commanded the "private sphere" of hearth and home where her nurturing instinct provided a safe haven for her family. Unsurprisingly, the medical profession went to great lengths to prove that woman's natural state was to be biologically and sexually passive. The luckiest women, some doctors argued, were those who felt no pleasure in sex at all. They were the highest on the evolutionary chain.

Women were not completely subjugated by men, however. They were not necessarily repressed victims, as some historians contend. The evidence is clear that women, too, subscribed to the notion of their inherent moral superiority. They also saw themselves as "safe and calm harbours." Controlling oneself was perceived as a cardinal virtue, especially in Protestant societies, and medical evidence suggested that women were more capable of doing so than men and would therefore not only provide calmness but be role models to their men and to the wider society. An active female sex life with personal pleasure as a motive was therefore anathema.

Controlling sexual urges also facilitated smaller families, which typically allowed for a higher standard of living. For the middle classes it separated them from "the lower orders" through their morally "superior" restrictive practices. In their eyes sexual control separated man from beast, and the Victorians were very keen to justify their self-imposed place on the top rung of the animal kingdom. Finally, sexual control equated to social control. There was a strong belief that sexual purity kept the race pure too. It is not by chance that a later edition of *Searchlight on Health*... (from which the following excerpt comes) was entitled *Practical Eugenics*. "Control" was not necessarily "repression." It was instead a way to moderate and avoid extremes and to maintain superiority.

Scientific knowledge of the human body was remarkably inaccurate in the late Victorian period. Doctors, for example, thought that the ripest time for conception was just before menstruation. Equally, they believed that men had finite amounts of sperm, known as the "life force," which must therefore be carefully and judiciously husbanded and certainly not wasted. This obviously explains the physiological case against masturbation. Physiology or not, however, it was the normative social values that inspired much of the literature, and the great challenge for Canadian doctors was to mate their square peg of medical knowledge with the round hole of social values. It begs the question, though: how did doctors become the custodians of moral and medical knowledge whom Canadians trusted and to whom they increasingly turned?

Several separate developments during the nineteenth century coalesced to produce a situation where doctors, by the end of that century, became the acknowledged fountains of wisdom and gained a commensurate social prestige they previously lacked. Early in the century, and during the preceding eras, medicine had neither status nor much credibility. This was partly because medicine, as a practice, remained in its infancy and because there was essentially no regulation of the profession. Thus anyone could, and often did, set himself up as a doctor, regardless of his training or knowledge. Complete quacks worked alongside *bone fide* doctors. The fact that non-medical people often performed what later became "medical" tasks further explains why doctors had little esteem. Barbers, after all, did dentistry, and midwives obstetrics. Over the century, however, those doctors who had served apprenticeships under others, typically for five years, began to organize and to exclude those who were perceived as practicing medicine outside the "standard" milieu. With numbers came strength. By the latter part of the nineteenth century, the Canadian public accepted the university-trained doctor as the purveyor of professional medical care and knowledge—which did not prevent them from buying gallons of home cures sold by quacks through the back pages of magazines.

The other revolution boosting doctors' status was the melding of science with medicine. The two were distinctly separate until the mid-nineteenth century. Medicine used to be about returning the imbalance of a sick body to balance, an act that had little to do with objective science and more with unsubstantiated tradition and downright hocus-pocus. Meanwhile, scientists expanded their horizons with instruments like the microscope, which allowed them to explore life to an unprecedented degree. Then came the germ theory purveyed by men such as Pasteur and Lister, and the invention of first ether and then chloroform as an anesthetic. Doctors could now explore living bodies and make objective observations based upon what they saw, sometimes fix the problem, and stitch the patient back together with a reasonable expectation that he would survive. The doctor became a highly trained specialist, a healer, an objective scientist, and thereby the fountain of wisdom in a world progressively dominated by science.

Doctors' prestige further grew as a result of a decline, or at least a questioning, of traditional religious dogma. Canadians increasingly puzzled over the efficacy of stories like Adam and Eve, especially in the face of scientific evidence from men such as Charles Darwin. They began to seek answers to the puzzling questions of life from those they now perceived as objective men of science: doctors. It further helped that the Victorians developed philosophies of positivism, which insisted that all life was scientifically quantifiable and could be understood objectively. This was a direct challenge to the traditional biblical "leap of faith" and again inclined the Victorian toward the doctor, rather than the priest, when he was perplexed about the great questions of life. For their part, doctors responded in what they believed to be a scientific, objective, and rational manner. The evidence, however, suggests that they could not separate science and morality, medicine from social convention—the two were inextricably linked. That did not matter to a knowledge-hungry public that lapped up their medical prognostications.

DISCUSSION POINTS

1. Based upon these documents, what constituted proper sexual conduct in the Victorian era?

2. To what degree, if any, did religious concerns conflict with science when it came to sex advice?

3. What specific sex advice demonstrated gender inequality during this era?

4. Whether sex education belongs in the home or in school still remains a controversial topic. Would sex advice have been more effective if it had been taught in the schools rather than found in books and journals only accessible to well-educated Canadians?

DOCUMENTS

1. Benjamin Jefferis and James Nichols, *Searchlights on Health, Light on Dark Corners: A Complete Sexual Science and A Guide to Purity and Physical Manhood, Advice to Maiden, Wife and Mother, Love, Courtship and Marriage*, 1894

Benjamin Grant Jefferis (1851–1929) was a medical doctor, professor, and prolific writer from Illinois. His book Searchlights on Health *… went through at least 41 editions, including several Canadian, and sold well over a million copies. Among his many titles were* The Domestic Cyclopedia: A Practical Family Physician *(Toronto, 1894) and* Sex and Dating: Advice to Maidens and Young Men *(1894). His motto was "Fight social diseases with facts, not sentiments; study the problem of venereal infection for information, not sensation; combat social evils with science, not mystery. This is the keynote of our campaign to train men, women and children to think straight along the line of social hygiene."*

James Lawrence Nichols (circa 1851–95) co-authored many of Jefferis's books. He rose from humble orphan beginnings to become a professor at North Central College in Naperville, Illinois, a very successful author, and a book publisher. As well as books on health and sexuality, Nichols wrote on business and left sufficient money for the town of Naperville to build the "Nichols Library."

Reading Novels. How often have I seen girls not twelve years old, as hungry for a story or a novel as they should be for their dinners! A sickly sentimentalism is thus formed, and their minds are sullied with impure desires. Every fashionable young lady must of course read every new novel, though nearly all of them contain exceptionable allusions, perhaps covered with a thin gauze of fashionable refinement.... Shame on novel-reading females for they cannot have pure minds and unsullied feelings.

Theatre-going. Theaters and theatrical dancing also inflame the passions, and are "the wide gate" of "the broad road" of moral impurity. Fashionable music is another, especially the verses set to it, being mostly over-sick ditties or sentimental odes, breathing this tender passion in its most melting and bewitching strains.

Improper prints often do immense injury in this respect, as do also balls, parties, annuals, newspaper articles...

Scarcely one in a hundred of the girls attending these balls preserve their purity. They meet the most desperate characters, professional gamblers, criminals and the lowest debauchees. Such an assembly and such influence cannot mean anything but ruin for an innocent girl.

Vile Women. The public ball is always a resort of vile women who picture to innocent girls the ease and luxury of a harlot's life, and offer them all manner of temptations to abandon the paths of virtue. The public ball is the resort of the libertine and the adulterer, and whose object is to work the ruin of every innocent girl that may fall into their clutches.

The Question. Why does society wonder at the increase of prostitution, when public balls and promiscuous dancing is so largely endorsed and encouraged?

Working Girls. Thousands of working girls enter innocently and unsuspectingly into the paths which lead them to the house of evil, or who wander the streets as miserable outcasts all through the influence of the dance. The low theatre and dance halls and other places of unselected gatherings are the milestones which mark the working girl's downward path from virtue to vice, from modesty to shame.

The Saleswoman, the seamstress, the factory girl or any other virtuous girl had better, far better, die than take the first step in the path of impropriety and danger. Better, a thousand times better for this life, better for the life to come, an existence of humble, virtuous, industry than a single departure from virtue, even though it were paid with a fortune.

Temptations. There is not a young girl but who is more or less tempted by some unprincipled wretch who may have the reputation of a genteel society man. It behooves parents to guard careful the morals of their daughters, and be vigilant and cautious in permitting them to accept the society of young men. Parents who desire to save their daughters from a fate worse than death, should endeavour by every means in their power to keep them from falling into traps cunningly devised by some cunning lover. There are many good young men, but not all are safe friends....

It is not uncommon to see girls at the tender age of thirteen or fourteen—mere children—hardened courtesans, lost to all sense of shame and decency. They are reared in ignorance, surrounded by demoralizing influences, cut off from the blessing of church and Sabbath school, see nothing but licentiousness, intemperance and crime. These young girls are lost forever. They are beyond the reach of the moralist or the preacher and have no comprehension of modesty and purity. Virtue to them is a stranger, and has been from the cradle.

A Great Wrong. Parents too poor to clothe themselves bring children into the world, children for whom they have no bread, consequently the girl easily falls victim in early womanhood to the heartless libertine. The boy with no other schooling but that of the streets soon masters all the qualifications for a professional criminal. If there could be a law forbidding people to marry, who have no visible means of supporting a family, or if they should marry, if their children could be taken away from them and properly educated by the State, it would cost the country less and be a great step in advancing our civilization.

The First Step. Thousands of fallen women could have been saved from lives of degradation and deaths of shame had they received more toleration and loving forgiveness in the first steps of error. Many women naturally pure and virtuous have fallen to the lowest depths because discarded by friends, frowned upon by society, and sneered at by the world, after they had taken a single misstep. Society forgives man, but woman never...

Know Thyself.... All are born with the desire to become attractive—girls especially want to grow up, not only attractive, but beautiful. Some girls think that bright eyes, pretty hair and fine clothes alone make them beautiful. This is not so. Real beauty depends upon good health, good manners and a pure mind....

...God made the sexual organs so that the race should not die out. He gave them to us so that we may reproduce life, and thus fill the highest position in the created universe. The purpose for which they are made is high and holy and honorable, and if they are used only for this purpose—and they must not be used at all until they are fully matured—they will be a source of the greatest blessing to us all...

As in the Boy, so in the Girl, self-abuse causes an undue amount of blood to flow to those organs, thus depriving the body of its nourishment.... The bloodless lips, the dull, heavy eye surrounded with dark rings, the nerveless hand, the blanched cheek, the short breath, the old, faded look, the weakened memory and silly irritability tell the story all too plainly. The same evil results follow, perhaps ending in death, or worse, in insanity. Aside from the injury the girl does herself by yielding to this habit, there is one other reason which appeals to the conscience, and that is that self-abuse is an offence against moral law—it is putting to a vile, selfish use the organs which were given for a high, sacred purpose.

Let Them Alone.... They were given to you that you might become a mother, the highest office to which God has ever called one of His creatures. Do not debase yourself and become lower than the beasts of the field. If this habit has fastened upon any of our readers, stop it now. Do not allow yourself to think about it, give up all evil associations, seek pure companions, and go to your mother, older sister, or physician for advice....

Teach [the boy] that when he handles or excites the sexual organs all parts of the body suffer, because they are connected by nerves that run throughout the system; this is what is called "self-abuse." The whole body is abused when this part of the body is handled or excited in any manner whatsoever. Teach them to shun all children who indulge in this loathsome habit, or children who talk about these things. The sin is terrible and is, in fact, worse than lying or stealing. For, although these are wicked and will ruin their souls, yet this habit of self-abuse will ruin both soul and body....

It lays the foundation for consumption, paralysis and heart disease. It weakens the memory, makes a boy careless, negligent and listless. It even makes many lose their minds; others, when grown commit suicide. How often mothers see their little boys handling themselves, and let it pass, because they think the boy will outgrow the habit, and do not realize the strong hold it has upon them....

Sensuality. Lust crucifies love. The young sensual husband is generally at fault. Passion sways and the duty to bride and wife is not thought of, and so a modest young wife is often actually forced or assaulted by the unsympathetic haste of her husband. An amorous man in that way soon destroys his love, and thus laid the foundation for many difficulties that soon develop.... Many a young husband often lays the foundation of many diseases of the womb and of the nervous system in gratifying his unchecked passions without proper regard for his wife's exhausted condition....

The First Conjugal Approaches are usually painful to the new wife and no enjoyment to her follows. Great caution and kindness should be exercised. A young couple rushing together in their animal passion soon produce a nervous and irritation condition, which ere long brings apathy, indifference, if not dislike. True love and a high regard for each other will temper passion with moderation....

The Time for Indulgence. The health of the generative functions depends upon exercise, just the same as with any other vital organ. Intercourse should be absolutely avoided just before or after meals, or just after mental excitement or physical exercise. No wife should indulge her husband when he is under the influence of alcoholic stimulants, for idiocy and other serious maladies are liable to be visited upon the offspring.

Passions. Every healthful man has sexual desires, and he might as well refuse to satisfy his hunger as to deny their existence. The Creator has given us various appetites, intended they should be indulged, and has provided the means....

Committing Adultery in the Heart. A young man who allows his mind to dwell upon the vision of nude women will soon become the victim of ruinous passion, and either fall under the influence of lewd women or resort to self-abuse. The man who has no control over his mind and allows impure thoughts to be associated with the name of every female that may be suggested to his mind, is but committing adultery in his heart, just as guilty at heart as though he had committed the deed....

The Practice of Abortion. That we have the practice of abortion reduced in modern times to a science, and almost to a distinct profession. A large part of the business is carried on by the means of medicines advertised in obscure but intelligible terms as embryo-destroyers or preventives of conception. Every large city has its professional abortionist. Many ordinary physicians destroy the embryos to order, and the skill to do this terrible deed has even descended among the common people....

2. "Female Cyclists," *Dominion Medical Monthly and Ontario Medical Journal* VII, 3 (September 1896)

The Dominion Medical Monthly and Ontario Medical Journal *was published every month from July 1895 to December 1921 and served as a medical journal aimed at doctors studying hygiene and public welfare. It was created by the amalgamation of the* Dominion Medical Monthly *with the* Ontario Medical Journal, *and was superseded by the* Journal of National Hygiene and Public Welfare. *It prided itself on being unaffiliated to any corporate or other interests, thereby championing its objectivity.*

Possibly no craze has taken so complete a hold on the people as cycling. It seems to be the ambition of every person, male and female, from the time they walk until they have reached the age of discretion, say, about seventy-five or eighty, to own a bicycle. Much of this is undoubtedly due first to the introductions of what is known as the safety bicycle, second to the booming methods of bicycle manufacturers, and third the feature with which we have to deal, the general introduction of bicycle riding among women. There are two classes of people who object to this, those holding the opinion that bicycle riding is good for women, and those who declare that it is injurious and should not be tolerated. The latter class may be properly divided into those who object to bicycle riding on the grounds of propriety. As far as these latter are concerned, what is and what is not propriety is largely a matter of opinion and custom, and with it we have very little to do. The others are those who object to it because it is injurious to the rider herself and decidedly immoral in its tendencies. While we may admit everything that has been said in regard to the advantages to women of getting out in the open air and having healthful exercise, we object to this particular form of it. We are of the opinion that there never has been any law that we know of which prevented women in Christianized countries from getting out in the open air as much as they pleased so long as it was compatible with the ordinary duties for which they were intended, raising a family and making a home comfortable. As far as exercise is concerned, the average woman will readily admit that she gets about all the exercise she wants in looking after her home.... We now propose to consider directly and plainly, as far as experience has informed us of the immoral and injurious effect of bicycle riding upon women. To first consider the position in which a woman is placed on a bicycle, we have a saddle so constructed that it fits more or less accurately the perineum and adjacent parts. In the saddle as used by men, and there is practically very little difference if any between the saddles for the respective sexes, the general report is that all the pressure comes on the soft part of the buttock between the tuberosities of the ischium on the perineum and forward towards the scrotum, the latter being produced by the stooping position in which the person rides; and as they explain it, they have got "to hinch backward" occasionally in order to relieve the pressure and irritation along the urethra. All of which brings us directly to the point that the strong pressure upon the like parts of the female goes a long way towards, as one of our exchanges expresses it, "filling a long felt want." While this, of course, expresses the effect produced it would be absurd to suppose that it was the primary reason for bicycling, nonetheless the consensus of opinion is increasingly overwhelmingly day by day that the bicycle produces in the female a distinct orgasm. We know a number of lady riders who have been compelled to give up the use of the bicycle on this account; and even if an orgasm is not produced the continued erethism is decidedly more injurious and tends to produce nervous diseases, and the general breaking down of the system.... in one place where cycling is taught the saddle has been purposely raised to aggravate this condition, and that the attendants who steer innocent maidens around on their wheels find that at first erethism and then orgasm is produced; the lady complains of being tired and gets off her wheel, a condition so scandalous and abominable deserves the attention of every man who trusts his female relative to bicycle riding, and if men are found who would purposely do this sort of thing, as there is no doubt some have done it, a term in the penitentiary with an occasional application of the cat [whip] would be a mild punishment.

We would say, in conclusion, that in bicycle riding we have a woman pedaling ways in much the same manner as running a sewing machine, and we know what this has been accused of in the way of producing female complaints. But add to all this the working with contracted chest in a stooped position with all the abdominal organs pressed downwards, subjected to continued erethism, as well as the occasional orgasm and you have a condition of affairs which will take a better authority than the bicycle manufacturer to prove to us that bicycle riding is a healthful exercise for women. It is not necessary to point out to physicians the relaxed nervous and moral stamina produced in a girl taking a ride out into the country. We hope physicians will look earnestly into this matter, and our colleagues will be open for them to report. We have a number of cases now which have been carefully looked into by physicians of our staff and we are absolutely satisfied, as far as we are concerned, that female bicycling must be sharply looked after, and care taken in its indulgence.

3. *The Ladies Book of Useful Information Compiled from Many Sources*, 1896

Nothing is known about The Ladies Book of Useful Information Compiled from Many Sources *except that it was published anonymously in London, Ontario, in 1896.*

SEXUAL INTERCOURSE — ITS LAWS AND CONDITIONS — ITS USE AND ABUSE

There is an increasing prevalence of nervous ailments and complicated disorders that could be traced to have their sole origin from this source. Hypochondria, in its various phases, results from the premature and unnatural waste of the seminal fluid. This speedily ensues a lack of natural heat, deficiency of vital power, and consequently indigestion, melancholy, languor, and dejection ensue; the victim becomes enervated and spiritless, loses the very attributes of man, and premature old age soon follows.

It is a prevalent error that it is necessary for the semen to be ejected at certain times from the body; that its retention is incompatible with sound health and vigor of body and mind. This is a very fallacious idea. The seminal fluid is too precious, nature bestows too much care in its elaboration for it to be used in this unproductive manner. It is intended, when not used for the purpose of procreation, to be reabsorbed again into the system, giving vigor of body, elasticity and strength to the mind, making the individual strong, active, and self-reliant.

When kept as nature intended, it is a perpetual fountain of life and energy—a vital force which acts in every direction, a motive power which infuses manhood into every organ of the brain and every fiber of the body.

The law of sexual morality for childhood is one of utter negation of sex. Every child should be kept pure and free from amative excitement and the least amative indulgence, which is unnatural and doubly harmful. No language is strong enough to express the evils of amative excitement and unnatural indulgence before the age of puberty.

Men expect that women shall come to them in marriage chaste and pure from the least defilement. Women have a right to expect the same of their husbands. Here the sexes are upon a perfect equality...

Every man and every woman living simply, purely, and temperately—respecting the laws of health in regard to air, food, dress, exercise and habits of life—not only can live in the continence of a pure virgin life when single, and in the chastity which should be observed by all married partners, but be stronger, happier, and in every way better by so living.

Chastity is the conservation of life, and the consecration of its forces to the highest use. Sensuality is the waste of life, and the degradation of its forces to pleasure divorced from use. Chastity is life, sensuality is death.

From the age of puberty to marriage the law is the same for both sexes—full employment of mind and body, temperance, purity, and perfect chastity in thought, word and deed....

The child has its rights, and every child has the right to be born in honest, respectable wedlock, of parents about to give it a sound constitution and the nurture and education it requires. The child who lacks these conditions is grievously wronged by both father and mother....

4. J.E. Hett, *The Sexual Organs, Their Use and Abuse the Subject upon Which Men and Women Know Least, Yet Ought to Know the Most: Guide to Man,* 1899

Dr. John E. Hett (1870-1956) was the son of German immigrants. He graduated as a medical doctor from the University of Toronto in 1891 and established his practice in Kitchener, Ontario. There he became active in the community, serving on the school board, as a member of the Board of Education, and as mayor from 1915 to 1916. Hett was a staunch socialist who ran unsuccessfully for the Independent Labour Party in the 1917 election and who advocated the nationalization of medicine. In 1899 he self-published the book from which the following is excerpted.

...The secrets of life lie in the control of the sexual organs and the turning of those thoughts into spirituality.

I am absolutely positive, if men endeavour to curb their sexual thoughts, they will not give way to drunkenness or other vices. The future prospects of humanity rest in the domain of those now living. The degradation of the race today lies more in the sexual line than in all the other forms of vices put together, and the sooner men and women will appreciate the great truths concerning the law of creation, as inherent in themselves, the better will it be for themselves, their children, their neighbors and their Christianity. It is really too bad that so little attention has been paid to the domain of sex, for after all it is the greatest divine principle in Religion.

Can a man be a true Christian who often has sexual intercourse with his wife whilst she is pregnant? Yet this is being done by far the greater majority of them. They haven't been taught differently, and since they do not realize the great wrongs they are doing by implanting that stain upon their offspring, is it any wonder then, that the children of Christians will sow wild oats...

Some men who read this book will think that it may arouse his sons and draw their attention to sexual thoughts. They may think that harm may result from the perusal of this book, but let me assure all that such fears are without foundation.... A father who places this work in the hands of his sons is very wise and it may save him countless troubles. How much more important is it for men to think, speak and discuss the various topics in these pages than to allow their thoughts to run away with their passions?

...Young men and women today are becoming educated in the methods of preventing conception, and when the truth is known it is remarkable how much they know of this dirty work. Abortions are frightfully on the increase and our women are becoming adept in the manipulations of the same.

Various instruments to prevent conception are also being peddled throughout the country. Every physician knows this to be the case, and since the writer has met with thousands of cases of sexual abuse, it becomes his sacred duty to say a few words upon this subject with the hope of enlightening our young men and women of the true sexual functions....

In the ideal state of marriage the organs of sex should be used solely for the purpose of reproduction, and the closer married people live in the exchanging of their wisdom and love, the nobler and more Christ-like will they become....

The sexual propensities which are everywhere so plainly manifested today in our young people exist because they have been born with those desires, and since there is so little stress laid upon these subjects by the parents, the church, and the state, it is certainly no wonder that so much licentiousness and vice prevails in our midst....

Sex worship is carried on in a frightful way at present. Instead of worshipping God in spirit and truth, the masses are continually indulging in lustful thoughts, words and actions. May the attention of the coming races be diverted from this false worship and may their forces and energies be turned to higher ideals in manhood and womanhood....

Now, since there is less manual labor than there was fifty years ago, and since the mentality of the race is being developed, we find also that there is more abuse of the sexual organs now than then....

If a man works hard, he is not as sensual as when he does not... farmers who work hard are less sensual than others. In spite of the progress of our race there is greater sensuality also. The church is powerless at the present to check it, and we sincerely hope that clergymen will recognize the importance of educating our people upon these important questions....

When once the sexual appetite has been awakened, the spark is kindled. This begins to play upon his fancy and his thoughts will revel in sexual matters, and soon again the same act will be repeated. Then follows the third, then the fourth and then others in quick succession.

After the first intercourse the youth may feel a little shame and may argue with himself concerning the right or wrong of it, but his mind becomes shifted on a scale, as it were, until he meets the same girl, or a similar one, and then the balance is quickly drawn down by the lascivious thoughts of the tempter.

After a few acts, the mind thinks little of right or wrong, but simply follows the sensual notions, and reason is out of the question. Reason becomes blunted, and this blunting process follows man continually until he becomes entirely lost. Often has the word been spoken to "sports" about the awful condition and slavery they were in, whereupon they simply replied, "You don't know the fun you are missing." The state of their reason is here shown. The further down men and women shall fall, the less and less reason will they have. Now, what can be man's judgment when his brain is inflated with passion? They think and act according to their standpoint of judgment. Is it any wonder that so many wrongs exist in the world?

...There are many different houses of ill-fame in which merchandise is made of the polluting embrace with all its evils. It is a common thing to hear "up to date sports" say that they feel themselves safe in going to the better class of sporting houses since it is the business of the girls to keep themselves clean. Undoubtedly they are less liable to contract venereal disease from a professional "sport" than from an immoral servant girl or street strumpet, and then they are also less liable to get into trouble through blackmail or by the woman or girl becoming pregnant. It is likewise true also, that the sin which man inflicts upon the public prostitute is not as great as upon another women, for it is rather difficult to spoil a rotten egg as it were.

It is however right in the fashionable brothels where men very often contract venereal disease, which at times follows them all their lives. If a prostitute is closely examined, she is a very repulsive object, and especially is this the case when she is closely examined by the scrutinizing eye of the physician. If men could but realize the filthy places in which they have their enjoyment, they wouldn't feel like digging their graves in such dirty localities. This is what millions of men are continually doing every year.

Men, who are frequenters of these brothels never reason, and simply go by the impulses of their passions. If they would only think how many other men co-habit with the same girls which they caress (for it takes many as a rule to keep these unfortunate in board and clothes), they would perhaps have enough. If they would only see the dirty specimens of men who have their indulgences in the very same places as they do, they would not feel like co-habiting with such women.

Prostitutes are very fond of perfume, which assists them in covering up their filth and charming their frequenters with the idea that they are beautiful. In speaking of prostitutes we can easily say, "The way of the transgressor is hard." Women who work nothing and simply earn their living by selling their bodies, their minds and their souls to dirty men are objects of pity. How few are the missionaries that come to them and say "Sin no more"! Who comes to them and tries to reform them by instructing them that the secret of life lies in the control of the organs of sex and the doing of one's duty! Who comes to them and shows them the purity of Religion! Ah! Alas, they verily are in a hell into which clergymen are afraid to tread.

From a careful study of prostitution, I am absolutely positive that if clergymen would endeavour to reform them, their efforts would be in vain. When a woman has once entered into a house of prostitution she is beyond the reach of the methods of reformation at the present time. If anything ever can be accomplished, it can only be done when clergymen will truly understand the organs of sex, their use and abuse, and when they make that study a part of their teachings.

Prostitutes think that almost everybody is as licentious as they are themselves. Often have I heard such statements. They consider themselves just as good as the men who co-habit with them, and in that thought they are not so very far astray. Their minds are filled with nothing but obscene matters. When they look at anything, they look at it through obscene eyes. Nearly all prostitutes are hysterical and since they do not possess a strong will, they roll along in the maelstrom of destruction, which verily is a frightful hell. Many loose women are beautiful and kind-hearted, and if the world would know the causes which made them seek shelter in a house of ill-fame, moral people would hesitate in treading them under their feet....

The causes which make women public prostitutes are many.... The greatest cause of all is that children have fornication born within themselves; the sons of the land create a demand for prostitutes; the awful responsibility that falls upon a man who robs a girl of her virginity, is not thought of at all in the true light. Under the present system of laws a man may rob the virtue of dozens of women, who afterwards are cast upon the road of degradation, whilst he himself receives no punishment from the state, and may associate with the best society in the land. The world as yet cannot see that he is punished by the eternal laws of God.... Besides the causes which are at work within a person, we have other causes which are responsible. Thus we have alcohol, our erroneous system of education, our sweat shops with starvation wages, the accumulation of wealth in the hands of the few at the expense of the poor masses, thus debarring the latter from education and allowing ignorance and passion to rule their minds, and a host of other selfish notions....

Very rarely does woman enter upon life in a brothel simply from choice, but she is forced or led into it by misfortune and ignorance. Temptations surround our poor girls on all sides; the appearance of a gay life, flirtations, jewelry, and fine dresses extend to them the hand of enchantment with all its snares. Little do the poor unfortunate women realize the misery, the sickness, and the horror of the hells that surely line not far off. The average life of a prostitute is very short; by some it is claimed that it lasts no more than four years....

...There are many evils resulting from the over-indulgence in alcohol, but the evil effects from the misuse of the sexual organs are a thousand times worse than those resulting from alcohol.

Since no law can be enforced which will prevent adulteries and all the vice and licentiousness resulting from fornication, the only way that these evils can be overcome is by educating men and women in the physiology of the sexual organs and the divine laws of creation.

Intemperance today is overcome to a great extent by showing people that alcohol, excessively used, is injurious. Thousands of men, however, may be around hotels, saloons, etc., and yet will never become intoxicated. They know better; for they have sufficient common sense to know when they have enough. Likewise, our men and women should be instructed about the evil effects of the perversion of their sacred organs, and then there would be established the kingdom of heaven within themselves....

Death frequently follows abortion and little does the world ever dream of the suffering which often precedes this fatal ending. Statistics show fifteen deaths from abortion to one from natural labor.... About two-thirds of all the female complaints are due to abortions, whilst shattering the nervous system, which gives rise to nervous prostration and insanity, is a very frequent effect.

Women think very little of the risks they are running in these matters, and if they could but see all the possible complications, as a physician does, then we would hear rarely of these cold blooded murders. Aside from death, the terrible sufferings are frightful, and the sooner women will realize the awful crime and its evil consequences to their bodies and their minds, the better it will be for the world. If the physical and mental sufferings are so horrible, what will be the spiritual?

Many are of the opinion that abortions take place mostly amongst single women, but this is not the case. It is in the sanctum of the married families that they occur most frequently. Think of a woman destroying her nearest relative! The one in whose body verily flows the same blood as her own! For what cause is murder committed? What wrong has the child done to be put away? Who are these murderers? We find them all over, especially amongst the women of fashion wearing gems and jewels of precious worth to make them look beautiful. They can't be bothered with brats and at the same time attend fancy dress balls or go away on their trips.... The crime of abortion has found its way into all societies, and is frightfully on the increase....

Self-abuse is known by various names such as masturbation, onanism, self-abuse, solitary vice, secret evil, and a variety of other names. It is produced by playing or toying with the sexual organs, which creates an excited condition, until the fluid passes; then in a few moments all the apparently pleasant sensations vanish. Were it not for these apparently pleasant sensations, self-abuse would never be practiced, but it is owing to this sensation that the evils get hold of a person. Both boys and girls become afflicted. The sin of self-pollution is the most destructive evil practiced by fallen man. It is far worse than illegitimate sexual intercourse, yet strange to say that it is present mostly in the "apparently good" children, who would be shocked by the wickedness of sexual intercourse with a prostitute.

It is a far greater evil than diphtheria, scarlet fever or small pox, yet we allow this awful curse to destroy youths and maidens by the thousands, not by a genuine death, which even would be a blessing, but by a living death; which makes them imbeciles and deprives them of their reason, so that they are fit for nothing but the lunatic asylum. If all the secrets of the insane asylums were truly known, the world would be shocked at the large number of inmates whose reasons have been destroyed by this awful curse....

...The close connection between the organs of sex and the brain has been shown, consequently we should expect this most unnatural abuse to show itself in the reasoning faculties before affecting anything else. This is exactly what takes place, and, consequently when the dirty act has been performed for the first time, it will not be long before the victim will want to do it again. In a short time he wants to do it oftener, until at last he resorts to the dirty act very frequently....

FURTHER READINGS

M. Bliss, "'Pure Books on Avoided Subjects': Pre-Freudian Sexual Ideas in Canada." In *Studies in Canadian Social History*, ed. M. Horn and R. Sabourin. Toronto: McClelland and Stewart, 1974.

B. Curtis, "Illicit Sexuality and Public Education, 1840-1907." In *Sex in Schools: Canadian Education and Sexual Regulation*, ed. S. Prentice. Toronto: Our Schools/ Our Selves Education Foundation, 1994.

Dubinsky, K. *Improper Advances: Rape and Heterosexual Conflict in Ontario, 1880-1929.* Chicago: University of Chicago Press, 1993.

Dubinsky, K., and A. Givertz. "'It Was Only a Matter of Passion': Masculinity and Sexual Danger." In *Gendered Pasts: Historical Essays in Femininity and Masculinity in Canada*, ed. K. McPherson, C. Morgan, and N. Forrestell. Toronto: Oxford University Press, 1999.

Maynard, S. "'Horrible Temptations': Sex, Men and Working-Class Male Youths in Urban Ontario, 1880-1935." *Canadian Historical Association* 78 (June 1997): 191-235.

McLaren, A., and A. McLaren. *The Bedroom and the State: The Changing Practices and Politics of Contraception and Abortion in Canada, 1880-1980*. Toronto: McClelland and Stewart, 1986.

McLaren, J. "Chasing the Social Evil: Moral Fervour and the Evolution of Canada's Prostitution Laws, 1867-1917." *Canadian Journal of Law and Society* 1 (1986): 125-65.

Mitchinson, W. *The Nature of Their Bodies: Women and Their Doctors in Victorian Canada*. Toronto: University of Toronto Press, 1991.

Myers, T. *Caught: Montreal's Modern Girls and the Law, 1869-1945*. Toronto: University of Toronto Press, 2006.

Nilsen, D. "The Social Evil: Prostitution in Vancouver, 1900-1920." In *Not Just Pin Money*, ed. B. Latham and R. Pazdro. Victoria: Camosun College, 1980.

Sangster, J. *Regulating Girls and Women: Sexuality, Family, and the Law in Ontario, 1920-1960*. Toronto: Oxford University Press, 2001.

Snell, J. "The White Life for Two: The Defence of Marriage and Sexual Morality in Canada, 1800-1914." *Histoire Social* 16, 31 (1983): 111-28.

Strange, C. *Toronto's Girl Problem: The Perils and Pleasures of the City, 1880-1930*. Toronto: University of Toronto Press, 1995.

Valverde, M. *The Age of Light, Soap, and Water: Moral Reform in English Canada, 1885-1925*. Toronto: McClelland and Stewart, 1991.

Valverde, M. "'When the Mother of the Race Is Free': Race, Sexuality, and Reproduction in First-Wave Feminism." In *Gender Conflicts: New Essays in Women's History*, ed. F. Iacovetta and M. Valverde. Toronto: University of Toronto Press, 1992.

"Two Distinct Personalities"

THE QUESTION OF RIEL'S SANITY

INTRODUCTION

The enigmatic Louis Riel still stirs controversy over a century after his execution in the Regina police barracks. The man, his legacy, and his place in the national pantheon continue to foment debate, historical papers, and letters to editors. Riel has, since his death, metamorphosed in the public perception from traitor to a hero of Canadian minority rights and one of the Fathers of Confederation. He remains a lightning rod for issues of social justice and for civil and minority rights versus government rights.

The question of Riel's sanity before, during, and after the Northwest Rebellion of 1885 generated considerable debate. What would it say about the Métis, for example, if they willingly followed a *bone fide* lunatic? Did that not imply that they, as a people, were either equally crazy, hopelessly gullible, or both? The federal government, meanwhile, could be justified for its action, or inaction, before and during the rebellion if Riel were insane — but then he should not have been hanged. Conversely, finding him sane, even in retrospect, justified his execution yet simultaneously legitimized his cause, making the federal government the "bad guy." The Catholic Church, too, discussed the issue of Riel's sanity. Was he indeed a mad heretic to be pitied, dismissed, or excommunicated? Perhaps, but many Catholics believed then, and still believe, that Riel, like Joan of Arc, deserves ecclesiastical recognition as a martyr and saint, not a lunatic.

Tackling the issue from an entirely different perspective, some debate whether Riel's sanity is a legitimate issue at all or simply a red herring conjured to deflect people's attention from the truly significant matters arising from the Northwest Rebellion. If not a red herring, could historical and contemporary efforts to brand Riel a madman arise from those who, both then and now, want to discredit Natives who dared oppose colonization?

Establishing Riel's guilt as a traitor posed few problems in the narrow eyes of British common law. The evidence overwhelmingly proved that he broke the Elizabethan Statute of Treasons by "most wickedly and traitorously [making] war against our said lady the Queen." Where the issue became ambiguous was whether he knew he broke the law and whether, if he did, he knew it was wrong to do so. An affirmative answer to either indicated sanity: he knew what he was doing. This made him guilty of intent, for which the state had every right to punish him. If, on the other hand, he did not know what he was doing, or did not recognize his actions as wrong, then he could not be held responsible by virtue of insanity, and a jury must acquit him. The conundrum, of course, lay in interpreting the word "wrong" because legal and moral "wrongs" were, and are, not necessarily the same thing. Riel, after all, did not believe it morally "wrong" to defend his people against federal incursion, despite it being legally "wrong" to do so through armed struggle.

British common law recognized insanity through a series of precedent setting cases and accepted the notion that an insane criminal must be pitied, not punished, because "they knew not what they did." "Pity" ironically meant indefinite incarceration in an insane asylum which, considering conditions in the nineteenth century, was harsh punishment indeed—but it wasn't dangling from a noose. The difficulty lay in developing criteria for testing and definition because "sanity" was subjective and interpretive: one man's visionary is another's lunatic. To address this, British judges in the 1840s created a set of cognitive tests, known as the McNaughten Rules, to establish an accused's sanity. The individual answered a series of questions that purportedly ascertained his or her ability to distinguish right from wrong. Though controversial and rejected by many in the fledgling psychiatric community, the McNaughten Rules remained in force throughout the empire and for the rest of the century. Very few successfully pleaded insanity under these rules.

Interested parties at the time of his trial interpreted "facts" in their effort to plead their view of Riel's mental status. Riel indeed spent time in insane asylums twice during the 1870s but was released as "cured" in both cases—which, of course, could "prove" either his sanity or insanity. Riel readily admitted hearing divine voices directing him to lead the Métis people under new religious tenets. Though erratic and with unorthodox religious views, he did enjoy support from Métis, Native people, and white settlers. Several hundred men, after all, freely followed him into battle in 1885. Throughout his trial Riel insisted on his sanity, a claim that his defence team ironically used as proof of his insanity.

The case became particularly awkward for the federal government when the jury returned a guilty verdict, implying sanity, but recommended clemency. Because a prime minister could grant clemency, this placed the case back into John A. Macdonald's hands, where he did not want it. It put him in the unenviable political position of juggling Ontario's wish for "Riel's head in a sack" against the court's and Quebec's call for mercy. Clemency also implied at least some federal culpability in the rebellion, which Macdonald found unacceptable. The prime minister opted for a set of maneuvers that, though legal, pushed the envelope of justice and interpretations of "wrong." A series of carefully orchestrated medical examinations found Riel sane and therefore criminally eligible for execution.

Louis Riel walked peacefully to the scaffold at dawn on November 16, 1885. Tradition stipulated that the family of the condemned receive the body immediately after execution. In this case, authorities buried Riel in the prison courtyard and forbade his exhumation until some six weeks later.

DISCUSSION POINTS

1. Based upon the documents in this chapter, should the jury have found Riel sane or insane?

2. Since some argue that prayer is still a common means of communicating with God, should Riel's divine communications be taken as evidence of instability? Would this behaviour have been more acceptable in the nineteenth century than today?

3. How consistent was the evidence provided by the medical examiners?

4. Is there any evidence to suggest that the whole issue of insanity was designed to take the focus away from other issues such as the federal government's administration of the West?

DOCUMENTS

1. François Roy, Testimony, *The Queen v. Louis Riel*, 1885

François-Elzéar Roy (1837-87) came from a prosperous French-Canadian family, was an enthusiastic classicist, Justice of the Peace, and medical superintendent of the Beauport Asylum in Quebec. The hospital was very progressive and subscribed to rehabilitation through fresh air and physical work, rather than the normal brutal incarceration. Roy travelled to the United States, and possibly to Europe, to study psychiatric hospitals and treatment. Prosecutors accused him of prolonging Riel's hospitalization for financial gain since Quebec mental hospitals were privately owned and received provincial funding according to their patient population.

Q. What is your position in Quebec? A. For a great number of years I have been medical superintendent and one of the proprietors of the lunatic asylum at Beauport.

Q. How long have you been connected with the asylum as superintendent? A. More than fifteen or sixteen years.

Q. You are also a member of the society of America—of the Society of the Superintendents of the Insane Asylums of America? A. Yes.

Q. During these fifteen or sixteen years your duties caused you to make a special study of diseases of the brain? Is it not true that it has been necessary for you to make a special study of diseases of the brain? A. Yes; it was my duty to go to the principal asylums in the United States and see how the patients were treated there.

Q. Had you any connection with the asylum of Beauport in 1875 and 1876? A. Yes.

Q. You were at that time superintendent of the asylum? A. Yes.

Q. In those years, or about that time, did you have occasion to see the prisoner? A. Certainly; many times.

Q. Where did you see him? A. In the asylum.

Q. Can you tell the date? A. Yes, the date was taken from the register when I left Quebec.

Q. What date is that? A. I took the entry from the register in the hospital in the beginning of this month.

Q. Was he admitted with all the formalities required by law? A. Yes.

Q. Will you tell me what time he left the asylum? A. He was discharged about the 21st of January, after a residence in the house of about nineteen months.

Q. Had you occasion to study at that time the mental disease by which the prisoner was affected at that time? A. Yes.

Q. Did you have relations with him during that time, and did you watch him carefully during that time? A. Not every day, but very often.

Q. Can you say now what mental disease the prisoner was then suffering from? A. He was suffering from what is known by authors as megalomania.

Q. Will you speak from memory or by referring to the authors, what are the other symptoms of this disease? A. They sometimes give you reasons which would be reasonable if they were not starting from a false idea. They are very clever on those discussions, and they have a tendency to irritability when you question or doubt their mental condition, because they are under a strong impression that they are right and they consider it to be an insult when you try to bring them to reason again. On ordinary questions they may be reasonable and sometimes may be very clever, in fact without careful watching they would lead one to think that they were well.

Q. Was he there some weeks or months before you ascertained his mental condition? A. Yes. I waited till then to classify him as to his mental condition. We wait a few weeks before classifying the patient.

Q. Does a feeling of pride occupy a prominent position in that mental disease? A. Yes, in different forms, religion, and there are a great many with pride; we have kings with us.

Q. Is the question of selfishness or egotism prominent in those cases? A. Yes.

Q. Are they liable to change in their affections rapidly? A. Yes, because they are susceptible to the least kind of attraction.

Q. In that particular malady are the patients generally inclined to be sanguine as to the success of their projects? A. The difficulty is to make them believe that they will not have success; you cannot bring them to change that, it is a characteristic of the disease.

Q. Are people who suffer from this particular form of disease liable to be permanently cured or are they liable to fall back into the old malady? A. Generally they remain in that condition; they may have sensible moments and then intermission would interfere.

Q. In a case of this kind could a casual observer without any medical experience form an estimate as to the state of the man's mind? A. Not usually, unless he makes a special study of the case; there is more or less difference in each case.

Q. What is the position of the mind of a man suffering from this disease in reference to other subjects which do not come within the radius of his mania? A. They will answer questions as any other man with the sense of reason; it is only when they touch the spot of their monomania that they become delirious.

Q. You stated that the prisoner left the asylum in 1878? A. In January 1878.

Q. Have you ever seen him from that time till yesterday? A. No, never.

Q. Do you recognize him perfectly as the same person who was in your asylum in 1876 and 1878? A. Yes.

Q. Were you present at the examination of the witnesses that took place today and yesterday? A. Partly.

Q. Did you hear the witnesses describing the actions of the prisoner as to his peculiar views on religion in reference to his power, to his hoping to succeed the Pope, and as to his prophecies, yesterday and today? A. Yes.

Q. From what you heard from these witnesses and from the symptoms they prove to have been exhibited by the prisoner, are you now in a position to say whether or not at that time he was a man of sound mind? A. I am perfectly certain that when the prisoner was under our care he was not of sound mind, but he became cured before he left, more or less. But from what I heard here today I am ready to say that I believe on these occasions his mind was unsound....

Q. Do you believe that under the state of mind as described by the witnesses and to which you referred that he was capable or incapable of knowing the nature of the acts which he did? A. No, I do not believe that he was in a condition to be the master of his acts, and I positively swear it and I have people of the same character under my supervision.

Q. Will you swear from the knowledge you have heard? A. From the witnesses.

Q. That the man did not know what he was doing or whether it was contrary to law in reference to the particular delusion? A. No, and for another reason the same character of the disease is shown in the last period, the same as when he was with us, there is no difference, if there was any difference in the symptoms I would have doubts, but if it was of the same character so well described by Dagoust, who is taken as an authority and has been adopted in France as well as in America and England.

Q. The opinion you have formed as to the soundness of his mind is based upon the fact that the symptoms disclosed by the witnesses here yesterday and today are to a large extent identical with the symptoms of his malady as disclosed while he was at your asylum? A. Yes.

2. Sir Charles Fitzpatrick, "Address of Defense Counsel,"
The Queen v. Louis Riel, 1885

Sir Charles Fitzpatrick (1853-1942) was born in Quebec City, studied law at Laval University, and was called to the bar in 1876, after which he quickly made a name for himself as a criminal lawyer and founded the law firm of Fitzpatrick and Taschereau. He later joined the Supreme Court as Chief Justice and was instrumental in creating the provinces of Saskatchewan and Alberta.

...We have stated that this man was suffering from that form of disease known as megalomania. It is not necessary for me to tell you more than that the characteristic symptom of this disease is an insane, an extraordinary love of power and extraordinary development of ambition, a man that is acting under the insane delusion that he is either a great poet or a god or a king or that he is in direct communication with the Holy Ghost; and it may be well for me here to remind you that I do not speak here of my own authority. I tell you here that from books, the most reputed authorities on this subject, one of the distinguishing characteristics of this disease is that the man might reason perfectly and give perfect reasons for all that he does and justify it in every respect, subject always to the insane delusion. They are naturally irritable, excitable, and will not suffer that they can be contradicted in any respect...

But, gentlemen, if his conduct is entirely inconsistent with the possession of a sound mind, is it not consistent with the possession of an unsound mind? And here I may as well tell you that you are entire masters of the fact in this case, that all the evidence given here is given for the purpose of enabling you to arrive at a conclusion, that you are not to take your verdict from me, from the Crown nor from the court; that the oath which you have taken, as you understand thoroughly, obliged you, when you came into the box, to stand indifferent as you stood unsworn, and the true deliverance made between our Sovereign Lady the Queen and the prisoner at the bar, according to your conscience and to your judgment.

Therefore, gentlemen, you have these facts in evidence, that this man, laboring under the insane delusion that he at some future day would have the whole of the North-West Territories under his control, and being thoroughly convinced that he was called and vested by God, for the purpose of chastising Canada and of creating a new country and a new kingdom here, acting under that insane delusion, what do we find him doing? We find him then taking such steps as would enable him to carry out the object which he then had in view. We find this man believing himself to be inspired by God and believing himself to be in direct communication with the Holy Ghost, believing himself to be an instrument in the hands of the Lord of Hosts. We find him with forty or fifty men going out to do battle against the force of Canada. If the man was sane, how is it possible for you to justify such conduct as that? If the man was insane you know it is one of the distinguishing characteristics of his insanity that he could see no opposition of his objects, that he believed himself to be under the guidance of the Lord of Hosts ... that the All Powerful will necessarily give him the victory no matter what may be the material that may be placed in his hands, no matter how inadequate that material may appear to a sane man, I, knowing that I am inspired by the Almighty, knowing that I am the instrument in the hands of God, I know that I will necessarily gain the victory; and he goes forth and gives battle with these men. Therefore, gentlemen of the jury, you have one illustration of the insanity, of the unsoundness of this man's mind in those very facts.

... Now, gentlemen, I say that the conduct of Louis Riel throughout the whole of this affair is entirely inconsistent with any idea of sanity, but is entirely consistent with his insanity. As I said to you a moment ago in speaking at the opening of this case, the fact of his delivering himself up is one of the characteristics of a man suffering from the insanity from which he is suffering, because he cannot appreciate the danger in which he is placed. It is impossible for him to appreciate the danger in which he places himself, and he never sees that there is any possibility that any harm can happen to him. If that man was perfectly sane, gentlemen, if that man was perfectly sane in doing as he did do, then you have to say whether or not, as I said before, there are not some redeeming features about this man's character, in the heroic act which he did in delivering himself up to Middleton. On the other hand if he is insane, as I contend he is, you see then the proof, for any man of ordinary prudence knows that this man could have escaped and could have evaded the officers of the law and the soldiers. Notwithstanding all that, he comes and gives himself over to General Middleton and is prepared to take the consequences, no matter what they are. I say that that is one of the characteristics of his malady, that that is one of the proofs of his insanity and that is one of the characteristics which are laid down in all the books, as being characteristic of the disease of those men who believe themselves to be in constant intercourse with God, because they think God is always around them, that He is constantly taking care of them and that no harm of any kind can befall them....

3. Mr. Robinson, "Address of Crown Counsel," *The Queen v. Louis Riel*, 1885

Christopher Robinson (1828–1905) served as senior Crown Counsel in the Riel trial. Born into Toronto's elite, he attended Upper Canada College and King's College, where he studied law. He was called to the bar in 1850, specializing in commercial law. After being appointed Queen's Counsel in 1863 he successfully argued a number of high profile cases on the Crown's behalf. During that time he also compiled and published reviews on constitutional law and became an acknowledged expert in the area. His reputation for loyalty and shrewdness made him a logical choice to prosecute the government's case against Riel, which explains why Justice Minister Sir Alexander Campbell and Prime Minister John A. Macdonald picked him for the job.

My learned friends must make their choice between their defences. They cannot claim for their client what is called a niche in the temple of fame and at the same time assert that he is entitled to a place in a lunatic asylum. I understand perfectly well the defence of insanity; I understand perfectly the defence of patriotism, but I am utterly unable to understand how you can be told in one breath a man is a noble patriot and to be told in the next breath that every guiding motive of his actions, every controlling influence which he is bound by his very nature to give heed to, is that of overweening vanity, a selfish sense of his own importance and an utter disregard to everything but his own insane power. There must be either one defence or the other in this case.

Unfortunately it becomes my duty to show to you, that the case which the Crown believes it has made out is, that this prisoner at the bar is neither a patriot nor a lunatic.

But before I proceed further as to that, I would ask you in all seriousness, as sensible men: do you believe that a defence of insanity could have any conceivable or possible applicability to a case of this description?...

Now, gentlemen, just remember what you are told and what you are asked to believe: The half-breeds of this district number, I understand, some 600 or 700. I am speaking entirely of the French half-breeds. I believe the English half-breeds are more numerous than that.

In July 1884, the French half-breeds, believing that the prisoner at the bar was a person in whose judgment, whose advice, whose discretion they could trust and rely upon, sought him out in the place where he was then living with a view of getting him to manage for them their affairs, and to represent their grievances, and to endeavor to obtain for them those rights and that justice which they believed to be theirs.

They sent men, I suppose, in whom they had confidence to ask the prisoner to come for that purpose. They, in their intercourse with him, discovered nothing wrong in his mind, no unsoundness in his reason. The prisoner came here. He remained here from July 1884, till March 1885, and during all that time he was before the public; he addressed, I think we have been told, seven meetings, and there were, I suppose, many more in which he also participated. There was in the district a population of at least 2,000 altogether, for there were six or seven hundred French half-breeds and the English half-breeds outnumbered them. There can be no question, I say, that the prisoner at the bar addressed on public affairs at least two thousand people.

During that time was there ever a whisper of his insanity heard? Have you had one single soul who heard him during that time, one single person of the community among which he lived, and which believed in him; have you heard, I say, one single suspicion from any of them that the prisoner was insane?

The next thing we find in regard to these men is that under the guidance of the prisoner they embark in an enterprise full of danger and gravity. They place their lives and property under his control and direction, and trusting in his judgment they risk both in obedience to his advice, and we have not heard from any one of them that during all that time there was the smallest suspicion he was affected with any unsoundness of mind whatever.

Now, gentlemen, am I speaking reason or am I not speaking reason? Unless all reason and common sense has been banished from the land is it possible that a defence of insanity can be set up in the case of a person of that description? If so, I should like to know what protection there is for society, I should like to know how crimes are to be put down. I should like to know more; I should like to know if the prisoner at the bar is not in law to be held responsible for this crime, who is responsible? He was followed by some six or seven hundred misled and misguided men. Are we to be told that the prisoner at the bar was insane but that his followers were sane? Is there any escape from the one inevitable conclusion either that the prisoner at the bar was perfectly sane and sound in mind or that all the half-breed population of the Saskatchewan were insane. You must have it either one way or the other.

What in reality is the defence set up here; what in reality is the defence which you, as sensible men, are asked to find by your verdict? You are asked to find that six or seven hundred men may get up an armed rebellion with its consequent loss of life, its loss of property, that murder and arson and pillage may be committed by that band of armed men, and we are to be told they are all irresponsible lunatics....

There are, I say, other features connected with the prisoner's conduct which I think ought to be submitted to you to show that his mind was strong and clear, that he was not merely a man of strong mind but unusually long-headed, that he was a man who calculated his schemes and drew his plans with shrewdness, and was controlled by no insane impulse.

In the first place do you think his treatment with regard to the rising of the Indians is a piece of insanity?... Do you think the communications which he sent them were suited to their purpose, were adapted to answer the object he had in view? Or do you think you can discover in any one of these communications the insane ravings of an unsound mind? I shall come to this on another branch of the case in a few minutes....

The only peculiarity in this case is that some eight or nine years ago the prisoner was in a lunatic asylum, and I cannot help saying that the evidence we have had here on that subject was to my mind unsatisfactory. I should like to have known how, and under what circumstances, the prisoner was placed in that asylum, under an assumed name. I should like to know who were responsible for his being placed there. I should like to have seen the register and records which are kept in every asylum from week to week, and I should like to have seen not only why he was received into that asylum, but how he came to be discharged....

I have nothing more to say in that respect except this: It has been said by learned judges over and over again that insanity is not a question which is only decided by experts. Any man of intelligence and sense, and ordinary capacity is said to be a perfectly good witness, and in many respects as capable to decide on cases of insanity as medical experts can be....

The medical experts have none of them had any opportunity of observing the prisoner at the bar and his state of mind at the only time when his state of mind is in question, at the time when his crimes were planned and carried out. Our witnesses are men who saw him at that very time and who observed his demeanor, who had much better opportunities of observing him ...

Gentlemen, as to latent insanity, all I can say is this: There are cases of latent insanity; human nature is always fallible, but if it be possible in any civilized community for a man to go through the career which the prisoner at the bar has had, for a man to exercise all that influence over his fellow-creatures which he has exercised, and if sensible men are then to be told that during that time he was practically irresponsible, then all I can say is that there is no safety for society—can be no safety for society at all. If we are to be told that these six or seven hundred men who entrusted themselves to his guidance were all a band of lunatics, following a lunatic leader, and that they are not responsible for murder, pillage, arson, spread throughout this country, then all we can say is that it is not a country for human beings to live in.

4. Louis Riel, "Statement," *The Queen v. Louis Riel*, 1885

From a Catholic St. Boniface, Manitoba, Métis family, Louis Riel (1844–85) entered a Quebec seminary in 1858 but left in 1864. Returning to Red River in 1868 and insisting on Métis rights, he led the Métis against the transfer of the Hudson's Bay Company's lands to the Canadian government, which ultimately created the province of Manitoba in 1870. Riel fled, fearing arrest for his part in the execution of Thomas Scott that March. Increasing mental instability led to his hospitalization in 1876. Meanwhile, Ottawa offered him amnesty with banishment for five years. Riel became an American citizen in 1883. Persuaded to return to Canada in 1884 to help the Métis in Saskatchewan, he formed a provisional government there on March 19, 1885 but was defeated and surrendered on May 15.

Your Honors, gentlemen of the jury: It would be easy for me today to play insanity, because the circumstances are such as to excite any man, and under the natural excitement of what is taking place today (I cannot speak English very well, but am trying to do so, because most of those here speak English), under the excitement which my trial causes me would justify me not to appear as usual, but with my mind out of its ordinary condition. I hope with the help of God I will maintain calmness and decorum as suits this honorable court, this honorable jury ...

It is true, gentlemen, I believed for years I had a mission, and when I speak of a mission you will understand me not as trying to play the roll of insane before the grand jury so as to have a verdict of acquittal upon that ground. I believe that I have a mission, I believe I had a mission at this very time. What encourages me to speak to you with more confidence in all the imperfections of my English way of speaking, it is that I have yet and still that mission, and with the help of God, who is in this box with me, and He is on the side of my lawyers, even with the honorable court, the Crown and the jury, to help me, and to prove by the extraordinary help that there is a Providence today in my trial, as there was a Providence in the battles of the Saskatchewan ...

Today when I saw the glorious General Middleton bearing testimony that he thought I was not insane, and when Captain Young proved that I am not insane, I felt that God was blessing me, and blotting away from my name the blot resting upon my reputation on account of having been in the lunatic asylum of my good friend Dr Roy. I have been in an asylum, but I thank the lawyers for the Crown who destroyed the testimony of my good friend Dr Roy, because I have always believed that I was put in the asylum without reason. Today my pretension is guaranteed, and that is a blessing too in that way. I have also been in the lunatic asylum at Longue Pointe, and I wonder that my friend Dr Lachapelle, who took care of me charitably, and Dr Howard are not here.

Even if I was going to be sentenced by you, gentlemen of the jury, I have this satisfaction if I die—that if I die I will not be reputed by all men as insane, as a lunatic. A good deal has been said by the two reverend fathers, André and Four-mand. I cannot call them my friends, but they made no false testimony. I know that a long time ago they believed me more or less insane. Father Fourmand said that I would pass from great passion to great calmness. That shows great control under contradiction, and according to my opinion and with the help of God I have that control.

As to religion, what is my belief? What is my insanity about that? My insanity, your Honors, gentlemen of the jury, is that I wish to leave Rome aside, inasmuch as it is the cause of division between Catholics and Protestants. I did not wish to force my views, because in Batoche to the half-breeds that followed me I used the word, *carte blanche*. If I have any influence in the new world it is to help in that way and even if it takes 200 years to become practical, then after my death that will bring out practical results, and then my children's children will shake hands with the Protestants of the new world in a friendly manner. I do not wish these evils which exist in Europe to be continued, as much as I can influence it, among the half-breeds. I do not wish that to be repeated in America. That work is not the work of some days or some years, it is the work of hundreds of years.

My condition is helpless, so helpless that my good lawyers, and they have done it by conviction (Mr Fitzpatrick in his beautiful speech has proved he believed I was insane) my condition seems to be so helpless that they have recourse to try and prove insanity to try and save me in that way. If I am insane, of course I don't know it, it is a property of insanity to be unable to know it. But what is the kind of mission that I have? Practical results. It is said that I had myself acknowledged as a prophet by the half-breeds. The half-breeds have some intelligence. Captain Young who has been so polite and gentle during the time I was under his care, said that what was done at Batoche, from a military point of view was nice, that the line of defence was nice, that showed some intelligence.

It is not to be supposed that the half-breeds acknowledged me as a prophet if they had not seen that I could see something into the future. If I am blessed without measure I can see something into the future, we all see into the future more or less. As what kind of a prophet would I come, would it be a prophet who would all the time have a stick in his hand, and threatening, a prophet of evil? If the half-breeds had acknowledged me as a prophet, if on the other side priests come and say that I am polite, if there are general officers, good men, come into this box and prove that I am polite, prove that I am decent in my manner, in combining all together you have a decent prophet. An insane man cannot withhold his insanity, if I am insane my heart will tell what is in me ...

If it is any satisfaction to the doctors to know what kind of insanity I have, if they are going to call my pretensions insanity, I say humbly, through the grace of God, I believe I am the prophet of the new world.

I wish you to believe that I am not trying to play insanity, there is in the manner, in the standing of a man, the proof that he is sincere, not playing. You will say, what have you got to say? I have to attend to practical results. Is it practical that you be acknowledged as a prophet? It is practical to say it. I think that if the half-breeds have acknowledged me, as a community, to be a prophet, I have reason to believe that it is beginning to become practical. I do not wish, for my satisfaction, the name of prophet, generally that title is accompanied with such a burden, that if there is satisfaction for your vanity, there is a check to it ...

If you take the plea of the defence that I am not responsible for my acts, acquit me completely since I have been quarrelling with an insane and irresponsible Government. If you pronounce in favor of the Crown, which contends that I am responsible, acquit me all the same. You are perfectly justified in declaring that having my reason and sound mind, I have acted reasonably and in self-defence, while the Government, my accuser, being irresponsible, and consequently insane, cannot but have acted wrong, and if high treason there is it must be on its side and not on my part.

... Up to this moment I have been considered by a certain party as insane, by another party as a criminal, by another party as a man with whom it was doubtful whether to have any intercourse. So there was hostility, and there was contempt, and there was avoidance. Today, by the verdict of the court, one of those three situations has disappeared.

I supposed that after having been condemned, I will cease to be called a fool, and for me, it is a great advantage. I consider it as a great advantage. If I have a mission—I say "if," for the sake of those who doubt, but for my part it means "since," since I have a mission, I cannot fulfil my mission as long as I am looked upon as an insane being—human being, as the moment I begin to ascent that scale I begin to succeed.

You have asked me, your Honors, if I have anything to say why my sentence should not be passed. Yes, it is on that point particularly my attention is directed.

Before saying anything about it, I wish to take notice that if there has ever been any contradiction in my life, it is at this moment, and do I appear excited? Am I very irritable? Can I control myself? And it is just on religion and on politics, and I am contradicted at this moment on politics, and the smile that comes to my face is not an act of my will so much as it comes naturally from the satisfaction that I proved that I experienced seeing one of my difficulties disappearing. Should I be executed—at least if I were going to be executed—I would not be executed as an insane man. It would be a great consolation for my mother, for my wife, for my children, for my brothers, for my relatives, even for my protectors, for my countrymen. I thank the gentlemen who were composing the jury for having recommended me to the clemency of the court . . .

Besides clearing me of the stain of insanity, clearing my career of the stain of insanity, I think the verdict that has been given against me is a proof that I am more than ordinary myself, but that the circumstances and the help which is given to me is more than ordinary, are more than ordinary, and although I consider myself only as others, yet by the will of God, by his Providence, by the circumstances which have surrounded me for fifteen years, I think that I have been called on to do something which, at least in the North-West, nobody has done yet. And in some way I think, that, to a certain number of people, the verdict against me to-day is a proof that maybe I am a prophet, maybe Riel is a prophet, he suffered enough for it.

5. Dr. François-Xavier Valade, "Report on the Sanity of Louis Riel," 1885

François-Xavier Valade (1847?–?) was a well-known French-Canadian doctor in Ottawa. Valade was on the federal government payroll after 1884, earning over $1,000 per year testing food samples for the Inland Revenue Department. His testimony on Riel's sanity contradicted his colleagues' and was falsified by the Ministry of Justice in the report submitted to Parliament in 1886 to make it appear that he agreed with the two other examining doctors who found Riel sane.

On the thirty first of October last I was appointed to a medical commission named to investigate the then mental condition of Louis Riel, lying under sentence of death for the crime of High Treason.

. . . On the same afternoon I had occasion to spend about one hour and a half with the prisoner. During this visit after much conversation and having questioned him at length in regard to the northwest troubles and many other matters entirely foreign to that question, I established that Riel was suffering from religious and political hallucinations. Although he was very clear I may even say very rational upon certain questions foreign to what was engrossing his mind, still I assert positively that it was impossible for him to keep up any serious conversation with sustained attention, or to speak upon any moral or philosophical matter without travelling off into vagaries to say the least of it. His prophetic themes, his divine mission, his revelations in regard to the regeneration of the whole world, of the different governments and the northwest in particular, the voices that were speaking to him, and in one word his wild fantasies completely absorbed him ...

He came to us with his book of prophecies wherein he had noted down all his revelations, and with several other documents, two of which I shall quote since they establish to my mind a well defined proof of the politico-religious monomania under which he was really and unfeignedly labouring. Dr. Lavell and I questioned him in turn, upon the northwest troubles and other matters, as we had done on the preceding day. Then as usual, according to the evidence mentioned above, he was at times lucid, rational, and even logical on certain points, but this lucidity and logic lasted for a moment only, his mind would wander at once to his favorite topics and it was then impossible to bring him back to the points. Thus upon Dr. Lavell asking why he had proposed giving up the rebellion if the government would pay him the sum of thirty five thousand dollars, he answered: "Do I inquire of you how you employ your money? Have I not children to educate and provide for?" And on my asking if it were not his intention to return to the States and establish there a great newspaper, "Oh yes," he exclaimed. "This is my divine mission. I must establish a paper for the spread of my views and plans, and with it I must raise an army of twenty or thirty thousand men to carry out my vocation as a Prophet and to reconquer the northwest which I have been chosen to govern." ...

Let us now examine genuine insanity:

1st — From the best information I could collect there have been cases of folly in Louis Riel's family. His mother even is subject to hallucinations.

2nd & 3rd — Riel was confined for four years in two lunatic asylums, which clearly indicates some premonitory symptoms in his case.

4th — These are well defined characteristics of politico-religious monomania.

5th — Riel has on every occasion maintained that he was of thoroughly sound mind, and would become indignant on this point being questioned.

6th — He never attempted to escape, he did the very reverse, and he was constantly proclaiming that he had been unable to prevent the committal of the crime for which he was condemned, since it was in fulfilment of his divine mission.

7th—He constantly argued on the same political and religious questions in presence of doctors and other visitors. Dr. Jukes testifies that he never spoke to him on outside matters.

8th—He was generally indifferent to disastrous consequences of his doings as Dr. Jukes has stated on his testimony, viz: there is one point which struck me: he has given up all interest in anything.

9th—In my opinion there was a marked expression of insanity in his look and manner. In fact, these various signs of insanity were strongly marked in Louis Riel's case.

The lengthy interviews we had together, the perusal of some of his papers besides those cited above, the prisoner's evident and unfeigned conviction in the truth of his revelations, his faith in his prophecies, his excitement, the wildness of expression about his eyes, his excessive action, his dissertations and speeches on the two favorite topics, religion and politics, which were ever uppermost in his thoughts, all this together was sufficient to convince me that Riel was suffering from uncontrollable politico-religious hallucinations....

We have observed and discovered in the conversation and conduct of the prisoner Riel the evidence of fixed delusions, the expressions of which could by no logical sequence be linked on to ideas previously expressed. It is of no consequence that he manifested lucid intervals, and that he could even talk like a philosopher; nor is it of any importance that taking his fixed delusion as a starting point, he could reason logically in that direction; this would only go to prove that the reasoning faculty was not entirely destroyed. A railway train running off the track keeps going for some time.

Besides do not maniacs sometimes give utterance to sensible and even deep sayings in the midst of their ravings: even idiots have now and then lucid intervals. While conversing with monomaniacs they suddenly become incoherent and wild, when a moment before they were rational. It is because they have entered upon the ground of their delusions in spite of every effort to keep them from it. This was precisely Louis Riel's case. It was useful to attempt by interruptions or questions asked in the midst of his disposition on politics and religions, and entirely foreign to these matters, to turn away his thoughts, he was invariably and fatally recalled to his fixed delusion which was ever pursuing and worrying him. Reason and Justice and science agree as to the responsibility of an insane man, calling himself a monomaniac when he acts outside of the range of his delusion but they also agree to free him from all responsibility when he has committed a crime deriving from the very delusion itself.

In conclusion we may state that for the advocates of partial responsibility there exists in the monomaniac two distinct personalities, the one sane, the other insane: now the latter alone is not answerable for his acts, since he has been pushed to commit them by a hallucination, a delirious conception or a delusion.

I have stated that Louis Riel was suffering from political-religious hallucinations but on all other matters, he was responsible for his acts, and could distinguish right from wrong. All this means and meant very clearly that in the sphere of the fixed delusions which were constantly occupying his mind and which were the one theme of his writings, speeches, and conversations, he was not fit to perceive the crime of High Treason of which he had been guilty; and that when I examined him he could not in my humble opinion, distinguish between right and wrong on politico-religious questions.

6. Dr. Daniel Clark, "A Psycho-Medical History of Louis Riel," *Journal of Insanity*, July 1887

Dr. Daniel Clark (1830–1912) came to Upper Canada from Scotland in 1841 and, after a career as a gold miner in California and trainee minister in the Presbyterian church, he completed his medical education and began practicing in 1859. Because of his skill in treating the insane, Clark became medical superintendant of the Asylum for the Insane in Toronto in 1875, a position he held for 30 years. A stickler for detail and evidence, Clark was an esteemed forensic psychiatrist and acted as an expert witness in several cases prior to Riel's case. Clark declared Riel insane and presented a paper on this to the Association of Medical Superintendents of American Institutions for the Insane in 1887.

On July 28, 1885, the writer made a first visit to Riel in the prison at Regina, Northwest Territory. He was found to be a stoutly built man and of splendid physique. He was in good health, about forty-two years of age. He had a swarthy complexion and black eyes of great brilliancy, restless and searching. His movements were nervous, energetic and expressive as are so characteristic of the French. This was evidently a normal condition and not from apprehension as to his fate. He was very talkative, and his egotism made itself manifest, not only in his movements, but also in his expressed pleasure in being the central figure of a State trial, which was likely to become historic. The writer stated to him that his lawyers were trying to save his life by proving that he had been insane. At this statement he got very much excited, and paced up and down his cell like a chained animal until his irons rattled, saying with great vehemence and gesticulation, "My lawyers do wrong to try to prove I am insane. I scorn to put in that plea. I, the leader of my people, the centre of a national movement, a priest and prophet, to be proved to be an idiot. As a prophet, I know beforehand, the jury will acquit me. They will not ignore my rights. I was put in Longue Pointe and Beauport Asylums by my persecutors, and was arrested without cause when discharging my duty. The Lord delivered me out of their hands."

I questioned him very closely as to his plans in the past, but he did not seem to be communicative on these points. He said he would insist on examining the witnesses himself. He did not feel disposed to allow his lawyers to do it for him, if they were determined to try to prove he was insane. During the trial he made several attempts to take the case into his own hands, as in the questioning of witnesses, his importance seemed to be ignored by his counsel. I asked him if he thought he could elicit more on his own behalf than men expert in law could. He proudly said: "I will show you as the case develops." During a long conversation with him, I found him quite rational on subjects outside of those connected with his "mission" and personal greatness. He walks about a good deal as he talked, at the same time putting on his hat and taking it off in a nervous way. His fidgety way, his swagger, his egotistic attitudes, his evident delight at such a trying hour—in being so conspicuous a personage—impressed me very strongly as being so like the insane with delusions of greatness, whether paretics or not. A hundred and one little things in appearance, movement and conversation, which cannot be described in writing, are matters of every day observation by asylum medical officers. I may say they are almost intuitions in this respect. Such knowledge as this, which we acquire by every day acquaintance of the insane, would be laughed out of court by the legal profession, who cannot discern any valid evidence that does not tally with a metaphysical and obsolete definition.

It was evident to me that Riel was concealing to some extent the inner workings of his mind, and that he had an object in view in hiding his thoughts. I endeavored to make him angry by speaking contemptuously of his pretensions. He only shrugged his shoulders and gave me a smile of pity at my ignorance. I touched upon his selfishness in asking $35,000 from the government, and on receipt of it, to cease agitation. He smiled at my charge, and said that the money had been promised to him and was due to him. Had he received it he would have established a newspaper to advocate the rights of his kindred. It would have been a glorious work for him to be able to control a newspaper, and to promulgate in print his mission to the world.

Dr. Roy and myself had a second examination of Riel at the Police Barracks, on the evening of the 28th of July. He was closely catechised by Dr. Roy in French, and by me in English. He evaded giving direct answers to our questions, although he knew we were to give evidence for the defense, if his insanity were a fact. He thanked us for our kindly interest in him, but repudiated our plea with scorn. We took that ground to possibly put him off his guard, but in this he was consistent with himself and his record. We elicited little from him except that great developments, of a national character, were near at hand, according to his prophecy, and he was to be the central moving power. The insanity plea was abhorrent to him, and he scorned to take that ground, even to save his life. Friends and foes were convinced of his honesty and candor in his repudiation of this defense. He would rather die as a deliverer than live as a lunatic.

I had a third visit alone with Riel, in his cell, on the 29th of July. He was very much excited, and paced his narrow enclosure like an enraged tiger would, yet in this mood he said nothing. I accused him of hiding his motives to his own hurt, and told him that his friends from Quebec could do nothing for him because of his obstinacy. Suddenly he calmed down and with great self-possession said: "His legal friends had mistaken his mission. At present he was an important State prisoner, and he was suffering, not only for himself, but also for others." He also told me that he wrote a book which was still in existence. In it he clearly proved that he was a great prophet, and as a prophet he *knew* beforehand that a verdict would be given in his favor. I closely questioned him as to why he thought so, but his only reply was in putting his hand over his heart and saying pathetically, "It is revealed to *me*." I informed him that there was a bitter feeling hostile to him outside, and that so far the evidence was strongly against him and that he would probably be hanged as a felon. He smiled cynically at my ignorance, but the alternative did not seem to affect him. I told him the feeling had not subsided for the murder of Scott, in 1879. In reply he said the Northwest Council sentenced Scott to death for treason. He was only one of thirteen. He suddenly broke away from this subject and began to pour out a torrent of vigorous language on the head of Dr. Steultze, of Winnipeg, whom he associated in some way with Scott and the rebellion of 1870. Before I left he came back to the fulcrum idea that he was yet to be a great political and religious leader, who would revolutionize the world.

These were the notes I took at the time. To me they were significant, but as legal evidence they would be considered of little value.

I wish again to repeat the statement which is a truism to alienists. He had a look and movement so characteristic of insane people, which it is impossible to put in words, but known so well to us. He had that peculiar appearance, which is hard to be described, of a man who is honest and sincere in his insane convictions and statements. There could be no doubt he was stating what he himself believed to be true. In acting as he did he was not a pretender, and did not assume those feelings to his own hurt for the occasion. The most cunning deceiver could not simulate the appearance and actions which he presented. A malingerer would never utter so much wisdom, mixed with so much that showed insanity. Riel's great aim, even at the trial, was to falsify the charge of insanity, and to show by his words his mental capacity to be a leader of men. Anyone who has read his letters and addresses to the jury will see that a great deal of shrewdness, and irony, and sarcasm, of rather an intelligent kind, were mingled with his delusions of greatness. This is perfectly consistent with his form of insanity. Every asylum could produce men and women just as clever, cunning, and able to write as good letters as Riel did, and even hide their delusions when it suits their purpose so to do. His frowns, facial disgust and deprecatory shakes of the head when evidence was given to prove his insanity, and his egotistic walking up and down the dock, with swinging arms and erect head when his sanity was witnessed to, were no actor's part. His actions and speeches carried conviction of their genuineness even to the minds of many who were bitterly hostile to him. Much evidence was given by the Crown after mine was rendered. His two speeches made to the jury and much of his excited conduct in the dock towards the end of his trial impressed me very strongly as to the prisoner's mental unsoundness. His whole aim was to show that he was responsible in all his conduct, and not demented. He was a saviour and leader of his people, and this glorious position was to be taken from him by his friends trying to prove his insanity. He repudiated the plea with scorn....

... It is recorded in law books, and was asserted by a learned Queen's Counsel at the trial, that any ordinary common sense man could detect an insane man as easily as could an expert. Had this sweeping assertion been made of cases of acute mania, there might have been some force in it; but any one who has even a limited experience of the insane knows that there are many phases of insanity in all our asylums which in their subtility and masked form, would baffle the common sense but inexperienced man, and even the legal theorist, with his ethical and antiquated absurdities of definition. I have seen judges, lawyers, and members of grand juries trying their mental acumen at selecting the sane from the insane in our wards, with most ludicrous results. Only a few days before his execution he wrote to his clerical friend in Winnipeg a farewell epistle. It is closely written in French, and contains fourteen pages of foolscap. He knew that his day of doom had come, yet it is full of the old delusions of prophecy and other rubbish concerning his power and greatness. One sentence will suffice as a specimen. He says: "The pope of Rome is in bondage and is surrounded by wicked counsellors. He is, however, not infallible, and the centre of the hierarchy should be located on this continent. I have elected Montreal as its headquarters. In a year of weeks after this change the Papal Sea will be centred in St. Boniface, Manitoba. The new order of things will date from December 8, 1875, and will last four hundred and seventy-five years."

Then again: "Archbishop Bourget told me of my supernatural power on the 18th of December, 1874. I felt it on that day, while I was standing alone on a high hill, near Washington, D.C. A spirit appeared to me and revealed it out of flames and clouds. I was speechless with fear. It said to me, 'Rise, Louis *David* Riel. You have a mission to accomplish for the benefit of humanity.' I received my divine mission with bowed head and uplifted hands. A few nights before this the same spirit told me that the apostolic spirit which was in the late Archbishop Bourget, and who was the pope of the new world, had taken possession of Archbishop Taché. It is to remain with the latter until his death, and then will re-enter the archbishop of Montreal. It will remain in him and his successors for one hundred and fifty-seven years. At the end of that time it will return to the ecclesiastical head of St. Boniface and his successors for 1,876 years."

Such delusional and egotistic nonsense could be quoted to any extent. Enough has been transcribed, not only to show the groove in which his mind ran when these frenzies took hold of him, but also to indicate how consistent throughout his whole career of over a quarter of a century, his mental activity was in respect to the uniformity of these vagaries.

Archbishop Taché, in speaking of Riel and his condition, said: "For many years I have been convinced beyond the possibility of a doubt, that, while endowed with brilliant qualities of mind and heart, the unfortunate leader of the Metis was a prey to what may be termed 'megalomania' and 'theomania,' which alone can explain his way of acting up to the last moments of his life."

The prosecution brought forward a number of witnesses to show that such had known Riel and had conversations with him, but saw no signs of insanity. It need scarcely be said that such *negative* evidence is worthless. A person may be insane and yet *rational*. Such having delusions can mask them with a great deal of shrewdness in ordinary conversation. All asylums have this experience, until some pertinent remark or favorable condition evokes and brings into prominence and activity the abnormal and diseased mental bias. A thousand persons may see no insanity in a patient, but one reliable witness who has seen indubitable evidence of mental alienation, will cancel the whole negation. Leaving out the evidence for the defense altogether, the witnesses for the crown gave facts enough to establish the prisoner's mental unsoundness, at least in the estimation of the writer.

There is no doubt that Riel was responsible for some years, up to the time of the Duck Lake fight. The excitement of that fight caused another attack of insanity, and from that time there is no evidence that he was accountable for what he did. While he was suffering from these attacks he was not responsible for anything he did. I spoke to some of the half-breeds who were in all the engagements with Riel, and they uniformly said he was not the same man after the first fight. He seemed to have changed entirely, and became frenzied. He organized no opposition after this time, did no fighting, but was looked upon as inspired by his deluded followers, and ran about from rifle pit to rifle pit, holding aloft a crucifix, and calling upon the Trinity for aid. The military organizers, leaders and fighters were Dumont and Dumais. These sane, shrewd and brave rebels have been amnestied by our government, but the mental weakling was hanged....

The writer challenged the government to hold a *post mortem* on Riel's brain, and submit it to the examination of any competent pathologist. He was prepared to abide by the opinion and verdict of such an expert. This challenge was made through the press, and especially through the government organ. The writer was sure that organic changes would be found in Riel's brain, even of a gross nature, after such mental storms of a lifetime. The footprints of disease were there, and within that skull was evidence of the prisoner's aberrations. Two medical men were present at his execution, but they also were government officers, under instructions. No *post mortem* of the brain was made. He was buried beside the scaffold where he bravely died. His body was kept under military supervision for about four weeks, and at the expiration of that time it was delivered up to friends. Decomposition had set in, and so the brain records were forever destroyed....

FURTHER READINGS

Barron, F., and J. Waldram. *1885 and After: Native Society in Transition*. Regina: University of Regina Press, 1986.

Beal, B., and R. Macleod. *Prairie Fire: The 1885 North-West Rebellion*. Edmonton: Hurtig, 1984.

Bingaman, S. "The Trials of the 'White Rebels' 1885." *Saskatchewan History* 25 (1972): 41-80.

Brown, D. "The Meaning of Treason in 1885." *Saskatchewan History* 28, 2 (1975): 65-73.

Bowsfield, H., Ed. *Louis Riel: Rebel of the Western Frontier or Victim of Politics and Prejudice?* Toronto: Copp Clark, 1969.

Bowsfield, H., Ed. *Louis Riel: Selected Readings.* Toronto: Copp Clark Pitman, 1988.

Flanagan, T. *Louis "David" Riel: Prophet of the New World.* Toronto: University of Toronto Press, 1979.

Flanagan, T. "Louis Riel: Insanity and Prophecy." In *The Settlement of the West*, ed. H. Palmer. Calgary: Comprint, 1977.

Flanagan, T. *Riel and the Rebellion: 1885 Reconsidered.* Saskatoon: Western Producer, 1983.

Flanagan, T., and N. Watson. "The Riel Trial Revisited." *Saskatchewan History* 34, 2 (1981): 57-73.

Goulet, G. *The Trial of Louis Riel: Justice and Mercy Denied.* Calgary: Tellwell, 1999.

Lee, D. "The Militant Rebels of 1885." *Canadian Ethnic Studies* 21, 3 (1989): 1-19.

McLean, D. *1885: Métis Rebellion or Government Conspiracy?* Winnipeg: Pemmican, 1985.

Morton, D., Ed. *The Queen v. Louis Riel.* Toronto: University of Toronto Press, 1974.

Sprague, D. *Canada and the Métis, 1869-1885.* Waterloo: University of Waterloo Press, 1988.

Stanley, G. *The Birth of Western Canada: A History of the Riel Rebellions.* 3rd ed. Toronto: University of Toronto Press, 1970.

Stanley, G. *Louis Riel.* Toronto: McGraw Hill Ryerson, 1963.

Thomas, L. "A Judicial Murder: The Trial of Louis Riel." In *The Settlement of the West*, ed. H. Palmer. Calgary: Comprint, 1977.

Verdun-Jones, S. "'Not Guilty by Reason of Insanity': The Historical Roots of the Canadian Insanity Defence, 1843-1920." In *Crime and Criminal Justice in Europe and Canada*, ed. L. Knafla. Waterloo: Wilfrid Laurier University Press, 1981.

CHAPTER 3

"Broken Promises"

TREATIES IN THE FAR NORTH

INTRODUCTION

Graphic confrontational scenes from Oka in Quebec to Gustafson Lake in British Columbia remind Canadians that all is not well between the federal government and Canada's First Nations. Much of the problem stems either from the absence of treaties, as in British Columbia, or over the exact terms of what was promised in them where they exist. What did Natives concede? Who controlled the negotiations? Were one culture's concepts successfully transmitted to the other? Was the process equitable? Many Natives now categorically state that treaty-making constituted sanctioned robbery and is therefore illegitimate and invalid. The Manitoba Indian Brotherhood, for example, calls treaties "legal fraud in a very sophisticated manner committed upon unsophisticated, unsuspecting, illiterate, uninformed natives." Others argue that the federal government dealt generously and honourably with Canada's Native people and wished to do right by them, crafting fair treaties under conditions appropriate to the time.

Unsurprisingly, the root of the problem revolves around land ownership, but this concept, in itself, opens a Pandora's box of interpretative problems: how to define what is ostensibly a simple concept, that of "land ownership." Most Native North Americans, and particularly nomadic ones, did not have concepts of "ownership," or possession, in the European sense of the word. Instead, they perceived themselves as custodians of particular pieces of land, which they must pass on, healthy and intact, to future generations of their own people. Stewardship did not mean, according to Indigenous law and custom, that all comers had the right of trespass onto land patrolled by a particular band. On the contrary, apportioned and negotiated land stewardship was every bit as sensitive and complex as European nation-states with their borders, frontier lands, treaties, and disputed bits of territory. The singular difference was that Native people did not perceive that the land they cared for "belonged" to them. Land, to them, could not "belong" to anyone. To European eyes, however, these Natives were not owners—which meant that the land they stewarded was open for settlement.

Europeans believed that all land belonged to *somebody* through inheritance, purchase, secession, conquest, or by any number of other methods.... An owner had proprietary rights to do with his land as he saw fit and, in particular, could prevent ingress of anyone but the invited. That right could be enforced at gunpoint, through the police, or with the national army in sufficiently serious cases.

A cultural clash like this was bound to have a more negative impact on the group for whom "land ownership" *did not* exist because those for whom it *did* had a much easier task of obtaining and holding it. By the time Native people understood the cultural differences it was too late and much of the land they formerly held in trust, as per Native tradition, now belonged to someone else who held it with all the force of British common law. Nor, in European eyes, was the process malicious or illegal. Settlers simply occupied and claimed "un-owned" land.

The process of treaty-making essentially dates to the Royal Proclamation of 1763, which many Native people still perceive as their *Magna Carta*—their guarantee of certain inalienable rights. George III signed the Proclamation after Britain's victory over France in the Seven Years' War. It codified the idea that Native North Americans were the original inhabitants. The importance of this, according to European rules of land ownership, was that unless those original owners willingly gave up that land, it still belonged to them. This concept was further buttressed in the Proclamation when the British Parliament set aside a huge area of land, called the "Indian Territory," for exclusive Native use in perpetuity. The territory encompassed much of present-day central Quebec, the entire Great Lakes basin, and a huge sickle-shaped wedge encircling the New England colonies on the western side of the Appalachian Mountains.

The new United States of America, of course, refused to recognize the Indian Territory, and it disappeared under the feet of hundreds of thousands of Americans tramping west for arable land. British North America, however, continued to live by the

Proclamation in theory. It meant, for example, that when the federal government, immediately after Confederation, wished to settle the prairies with "actual settlers," it first negotiated with the original inhabitants, the Natives living there. The government had to create a document between itself and the various prairie tribes in which the Native people relinquished their right to the land and passed it on to the government in return for promises of land reserved for them ("reservations"), protection from want, medical assistance, and other guarantees of support. These so-named Numbered Treaties essentially transferred the Canadian prairies to government ownership during and after the 1870s and paved the way for Ottawa to go the next step and grant its new land to the flood of immigrants about to pour into the area.

That begs the question: why did Natives peaceably relinquish their entitlement to the land when their compensation seemed such a pittance compared to the millions of acres they gave up? By the end of the nineteenth century, Native people simply did not have a choice. They had no bargaining power. They came to the treaty table facing a much more powerful opponent. A combination of disease and the eradication of the primary food source, the buffalo, meant that the population of prairie Natives was perhaps half what it was at its peak and still declining. The impact of this was both physically and psychologically devastating. On top of that, the Canadian Pacific Railroad now crossed the west, settlers arrived by the thousands, and Canadian Natives saw what happened to their American brethren who tried to resist the westward tide. They died by the thousands in the "Indian Wars," which pit men like Chief Sitting Bull against the American cavalry.

Thus did Canadian Natives agree to transfer their ownership of land. It was not happily, willingly, or without deep suspicion directed at what they perceived as an imperializing power that had brought them to the brink of collapse. It was not by chance that they demanded protection from disease and starvation. These were, after all, the killers that destroyed any chance they had of meeting the federal government as equals around the negotiating table.

Natives who "took treaty" were not compelled to live on the new reservations set aside for them. They were free to leave and to integrate into mainstream society, but doing so lost them many of their treaty guarantees. This was logical because the government keenly sought to "destroy the Indian in the Indian," for his own good, and have him assimilate into European society. Leaving "the res" and renouncing Indian Status, for example, meant gaining the right to vote, that powerful symbol of equality, and receiving land as freehold, just like any other settler. Interestingly though, it did not grant the right to buy alcohol.

Those who took treaty and lived on the new reservations received their treaty guarantees from the local Indian Agent, a bureaucrat appointed by the federal government to administer the treaty for that particular tribe in accordance with the deal it made.

These agents became powerful because they administered federal financial support and implemented the policies of the Department of Indian Affairs. Natives were, for example, encouraged to become farmers and received assistance in the form of tools and cattle to do so. The goal was laudable: self-sufficiency. Further "encouragement" to achieve this was to have treaty guarantees, such as food and medicine, withheld by the local Indian Agent until Natives showed a genuine commitment to farm.

Herein lies one of the perennial problems with treaty-making. The process was, and remains, very paternalistic. George III set the tone in 1763 by referring to the Natives as "my children," and that sentiment remains. Reserve land is still held in trust for Native people by the federal government and does not "belong" to them, except in a very few isolated cases. Thus, Native people do not have the right to do with it as they see fit. This makes them vulnerable and at the mercy of a federal government they see as patronizing, unsympathetic, and capricious.

Treaty-making in Canada's north came later than most elsewhere (except in British Columbia where treaties continue to be negotiated at glacial speed). Why? Because the north was settled as a last resort. It was simply too harsh an environment for all but the hardiest settlers. That meant that northern Native people could look over their shoulders to the precedents set by treaties formulated earlier and hopefully learn from their brethren's mistakes. This helps explain the canniness of Native negotiators and their obvious suspicion toward the dependability of the promises made. The northern economy, too, was very different than elsewhere, being largely dependent on harvesting the area's disappearing fauna rather than flora. This permitted a traditional trap-line lifestyle but generated environmental concerns because of the fragile ecosystem. No wonder later gas exploration became such a contentious issue in areas such as the Mackenzie Delta.

The Métis, too, posed a unique dilemma for treaty-makers. These "Half-breeds" were, after all, not "Natives" and therefore did not fall under the rubric of the Royal Proclamation. Nor were they "original inhabitants." On the other hand, to suggest that they were "European" was ludicrous because most of the northern Métis lived lives more akin to Natives than to Europeans. To compound the complication, Métis and Natives tended to distrust and dislike each other. Thus, at a time when the two groups would have been well served by marshalling their collective strength, they instead divided against each other. This division, of course, assisted the federal government's task.

DISCUSSION POINTS

1. Compare the Treaty Commissioners' perspective of the treaty with the Native understanding of the spirit and terms of the negotiations.

2. Were northern Native people exploited by the treaty process?

3. Based upon prior occupation, Native people insist upon distinct rights, which include variations of local self-government and Indigenous justice systems. Should Canada recognize a unique Native status or is doing so inherently discriminatory and racist?

DOCUMENTS

1. Charles Mair, *Through the Mackenzie Basin*, 1908

Charles Mair (1838 or 1840-1927) was a poet and Canadian nationalist who helped strengthen the Canada First movement and strongly opposed Louis Riel's two rebellions in the Canadian west. Unlike many "Canada Firsters" who wanted Canada to separate from Britain and become completely independent, Mair believed that Canada must remain connected to its former motherland as a mutually supporting partner rather than as a junior quasi-colony. Mair acted as the recording secretary for the scrip commissioners during the 1899 treaty-making process.

...The more immediate motive for treating with the Indians of Athabasca has been already referred to, viz., the discovery of gold in the Klondike, and the astonishing rush of miners and prospectors, in consequence, to the Yukon, not only from the Pacific side, but, east of the mountains, by way of the Peace and Mackenzie rivers. Up to that date, excepting to the fur-traders and a few missionaries, settlers, explorers, geologists and sportsmen, the Peace River region was practically unknown; certainly as little known to the people of Ontario, for example, as was the Red River country thirty years before. It was thought to be a most difficult country to reach—*a terra incognita*—rude and dangerous, having no allurements for the average Canadian, whose notions about it, if he had any, were limited, as usual, to the awe-inspiring legend of "barbarous Indians and perpetual frost."... The gold-seekers, chiefly aliens from the United States, plunged into the wilderness of Athabasca without hesitation, and without as much as "by your leave" to the native. Some of these marauders, as was to be expected, exhibited on the way a congenital contempt for the Indian's rights. At various places his horses were killed, his dogs shot, his bear-traps broken up. An outcry arose in consequence, which inevitably would have led to reprisals and bloodshed had not the Government stepped in and forestalled further trouble by a prompt recognition of the native's title. Hitherto he had been content with his lot in these remote wildernesses, and well might he be!...

But the spirit of change was brooding even here. The moose, the beaver and the bear had for years been decreasing, and other fur-bearing animals were slowly but surely lessening with them. The natives, aware of this, were now alive, as well, to concurrent changes foreign to their experience. Recent events had awakened them to a sense of the value the white man was beginning to place upon their country as a great storehouse of mineral and other wealth, enlivened otherwise by the sensible decrease of their once unfailing resources. These events were, of course, the Government borings for petroleum, the formation of parties to prospect, with a view to developing, the minerals of Great Slave Lake, but, above all, the inroad of gold-seekers by way of Edmonton.

The latter was viewed with great mistrust by the Indians, the outrages referred to showing, like straws in the wind, the inevitable drift of things had the treaties been delayed. For, as a matter of fact, those now peaceable tribes, soured by lawless aggression, and sheltered by their vast forests, might easily have taken an Indian revenge, and hampered, if not hindered, the safe settlement of the country for years to come. The Government, therefore, decided to treat with them at once on equitable terms, and to satisfy their congeners, the half-breeds, as well, by an issue of scrip certificates such as their fellows had already received in Manitoba and the organized Territories.

To this end adjustments were made by the Hon. Clifford Sifton, then Minister of the Interior and Superintendent-General of Indian Affairs, during the winter of 1898-9, and a plan of procedure and basis of treatment adopted, the carrying out of which was placed in the hands of a double Commission, one to frame and effect the Treaty, and secure the adhesion of the various tribes, and the other to investigate and extinguish the half-breed title. At the head of the former was placed the Hon. David Laird, a gentleman of wide experience in the early days in the North-West Territories, whose successful treaty with the refractory Blackfeet and their allies is but one of many evidences of his tact and sagacity....

On the 19th of June our little fleet landed at Willow Point....Tepees were to be seen in all directions from our camp—the lodges of the Indians and half-breeds. But no sooner was the treaty site apparent than a general concentration took place, and we were speedily surrounded by a bustling crowd, putting up trading tents and shacks, dancing booths, eating-places, etc., so that with the motley crowd, including a large number of women and children...

During the previous winter, upon the circulation in the North of the news of the coming treaty, discussion was rife, and every cabin and tepee rang with argument. The wiseacre was not absent, of course, and agitators had been at work for some time endeavouring to jaundice the minds of the people — half-breeds, it was said, from Edmonton, who had been vitiated by contact with a low class of white men there — and, therefore, nothing was as yet positively known as to the temper and views of the Indians. But whatever evil effect these tamperings might have had upon them, it was felt that a plain statement of the proposals of the Government would speedily dissipate it, and that, when placed before them in Mr. Laird's customary kind and lucid manner, they would be accepted by both Indians and half-breeds as the best obtainable, and as conducing in all respects to their truest and most permanent interests...

The crowd of Indians ranged before the marquee had lost all semblance of wildness of the true type. Wild men they were, in a sense, living as they did in the forest and on their great waters. But it was plain that these people had achieved, without any treaty at all, a stage of civilization distinctly in advance of many of our treaty Indians to the south after twenty-five years of education. Instead of paint and feathers, the scalp-lock, the breech-clout, and the buffalo-robe, there presented itself a body of respectable-looking men, as well dressed and evidently quite as independent in their feelings as any like number of average pioneers in the East. Indeed, I had seen there, in my youth, many a time, crowds of white settlers inferior to these in sedateness and self-possession. One was prepared, in this wild region of forest, to behold some savage types of men; indeed, I craved to renew the vanished scenes of old. But, alas! one beheld, instead, men with well-washed, unpainted faces, and combed and common hair; men in suits of ordinary "store-clothes," and some even with "boiled" if not laundered shirts. One felt disappointed, almost defrauded. It was not what was expected, what we believed we had a right to expect, after so much waggoning and tracking and drenching, and river turmoil and trouble. This woeful shortcoming from bygone days attended other aspects of the scene. Instead of fiery oratory and pipes of peace — the stone calumets of old — the vigorous arguments, the outbursts of passion, and close calls from threatened violence, here was a gathering of commonplace men smoking briar-roots, with treaty tobacco instead of "weed," and whose chiefs replied to Mr. Laird's explanations and offers in a few brief and sensible statements, varied by vigorous appeals to the common sense and judgment, rather than the passions, of their people. It was a disappointing, yet, looked at aright, a gratifying spectacle. Here were men disciplined by good handling and native force out of barbarism — of which there was little to be seen — and plainly on the high road to comfort; men who led inoffensive and honest lives, yet who expressed their sense of freedom and self-support in their speech, and had in their courteous demeanour the unmistakable air and bearing of independence. If provoked by injustice, a very dangerous people this; but self-respecting, diligent and prosperous in their own primitive calling, and able to adopt agriculture, or any other pursuit, with a fair hope of success when the still distant hour for it should arrive.

The proceedings began with the customary distribution of tobacco, and by a reference to the competent interpreters who had been appointed by the Commission, men who were residents, and well known to the Indians themselves, and who possessed their confidence. The Indians had previously appointed as spokesman their Chief and head-man, Keenooshayo and Moostoos, a worthy pair of brothers, who speedily exhibited their qualities of good sense and judgment, and, Keenooshayo in particular, a fine order of Indian eloquence....

Mr. Laird then rose, and having unrolled his Commission, and that of his colleagues, from the Queen, proceeded with his proposals. He spoke as follows:

"Red Brothers! we have come here to-day, sent by the Great Mother to treat with you, and this is the paper she has given to us, and is her Commission to us signed with her Seal, to show we have authority to treat with you. The other Commissioners, who are associated with me, and who are sitting here, are Mr. McKenna and Mr. Ross and the Rev. Father Lacombe, who is with us to act as counsellor and adviser. I have to say, on behalf of the Queen and the Government of Canada, that we have come to make you an offer. We have made treaties in former years with all the Indians of the prairies, and from there to Lake Superior. As white people are coming into your country, we have thought it well to tell you what is required of you. The Queen wants all the whites, half-breeds and Indians to be at peace with one another, and to shake hands when they meet. The Queen's laws must be obeyed all over the country, both by the whites and the Indians. It is not alone that we wish to prevent Indians from molesting the whites, it is also to prevent the whites from molesting or doing harm to the Indians. The Queen's soldiers are just as much for the protection of the Indians as for the white man. The Commissioners made an appointment to meet you at a certain time, but on account of bad weather on river and lake, we are late, which we are sorry for, but are glad to meet so many of you here to-day.

"We understand stories have been told you, that if you made a treaty with us you would become servants and slaves; but we wish you to understand that such is not the case, but that you will be just as free after signing a treaty as you are now. The treaty is a free offer; take it or not, just as you please. If you refuse it there is no harm done; we will not be bad friends on that account. One thing Indians must understand, that if they do not make a treaty they must obey the laws of the land — that will be just the same whether you make a treaty or not; the laws must be obeyed. The Queen's Government wishes to give the Indians here the same terms as it has given all the Indians all over the country, from the prairies to Lake Superior. Indians in other places, who took treaty years ago, are now better off than they were before. They grow grain and raise cattle like the white people. Their children have learned to read and write.

"Now, I will give you an outline of the terms we offer you. If you agree to take treaty, everyone this year gets a present of $12.00. A family of five, man, wife and three children, will thus get $60.00; a family of eight, $96.00; and after this year, and for every year afterwards, $5.00 for each person forever. To such chiefs as you may select, and that the Government approves of, we will give $25.00 each year, and the counsellors $15.00 each. The chiefs also get a silver medal and a flag, such as you see now at our tent, right now as soon as the treaty is signed. Next year, as soon as we know how many chiefs there are, and every three years thereafter, each chief will get a suit of clothes, and every counsellor a suit, only not quite so good as that of the chief. Then, as the white men are coming in and settling in the country, and as the Queen wishes the Indians to have lands of their own, we will give one square mile, or 640 acres, to each family of five; but there will be no compulsion to force Indians to go into a reserve. He who does not wish to go into a band can get 160 acres of land for himself, and the same for each member of his family. These reserves are holdings you can select where you please, subject to the approval of the Government, for you might select lands which might interfere with the rights or lands of settlers. The Government must be sure that the land which you select is in the right place. Then, again, as some of you may want to sow grain or potatoes, the Government will give you ploughs or harrows, hoes, etc., to enable you to do so, and every spring will furnish you with provisions to enable you to work and put in your crop. Again, if you do not wish to grow grain, but want to raise cattle, the Government will give you bulls and cows, so that you may raise stock. If you do not wish to grow grain or raise cattle, the Government will furnish you with ammunition for your hunt, and with twine to catch fish. The Government will also provide schools to teach your children to read and write, and do other things like white men and their children. Schools will be established where there is a sufficient number of children. The Government will give the chiefs axes and tools to make houses to live in and be comfortable. Indians have been told that if they make a treaty they will not be allowed to hunt and fish as they do now. This is not true. Indians who take treaty will be just as free to hunt and fish all over as they now are.

"In return for this the Government expects that the Indians will not interfere with or molest any miner, traveller or settler. We expect you to be good friends with every-one, and shake hands with all you meet. If any whites molest you in any way, shoot your dogs or horses, or do you any harm, you have only to report the matter to the police, and they will see that justice is done to you. There may be some things we have not mentioned, but these can be mentioned later on. Commissioners Walker and Cote are here for the half-breeds, who later on, if treaty is made with you, will take down the names of half-breeds and their children, and find out if they are entitled to scrip. The reason the Government does this is because the half-breeds have Indian blood in their veins, and have claims on that account. The Government does not make treaty with them, as they live as white men do, so it gives them scrip to settle their claims at once and forever. Half-breeds living like Indians have the chance to take the treaty instead, if they wish to do so. They have their choice, but only after the treaty is signed. If there is no treaty made, scrip cannot be given. After the treaty is signed, the Commissioners will take up half-breed claims. The first thing they will do is to give half-breed settlers living on land 160 acres, if there is room to do so; but if several are settled close together, the land will be divided between them as fairly as possible. All, whether settled or not, will be given scrip for land to the value of $240.00, that is, all born up to the date of signing the treaty. They can sell that scrip, that is, all of you can do so. They can take, if they like, instead of this scrip for 240 acres, lands where they like. After they have located their land, and got their title, they can live on it, or sell part, or the whole of it, as they please, but cannot sell the scrip. They must locate their land, and get their title before selling.

"These are the principal points in the offer we have to make to you. The Queen owns the country, but is willing to acknowledge the Indians' claims, and offers them terms as an offset to all of them. We shall be glad to answer any questions, and make clear any points not understood. We shall meet you again to-morrow, after you have considered our offer, say about two o'clock, or later if you wish. We have other Indians to meet at other places, but we do not wish to hurry you. After this meeting you can go to the Hudson's Bay fort, where our provisions are stored, and rations will be issued to you of flour, bacon, tea and tobacco, so that you can have a good meal and a good time. This is a free gift, given with goodwill, and given to you whether you make a treaty or not. It is a present the Queen is glad to make to you. I am now done, and shall be glad to hear what any one has to say."

KEENOOSHAYO (The Fish): "You say we are brothers. I cannot understand how we are so. I live differently from you. I can only understand that Indians will benefit in a very small degree from your offer. You have told us you come in the Queen's name. We surely have also a right to say a little as far as that goes. I do not understand what you say about every third year."

MR. MCKENNA: "The third year was only mentioned in connection with clothing."

KEENOOSHAYO: "Do you not allow the Indians to make their own conditions, so that they may benefit as much as possible? Why I say this is that we to-day make arrangements that are to last as long as the sun shines and the water runs. Up to the present I have earned my own living and worked in my own way for the Queen. It is good. The Indian loves his way of living and his free life. When I understand you thoroughly I will know better what I shall do. Up to the present I have never seen the time when I could not work for the Queen, and also make my own living. I will consider carefully what you have said."

MOOSTOOS (The Bull): "Often before now I have said I would carefully consider what you might say. You have called us brothers. Truly I am the younger, you the elder brother. Being the younger, if the younger ask the elder for something, he will grant his request the same as our mother the Queen. I am glad to hear what you have to say. Our country is getting broken up. I see the white man coming in, and I want to be friends. I see what he does, but it is best that we should be friends. I will not speak any more. There are many people here who may wish to speak."...

THE CAPTAIN (an old man): "I accept your offer. I am old and miserable now. I have not my family with me here, but I accept your offer."

MR. LAIRD: "You will get the money for all your children under age, and not married, just the same as if they were here."

THE CAPTAIN: "I speak for all those in my part of the country."

MR. LAIRD: "I am sorry the rest of your people are not here. If here next year their claims will not be overlooked."

THE CAPTAIN: "I am old now. It is indirectly through the Queen that we have lived. She has supplied in a manner the sale shops through which we have lived. Others may think I am foolish for speaking as I do now. Let them think as they like. I accept. When I was young I was an able man and made my living independently. But now I am old and feeble and not able to do much."

MR. ROSS: "...Keenooshayo has said that he cannot see how it will benefit you to take treaty. As all the rights you now have will not be interfered with, therefore anything you get in addition must be a clear gain. The white man is bound to come in and open up the country, and we come before him to explain the relations that must exist between you, and thus prevent any trouble. You say you have heard what the Commissioners have said, and how you wish to live. We believe that men who have lived without help heretofore can do it better when the country is opened up. Any fur they catch is worth more. That comes about from competition. You will notice that it takes more boats to bring in goods to buy your furs than it did formerly. We think that as the rivers and lakes of this country will be the principal highways, good boatmen, like yourselves, cannot fail to make a good living, and profit from the increase in traffic. We are much pleased that you have some cattle. It will be the duty of the Commissioners to recommend the Government, through the Superintendent-General of Indian Affairs, to give you cattle of a better breed. You say that you consider that you have a right to say something about the terms we offer you. We offer you certain terms, but you are not forced to take them. You ask if Indians are not allowed to make a bargain. You must understand there are always two to a bargain. We are glad you understand the treaty is forever. If the Indians do as they are asked we shall certainly keep all our promises. We are glad to know that you have got on without any one's help, but you must know times are hard, and furs scarcer than they used to be. Indians are fond of a free life, and we do not wish to interfere with it. When reserves are offered you there is no intention to make you live on them if you do not want to, but, in years to come, you may change your minds, and want these lands to live on. The half-breeds of Athabasca are being more liberally dealt with than in any other part of Canada. We hope you will discuss our offer and arrive at a decision as soon as possible. Others are now waiting for our arrival, and you, by deciding quickly, will assist us to get to them.". . .

KEENOOSHAYO: "Are the terms good forever? As long as the sun shines on us? Because there are orphans we must consider, so that there will be nothing to be thrown up to us by our people afterwards. We want a written treaty, one copy to be given to us, so we shall know what we sign for. Are you willing to give means to instruct children as long as the sun shines and water runs, so that our children will grow up ever increasing in knowledge?"

MR. LAIRD: "The Government will choose teachers according to the religion of the band. If the band are pagans the Government will appoint teachers who, if not acceptable, will be replaced by others. About treaties lasting forever, I will just say that some Indians have got to live so like the whites that they have sold their lands and divided the money. But this only happens when the Indians ask for it. Treaties last forever, as signed, unless the Indians wish to make a change. I understand you all agree to the terms of the Treaty. Am I right? If so, I will have the Treaty drawn up, and to-morrow we will sign it. Speak, all those who do not agree!"

MOOSTOOS: "I agree."

KEENOOSHAYO: "My children, all who agree, stand up!"

The Reverend Father Lacombe then addressed the Indians in substance as follows: He reminded them that he was an old friend, and came amongst them seven years ago, and, being now old, he came again to fulfil another duty, and to assist the Commission to make a treaty. "Knowing you as I do, your manners, your customs and language, I have been officially attached to the Commission as adviser. To-day is a great day for you, a day of long remembrance, and your children hereafter will learn from your lips the events of to-day. I consented to come here because I thought it was a good thing for you to take the Treaty. Were it not in your interest I would not take part in it. I have been long familiar with the Government's methods of making treaties with the Saulteaux of Manitoba, the Crees of Saskatchewan, and the Blackfeet, Bloods and Piegans of the Plains, and advised these tribes to accept the offers of the Government. Therefore, to-day, I urge you to accept the words of the Big Chief who comes here in the name of the Queen. I have known him for many years, and, I can assure you, he is just and sincere in all his statements, besides being vested with authority to deal with you. Your forest and river life will not be changed by the Treaty, and you will have your annuities, as well, year by year, as long as the sun shines and the earth remains. Therefore I finish my speaking by saying, Accept!"...

At three p.m. on Wednesday, the 21st, the discussion was resumed by Mr. Laird, who, after a few preliminary remarks read the Treaty, which had been drafted by the Commissioners the previous evening. Chief Keenooshayo arose and made a speech, followed by Moostoos, both assenting to the terms, when suddenly, and to the surprise of all, the chief, who had again begun to address the Indians, perceiving gestures of dissent from his people, suddenly stopped and sat down. This looked critical; but, after a somewhat lengthy discussion, everything was smoothed over, and the chief and head men entered the tent and signed the Treaty after the Commissioners, thus confirming, for this portion of the country, the great Treaty which is intended to cover the whole northern region up to the sixtieth parallel of north latitude. The satisfactory turn of the Lesser Slave Lake Treaty, it was felt, would have a good effect elsewhere, and that, upon hearing of it at the various treaty points to the west and north, the Indians would be more inclined to expedite matters, and to close with the Commissioner's proposals....

On the 8th July, Mr. Laird secured the adhesion of the Crees and Beavers at Fort Vermilion, and Messrs. Ross and McKenna of those at Little Red River, the headman there refusing to sign at first because, he said, "he had a divine inspiration to the contrary"! This was followed by adhesions taken by the latter Commissioners, on the 13th, from the Crees and Chipewyans at Fort Chipewyan.

"Here it was," Mr. McKenna writes me, "that the chief asked for a rail-way—the first time in the history of Canada that the red man demanded as a condition of cession that steel should be laid into his country. He evidently understood the transportation question, for a railway, he said, by bringing them into closer connection with the market, would enhance the value of what they had to sell, and decrease the cost of what they had to buy. He had a striking object-lesson in the fact that flour was $12 a sack at the Fort. These Chipewyans lost no time in flowery oratory, but came at once to business, and kept us, myself in particular, on tenterhooks for two hours. I never felt so relieved as when the rain of questions ended, and, satisfied by our answers, they acquiesced in the cession."

Next morning these Commissioners left for Smith's Landing, and, on the 17th, made treaty with the Indians of Great Slave Lake. Meanwhile Mr. Laird had proceeded to Fond du Lac, at the eastern end of Lake Athabasca, and there, on the 27th, the Chipewyans adhered, whilst Messrs. Ross and McKenna, in order to treat with the Indians at Fort McMurray and Wahpooskow, separated. The latter secured the Chipewyans and Crees at the former post, and Mr. Ross the Crees at Wahpooskow, both adjustments, by a coincidence, being made on the same day....

There were, of course, many Indians who did not or could not turn up at the various treaty points that year, viz., the Beavers of St. John, the Crees of Sturgeon Lake, the Slaves of Hay River, who should have come to Vermilion, and the Dog-Ribs, Yellow-Knives, Slaves, and Chipewyans, who should have been treated with at Fort Resolution, on Great Slave Lake.

Accordingly, a special commission was issued to Mr. J. A. Macrae, of the Indian Office in Ottawa, who met the Indians the following year at the points named, and in May, June, and July, secured the adhesion of over 1,200 souls, making, with subsequent adhesions, a total of 3,568 souls to the 30th June, 1906.

The largest numbers were at Forts Resolution, Vermilion, Fond du Lac, and Lesser Slave Lake, the latter ranking fourth in the list...

2. "Report of the Treaty Commission," September 22, 1899

From May 29, 1899 and through that summer, the federal government's Treaty Commission travelled through northern Alberta and the Northwest Territories making treaties with local Native bands. David Laird, the former Minster of Indian Affairs and Lieutenant-Governor of the Northwest Territories, led the Commission, which also included James Ross and J.A. McKenna. Scrip commissioners were J.A. Cote and Major James Walker with Charles Mair as secretary; they were accompanied by other officials and observers. What follows is part of the Commission's final report.

SIR, ... We met the Indians on the 20th, and on the 21st the treaty was signed.... There was a marked absence of the old Indian style of oratory. Only among the

Wood Crees were any formal speeches made, and these were brief. The Beaver Indians are taciturn. The Chipewyans confined themselves to asking questions and making brief arguments. They appeared be more adept at cross-examination than at speech-making, and those at Fort Chipewyan displayed considerable keenness of intellect and much practical sense in pressing the claims of his band. They all wanted as liberal, if not more liberal terms, than were granted to the Indians of the plains. Some expected to be fed by the Government after the making of treaty, and all asked for assistance in seasons of distress and urged that the old and indigent who were no longer able to hunt and trap and were consequently often in distress should be cared for by the Government. They requested that medicines be furnished. At Vermilion, Chipewyan and Smith's Landing, an earnest appeal was made for the services of a medical man. There was expressed at every point the fear that the making of the treaty would be followed by the curtailment of the hunting and fishing privileges, and many were impressed with the notion that the treaty would lead to taxation and enforced military service. They seemed desirous of securing educational advantages for their children, but stipulated that in the matter of schools there should be no interference with their religious beliefs.

We pointed out that the Government could not undertake to maintain Indians in idleness; that the same means of earning a livelihood would continue after the treaty as existed before it, and that the Indians would be expected to make use of them. We told them that the Government was always ready to give relief in cases of actual destitution, and that in seasons of distress they would without any special stipulation in the treaty receive such assistance as it was usual to give in order to prevent starvation among Indians in any part of Canada; and we stated that the attention of the Government would be called to the need of some special provision being made for assisting the old and indigent who were unable to work and dependent on charity for the means of sustaining life. We promised that supplies of medicines would be put in the charge of persons selected by the Government at different points, and would be distributed free to those of the Indians who might require them. We explained that it would be practically impossible for the Government to arrange for regular medical attendance upon Indians so widely scattered over such an extensive territory. We assured them, however, that the Government would always be ready to avail itself of any opportunity of affording medical service just as it provided that the physician attached to the Commission should give free attendance to all Indians whom he might find in need of treatment as he passed through the country.

Our chief difficulty was the apprehension that the hunting and fishing privileges were to be curtailed. The provision in the treaty under which ammunition and twine is to be furnished went far in the direction of quieting the fears of the Indians, for they admitted that it would be unreasonable to furnish the means of hunting and fishing if laws were to be enacted which would make hunting and fishing so restricted as to render it impossible to make a livelihood by such pursuits. But over and above the provision, we had to solemnly assure them that only such laws as to hunting and fishing as were in the interest of the Indians and were found necessary in order to protect the fish and fur-bearing animals would be made, and that they would be as free to hunt and fish after the treaty as they would be if they never entered into it.

We assured them that the treaty would not lead to any forced interference with their mode of life, that it did not open the way to the imposition of any tax, and that there was no fear of enforced military service. We showed them that, whether treaty was made or not, they were subject to law, bound to obey it, and liable to punishment for any infringements of it. We pointed out that the law was designed for the protection of all, and must be respected by all the inhabitants of the country, irrespective of colour or origin; and that, in requiring them to live at peace with white men who came into the country, and not to molest them in person or in property, it only required them to do what white men were required to do as to the Indians.

As to education, the Indians were assured that there was no need of any special stipulation, as it was the policy of the Government to provide in every part of the country, as far as circumstances would permit, for the education of Indian children, and that the law, which was as strong as a treaty, provided for non-interference with the religion of the Indians in schools maintained or assisted by the Government.

We should add that the chief of the Chipewyans of Fort Chipewyan asked that the Government should undertake to have a railway built into the country, as the cost of goods which the Indians require would be thereby cheapened and the prosperity of the country enhanced. He was told that the Commissioners had no authority to make any statement in the matter further than to say that his desire would be made known to the Government.

When we conferred, after the first meeting with the Indians at Lesser Slave Lake, we came to the conclusion that it would be best to make one treaty covering the whole of the territory ceded, and to take adhesions thereto from the Indians to be met at the other points rather than to make several separate treaties. The treaty was therefore so drawn as to provide three ways in which assistance is to be given to the Indians, in order to accord with the conditions of the country and to meet the requirements of the Indians in the different parts of the territory.

In addition to the annuity, which we found it necessary to fix at the figures of Treaty Six, which covers adjacent territory, the treaty stipulates that assistance in the form of seed and implements and cattle will be given to those of the Indians who may take to farming, in the way of cattle and mowers to those who may devote themselves to cattle-raising, and that ammunition and twine will be given to those who continue to fish and hunt. The assistance in farming and ranching is only to be given when the Indians actually take to these pursuits, and it is not likely that for many years there will be a call for any considerable expenditure under these heads. The only Indians of the territory ceded who are likely to take to cattle-raising are those about Lesser Slave Lake and along the Peace River, where there is quite an extent of ranching country; and although there are stretches of cultivable land in those parts of the country, it is not probable that the Indians will, while present conditions obtain, engage in farming further than the raising of roots in a small way, as is now done to some extent. In the main the demand will be for ammunition and twine, as the great majority of the Indians will continue to hunt and fish for a livelihood. It does not appear likely that the conditions of the country on either side of the Athabasca and Slave Rivers or about Athabasca Lake will be so changed as to affect hunting or trapping, and it is safe to say that so long as the fur-bearing animals remain, the great bulk of the Indians will continue to hunt and to trap.

The Indians are given the option of taking reserves or land in severalty. As the extent of the country treated for made it impossible to define reserves or holdings, and as the Indians were not prepared to make selections, we confined ourselves to an undertaking to have reserves and holdings set apart in the future, and the Indians were satisfied with the promise that this would be done when required. There is no immediate necessity for the general laying out of reserves or the allotting of land. It will be quite time enough to do this as advancing settlement makes necessary the surveying of the land. Indeed, the Indians were generally averse to being placed on reserves. It would have been impossible to have made a treaty if we had not assured them that there was no intention of confining them to reserves. We had to very clearly explain to them that the provision for reserves and allotments of land were made for their protection, and to secure to them in perpetuity a fair portion of the land ceded, in the event of settlement advancing…

The Indians with whom we treated differ in many respects from the Indians of the organized territories. They indulge in neither paint nor feathers, and never clothe themselves in blankets. Their dress is of the ordinary and many of them were well clothed. In the summer they live in teepees, but many of them have log houses in which they live in winter. The Cree language is the chief language of trade, and some of the Beavers and Chipewyans speak it in addition to their own tongues. All the Indians we met were with rare exceptions professing Christians, and showed evidences of the work which missionaries have carried on among them for many years. A few of them have had their children avail themselves of the advantages afforded by boarding schools established at different missions. None of the tribes appear to have any very definite organization. They are held together mainly by the language bond. The chiefs and headmen are simply the most efficient hunters and trappers. They are not law-makers and leaders in the sense that the chiefs and headmen of the plains and of old Canada were. The tribes have no very distinctive characteristics, and as far as we could learn no traditions of any import. The Wood Crees are an off-shoot of the Crees of the South. The Beaver Indians bear some resemblance to the Indians west of the mountains. The Chipewyans are physically the superior tribe. The Beavers have apparently suffered most from scrofula and phthisis, and there are marks of these diseases more or less among all the tribes.

Although in manners and dress the Indians of the North are much further advanced in civilization than other Indians were when treaties were made with them, they stand as much in need of the protection afforded by the law to aborigines as do any other Indians of the country, and are as fit subjects for the paternal care of the Government...

3. Susie (Joseph) Abel

Susie (Joseph) Abel (1888–1968 or 1969) was a Dogrib chief. He lived in the Yellowknife area. No further information is available.

...The Agent walked up to meet us. He said, "I'm pleased to see all this bunch. It is late in the season. I was afraid everyone had left for the bush. On the Queen's word I have come with money. I'm going to issue the money to all the Indians. I am pleased that lots of people are still here." And one of the Indian leaders told the Agent, "You are glad to meet us. But everyone is pretty near starving. We were supposed to leave the fort. But we heard you were coming, so we've been waiting without food." The Agent said, "I haven't got much food, but I brought some flour and bacon. I can give you some flour and bacon for the kids and old people. It is late now, so we won't talk more. But I will give you 700 pounds of flour and 300 pounds of bacon. You can divide it among yourselves."

So the Indians took the flour. One of the leaders gave it out to all the people. They opened the sacks and gave a cup to every person. In those days we didn't have many dishes. So some guys took their shirts off and they took the flour in their shirts. But some, even in their camp had nothing to put the flour in. Some women—in those days they wore aprons—they picked up their aprons to put the flour in. Someone cut the bacon. They threw it in the apron on top of the flour. When they had given out all the flour and bacon, everyone was so happy, they were frying bacon and cooking bannock. You could hardly see all night from the smoke of the frying bacon.

The Agent said, "Tomorrow, I am going to put up a tent. We will have a meeting before I give money. Everyone—old, young—has got to come and hear what is said." So the Indians went back to their tents, and the Agent went back to the scow. . . .

In the morning, the Agent put up a tent. We had never seen a one-pole tent before. It was a great big one. Everyone went over to listen. When we got to the tent there was a table and chairs for the Agent and the interpreter. We sat on the ground on one side. The Treaty Commissioner said, "We don't come to make trouble. We come for peace and to talk about money. We come for peace. From now on, there will be lots of White men. So if the White men come you will treat them just like your own brothers. And the White men, if they see a poor Indian in trouble, they will help, just like he was their own brother. That is why we came here. There will be lots of Metis later on. From now on White men and Indians are going to be like one family. That is why I tell you this. We have never talked about this before, and you will remember it. That is why I brought this money."

An Indian by the name of N'doah said, "Funny, this is the first time we have gotten free money." None of the Indians liked the way N'doah sounded (they were afraid he would make trouble). So they said that they were going to take another man to speak. So they took Old Drygeese for the Indians. The old people said, "Andare Wetah (Old Drygeese) is the man to talk for us." And Andare Wetah said, "All right, I will talk for you."

Drygeese said, "This money never happened before, so we want to know if something will be changed later. If it is going to change, if you want to change our lives, then it is no use taking treaty, because without treaty we are making a living for ourselves and our families."

The Agent said, "We are not looking for trouble. It will not change your life. We are just making peace between Whites and Indians for them to treat each other well. And we do not want to change your hunting. If Whites should prospect, stake claims, that will not harm anyone. I have come here to issue this money that is all."

So Drygeese said, "All right, if you're going to give us money. But before you issue money I want you to sign what you said and let me have one copy of what you sign."

Big Michel, Michel Mandeville, was interpreter. He was a good interpreter.

Drygeese said, "We won't stop you from giving us treaty, but we are going to have a meeting amongst ourselves, especially the old people, today. So if you want to give treaty, it will have to be tomorrow."

So everyone went home. The old people were talking amongst themselves. I [Susie Abel] didn't follow the old people, because I was just a young man, so I didn't know what they talked about.

The next day they came back to the tent for treaty. When they had all gathered, Drygeese spoke to the Agent, "Don't hide anything that I don't hear. Maybe later on you are going to stop us from hunting or trapping or chopping trees down or something. So tell me the truth. I want to know before we take treaty." The Agent said, "I do what I am told—give you fellows money. There will be no trouble for anybody. We will not stop anything."

Drygeese said, "If that's the way it is, I want to tell you something. As you have said, 'As long as the world does not change, the sun does not change, the river does not change, we will like to have peace—if it is that way, we will take the money and I want you the Agent to sign that that is the way it is going to be." ... "I would like a written promise from you to prove you are not taking our land away from us." ... Then Chief Drygeese said, "There will be no closed season on our land. There will be nothing said about the land. I may be the Chief, but I would like to hear what my people have to say." All the people agreed.

The Agent said, "OK." So he signed the paper. So they gave us the money now.

The Agent gave Drygeese one sheet, and there was a sheet for the Agent, and one for the Hudson's Bay man to keep. The Agent signed four sheets.

That was the first time we saw money. Every person got $12.00, even the kids. [I] was a young man then—and in those days, if your dad was alive you were not the boss and your Dad did all the trading—that is, collected the money in this case.

In those days, we never saw cash before, we just traded. We didn't know how to use it. So the trader told the Indians, "If you want to spend money in here, the money you got for your whole family, if you spend it here (in my store), I'm going to give you extra goods, maybe $10 or $15 extra."

There were two stores, Northern Traders, and the Hudson's Bay Company. So the Indians didn't know how to handle the money. They just took $1 to buy this, another $1 to buy that. So that's why the trader offered us maybe $25 or so in extra goods, if we spent it all in his store.

So they gave us treaty. And they picked up all the Chiefs and Councillors from all over. They put Drygeese as head Chief [that is, for the Dogrib Band], and next is Benaiyah, and the next is Sek'eglinan. These were the three Chiefs for Wuledeh [Yellowknife River Dogrib Band].

4. Ted Trindel, Testimony on Treaty #11 Signed at Fort Simpson, July 11th, 1921

Ted Trindel (1901–?) was a Métis from the Mackenzie. He and three other Fort Simpson residents later testified before Justice Morrow on the creation of Treaty 11, signed between 347 Natives from the Fort Simpson area and the federal government on July 11, 1921. No further information is known about him.

In those days, if you promise an Indian something for nothing, he'll jump at it. He doesn't think of tomorrow as Today. The Treaty had been going on in the South already, with all the laws and acts and everything was already marked which they didn't show to these Indians. All they wanted was to give them five dollars to protect them against the White man when the White man comes into the country like what is happening now. And I don't see any protection yet.... They [the Indians] didn't know what the White man was or anything else. So I don't see how you can judge those days with all the laws and stuff today. It was just like taking candy from a baby.

And old Norwegian they wanted him to be the Chief to take the Treaty, but he said no because he didn't understand what it was all about.

There was ... old Nakekon ... when they promised him an outfit or that they would take good care of him, that was just in line with him.

The Indians didn't know what treaty was. In fact, I swear they didn't know what it was all about. All they knew was, sort of peace way, so that there would be no more fighting. Finally they took the Treaty and the Treaty party told them that they could carry on hunting as they wished. But then again in the Treaty book it says that you'll be subject to the Law, and it says that after the Treaty you had to abide by whatever rules come along, but at Treaty time the Treaty party didn't tell them that. It was still your country. The Treaty was more or less to keep peace in the family. In fact the Indians didn't realize that they were signing their rights over. In other words, can you make a deal with a five year old baby? The Indian was smart in the bush, but as far as civilization was concerned, he had no more idea than a two year old baby. At the time of the Treaty in the North I would swear that the Indian didn't know what he was doing. But the White man knew what he was doing.

The Treaty meeting lasted about a week. Fort Providence was the same. Like old Squirrel told me, the Indians asked the Treaty party why they gave them treaty but Conroy wouldn't tell them why. They got treaty but they wouldn't tell them why. How can an Indian accept anything when he knows nothing about the White man. The Indian is just a bush man.

Archie Gardner was the interpreter. And Bishop Breynat was there. Archie was a good interpreter. Naturally the Indians had his influence. I don't know what Bishop Breynat said or did, but there were a lot of Catholics so when the Bishop told them it was O.K. I guess they agreed that it was O.K.

All the people knew was that they got treaty and that they would be helped. That's all there was to it. They weren't convinced one way or the other ...

I'm just saying what I think. I'm not for and I'm not against it. Even if I was Treaty, what could I do?

To a White man, yes, the deal is there. But for an Indian, what did he know about that? Because he had no idea of what was going on, he didn't know what law was, he didn't know what a deal was, he didn't know what a contract was.

It's a big thing as far as I'm concerned. We were told about the Treaty to protect us against the invasion. And that's all it was—to protect the Indians and to keep them. That was the deal. But overall, as far as land, they didn't know that they were signing their rights over, they didn't know anything about minerals, oil or gold. If they'd seen gold they wouldn't know what it was.

At the time, people like me didn't realize what was going on. They had been paying in the South. All the rules, acts and laws were already ready. And they go by that, come down here—what did Mr. Indian in the Mackenzie know about law or treaty or anything else?

In fact I remember when there was no policeman here, no law. You just lived as you were. So the people who took the Treaty pretty well didn't know anything about the White man's way, law, or anything else.

FURTHER READINGS

Aasen, W. *The Spirit and Intent of Treaty 8 in the Northwest Territories: As Long As the Sun Shines, the River Flows, and the Grass Grows*. Yellowknife: Treaty 8 Tribal Council, 1994.

Abel, K. *Drum Songs: Glimpses of Dene History*. Montreal and Kingston: McGill-Queen's University Press, 1993.

Alberta. *As Long As the Sun Shines, the Rivers Flow, and the Grass Grows*. Edmonton: Government of Alberta, 1977.

Bell, C. "*R. v. Badger*: One Step Forward and Two Steps Back?" *Constitutional Forum* 8 (1997): 21-26.

British Columbia Hydro and Power Authority. *Indian Reserves and Indian Treaty Problems in Northeastern BC*. British Columbia: British Columbia Hydro and Power Authority, 1981.

Brody, H. *Maps and Dreams: Indians and the British Columbia Frontier*. Vancouver: Douglas and McIntyre, 1988.

Cardinal, H. *Treaty 8: A Case Study*. Ottawa: Royal Commission on Aboriginal Peoples, 1993.

Coates, K. *Best Left As Indians: The Federal Government and the Indians of the Yukon, 1894-1950*. Montreal and Kingston: McGill-Queen's University Press, 1991.

Coates, K. "Best Left As Indians: The Federal Government and the Indians of the Yukon, 1894-1950." *Canadian Journal of Native Studies* 4, 2 (1984): 179-204.

Coates, K., and W. Morrison. *Treaty Research Report: Treaty Eleven (1921): Rapport D'étude Sur Les Traités: Traité No 11 (1921)*. Ottawa: Treaties and Historical Research Centre, Department of Indian Affairs and Northern Development, 1987.

Crerar, D., and J. Petryshyn, Eds. *Treaty 8 Revisited: Selected Papers on the 1999 Centennial Conference*. Grand Prairie: Lobstick, 2000.

Deh Cho Tribal Council. *"It Was Only A Treaty": Treaty 11 According to the Dene of the Mackenzie Valley.* Ottawa: Royal Commission on Aboriginal Peoples, 1993.

Drees, L. "Citizenship and Treaty Rights: The Indian Association of Alberta and the Canadian Indian Act, 1946-1948." *Great Plains Quarterly* 20, 2 (2000): 141-58.

Dyck, N. "The Negotiation of Indian Treaties and Land Rights in Saskatchewan." In *Aborigines, Land, and Land Rights*, ed. Nicolas Peterson and Marcia Langton. Canberra: Australian Institute of Aboriginal Studies, 1983.

Ens, G. *Treaty Eight and Métis Scrip: A Historical Report.* Edmonton: University of Alberta Press, 1999.

Ferreira, D. "Oil and Lubicons Don't Mix: A Land Claim in Northern Alberta in Historical Perspective." *The Canadian Journal of Native Studies* 12, 1 (1992): 1-35.

Fisher, R. *Contact and Conflict: Indian-European Relations in British Columbia, 1774-1890.* Vancouver: University of British Columbia Press, 1977.

Fumoleau, R. *As Long As This Land Shall Last: A History of Treaty 8 and 11, 1870-1939.* Toronto: McClelland and Stewart, 1973.

Gulig, A.G. *Shifting Sands: Treaty Rights and Fish and Game Law Enforcement in Northern Saskatchewan, 1920-1945.* Whitewater: University of Wisconsin Press, 2000.

Irwin, R. "Treaty 8: An Anomaly Revisited." *BC Studies* 127 (2000): 83-101.

Korsmo, F. "Claiming Memory in British Columbia: Aboriginal Rights and the State." *American Indian Culture and Research Journal* 20, 4 (1996): 71-90.

Lamothe, R.M.J. *It Was Only a Treaty: Treaty 11 According to the Dene of the Mackenzie Valley.* Ottawa: Royal Commission on Aboriginal Peoples, 1993.

Leonard, D., and B. Whelan, Eds. *On the North Trail: The Treaty 8 Diary of O.C. Edwards.* Edmonton: Historical Society of Alberta, 1998.

Madill, D. *British Columbia Indian Treaties in Historical Perspective*. Ottawa: Treaties and Historical Research Centre, Department of Indian Affairs and Northern Development, 1984.

Madill, D. *Treaty Research Report: Treaty Eight*. Ottawa: Treaties and Historical Research Centre, Department of Indian Affairs and Northern Development, 1987.

Maguire Group. *Treaties One to Eleven: A Synthesis of the Study 1971-1976 on the History of the Fulfilment of the Crown's Obligations*. Ottawa: Treaty Policy Directorate, Department of Indian Affairs and Northern Development, 1994.

McCardle, B. *Indian Land Holdings in Severalty Under Treaty Eight and the Indian Acts, 1899-1930: A Preliminary Discussion*. Ottawa: Treaty and Aboriginal Rights Research of the Indian Association of Alberta, 1977.

McCardle, B., and R. Daniel. *Development of Farming in Treaty 8, 1899-1940*. Edmonton: Treaty and Aboriginal Rights Research of the Indian Association of Alberta, 1976.

Melville, J. *Indian Reserves and Indian Treaty Problems in Northeastern BC*. Vancouver: British Columbia Hydro and Power Authority, 1981.

Murray, J. "Hard Bargains: The Making of Treaty 8." *Archivist: Magazine of the National Archives of Canada* 117 (1998): 38-45.

Potyondi, B. *Treaty No. 8: Economic Benefits and Four Dene First Nations in the Northwest Territories 1899-1965*. Ottawa: Department of Indian Affairs and Northern Development, Treaty Land Entitlement, 1996.

Pratt, A. *Discussion Paper Regarding the Natural Resources Transfer Agreements of the Prairie Provinces: The Numbered Treaties and Extinguishment: A Legal Analysis*. Ottawa: Royal Commission on Aboriginal Peoples, 1993.

Price, R., Ed. *New Perspectives on the Alberta Indian Treaties*. Edmonton: Indian Association of Alberta, 1976.

Price, R., Ed. *Spirit and Terms of Treaties 6, 7 and 8: Alberta Indian Perspectives*. Edmonton: Indian Association of Alberta, 1975.

Price, R., Ed. *The Spirit of the Alberta Indian Treaties*. Edmonton: Pica Pica Press, 1987.

Price, R., and S. Smith. "Treaty 8 and Traditional Livelihoods: Historical and Contemporary Perspectives." *Native Studies Review* 9, 1 (1993-94): 51-92.

Ray, A. "Commentary on the Economic History of the Treaty 8 Area." *Native Studies Review* 10, 2 (1995): 169-95.

Ray, A. "Treaty 8: A British Columbian Anomaly." *BC Studies* 123 (1999): 5-58.

Ray, A., J.R. Miller, and F. Tough, Eds. *Bounty and Benevolence: A History of Saskatchewan Treaties*. Montreal and Kingston: McGill-Queen's University Press, 2000.

Tennant, P. *Aboriginal Peoples and Politics: The Indian Land Question in British Columbia*. Vancouver: University of British Columbia Press, 1990.

Tough, F. "Aboriginal Rights Versus the Deed of Surrender: The Legal Rights of Native Peoples and Canada's Acquisition of the Hudson's Bay Company Territory." *Prairie Forum* 17, 2 (1992): 225-50.

Voyageur, C. "A Media Account of the Government's Acquisition of Treaty 8 Lands." *Prairie Forum* 25, 2 (2000): 271-82.

Ware, R. *Treaty 8 in British Columbia*. Vancouver: Union of British Columbia Indian Chiefs, 1974.

Whitehouse, D. "The Numbered Treaties: Similar Means to Dichotomous Ends." *Past Imperfect* 3 (1994): 25-45.

CHAPTER 4

"The Unfriendly Reception"

IMMIGRATION

INTRODUCTION

"Come to Canada" said the pamphlets circulating through Europe. In 1900 the federal Immigration Branch published and distributed over one million of these pamphlets in many languages, extolling the Canadian west to Europeans anxious for a fresh start on a young continent far from the stultifying social inertia, poverty, and perpetual turmoil of their homelands. Though earlier Canadian immigration policy favoured British Isles residents to the virtual exclusion of others, Prime Minister Wilfrid Laurier and his Minister of the Interior, Clifford Sifton, boldly invited immigrants from east and central Europe too—to the considerable consternation of those wishing to perpetuate the traditional Anglo-Saxon temper of Canada.

Sifton understood that ignoring majority sentiment, especially over issues as sensitive as immigration, could mean political suicide. He therefore sought to change popular perception of prospective settlers. Mainstream Canadians, he knew, judged immigrants' desirability like the concentric rings from a pebble tossed in a pond: London represented the epicentre and the closer the ring to it, the better the immigrant. British, Scandinavians, and North Germans were fine, as were the Dutch. And France, a mere stone's throw across the English Channel? French immigrants were acceptable to the Québécois, but Sifton wanted a unicultural Anglo-Saxon prairies in a bid to prevent recurrence of the nineteenth-century Métis problems. Thus, immigration officers steered away from France, whose government dissuaded them anyway. Rings radiating further outward were problematic. Ones representing Mediterranean nations were really too remote to be desirable. Italians and other "Latins," after all, were too lascivious and passionate, and East European rings too Slavic for mainstream acceptability. Sifton agreed with the former but disputed the later. He argued that a "stalwart peasant in a sheepskin coat with a stout wife" from Eastern Europe would develop the Canadian northwest better than a prospective immigrant from Britain. Unlike their British counterparts, Slavs lived in a similar environment to the Canadian prairies. To assuage xenophobic fears, Sifton assured Canadians that a Ukrainian settler would soon assimilate and become indistinguishably Britannic. And what of the far-flung rings representing prospective immigrants of colour: Africans, Indians, and Asians?

Many Canadians viewed non-white newcomers with concern and hostility. This was particularly true in British Columbia where a disproportionate number of prospective immigrants arrived from non-Caucasian countries such as Japan, China, and India. Those settlers bore the brunt of stereotyping and usually found their presence unwelcome—except when it served employers' needs. Though the basis for racism in British Columbia was multifaceted, it was largely economic and emanated mainly from working-class residents, who worried that visible minority immigrants would arrive *en masse* and take over because they accepted lower living standards and wages, both of which would then be driven down for everyone.

Federal and provincial governments responded to local anxieties and soon erected barriers against those immigrants deemed "undesirable." And if the barriers were too low? Raise them. Do whatever was necessary. Thus, Chinese immigrants paid head taxes upon arrival, taxes that rose from an initial $50, to $100, and finally to $500—far beyond the means of most would-be applicants. The federal government created a "gentleman's agreement" with Japan whereby the Japanese government forbade all but a handful of its citizens from travelling to Canada. India and Indian emigrants, however, posed a special conundrum. Members of the British Empire had legal rights to travel and live anywhere within the Empire. Thus, Indians could legally immigrate to Canada if they so wished, and, much to the dismay of many in British Columbia, a growing number did. In response, the federal government enacted the Continuous Passage Act that neatly circumvented legal niceties by requiring prospective Indian immigrants to travel by continuous passage from India to Canada—which was impossible. Efforts to challenge the act came to a head in the summer of 1914 when the *Komagata Maru* and its nearly 400 Indian passengers sailed from Calcutta to Vancouver. Stuck on board and anchored in the middle of Vancouver's harbour when the ship was forbidden docking rights, the 400 immigrants sweltered in increasingly deplorable conditions in the summer heat. Nearly two months later, and after the ship had become something of a local attraction, Canadian soldiers escorted it out of Canadian waters at gunpoint and without disembarking its passengers.

Sifton's settlement of the prairies proceeded at a rapid pace and with less anti-immigrant hostility than on the West Coast. The Canadian west's population of 300,000 before 1896 grew to 1.5 million by the eve of World War I in 1914. The prairies ceased being primarily Native and Métis homelands and instead developed a multicultural milieu unlike any other in the country. Winnipeg, as the gateway to the prairies, had far more foreign than native-born citizens, and they came from all over Europe. Settlement was not easy, however. Certainly the prairies offered better opportunities and more potential than their original homelands, but life proved much harsher than immigrants expected. Canadian government propaganda, after all, only described success stories, never failures. Pamphlets failed to mention the expectation of assimilation, racism, bigotry, and discrimination. Immigration agents in Europe never warned about homesickness, loneliness, or any of the other traumas so common to new immigrants. The Canadian Pacific Railroad, which played a major part in recruiting and transporting immigrants, even failed to mention winter or snow in its promotional advertisements extolling the virtues of life on the Canadian prairies.

DISCUSSION POINTS

1. Would you agree with Scott's description of the federal government's immigration policies as "just and humane"? If not, how would you define them?

2. On what basis did Canada rank immigrants?

3. Compare the experiences of visible minorities such as the Chinese and Sikhs with those of Adamowska.

4. Did the federal government take advantage of newly arrived immigrants? Did it have an obligation to provide more support to these people?

5. Three decades passed between Adamowska's initial immigration experience and its publication. Would her description have been different if it had been recorded earlier? What distinguishes "history" from "memory"?

6. Scott's account contains many racial stereotypes and demeaning images of ethnic groups. Should we reprint and study these types of documents? Do they qualify as hate literature?

DOCUMENTS

1. W.D. Scott, "The Immigration by Races," 1914

William Duncan Scott (1861–1925) studied law but quit to become a land agent in Manitoba. He joined Manitoba's immigration office in Toronto in 1889 as a promoter for Canadian migration westward. From 1900 to 1902 he toured northern Europe and the British Isles for the federal government, successfully promoting western Canada to prospective immigrants. This led to his appointment as the federal Superintendent of Immigration from 1906 to 1923, in which capacity he developed and implemented immigration policy. He also became chief controller of Chinese immigration in 1911. Scott was well respected and known for his kindly disposition. The following document was unofficial, but it reflects the basic rationale behind Canada's immigration policy.

… Compared with other European settlers the British start with the advantage of having the same mother tongue as Canadians; with this exception they are on an equal footing with all others and must be prepared to compete on these terms. Much is said of the preference which Canada should give to persons from the mother country, but there is little sentiment in business, and if an Italian immigrant can do more work than an Englishman, the Italian "gets the job." Fortunately for Canada and for the immigrants there is usually work for both.

Considering the immense number of British immigrants arriving—some 674,000 in the first decade of the century—it speaks well for them and well for the country that so few have failed. Those who do not succeed are the exception. Although the success is of varying degree, it is as a rule according to the energy and tenacity of purpose displayed. There are few British immigrants in Canada who are not in a position much superior to that which they would now be occupying had they remained at home.

For the last twelve fiscal years, 1901-12, the immigration from Great Britain and Ireland amounted to 823,188 in the following proportion: English and Welsh, 601,963; Scottish, 171,897; Irish, 49,328. The largest number in any one year was for the twelve months ending March 31, 1912, when the total reached the immense figure of 138,121, made up of 96,806 English and Welsh, 32,988 Scottish and 8,327 Irish.

United States Immigration

The people from the United States most readily adapt themselves to Canadian conditions. The greater portion come from the Northern and Western States, where climatic and agricultural conditions closely resemble those of the Dominion. As they are largely of the agricultural class and come to Canada to take up farming, they know the proper course to adopt immediately upon arrival. United States immigrants may be considered the most desirable for a number of reasons. They understand Canadian conditions so well that their success in the so called dry belt of Alberta has been greater than that of the Canadian born; immediately on arrival they put large tracts under cultivation, and induce the railway companies to provide transportation facilities in the districts where they settle; they use the most recent machinery and labour-saving devices, and are thus an object-lesson, more especially to foreign settlers, who, without this clear proof of the value of improved machinery, would be slow in commencing its use; and, lastly and most important of all, they employ upon their farms large numbers of the immigrants of all races, who yearly arrive without sufficient capital to commence operations at once on their own account, and who must seek employment with others until they have saved enough to begin work on their free homesteads.

Much is spoken and written of the danger that Western Canada may become Americanized. The force of such arguments depends upon what is meant by "Americanized." If it is to be taken to mean the growing up of a sentiment in favour of annexation with the United States, the charge is groundless; if it means that the progressiveness of the American will be copied by the Canadian, the more rapid the Americanization the better. The Western Canadian is never averse to learning, no matter who may be his teacher. Sometimes the American settler finds in turn that in many things he may safely follow the lead of his Canadian neighbour.

When speaking of the possibility of annexation to the United States it is well to remember that probably not more than 50 percent of the immigrants from the United States were born there, and that, in addition to the 10 percent of the immigrants who are Canadians returning to the Dominion, which they left when the conditions were adverse, there are numbers who, while born in the States, are children of Canadian parents, and look upon themselves as really Canadians. Nor must it be forgotten that a considerable portion were born in the British Islands, and, coming again under the same flag, immediately upon arrival look upon themselves as Canadians.

The immigrants from the United States become naturalized at the earliest opportunity, while those who may be repatriated upon a three months' residence are quick to avail themselves of the opportunity. Generally speaking, the Americans are staunch supporters of the Canadian system of government, and are ever ready to point out wherein it is superior to that which they have left. More especially is this true with regard to the Canadian system of judiciary. No warmer advocate of the appointive system of judges exists than the American, who has had experience of the elective system ...

Austro-Hungarians

One of the largest contributors of immigrants to Canada of late years has been Austria-Hungary. The term Austro-Hungarian, however, has no very definite meaning. Such words as English, French, German, Norwegian convey to the mind a class of persons of certain language, type, appearance and peculiarities. Not so with the term Austro-Hungarian. Austria-Hungary is not a country wherein dwells a particular class of people, but is a certain area under two constituted governments, ruled over by one sovereign. The population is made up of a number of races with different languages, religions and social ideals. Divided into a large number of provinces, the country as a whole has an area of 240,942 square miles and a population of about fifty million. Of these 45 percent are Slavs, 25 percent Germans, 16 percent Magyars; the remainder consist of Romanians, Croatians, Ruthenians, Ser[b]ians, Poles, Bohemians, Jews and numerous other races. Of the different races the Germans are the most desirable in every respect, their educational standard being much higher, their industry more noticeable, and their ideals more closely approaching those of Canadians than is the case with the other races. The provinces which have contributed most largely to the movement of immigrants to Canada are Galicia and Bukowina. The North Atlantic Trading Company, which will be mentioned later, brought Canada to the attention of the people in these two provinces especially, and the movement once commenced continued through the indirect immigration work carried on by those who were successful in their new homes. The census of 1901 showed 28,407 persons in Canada who had been born in Austria-Hungary, and 18,178 of these were classified as Austro-Hungarians, the balance presumably being of German origin. Since that date the immigration movement has been large, nearly 140,000 arriving in the years 1901-12.

Coming from a country where agriculture is the principal industry, the Galicians and others from Austria-Hungary are fitted in some ways to make suitable settlers in Canada. They have been, however, embarrassed for want of capital. They have, moreover, preferred to settle on lands well covered with timber, and the cost of clearing the land and bringing it under cultivation has been higher than that of cultivating prairie land. In the majority of cases when the $10 entry fee for a homestead was paid and a not very habitable house erected, the head of the family, together with any other members able to act as wage-earners, found it necessary to seek work in order to secure funds to purchase stock and machinery. Employment could generally be secured with farmers in the harvesting season, with threshing outfits during the autumn, and in the bush during the winter. In this way the men have secured some knowledge of the English language, as have also some of the women who have become domestic servants.

The Galicians and other Austro-Hungarians are settled largely in the eastern portion of Manitoba and the northern sections of Saskatchewan and Alberta. They have improved their positions by coming to Canada, but whether or not they are a valuable acquisition to the Dominion is an open question. They are slow to assimilate and adopt Canadian customs, and, after all is said, this should be the final test as to the desirability of any class of immigrants. If they will not aid in forming a people united in customs and ideals, their room should be more acceptable than their company. Time will, no doubt, work wonders in their case, as it has in the case of other nationalities, and eventually it is hoped that they will make good Canadians. The process, however, will be slow.

What has already been said refers to those who have gone upon farms in Canada. Those who have settled in the cities form an entirely different problem. Living as they do in crowded, insanitary and usually filthy quarters, existing upon food and under conditions which a self-respecting Canadian would refuse to tolerate, they enter into unfair competition with the wage-earners of Canada and constitute a source of danger to the national life. Crime is all too common among them, and it is without doubt the city element of this people which has brought about the prejudice which exists against Galicians in the minds of Canadians. Since 1906 no effort has been made by the Canadian government to secure further immigration of this class. But, although all the restrictive regulations mentioned later on are enforced against them, large numbers still arrive, and are likely to arrive for years to come. A flow of any particular class of immigrants is usually difficult to start, but when once commenced it is often just as difficult to check.

The Italians

According to the 1901 census there were then in Canada 6,854 persons born in Italy and 10,834 persons of Italian origin. Between the fiscal years 1901-2 and 1911-12 nearly 62,000 immigrants arrived from Italy. The large majority of the Italians cannot, however, in the true sense be classed as immigrants, for they do not come with the intention of making permanent homes. They are "hewers of wood and drawers of water" who, by living at the lowest possible expense and by working diligently, hope to accumulate sufficient wealth to enable them to live comfortably in "Sunny Italy." They arrive with little that cannot be carried tied up in a handkerchief, and leave with a travelling outfit of about the same dimensions. Stored about their persons, or transmitted already to their native land, is the money they have earned during their sojourn here.

If we except the hand-organ man and the fruit-dealer, practically all are engaged at work as navvies. In every city you see them digging drains; on railway construction from the Atlantic to the Pacific their services are eagerly sought. The Italian is a good navvy. He obeys the orders of the "boss." He is anxious [not] to go on strike, as he counts that any increase in wages would in the short period he intends to remain in the country no more than reimburse him for the wages lost while the strike was on. At construction work he boards himself, or, if eating at the contractor's boardinghouse, is likely to be satisfied with whatever fare is furnished. He has no desire to insist upon exceptionally clean sleeping quarters, and, in a word, is exactly the class of help which contractors desire for the rough work of railway construction. When times are slack the Italians flock to the cities, and in their little colonies in Montreal, Toronto, Winnipeg and Vancouver huddle into their cheap boarding houses and live under appalling conditions, at a rate so low as almost to shatter belief in the much talked of "increased cost of living." When work is again available they are shipped off by employment agents to points at which their services are needed.

They have arrived from their native land with the idea that it is for them to right their own wrongs in person. Thus, while crimes committed by them against other than Italians are uncommon, stabbing and shooting affrays are all too common where men of their own race are the victims. Edward A. Steiner, in his book *On the Trail of the Immigrant*, writes thus of the Italian attitude towards crime:

> The worst thing about the Italians is that they have no sense of shame or
> remorse. I have not yet found one of them who was sorry for anything

except that he had been caught; and in his own eyes and in the eyes of his friends he is "unfortunate" when he is in prison and "lucky" when he comes out. "He no bad," his neighbour says. "He good, he just caught." And when he comes out he is received as a hero.

Of the Black Hand societies, of which we hear so much in the large cities of the United States, little as yet has been heard in Canada. That they exist is admitted by those most familiar with the Italian in the Dominion, but as their threats are invariably addressed to members of their own race, information is unlikely to be furnished to the courts, or even to creep into the press of the country.

That labour is necessary to carry on the large public works throughout the Dominion is admitted; that, if not on hand, it must be brought to the country is conceded. We may, however, hold that the help should be secured from such immigrants as are considered desirable, so that the country may have as its labourers those who intend to become permanent residents. The Italians are not of this class. They merely save money with which to return to their native land.

The enforcement of the regulation requiring Italians upon arrival to present their penal certificates has resulted in the rejection of many. A penal certificate is a civil document showing the number of convictions registered against the person to whom it is issued. As each Italian is supposed by the laws of his own country to possess one, the fact that he is without one is taken as evidence that he does not wish it seen, or, in other words, that it shows him to have been convicted of crime. As many have been rejected, either on account of information furnished on the penal certificate or through not possessing a penal certificate, it is evident that many of the Italians attempting to come to Canada (and the same is true of the United States) belong to the criminal class. The government has never encouraged immigration from Italy, except, for a very brief period, in the case of some northern Italians. The large number of arrivals from Italy is accounted for simply by the fact that those emigrating desire work, and that the work awaits them in Canada.

The French

With the population of France at a standstill and the people prosperous, it is not to be expected that any great movement of settlers should take place from that country; nevertheless, since the beginning of the twentieth century there has been a steady flow of emigration to Canada. The number for the years 1901-12 was 17,970. As in 1901 there were only 7,944 persons in Canada who had been born in France, this class of population has more than doubled in the last decade.

The French coming to Canada have settled largely in Quebec, Ontario and the western provinces. There are several very progressive colonies in Saskatchewan. The French are an industrious and thrifty people, and will make a success of agricultural work in the Dominion.

More important than the movement from France is that of "Returned Canadians" from the Eastern States. These people left Quebec when Canada was far from being as prosperous as it now is, and are returning to Canada to take up free homesteads in the prairie provinces, or to secure crown lands in Quebec or Ontario....

The Germans

In Canada in 1901 there were only 27,300 persons who had been born in Germany; there were, however, 310,501 of German origin, or almost 6 percent of the total population of the Dominion. In the early days ... Canada received considerable German immigration both directly from the Fatherland and indirectly from the German settlements in the United States. The descendants of these settlers form the greater part of the present population of German origin. The immigration from Germany during the years 1901-12 was about 25,000. In addition to the above a considerable portion of the immigration from Austria-Hungary and Russia is of German origin. For the fiscal years 1909-10 and 1910-11 the unnaturalized Germans from the United States numbered 2,378 and 1,123 respectively.

Sturdy, intelligent, honest and industrious, the German makes an ideal farmer, and he is in other walks of life a good citizen. Although he clings to his language he also acquires English, and the younger people especially adopt Canadian customs. They are amongst Canada's best settlers, and it is to be regretted that the laws of Germany prohibit the active immigration propaganda which would enable the Dominion to secure a much larger number than are now arriving.

The Scandinavians

... As of [Icelanders], so of the other Scandinavian races—Swedes, Norwegians, and Danes—nothing but good can be said. The larger part of the immigrants of these races go on the land; but whether they engage in agriculture or take up employment in the cities they prove hard-working, honest, thrifty and intelligent settlers of whom any country might be proud. In addition to those coming direct from the homeland many have been moving for years past from the Western States into Saskatchewan and Alberta, and are there looked upon as amongst the most progressive settlers. They readily acquire the English language, become naturalized at the earliest possible moment, take an interest in the political questions affecting their new homes, and, in a word, "become Canadians." In 1901 there were in Canada 2,075 Danes and 10,256 Norwegians and Swedes. Between 1901-1902 and 1911-12 over 4,700 Danes and over 36,500 Norwegians and Swedes arrived in the Dominion. With the Scandinavian race there is really no question of assimilation. They are sprung largely from the same stock as are the English, and, when they have acquired the language and become acquainted with Canadian customs, they will be as other Canadians. True, the first generation will be distinguished by their accent, but even this disappears in the second generation.

Turks, Armenians, and Syrians

Turkey, Armenia and Syria supply some of Canada's most undesirable immigrants. With them assimilation is out of the question and, except rarely, they are not producers. The Italians have their faults; Canadians may not approve of the manner in which the Poles and many other Eastern European races live. But these people are at least workers. If they take money out of the country when they go back to their homes, they leave behind them tasks performed, for which as a rule they have received no more than they have earned. But with the Turks, Syrians and Armenians it is different. They live under conditions which are a menace to the country, and their time is spent in trade and barter. Like the Gypsies, they are quick to avail themselves of naturalization, not that they admire Canada's form of government or take any interest in political events, but merely because of the extra protection which naturalization affords or which they imagine it affords. They are of a wandering nature, and many of them have lived on both sides of the international boundary. It is not uncommon to meet people of these classes who carry with them when travelling naturalization papers from both Canada and the United States. They find them of value in passing from one country to the other. There were 1,571 Turks and Syrians in Canada in 1901, and of these 481 were naturalized. Since that date there have arrived 2,456 Turks, 5,229 Syrians and 1,473 Armenians. Pedlars are no great acquisition to any country, and there are few people in the Dominion who would care to see the day arrive when people of these races might be pointed out as fair samples of Canadian citizens.

Greeks, Macedonians, and Bulgarians

The Greeks, Macedonians and Bulgarians are all dwellers in cities when that is possible. If city work is not available they take railway construction work, and, as they can live on very little, they are able to save a large part of their earnings. The Greek is rapidly branching out into two new callings, shoe-polishing and confectionery. Amongst the Macedonians and Bulgarians the highest ambition seems to be to keep small stores where they sell the necessaries of life, even if in a small way, as it gives them a better opportunity to prey upon their countrymen.

The modern Greek, Macedonian and Bulgarian have far from a high sense of truthfulness. The writer has seen squads of forty or fifty examined at the ocean port. Each one gave an address to which he was proceeding, and gravely informed the inspector that the person he was going to join was his brother. Each one gave the same address. When asked if he had any relatives accompanying him, each stated that he had none. When confronted with the statements of others of the party these dissemblers would then change their story and claim to be cousins, brothers-in-law, or to have any other convenient relationship to the one already in the country. A recent case occurred in which a Macedonian naturalized in Canada sent his naturalization papers to a friend in the United States who desired to come to the Dominion. This person, when stopped by an immigration official, demanded entry as a Canadian citizen. The fraud was discovered, the would-be immigrant was fined and deported, and the Macedonian Canadian citizen was fined $250 for aiding and abetting the entry of an undesirable.

Practically all these three classes in the Dominion have arrived since the beginning of the present century, the Greek and Macedonian immigration numbering 3,997 in the first decade and the Bulgarian 4,484 in the same time. Since the 1910 Immigration Act came into force the rejections amongst these classes have been very heavy. None are now admitted if they can be legally kept out.

The Chinese

Chinese immigration has undergone many changes. It was openly encouraged in the early eighties when Chinese labourers were needed in the construction of the Canadian Pacific Railway. In 1886 an agitation carried on by trade unions resulted in the imposing of a head tax of $50 on this class of immigrants. In 1901 this was increased to $100 and in 1904 to $500. In 1901 there were 17,043 persons in Canada who had been born in China. The number of those of Chinese origin was probably somewhat larger. Between 1901 and 1912 upwards of 30,000 entered Canada. Very few of the Chinese arriving in Canada come on their own initiative. Their fares and head tax are paid by "tyees" or contractors, who hold them practically in bondage until they repay the expense entailed in bringing them to Canada, together with an exorbitant profit. They are industrious workers, very thrifty, live well according to their standards, and insist upon receiving the highest rate of remuneration which their services can secure.

The Chinese in Canada may be divided into four classes: merchants, dealing largely in teas, silks, opium and other Oriental products; gardeners who devote their attention almost entirely to garden products, and who in British Columbia appear able to make large profits after paying a yearly rental of $25 an acre for their land; restaurant keepers and laundrymen; and, lastly, domestic servants. In the last-mentioned occupation they give excellent satisfaction to their employers, but as their wages have doubled since the imposition of the $500 head tax, it is their proud boast that it is the Canadians and not themselves who are mulcted. For this boast they apparently have good grounds.

Generally speaking the Chinamen are quiet, inoffensive, law-abiding people, if we leave out of account their tendency to gamble and to indulge in opium. Many missions exist for their conversion to Christianity. It is true, however, that while large numbers profess conversion some will admit to their intimate friends that they have done so because, as they say, it is "good for bizness." When gambling they are not averse to deception, but in business transactions they are credited with having a strict sense of honour; many who know them best say that a Chinaman's word is as good as his bond.

The large increase in numbers arriving during 1910-11 is reported to have been caused by the circulation of a report in China that the Canadian government intends raising the head tax to $1,000. Although not popular, the Chinaman may be said to be now the least hated Oriental on the western coast. As the desire of the Chinese is to accumulate wealth to take back to their native land, and as assimilation is out of the question, they cannot be classed as desirable, but, unless the numbers arriving increase very largely, they cannot be said to constitute any great menace to Canada.

The Japanese

The Japanese are, from a Canadian standpoint, the most undesirable of the Orientals. Belonging to an emigrating race, filled with patriotism for their own country, and living within such easy reach of Canada's western coast, they might, if allowed to come, flood the Province of British Columbia and dominate not only the labour market, but, through the investment of capital, the principal industries as well. That they are industrious and capable is admitted by all acquainted with them. They would, however, never become Canadians, and their arrival in large numbers is, therefore, a contingency which should be carefully guarded against.

Unlike the other Orientals, they are not content to remain "hewers of wood and drawers of water." Possibly this desire to figure in all walks of life is not unconnected with the dislike which the white races bear towards them. There were about 4,700 Japanese in Canada in 1901. Between 1901 and 1912 about 15,000 entered the Dominion, the heaviest immigration being in 1907-8, when 7,601 arrived. There was a great falling off in the numbers (495) arriving in 1908-9 as compared with 1907-8; this was the result of an arrangement between Canada and Japan, whereby the Japanese coolies arriving in any one year were to be restricted to a certain number. Japan has kept well within the number arranged for. So long as this arrangement remains in force Japanese immigration need cause no anxiety to Canada.

The Hindus

Of the different immigration problems which from time to time have faced the Dominion, that of the influx of Hindus appeared for a time to be possibly the most serious. This movement commenced in 1905. The arrivals up to the close of the fiscal year 1911-12 were 5,203. British Columbia, the nearest province to the Orient and the one possessing the climate most closely resembling that of their native land, was the ultimate destination of these unwelcome comers, and British Columbia was not slow in expressing her disapproval of them. "A White Canada" was her cry. That these immigrants were British subjects; that many had fought for the Empire; that many expressed their willingness to do so again should occasion arise — all this in no way lessened the antipathy of the white race towards them.

True, there were some imperialists who, recognizing in the Hindus subjects of the same sovereign, argued that they were entitled to enter the Dominion as a matter of right, and that any action towards restricting their movements from one part of the British domain to another would endanger the existence of the Empire. But the counsels of the advocates of "A White Canada" finally prevailed, and an order-in-council was passed providing that persons of Asiatic origin, other than Chinese and Japanese, must have in their possession $200 at the time of landing in Canada. This came into force in 1908, and the numbers arriving immediately dropped from 2,623 in that year to almost nothing.

The Hindus who came to Canada were largely from the Punjab and, physically, were a fine set of men. The term Hindu as here applied is a misnomer, denoting as it does a religious sect rather than a race of people. In religion they were divided, some being Hindus, others Buddhists and others Mohammedans. It is doubtful whether with their constitutions, suitable for the country and climate from which they came, they will ever become thoroughly acclimatized in Canada. Pneumonia and pulmonary troubles have already resulted in the death of no small number. Their bodies were disposed of by cremation, the burial method of their own country; possibly this is the only one of their customs which might with advantage be adopted.

Sawmills and railway construction work afforded employment to the Hindus. While they were able at most times to secure employment, it was at a lower rate than that paid to white men or even to Japanese or Chinese. They were unaccustomed to Canadian methods, and though able to speak a little English were slow to learn more. Their greatest disadvantage, however, is their caste system, which prevents them from eating and sometimes even from working with white men, or even with others of their own race who belong to a different social scale — for this is practically the meaning of caste. Now that the influx is checked the Hindu problem is ended. . . .

The Jews

Scattered over the face of the earth, a people but not a nation, the Jews seek the land where they may hope to reap a harvest from their labours. Canada, in common with the United States, has proved a loadstone to draw these wanderers from the ends of the earth. . . .

Efforts at colonization on the land have been made. Two of the most important were at Wapella and Hirsch. Neither has proved a conspicuous success. More recently the Jews have attempted the cultivation of the finer grades of tobacco in the Province of Quebec, and although their efforts are apparently meeting with success it is as yet too soon to predict the final result. They cannot be classed as agriculturalists, and the number who have engaged in this occupation is small compared with those engaged in trade and barter or who take up manufacturing.

The Jews are preeminently dwellers in cities. The clothing trade in its various branches provides employment for many; other occupations that attract them are cigar and cigarette making, shoe-repairing, fruit-dealing and vegetable-dealing, and rag and other varieties of peddling.

The increase in the Hebrew population has been very rapid in Canada, rising from 667 in 1881 to 16,131 in 1901; since then the immigration of this race has amounted to over 50,000. According to the census of 1901, of the 16,131 Jews then resident in Canada 13,470 lived in twelve cities. In Montreal, Toronto and Winnipeg the conditions under which some, especially the Russian Jews, live are far from satisfactory, either as respects air-space, ventilation or cleanliness.

Sweatshops have not yet reached in Canada the deplorable condition found in the United States, but the tendency is in that direction, and the Jews are one of the strongest factors in bringing this about. No effort is or ever has been made by the government of Canada to induce Jewish immigrants to come to the Dominion, and the influx has been entirely unsolicited. In their movements to America they are aided largely by their philanthropic societies. These also do useful work amongst their own people by looking after those unable to support themselves....

THE IMMIGRATION POLICY OF CANADA

The immigration policy of the government of Canada at the present time is, and for many years past has been, to encourage the immigration of farmers, farm labourers and domestic servants from countries which are classed as desirable. The list of countries had undergone change from time to time, and at the present includes the United States, the British Isles, France, Belgium, Holland, Switzerland, Germany, Denmark, Norway, Sweden and Iceland.

On the other hand, it is the policy of the government to do all in its power to keep out of the country undesirables, who may be divided into three classes:

1. Those physically, mentally or morally unfit whose exclusion is provided for by the immigration act already quoted.

2. Those belonging to nationalities unlikely to assimilate and who, consequently, prevent the building up of a united nation of people of similar customs and ideals.

3. Those who from their mode of life and occupations are likely to crowd into urban centres and bring about a state of congestion which might result in unemployment and a lowering of the standard of Canadian national life.

While neither the Immigration Act nor the orders-in-council passed thereunder prohibit the landing in Canada of persons belonging to the second and third classes above mentioned, still their entry has been made difficult. Their coming is discouraged in a number of ways. Chinese are subject to a head tax of $500. The number of Japanese coolies has been limited by arrangements between the two countries. Orders-in-council have been passed requiring (1) Asiatic arrivals to have $200 in cash at the time of landing; (2) the production of passports and penal certificates by persons coming from the countries which issue these; (3) the continuous journey of all immigrants from the country of their birth or citizenship on tickets purchased in that country or purchased or prepaid in Canada. All these regulations put obstacles in the way of immigrants from Asia and Southern and Eastern Europe, and, consequently, the numbers coming or likely to come from those countries are correspondingly diminished.

Briefly, this is the immigration policy of the government. In so far as the administration of the restrictive part of the policy is concerned the Immigration department has at all times endeavoured to be both just and humane, bearing in mind, however, that its duty is to Canada and to Canada only, and that while every applicant for admission who is likely to be an acquisition to the country shall be admitted if the law will permit it, on the other hand, every person who is likely to be a detriment to the country must be rejected if the law will allow it.

It may be here stated that until 1903 immigrants, upon arrival in Canada, underwent no medical examination which might result in their rejection through physical or mental unfitness. In 1903, however, a medical examination was commenced, and from that year rejections at the ocean ports have been frequent, both upon medical and civil grounds. The rejections at border points between Canada and the United States commenced in 1908-9. During the fiscal years 1902-12 8,500 rejections were recorded at ocean ports and 51,015 at border stations on the United States boundary. Even with the care exercised in the rejection of undesirables when they apply for admission, a certain percentage enter Canada who prove failures and who are deported. During the years 1902-12 5,626 such deportations were made ...

THE PROBLEM OF FUTURE IMMIGRATION

At the present time there is no large number of persons in Canada whose presence is a menace to the country from a political, moral or economic point of view. The reason for the absence of such a problem is that representatives of undesirable nationalities have as yet come in small number only. Who would care to see Alberta a second Mississippi or Georgia, as far as population is concerned? Who would wish to see the day arrive when British Columbia could be termed the "Second Flowery Kingdom," as might easily happen if the doors were thrown open to the Japanese? Who would not regret to see the ghettos and slums of New York, with her hived population and her reeking sweatshops, duplicated in Montreal, Toronto and Winnipeg? These are the questions which today confront Canadians, and this is the problem of the future. More important than the drilling of armies, more important than the construction of navies, more important even than the fiscal policy of the country is the question of who shall come to Canada and become part and parcel of the Canadian people.

Fifty years ago the United States was receiving practically the class which is today coming to Canada. With the disappearance of free lands the character of the immigration to the United States has changed, and now Southern and Eastern Europe are furnishing most of her new settlers, and a large percentage of her immigrants remain in the cities. The people of the republic are now awake to the danger which this involves, and anti-immigration leagues and similar organizations are being formed to bring the question prominently before the public. Canada, with this object-lesson before her, has no excuse if she allows the same evils to grow. Much has already been done to prevent this. One suggestion for further checks is the introduction of educational tests. It is, for instance, suggested that no one over ten years of age shall be admitted who is unable to speak, read and write either English, Welsh, Gaelic, French, German, Dutch, Danish, Norwegian, Swedish or Icelandic. This would practically confine immigration to the countries where immigration work is now carried on ...

In checking undesirable immigration it must be decided what constitutes an undesirable, and the following definition is put forward for consideration: undesirable immigrants are those who will not assimilate with the Canadian people, or whose presence will tend to bring about a deterioration from a political, moral, social or economic point of view.

2. W.A. Cum Yow, Testimony before the *Royal Commission on Chinese and Japanese Immigration*, 1903

Won Alexander Cum Yow (1861–1955) was reputedly the first ethnic Chinese person born in Canada, at Port Douglas in British Columbia to Chinese parents who arrived from Canton via San Francisco during the gold rush of 1858. His father operated various businesses on Harrison Lake servicing the miners. Mr. Cumyow was trilingual in Chinese, English, and Chinook, skills which served him well as the Court Interpreter in New Westminster. Though a trained lawyer, he could not practice because only registered voters could be called to the bar. Since 1877 the Chinese had been officially denied the right to vote. Mr. Cumyow also became a prominent merchant, labour contractor, and community leader; founded the Chinese Empire Reform Association of Canada; and was president of the Chinese Benevolent Association.

I was born at Port Douglas in this province in the year 1861. My parents are both Chinese. They have lived in the province for nearly 45 years. I was educated in the province. I am corresponding foreign secretary of the Chinese Empire Reform

Association of Canada. I have been in close touch with the Chinese all my life, and I am familiar with their modes of living and of doing business. There has been no systematic importation of Chinese into this province since the construction of the Canadian Pacific Railway. At that time a large number were engaged and brought over. This was done by the Chinese contractors who were working under Mr. Onderdonk. Some of these men went back, but others had no means to pay their way back, and many who remained were in great straits for a long time. These men were all voluntarily hired, and were in no sense serfs. Serfdom is not practiced among the Chinese. All who come here come free men and as a rule pay their own boat fare and entry tax. These are paid in Hong Kong to the steamboat agents before they start. I am certain none of the Chinese labour contractors here have sent money to pay for a number of Chinamen to come here. Occasionally, Chinamen have sent money to bring out relatives or personal friends, but that is the extent to which this is done. There is never any bond given for repayment of such advances, but where there is an understanding that repayment will be made it is always faithfully done. Chinese merchants have sometimes taken action to limit the number of those coming when they find there are too many here. They do this by communicating with the merchants in China, who have great influence with the labouring classes. They took this course two years ago when the labour market was over-supplied owing to the number of Japs who had come in. There are not so many Chinamen or Japs here at present as there were a year ago. Many of those who were here have gone over to the States where liberal wages are being paid them, and they can do much better than here. Others have gone to the West Indies and settled there. Many of the Chinamen who previously went to the West Indies have made lots of money, and some of them have intermarried with the native races. There have been cases of importation of Chinese girls for immoral purposes, but not many. This has been the work of unscrupulous men, who, by gross misrepresentations, and free use of money have led poor people to entrust them with the care of their daughters. Proportionately, I believe, there is nothing like the same number of such cases among the Chinese as among white people, but there are wicked and unscrupulous men among the Chinese as among other races. I do not think any Chinese parents would willingly give up their daughters for such purposes. The Chinese who are here usually congregate in one part of the city. The chief reason for this is for companionship. Besides the Chinese know that the white people have had no friendly feeling towards them for a number of years. This has been most apparent since the Canadian Pacific Railway construction days, and it has been accentuated by those who since then have come into the province from all parts of the world, many of whom were not in touch with the Chinese before. This unfriendliness and want of respect has caused a feeling of want of confidence among the Chinese, and it certainly has not tended to induce them to abandon their own ways and modes of life. It was very different before the date referred to, when a feeling of mutual confidence and respect prevailed, and all were able to work in harmony. This system of doing business also tends to keep them together, as it enables them the better to have their own social functions and meetings. They have their own Board of Trade and other meetings as to their trade interests. We have not here the faction element which prevails to some extent in San Francisco. There are now in this province strong branches of the Chinese Empire Reform Association of Canada. This association has been incorporated. Its objects are duly set forth in the accompanying copy of the constitution and bylaws. The Reform Association has branches all over the world where there are Chinamen. They wish to elevate the Chinese and to promote the prosperity of the old land. The work is carried on here largely by public meetings and addresses. Some of the members are most eloquent speakers. This work cannot be carried on yet in China itself, but we hope for great good to China from the movement, and also to be able to do something for the good of the Chinese who are here. The association has also arranged for the translation of some of the best books in the English language into Chinese for distribution among Chinamen in China and other parts of the world. They are also sending students to different seats of learning to be educated. The Chinese have always a very high regard to their home land, and a strong filial affection. They sacrifice a great deal for themselves to be able to send money home to sustain their parents or their families, and if by any piece of good fortune or by success in gambling they make a large sum at any time, the larger part of that money will usually be sent to China for the use of their families. They do not spend it on themselves. There is proportionately a large amount of gambling among the Chinese. Some do gamble for large amounts, but more commonly the play is for amusement only, and for small sums to pass the time, as this is done in the common room of the boarding house, where all assembled, though differently occupied. If a police raid is made and any are caught playing, all are arrested for gambling or looking on. . . . Chinese use intoxicating liquors, but not often, and usually in moderation. They use all kinds of liquor. They sometimes use a Chinese wine, which serves as a tonic for the system. They very seldom get drunk or drink to excess. They regard all who are excessive drinkers as barbarians and beneath contempt. So strong is the feeling among them, that if any one should indulge too freely, they are heartily ashamed of it, and they at once go to bed. A certain number indulge in opium smoking, but only a small percentage of the whole. The habit is induced by companionship with those who use it. I have seen white men in the Chinese quarter using opium, but not many of them here. The opium smokers realize the evil of the habit, but they are unable to break it off. The Chinese have a hospital for the treatment of sick men who are without means. It is a charitable institution, and is supported by voluntary subscriptions, contributed chiefly by the merchants. They have a Chinese doctor of their own, and he does the work for charity. The patients are cared for by the janitor of the hospital, and by their own friends. I have known of some cases of recovery there, but they generally go there as a last resort, hence the large percentage of deaths. In the boarding houses the attention is given to the sick. Of course those who have money secure better treatment than those who have none. It is not the case that any of the sick are neglected. They are cared for up to the ability of their friends, and after death they are given a proper burial by the undertakers at the friends' expense. I have never known a case of concealment of infectious disease among them.

The Chinese have a very high regard for the marriage relationship. They usually marry at from sixteen to twenty years of age. Many of those who are here are married and have wives and children in China. A large proportion of them would bring their families here, were it not for the unfriendly reception they got here during recent years, which creates an unsettled feeling. Both spouses are, as a rule, faithful to each other, and the wife stays with the husband's relations, the money sent home by the husband is of use to them all. Often the family property has to be mortgaged to help the son to come here, and the first thing he does is to try to lift the mortgage. Divorce is unknown in China, and it is a very uncommon thing for spouses to separate their relations on any ground. As a nation, the Chinese are very anxious that their children be well educated. There has been no serious attempt in China to teach other than the Chinese language until recently. Now English is largely taken up, as they are coming more and more into contact with the English speaking people. The desire to learn is not confined to any one class. The laboring or farming class are as anxious for education as the others, and they stand the same show to get it. The Chinese here are all anxious to have their children taught the same as other children are taught here. Regarding prospects of assimilation, I do not think this will be easily or soon brought about. I do not favor the idea of intermarriage, as the modes of life of the races are different in several respects, and it would not conduce to happiness. There are exceptional cases, such as where the parties have been brought up together or under similar conditions, but this seldom happens. Assimilation can only come through those who are born here, or at least are brought here in infancy, and are separated from the ideas of the old land and the mode of life there. For work, the Chinese are not so physically strong as the white people. This is due to the diet they take, but they are very patient and persevering workers, and they are quick in action. It therefore follows, that for light work they excel the white people, but for heavy work white men have the advantage. Their wages vary considerably. In the canneries they get from $45 to $50 a month, but the month must consist of 26 days of 10 hours each of actual work. As day labourers they get about $1 per day. Chinese farmers and laundrymen usually get from $10 to $20 per month and their board and lodging. In the cannery boardinghouse the bosses supply the food and each is charged in proportion to the cost of it. This will amount to from $9 to $10 per month for each. The rule in regard to laundries applies to some other lines of light work. The boots and shoes and a large proportion of the clothing used by Chinamen are made in Canada or the United States. The silk goods and silk shoes come from China. They get some of their food stuffs from China, such as rice, which cannot be grown here. Rice is one of the essential parts of their diet. The Chinese are especially suited for such light work as in the laundries, cooks in hotels or camps and in domestic service. They have been engaged in such work as long as I can remember, and always received with favour by the employers. They are quick in action, and ready to do what they are told, and able to do a greater variety of work than a girl can do in domestic service. In all my experience I have not heard of a Chinaman being indecent in his relation to the household where he works. As a rule they can be relied on and are very attentive to duty. The Chinese have been engaged largely in market gardening in this province for over thirty-five years, and they have during all those years been the chief source of supply of vegetables for our markets. They work late and early on their ground, and have it in a high state of cultivation, hence they can make a good living off ten acres of land. They have been engaged in the fish-canning work since the beginning of the industry over twenty-five years ago. They are thoroughly trained in all the different inside departments. I cannot see how they can be dispensed with, as so many hands are required, and all need a special training for the work. As a fact it would take years to train a sufficient number of white men or children. These could better do the work now done by Indians, but of course the Indians would resent this inroad on them. A great feature of their character is their frugality. In fact this is one of the chief complaints against them. They are trained to be frugal, and it seems to me a virtue rather than a cause of offence. True it enables them to save money and to send some of it to China to help their families there, but that is also a virtue. They are willing also to undertake work at a small wage rather than be idle, and they are very careful to live within their income, whether it be large or small, that they may have some provision for idleness or illness. In this respect it seems to me, that they are superior to many white men who will not work unless they get a high pay, and are extravagant and even reckless in their expenditure of the money they earn, who never think of providing for the future, and have very little consideration, even for their own wives and families. To some extent this may be due to the privileges the white men have of friendly and charitable societies to rely upon which are not available for the Chinaman. My opinion is, that if the Chinese were accorded the same respect as others here, they would prove themselves to be good citizens, and they would settle in the land with their wives and families. Being thrifty they would save money, and that money would be judiciously used in the country. Certainly, if their families were here, they would have no occasion to send their money away. It is not pleasure for them to be separated from their families (in a good many cases for 15, 20 and 25 years). They come here to improve their circumstances, and they would only be too glad to have their families to enjoy with them any improvements that are available. Many of the chief opponents of the Chinese are comparatively new arrivals in the province, who have very little idea of the facts of the case. Some of these men are unwilling to work themselves, and they misspend the earnings they do make, yet they are eager to run down the Chinese who are willing to work and who do work hard, and are very careful of their hard-earned money. Men are coming here from all parts of the world and of all nationalities. As regards industry and thrift, the Chinese will compare favourably with any of them. In many respects they are greatly superior to many of the men who come here during the canning season and claim the privilege of being British subjects. Some of these are wild, lawless drinking men who are a discredit to any community. During the canning season, though a large number of Chinese congregate at Steveston and other points, they are all very orderly and obedient to the laws. Referring to cannery work, it is well known that the Chinese contractors each year enter upon very onerous contracts with the canners for labour, and that under these contracts large advances are made by the canners to the contractors before the work of the season begins. I do not know of one single instance where a Chinese contractor failed to carry out his contract in full. I know of many instances where they have done it at a heavy loss to themselves, but they did it honourably. As regards further immigration, I think the matter will always fully regulate itself. The Chinese merchants will always take care that too many do not come. It is a serious burden on them if they come and do not get plenty of work. The head tax also presents a substantial barrier against them coming in present circumstances.

I do not favour the existence of this tax. I think the same end could have been reached by diplomacy, as was done by the United States. I quite approve of certain conditions being attached to the granting of the franchise, such as are provided in the Natal Act, and that it be applicable to Japanese, Galicians, Italians and others all alike. I do think however, that if the Chinese pay admission to this country, and if they have educational qualifications they should not only be allowed the privilege of the franchise, but be treated otherwise as men and as British citizens. Already the Chinese have done good work in placer mining, as they are content to work up claims deserted by the white minters, if they yield even $1.25 to $2 per day. There are great areas of such properties, and the reclamation of this gold is a valuable provincial asset, which would otherwise remain worthless. Besides mining this province has a vast territory, and many other undeveloped resources. It has, therefore, opening for a very large industrial population, and as the Chinese are, as already stated, industrious, thrifty and persevering, and always amenable to the laws of the land, as far as they understand them, they should make valuable citizens and greatly aid in the development of this great country. This is particularly true of the opening up of the agricultural land, as the Chinese are born agriculturists and are accustomed to make the very best of the soil. Their experience should therefore in agriculture be most valuable to enable this province to provide for its own want as well as to become an exporting country. In view of the agitation being carried on by politicians and professional agitators against the Chinese here, it is a mystery to me as it must be to other observers that so many people in all ranks of life are so ready to employ Chinamen to do their work. Many of them are thus employed, and some at fairly high salaries, and this seems to nullify the allegations that they are either offensive or detrimental to the development of the country. It is as a fact a valuable testimonial of merit and proves that they are needed in the country.

In conclusion, my firm conviction is that the agitation which has arisen in connection with the orientals is more directed against the capitalists than against the Chinese themselves. They seem to think that the capitalists are benefiting from the labour of the orientals in a special manner; whereas it seems to me that the orientals are enabling the capitalists to carry on business which directly benefits all classes in the community. It is true there are also those who seem to dislike the appearance of the Chinamen and their oriental ways of living and dressing, and there is a large unthinking class who condemn them because it has become a custom to do so. I have always urged the Chinamen to adopt the British mode of dress and living; and, judging from the experience of the Japanese, I am satisfied the Chinese would greatly benefit if they did so.

3. Dr. Sundar Singh, *Addresses Delivered to the Members during the Session of 1911–12*, Empire Club of Canada

Dr. Sundar Singh (dates unknown) entered Canada illegally through Halifax in 1909. Dr. Singh co-owned British Columbia's only Punjabi newspaper, The Sansar. *He also founded the Hindustanee Association and the Hindu Friend Society, but was apparently the sole member of both. A publicist, he claimed to represent the Indian community, but in fact he had little local support. A Sundar Singh returned to India aboard the* Komagata Maru *in 1914. Still another Sundar Singh arrived in India in 1915 after having been deported from the United States where he allegedly sought work after leaving Canada. It is unclear whether either of these subsequent events were experienced by the Dr. Singh who addressed the Empire Club of Canada, the country's premier speaker's forum established in 1903.*

Some few years ago a few troops of the Sikhs passed through Canada on their way to the jubilee of the late Queen Victoria, and the gentlemen who were in charge of them spoke very highly of them. These Sikhs went back home and they spoke of the vast prairies where they saw wheat growing the same as we grow wheat. The consequence was that a score of them came out in 1905—about forty of them came in that year and the next, and this went on till in 1909 there was quite a strong body of them, about 4,000 in all, engaged in agriculture; they were farmers in India, and of course they naturally took to farming when they came to this country.

They are British subjects: they have fought for the Empire; many of these men have war medals; but, in spite of this fact, they are not allowed to have their families with them when they come to this country; in spite of their being British subjects, they are not allowed to have their wives here. People talk about these Oriental races, and the phrase is understood to include not only the Chinese and the Japanese, but the Sikhs as well, which is absurd. Letters giving inaccurate statements are appearing in the press all the time. I do not know why all this objection should be directed against the Sikhs—against that people, more than against any other Oriental people.

These people are here legally; they have satisfied every process of law; they have been here over five years; they have been good to their employers—Colonel Davidson employs 350 of them in his mills in New Westminster—their work is equal to that of other labourers; their quarters are better, and they are making more wages now; they have fitted into the situation here; they have made good.

In spite of this, there are these letters going through the papers, and there are attacks upon these men; yet, although they are British subjects, nobody stands up for them. We appeal to you of the Empire Club, for we are only 4,000 in number, to help us in this matter, and to see that justice is done to these subjects of our King.

We are subjects of the same Empire; we have fought, we have sacrificed. We have fought for the Empire and we bear her medals; we have an interest in this country: we have bought about $2,000,000 of property in British Columbia; we have our church and pay our pastor, and we mean to stay in this country. I understand that there is a society called the Home Reformation Society and that it says that it is better for a man to have a wife and family. To others you advance money to come here, and yet to us, British subjects, you refuse to let down the bars. All we are asking of you is justice and fair play, because the Sikhs have believed in fair play, and have believed all the time that they will get justice; that ultimately they will get justice from the British people.

Many people have been telling me that it is useless my trying to bring this question before the Canadian people, but I am firmly persuaded that, if the question, is properly brought before right-minded Canadians, that they will say that the same rights should be given to the Sikh people as are given to any other British subjects.

Some people have spread the false statement that the Sikhs are polygamous; they are monogamous in India, and are not more polygamous than you are. They are strictly monogamous by their religion, and it is useless to spread these false stories. There are officers in India—perhaps some have come from Canada—and they can take their families to India to our people; are the laws made so invidious that it cannot work both ways! That law was meant to shut out the Japanese, yet, in the year 1908, 5,000 came from Honolulu, and they let them in. We do know that we are British subjects and we ask for our rights; if you can allow the alien to come over here, surely a British subject ought to have the same rights as an alien.

The position cannot hold good; it is inevitable that it cannot hold good. These Sikhs are the pick of their villages, they are not out here like the Japanese and Chinese. The Japanese has to show only 50 cents when he arrives, but the Sikh has to show $200, and, if he cannot, he is sent away. Of course you can understand what the reflex action of this treatment might be in the present state of India. These people who are here, are here legally; if they were new people coming in, it would be a different matter; but as such they have rights, and I think those rights ought to be respected.

It is only a matter of justice. If this Empire is to be and continue to be a great Empire, as it is sure to be, then it must be founded on righteousness and justice; your laws cannot be one thing for one set and a different thing for the rest of us.

These Sikhs are quite alone; they do the roughest labour; they do not come into competition with other labour, and yet this is the treatment they receive. They are plainly told: "We do not want you to bring your wives in." You cannot expect people to be moral, if you debar them from bringing in their wives and children. They can travel in Japan, they can travel in Europe; they can travel anywhere under the British flag, except here.

Just at present there are two Sikh women confined on board a boat at Vancouver; they came on the 22nd. One is the wife of a merchant, the other is the wife of a missionary. These men have been settled in this country for five years, and are well spoken of. They went back some time ago to bring out their wives and children. They asked the steamship company to sell them tickets, and the company told them that they would be refused admission. They came to Hong Kong, and the steamship company refused to sell them tickets; they waited ever since last March and last month the C.P.R. sold them tickets. On the 22nd, they arrived here, and the men were allowed to land, but the ladies are still confined as if they were criminals.

Now, if these men were allowed to land, why not their wives; why should they not be allowed to land, too? That is what they do not understand, and, although they are well versed in the occult sciences and mystical philosophy, why this should be so, they cannot see.

We have the promise of Queen Victoria that all British subjects, no matter what race or creed they belong to, shall be treated alike. These promises have been confirmed by King Edward, and by His Majesty King George the Fifth. When he was in India, he granted their full rights to the Hindoo people. The Indian people are loyal British subjects. They are as loyal as anybody else. Why should there be such a difference in the treatment of these loyal people?

We appeal to you, gentlemen, to say that in any country, under any conditions, the treatment that the Sikhs are receiving is not fair. We appeal to your good sense and to your humanity to see that justice is done, that this thing is not continued, for it has been going on for quite a long time. You may well imagine the feeling of these two men, who are suffering as I have described, for no fault at all, except that they are Sikhs.

4. Maria Adamowska, "Beginnings in Canada," 1937 and 1939

Maria Adamowska (1890-1961) arrived in Canada from the Ukraine in 1899 and, over the years, wrote a number of poems and articles about her experiences as an immigrant. This material appeared as articles in the Almanac of the Ukrainian Voice *in 1937 and 1939.*

... Finally, we sailed into port Halifax. On the shore, a crowd of people stared at us, some out of curiosity, some out of contempt. Our men, particularly those from Galicia, were dressed like gentlemen for the voyage, but the women and children traveled in their everyday peasant costumes. The older men from Bukovina attracted attention to themselves by their waist-length hair—greased with reeking lard—and by their smelly sheepskin coats. Perhaps that was the reason why the English people stopped their noses and glued their eyes upon us—a strange spectacle, indeed.

In Halifax, we boarded a train and continued on our journey. As we sped across Ontario with its rocks, hills, and tunnels, we were afraid we were coming to the end of the world. The heart of many a man sank to his heels, and the women and children raised such lamentation as defies description.

At last we arrived in Winnipeg. At that time, Winnipeg was very much like any other small farmers' town. From the train we were taken to the immigration home....

One must remember that times were different then. Nowadays when an immigrant arrives in Canada, he feels more or less at home. Here he can find his own people everywhere and hear his own language. But in those days you had to wander far and wide before you could meet one of your countrymen. No matter what direction you turned, all you could see was the prairie like a vast sea on which wild animals howled and red-skinned Indians roamed. It was not until after our arrival that the mass immigration of Ukrainians to Canada began ...

From Winnipeg, we went to Yorkton, Saskatchewan. There we hired a rig which took us more than thirty miles farther north. At long last, after a miserable trip—we were nearly devoured alive by mosquitoes—we managed to reach our destination, the home of our acquaintances.

Our host, who had emigrated to Canada a year or two before, had written us to boast of the prosperity he had attained in such a short time. He said that he had a home like a mansion, a large cultivated field, and that his wife was dressed like a lady. In short, he depicted Canada as a country of incredible abundance whose borders were braided with sausage like some fantastic land in a fairy tale.

How great was our disenchantment when we approached that mansion of his and an entirely different scene met our eyes! It was actually just a small log cabin, only partly plastered and roofed with sod. Beside the cabin was a garden plot which had been dug with a spade. The man's face was smeared with dirt from ear to ear, and he looked weird, like some unearthly creature. He was grubbing up stumps near the house, and his wife was poking away in the garden. She reminded us of Robinson Crusoe on an uninhabited island. She was suntanned like a gypsy and was dressed in old, torn overalls. A wide-brimmed hat covered her head.

When mother saw this scarecrow, she started crying again. Later on, father reprimanded the man for writing us such nonsense. But his only answer was, "Let someone else have a taste of our good life here."...

Our troubles and worries were only just beginning. The house was small, and there were eighteen of us jammed within its four walls. What was one to do?

My father had brought some money with him, and with it he bought a cow and, later, a horse. Needless to say, I was the cowherd....

Winter was setting in. Dreading the idea of having to spend the season in such cramped quarters, my father dug a cave in a riverbank, covered it with turf, and there was our apartment, all ready to move into. Oh, how fortunate we felt! We would not have traded that root cellar for a royal palace. To this spot, we carried hay in bed sheets on our backs and stacked it. We also dragged firewood on our backs and made other preparations.

Day by day, our provisions ran lower and lower. The older folk were able to put up with hunger, but the famished children howled pitifully, like wolves.

One day I sneaked into our hostess' garden and pulled a turnip. Then I slipped out of the patch and ran as fast as I could into a gorge where I planned to hide myself in the tall grass and enjoy a real treat. Unfortunately, our hostess spied me, grabbed a club, and chased after me with the speed of a demon. To escape, I hid in some tall grass, but this heartless woman searched until she found me. There she stood over me and, as she raised her club, hissed, "You detestable intruder! One blow with this, and you'll be dead like a dog."

Fear of death made me forget about the turnip. It did not matter now how hungry I was: life was still sweet. And the woman was so ferocious that one blow of that club would certainly have meant the end of my life.

With tears in my eyes I began to plead, "Auntie darling, forgive me. I'll never again set my foot in your garden as long as I live."

Spitting at me with disgust the woman said, "Remember! Write that down on your forehead."

And so, for a piddling turnip, I almost paid with my life.

Came winter. Our cow stopped giving milk. Aside from bread, there was nothing to eat at home. Was one to gnaw the walls? One time I happened to notice tears rolling down mother's cheeks as she sipped something from a small pot. We children began to weep with her, "Mother, why are you crying? Won't you let us taste what you're eating?"

Mother divided the gruel among us. She tried to say something, but all she could manage was "My chil—"; further words died on her lips. Only a moan of anguish escaped from her breast. We learned afterwards that, late in the fall, mother had visited the garden of our former host and painstakingly raked the ground for potatoes that had been too small to be worth picking at potato-digging time. She had found a few tiny ones, no larger than hazel nuts. From these potatoes, she had made a gruel that tasted like potato soup, and it was this gruel which we children shared, tears flooding our eyes. Who knows how we would have managed if father had not brought his gun from the old country. With it he went hunting, and we had game all winter.

Before spring arrived, father went to look for a farm. He found one some fifteen miles to the west of us, and we began to build a house. We dug a round pit in the ground about five yards in diameter, just deep enough to scrape the black earth off the top and reach clay underneath. We mixed hay and water with the clay and kneaded it with our bare feet. With this clay, we plastered our house. In the spring, we moved into it. By that time, all our provisions had run out.

And so it was that father left home one day, on foot, prepared to tramp hundreds of miles to find a job. He left us without a piece of bread, to the mercy of fate.

While father was away, mother dug a plot of ground and planted the wheat she had brought from the old country, tied up in a small bundle. Every day, she watered it with her tears.

That done, there was no time to waste; every moment was precious. Mother and I began to clear our land. But since I was hardly strong enough for the job, I helped by grabbing hold of the top of each bush and pulling on it while mother cut the roots with the ax. Next we dug the ground with spades. How well did I do? At best, I had barely enough strength to thrust half the depth of the blade into the ground, no deeper. But that did not excuse me from digging. Where the ground was hard, mother had to correct my work, and thus the two of us cleared and dug close to four acres of land.

We lived on milk. One meal would consist of sweet milk followed by sour milk; the next meal would consist of sour milk followed by sweet milk. We looked like living corpses.

In the beginning of our life in Canada, old and young alike had to work grievously hard, often in the cold and in hunger. The effects of this hard work can now be painfully felt in even the tiniest bones of our bodies....

Our Rumanian neighbor, who lived a mile from our place, had made himself a small handmill for grinding wheat into flour. In the fall, when our wheat was ripe, mother reaped it very thoroughly, every last head of it, rubbed the kernels out, winnowed the grain, and poured it into a sack. Then she sent me with this grain—about eight pounds of it—to have it ground at our neighbor's mill.

It was the first time I had ever been to his place. As soon as I entered the vestibule of the house, I could see the hand mill in the corner. Now a new problem faced me: I had not the faintest idea how to operate the mill, and there was no one around to show me. I sat down and began to cry. After a while, the neighbor's wife showed up and spoke to me, but I could not understand her so I just kept on crying. I had the feeling that she was scolding me for sneaking into her house. I pointed to the bag of wheat. She understood what I wanted, pointed to the hand mill, and went inside the house, leaving the door open. She sat down at the table, picked up a piece of bread which was as dark as the ground we walked on, dipped it in salt, and munched away at it.

As I watched her, I almost choked with grief. Oh, how strong was my urge to throw myself at her feet and plead for at least one bite of that bread. But, as she obviously was not thinking of me, I got ahold of myself. That piece of bread might well have been the last she had in the house. That experience gave me the most profound shock of my entire life. No one can fully appreciate what I went through unless he has lived through something similar himself.

Continually swallowing my saliva, I kept grinding the wheat until I had finished. Then I ran home with that little bit of flour, joyfully looking forward to the moment when we, too, would have bread.

But my joy quickly evaporated. Mother pondered a moment and said, "This will make two or three loaves of bread, and the flour will be all gone. Not enough to eat and not enough to feast our eyes upon. I'm going to cook cornmeal for you; it will last longer." And so we teased ourselves with cornmeal for some time.

On his way home from the other side of Brandon, where he'd been working, father stopped at Yorkton and bought a fifty-pound sack of flour. He carried it home on his back every inch of the twenty-eight miles. When we saw him coming home, we bounced with excitement and greeted him with joyous laughter mixed with tears. And all this excitement over the prospect of a piece of bread! Father had not earned much money, for he had lost a lot of time jobhunting. Then, at work, he had fallen from a stack onto the tines of a pitchfork and been laid up for a long time. But he had managed to earn something like twenty dollars, enough for flour to last us for a time.

The coming of winter presented new problems. We had nothing to wear on our feet. Something had to be done about that. Mother had brought a couple of woolen sheets from the old country. From these she sewed us footwear that kept our feet warm all winter.

That winter our horse died. We were now left with only one horse and he was just a year-old colt, though he looked like a two-year old. Father made a harness from some ropes, and a sled, and began to break him in.

... Even in winter we had no rest. We had settled in a low-lying area. In the summertime, water lay everywhere, and the croaking of frogs filled the air. And it never rained but poured in those days. Often the downpour continued for two or three weeks without a letup. In the winter, the water in the lakes froze up, the wells — always few in number — dried up, and there was nothing one could do about it. We were concerned not so much about ourselves as about our few head of livestock, which would have no water. We could not let them die; a way had to be found to obtain water for them.

Father found a piece of tin somewhere, shaped it into a trough, built an enclosure out of stones, placed the trough over it, built a fire in the enclosure under the trough, kept the trough filled with snow, and, as the snow melted, collected the water in a tub at the bottom end of the trough. But this was not the best way to water cattle. A cow could drink up a couple of tubs of water at a time and then look around and moo for more.

As a result, we messed around with snow all winter long, until at times the marrow in our bones was chilled. And talk about snow in those days! Mountains of it! Your cattle might be lowing pitifully in the stable, and you could not get to them because heaps of snow blocked your way. It might take a hard morning's work before a tunnel could be dug to the stable, and the cattle fed....

Ours was a life of hard work, misery, and destitution. Things got a little better only after we acquired a yoke of oxen to work with. But when we first got them, we experienced some unhappy and frustrating moments....

With each day of labor, our poor settlers could see some progress. They now lived in hastily built houses, as everyone was sick and tired of living in damp, smelly root cellars. Although these houses lacked in comfort, there was at least fresh air in them. By now, each settler had dug up a piece of land and owned a few head of cattle and other livestock....

In the spring, father was able to get some seed wheat. When he finished seeding our tiny, little field, he left home to look for a job again. At home, the family buckled down to clearing, digging, and haying. Mother mowed the hay with a scythe, and we children raked it, carried it home on our backs, and stacked it. We also brought a supply of wood for the winter.

In the meantime, the people from the old country had arrived. This added a touch of brightness to our social life. The newcomers, Mrs. D.F. Stratychuk and Mrs. P. Denys, even helped us to harvest our crop....

That autumn father's earnings were a little more substantial. He was able to buy another cow and another steer. And he bought me a pair of shoes and material for a skirt. Those shoes meant more to me than any ordinary ones....

As for their durability, suffice it to say that when one of us girls got married, she handed the shoes down to the younger sister, and the process was repeated until four of us had worn them, each for a few years. And who knows how many more generations those shoes would have survived if it had not been for mother. She got so disgusted with them that she threw them into the stove one day and burned them.

As for my skirt, it was made of the finest quality "silk," the kind used for making overalls. So one can imagine how I looked in that gorgeous costume. But, poor me, I was quite happy with it.

In the wintertime, father used to ask some of his neighbors to give him a hand in threshing his wheat with flails. Once the threshing was done, he had other work to do, such as making a yoke for the oxen and repairing the harrow and the plow, so that everything would be ready for spring work....

In our neighborhood, there were settlers of other nationalities, mainly Rumanian. One of them put on a wedding for his daughter and invited us to attend. We accepted first because there had not been such an event in the few years that we had been in Canada, and second, out of simple curiosity to see a Rumanian ceremony....

The town of Canora was founded five miles from our place. Our people were quite happy about that, and they were happy when its first store was opened by a Jewish merchant. For one thing, we were fed up with traveling all that distance to Yorkton to do our shopping. Secondly, with a Jew we could always speak in our own language, for at that time how many of us immigrants could speak English? When we did try, it was only by means of sign language ...

Year by year the cultivated area of our farm grew in size. And when the field got too large to be harvested with sickles, father had to buy a binder. For the first couple of years we used it, we hitched our oxen to it. That was a miserable experience. Cutting grain of medium height posed no problem, but if it was heavy or lying flat and you had to give the binder a little more speed, you could not make the oxen move faster even by lighting a fire under them. They kept to the same slow pace no matter what. The only way to cope with this problem was to buy another horse. A team of horses made harvesting so much easier.

During the long winter evenings, I taught younger children to read in Ukrainian. Among my students were a girl [of] non-Ukrainian descent and an elderly gentleman. There were no schools anywhere around in those days. Children grew up like barbarians....

We had quite a few books at home. Father had brought a lot of them from the old country, all on serious subjects. Later on, when Ukrainian newspapers began to be published, none of them escaped father's attention. Even if he had to go without food and live on water for a whole week, he found the money for newspaper subscriptions. Since there were several literate people in our community, they used to get together at our home on the long winter evenings, to read the papers and discuss their contents. Many a sunrise found these men, though weary from the previous day's hard toil, going without a wink of sleep to forge a happier lot for themselves and their children.

Those sleepless nights were not spent in vain. In 1904-05, thanks to the efforts of our pioneer fathers, a small but beautiful school was built. Its first teacher was the scholarly and patriotic Ukrainian, the late Joseph Bychynsky....

As for churches or Ukrainian priests, you could not have found one if you'd searched the country with a fine-tooth comb. Occasionally a priest would stray our way, but he was what we called an "Indian priest," and we could not understand him, nor he us. Our poor settlers consulted among themselves and decided to meet every Sunday and sing at least those parts of the liturgy that were meant to be sung by the cantor. Since our house was large enough, that was where the meetings were held. On Sunday morning, everyone hurried to our house the way one would to church....

In due course, the Bukovinians built themselves a church in which services were at first conducted by a visiting Russian priest. Often we were invited to attend but we could not understand their service, which was in Rumanian ...

That year Easter came very early. It was the Saturday before Easter, but only here and there was the snow beginning to melt. The day before, a severe blizzard had piled up banks of snow and drifted over all the roads. But there was no power on earth which could have stopped us from carrying out our plans....

Whatever the course of later events, it must be recognized that, in the beginning, the pioneer priests contributed a great deal to the cultural development of our people here, in what was then a foreign land to them. And for their efforts and troubles, they sought no favors from anyone. They suffered the same woes and miseries as did everyone else. In short, they proved themselves to be true sons of the Ukrainian people....

In those days, no one dreamed of such luxuries as paint or lime. For white-washing jobs, people used a kind of ash-gray clay found under the surface of the ground cover in swampy areas. They dug this clay, pressed it into flat cakes, and dried it. Dissolved in water, it was used for whitewashing.

Bitter and unenviable were our beginnings, but by hard work and with God's help, we gradually got established. Not very far from our place a few neighbors pooled their resources and bought a steam threshing outfit in partnership. Father decided it was time, we, too, had our threshing done by a threshing machine....

In 1908, father traded farms with an Englishman, and our family moved thirty miles farther north, to the Hyas district....

By moving to Hyas, we had to start all over again and suffer the same hard-ships as in the beginning. But hope of better times lifted our spirits and gave us courage and strength to face future labors.

Such were the tremendous hardships our people had to endure in the early days of immigration. Since there were as yet no railways, they were compelled to travel hundreds of miles on foot. Toiling in cold and hunger, they cleared the forests, [cleaned] the land of rocks, and converted the inaccessible areas into fertile fields. Many of the pioneers who came here in the prime of their lives are no longer with us. Those who are still with us are stooped with age; tomorrow it will be their turn to leave us for their eternal rest....

FURTHER READINGS

Anderson, K. *Vancouver's Chinatown: Racial Discourses in Canada, 1875-1980.* Montreal and Kingston: McGill Queen's University Press, 1991.

Avery, D. *Dangerous Foreigners: European Immigrant Workers and Labour Radicalism in Canada.* Toronto: McClelland and Stewart, 1979.

Avery, D. *Reluctant Hosts: Canada's Response to Immigrant Workers, 1896-1994.* Toronto: McClelland and Stewart, 1995.

Burnet, J., Ed. *Looking into My Sisters' Eyes: An Exploration in Women's History.* Toronto: Multicultural History Society of Ontario, 1986.

Dunae, P. *Gentlemen Immigrants: From British Public Schools to the Canadian Frontier.* Vancouver: Douglas and McIntyre, 1981.

Hall, D. *Clifford Sifton.* Vancouver: University of British Columbia Press, 1985.

Jackel, S., Ed. *A Flannel Shirt and Liberty: British Emigrant Gentlewomen in the Canadian West, 1880–1914.* Vancouver: University of British Columbia Press, 1982.

Johnston, H. *The Voyage of the Komagata Maru: The Sikh Challenge to Canada's Colour Bar.* Delhi: Oxford University Press, 1979.

Lehr, J. "Government Coercion in the Settlement of Ukrainian Immigrants in Western Canada." *Prairie Forum* 8 (1983): 179-94.

Lehr, J. "Kinship and Society in the Ukrainian Pioneer Settlement of the Canadian West." *The Canadian Geographer* 29, 3 (1985): 207-19.

Lindstrom-Best, V. *Defiant Sisters: A Social History of Finnish Immigrant Women in Canada.* Toronto: University of Toronto Press, 1988.

Luciuk, L., and S. Hryniuk, Eds. *Canada's Ukrainians: Negotiating an Identity.* Toronto: University of Toronto Press, 1991.

Lupul, M., Ed. *A Heritage in Transition: Essays in the History of Ukrainians in Canada.* Toronto: McClelland and Stewart, 1982.

Martynowych, O. *Ukrainian Canadian: The Formative Years 1891–1924.* Edmonton: Canadian Institute of Ukrainian Studies, 1991.

Palmer, H. *Patterns of Prejudice: A History of Nativism in Alberta.* Toronto: McClelland and Stewart, 1982.

Palmer, H., Ed. *Immigration and the Rise of Multiculturalism.* Toronto: Copp Clark, 1975.

Parr, J. *Labouring Children: British Immigrant Apprentices to Canada, 1869–1924.* 2nd ed. Toronto: University of Toronto Press, 1994.

Petryshyn, J. *Peasants in the Promised Land: Canada and the Ukrainians, 1891-1914.* Toronto: James Lorimer, 1985.

Potrobenko, H. *No Streets of Gold: A Social History of Ukrainians in Alberta.* Vancouver: New Star, 1977.

Ramirez, B. *On the Move: French-Canadian and Italian Migrants in the North Atlantic Economy, 1860-1914.* Toronto: McClelland and Stewart, 1991.

Roberts, B. "A Work of Empire': Canadian Reformers and British Female Immigration." In *A Not Unreasonable Claim: Women and Reform in Canada, 1880s-1920s,* ed. L. Kealey. Toronto: Women's Press, 1979.

Roberts, B. *Whence They Came: Deportation from Canada 1900-1935.* Ottawa: University of Ottawa Press, 1988.

Roy, P. *A White Man's Province: British Columbia Politicians and Chinese and Japanese Immigration, 1858-1914.* Vancouver: University of British Columbia Press, 1989.

Swyripa, F. *Wedded to the Cause: Ukrainian-Canadian Women and Ethnic Identity 1891-1991.* Toronto: University of Toronto Press, 1993.

Ward, P. *White Canada Forever: Popular Attitudes and Public Policy Towards Orientals in British Columbia.* Montreal and Kingston: McGill-Queen's University Press, 1978.

CHAPTER 5

"Perfect Justice and Harmony"

VOTES FOR WOMEN

INTRODUCTION

Statistical data definitively proves that Canadian women still struggle for political and social equality in our new century, and the evidence even suggests regression in some areas. Though they are hardly shoeless and pregnant in the kitchen, a glimpse at the House of Commons, any university engineering faculty, or corporate boardroom graphically illustrates that women do not share power commensurate to their proportion of the population. On average women still earn three-quarters as much as men—though this is a significant improvement over the early part of the twentieth century when they could expect half, at best. Social issues that directly affect women, such as a national day-care policy, remain unaddressed. Unfortunate as the present situation may be, it bears remembering that less than 100 years ago women could not even vote, let alone run for Parliament. Engineering faculties in 1900 forbade their admission, and they entered national boardrooms as stenographers, not executives. There has been progress. The question remains, however: why was it so difficult to obtain the vote? And to what degree, if any, did enfranchisement actually fulfill women's hopes and promises?

The Canadian feminist movement emerged simultaneously with those in the United States and Britain but, unlike the latter, never became violent. First-wave feminism sprang from the ideological and social dilemmas posed by industrialization, urbanization, and a perceived threat to the family. As such, it shared ties with general reformist ideas challenging the exploitive excesses of modern capitalism. For much of its history in Canada, the core of the movement remained in Toronto, which served as the headquarters for groups such as the Dominion Women's Emancipation Association, the Dominion Enfranchisement Association, and the Canadian Suffrage Association. While claiming to be national in outlook, these organizations had little impact outside that city, and most suffrage campaigns began as intensely provincial, not national, movements. Nor did they represent a cross-section of Canadian womanhood. The associations were thoroughly upper class — often snobbishly so — urban, English, and led by women with leisure time to study and organize — of whom there were few.

Most national organizations supposed that women's voting and political participation would spread biologically based maternal qualities to the society at large. This "maternal" feminist strain cared little about equality, believing instead that inasmuch as women perform different roles in society than men, they must champion those nurturing qualities from which the whole nation would benefit. For this group, achieving the vote was a means to social reform, not an end in itself. Thus, it is hardly surprising that maternal feminists formed the vanguard of the prohibition movement. The other branch of feminism, the "equal rights" feminists, disagreed with their "maternal" sisters and argued in favour of the vote on the ideological principle that women, as equals to men, deserved equal political power. This group, in fact, saw "maternal feminists" as misguided.

Both feminist groups judged that Canadian women voters would significantly improve the social fabric by pressuring male parliamentarians in areas they apparently ignored. Social policy issues such as child labour, day care, education, welfare, prohibition, and protection for women must be addressed; this, they argued, would only occur if women gained a direct political voice. Enfranchised women, by constituting half the voting population, would force change by electing candidates, male or female, who promised to push appropriate legislation through the provincial and federal corridors of power. Thus, a sense of "women-as-national-saviours" permeated both branches of the suffrage movement.

Many men and women, however, argued that getting the vote would affect nothing, either for women or the nation. Power and the ability to enact change, they said, did not lie in political gender balance but elsewhere. This was a popular and effective weapon in the anti-suffrage arsenal and led to a certain smugness when female voters and legislators enjoyed limited success in the post-enfranchisement period, particularly compared to their high hopes and expectations. Today the narrow first-wave agenda earns dismissal or derision from those who argue that its motivation had little to do with emancipating Canadian women.

Why did it take so long for Canadian women to gain the vote in the first place? Actually it didn't, at least not in relative terms. Canada compares very well to the rest of the world, both then and now, when it comes to implementing women's rights. Still, there is no denying the protracted struggle Canadian women experienced in their march to the ballot box. In the final analysis, the patriarchal nature of Canadian society ensured that men wielded legislative power, and it was they who had to change, and they who had to accept the idea of women's suffrage for it to occur. Sharing, especially sharing power, did not come naturally or easily, and most men initially resented or feared the suffrage movement. Male farming associations in the prairies first broke the patriarchal mold by endorsing women's political rights, perhaps because prairie women so often worked as equals to their husbands as they co-operatively struggled to hew new lives from the unyielding prairie. Manitoba granted women the franchise in 1916, the first province to do so, and the other prairie legislatures soon followed. Ottawa granted women the right to vote federally in 1918. On the other hand, the vote did not make Canadian women legally "persons," and in 1922, 44,259 Quebec women petitioned *against* giving women the vote. They remained disenfranchised there until 1940; Swiss women didn't get the vote until 1971.

DISCUSSION POINTS

1. Summarize the arguments in these documents made for and against women getting the vote.

2. Leacock and H.D.P. all cast doubt upon the significance of women gaining the right to vote. Were they right? Was the original feminist movement misdirected?

3. While western Canada became the chief centre of support for suffrage, Quebec lagged far behind. Why?

DOCUMENTS

1. Hon. John Dryden, Minister of Agriculture, "Womanhood Suffrage," Speech, Ontario Legislature, May 10, 1893

Hon. John Dryden (1840-1909) was a successful farmer known for progressive and quality livestock breeding efforts on his 420-acre farm in southern Ontario. His political career began as secretary of the local school board, progressed to town councillor in 1863, and in 1879 to election as a Liberal to the Ontario provincial legislature, in which capacity he served until 1905. Dryden's political acumen and agricultural expertise made him a logical agriculture minister, a post he accepted in 1890. He believed very strongly in education for Ontario's farmers and was deeply committed to the Ontario Agricultural College. He had three sons, two of whom died in infancy, and five daughters.

... An advocate of women's suffrage openly repudiates the Bible on the ground that "its teachings oppose that liberty of speech and action which she as a representative woman demands." Another lady writer states that "if the Bible stands in the way of women's rights then the Bible and religion must go." These are strong statements, which will not be endorsed by many who support this Bill in this Legislature or outside of it.

...I am free to say to you that these convictions as to whether this measure is right or wrong, have been formed from a careful study of the teachings of the Bible which bear upon it. I accept these teachings as of divine origin, and they cannot, therefore, change from age to age...

If we go back to the account of creation, we shall find that man being created, the various animal creations which had been brought into existence were brought before him in order that he might name them. But among them all there did not appear any that could be utilized as his associate—after they have all passed before him he is still left alone and has no companion. Then the statement is made that "It is not good for man to be alone; we will make an help-meet for him." And in after ages, when the apostles made reference to this statement they used these words: "Man was made and then the woman; the man was not made for the woman, but the woman for the man."

The point I want to emphasize in this regard is that woman was formed to be an associate, a companion, a helper of man, and not to usurp authority or control over him. They are two persons, yet they are spoken of as one—of the same flesh, one the complement of the other. The same rule applies in their formation as in the animal creation everywhere. Man's appearance indicates force, authority, decision, self-assertion, while that of a woman shows exactly the opposite, and indicates instead trust, dependence, grace and beauty. In other words, man was made in such a form when compared to woman as stamps him with the attributes of authority, government and control ...

In view of these statements, and others which might be quoted, I therefore conclude that woman's place in accordance with Bible teaching is to be in submission to man, and not to assume the place of authority. When my honorable friend seeks to give them the ballot he in effect says, "I propose to give woman control of public affairs; I wish to place in her hands governing power to compel man to accept her dictation." That proposition, according to my argument, is against the teaching of Scripture, and therefore is not and cannot be right....

Women have exercised and will exercise more power without the ballot than with it in matters of this kind. What has changed the drinking customs of this country from the drunken revels of the past to the orderly, sober conduct of today? It is largely due to the influence of women. How has this influence been exercised? Not by force, not by control, nor by authority, but by the strongest of all forces, loving persuasion. Women today can do much more in this direction than they have ever done in the past if they will unite in creating a sentiment in favor of sobriety and right conduct. Woman has in this regard immense power over man if she is willing to exercise it....

I notice that Mrs. Rockwell, the lady who seems to stand at the head of this movement in this country, writes in one of the public papers that man cannot legislate for woman, and that woman, therefore, needs the franchise for her own protection. In that statement you have an utter repudiation of woman's dependence upon man; it is an assertion of independence; it is a desire to live and work separately. She says, "Give us the franchise and we will protect ourselves and our sex." Now, I repudiate entirely this doctrine. Do what you will you cannot, and you ought not if you could, reverse nature's law. Woman always was and always will be dependent upon man, and whether some women who are manhaters like it or not it cannot be changed. This lady's statement means that man has no regard for wife, mother, sister or daughter—that he, their rightful protector, will see them injured and refuse to come to their aid....

This same lady tells us that women do not receive equal pay with men for equally good work. How can the ballot correct this? Can you compel by law the payment of a higher scale of wages? So long as women are willing and anxious to work for less wages than men, so long will they be paid less. Would the use of the ballot compel the mistress on Bloor street to give her servants higher wages? Would it insure the dressmaker down town more wage for her work? All this is regulated by the law of supply and demand, and is in no way affected by the ballot.

TO REFINE POLITICS

The advocates of Women's Suffrage tell us that the ballot is wanted in order to refine politics, in order to bring better candidates before the public. That depends on what you consider better candidates. Is it better looking men who are required? I can easily understand looking around this Assembly, if a few, especially in this corner, were excluded, including the Attorney-General and perhaps the leader of the Opposition, it is possible better candidates in this regard might be secured. But speaking for myself, I am not aware that there is any particular necessity for refining politics in this country. I believe that our political campaigns in these days are conducted in a very orderly manner already....

But my strongest objection to the Bill of my hon. friend is the evil effects which in my judgment would result to society and to woman herself. These results would not be seen immediately; they would not be observed at the first few elections, they probably would take years to work out, but in the end the result would be evil, and evil alone. The right to cast the ballot carries with it the right to be elected by the ballot. If woman is part of the people, as is alleged, if she stands on an equality with man, having the same rights in the body politic, having equal intelligence, equal education, equal business training, by what process of reasoning can you show that the right to vote in her case does not carry with it the right to be voted for? ... The right to vote for a member of the Legislative Assembly would carry with it the right to be elected a member of this Assembly, the right to preside here, the right to take part here in all its deliberations. I think I hear the question coming to my ears. And why should they not take part? My answer is, not because woman is not intelligent, nor because she is not sufficiently educated, but because she is woman, because by putting her thus out of her sphere you unsex her, you are seeking to make her a man, to induce her to fill the place of a man; to seat her in Parliament making laws and governing the stronger sex—sitting as judge on the bench and as juror in the box.

A LOW TYPE OF WOMANHOOD

I am well aware that this is the ambition of some women, masculine in character, disliking their own sex, having only selfish ambitions, deploring the fate that brought them into the world as women, and determined at all hazards to break the bonds of womanhood, and to take the part of a man. Such a woman says, "give me a chance and I will show you that I am not dependent; I refuse to take the place of humble submission which nature has assigned me; I am as able as any man; I can fill his place anywhere." Such a person I describe as a manly woman—the lowest type of true womanhood. An effeminate man or a manly woman is not the ideal type of humanity. They are nowhere in demand. The masculine, manly woman is not respected by her own sex—they generally despise and mock her—and I am certain that she is not strongly admired by many men either. It is not her misery that she cannot be a man, but rather that she cannot be a woman.

I appeal to true womanhood if its highest joy is not to know that in man they have a protector, one who loves them, provides for their needs, not by force, but willingly, because he delights to do it, and I appeal to true manhood if the strongest incentive to active exertion to do their best in every way is not the fact that there is dependent upon them a loving, dutiful wife, or a mother, daughter or sister.

INJURY TO HOME

Can you not see that when you have brought women into the rightful sphere of man you will have revolutionized society, and so changed altogether the relation-ship of man and woman? Will such a course bring greater harmony? Will the happiness of the people be thereby increased? Will, as these people imagine, all sin thus be stamped out? How will such a course affect the home life? Suppose that men and women voted differently, the mother against the son, the husband against the wife, and so on. If they did not thus vote differently, according to the argument, all these supposed wrongs could never be righted, and no object would be gained by adding this enormous number to the list of voters. If they did vote differently, is it possible that this would add to the joy of the home? Will it permit in many cases harmony and love to continue?

Women are more strongly partizan than men; they admire more strongly, and when one has become the idol of their choice there is nothing they would not do to secure his election.... Imagine the female portion of a household the mem-bers of one partizan committee and the men arrayed on the other side. Imagine the men of the opposite party holding consultations with the women of one's own household in the heat of a party contest. It is impossible under such circumstances that bitterness should not come into that home. Its harmony would be gone; it would no longer be a place of joy and love and trust; these would certainly give place to jealousy, hatred and malice.

I am firmly convinced that one of the curses of this age is that there is not enough of home life. I think that home life is the strength of any nation.... The demand for woman suffrage is a blow at this power. If I had the privilege, and wished to bring the greatest blessing possible to our people, I should choose to increase and develop the influence of the home, to endeavour to change the tendency of the times, and to encourage young people together to build homes where mutual companionship, harmony and love might prevail: such homes as would prove a greater attraction than the street parade, the saloon or the theatre: homes where character would be built which would increase right conduct and prove a shield from temptation.

WOMEN WITHOUT HOMES

One reason urged why woman suffrage should be granted is because so many women are without homes. I know that this is true, and that the tendency in that direction is increasing, but it is largely the result of the prevailing fashion among young people to desire neither to be mistress of a home nor to work in the home of another. They choose in preference the factory, the counter of a store, and the tailor shop: anywhere to be entirely independent and to live unto themselves. I have no quarrel with them if they wish to do this, but I want to say that it is certainly not conducive to increasing morality. Intemperance is spoken of as the greatest evil, but I ask those who have observed more closely the workings of society whether or not the tendency to forsake home and home life does not lead directly to that end? I ask whether the prevailing vices of our cities and towns are not the direct outcome of forsaken homes, and do not lead directly in the way of the saloon and the grog shop? To introduce women into the political arena is to add to this tendency, and those who advocate it are incurring a great responsibility. I certainly shall not be one of them. The home is woman's place of power; if she is a true woman she rules there, although she does not assume that authority. This is her queenly station in every Christian country. Here her nobility, grace and moral power can be felt, and will always wield a greater influence on the nation than she ever could by assuming to take control in the political world.

DEGRADING WOMAN

I have already stated that woman is most respected in Christian and civilized countries. Introduce her into politics; make her an active agent, an active canvasser in political campaigns; bring her upon the platform and let her try her hand at sarcasm and ridicule; let her drop her winning ways and patient persuasion; let her shake her fist in man's face; let her undertake to fight her way thus to fancied freedom, and declare her power to compel him to submit to her dictation, and what inevitably must be the result? Shall I still be expected to lift my hat in respectful deference? Will man anywhere give place to her, in the car or on the street? In so doing she declares her equality, and constantly states that she is not dependent. She will in the end be taken by most men at her word and left in public to look after herself....

Example is given us of women in history who have figured as rulers of nations. We are frequently pointed to queens who have taken a notable place in history, but it will be observed always that these women have occupied this position only because they appeared in the direct line of descent, and because there was no male to fill the place. Our own Queen is pointed to as an example of what a woman can do in ruling a great nation. She has won the respect and admiration, not only of her own people, but of the whole civilized world. But how has she done this? Is it because she has assumed the position that these persons desire women generally to take? Has she assumed the position of a dictator, that she might have her will and her way? I think not.

She has always shown her dependence upon men by choosing from among her people the wisest and best men upon whom to place the responsibility of the great work of governing her vast empire. She is admired to-day, not because she is a ruler, but because, in the midst of all her queenly duties she still maintains the womanly part; she is esteemed because of the admirable example she has placed before her people as a dutiful wife and an affectionate mother.

I do not wish to be misunderstood by anyone. I am conscientious in my statement of the case. I am not seeking to degrade woman, but am anxious, rather, that she should maintain her present high place, and be beloved still more, if possible. What I have said here I have said in her defence. I am here to defend my wife and my daughters; I am here to stand in defence of our home; to stand in defence of the influence and power of woman in the home, in the church and in society, and I call upon the hon. members of the Legislature not to treat this matter as a trifling question, to pass it by with a smile and vote for the Bill because they think they are thus paying a compliment to woman. It is not a compliment to them to vote in favor of my hon. friend's proposition. I call upon them to take the manly part; to join with me in defending woman from the degrading influences which are sure to follow if she takes part in political warfare.

2. James L. Hughes, *Equal Suffrage*, 1910

James Laughlin Hughes (1846–1935) grew up near Bowmanville, Ontario, became a teacher at age 18, and school principal at 24. He was appointed inspector of public schools for Toronto in 1874, eventually becoming chief inspector. During his tenure he enacted many reforms to the public school system, including the introduction of kindergarten and manual training courses. In 1890 he was defeated in the Ontario provincial election as the pro-suffragist equal rights candidate for Peel County. Hughes was an active Orangeman, Methodist, and athlete. He also wrote a number of school texts and several volumes of poetry.

... 3. *"Women would not vote if they had the opportunity."* Women do vote when they get the opportunity to do so. In all countries where they have the parliamentary franchise they vote quite as well as men. In some countries even a larger percentage of women vote than of men.

There is no use in theorizing about the question. Men proved conclusively that locomotives could not run on smooth rails, but they ran, and that settled the discussion. Women do vote in Church matters, in school elections, in municipal elections and in parliamentary elections wherever they have the legal right to do so. If women would not vote, no harm could come from making the experiment of granting woman suffrage.

4. *"All women do not wish to vote."* True. Neither do all men. It would, therefore, be as logical to refuse to let men vote because some men do not care to vote as to refuse to let women vote because some of them do not yet wish to vote. Less than half the men vote at ordinary municipal elections in many places. It would be utterly unjust on this account to disfranchise those who wish to vote. If only one hundred women in Canada believed it to be their right and duty to vote, there is no spirit of justice, human or divine, that would prevent their voting merely because other women do not wish to vote. Not one woman in a hundred wishes to teach school. The same argument would prohibit all women from teaching because all women do not wish to teach. The logical outcome of this argument allows no woman to do anything unless all women desire to do it. Many women do vote in municipal matters, and desire the right to vote on other questions. The indifference of women not yet aroused cannot affect the rights of those who are awake. The ballot was given to the negroes not because all negroes wanted it, but because it was right that they should have it. Duty is the broad ground on which the question rests. Thousands of true, pure, home-loving women sincerely believe it to be their duty to vote in order to help to decide great social and national

questions that affect the well-being of their country and their homes. They surely have as well-defined a right to desire to vote as other women have to oppose woman's enfranchisement. The women who wish to vote do not try to compel those women to vote who oppose woman suffrage. This is an age of individual liberty. Right and duty and conscience should guide us. Each woman should be at liberty to decide for herself....

10. "*Woman's mental nature is different from man's.*" However it may be expressed, this is precisely the strongest reason why they should vote. God made man and woman different in characteristics, but He made the one the complement of the other. Perfect unity is wrought out of different but harmonious elements. Legislation will be essentially one-sided until man's ideals are balanced by woman's. Woman's individuality does differ from man's, and her individuality is necessary to perfect justice and harmony in the senate as well as in the home.

Woman's different mental attitude makes her vote valuable. She is the complement of man in the divine conception of humanity. Her vote should therefore be the complement of man's vote. The unity of related diversity produces harmony. The male and female elements of intellect and character when balanced produce the grandest unities of human intelligence. The enfranchisement of a sex means more than the liberation of a class chiefly because it brings a distinct and hitherto unrepresented element into the voting power of the world. There would be only a partial hope in securing woman suffrage if it would simply increase the number of voters. It will do much more than this. It will not only enlarge the voting power; it will enrich it.

11. "*Politics will degrade women.*" "*It is because women have kept out of politics and generally out of the contentious arena, that they have remained gentle, tender and delicate women.*" Politics should not be degrading. It is discreditable to men that the sacred duty of statecraft should be associated with any processes or experiences of a debasing character. But the presence of woman purifies politics. The women of Wyoming are as womanly and as gentle as those in the neighboring States where women do not vote. The women who lead in municipal reforms in England, or who champion the cause of woman's enfranchisement there, are as true and pure and sweet-voiced as those who are conventional models. Politics should mean high thinking on social and national questions, and the carrying out of calm decisions by voting for right measures. Thinking about her country's history and present condition and hopes and relationships to other countries, need not destroy a woman's gentleness. Strength of character does not rob woman of her witching charm. The condition of politics, as admitted by this objection, indicates the need of woman's elevating, purifying influence.

Wendell Phillips crystallized the reply to this argument when he said, "Women will make the polling booth as pure as the parlor," and there is every reason to believe with Mr. Phillips that instead of politics degrading women, women would elevate politics. Why should it degrade a woman to do her part in making the laws of her country harmonize with her purest feelings and her highest thought? It is impossible to believe that such a result could follow such action. Character is not ennobled by thinking good thoughts, but by executing them. History proves conclusively that men have always risen to a higher dignity of manhood after being entrusted with the ballot. The result would inevitably be the same in the case of woman. The sense of responsibility would define and strengthen her character.

If politics are really degrading in themselves, men should be prohibited from taking part in them as well as women, but they are not necessarily degrading either to men or women. It is not necessary to theorize about this question, however. The test has been made for nearly forty years in Wyoming, and there has been no degradation of the women there, no unsexing, no loss of the sweetness and tenderness of woman's character....

14. *"Wives might vote against their husbands, and thus destroy the harmony of the home."* It is a strange conception of family harmony that husband and wife must think alike in regard to all subjects. This would not be true harmony, it would be mere sameness; and it is only logically conceivable on the surrender of the individuality of one to that of the other. This can never be done without degradation to the one who has to submit. Woman has had too much of such degradation. Why should two reasonable beings cease to recognize each other's right to independent judgment because they are married to each other? Woman suffrage will elevate the condition of both husband and wife. The wife will be emancipated from a subjection pronounced by God to be a curse, and the husband will be saved from the debasing selfishness of believing himself to be the only member of his household worthy of being entrusted with the dignity of voting.

It would be a great advantage if the drunkard's wife and the moderate drinker's wife could vote in opposition to their husbands. Such opposition would result in ultimate peace and not discord....

21. *"The transfer of power from the military to the unmilitary sex involves a change in the character of a nation. It involves, in short, national emasculation."* The "war" argument is a very old one often answered. Women suffer as much as men from war. Their hardships at home are often equal, and their anxieties greater than those of the soldiers on the field or in the camp. Those soldiers are husbands, sons, brothers or lovers of sorrowing women. Many women labor in hospitals and

various other ways for the soldiers. Woman's work is not man's work, nor man's work woman's, in war or in peace; but her work is quite as needful to the world's advancement, both in peace and war, as man's is. The time cometh, too, when "war shall be no more," and however man may sneer at woman suffrage, woman's work will aid in the fulfilment of this prophecy.

Then, too, very few men ever really fight for their country. The "war argument" would, therefore, disqualify most of the very men who use it from voting, and, carried to its logical limit, it would confine suffrage to soldiers alone. If the function of the State be only to raise armies and build court-houses and jails, woman may safely be refused the ballot; but if the State should deal with education, with moral, social, and industrial evolution, with art, science, charity, justice, manufactures and commerce, woman is entitled to her share in guiding the affairs of State.

22. *"Man alone can uphold government and enforce the law. Let the edifice of law be as moral as you will, its foundation is the force of the community, and the force of the community is male. Laws passed by the woman's vote will be felt to have no force behind them. Would the stronger sex obey any laws manifestly carried by the female vote in the interests of woman against man? Man would be tempted to resist woman's government when it galled him."* Women have made no proposal to establish a government by women. They strongly object to government by one sex, either male or female. It is not possible to have all the men voting on one side, and all the women on the other. All women do not think alike, nor will they ever vote unanimously any more than do the men. It is purely imaginary to speak of woman's government. Government will always be maintained by a majority composed of the united votes of men and women. Moreover votes are now cast in the ballot box, and it will not be possible to find out whether the majority consists chiefly of men or of women. Therefore it is clear that the question of force cannot be brought into the suffrage discussion. The force of a nation must remain on the side of the majority. But modern governments do not rely on force for their existence or for the execution of their laws. The edicts of despots had to be forced on unwilling people. Rebels today know that their rebellion is not against kings or governments, but against the will of the people. Men submit to laws because they have shared in making them....

27. *"Woman is weaker than man physically."* Has she strength enough to go to the polls and vote? If she has, the question of strength has nothing more to do with deciding the question of suffrage.

Men are allowed to vote who are carried in bed to the polls, so that by man's own physical standard set for himself, woman is competent to vote. No physical test has been adopted for men; none must be fixed for women. The strength test, and the sex test cannot be the same.

28. *"Woman's brain is not so large as man's, therefore she should not vote."* Size of brain has never been made a test in deciding man's right to vote, so this objection is irrelevant. No one ever saw an official at a polling booth with a tapeline to measure men's heads to decide whether they should vote or not. It is therefore perfectly illogical to raise the question of the size of woman's head in discussing her right to vote. If a standard could be fixed for the size of a voter's head, and applied in the case of men as well as women, there would be justice in the rule, but little sense. Only small-headed men, with their largest development in the back of their heads near the top, could be illogical enough to propose such a test. Quality of brain is more important than size of brain. Thousands of men vote in every country who are not equal in intelligence to the average woman. The great body of men most uniformly opposed to equal suffrage are not only small-headed, but small-hearted....

30. *"Women are more nervous than men, and the excitement of elections would undermine their constitutions and tend to unbalance them."* Thousands of men vote whose nervous systems are in a worse condition than the nervous system of the average woman. Men indulge in smoking, in the drink habit and in other habits exhaustive to the nervous system more than women do, so men should take care lest, by suggesting a nervous test, they may be establishing a principle that will disfranchise the male sex at no distant date. If humanity demands that woman should be prohibited from voting in order to prevent her physical deterioration in consequence of her present weakness, surely the same principle would prohibit those men from voting who are weaker than women, in order to prevent the further deterioration of their already enfeebled bodies.

It is very satisfactory to note that men as well as women are becoming aroused in regard to the physical deterioration of women under false conditions, and that widespread efforts are being made to improve the conditions of training and living so that woman may have the opportunity to develop vigor and endurance as freely as man.

Woman has been restricted in her physical development by conventionalities and erroneous notions that proscribed outdoor games as improper for her. She has, by custom, been confined to the house. Men have made it popular with women to be somewhat delicate, because they have too often shown a decided tendency to admire the frail, timid, dependent, "clinging little creatures." Robustness was really a disadvantage to a woman, and was likely to gain for her a reputation for masculinity....

Sensible men and women have ceased to regard weakness as an essential characteristic of true womanhood. Women are freeing themselves from the tyranny of social customs which injure their health, and they are rapidly regaining the individuality which enables them to discard modes of dress that prevent the full and natural growth of their vital organs. Popular opinion and popular sentiment are removing the ban from girls and young women which made it immodest for them to play at outdoor sports, and so the women of the future are likely to get a fair chance to have better bodies. They need boating, the ball games, the running games and all sports that make energetic physical effort an essential to success quite as much as boys do, they need them more, indeed, to help to overcome the false training of centuries....

3. H. Bate, "Are Women to Blame?," *Grain Grower's Guide*, March 1, 1911

H. Bate's history remains unknown. According to 1911 census records, there was no "H. Bate" in either Alberta or Saskatchewan, but two, Humphrey (aged 70) and Harry (aged 55) in Manitoba. The Grain Grower's Guide, *to which this person wrote in 1911, served the grain grower's associations on the Canadian prairies and championed education reform, temperance, the co-operative movement, and the Social Gospel. Prominent members of the women's suffrage movement contributed regularly to its pages.*

It is with interest, amusement and disgust that I read the arguments in favor of women's suffrage as advanced by contributors to your department of THE GUIDE. In the first place, I doubt very much if a majority of women are in favor of suffrage. It is a matter that should be decided for women by women. If it can be proven that the majority of women really desire so-called equal rights with men, I say let them have them at once.

I have taken the trouble to inquire to the different classes, professional, domestic and leisured women of my acquaintance and I find that 75 per cent do not bother their heads about it, and half of the other 25 per cent are in disfavor of the suffrage movement. I think I am safe in saying that these women are as intellectual, cultured and as up-to-date as the average.

It amuses me to see the horrible pictures that these suffrage exponents draw of mere man as a monster of oppression, and it leads me to mention that as women had the bearing and rearing of man, as they had the first chance to mold and form his character, why did they not make a better job of it? To my mind their arguments are an attempt at face saving, and a way they have of covering up their botch-work. According to the reasoning of a great many of the leading suffragists on account of the injustice and oppression of man in the past, it was impossible that our grandmothers and mothers could have been women of intellect, culture, virtue and purity. They must have been mere child-bearing, dish-washing, cooking machines. The suffragist has yet, I think, to advance arguments that will convince the world that the noble women of the past would have been more noble than they were if they had the privilege of so-called equal rights. They have yet to show me how so-called equal rights will cause the women of today to be able to rear more noble sons than Christ, Luther, Knox, Lincoln, or the great many other honorable and just men who lived in the past—who live today. How can it cause the women of today to bear and rear more beautiful and better daughters than Mary, Mother of Christ, Martha, Florence Nightingale or Queen Victoria, or our mothers, who we all agree were as pure and noble, as much a power for good in the world, as if they had had these so-called equal rights. If it can with logic and reason be proven to me that suffrage will cause the world to be richer in more honorable, Christ-like men, or more pure and virtuous women than the above, I am prepared to became a champion of woman's rights for all time.

It is a fact admitted by all who have made a study of the matter that it takes the average person a lifetime to make a success of any one thing. The average person cannot do two things well. I believe the all-wise Creator intended men for the sphere outside the home; women for the sphere inside of the home. If not we would have been made more alike in temperament. If the average woman is going to be a successful homekeeper she will find her life well and satisfactorily filled as our mothers did. In winning a satisfactory living from the world, no matter in what line of labor or endeavor, the average man will find his life well and satisfactorily filled as our fathers did. Outside the home women have not attained the heights of worldly endeavor as a Cromwell, Washington, Karl Marx, Lloyd-George, etc., did. They were not created of the same stuff or with that end in view.... It is true if the vote was given to women it might down the liquor traffic the sooner, but if we do not become temperate in all things what is the use? When the windows need washing we do not scrub up one pane of glass and call the job done; we wash them all.

When we see as we often do these reformer women wearing hats decorated with the innocent little birds and preaching the cause of humanity, we can only come to the conclusion that after all women are subject to the same inconstancies and errors that men have been. Let the women of today learn less worldliness and more of that good old book, the Bible, that our mothers and grandmothers knew

so well and the result will be that both sexes will become more free and a force
for good in the world to any extend they desire.

4. Nellie McClung, *In Times Like These*, 1915

*McClung (1873–1951) grew up on farms in Ontario and Manitoba, became a teacher
at age 16, and married a pharmacist. Her efforts as writer and activist earned her a
reputation as a dogged, but uncharacteristically humorous proponent of temperance
and women's suffrage. She played a significant role assisting Manitoba women to gain
the vote in 1916. She and her family moved to Alberta in 1914, where she continued
to work for women's voting rights. She succeeded and was personally elected to the
Alberta legislature in 1921. McClung was among the "Famous Five" who fought for
legal recognition of women as "persons," which finally occurred in 1929, but not before
defeat by the Canadian Supreme Court and an appeal to the Privy Council in London.*

Any man who is actively engaged in politics, and declares that politics are too
corrupt for women, admits one of two things, either that he is a party to this corruption, or that he is unable to prevent it—and in either case something should
be done. Politics are not inherently vicious. The office of lawmaker should be the
highest in the land, equaled in honor only by that of the minister of the gospel.
In the old days, the two were combined with very good effect; but they seem to
have drifted apart in more recent years.

If politics are too corrupt for women, they are too corrupt for men; for men
and women are one—indissolubly joined together for good or ill. Many men have
tried to put all their religion and virtue in their wife's name, but it does not work
very well. When social conditions are corrupt women cannot escape by shutting
their eyes, and taking no interest. It would be far better to give them a chance
to clean them up.

What would you think of a man who would say to his wife: "This house to
which I am bringing you to live is very dirty and unsanitary, but I will not allow
you—the dear wife whom I have sworn to protect—to touch it. It is too dirty
for your precious little white hands! You must stay upstairs, dear. Of course the
odor from below may come up to you, but use your smelling salts and think no
evil. I do not hope to ever be able to clean it up, but certainly you must never
think of trying."

Do you think any woman would stand for that? She would say: "John, you are
all right in your way, but there are some places where your brain skids. Perhaps
you had better stay downtown today for lunch. But on your way down please call

at the grocer's, and send me a scrubbing brush and a package of Dutch Cleanser, and some chloride of lime, and now hurry." Women have cleaned up things since time began; and if women ever get into politics there will be a cleaning-out of pigeon-holes and forgotten corners, on which the dust of years has fallen, and the sound of the political carpet-beater will be heard in the land.

There is another hardy perennial that constantly lifts its head above the earth, persistently refusing to be ploughed under, and that is that if women were ever given a chance to participate in outside affairs, that family quarrels would result; that men and their wives who have traveled the way of life together, side by side for years, and come safely through religious discussions, and discussions relating to "his" people and "her" people, would angrily rend each other over politics, and great damage to the furniture would be the result. Father and son have been known to live under the same roof and vote differently, and yet live! Not only to live, but live peaceably! If a husband and wife are going to quarrel they will find a cause for dispute easily enough, and will not be compelled to wait for election day. And supposing that they have never, never had a single dispute, and not a ripple has ever marred the placid surface of their matrimonial sea, I believe that a small family jar—or at least a real lively argument—will do them good. It is in order to keep the white-winged angel of peace hovering over the home that married women are not allowed to vote in many places. Spinsters and widows are counted worthy of voice in the selection of school trustee, and alderman, and mayor, but not the woman who has taken to herself a husband and still has him.

What a strange commentary on marriage that it should disqualify a woman from voting. Why should marriage disqualify a woman? Men have been known to vote for years after they were dead!

Quite different from the "family jar" theory, another reason is advanced against married women voting—it is said that they would all vote with their husbands, and that the married man's vote would thereby be doubled. We believe it is eminently right and proper that husband and wife should vote the same way, and in that case no one would be able to tell whether the wife was voting with the husband or the husband voting with the wife. Neither would it matter. If giving the franchise to women did nothing more than double the married man's vote it would do a splendid thing for the country, for the married man is the best voter we have; generally speaking, he is a man of family and property—surely if we can depend on anyone we can depend upon him, and if by giving his wife a vote we can double his—we have done something to offset the irresponsible transient vote of the man who has no interest in the community.

There is another sturdy prejudice that blooms everywhere in all climates, and that is that women would not vote if they had the privilege; and this is many times used as a crushing argument against woman suffrage. But why worry? If women do not use it, then surely there is no harm done; but those who use the argument seem to imply that a vote unused is a very dangerous thing to leave lying around, and will probably spoil and blow up. In support of this statement instances are cited of women letting their vote lie idle and unimproved in elections for school trustee and alderman. Of course, the percentage of men voting in these contests was quite small, too, but no person finds fault with that.

Women may have been careless about their franchise in elections where no great issue is at stake, but when moral matters are being decided women have not shown any lack of interest....

"Why, Uncle Henry!" exclaimed one man to another on election day. "I never saw you out to vote before. What struck you?"

"Hadn't voted for fifteen years," declared Uncle Henry, "but you bet I came out today to vote against givin' these fool women a vote; what's the good of givin' them a vote? They wouldn't use it!"

Then, of course, on the other hand there are those who claim that women would vote too much—that they would vote not wisely but too well; that they would take up voting as a life work to the exclusion of husband, home and children. There seems to be considerable misapprehension on the subject of voting. It is really a simple and perfectly innocent performance, quickly over, and with no bad after-effects.

It is usually done in a vacant room in a school or the vestry of a church, or a town hall. No drunken men stare at you. You are not jostled or pushed—you wait your turn in an orderly line, much as you have waited to buy a ticket at a railway station. Two tame and quiet-looking men sit at a table, and when your turn comes, they ask you your name, which is perhaps slightly embarrassing, but it is not as bad as it might be, for they do not ask your age, or of what disease did your grandmother die. You go behind the screen with your ballot paper in your hand, and there you find a seal-brown pencil tied with a chaste white string. Even the temptation of annexing the pencil is removed from your frail humanity. You mark your ballot, and drop it in the box, and come out into the sunlight again. If you had never heard that you had done an unladylike thing you would not know it. It all felt solemn, and serious, and very respectable to you, something like a Sunday-school convention. Then, too, you are surprised at what a short time you have been away from home. You put the potatoes on when you left home, and now you are back in time to strain them.

In spite of the testimony of many reputable women that they have been able to vote and get the dinner on one and the same day, there still exists a strong belief that the whole household machinery goes out of order when a woman goes to vote. No person denies a woman the right to go to church, and yet the church service takes a great deal more time than voting. People even concede to women the right to go shopping, or visiting a friend, or an occasional concert. But the wife and mother, with her God-given, sacred trust of molding the young life of our land, must never dream of going round the corner to vote. "Who will mind the baby?" cried one of our public men, in great agony of spirit, "when the mother goes to vote?"

... Father comes home, tired, weary, footsore, toe-nails ingrowing, caused by undarned stockings, and finds the fire out, house cold and empty, save for his half-dozen children, all crying.

"Where is your mother?" the poor man asks in broken tones. For a moment the sobs are hushed while little Ellie replies: "Out voting!"

Father bursts into tears.

Of course, people tell us, it is not the mere act of voting which demoralizes women — if they would only vote and be done with it; but women are creatures of habit, and habits once formed are hard to break; and although the polls are only open every three or four years, if women once get into the way of going to them, they will hang around there all the rest of the time. It is in woman's impressionable nature that the real danger lies.

Another shoot of this hardy shrub of prejudice is that women are too good to mingle in everyday life — they are too sweet and too frail — that women are angels. If women are angels we should try to get them into public life as soon as possible, for there is a great shortage of angels there just at present, if all we hear is true.

Then there is the pedestal theory — that women are away up on a pedestal, and down below, looking up at them with deep adoration, are men, their willing slaves. Sitting up on a pedestal does not appeal very strongly to a healthy woman — and, besides, if a woman has been on a pedestal for any length of time, it must be very hard to have to come down and cut the wood.

These tender-hearted and chivalrous gentlemen who tell you of their adoration for women, cannot bear to think of women occupying public positions. Their tender hearts shrink from the idea of women lawyers or women policemen, or even women preachers; these positions would "rub the bloom off the peach," to use their own eloquent words. They cannot bear, they say, to see women leaving the sacred precincts of home — and yet their offices are scrubbed by women who do their work while other people sleep—poor women who leave the sacred precincts of home to earn enough to keep the breath of life in them, who carry their scrub-pails home, through the deserted streets, long after the cars have stopped running. They are exposed to cold, to hunger, to insult—poor souls—is there any pity felt for them? Not that we have heard of. The tender-hearted ones can bear this with equanimity. It is the thought of women getting into comfortable and well-paid positions which wrings their manly hearts.

Another aspect of the case is that women can do more with their indirect influence than by the ballot; though just why they cannot do better still with both does not appear to be very plain. The ballot is a straight-forward dignified way of making your desire or choice felt. There are some things which are not pleasant to talk about, but would be delightful to vote against. Instead of having to beg, and coax, and entreat, and beseech, and denounce as women have had to do all down the centuries, in regard to the evil things which threaten to destroy their homes and those whom they love, what a glorious thing it would be if women could go out and vote against these things. It seems like a straight-forward and easy way of expressing one's opinion.

But, of course, popular opinion says it is not "womanly." The "womanly way" is to nag and tease. Women have often been told that if they go about it right they can get anything. They are encouraged to plot and scheme, and deceive, and wheedle, and coax for things. This is womanly and sweet. Of course, if this fails, they still have tears—they can always cry and have hysterics, and raise hob generally, but they must do it in a womanly way. Will the time ever come when the word "feminine" will have in it no trace of trickery?

Women are too sentimental to vote, say the politicians sometimes. Sentiment is nothing to be ashamed of, and perhaps an infusion of sentiment in politics is what we need. Honor and honesty, love and loyalty, are only sentiments, and yet they make the fabric out of which our finest traditions are woven....

For too long people have regarded politics as a scheme whereby easy money might be obtained. Politics has meant favors, pulls, easy jobs for friends, new telephone lines, ditches. The question has not been: "What can I do for my country?" but: "What can I get? What is there in this for me?" The test of a member of Parliament as voiced by his constituents has been: "What has he got for us?" The good member who will be elected the next time is the one who did not forget his friends, who got us a Normal School, or a Court House, or an Institution for the Blind, something that we could see or touch, eat or drink. Surely a touch of sentiment in politics would do no harm....

There are people who tell us that the reason women must never be allowed to vote is because they do not want to vote, the inference being that women are never given anything that they do not want....

That fact that many women are indifferent on the subject does not alter the situation. People are indifferent about many things that they should be interested in. The indifference of people on the subject of ventilation and hygiene does not change the laws of health. The indifference of many parents on the subject of an education for their children does not alter the value of education. If one woman wants to vote, she should have that opportunity just as if one woman desires a college education, she should not be held back because of the indifferent careless ones who do not desire it. Why should the mentally inert, careless, uninterested woman, who cares nothing for humanity but is contented to patter along her own little narrow way, set the pace for the others of us? Voting will not be compulsory; the shrinking violets will not be torn from their shady fence-corner; the "home bodies" will be able to still sit in rapt contemplation of their own fireside. We will not force the vote upon them, but why should they force their votelessness upon us?

5. Stephen Leacock, "The Woman Question," *Essays and Literary Studies*, 1916

Stephen Leacock (1869–1944) is best known as a humourist, but he was also a brilliant academic with a Ph.D. in political science from the University of Chicago and had a long career writing scholarly monographs and teaching at the university level. Herein lies the problem for historians assessing Leacock's comments on womens' rights: was he kidding? He coaxes readers along masterfully developed and brilliantly written arguments that inevitably lead to outrageous conclusions that blur the distinction between irony and genuine belief. He certainly did not believe in higher education for women and did indeed exhibit a strong misogynist streak, but did he really believe that a woman's freedom came from limiting her universe to her work in the home?

... "Things are all wrong," she screamed, "with the *status* of women." Therein she was quite right. "The remedy for it all," she howled, "is to make women 'free,' to give women the vote. When women are free everything will be all right." Therein the woman with the spectacles was, and is, utterly wrong.

The women's vote, when they get it, will leave women much as they were before ...

For when the vote is reached the woman question will not be solved but only begun. In and of itself, a vote is nothing. It neither warms the skin nor fills the stomach. Very often the privilege of a vote confers nothing but the right to express one's opinion as to which of two crooks is the crookeder.

But after the women have obtained the vote the question is, what are they going to do with it? The answer is, nothing, or at any rate nothing that men would not do without them. Their only visible use of it will be to elect men into office. Fortunately for us all they will not elect women. Here and there perhaps at the outset, it will be done as the result of a sort of spite, a kind of sex antagonism bred by the controversy itself. But, speaking broadly, the women's vote will not be used to elect women to office. Women do not think enough of one another to do that. If they want a lawyer they consult a man, and those who can afford it have their clothes made by men, and their cooking done by a chef. As for their money, no woman would entrust that to another woman's keeping. They are far too wise for that.

So the woman's vote will not result in the setting up of female prime ministers and of parliaments in which the occupants of the treasury bench cast languishing eyes across at the flushed faces of the opposition. From the utter ruin involved in such an attempt at mixed government, the women themselves will save us. They will elect men. They may even pick some good ones. It is a nice question and will stand thinking about.

But what else, or what further can they do, by means of their vote and their representatives to "emancipate" and "liberate" their sex?

Many feminists would tell us at once that if women had the vote they would, first and foremost, throw everything open to women on the same terms as men. Whole speeches are made on this point, and a fine fury thrown into it, often very beautiful to behold.

The entire idea is a delusion. Practically all of the world's work is open to women now, wide open. *The only trouble is that they can't do it.* There is nothing to prevent a woman from managing a bank, or organising a company, or running a department store, or floating a merger, or building a railway—except the simple fact that she can't. Here and there an odd woman does such things, but she is only the exception that proves the rule. Such women are merely—and here I am speaking in the most decorous biological sense—"sports." The ordinary woman cannot do the ordinary man's work. She never has and never will. The reasons why she can't are so many, that is, she "*can't*" in so many different ways, that it is not worthwhile to try to name them.

Here and there it is true there are things closed to women, not by their own inability but by the law. This is a gross injustice. There is no defence for it. The province in which I live, for example, refuses to allow women to practise as lawyers. This is wrong. Women have just as good a right to fail at being lawyers as they have at anything else. But even if all these legal disabilities, where they exist, were removed (as they will be under a woman's vote) the difference to women at large will be infinitesimal. A few gifted "sports" will earn a handsome livelihood but the woman question in the larger sense will not move one inch nearer to solution.

The feminists, in fact, are haunted by the idea that it is possible for the average woman to have a life patterned after that of the ordinary man. They imagine her as having a career, a profession, a vocation—something which will be her "life work"—just as selling coal is the life work of the coal merchant.

If this were so, the whole question would be solved. Women and men would become equal and independent. It is thus indeed that the feminist sees them, through the roseate mist created by imagination. Husband and wife appear as a couple of honourable partners who share a house together. Each is off to business in the morning. The husband is, let us say, a stock broker: the wife manufactures iron and steel. The wife is a Liberal, the husband a Conservative. At their dinner they have animated discussions over the tariff till it is time for them to go to their clubs.

These two impossible creatures haunt the brain of the feminist and disport them in the pages of the up-to-date novel.

The whole thing is mere fiction. It is quite impossible for women—the average and ordinary women—to go in for having a career. Nature has forbidden it. The average woman must necessarily have—I can only give the figures roughly—about three and a quarter children. She must replace in the population herself and her husband with something over to allow for the people who never marry and for the children that do not reach maturity. If she fails to do this the population comes to an end. Any scheme of social life must allow for these three and a quarter children and for the years of care that must be devoted to them. The vacuum cleaner can take the place of the housewife. It cannot replace the mother. No man ever said his prayers at the knees of a vacuum cleaner, or drew his first lessons in manliness and worth from the sweet old-fashioned stories that a vacuum cleaner told. Feminists of the enraged kind may talk as they will of the paid attendant and the expert baby minder. Fiddlesticks! These things are a mere supplement, useful enough but as far away from the realities of motherhood as the vacuum cleaner itself. But the point is one that need not be laboured. Sensible people understand it as soon as said. With fools it is not worthwhile to argue.

But, it may be urged, there are, even as it is, a great many women who are working. The wages that they receive are extremely low. They are lower in most cases than the wages for the same, or similar work, done by men. Cannot the woman's vote at least remedy this?

Here is something that deserves thinking about and that is far more nearly within the realm of what is actual and possible than wild talk of equalising and revolutionising the sexes.

It is quite true that women's work is underpaid. But this is only a part of a larger social injustice.

The case stands somewhat as follows: Women get low wages because low wages are all that they are worth. Taken by itself this is a brutal and misleading statement. What is meant is this. The rewards and punishments in the unequal and ill-adjusted world in which we live are most unfair. The price of anything — sugar, potatoes, labour, or anything else — varies according to the supply and demand: if many people want it and few can supply it the price goes up: if the contrary it goes down. If enough cabbages are brought to market they will not bring a cent a piece, no matter what it cost to raise them.

On these terms each of us sells his labour. The lucky ones, with some rare gift, or trained capacity, or some ability that by mere circumstance happens to be in a great demand, can sell high. If there were only one night plumber in a great city, and the water pipes in a dozen homes of a dozen millionaires should burst all at once, he might charge a fee like that of a consulting lawyer. . . .

So it stands with women's wages. It is the sheer numbers of the women themselves, crowding after the few jobs that they can do, that brings them down. It has nothing to do with the attitude of men collectively towards women in the lump. It cannot be remedied by any form of woman's freedom. Its remedy is bound up with the general removal of social injustice, the general abolition of poverty, which is to prove the great question of the century before us. The question of women's wages is a part of the wages' question.

To my thinking the whole idea of making women free and equal (politically) with men as a way of improving their *status*, starts from a wrong basis and proceeds in a wrong direction.

Women need not more freedom but less. Social policy should proceed from the fundamental truth that women are and must be dependent. If they cannot be looked after by an individual (a thing on which they took their chance in earlier days) they must be looked after by the State. To expect a woman, for example, if left by the death of her husband with young children without support, to maintain herself by her own efforts, is the most absurd mockery of freedom ever devised. Earlier generations of mankind, for all that they lived in the jungle and wore coconut leaves, knew nothing of it. To turn a girl loose in the world to work for herself, when there is no work to be had, or none at a price that will support life, is a social crime....

I leave [readers] with the thought that perhaps in the modern age it is not the increased freedom of woman that is needed but the increased recognition of their dependence. Let the reader remain agonised over that till I write something else.

6. H.D.P., "The Failure of the Suffrage Movement to Bring Freedom to Women," *The Woman Worker*, December 1928

While nothing is know about H.D.P., The Woman Worker *was published by the Canadian Federation of Women's Labour Leagues. It claimed to "champion the Protection of Womanhood, and the cause of the Workers generally." Its editor, Florence Custance, was a leading member of the Communist Party of Canada.*

The great activity shown when occasion demands by political parties in their efforts to get the woman vote, brings to mind many of the promises and prophesies which were made by friends and foes in those not distant days when it required a little courage to wear a "votes for women" button.

Of course the "Antis" sounded their usual alarm—the home would be destroyed—and one admits that many suffragists also showed their ignorance of the "world process" by their optimistic arguments along opposite lines: And after it was all over what happened?

In the first place, the anti-suffragists who were loudest in proclaiming that "woman's place is the home" were the very first to step out and seek political and other offices. And of all the others who fought so well for this right of self-expression, only one or two, here and there over the whole country, saw that this was not the end of the struggle, but only a very small beginning.

To be sure, it was not a working class movement. The majority in it were middle class and fairly satisfied with conditions—as one well known club woman said to me "It seems so absurd that my gardener can vote and I can't." It was just a matter of status with her.

They were the sort who used to get up in meetings and enquire anxiously— "but who will do the menial work," when one was trying to picture a better social order. Evidently, if it meant work and responsibility for all, they were not going to stand for it. But they were mostly nice, kind ladies, and they often meant well, as on the occasion when one of them undertook to investigate conditions in a certain workshop, she brought back an excellent report, and when asked from whom she got her information, she said, "Oh, I went right to the manager!" And how they wanted to supervise the spending of working class housewives at the beginning of the war. It seems that some of these wasteful creatures were discovered buying oranges and pickles—and later on it was gramophones and pianos!

But when election time came these same fine ladies were very busy calling on women in various working class districts, and acting so "perfectly lovely," that many a foolish woman voted against her own interests and against her family and her class, because she was so flattered she was easily deceived.

In the U.S.A. a group of influential ones, called "The Women's National Party," are now going before Congress—supported by members of the employer's association—and opposing legislation that would aid great numbers of women to an approach to economic equality with men. They call it, asking for "equal rights." If, for instance, men are working ten hours a day in certain places, women employed there must also have the "right" to work ten hours a day. If successful, they will nullify the work of years done by trade unions and labor groups for the betterment and relief of working women. It may be that they do not grasp the serious problems of the woman worker, but, anyway, they are proving again that the business of fair play for all who work for wages is the worker's own task.

Another reason why the vote has been of so little use to us is the fact that hundreds of thousands are always disfranchised.

The law requires certain conditions and the worker following his job or moving about in search of employment is thus automatically off the voters' list.

And the working class generally is suffering today in "mind, body, and estate" because we've been too confiding, too good natured, too patient. We have failed to see that whatever value there was in the vote was lost entirely unless used for ourselves. And if this be intelligent selfishness there's little to argue about.

Certainly the so-called "dignity of labor" is only an election phrase, but there are enough workers to give it real meaning. We could very well take a lesson from the conduct of those in authority over us. They realize what class loyalty means, even though they may not like or in any way approve of each other individually. Yet they are rarely so silly as to be caught voting or acting in any way against their class interests. They stick together.

And since we have in Canada such a high class paper as "The Woman Worker" it must be now much easier to get together in great numbers with one common denominator—working class freedom.

If we meet just as working women, with no handicaps because of race, creed or color, it will speed up the day when voting will not be the force it now is, when governments will not be something remote and threatening, when the ruling of peoples will give place to the administration of things "for the wellbeing of all."

FURTHER READINGS

Bacchi, C. *Liberation Deferred? The Ideas of the English Canadian Suffragists, 1877-1918.* Toronto: University of Toronto Press, 1983.

Cleverdon, C. *The Woman's Suffrage Movement in Canada: The Start of Liberation.* 2nd ed. Toronto: University of Toronto Press, 1974.

Cohen, Y. *Femmes de Parole: L'Histoire de Cercles de Fermières du Quebec, 1915-1990.* Montreal: Le Jour, 1990.

Cook, R., and W. Mitchinson, Eds. *The Proper Sphere: Women's Place in Canadian Society.* Toronto: Oxford University Press, 1974.

Crowley, T. "Adelaide Hoodless and the Canadian Gibson Girl." *Canadian Historical Review* 67, 4 (December 1986): 520-47.

Crowley, T. *Agnes Macphail and the Politics of Equality.* Toronto: James Lorimer, 1990.

Cramner, M. "Public and Political: Documents of the Women's Suffrage Campaign in British Columbia, 1871-1917: The View from Victoria." In *In Her Own Right: Selected Essay on Women's History in BC*, ed. B. Latham and C. Kess. Victoria: Camosun College, 1980.

Flemengo, J. "A Legacy of Ambivalence: Responses to Nellie McClung." *Journal of Canadian Studies* 34, 4 (Winter 1999-2000): 70-87.

Forbes, E. "Battles in Another War: Edith Archibald and the Halifax Feminist Movement." *Challenging the Regional Stereotype: Essays on the 20th Century Maritimes.* Fredericton: Acadiensis Press, 1989.

Hallet, M., and M. Davis. *Firing the Heather: The Life and Times of Nellie McClung.* Calgary: Fifth House, 1993.

Kealey, L., Ed. *A Not Unreasonable Claim: Women and Reform in Canada, 1880s-1920s.* Toronto: Women's Press, 1979.

Kealey, L., and J. Sangster, Eds. *Beyond the Vote: Canadian Women and Politics*. Toronto: University of Toronto Press, 1989.

Kinnear, M., Ed. *First Days, Fighting Days: Women in Manitoba History*. Regina: Canadian Plains Research Centre, 1989.

Latham, B., and R. Pazdro, Eds. *Not Just Pin Money: Selected Essays in the History of Women's Work in British Columbia*. Victoria: Camosun College, 1984.

Lavigne, M., and Y. Pinard, Eds. *Travailleuses et Feministes: Aspects Historiques*. Montreal: Boreal Express, 1983.

Le Clio Collectif. *L'Historie des Femmes au Québec depuis Quatre Siècles*. Montreal: Women's Press, 1991.

Light, B., and J. Parr, Eds. *Canadian Women on the Move, 1867-1920*. Toronto: New Hogtown Press, 1984.

Newton, J. *The Feminist Challenge to the Canadian Left, 1900-1918*. Montreal and Kingston: McGill-Queen's University Press, 1995.

Roberts, W. *Honest Womanhood: Feminism, Femininity, and Class Consciousness among Toronto Working Women 1893-1914*. Toronto: New Hogtown Press, 1976.

Sangster, J. *Dreams of Equality: Women on the Canadian Left, 1920-1950*. Toronto: McClelland and Stewart, 1987.

Silverman, E. *The Last Best West: Women on the Alberta Frontier, 1880-1930*. Montreal: Eden Press, 1984.

Strong-Boag, V. "'Ever a Crusader': Nellie McClung, First Wave Feminist." In *Rethinking Canada: The Promise of Women's History*, 2nd ed., ed. V. Strong-Boag and A. Fellman. Toronto: Copp Clark Pitman, 1991.

Strong-Boag, V. *The New Day Recalled: Lives of Girls and Women in English Canada, 1919-1939*. Toronto: Copp Clark Pitman, 1988.

Strong-Boag, V. *The Parliament of Women. The National Council of Women of Canada 1893–1929.* Ottawa: National Museums of Canada, 1976.

Trofimenkoff, S. "Henri Bourassa and the 'Woman Question.'" *Journal of Canadian Studies* 10 (November 1975): 3-11.

Warne, R. *Literature as Pulpit: The Christian Social Activism of Nellie L. McClung.* Waterloo: Wilfrid Laurier Press, 1988.

CHAPTER 6

"What Is Our Duty?"

MILITARY SERVICE IN WORLD WAR I

INTRODUCTION

Canada did not have a strong military tradition and was unprepared, psychologically and materially, when war broke out in the summer of 1914. Just the same, the nation responded with aplomb to the British Declaration of War. This was not a matter of choice. Under the British North America Act, Britain still chose the Dominion's friends and enemies, and the British Declaration of War automatically included Canada—which suited most Canadians just fine. The war, however, turned out to be far less glorious and romantic than its billing. Modern mechanized warfare dehumanized combat to the point where the enemy was an invisible foe unleashing relentless barrages of lethal shells, hour after hour, day after day. There was mustard gas, barbed wire, and hopeless charges into no-man's land. Living conditions at the front degenerated into raw survival in rat-infested, stinking, water-filled trenches. Soldiers were cold, hungry, flea-ridden, bored, terrified, and often deeply disillusioned. In total, some 620,000 Canadian men and several thousand women actively served over the four years of the conflict, and over 60,000 died. Those enormous numbers, from a population of a mere 8 million in

1914, may tempt Canadians to believe that the nation gave a disproportionate number of its young to the war. Canada indeed made huge sacrifices, but its efforts were, in fact, proportionally smaller than some other members of the Empire, because of the difficulty of maintaining and increasing the size of its manpower contribution.

Recruiting initially proceeded very successfully, with young men across Canada flocking to the recruiting stations. For many, the real fear was that the war would be over before they got there: that they would miss "the show." The flood of volunteers, however, dried to a trickle by 1916 when descriptions of the Western Front reached home and patriotic enthusiasm evaporated. The federal government responded with an intense and relatively crude propaganda campaign geared to encourage recalcitrant young men to sign up. Prime Minister Robert Borden wanted 500,000 men in uniform, which called for aggressive recruitment indeed. The essence of the campaign was simple: any young, able-bodied man not in uniform was presumably shirking his responsibility to Canada and the Empire, and so he must be "encouraged" to sign up. This could be done by humiliating him through "white-feathering"—that is, by publicly presenting him with the white feather that represented cowardice—appealing to his sense of duty, warning him of social stigmas if he did not volunteer, and by any other means the government thought might work. Propaganda posters glamorized the soldier's life and boldly implied that the war was a grand and righteous adventure, despite what anyone said to the contrary.

French Canadians came under an especially withering propaganda barrage, which is hardly surprising. French-Canadian voluntarism, at 5 per cent of total volunteers, lagged far behind its Anglo-Canadian counterpart throughout the war. Why? There were likely as many reasons as there were men who refused to sign up, but distinct trends emerge. Some assumed that because English Canada still venerated its mother country, French Canada would support France—Britain's ally. French Canadians, in fact, had few ties to France. The Conquest ended in 1763, some 150 years previously, and many Québécois blamed France for that loss. French-Canadian feelings of antipathy toward the rest of Canada also lingered over the country's role in the Boer War, French language rights, and separate schools in both Ontario and Manitoba. Then there was the organization of the Canadian army: few officers spoke French; chances of promotion for Québécois enlisted men remained very limited; a unilingual Anglican minister headed official recruiting in Quebec; and there was no French-speaking regiment until 1917 when the Vandoo (Royal 22nd) was created. Finally, the Québécois argued that they had proportionately greater family obligations impinging on their liberty to sign up.

Close scrutiny of the recruitment data indicates that the Québécois were not, in fact, the only reluctant volunteers. Western Canadians and Maritimers also demonstrated a lack of commitment compared to areas with large pockets of recent British immigrants, many of whom were single men without family responsibilities. Large numbers of western

Canadians were first-generation immigrants who had fled Europe precisely to avoid repressive governments that forced young men to fight their wars. They would hardly return, or send their sons, after just escaping to more congenial climes. They also argued that their place was on Canada's farms where they and their families contributed as much, if not more, to the war effort than by donning uniforms.

Lack of recruits and an appalling casualty rate eventually led Prime Minister Borden to introduce conscription in 1917, an act of Parliament as contentious and divisive as anything since Confederation. It so badly divided the country that for the first and only time in Canadian history the two main federal political parties split along ethnic lines, French-Canadian members of Parliament, be they Liberal or Conservative, rallying to Laurier's anti-conscription Liberals. Borden, meanwhile, created the new Union party from pro-conscription English-Canadian Liberals and Conservatives. The ensuing election was terribly divisive, with violence, unscrupulous political manipulation, intimidation, and propaganda on both sides. Borden won, and his Military Service Act led to clashes between troops and French Canadians in Quebec that killed five civilians. In response the Quebec National Assembly discussed a resolution to secede from Canada.

Why was conscription so contentious? The country had little military experience and many Canadians found the concept of conscription foreign. Canada traditionally relied upon voluntarism for its armed forces. Many thought that World War I simply was not Canada's fight: that it had nothing to do with them. Some, on moral principles, could not accept the notion of the state forcing its citizens into arms. But what about duty, others wondered? Canada, after all, belonged to the British Empire, and like it or not, club membership entailed responsibilities as well as privileges. And if not to the Empire, surely the rights of Canadian citizenship also involved obligations. Thus, they argued, if Canada was in trouble but low on volunteers, the government must make up the deficit by conscripting its citizens.

DISCUSSION POINTS

1. Summarize the arguments for and against increased Canadian participation in World War I.

2. Based on these accounts, how ideologically motivated were Canadians? Did they understand what was at stake in the war?

3. Should governments have the power to coerce their citizens into military service? Should military service be considered a duty of citizenship?

4. Explain the "conscription of wealth." Should it have taken place before or alongside the conscription of men? Was it even realistic?

DOCUMENTS

1. Peter McArthur, "Country Recruits," *Globe*, January 30, 1915

Peter McArthur (1872-1934) grew up on a farm in County Middlesex, Ontario. His upbringing left such an indelible impression on him that he spent the rest of his life writing about the virtues of farm life and nature. He attended the University of Toronto and in 1889 joined the staff of the Toronto Globe *as a journalist. From 1890 to 1908 McArthur lived in the United States and Britain working as a journalist or in publishing. He returned to the family farm in 1908. McArthur published at least four books of essays and poetry, as well as articles for many magazines including* Punch, Saturday Night, Harper's Monthly, *and* Atlantic Monthly. *He and his wife had one daughter and four sons, one of whom served in the 56th Overseas Battery.*

With all the papers lamenting the fact that the rural districts are not contributing a satisfactory number of recruits to the war, it is perhaps unsafe for me to point out a few facts about rural conditions, for the last time I did so I was accused in a section of the press of preparing a defence for people who lack patriotism. I have surely put myself on record often enough as believing that the war must be supported to the utmost, but I am not going to let that belief make me unjust. I have told you how scarce men of military age are in this district and that if they enlist there can be none of the increased production that is being urged as an expression of patriotism. The Department of Agriculture is proclaiming that the man who produces more foodstuffs is doing a man's work for the Empire, and the few young men who are on the farms are practically all producers. Each one who went to the front would leave a hundred acres untilled.

It is high time that the Department of Militia and the Department of Agriculture got together and decided on a definite policy. If a man is doing his duty by producing more, he should not be open to criticism if he does not enlist. To show you how shorthanded this district is it is only necessary to point out that during the past ten years the population of the county of Middlesex has been so greatly reduced that at the recent redistribution one riding was wiped out. I have not the figures by me, but I understand that the population has fallen off something over ten thousand. This decrease is largely due to the exodus of young men to the west and to the cities. If the country had been at war for the past ten years we could not have lost a greater proportion of our population. If every young man of military age enlisted, the county could hardly make a fair showing and it would fall behind in production. Will those who are condemning the rural districts for not sending more recruits kindly tell what should be done in the case of Middlesex county?

While the above paragraph was in course of preparation I received a letter from a correspondent in Castorville which reports a similar condition. The writer says

"While reading *The Globe* last evening I noticed a considerable complaint that the country districts are not responding very heartily to the call for volunteers to go to the war. In thinking the matter over I felt that there is a danger of not giving the country due consideration for this seeming shortcoming.

"I do not wish to excuse the country where it is lacking patriotism but I feel that the conditions of farmers are not fully comprehended which I will note briefly:

"(1) The smallness of families in farming districts these days is noticeable. There used to be five and six boys in a family on the farm. Today there are only one or two.

"(2) The spare boy that could be gotten along without has gone to the city or the west, and now not one farm in three has even one boy or man eligible to be a volunteer.

"(3) Help is scarce on the farms and in the farming districts. Most of the farmers are and have been running their farms with as little help as possible, and even when we feel we would like to have someone to help it is almost impossible to get it for there are no spare hands in the community.

"(4) If Canada is to provide bread, beef, horses, etc. for the war, the farmer must have sufficient help to do it.

"(5) The overflow of country population has gone to the cities or west.

The congestion in the labour market at the present time is found in the cities, therefore it is not surprising that the majority of volunteers should come from that quarter."

This letter is of interest because it shows that conditions in other parts of the country are the same as I find them here in Middlesex. The farmers cannot both increase production and give volunteers to the army.

There is a thought that suggests itself in connection with this state of affairs. In the present national crisis we have a right to expect every man who is capable of rendering service to do so patriotically. The man who enlists to go to the front is making the supreme sacrifice that it is possible for a man to make. He is offering to give his life for his country. The man who is eligible to give similar service but feels that his call of duty is to stay at home and help his country with increased products should also be prepared to make many and great sacrifices. He is not offering his life, and therefore he should not stint in offering his means. If the young men who avoid military service do so because they think that during war times farming will yield them increased profits they must expect to take their profits with a share of public contempt. Never before has the call for unselfish service been so urgent and so great. Those who elect to serve their country as producers must be prepared to give to their full capacity. Even if they give all, they will not be giving so much as those who are offering their lives. As the war progresses public sentiment will probably be educated to a point where men in all walks of life who try to make profits from the unhappy condition of their country will be scorned for their selfishness. If we cannot serve at the front we must be prepared to serve unselfishly at home. As a matter of fact, I think it would be quite justifiable to ask the young married men of military age who are not enlisting what proportion of their products they will give for patriotic purposes over and beyond what they will have to pay in the form of taxes. When the survivors of those who volunteer for service at the front come back wounded and broken the young men who stay at home cannot feel much self-respect if they have spent the time in accumulating profits. This should show definitely whether their "patriotism of production" is real or only an excuse.

2. Talbot M. Papineau, "An Open Letter from Capt Talbot Papineau to Mr. Henri Bourassa," March 21, 1916

The bilingual Talbot Mercer Papineau (1883–1917) was born in Montebello, Quebec, and was a great-grandson of French Canada's most famous reformer, Louis Joseph Papineau. His mother was American, from a prominent Philadelphia family, and most of his upbringing was in English. After attending McGill University in Montreal, he became one of Canada's first Rhodes Scholarship recipients, receiving a B.A. from Oxford in 1908. Papineau returned to Canada and practiced law before volunteering for the Princess Patricia Light Infantry at the outbreak of war in August 1914. Awarded the Military Cross for exemplary gallantry, and promoted to the rank of major, Papineau was killed in October 1917 at Passchendaele, where Canada suffered 16,000 casualties.

In the Field, France.

My dear Cousin Henri, —

... Too occupied by immediate events in this country to formulate a protest or to frame a reasoned argument, I have nevertheless followed with intense feeling and deep regret the course of action which you have pursued. Consolation of course I have had in the fact that far from sharing in your views, the vast majority of Canadians, and even many of those who had formerly agreed with you, were now strongly and bitterly opposed to you. With this fact in mind, I would not take the time from my duties here to write you this letter did I not fear that the influence to which your talent, energy, and sincerity of purpose formerly entitled you, might still be exercised upon a small minority of your fellow countrymen, and that your attitude might still be considered by some as representative of the race to which we belong.

Nor can I altogether abandon the hope — presumptuous no doubt but friendly and well-intentioned — that I may so express myself here as to give you a new outlook and a different purpose, and perhaps even win you to the support of a principle which has been proved to be dearer to many Canadians than life itself.

I shall not consider the grounds upon which you base your opposition to Canadian participation in this more than European — in this World War. Rather I wish to begin by pointing out some reasons why on the contrary your whole-hearted support might have been expected.

And the first reason is this. By the declaration of war by Great Britain upon Germany, Canada became "ipso facto" a belligerent, subject to invasion and conquest, her property at sea subject to capture, her coasts subject to bombardment or attack, her citizens in enemy territory subject to imprisonment or detention. This is not a matter of opinion — it is a matter of fact — a question of international law. No arguments of yours at least could have persuaded the Kaiser to the contrary. Whatever your views or theories may be as to future constitutional development of Canada, and in those views I believe I coincide to a large extent, the fact remains that at the time of the outbreak of war Canada was a possession of the British Empire, and as such as much involved in the war as any county in England, and from the German point of view and the point of view of International Law equally subject to all its pains and penalties. Indeed proof may no doubt be made that one of the very purposes of Germany's aggression and German military preparedness was the ambition to secure a part if not the whole of the English possessions in North America.

That being so, surely it was idle and pernicious to continue an academic discussion as to whether the situation was a just one or not, as to whether Canada should or should not have had a voice in ante bellum English diplomacy or in the actual declaration of war. Such a discussion may very properly arise upon a successful conclusion of the war, but so long as national issues are being decided in Prussian fashion, that is, by an appeal to the Power of Might, the liberties of discussion which you enjoyed by virtue of British citizenship were necessarily curtailed and any resulting decisions utterly valueless. If ever there was a time for action and not for theories it was to be found in Canada upon the outbreak of war.

Let us presume for the sake of argument that your attitude had also been adopted by the Government and people of Canada and that we had declared our intention to abstain from active participation in the war until Canada herself was actually attacked. What would have resulted? One of two things. Either the Allies would have been defeated or they would not have been defeated. In the former case Canada would have been called upon either to surrender unconditionally to German domination or to have attempted a resistance against German arms.

You, I feel sure, would have preferred resistance, but as a proper corrective to such a preference I would prescribe a moderate dose of trench bombardment. I have known my own dogmas to be seriously disturbed in the midst of a German artillery concentration. I can assure you that the further you travel from Canada and the nearer you approach the great military power of Germany, the less do you value the unaided strength of Canada. By the time you are within fifteen yards of a German army and know yourself to be holding about one yard out of a line of five hundred miles or more, you are liable to be enquiring very anxiously about the presence and power of British and French forces. Your ideas about charging to Berlin or of ending the war would also have undergone some slight moderation.

No, my dear Cousin, I think you would shortly after the defeat of the Allies have been more worried over the mastery of the German consonants than you are even now over a conflict with the Ontario Anti-bilinguists. Or I can imagine you an unhappy exile in Terra del Fuego eloquently comparing the wrongs of Quebec and Alsace.

But you will doubtless say we would have had the assistance of the Great American Republic! It is quite possible. I will admit that by the time the American fleet had been sunk and the principal buildings in New York destroyed the United States would have declared war upon Europe, but in the meantime Canada might very well have been paying tribute and learning to decline German verbs, probably the only thing German she *could* have declined....

A COUNTRY NOURISHED ON SELF-DOUBT

Nor disappointed as I am at the present inactivity of the States will I ever waiver in my loyal belief that in time to come, perhaps less distant than we realise, her actions will correspond with the lofty expression of her national and international ideals.

I shall continue to anticipate the day when with a clear understanding and a mutual trust we shall by virtue of our united strength and our common purposes be prepared to defend the rights of humanity not only upon the American Continent but throughout the civilised world.

Nevertheless we are not dealing with what may occur in the future but with the actual facts of yesterday and today, and I would feign know if you still think that a power which without protest witnesses the ruthless spoliation of Belgium and Serbia, and without effective action the murder of her own citizens, would have interfered to protect the property or the liberties of Canadians. Surely you must at least admit an element of doubt, and even if such interference had been attempted, have we not the admission of the Americans themselves that it could not have been successful against the great naval and military organisations of the Central Powers?

May I be permitted to conclude that had the Allies been defeated Canada must afterwards necessarily have suffered a similar fate.

But there was the other alternative, namely, that the Allies even without the assistance of Canada would *not* have been defeated. What then? Presumably French and English would still have been the official languages of Canada. You might still have edited untrammelled your version of Duty.... In fact Canada might still have retained her liberties and might with the same freedom from external influences have continued her progress to material and political strength.

But would you have been satisfied—you who have arrogated to yourself the high term of Nationalist? What of the Soul of Canada? Can a nation's pride or patriotism be built upon the blood and suffering of others or upon the wealth garnered from the coffers of those who in anguish and with blood-sweat are fighting the battles of freedom? If we accept our liberties, our national life, from the hands of the English soldiers, if without sacrifices of our own we profit by the sacrifices of the English citizen, can we hope to ever become a nation ourselves? How could we ever acquire that Soul or create that Pride without which a nation is a dead thing and doomed to speedy decay and disappearance.

If you were truly a Nationalist—if you loved our great country and without smallness longed to see her become the home of a good and united people—surely you would have recognised this as her moment of travail and tribulation. You would have felt that in the agony of her losses in Belgium and France, Canada was suffering the birth pains of her national life. There even more than in Canada herself, her citizens are being knit together into a new existence because when men stand side by side and endure a soldier's life and face together a soldier's death, they are united in bonds almost as strong as the closest of blood-ties.

There was the great opportunity for the true Nationalist! There was the great issue, the great sacrifice, which should have appealed equally to all true citizens of Canada, and should have served to cement them with indissoluble strength—Canada was at war! Canada was attacked! What mattered then internal dissentions and questions of home importance? What mattered the why and wherefore of the war, whether we owed anything to England or not, whether we were Imperialists or not, or whether we were French or English? The one simple commending fact to govern our conduct was that Canada was at war, and Canada and Canadian liberties had to be protected.

To you as a "Nationalist" this fact should have appealed more than to any others. Englishmen, as was natural, returned to fight for England, just as Germans and Austrians and Belgians and Italians returned to fight for their native lands.

But we, Canadians, had we no call just as insistent, just as compelling to fight for Canada? Did not the *Leipzig* and the *Gneisnau* possibly menace Victoria and Vancouver, and did you not feel the patriotism to make sacrifices for the protection of British Columbia? How could you otherwise call yourself Canadian? It is true that Canada did not hear the roar of German guns nor were we visited at night by the murderous Zeppelins, but every shot that was fired in Belgium or France was aimed as much at the heart of Canada as at the bodies of our brave Allies. Could we then wait within the temporary safety of our distant shores until either the Central Powers flushed with victory should come to settle their account or until by the glorious death of millions of our fellowmen in Europe, Canada should remain in inglorious security and a shameful liberty?

I give thanks that that question has been answered not as you would have had it answered but as those Canadians who have already died or are about to die here in this gallant motherland of France have answered it.

It may have been difficult for you at first to have realised the full significance of the situation. You were steeped in your belief that Canada owed no debt to England, was merely a vassal state and entitled to protection without payment. You were deeply imbued with the principle that we should not partake in a war in the declaration of which we had had no say. You believed very sincerely that Canadian soldiers should not be called upon to fight beyond the frontier of Canada itself, and your vision was further obscured by your indignation at the apparent injustice to a French minority in Ontario.

It is conceivable that at first on account of this long held attitude of mind and because it seemed that Canadian aid was hardly necessary, for even we feared that the war would be over before the first Canadian regiment should land in France, you should have failed to adapt your mind to the new situation and should for a while have continued in your former views;—but now—now that Canada has pledged herself body and soul to the successful prosecution of this war—now that we know that only by the exerci[s]e of our full and united strength can we achieve a speedy and lasting victory—now that thousands of your fellow citizens have died, and alas! many more must yet be killed—how in the name of all that you hold most sacred can you still maintain your opposition? How can you refrain from using all your influence and your personal magnetism and eloquence to swell the great army of Canada and make it as representative of all classes of our citizens as possible?

Could you have been here yourself to witness in its horrible detail the cruelty of war—to have seen your comrades suddenly struck down in death and lie mangled at your side, even you could not have failed to wish to visit punishment upon those responsible. You too would now wish to see every ounce of our united strength instantly and relentlessly directed to that end. Afterwards, when that end has been accomplished, then and then only can there be honour or profit in the discussion of our domestic or imperial disputes.

And so my first reason for your support would be that you should assist in the defence of Canadian territory and Canadian liberties....

The third reason is this: You and I are so called French-Canadians. We belong to a race that began the conquest of this country long before the days of Wolfe. That race was in its turn conquered, but their personal liberties were not restricted. They were in fact increased. Ultimately as a minority in a great English speaking community we have preserved our racial identity, and we have had freedom to speak or to worship as we wished. I may not be, like yourself, "un pur sang," for I am by birth even more English than French, but I am proud of my French ancestors, I love the French language, and I am as determined as you are that we shall have full liberty to remain French as long as we like. But if we are to preserve this liberty we must recognise that we do not belong entirely to ourselves, but to a mixed population, we must rather seek to find points of contact and of common interest than points of friction and separation. We must make concessions and certain sacrifices of our distinct individuality if we mean to live on amicable terms with our fellow citizens or if we are to expect them to make similar concessions to us. There, in this moment of crisis, was the greatest opportunity which could ever have presented itself for us to show unity of purpose and to prove to our English fellow citizens that, whatever our respective histories may have been, we were actuated by a common love for our country and a mutual wish that in the future we should unite our distinctive talents and energies to create a proud and happy nation.

That was an opportunity which you, my cousin, have failed to grasp, and unfortunately, despite the heroic and able manner in which French Canadian battalions have distinguished themselves here, and despite the whole-hearted support which so many leaders of French Canadian thought have given to the cause, yet the fact remains that the French in Canada have not responded in the same proportion as have other Canadian citizens, and the unhappy impression has been created that French Canadians are not bearing their full share in this great Canadian enterprise. For this fact and this impression you will be held largely responsible. Do you fully realise what such a responsibility will mean, not so much to you personally—for that I believe you would care little—but to the principles which you have advocated, and for many of which I have but the deepest regard. You will have brought them into a disrepute from which they may never recover. Already you have made the fine term of "Nationalist" to stink in the nostrils of our English fellow citizens. Have you caused them to respect your national views? Have you won their admiration or led them to consider with esteem, and toleration your ambitions for the French language? Have you shown yourself worthy of concessions or consideration?

After this war what influence will you enjoy—what good to your country will you be able to accomplish? Wherever you go you will stir up strife and enmity—you will bring disfavour and dishonour upon our race, so that whoever bears a French name in Canada will be an object of suspicion and possibly of hatred.

And so, in the third place, for the honour of French Canada and for the unity of our country, I would have had you favourable to our cause.

I have only two more reasons, and they but need to be mentioned, I think to be appreciated.

Here in this little French town I hear about all me the language I love so well and which recalls so vividly my happy childhood days in Montebello. I see types and faces that are like old friends. I see farm houses like those at home. I notice that our French Canadian soldiers have easy friendships wherever they go.

Can you make me believe that there must not always be a bond of blood relationship between the Old France and the New?

And France—more glorious than in all her history—is now in agony straining fearlessly and proudly in a struggle for life or death.

For Old France and French civilisation I would have had your support.

And in the last place, all other considerations aside and even supposing Canada had been a neutral country, I would have had you decide that she should enter the struggle for no other reason than that it is a fight for the freedom of the world—a fight in the result of which like every other country she is herself vitally interested. I will not further speak of the causes of this war, but I should like to think that even if Canada had been an independent and neutral nation she of her own accord would have chosen to follow the same path of glory that she is following today.

Perhaps, my cousin, I have been overlong and tedious with my reasons, but I shall be shorter with my warning—and in closing I wish to say this to you.

Those of us in this great army, who may be so fortunate as to return to our Canada, will have faced the grimmest and sincerest issues of life and death—we will have experienced the unhappy strength of brute force—we will have seen our loved comrades die in blood and suffering. Beware lest we return with revengeful feelings, for I say to you that for those who, while we fought and suffered here, remained in safety and comfort in Canada and failed to give us encouragement and support, as well as for those who grew fat with the wealth dishonourably gained by political graft and by dishonest business methods at our expense—we shall demand a heavy day of reckoning. We shall inflict upon them the punishment they deserve—not by physical violence—for we shall have had enough of that—nor by unconstitutional or illegal means—for we are fighting to protect not to destroy justice and freedom—but by the invincible power of our moral influence.

Can you ask us then for sympathy or concession? Will any listen when you speak of pride and patriotism? I think not.

Remember too that if Canada has become a nation respected and self-respecting she owes it to her citizens who have fought and died in this distant land and not to those self-styled Nationalists who have remained at home.

Can I hope that anything I have said here may influence you to consider the situation in a different light and that it is not yet too late for me to be made proud of our relationship?

At this moment, as I write, French and English-Canadians are fighting and dying side by side. Is their sacrifice to go for nothing or will it not cement a foundation for a true Canadian nation, a Canadian nation independent in thought, independent in action, independent even in its political organisation—but in spirit united for high international and humane purposes to the two Motherlands of England and France?

I think that is an ideal in which we shall all equally share. Can we not all play an equal part in its realisation?

I am, as long as may be possible,
Your affectionate Cousin,
TALBOT M. PAPINEAU.

3. Henri Bourassa, "Mr. Bourassa's Reply to Capt. Talbot Papineau's Letter," August 2, 1916

Henri Bourassa (1868-1952) was also a grandson of Quebec's reformer, Louis Joseph Papineau. He studied at Montréal's École Polytechnique and in Massachusetts, and became mayor of Montebello, Quebec, at age 22. Elected to the House of Commons in 1896, he resigned in 1899 over Canada's aid to Britain in the Boer War. In 1903 he created the Nationalist League to promote an independent and autonomous Canada within the British Empire. He accepted the idea of a Canadian navy as long as it was solely under Canadian control. In 1910 he founded the newspaper Le Devoir *in order to publicize his ideas.*

... As early as the month of March 1900, I pointed out the possibility of a conflict between Great Britain and Germany and the danger of laying down in South Africa a precedent, the fatal consequence of which would be to draw Canada into all the wars undertaken by the United Kingdom. Sir Wilfrid Laurier and the liberal leaders laughed at my apprehensions; against my warnings they quoted the childish safeguard of the "no precedent clause" inserted in the Order in Council of the 14th of October 1899. For many years after, till 1912, and 1913, they kept singing the praises of the Kaiser and extolling the peaceful virtues of Germany. They now try to regain time by denouncing vociferously the "barbarity" of the "Huns." Today, as in 1900, in 1911, and always, I believe that all the nations of Europe are the victims of their own mistakes, of the complacent servility with which they submitted to the dominance of all Imperialists and traders in human flesh, who, in England as in Germany, in France as in Russia, have brought the peoples to slaughter in order to increase their reapings of cursed gold. German Imperialism and British Imperialism, French Militarism and Russian Tsarism, I hate with equal detestation; and I believe as firmly today as in 1899 that Canada, a nation of America, has a nobler mission to fulfill than to bind herself to the fate of the nations of Europe or to any spoliating Empire—whether it be the spoliators of Belgium, Alsace, or Poland, or those of Ireland or the Transvaal, of Greece or the Balkans.

Politicians of both parties, your liberal friends as well as their conservative opponents, feign to be much scandalised at my "treasonable disloyalty." I could well afford to look upon them as a pack of knaves and hypocrites. In 1896, your liberal leaders and friends stumped the whole province of Quebec with the cry "WHY SHOULD WE FIGHT FOR ENGLAND?" From 1902 to 1911, Sir Wilfrid Laurier was acclaimed by them as the indomitable champion of Canada's autonomy against British Imperialism. His resisting attitude at the Imperial Conferences of 1902 and 1907 was praised to the skies. His famous phrase on the "vortex of European militarism," and his determination to keep Canada far from it, became the party's byword—always in the Province of Quebec, of course. His Canadian Navy scheme was presented as a step towards the independence of Canada....

By what right should those people hold me as a "traitor," because I remain consequent with the principles that I have never ceased to uphold and which both parties have exploited alternately, as long as it suited their purpose and kept them in power or brought them to office?

Let it not be pretended that those principles are out of place, pending the war. To prevent Canada from participating in the war, then foreseen and predicted, was their very object and *raison d'être*. To throw them aside and deny them when the time of test came, would have required a lack of courage and sincerity, of which I feel totally incapable. If this is what they mean by "British loyalty" and "superior civilisation," they had better hang me at once. I will never obey such dictates and will ever hold in deepest contempt the acrobats who lend themselves to all currents of blind popular passion in order to serve their personal or political ends....

I will not undertake to answer every point of the dithyrambic plea of my gallant cousin. When he says that I am too far away from the trenches to judge of the real meaning of this war, he may be right. On the other hand, his long and diffuse piece of eloquence proves that the excitement of warfare and the distance from home have obliterated in his mind the fundamental realities of his native country. I content myself with touching upon one point, on which he unhappily lends credit to the most mischievous of the many anti-national opinions circulated by the jingo press. He takes the French-Canadians to task and challenges their patriotism, because they enlist in lesser number than the other elements of the population of Canada. Much could be said upon that. It is sufficient to signalise one patent fact: the number of recruits for the European war, in the various Provinces of Canada and from each component element of the population, is in inverse ratio of the enrootment in the soil and the traditional patriotism arising therefrom. The newcomers from the British Isles have enlisted in much larger proportion than English-speaking Canadians born in this country, while these have enlisted more than the French-Canadians. The Western Provinces have given more recruits than Ontario, and Ontario more than Quebec. In each Province, the floating population of the cities, the students, the labourers and clerks, either unemployed or threatened with dismissal, have supplied more soldiers than the farmers. Does it mean that the city dwellers are more patriotic than the country people? or that the newcomers from England are better Canadians than their fellow citizens of British origin, born in Canada? No; it simply means that in Canada, as in every other country, at all times, the citizens of the oldest origin are the least disposed to be stampeded into distant ventures of no direct concern to their native land. It proves also that military service is more repugnant to the rural than the urban populations.

There is among the French-Canadians a larger proportion of farmers, fathers of large families, than among any other ethnical element in Canada. Above all, the French-Canadians are the only group exclusively Canadian, in its whole and by each of the individuals of which it is composed. They look upon the perturbations of Europe, even those of England or France, as foreign events. Their sympathies naturally go to France against Germany; but they do not think they have an obligation to fight for France, no more than the French of Europe would hold themselves bound to fight for Canada against the United States or Japan, or even against Germany, in case Germany should attack Canada without threatening France.

English Canada, not counting the *blokes*, contains a considerable proportion of people still in the first period of national incubation. Under the sway of imperialism, a fair number have not yet decided whether their allegiance is to Canada or to the Empire, whether the United Kingdom or the Canadian Confederacy is their country.

As to the newcomers from the United Kingdom, they are not Canadian in any sense. England or Scotland is their sole fatherland. They have enlisted for the European war as naturally as Canadians, either French or English, would take arms to defend Canada against an aggression on the American continent.

Thus it is rigorously correct to say that recruiting has gone in inverse ratio of the development of Canadian patriotism. If English-speaking Canadians have a right to blame the French Canadians for the small number of their recruits, the newcomers from the United Kingdom, who have supplied a much larger proportion of recruits than any other element of the population, would be equally justified in branding the Anglo-Canadians with disloyalty and treason. Enlistment for the European war is supposed to be absolutely free and voluntary. This has been stated right and left from beginning to end. If that statement is honest and sincere, all provocations from one part of the population against the other, and exclusive attacks against the French-Canadians, should cease. Instead of reviling unjustly one-third of the Canadian people—a population so remarkably characterised by its constant loyalty to national institutions and its respect for public order,—those men who claim a right to enlighten and lead public opinion should have enough good faith and intelligence to see facts as they are and to respect the motives of those who persist in their determination to remain more Canadian than English or French.

... The most that can be said is, that the backward and essentially Prussian policy of the rulers of Ontario and Manitoba gives us an additional argument against the intervention of Canada in the European conflict. To speak of fighting for the preservation of French civilisation in Europe while endeavouring to destroy it in America, appears to us as an absurd piece of inconsistency. To preach Holy War for the liberties of the peoples overseas, and to oppress the national minorities in Canada, is, in our opinion, nothing but odious hypocrisy.

Is it necessary to add that, in spite of his name, Capt. Papineau is utterly unqualified to judge of the feelings of the French-Canadians? For most part American, he has inherited, with a few drops of French blood, the most *denationalised* instincts of his French origin. From those he calls his compatriots he is separated by his religious belief and his maternal language. Of their traditions, he knows but what he has read in a few books. He was brought up far away from close contact with French-Canadians. His higher studies he pursued in England. His elements of French culture he acquired in France. The complexity of his origin and the diversity of his training would be sufficient to explain his mental hesitations and the contradictions which appear in his letter....

4. "No More Canadians for Overseas Service: This Young Dominion Has Sacrificed Enough," *Sault Express*, June 23, 1916

The Sault Express was one of two daily newspapers in Sault Ste. Marie, a small town in northern Ontario on the St. Mary's River between Lake Superior and Lake Huron. Located across the river from the United States, "the Sault," as it is commonly called, had a large European immigrant community, particularly Italian. The following article resulted in the paper being banned by the chief censor of Canada.

The *Express* in its limited sphere has been advocating peace among the warring nations of Europe, but save in the undercurrent of Canadian sentiment which we know exists in the heart of many of our people there appears to be no desire for a termination of hostilities until the Germanic power in Europe has been utterly destroyed and many of the old world wrongs have been made right. We fear that if Canada is to continue to shed her life blood until that day arrives there will not be many Canadians remaining to celebrate the conquest, and the high purposes for which our forefathers on this continent strove will all have been in vain. And more than that, we have grave fears that if this horrible conflict goes on for another two years we shall not have our United Empire to cheer for. These words are spoken in the fullest consciousness of their meaning. The destruction of the Teutonic race is quite as impossible as the destruction of the Anglo-Saxon race, and the destruction of either would be nothing short of a catastrophe handed down to posterity as an example of our present day higher civilization. What our empire needs right now and what Canada needs right now is PEACE. But we have drifted away from what we started out to say, which was that this Dominion should not send any more of her sons overseas to engage in this frightful cataclysm. The truth is that there has already been too much Canadian bloodletting and the cost of British connection has been away and beyond what our people counted on. We have less than eight millions of population as against three hundred millions in India. If, as we are told, the shedding of blood overseas is the silicon which binds the steel of Empire, then why does England not draw upon her three hundred millions in India as she has drawn upon her seven millions in Canada?

"The Canadian troops made a most gallant stand;" "the soldiers from Canada well upheld the traditions of the race;" "thousands of our brave Canadian soldiers fell with honour," "we can never forget the heroism of those grand Canadians." That kind of salve from London does not bind up the hearts of the thousands of Canadian mothers and sisters whose loved ones sleep in a foreign land after dying for a foreign cause.

It is about time for Canadians to wake up and realize that they are living in America and not Europe; that old world empires rise and fall; that we are the last great land to the west on this great planet and that the Lord has so ordained; that our neighbors and we are of the same faith, our language is the same and there is a comity of blood existing between us which makes us brothers in the truest human sense. A century of peace exemplifies the silicon in the steel.

Canada will contribute more to the future greatness of the Anglo-Saxon race by pursuing her own ideals and minding her own business on this side of the Atlantic then by spending "her last son and her last dollar" across the water in a futile effort to adjust the wrongs which most of our ancestors left the old world to escape....

5. Robert Borden, House of Commons *Debates*, 1917

Robert Borden's (1854–1937) ancestors came to Nova Scotia from England via Rhode Island. A classics scholar, Borden taught before articling for law in 1874. In 1896 he became a Conservative Member of Parliament for Halifax and rose to lead the party in 1901. As an imperialist, Borden supported immediate help for Britain in its effort to out-build the German navy with more Dreadnought battleships and rejected free trade with the United States. He became prime minister in 1911. Borden responded enthusiastically to Britain's Declaration of War in 1914, which saw Canada automatically join, and promised manpower, money, and material for the conflict's duration.

I approached a subject of great gravity and seriousness, and, I hope, with a full sense of the responsibility that devolves upon myself and upon my colleagues, and not only upon us but upon the members of this Parliament and the people. We have four Canadian divisions at the front. For the immediate future there are sufficient reinforcements. But four divisions cannot be maintained without thorough provision for future requirements.... I think that no true Canadian, realizing all that is at stake in this war, can bring himself to consider with toleration or seriousness any suggestion for the relaxation of our efforts.... Hitherto we have depended upon voluntary enlistment. I myself stated to Parliament that nothing but voluntary enlistment was proposed by the Government. But I return to Canada impressed at once with the extreme gravity of the situation, and with a sense of responsibility for our further effort at the most critical period of the war. It is apparent to me that the voluntary system will not yield further substantial results. I hoped it would. The Government have made every effort within its power, so far as I can judge. If any effective effort to stimulate voluntary recruiting remains to be made, I should like to know what it is....

All citizens are liable to military service for the defence of their country, and I conceive that the battle for Canadian liberty and autonomy is being fought today on the plains of France and of Belgium. There are other places besides the soil of a country where the battle for its liberties and its institutions can be fought; and if this war should end in defeat, Canada, in all the years to come, would be under the shadow of German military domination. That is the very lowest at which we can put it....

Now the question arises as to what is our duty.... A great responsibility rests upon those who are entrusted with the administration of public affairs. But they are not fit to be trusted with that transcendent duty if they shrink from any responsibility which the occasion calls for.... The time has come when the authority of the state should be invoked to provide reinforcements necessary to maintain the gallant men at the front.... I bring back to the people of Canada from these men a message that they need our help, that they need to be sustained, that reinforcements must be sent to them. Thousands of them have made the supreme sacrifice for our liberty and preservation. Common gratitude, apart from all other considerations, should bring the whole force of this nation behind them. I have promised ... that this help shall be given. I should feel myself unworthy of the responsibility devolving upon me if I did not fulfil that pledge. I bring a message also from them, yes, a message also from the men in the hospitals, who have come back from the very valley of the shadow of death, many of them maimed for life.... But is there not some other message? Is there not a call to us from those who have passed beyond the shadow into the light of perfect day, from those who have fallen in France and in Belgium, from those who have died that Canada may live—is there not a call to us that their sacrifice shall not be in vain?

I have had to take all these matters into consideration and I have given them my most earnest attention. The responsibility is a serious one, but I do not shrink from it. Therefore, it is my duty to announce to the House that early proposals will be made to provide by compulsory military enlistment on a selective basis, such reinforcements as may be necessary to maintain the Canadian army in the field.... The number of men required not be less than 50,000, and will probably be 100,000 ...

It has been said of this Bill that it will induce disunion, discord and strife and that it will paralyze the national effort. I trust that this prophecy may prove unfounded. Why should strife be induced by the application of a principle which was adopted at the very inception of Confederation?...

It was my strong desire to bring about a union of all parties for the purpose of preventing any such disunion or strife as is apprehended. The effort was an absolutely sincere one, and I do not regret that it was made, although the delay which it occasioned may have given opportunity for increasing agitation and for excitement arising from misunderstanding. I went so far as to agree that this Bill should not become effective until after a general election, in the hope that by this means all apprehension would be allayed, and that there might be a united effort to fulfil the great national purpose of winning this war. What may be necessary or expedient in that regard, I am yet willing to consider, for ever since this war began I have had one constant aim and it was this: to throw the full power and effort of Canada into the scale of right, liberty and justice for the winning of this war, and to maintain the unity of the Canadian people in that effort....

God speed the day when the gallant men who are protecting and defending us will return to the land they love so well. Only those who have seen them at the front can realize how much they do love this dear land of Canada. If we do not pass this measure, if we do not provide reinforcements, if we do not keep our plighted faith, with what countenance shall we meet them on their return?...

They went forth splendid in their youth and confidence. They will come back silent, grim, determined men who, not once or twice, but fifty times, have gone over the parapet to seek their rendezvous with death. If what are left of 400,000 such men come back to Canada with fierce resentment and even rage in their hearts, conscious that they have been deserted or betrayed, how shall we meet them when they ask the reason? I am not so much concerned for the day when this Bill becomes law, as for the day when these men return if it is rejected.

6. Francis Marion Beynon, "Women's View of Conscription," *Grain Growers' Guide*, May 30, 1917

Francis Marion Beynon (1884–1951) was a prominent, powerful, and outspoken Winnipeg journalist and suffragist. Her career began as a teacher, then shifted to being one of the first female managers at Eaton's department store, but she is best remembered as editor of the women's section of the Grain Grower's Guide. *In that capacity, between 1912 and 1917, she achieved national recognition in the campaign for female political equality. Her simultaneous pacifist beliefs, attacks on nationalist ideology, and anti-conscriptionist stance, however, made her increasingly unpopular, even among women, and eventually forced her resignation in 1917 and her move to New York City.*

There are four objections to the government's announced intention of forcing conscription upon the people of Canada, the first and greatest being that the people have not been consulted about it, the second that it should include married as well as single men; third, that it should be accompanied by conscription of all wealth and all moneys invested in the war loans, and fourth, that the government of Great Britain no longer ago than last week closed out a motion saying that they were not fighting for imperialistic conquest or aggrandisement.

Before men are arbitrarily taken from their homes and put through the military machine, they and their mothers and fathers have a right to say that they are willing it should be done. More particularly is this the case since the killing or physical maiming of them is among the lesser evils that have befallen many of the Canadian boys who have gone to serve in the army. It was admitted in the British House of Commons the other day that in one Canadian camp alone there were seven thousand men suffering from venereal disease, and medical reports in Great Britain show that ten per cent of the forces are affected.

Of these thousands of men who have been ruined there are numbers who would not in any case have led a blameless life, but there are also thousands of clean-minded innocent young boys who would otherwise have been decent upright citizens who will now be nothing but a scourge to their country when they return and whose lives have been completely ruined. Their chances of marrying and having a happy home and healthy children have been taken away from them. Before any mother sees her son forcibly exposed to these temptations she has a right to say whether or not she is willing to have it so. When Everywoman's World took a vote of its women readers on the question of conscription recently it was defeated six to one. If this is any indication of public opinion it is certainly a minority decision the government has arrived at. If you feel at all strongly on this question, bombard Premier Borden with letters demanding a referendum, and write at once.

Although the government doubtless intends to follow the example of Great Britain of taking first the single men and then extending the principle to apply to the married men, as the demand increases, it seems fair to make it apply to both from the outset. If the good of the individual is to be set aside at the demands of the country, then the rights of the individual ought to be completely disregarded, and those men, married or single, left at home who are mostly useful to the country. There is nothing to be gained by deceiving ourselves, it means conscription for married men also, sooner or later, if the war goes on, as it seems likely to do, indefinitely. The Canadian government has followed so far, exactly the system that was followed in England at the beginning of the war, and it is likely that they will continue to follow it in every particular.

Then as regards the conscription of wealth. It has been said over and over again that this war will be won by the silver bullet, but instead of the government getting this silver bullet through war loans at five per cent and forever exempt from income tax, let them conscript the city houses and the bank accounts and the railways and the munition plants and the farms, and let all the citizens pay rent to the government. Then with this income pay a generous separation allowance to the wives of married men, and a liberal pension to their widows, and above all an especially generous pension to returned soldiers who are partially or completely disabled, so that these men who have faced death for their country may not need to be the objects of charity from people who have gotten rich out of war profits. Moreover it is obviously unjust to conscript the life of the poor working man, which is all that stands between his family and destitution, while another man can go to the front knowing that in the event of his complete disablement, neither he nor his family will have to eke out a miserable existence for years and years to come.

Finally, before men are compelled to go against their will to serve in the army they have a right to know what they are fighting for, whether it is indeed the principle of democracy, which they were assured at the beginning of the war it was, or whether it is for territory, the acquisition of which will lead to the shedding of the blood of hundreds of thousands of other men at a later date, as territory snatching almost invariably does …

Now as has been pointed out in this column over and over again there is no territory in the world that is worth the slaughter of human beings, and, moreover, this snatching of territory is a positively bad and wicked thing, sowing the seeds of other wars for other men to be slaughtered in. It is utterly opposed to the principle of democracy for which the British Empire is supposed to stand and for which men believe they are dying in this war. No group of people have a right to be transferred from one government to another without their own consent, in a fair referendum, and they ought not so to be transferred at any time, whether in war time or peace. Therefore before conscription comes into force in Canada the British government should be compelled to repudiate any desire for territorial aggrandisement. Men have no right to be forcibly killed and maimed to acquire a few acres of land.

FURTHER READINGS

Armstrong, E. *The Crisis in Quebec, 1914-1918*. Toronto: McClelland and Stewart, 1974.

Berger, C., Ed. *Conscription, 1917*. Toronto: University of Toronto Press, 1969.

Bray, R. "Fighting as An Ally: The English-Canadian Patriotic Response to the Great War." *Canadian Historical Review* 61, 2 (June 1980): 141-68.

Brown, R., and D. Loveridge. "Unrequited Faith: Recruiting the CEF, 1914-1918." *Revue Internationale d'Histoire Militaire* 54 (1982): 53-78.

Cook, R. "Frances Beynon and the Crisis in Christian Reformism." In *The West and the Nation: Essays in Honour of W.L. Morton*, ed. C. Berger and R. Cook. Toronto: McClelland and Stewart, 1976.

Gorham, D. "Vera Brittain, Flora MacDonald Denison, and the Great War: The Failure of Non-Violence." In *Women and Peace: Theoretical, Historical and Practical Perspectives*, ed. R. Pierson. London: Croom Helm, 1987.

Granatstein, J., and J. Hitsman. *Broken Promises: A History of Conscription in Canada*. Toronto: Oxford University Press, 1977.

Hyatt, A. "Sir Arthur Currie and Conscription: A Soldier's View." *Canadian Historical Review* 50, 3 (September 1969): 285-96.

Morton, D. "French Canada and War, 1868-1917: The Military Background to the Conscription Crisis of 1917." In *War and Society in North America*, ed. J. Granatstein and T. Cuff. Toronto: Nelson, 1970.

Robin, M. "Registration, Conscription, and Independent Labour Politics, 1916-1917." *Canadian Historical Review* 47, 2 (June 1966): 101-18.

Roberts, B. "Women Against War, 1914-1918: Francis Beynon and Laura Hughes." In *Up and Doing: Canadian Women and Peace*, ed. J. Williamson and D. Gorham. Toronto: Women's Press, 1989.

Socknat, T. "Canada's Liberal Pacifists and the Great War." *Journal of Canadian Studies* 8, 4 (Winter 1983-84): 30-44.

Socknat, T. *Witness Against War: Pacifism in Canada, 1900-1945*. Toronto: University of Toronto Press, 1981.

Walker, J. "Race and Recruitment in World War I: Enlistment of Visible Minorities in the Canadian Expeditionary Force." *Canadian Historical Review* 70, 1 (March 1989): 1-26.

Warne, R. "Nellie McClung and Peace." In *Up and Doing: Canadian Women and Peace*, ed. J. Williamson and D. Gorham. Toronto: Women's Press, 1989.

Willms, A. "Conscription 1917: A Brief for the Defence." *Canadian Historical Review* 37, 4 (December 1956): 338-51.

Young, W. "Conscription, Rural Depopulation, and the Farmers of Ontario, 1917-1919." *Canadian Historical Review* 53 (September 1972): 289-320.

CHAPTER 7

"Ruthless Butchers of Men and Morals"

THE DRUG TRAFFIC

INTRODUCTION

Democracy supposedly offers each citizen greater levels of liberty than other forms of government. It is, after all, a political structure based upon the supremacy of the individual and at least pays lip-service to the idea of equality. Senior democracies with stable and prosperous societies, such as Canada, tend to be smug and even condescending about their citizens' liberties and how little the state interferes in private lives. Ironically, however, reform-minded citizens and all levels of Canadian governments have, periodically, been at the vanguard of strident and repressive efforts at social control. Legislation limiting civil rights and freedoms invariably emerged as a way to protect the wider social fabric from those who purportedly threatened it. The crusaders set out, with a profound sense of righteousness on their side, to limit the liberties of the few in order to safeguard the many. Most citizens either did not object or indeed supported the new laws. This is perhaps not as surprising as it may seem. Canada is, after all, the nation of "Peace, Order, and Good Government" where citizens insist that the stability of the nation and its structure is paramount. "Life, Liberty, and the Pursuit of Happiness" is not for us.

The freedom of the individual to consume drugs versus the society's right to prevent it is a prime example of this dialectic between freedom and control.

Few Canadians even realized that the country had a drug problem when the issue emerged in the 1920s. Nor does anyone know how drug use began in Canada, though the consensus seems to be that it either arrived in British Columbia in the 1850s with Chinese miners during the Cariboo gold rush or with Chinese railway workers in the 1880s. This, of course, begs the questions: why was it previously so obscure and why did it suddenly become such a moral panic and *cause célèbre*? That it formerly elicited little interest is likely because it was a minor issue relegated either to Chinese subculture or to the few members of the middle and upper classes in Canadian society. Thus, it was perceived as a tolerable weakness in the individual, not a serious social crisis, and certainly neither pathological nor a real threat to the *status quo*. Nineteenth-century middle-class doctors prescribed opiates to ease stress, and upper-class women indulged because it was socially acceptable — in moderation and with discretion. The world, too, was full of patent medicines made of opium and its derivatives, and these were perceived as perfectly acceptable and beneficial medicinal solutions to health problems. Lest we forget, Coca-Cola contained cocaine until 1903.

Nonetheless, anti-drug legislation began to appear at the start of the twentieth century; the Opium Act passed in 1908 prohibited the manufacture, sale, or importation of opium for non-medical purposes and was a direct effort to curb Chinese opium smoking. Smoking opium was previously perfectly legal and carefully taxed by the federal government. That same year further acts restricted the use of opium in patent medicines and outlawed cocaine. In 1911 morphine, an opium derivative, joined the list of restricted drugs. Ironically, returning veterans from World War I likely once again triggered the drug-issue alarm bells. Many ex-soldiers returned to Canada addicted to morphine as a result of pain management efforts for their wounds, and all levels of government had to contend with this increasingly outcast class. In 1921 the federal government changed the law to increase the sentences for drug traffickers from one to seven years. The following year legislation passed to allow aliens convicted of drug offences to be deported. By 1923, the House of Commons introduced legislation for mandatory jail time for all those convicted of trafficking, and in 1925 doctors were prohibited from prescribing opiates to addicts. Control legislation against the drug trade culminated with the Opium and Narcotics Drug Act of 1929, which included long jail sentences and whipping for those convicted of selling to minors. The combination of legislation, police enforcement, and deportation seemed to work. Convictions for drug offences fell from a high of 1,858 in 1921-22 to 230 in 1932-33.

The simple explanation for the sudden vilification of drug use and why it became a fundamental issue of social control during the 1920s was because three factors coalesced: 1) the drug culture made spectacular journalistic copy for a public hungry for a good story;

2) it directly addressed issues of immigration and in particular the thorny question of Chinese immigration; and 3) drug use became intertwined with the perceived importance of social control for racial purity and preservation at a time when many Canadians saw the country's heritage threatened.

Weekly magazines, particularly for women, began running stories such as those authored by Emily Murphy in the 1920s. The cast of characters made for salacious reading, and Canadians bought them by the millions. There was inevitably the virginal white girl lured into the vortex of drug abuse. Who led her into temptation? The nefarious and Wily Oriental Gentleman—giving rise to the opprobrious epithet "WOG"—who cleverly never used "dope" himself but snared her in his net and eventually forced her into prostitution as she struggled to feed her addiction. Prostitution implied miscegenation—that innocent white victim would bed men of different races and would produce "mongrel" offspring who would lower the superiority of the Anglo-Saxon race. And, if not that, there was the scourge of venereal disease. There were the uncontrolled "dope fiends" quick to gun down upstanding RCMP officers trying to curb the trade and save the maiden, and there were forays into the hidden world of the opium den. There were even intimations that the problem was no longer limited to the urban slums, but was stealthily creeping into rural Canada, that bastion of moral rectitude. Hollywood could not have created a finer set of criteria to titillate the national imagination.

By the 1920s, increasing numbers of Canadians voiced concern over the supposed explosion of immigration from China. The peril was that Chinese were perceived as smarter and harder working than Caucasians, but they lacked the European's sense of morality and higher levels of cultural sophistication to hold them in check. This, of course, made them doubly dangerous because they could, and would, do anything to outwit the white race. Taken to its logical conclusion, this scenario led to the belief that the Chinese would eventually dominate the country. It is not by chance that interest in the drug issue declined after passage of the Chinese Exclusion Act in 1923, virtually stopped all immigration from China.

Issues of racial purity raged through Canada after World War I. The birth rate among middle-class Canadians dropped precipitously during the decade. Since this class was perceived (by itself) as the country's moral backbone, this decline, combined with immigration of undesirables, spelled deep trouble. The fact that the "inferior" working class of Canada maintained its high birth rate exacerbated the problem and may explain the subtle shift of the portrayal of the drug addict: he was no longer a social manifestation of the middle and upper classes but became a male working-class "dope fiend." Allowing those "fiends" to reproduce, so the story went, would result in a rapid deterioration of Canada's social fabric. This may also explain why offspring of white drug addicts were typically described as the "feeble minded" whom mainstream society suggested must be sterilized to save the strength and purity of the race. Again, it is not by chance that during this decade provincial governments enacted eugenic legislation that led to the sterilization of thousands of allegedly mentally challenged Canadians. Alberta, Emily Murphy's home, was the most draconian province, passing legislation in 1937 that allowed sterilization without patient, parental, or spousal consent.

DISCUSSION POINTS

1. To what degree, if any, was the analysis of the drug use marred by exaggeration and unfounded speculation?

2. At what point, if at all, should the state have the right to interfere with the liberty of the individual? Did the government overstep its bounds in relation to the drug issue in the 1920s?

3. Not until the 1950s was drug use defined as an illness worthy of medical treatment. Why was this not recognized earlier?

·· DOCUMENTS

1. Emily Murphy, *The Black Candle*, 1922

Emily Murphy (1868–1933) was a suffragist, equal rights activist, and eugenicist. A self-taught legal expert, she became the first woman judge in the British Empire. Murphy involved herself with the lives of the accused and endorsed rehabilitation, not just punishment. The results of drug abuse among convicts caused her great distress, and she became a tireless anti-narcotics crusader. During the early 1920s she familiarized Canadians with the issue through articles in Maclean's Magazine *in which she exposed the evils of the drug trade. Eventually these articles became the basis of her book* The Black Candle.

A while ago we said that America led the world in the narcotic drug traffic. This is quite true, but only during the past two years, for in 1919, before the Canadian Government recognized the necessity to taking immediate and drastic steps to remedy the condition, Canada held that direful distinction, if we will compute the population of this Dominion as thirteen times less than that of the United States.

The legitimate importations in narcotics for 1920 were reduced, in some instances, from 75% to 25% as against the previous year. This was due in a large measure to the establishing of the licensing system.

But, in spite of their bold and determined effort to grapple with the illicit or unlicensed traffic, and in spite of their large seizures of contraband narcotics, the Government have acknowledged that it is actually on the increase. The Department of Health says it would astound the people in this country, and the authorities in many towns and cities if the conditions as they exist were brought to light.

Indeed the unlicensed traffic has gained such a foot-hold in Canada that it has become most alarming. In one Western inland city with about thirty thousand of a population, the federal police found upon investigation that there were hundreds of young men and women, many of them not out of their teens, who were addicted to the drug habit.

This prairie town, which is typical of many others in the Dominion, would have indignantly denied this charge and there is no doubt the police, clergy, teachers and parents, not looking for addiction and not knowing the symptoms, would have said "Impossible! We do not know of any drug users, or not more than three or four."

Yet, before the federal police left this town they laid evidence before the local authorities which led to the conviction of nearly fifty persons, most of them peddlers.

The trouble in most cities appears to be that the police are untrained in the work, and, in some few instances, actually in league with the traffickers, thereby affording them a certain amount of indirect protection.

It is the opinion of the Government officials that this underground traffic continues to flourish in spite of the efforts which are being made by the Royal Canadian Mounted Police, and by the provincial and municipal police by reason of the fact that there are enormous quantities of these drugs available in European countries.

For the twelve months ending March 31st, 1922, the Federal Government prosecuted, under the provisions of the Opium and Drugs Act, twenty-three doctors, eleven druggists, four veterinary surgeons, one hundred and sixty-five illicit dealers, and six hundred and thirty four Chinamen, making a total of eight hundred and thirty-five convictions. The fines imposed amounted to $127,947.00. These figures do not include provincial municipal convictions.

The municipal drug convictions for Vancouver totalled 858 for the year 1921, having jumped from 293 in 1918. It is expected the convictions for 1922 will pass the one thousand mark.

By comparing these figures with those of the American cities on the Pacific Coast, it will be seen that in spite of their greater population, Vancouver leads San Francisco, Seattle and Los Angeles. Indeed with the exception of New York, and possibly Chicago, Vancouver leads all of the way.

Commenting on these convictions, a western editor says, "Some with the aid of purchased legal skill went scot free on pettifogging technicalities. A few of them went to jail, for the most part for pitifully insufficient periods. The vast majority of them were levied for a contribution to the city treasury in the form of a fine. All of them, in due course, became free to commit the same sin against society."

While undoubtedly seaport cities, like Vancouver and Montreal, have a greater incidence than the cities like Toronto and Winnipeg, still the difference is not as much as one might expect.

The Kiwanis Club of Vancouver, in the report of its medical sub-committee, has this to say about the matter: "It is the general belief of observers that the habit of drug addiction has been steadily on the increase in most civilized countries, especially during the last ten years. Vancouver and British Columbia have been no exception and the drug habit has undoubtedly been on the increase here as in other places. There are no reliable statistics available to indicate the actual increase, but the opinions of police authorities and other reliable observers is that the number of drug addicts is gradually increasing in Vancouver."

In 1918, the late Chief of Police McLennan, who was brutally murdered by a drug-fiend, called attention to the prevalence of the drug habit in this city [Vancouver] which he stated was then becoming alarming. The police authorities claim that although the drug habit has been growing here, it has certainly not been growing any more rapidly than in other cities proportionately to population, but the greater prominence has been given to Vancouver on account of the publicity given to the subject in the daily press, and also on account of the great activity and success of the police department in prosecuting drug traffickers and seizing drugs....

It is generally held that breaches of the opium and liquor laws are proportionately more frequent in the cities than in the country. It is on this assumption that the special American Committee compute the numbers of their addicts, although they state that in the rural districts or smaller cities little or no attention has been given to this subject, and where decreases are reported, it is quite possible that the opinions expressed by the officials are at variance with the conditions as they actually exist.

If it could be shown that physicians, druggists, veterinarians and dentists who are responsible for a vast amount of the traffic were more honourable and less avaricious in the country districts than in the city, we might assume that New York was more deeply narcotised, proportionately, than the smaller places in Texas or Idaho, but such is not the case. The functioning of the Liquor Act in which prescriptions are freely distributed shows—in Canada anyway—that exactly the opposite condition prevails. In the Province of Ontario, which is thickly populated, for the year 1920, only 5% of the physicians wrote out their full quota of fifty prescriptions, while in Alberta where the population is less than one person to the square mile, 75% of the physicians wrote over 75 prescriptions per month.

It is well known by those who study the subject that drug runners are pushing out into the rural districts where there is comparatively little police supervision and where they can sell out their whole stock of contraband drugs to coal-miners, lumbermen, railway navvies, and even to the threshermen. It was also found that among those who took advantage of the harvest excursions from East and West to the Prairie Provinces were a number of addicts and peddlers....

At a meeting in March of this year, the following figures were presented to the Trades' and Labour Council of Vancouver showing the magnitude of the traffic:—"The amount of narcotic drugs legitimately sold in Canada in 1921 was valued at $182,484, including 2,416 ounces of cocaine, 5,286 ounces of morphine and 1,440 pounds of opium. Drug addicts known to Vancouver police are estimated at three thousand. The amount of drugs used per addict per day is from one to fifteen dollars' worth. If each addict used only one dollars' worth per day, then in Vancouver alone the traffic would amount to $912,516 a year. The total amount sold in the Dominion per year legitimately being $182,484, the balance of drugs used by addicts in Vancouver alone would be valued at $730,032. The estimated number of addicts in Canada and the United States is two million, on the basis of one dollar per day per addict, the traffic represents on the continent about $672,000,000 annually...."

Because they are more keenly awake to the menace, the city of Vancouver, in 1921 circularized one hundred cities and towns in Canada asking these to join with them in a drug war against the drug traffic, and proposing that the Dominion Government be requested to amend the penalty clause in the Opium and Drugs Act, so that a person guilty of an offence under the Act might be liable, on indictment, to imprisonment for seven years, or if convicted upon a summary proceeding, to a fine of from $200.00 to $1,000.00, or to imprisonment for eighteen months, or to both fine and imprisonment.

As a result of this campaign, a very distinct tightening was made in the Act, although much better results would have been accomplished had it not been for the opposition of some few of the medical doctors who were members of the legislature.

Apart from this opposition, one of the greatest difficulties arises from the profits that accrue from the traffic. In Canada, many persons prominent in "the learned professions," in social and business circles, police officials, chemists and even newspaper men are engaged in this nefarious trade, the profits ranging all the way from one hundred to ten thousand per cent.

While insanity sometimes results in the advanced stages of drug-addiction, it is not nearly so common as the public suppose.

While insanity within the meaning of the Criminal Code is not so frequent among addicts, it must be borne in mind that through excessive use of narcotics, or by means of sudden withdrawal, the victim undergoes what the French call "a crisis of the nerves" which amounts to insanity, but which is only temporary.

When a man is criminally inclined, cocaine and heroin produce delusions which actually make him "insane and dangerous to be at large." These drugs also give him courage without reason; make his vision more acute, and steady his hand so that he may commit murder with ease.

"I have noticed" says Dr. J.B. McConnell of Winnipeg, writing in this connection, "that the majority of petty thieves and hold-up men are usually addicts and they are very dangerous, and if ever they ask you to throw up your hands, I would advise you to do so at once, because they have to get the money in order to get the drugs."

When the four murderers of Herman Rosenthal were being tried, it was discovered that three of them were drug addicts who, before committing the deed, had to be "charged up" with cocaine, and it was under the leadership of "Dopey Benny," a slum addict, that a band of twelve dope-fiends hired out their services to "beat-up" or murder any individual, their regular fee for assassination being $200.00....

Persons suffering from cocaine-insanity have deep-seated delusions concerning electricity. Their nights become a termless hell when, because of their disordered perceptions, electric needles play over their skin or an enemy pours "the juice" into their head...

During the year 1917, the cases which passed through the Vancouver jail numbered 3,863, and of these according to the Chief-Constable and others, a large proportion were drug addicts, and it is believed that the use of drugs is probably one of the chief contributors to crime in British Columbia, in that it diminishes the responsibility of those who are mentally or nervously subnormal or disordered.

It need scarcely be explained that a mentally abnormal person whose abnormality has been further augmented by the use of noxious drugs, can hardly be kept from committing crime. Indeed, one of the Western police magistrates in writing me on the subject says, "The taking of drugs is undoubtedly the cause of a great deal of crime because people under its influence have no more idea of responsibility of what is right or wrong than an animal."

Another says, "The spread of drug-addiction has been so insidious, and so rapid in its growth, that it is only within the last few years an enlightened public has begun to realize its menacing nature. People in every stratum of society are afflicted with this malady, which is a scourge so dreadful in its effects that it threatens the very foundations of civilization."

Opium and morphine users seldom commit the more brutal crimes. The offences committed by these, in order of their frequency are:—larceny, burglary, vagrancy, forgery, assault, and violation of the drug laws.

Speaking of the effect of addiction on morals, a certain report has declared, however, that "the opium or morphine addict is not always a hopeless liar, a moral wreck, or a creature sunk in vice and lost to all sense of decency, but may often be an upright individual except under circumstances which involve his effection, or the procuring of the drug of addiction. He will usually lie as to the dose necessary to sustain a moderately comfortable existence, and he will stoop to any subterfuge, and even to theft to achieve relief from bodily agonies experienced as a result of the withdrawal of the drug."

A prominent Government official in a letter from Winnipeg, Manitoba, said recently, "Many crimes are to our knowledge committed by persons while under the influence of drugs, and we have good grounds for believing that the recent murder in the town of St. Boniface, whereby two Provincial police officers came to their death, was caused by a cocaine fiend."…

While the Assyrians, Negroes and Greeks in Canada have become allies of the Chinese in carrying on the traffic, it is well known to the police and Government authorities that many Anglo Saxons, men prominent in social and business circles, as well as lawyers, physicians and druggists have also become engaged in the illicit sale, because of the enormous profits accruing therefrom. These profits range all the way from one hundred to ten thousand per cent…

It is the habit of these peddlers to playfully shake some "snow"—that is to say a combination of cocaine and powdered borax—on the back of the hand of their friends and suggest that they sniff it up the nostrils. The friend is immediately stimulated, and if tired, loses his weariness and becomes mentally and physically alert. This is why the powder is sometimes described as "Happy dust."

The interest and curiosity of the recipients are aroused and if they enquire where they can get it, they are offered a package for a dollar. Presently, the new addicts pass on the discovery to their particular friends, with the information as to where the drug can be obtained.

Older people falling victim to it neglect all that life has held sweet to them in order that they may follow the trail of the scintillating powder. Fiends in human guise buy cocaine from certain quarters; it is then split into small quantities, wrapped in brown paper, each little package being sold for twenty-five cents.

"A dollar's worth of cocaine makes over one hundred such packages. The profit is therefore over two hundred and forty per cent. The sales are certain. The first samples are distributed to children free. The sample creates a demand and the children come again. It is refused unless they bind themselves to absolute secrecy. A few doses and the habit has grown. The children must have their dope. All moral sense is lost and in a few months our boys and girls are ruined."

A probation officer of the Children's Aid Society in one of our large cities has this to say of the subject: "So great has this evil become that one constable has on his book one hundred and forty cases in one district. I, personally, know at least fifty cases, all children, between the ages of twelve and eighteen. Little boys of eleven and fourteen have been caught peddling cocaine in houses of ill-fame.

"The physical aspect I can but liken to consumption. The deadly work of the drug is done before either the victim or the relatives perceive it. It is usually taken in powdered form and snuffed up the nostrils. The result, particularly in young people, is that the bones of the nose decay and they are subject to hemorrhages. It is the most diabolical of all drugs on this account, and for this reason, I am told by a physician, it directly attacks the lining of the nose and brain. The victim becomes emaciated, extremely irritable, nervous, suspicious, fearful of noise and darkness, depressed, without ambition and bad tempered to the extent of viciousness. Boys and girls lose all sense of moral responsibility, affection and respect for their parents, their one thought being to get the dope and be with their friends.

"So degenerate do they become that the public parks, roadside or shed, is the same to them as a home. I know boys and girls, none of them over fifteen, all brought up of respectable parents and in good homes, who spent nights in sheds scarcely fit for a dog, and without food or change of clothing."

In both the Police and Juvenile Courts many young persons under eighteen are found to be suffering from the drug habit, and one, known to myself became violently insane. Most of these juveniles are brought for crime of some kind or other, and are found to be habituated to the use of deleterious drugs. Some of these have belonged to prominent families, but in all the cases their names are kept out of the papers in order that the children may have a chance to be restored to normality without the handicap of a bad reputation.

If these are well-advanced in addiction, we have no option but to send them to jail, there being no other place of detention where they may be kept away from the drug.

From records in our possession—these being to the police—we have the names of Canadian doctors who have, until the present, been prescribing, as high as 100 grains of cocaine in each prescription, or equal to four hundred quarter-grain tablets, or average adult doses.

In three months, this winter, it was found that a certain physician in a Western town had issued fifty-two prescriptions for sixty grains of morphine and three thousand grains of cocaine. His extravagance is by no means peculiar, several other doctors having records approximately high.

In this same period of three months, one man not any considerable distance from where we write, was able to get from a drug company, by means of a doctor's prescription, nearly seven thousand grains of opium.

The doctors claim these prescriptions were given to cure the victim on the "gradual reduction" or "ambulatory method," and were without charge. Most of us will refuse to credit their claim. Men who are "yellow" enough to supply addicts, however much they suffered, with narcotics in such large bulk, ought for a certainty to be breaking stones in some jail yard.…

The medical, pharmaceutical, dental and veterinarian associations, in all part of the continent, could do excellent service if, on their own initiative, they secured the evidence to prosecute those of their members who violate the federal, provincial or state narcotic enactments. Some associations are already performing this service although, up to the present, none can be charged as overly precipitate in action. There is no reason why these associations should not protect their own and the people's rights by prosecuting those renegade members of their profession—a minority, to be sure—who engage in so nefarious and disreputable a trade as poison vending.

Physicians could also help by drawing the attention of the public to the slum conditions which enable the Oriental peddler to ply his business in comparative safety. Entering these places in his daily practice, the physician can speak with more authority than anyone else. It is a thousand pities they are so generally inarticulate on the subject. The unsanitary conditions prevailing should alone be sufficient cause for their taking the lead for better housing, with more sunlight and fresh air.

Physicians could also do much to prevent the acquiring of the drug habit by agitating for the examination of children in schools, by a specialist, whereby psychopathic tendencies could be detected and, if possible, corrected.

The system of medical inspection of schools being already established, this work would only be an adjunct thereto.

In Canada, all persons who are arrested for trafficking in narcotics, whether convicted or not, in any city or town, should have their photograph and finger prints taken by the police, and forwarded to a central bureau, preferably at Ottawa, where these could be copied and sent broadcast to all police officers throughout the Dominion.

In this way the police could be on the lookout for these traffickers and, as soon as they arrive in a city or town, if occasion warranted, apprehend them.

At the present time when a person is convicted of an offence against the Opium and Drugs Act and pays his fine, or serves a term in jail, he is released, and as a rule, leaves for some other locality to again ply his illegal trade, and the authorities of the city to which he goes have no information concerning him. He may, therefore, be able to operate for months or years before eventually being caught....

... It is plainly palpable that the illicit traffic in our Dominion has grown to menacing proportions and, as yet it remains to be grappled with....

But, undoubtedly, Mr. W.L. MacKenzie King, in his report published in 1908 on "The Need for the Suppression of the Opium Traffic in Canada," struck the right note on this phase of the subject when he said:—

"Other instances of legislative enactments to suppress the opium evil, and to protect individuals from the baneful effect of this drug might be given, if further examples were necessary. What is more important, however, than the example of other countries, is the good name of our own. To be indifferent to the growth of such an evil in Canada would be inconsistent with those principles of morality which ought to govern the conduct of a Christian nation."

Mr. King wrote these words in 1908, when the Chinese residents had presented claims to the Federal Government for losses occasioned by the anti-Asiatic riots during which seven of their opium factories were destroyed.

Mr. King, then the Minister of Labour, further said that the amount consumed in Canada, if known, would probably appal the ordinary citizen who is inclined to believe that the habit is confined to the Orientals. The Chinese with whom he had conversed assured him that almost as much opium was sold to white people as to Chinese, and that the habit was making headway, not only among white men and boys, but among women and girls.

This was eleven years ago, and no particular attention was paid Mr. King's warning, with the result that all the provinces of Western Canada are, today, suffering immensely from this evil. In referring to the traffic in drugs, the Editor of the *Edmonton Journal*, said in December 1919:—

"It is known that vast forces are now engaged in peddling morphias, opiums, and lesser known and even more devilish narcotics and stimulants. A few days in the Edmonton police court would reveal the extent of the system here in the far north, and it is certain that a vast international organization is handling the importation and supply of huge quantities of every sort of vicious drug. Action cannot be taken too soon."

Anyone who has lived in British Columbia knows that where the Chinese have their own districts, much smoking is indulged in…

While the drug habit affects all classes of society in Canada, there would seem to be more addicts, per capita, of the population, in some districts than in others.

Sometimes, one is inclined to think otherwise, and that the seeming difference is due to the various methods adopted in its detection.

In Edmonton, Alberta, our morality squad, or "plain-clothes men," who find prohibited drugs in the possession of any person are awarded half the fine by the magistrate. Indeed, any informant is awarded this if a conviction be made.

In Toronto, Winnipeg and other cities, this procedure is not pursued. It is claimed that if it were generally practised, the detectives would do no other work….

But apart from the sharpening of the official senses where the ferreting out of drugs is concerned, a moiety of the fines ought to be paid to the men who trail down the addicts and the illicit vendors. The traffic in drugs is carried on with such strict secrecy that the utmost caution and patience are required to secure information and evidence. This being secured, to force an entry to a drug den at two o'clock in the morning when the "dopers" are irresponsible either wholly or in part, is an unpleasant and often a dangerous task. A man needs to take his courage in both hands for, generally speaking, infuriated dopers are no herd of sheep.

In smoking, the Chinaman reclines on a mattress on the floor, having beside him a pan which contains the opium "lay-out." The cracks of the windows and doors are packed with wet clothes that the odour of the smoke may not escape. For the same reason, the keyhole of the door is plugged, thus preventing its being locked with a key. The door is secured with a butcher knife driven into the door-jamb.

Finally, the available furniture is piled against the door to guard against surprises. It is the butcher knife in the door-jamb that constitutes the chiefest danger to the detectives who come with an order for search, although more than one officer has been killed by a bullet sent through the panel of the door. Two years ago, the Chief of Police at Vancouver and one of his men were murdered in this way while waiting in a hallway for a dope-fiend to give entry.

In Toronto, they tell us that the Chinese used to smoke openly, but since 1911 when the Opium and Drug Act came into force, open smoking ceased and, as a result, there are fewer convictions.

Knowing the Chinese temperament and habits, one conjectures whether smoking is not as freely indulged in as formerly, but with probably more careful precautions and safeguards.

But if Toronto pays no *douceur* to the morality squad, still it has given considerable attention to the examination of the books and prescriptions of the druggists. If a druggist is selling more narcotics than other druggists he must render an accounting or lose his license.

In Winnipeg, it is officially stated that the habit is growing rapidly, and that the police have on their lists the names and addresses of hundreds of persons who are inveterate users of narcotics.

It was recently declared by an investigating committee in California that the drug distribution centre for all America is in Western Canada. The evidence upon which this astounding assertion is based has not been made public but it is quite possible, even probable, that this assertion is true.

It is claimed that less adroitness is required to land contraband in Canada than in the States, and that it is brought here daily in many and various containers, even in musical instruments.

Other than the assumption made by government officials at Ottawa that opium was being smuggled into the States from Montreal, it had occurred to few of us, if any, that an immensely greater traffic might have gained foothold in Western Canada. We took for granted that the commerce in drugs was directly between the United States and China, not dreaming that Canada might be the intermediary in the same.

All drugs in Canada should be procured from the Government. What the Government does not prohibit, it must monopolize. There should be no profits on the products whatsoever.

If drugs were sold by the retailers on a system of triplicate order blanks, one of these going to the Federal Government, a complete check could be kept on sales, but, however managed, there should be a record on every grain from the time it leaves the importer till it reaches the ultimate consumer.

Illicit vendors in drugs should be handled sternly, whatever their status, and it would be well for the Government to consider whether or not these should be given the option of a fine. The profits from the traffic are so high that fines are not in any sense deterrent. Besides, these ruthless butchers of men and morals are entitled to no more delicate consideration than the white-slaver, the train-wrecker, house-breaker, or the perpetrator of any other head-long crime....

2. Tom MacInnes, "The Futile Fight against Dope," *Saturday Night*, October 3, 1925

Tom MacInnes (1867–1951) was born in Ontario and educated at Osgoode Hall. As a federal civil servant he drafted a report on Indian Title in Canada in 1909 and on the 1908 Opium Act, and acted for the Chinese victims in the Vancouver riots of 1907, but he is chiefly remembered for his poetry. His views on the Chinese became vitriolic and possibly stemmed from living in China off-and-on from 1916 to 1927. He called for the racial segregation of Canada in his 1927 book Oriental Occupation of British Columbia *and perhaps unsurprisingly became a member of the Nationalist League of Canada.*

The fundamental creed of a true freeman is that the ultimate best comes to the uttermost freedom of all, consistent with personal safety and preservation of property. Apart from politics the chief issue dividing the people of Canada today is one of liquor rather than religion. So let us begin with liquor, and the fight made against it, in order to consider the greater problem of dope.

When the best whiskey was to be had freely in Canada for half a dollar a gallon, drunkenness was never heard of among women; and on the rare occasion when any woman did make a mistake in the quantity the fact was decently covered and no more said about it. As for clandestine drinking at social gatherings by young persons, both sexes intermingling for the purpose in retired nooks and cloak-rooms—why, the thing was unthinkable. And when no restrictions whatsoever on the sale of narcotic or stimulant drugs there were no drug addicts among the youth. The few adults who indulged in such drugs were harmless to the community; and they could have no possible mercenary motive for adding innocents to their number. Because of the general contempt with which the drug-addict was regarded, unless of course he could produce some work of genius in excuse of himself, the fact of habitual drug indulgence was concealed like any other abnormality. The men of those days, our fathers who laid the foundations of Canada, held themselves for the most part in their own sense of honour and decency, with no need for prohibitive props and police. They were not moral invertebrates because there were no fences between them and full indulgence in anything as they pleased, short of felony or common-law misdemeanour. Our fathers could stand erect for right in their own power. But now, because of the unorganized mass of us who are yet disposed to freedom having yielded to the organized prohibiting minorities, we have almost lost our old liberties; and many of us have so far lost the sense and right of manhood of them that we would be aghast at the proposal to repeal all of the restrictive laws of the last twenty years; to be followed by stern and unsentimental enforcement of the good laws that would remain. What, venture to face again the conditions under which our fathers came to their great manhood? What, cheap wine and beer and liquor for all who chose to go openly and buy it? What, the open bar instead of the blind pig and the rich man's cellar? What, no tax or restriction whatever on the use of opium? We jelly fish would be afraid of such freedom. We cannot think of ourselves living decently as our fathers did amid such liberties. Depending on the outer in the way of enactments rather than upon any power of our own within we wonder how Mahometans living all their days where wine and pork are freely sold do yet without aid or secular law obey cheerfully the decrees of the Prophet of God as given to them in these matters. But now, leaving aside, how shall we deal with the evil of dope, and come back to the general inner freedom from it which prevailed till less than twenty years ago.

Up to the year 1908 opium for smoking was prepared in factories owned by Chinese in British Columbia. The industry had been encouraged by the Dominion government from its inception; because a high import duty was imposed on all opium brought to Canada in the prepared state for smoking, but no duty was imposed on crude opium to be treated or manufactured for any purpose whatever. Trusting this tacit declaration of the Government the Chinese invested about a quarter of a million dollars at Victoria and Vancouver in plant and stock of crude opium. Opium smokers are steady in their habit and the quantity does not increase with the years and constant usage, as it is like to do with one who takes opium derivatives or other drugs. Not more than ten per cent of the Chinese in British Columbia smoked opium; and little harm it did to most of them as compared with other habits now being acquired because of not being able to smoke. The smoking of one or two drops, or pills, of the thick sirup [sic] was a long drawn out and pleasing performance because of the meticulous details with which it was accomplished. There was much then in the anticipation; ... But now the Chinese fear the prolonged ceremony of opium smoking. The police are liable to break in at any time and upset the romance of it. So the procedure now is a quick shot in the arm with morphine or heroin in some dark corner....

One time for a year or two, early in the century... I had occasion to know somewhat of the underworld of that port [Vancouver]. There was not opium smoking among youths in their teens or twenties. There was scarce any opium smoking by whites; even the broken down ones. But all that is changed now....

The typical American slogan is: "There ought to be a law!" All across Canada now we hear them shouting to each other; ... this puritan flu, has largely infected the unoriginal but evangelically impressible mentality of the average Canadian; especially such as may be of English and Protestant descent. But right here let me say that I do not wish to be misunderstood as minimizing the evil habit of habitual taking of narcotic or stimulant drugs. It is with the prevailing mode of attempting to prevent the evil that I quarrel. The dope habit as it is now called, is probably the most harmful and hopeless of all vices when carried to excess by those of depraved or criminal tendencies. But the majority of drug-addicts, unobtrusive and unknown, are neither depraved nor criminal in their tendencies. Among such the evil of drug addiction is much exaggerated; whatever certain physicians may tell you.... Any man fit to serve on a jury however, will find that the average drug addicts, barring those who would be abnormal or criminal in any event, are not looking for trouble if they can avoid it. They are generally quiet and pleasant persons. They are easy but seldom malicious liars; and rather unreliable, except where a stroke of brilliant skill or cunning is required. Then they may rise to the occasion far above the reach of the average. But they quickly relax. But drug addicts when deprived of their drug may resort to any method and suffer any indignity in order to secure a fresh supply of what has become necessary to their peace of mind. Yet opium will not twist the mind to crime. I know that of opium. And I think that while cocaine is undoubtedly tenfold more mind devastating and brain upsetting than morphine or heroin or hashish or even the Mexican mescal, yet the "cocaine rhythm leading to murder," and other lurid phrases of novelists and police-court reporters and paid propagandists for Geneva [the League of Nations], are sheer balderdash. If one has a natural tendency to crime and abnormal conduct such a tendency may be loosened in him by the drug; just as it may by sudden religious emotion or sudden prospect of gain, or sudden thrill on the edge of battle. It is the unexpected outlet; the quick turn, the swift expansion of consciousness: that turns the psychological trick in any such case....

Except where there has been great excess, ... the ordinary drug-addict is not betrayed to the inexperienced eye....

Drug addicts are found among Americans more than any other people, European or Oriental or African. This probably is mainly because Americans are now the most restrained and crowd compelled people in the world. And so it is that many of them will try anything which seems to offer a fair and safe outlet, if only for an hour, from the drab, soul-smothering sameness of life as they are forced to lead it. Deprived of the cheap and usually harmless solace of beer and wine ... he now takes to the costly and perilous drugs which are offered him as a substitute.

In a few cases the drug habit may be acquired by one who needs opiates to dull pain. But such cases are few and on the whole no great menace to the community comes that way. But here is one terrible menace to the community which our legislators in their prohibitive unwisdom have made possible and profitable. The appalling feature of drug addiction today is that the youth are deliberately seduced to it by peddlers, and the victim of peddlers, who make easy money by selling what is excessively costly and forbidden. Being forbidden naturally awakens curiosity. The most exaggerated stories are told of the thrills to be had and never found out, from the needle point or the sniff of "happy dust." And when the young are once caught in the web which is then woven around them escape seems impossible; and they go down in a way that does not often occur in the case of persons of middle age or more. Confronted only with these cases of drug addiction it is little wonder that some of our social workers grow hysterical and call for the lash and the death penalty against the dope peddler, who himself is often a victim of the stuff he sells. The traffic will never be stopped that way. There will always be new ones willing to take the risk, and be callous to the results of what they do so long as they may have the living they desire.

Take the profit from any traffic and the traffic dies. There is no other way; at least not in the case of dope. As soon as one source of the forbidden drug is destroyed, another will be opened up so long as there is any great profit in the handling of it. The world is too wide to effectively police every part against production, even if the world forces were united for the purpose; and they would never be so united in our time.

There is an International Dope Ring.... It is a world-girdling snake; and merciless. Its directors are more than a match for the wits and half-wits of Geneva.... This Dope Ring knows that it has so many possible sources of supply that the supply will never fail them; and the more the restriction the higher the price and the greater the profit. By all means I say that if every restriction on narcotics and stimulant drugs were withdrawn in the United States and Canada, … and if every import and revenue tax and need of medical certificate were lifted so that drugs might be had as easily and cheaply as shaving soaps and hair tonics; then the illicit would have no profit from the sale of habit forming drugs; and he would no longer engage in the seduction of the young and the weak. There would be no money in it for the covert peddler, nor the central supplier, nor smugglers from ship to land. And if there were not millions of dollars annually in the supply of forbidden drugs then the International Dope Ring would collapse like an exploded balloon. If all the restrictions and all the taxes were suddenly removed tomorrow with a stroke of the pen do you then think there would ensue a wild orgy of people plunging headlong into drug debauches? There would not. The drug addicts would be pleased; and go quietly about their business the smile of wonder on their faces. Many of them might go more happily and quickly out of this weary world. There would be no harm in that. But there would be no more drug peddlers; no more concealed supply centres in the cities; no more smugglers of drugs. … So far as Canadians were concerned not one in a million would smoke opium; and it would make half of those so sick at the first trial that they would never try it again.…

FURTHER READINGS

Boyd, N. "The Origins of Canadian Narcotics Legislation: The Process of Criminalization in Historical Context." *Dalhousie Law Journal* 8 (January 1984): 104-36.

Carstairs, C. "Deporting 'Ah Sin' to Save the White Race: Moral Panic, Racialization, and the Extension of Canadian Drug Laws in the 1920s." *Canadian Bulletin of Medical History* 16, 1 (1999): 65-88.

Carstairs, C. "Innocent Addicts, Dope Fiends, and Nefarious Traffickers: Illegal Drug Use in 1920s English Canada." *Journal of Canadian Studies* 33, 3 (Fall 1998): 145-62.

Carstairs, C. *Jailed for Possession*. Toronto: University of Toronto Press, 2006.

Chapman, T. "The Anti-Drug Crusade in Western Canada, 1885-1925." In *Law and Society in Canada in Historical Perspective*, ed. D. Bercuson and L. Knafla. Calgary: University of Calgary Press, 1979.

Chapman, T. "Drug Use in Western Canada." *Alberta History* 24 (Fall 1976): 18-27.

Comack, E. "The Origins of Canadian Drug Legislation: Labelling vs. Class Analysis." In *The New Criminology in Canada: Crime, State and Control*, ed. T. Fleming. Toronto: Oxford University Press, 1985.

Cook, S. "Canadian Narcotics Legislation, 1908-1923: A Conflict Model Interpretation." *Canadian Review of Sociology and Anthropology* 6, 1 (1969): 36-46.

Duffin, J. *Langstaff: A Nineteenth-Century Medical Life.* Toronto: University of Toronto Press, 1993.

Green, M. "A History of Canadian Narcotics Control: The Formative Years." *University of Toronto Faculty of Law Review* 42 (1979): 42-79.

Madison, T. "The Evolution of Non-Medical Opiate Use in Canada—Part I, 1870-1929." *Drug Forum* 5, 3 (1976-77): 237-65.

Malleck, D. "'Its Baneful Influences Are Too Well Known': Debates over Drug Use in Canada, 1867-1908." *Canadian Bulletin of Medical History* 14 (1997): 263-88.

Malleck, D. "'A State Bordering on Insanity': Identifying Drug Addiction in Nineteenth-Century Canadian Asylums." *Canadian Bulletin of Medical History* 16 (1999): 247-69.

Mosher, C., and J. Hagan. "Constituting Class and Crime in Upper Canada: The Sentencing of Narcotic Offenders, circa 1908-1953." *Social Forces* 72, 3 (March 1994): 626-41.

Murray, G. "Cocaine Use in the Era of Social Reform: The Nature of a Social Problem in Canada, 1880-1911." *Canadian Journal of Law and Society* 2 (1987): 29-43.

Small, S. "Canadian Narcotics Legislation, 1908-1923: A Conflict Model Interpretation." In *Law and Social Control in Canada*, ed. W. Greenaway and S. Brickley. Scarborough: Prentice Hall, 1978.

Soloman, R., and M. Green. "The First Century: The History of Nonmedical Opiate Use and Control Policies in Canada, 1870-1970." In *Illicit Drugs in Canada: A Risky Business*, ed. J.C. Blackwell and P.G. Erickson. Scarborough: Nelson, 1988.

Trasov, G. "History of Opium and Narcotic Drug Legislation in Canada." *Criminal Law Quarterly* 4 (1961-62): 274-84.

Warsh, C. *Moments of Unreason: The Practice of Canadian Psychiatry and the Homewood Retreat, 1883-1923*. Montreal and Kingston: McGill-Queen's University Press, 1989.

CHAPTER 8

"This Is My Last Chance"

DEPRESSION AND DESPAIR

INTRODUCTION

Unemployment rose to unprecedented levels when the Great Depression hit at the end of the 1920s, and Canada was among the nations worst affected, quickly skidding toward insolvency and social catastrophe. The economic situation was bad enough, with some 20 per cent of the population on relief over the worst years between 1933 and 1936. Environmental calamities on the southern prairies, however, exacerbated the problem by creating a dust bowl that thousands barely survived and many did not. Drought made conditions so unbearable that the International Red Cross declared parts of Saskatchewan as disaster areas. Social assistance, inevitably inadequate, barely existed for those desperate people, and it came at a high psychological cost. Collecting relief, after all, collided with the proud and independent spirit of those who believed in self-reliance, not charity. Applicants also knew that much of society still stigmatized them as failures who created their own misfortune or as layabouts who wanted free handouts. Solemnly swearing to a welfare officer that you had utterly failed to provide for your family, which was part of the application process, was not easy. And not only was the Great Depression deep, it also lasted longer in Canada than in most other countries—essentially a full decade. Britain, for example, began to emerge from the trough by 1934, years before Canada struggled back to its feet. It is hardly surprising that Canadian Depression survivors developed "depression mentalities"—they hoarded pieces of aluminum foil, twist-ties, and plastic bags for the rest of their lives.

The Great Depression, on the other hand, offered unprecedented increases in the standard of living for employed people who did not suffer pay cuts or for people with independent means. This, of course, worsened its impact by deepening and widening the financial and social gulf between the top and bottom of Canadian society. The Depression was, after all, a deflationary period when dollars, if one had them, bought more and more each day. Federal civil servants, for example, experienced a 25 per cent increase in their standard of living over this period, despite their wages being frozen. Services, goods, food, entertainment—almost all became cheaper for those with money.

The Depression was particularly hard on the aged, sick, marginalized, and young—those least able to fend for themselves. Though historians know the cold facts, statistics do not do the story justice. Statistics do not, for example, count those perched just above the poverty line because they were not officially "poor." Nor do the numbers include the thousands whose pride prevented them from seeking charity, despite their being below that line. Cold numbers do not show inspectors invading relief applicants' homes to search for "luxuries," such as telephones and drivers' licenses, the possession of which made the family ineligible. A person whose hours were cut by half for ten years was statistically "employed," period. Numbers cannot interpret a paranoid government encouraging people to inform on "relief cheats." Hard data cannot express a mother's humiliation as she exchanged her meagre food vouchers for goods under her neighbours' disapproving gaze.

Suspicious and cash-strapped governments stuck to the time-honoured belief that relief recipients created their own misfortune, that their impecuniousness derived from some sort of moral failing. They therefore purposefully made obtaining relief humiliating and preferred issuing vouchers in kind (redeemable for food, heat, and clothing) to cash, which profligate poor people would presumably squander—most likely on alcohol. Municipalities administering public relief made applicants work for their assistance too, on the principle that you don't get something for nothing. This created make-work schemes, such as street sweeping and wood chopping, which contributed little but further humiliation.

And for those without homes? Young men over 18 were ineligible for family relief because they were expected to care for themselves by that age and to live on their own. Relief recipients, however, had to fulfill a residency requirement before they were eligible, which caught the young in a particularly vicious Catch-22. It left thousands riding railway boxcars from town to town, city to city, drifting and unable to put down roots—they were marginalized. No wonder they began to organize, to join the Communist Party of

Canada, and to turn their backs on a mainstream society they felt betrayed them. The federal government, fearing this restive social sub-class and reacting to public complaints of vagrancy, enacted plans to contain it, but it only further alienated the men by establishing work camps in remote areas where they toiled for 20 cents per day at useless jobs under the watchful gaze of the Department of National Defence. Camp inmates even lost their right to vote and had their mail censored.

Ironically, Canadians elected the nation's first millionaire as prime minister in 1930. R.B. Bennett's annual income dropped considerably but never dipped below $150,000 per year during the Depression, a time when families lived comfortably on $25 per week. He promised to end unemployment through stiff tariffs that would protect and nurture Canadian industry, but they did more harm than good, especially in the agricultural sector, because they simply drove up prices. His administration, however, did provide extraordinary funds for destitute provincial coffers. Bennett hated the concept of relief, fearing that it promoted "idleness." Yet the economy had all but halted, and even he had to admit that jobs were scarce. Nor was he heartless. Bennett and his secretaries responded to virtually every letter he received, and he regularly dipped into his personal funds to alleviate particularly heart-wrenching stories. News of his philanthropy spread quickly, and the volume of mail increased to the point where he established a special donations fund to dole out his largesse, usually at $5.00 a time. The number of gifts peaked around election time in 1935.

Historians who originally published the following letters changed the senders' names and addresses in the interest of privacy. Thus, we do not know the writers' true identities. Leaving the original spelling and grammatical errors intact, they chose the most poignant correspondence for publication and attempted to balance the regional, ethnic, and occupational representation of the collection. Statistical analysis shows that Bennett and his staff had a slight preference for sending cash to youth, westerners, and Anglophones.

DISCUSSION POINTS

1. List the recurring themes of these letters. What do they say about the causes, conditions, and impact of poverty during the Depression?

2. Many claim that women have a unique culture and voice often overlooked by historians. Did men and women experience the Depression differently?

3. Were Canadian governments negligent in their treatment of the poor during the Depression?

4. Why did welfare seem dangerous or unadvisable to so many people?

5. The document "Experiences of a Depression Hobo" provides a rather different perspective from many of the Bennett letters. What would account for this?

DOCUMENTS

1. Mrs. Ernest Ferguson, Ferguson, New Brunswick, March 21, 1933

Hon. R.B. Bennett
Ottawa, Can.

Dear Sir,
The respectable people of this country are *fed up* on feeding the bums for that is all they can be called now. This "free" relief (free to the bums) has done more harm than we are altogether aware of. The cry of those who get it is "Bennett says he wont let anyone starve." They don't consider that the *people* (many poorer than themselves but with more spunk) have to foot the bill. The regulations (which are only a poor guide after all) were too loose from the start and *could be* and *were* easily side stepped many times.

Getting relief has become such a habit that the majority think only of how to get it regularly instead of trying to do without once in a while. Nearly all of them have dogs too which are fed by the country and are of no practical use. One family near me has three and another has two and others one and I know it is the same everywhere. I also know that food enough to keep one dog will keep at least four hens and keep them laying. The family that has the three dogs ate at least 550 pounds of meat from the second week in November until the first part of March. There are the parents, twins 10 years old and four children from one year to eight. Who but the dogs got a good part of that? Also dogs everywhere are chasing and catching deer but if a man tries to get one for the family he is either fined or jailed if found out. Or if he tries to get a few fish (he is mighty lucky if he succeeds above Newcastle on the Miramichi now) the wardens are right after him and he finds himself minus a net at the least.

Now the taxes are going to be forcibly collected to pay for the good-for-nothings for whom the debt was made. Those people should be made work and there wouldn't need to be much forcing for taxes. The taxpayers don't consider that they should keep people as well and sometimes better off than they are and their wives agree with them. We see plainly now that those being kept will not help themselves so long as they are fed for nothing.

Notice should be given at once to enable them to get crops in and so on and relief stopped altogether. The cost of that would pay for a good deal of work. Also please remember there are other people in the country who need your thought as well as those on relief as it is now though they are struggling along somehow. I think it only fair to state that if it continues or is considered for the future there will be a goodly number of Conservatives vote the other way for as I stated in the beginning we are sick and tired of being forced to keep the majority that are following the relief path. It hasn't been fair all through as any thoughtful man must know. I am not stating this idly because I have talked with many others many times and that is the general feeling. I think I can safely say too that the Liberals getting relief don't thank the Conservatives enough to give them a vote either because they nearly all say the country owes them a living and think no thanks are due.

I could write more but will let this suffice for this time but Please consider this question of relief as a very important one because a deal of trouble may brew from it.

2. Brief Presented by the Unemployed of Edmonton to the Hon. R.B. Bennett, December 30, 1933

Mr. R.B. Bennett
Prime Minister of Canada

For three long, weary years you, Mr Bennett and your Conservative Party have held undisputed and unmolested sway in Canada. You and your coleagues were elected primarily because you gave the people two great promises, (1) you would end unemployment, (2) you would blast your way to foreign markets. As to the first of these promises, you Mr. Bennett as the chief Economic Doctor, have failed, miserable failed, not only to cure the dangerous disease, but even to give it an unbiased diagnosis; and the only blasting that has been apparent has been the inhuman wrecking of millions of once happy homes. You have repeatedly reminded us of the sacredness of our British Institutions. Mr. Bennett, is not the home an institution? Then why do you callously stand by while it is being wantonly destroyed by the Molloch of Big business? We have this to say Mr. Bennett. Even a yellow dog will resist, to the death, the ruthless destruction of his most priceless possession.

Surely, in three years of full political power you could have found, if you had tried, a better method of dealing with unemployment than the Direct Relief System. In view of the fact that you have not we hereby give you the only solution which is applicable in society as at present constituted. Non-contributary Unemployment Insurance. It must be non-contributary, otherwise the million and a half already unemployed will receive no benefit. Pending the enactment of this Bill, Relief allowances must be raised. Seeing that we are not allowed to earn in wages sufficient to maintain us and our families, we demand adequate relief. The perpetual cry of Mayor Knott, and Premier Brownlee is "We can do nothing. We have no money." Without discussing the truthfulness of these statements, Mr. Bennett, we know that the contribution from the Federal Treasury must be doubled if it is designed to even remotely approach the need.... We have not words in our vocabulary sufficiently strong to properly condemn your method of dealing with unemployed single men. Those slave camps are a blot on the record of any civilized country. That young men, the very flower of the race, those who must make the next generation are forced, by economic necessity, to enter those isolated prisons, where there is neither proper physical food, nor mental stimulation, cries to Heaven for correction. What are you trying to do to our young men? Make a generation of physical wrecks and mental dolts? Or perhaps they will be used for cannon fodder? The militarization of those camps strongly points to this latter hypothesis as being the correct one ... placing the single men in camps under the control of the Department of National Defence is too apparent to be overlooked. We shall resist to the bitter end the slaughtering of those boys and young men in an Imperialist war. We demand that they be taken out of those camps and be given an opportunity to earn a civilized living, at a civilized wage, and live a normal life by taking a wife and raising a family. We protest against the increased appropriations for the National Defence. These monies should never be spent for these purposes, but instead, used to supplement the contribution to relief. The battleships and bombing planes, and big guns will never be used if it is left to the people to declare war. In this connection why has Japan been allowed to buy tremendous quantities of junk iron from Canada? Is it possible we shall again see and feel this iron in the form of bullets? If such a thing should come to pass, who is the butcher, the man behind the gun or the man who supplied him with the ammunition. We want it clearly understood that we consider the workers of Japan, Germany, France, Russia or any other country as nothing more nor less than brother workers and we strongly protest against the despicable and abominable part Canada is playing in hastening us toward another great Imperialist conflagration, the horrors of which were only too well forecast by the last World War.

Mr. Bennett, there was never a more damnable insult heaped upon a working class of any country than when armoured tanks and other highly perfected instruments of slaughter were sent into Stratford, Ontario. Are these the trying circumstances which will test the very best of our National fibre, which you mentioned upon your return from England? Why is it, that if our government is a Democratic institution, representing the whole people the armed forces of the nation is used to coerce the working class, who make up 95% of the population, and force them to submit to wage cuts and a general worsening of their living conditions? On the face of it, it appears that Big business, whose interest it is to force the working class into pauperism, is being protected and not we; that the minority is dictatorial machine, which our Democratic government allows to use the military power of the nation against the majority. Not only in Stratford does this phenomena manifest itself, but throughout the country, whenever the workers use the only economic weapon they have, the strike, the R.C.M.P. are rushed to the spot and club the workers into submission. We submit Mr. Bennett that we are a peaceful people. If you will send work at a living wage to strikers instead of tanks and machine guns your economic troubles will be considerably lessened. We protest against this Fascist terrorism, and demand the rights of free speech and free assemble. We protest against the policy of deporting foreign born workers simply because they can find no buyer for their labor power. The solidarity of the British Commonwealth of Nations is widely publicized, yet, we find workers born in the British Isles are subject to deportation. When a young and great country like Canada with only Ten million population finds itself in the position where it must deport labor power there must be something wrong with its economic system. Those workers, came to Canada in good faith, after being led to believe that this country was the land of their dreams. They did not come in order to get on Canada's Unemployed list. After promising them a Heaven, and then give them Hell is not a safe policy. The slightly lesser evil of the relief lists is, we feel, the worst that these people should be subject.

To sum up, Mr. Bennett, we are absolutely fed up with being on relief. The terrible waste that is implied in a million and a half idle man power is a crime against the human race. There is so much work to do, and here there are, unemployed. We don't know how the natural resources come to be where they are, but we do know, that neither you nor Big business created them. The material is here, land, lumber, iron, steel, etc. and so are we. If you can't supply the tokens of exchange that will bring us together, you had better resign and hand the country over to the workers. We may be ignorant uncouth men, belong to the lowest strata of a low society, but, and we don't boast, we will have enough sense to eat when there is food to eat, and work when there is work to be done and tools to work with.

3. R.D. to Canadian Government, December 1934

Canadian Govt. at Ottawa, Canada

Well Mr. R.B. Bennet, arnt you a *man* or are you? to be the cause of all this starvation and privation. You call us derelicts, then if we are derelicts *what else are you* but one too, only *a darn sight worse*. You said if you was elected, you would give us all work and wages, well you have been in the Prime Ministers shoes, now, for 4 years and we are *still looking for work and wages*. You took all our jobs away from us. We can't earn any money. You say a releif camp is good enough for us, then *its too good* for *you* Mr Bennet, you are on releif your own self. You put away your big govt salary, then ask the gov't. to pay for your big *feasts*, while *we* poor fellows starve. While *you* jazz around the hotel girls. You think people don't know anything well, even if we are "*derelicts*" "*as you called us*" and which we consider you as the leader of the derelicts Band you have fooled us a lot, in the last four years. We have lived on your hot air, so you may know you had to expell a *lot*. But you can't fool *all* of us, *all* the time.

… Well now Mr. Bennet, I hope this sinks clear down to your toes, and gives you swelled feet, instead of a swelled head. You have had a swelled head ever since you had the "Eddy" Match Co. signed to you by Mrs. Eddy, don't think people don't know anything.

P.S. this will take my last 3 cents, but we hope it goes to the bottom of *you*, and that you will hand us out *both work* and *living wages*. You have caused *lots* of people to kill their families and themselves rather than to slowly starve to death, or freeze to death. Try it you prime minister, just try it.

Now you are trying to get war going to make yourself richer. Well R.B. Bennet, I hope you get your share of the bullets.

We are going to give you a chance, (which you don't deserve) either you will stop this war, now, and give us fellows work and living wages enough to stop such starving, and freezing, because we *can't* buy any clothes, the doukabours are jailed because they wont wear any clothing while *we* are jailed trying to get clothing to wear. You say we live too extravagance, then you shall be able to hand out $5.00 to anyone and everyone, then we wont live so extravagant. You have heaps of money laid away. Well, it wont do you a bit of good if we have another war.

We are giving you this chance. We say again you do not deserve it at all. If we dont get work or wages, and "living wages" to, we are going to tell the Canadian government they have a "murderer," in the house at Ottawa. You said a rich uncle left you your wealth, bah. We know better. We are not trying to scare you, but we are tired, of relief camps and going hungry and cold. no homes, or any thing else.

4. P.R. Mulligan, Debden, Saskatchewan, March 3, 1934

Hon. Mr. R.B. Bennet
Ottawa, Canada

Dear Sir—

I am writing to see if you could not give me a little help. I hear you are going to destroy some thousands of tons of wheat to get rid of it; while my family & stock are starving to death. There is lots of wheat and other things here but I have no money to buy them with. I have been farming in Central Sask. since 1909 until a yr ago when I was forced off my farm. So last yr I could not get a place for to farm so could only get what I could by working out on farms. Which was not near enough to keep my family in food. In the fall I moved to the North hoping to be able to keep my stock alive and to be able to get a homestead. I had applied to have my stock sent to Spiritwood but by some mistake somewhere I was sent to Debden instead so then I had neither buildings or feed in reach and dead broke in bitter cold weather. So could not buy feed or take a homestead either. As the relief officer for this part was in town here at the time I asked him for relief & for feed. I could not get any feed whatever out of him until my four horses and seven head of cattle (my two best cows included) 16 pigs (some of them weighed over 100 lbs) and most of my poultry had actually starved to death. All that was necessary was an order to get some feed from the relief officer, but though I asked him several times & did not get any until that many were dead. Since then I have had orders amounting to 1500 (fifteen hundred) oat sheaves but nothing to feed a pig or chicken. If I had been given sufficient feed in the first place my stock would be alive and most of those hogs would now be ready for market. We would then have some meat for our table and the rest would have repaid the relief I needed and most likely would have left something to take me off the relief list for a time at least. Now we cannot farm the land I had rented because I haven't a horse left to farm with. We kept off relief as long as we had a cent to buy food or a rag of clothes that would hang together.

To date we have had $45.35 for food to feed ten of us from Dec 1st on until now, and I did relief bridge work to about that amount and was quite willing to do as much more as I would get the chance to do. But when I asked for a greater food allowance I was told that many were doing with much less as well as one insult upon another added thereto by the local relief officer. Yet I know several families right around here getting more relief according to the size of family and do not need relief at all but still they get it. I have 8 children ranging from 4 ½ yrs to 14 ½ yrs yet all we have had in the house for over a week has been dry bread and black tea and believe me Mr. Bennet it isn't very nice to listen hour after hr to young children pleading for a little butter or why can't we have some potatoes or meat or eggs. But how can I get it on what I have been getting when it takes most of it for flour alone. Because we were not sent where we asked to be sent to we have to live ten of us in cold one roomed shack instead of having a comfortable house to live in. We haven't a mattress or even a tick just simply have to sleep on a bit of straw and nearly every night we have to almost freeze because we haven't bed clothes. I did not ask relief to supply these but I did ask for pants, overalls and footwear for the children about two months ago, but to date we have had $15.95 of clothing (some of this had to be returned as it did not fit) and some of the children are at this time running barefooted & not one of them has either a pr. of pants or overalls to cover their nakedness. Neither can they go to school because they have no clothes and also because the local school board demand a tuition fee of $30 because we are not taxpayers as yet in this school and that after paying school taxes in this province for nearly 25 years. One result now is that the whole family have some kind of rash and running sores & I cannot take them to a Dr. as I have not the price to pay the Dr. or to buy the things that he would order. Also my wife has become badly ruptured and I can not have anything done about it for the same reason. I was born with one leg shorter than the other and am physically not a strong man but I have always done all I've been able to do and a lot more than many more able than I am and I am not in the habit of wasting any time or money on drinking, gambling or anything of the sort yet we have to sit here and see not only our stock starve but see my wife & children starve as well, and do the same myself. So for God's sake give us an order to get a few bus. of wheat to help us live and to raise a few chickens and pigs to eat at least and if we ever make enough to do it with I'll return it with interest too.

    Yours in need

5. Miss Elizabeth McCrae, Hamilton, Ontario, April 6, 1934

To His Excellency The Rt. Hon. R B Bennett, Parliament Buildings,
Ottawa Ontario.

Dear Sir:

I am writing you as a last resource to see if I cannot, through your aid, obtain a position and at last, after a period of more than two years, support myself and enjoy again a little independence.

The fact is: this day I am faced with starvation and I see no possible means of counteracting or even averting it temporarily!

If you require references of character or ability I would suggest that you write to T.M. Sanderson of Essex, Ontario. I worked as Stenographer and Bookkeeper with him for over three years in the office of the Sanderson-Marwick Co., Ltd., in Essex. I feel certain that you have made his acquaintance for he was President of the Conservative Association at the time of the Banquet held in your worshipful honour a few years ago.

I have received a high-school and Business-college education and I have had experience as a Librarian. My business career has been limited to Insurance, Hosiery, and Public Stenography, each time in the capacity of Bookkeeper and Stenographer—briefly, General Office work.

My father is a farmer at Pilot Mound, Manitoba and during the past years his income has been nil, so I cannot get any assistance from him. In fact, until I joined the list of unemployed I had been lending the folks at home my aid. To save my Mother from worry I have continually assured her that I am working and till the end I will save her from distress by sticking to this story.

When the Sanderson-Marwick Co., Ltd, went out of business I had saved a little money and there being no work there for me I came to Hamilton. Since then I have applied for every position that I heard about but there were always so many girls who applied that it was impossible to get work. So time went on and my clothing became very shabby. I was afraid to spend the little I had to replenish my wardrobe. Always the fear was before me that I would fail to get the position and then I would be without food and a roof over my head in a short time. Many prospective employers just glanced at my attire and shook their heads and more times than I care to mention I was turned away without a trial. I began to cut down on my food and I obtained a poor, but respectable, room at $1. per week.

First I ate three very light meals a day; then two and then one. During the past two weeks I have eaten only toast and drunk a cup of tea every other day. In the past fortnight I have lost 20 pounds and the result of this deprivation is that I am so very nervous that could never stand a test along with one, two and three hundred girls. Through this very nervousness I was ruled out of a class yesterday. Today I went to an office for an examination and the examiner looked me over and said; "I am afraid Miss, you are so awfully shabby I could never have you in my office."

I was so worried and disappointed and frightened that I replied somewhat angrily: "Do you think clothes can be picked up in the streets?"

"Well," he replied with aggravating insolence, "lots of girls find them there these days."

Mr. Bennett, that almost broke my heart. Above everything else I have been very particular about my friends and since moving here I have never gone out in the evening. I know no one here personally and the loneliness is hard to bear, but oh, sir, the thought of starvation is driving me mad! I have endeavoured to be good and to do what is right and I am confident I have succeeded in that score but I can name more than ten girls here in Hamilton who I am sure are not doing right and yet they have nice clothes and positions. That is what seems so unfair. They never think of God nor do they pray and yet they seem so happy and have so many things I would like, while I, who pray every night and morning have nothing!

Day after day I pass a delicatessen and the food in the window looks oh, so good! So tempting and I'm so hungry!

Yes I am very hungry and the stamp which carries this letter to you will represent the last three cents I have in the world, yet before I will stoop to dishonour my family, my character or my God I will drown myself in the Lake. However, I do not hint that I have the slightest intention of doing this for I am confident that you will either be able to help me find employment or God will come to my aid.

But in the meantime my clothing is getting shabbier and I am faced with the prospect of wearing the same heavy winter dress, that has covered me all winter, during the coming summer.

Oh please sir, can you do something for me? Can you get me a job anywhere in the Dominion of Canada. I have not had to go on relief during this depression but I cannot get relief even here. Moreover it is a job I want and as long as I get enough to live I shall be happy again.

I have tried to get work at anything and everything from housework up but I have been unsuccessful and now I am going to starve and in debt to my landlady. I wouldn't mind if I could just lay down and die but to starve, oh its terrible to think about.

Mr. Bennett, even if you can do nothing for me I want to thank you for your kindness in reading this letter and if I were jobless and semi-hungry for a lifetime I would still be a Conservative to the last, and fight for that Government.

Thanking you again for your very kind attention, I am,

Your humble servant,

6. L.M. Himmer, Blaine Lake, Saskatchewan, September 9, 1935

Hon. R.B. Bennett
Ottawa, Ont.

Dear Sir:

For some time I have been thinking what this new country of ours was coming to. I had the pleasure of talking with Mr. F.R. MacMillan M.P. of Saskatoon and Senator Hornor of Blaine Lake. They both insisted that I write you a line.

I wish to give my opinion of relief. First it is a shame for a strong young man to ask for relief in this country. To my mind the relief has helped out the C.C.F. and Social Credit. When you give an inch they take a foot. There are men, who have been on relief, now sitting on the street asking $2.50 and 3.00 per day. Many of them would not be worth a $1.00 per day to stook 60 ct wheat.

To my mind the poet is right nine times out of ten. The best thing that can happen to a young man is toss him overboard and compel him to sink or swim, in all my acquaintance I have never known one to drown who was worth saving.

When I hear young men, with their head full of book knowledge, complaining about no money no work. They say they'll try for relief and they get it, then they spend two or three months around a lake shore rolling in the sand and splashing in the water. When winter comes they have no preparations of any kind. They say they'll try for relief and they get it.

I say again a man must have a purpose in life if he hasn't he will never amount to much. He will eat that which he has not earned, he will clog the wheels of industry and stand in the way of progress. Thoughts of this kind should be empressed on the pupils by the teachers, and ministers, instead of the C.C.F. doctrine, and athletic sports. The people have gone silly over nonsense and it is our leaders that are teaching the younger generations to be useless.

I asked a young man to help me thresh, he said he would not pitch sheaves for less than $5.00 per day, he can get relief, no doubt. I have four young men four harvest and threshing, they blow their wages every Saturday night, some of them will be on relief this winter, if not all.

It takes hardship to make real men and women so cut out relief . . .

Relief is like a sixteen year old boy getting money from dad, when the old man gets wise and tightens up the boy gets mad and cuts a shine just as the relief strikers did.

There are some people in this country who are in hard circumstances, but I can safely say there is no one having the hardships that we pioneers had 28 and 30 years ago.

Yours truly

7. Mrs. Otto Brelgen, Dempster, Saskatchewan, April 15, 1935

R.B. Bennett Esq
Ottawa, Ont

Dear Friend,

I just can not stand for our treatment any longer without getting it off our chest. We came out here in Aug 1932 from Saskatoon on the Government Relief Plan. So you will understand that we have practically nothing as we had very little to start on, and we have worked very hard but have had terrible bad luck. We have lost 3 horses since coming out here so now are stranded with one horse which is on last legs. So how is it possible to go ahead and farm without help from somewhere. Last spring we had a neighbor break some for us. We have 15 acres now broke here, and my husband was working nearly all summer to pay the neighbor back so that certainly isn't going to put us somewhere we are going back fast. Still we are working like slaves, never have enough to eat and very little to wear. We have 5 children and our 2 selves. My baby was born up here without help of doctor or help in the house. Only what the neighbors felt like helping out. Now she is 16 month old and doesn't walk mostly lack of proper food. The other children all boys have been sick this winter, but how would it be possible to be healthy in such a condition. Last August our relief was cut down to $8.25 a month, but since Jan have recieved $11.65 so you see it is impossible to give the children proper foods. We had no garden at all everything froze to the ground as soon as it was started growing. We have about 20 chicken 1 cow. no meat or potatoes only what we buy many a meal around here is dry bread and milk when our cow is milking otherwise its water, butter is an extra luxury which we cannot afford. None of us have proper footwear now its not fit to be outside unless clothed properly. Its is a sin and a shame to be in such circumstance as that. It sure does grieve one when there nothing to eat or wear. We loan settler from the city's do not seem to be treated as well as those that moved in from the dried-out areas as they are fully equiped with live stock and also machinery, where we have nothing. I sure would like to know why that is. You maybe able to understand how it would be possible to feed our family on less 2 ½ cents each person each meal it is quite impossible as I have tried every way of getting by. But cannot make it go. My family don't live anymore we only exist. I think if the situation was more clearly put to the right parties they could help us more some less, as there are people who have cattle, garden, and could get by without gov. help still they receive assistance which does only makes it worse for those who really need it. I am looking forward that you may be able to help us in some way. We most certainly would like to be on the upward road. Just think how many families in these north woods are starving, trying to make things go. Such hard work without food to supply body energy. So first the body fails then the mind. I know Im very near a nerbous wreck. If we were allowed supose the doctor would tell me I had a nervous breakdown as it is I have to keep trudging along trying to make the best, but don't think I can stand the strain much longer. We never get out amongst any kind of entertainment as relief people are not allowed any recreation of any kind. We would be so thankful to you if you could help us in some way. Today is only the 15th of the month and our flour is all gone already and the stores will not give any credit out. So we'll all be quite hungry until the first of the month. Please give this your personal consideration and send me an answer of what could be done we are practally at the end of our rope now. Thanking you again for your attention

Your Faithfull Servant

8. Experiences of a Depression Hobo

I arrived in Toronto a week ago but have not got work yet. The trip down took 5 ½ days and I did not visit any jails. My total expenses were 50 cents but I ate and slept well.

On the Saturday night of April 15 my friend and I took the last street car out to Sutherland having previously found out that a freight train was leaving for Winnipeg during the early hours of Sunday morning. We slunk around the yards till we came upon a brakeman and asked when the freight for the East was pulling out. Before he could reply a torch light beamed in our faces and the "bull" asked "Where are you guys going?" "East"—"Winnipeg." "Well that freight won't pull out till seven tomorrow morning." We thanked the policeman for this information and retired to the shadow of a nearby Pool Elevator, lighted cigarettes and attempted keep warm. Even I, with 2 pairs underclothing, 2 shirts, a sweater, my brown suit, overalls, overcoat, winter cap & 2 pairs sox was getting chilly. Presently we became restless & walked out onto the tracks to spy an ancient looking empty coach with a light in it. Prowling lower we observed a notice on the side telling us it was for the use of stockmen only. A brakeman informed us that the coach was to be put on the freight to Winnipeg for the use of some stockman travelling. We entered the coach, found a fire burning in the stove, wiped the dust off the seats, spread them out bed fashion & were soon asleep. We were suddenly awakened by the guard who informed us that the train was pulling out in 5 minutes and that a "bull" was going to travel with the train. Observing the "bull" walking down the side of the train we waited till he rounded the end before ourselves, hopping out, walked after him & inspected the box cars. All but one were sealed, this "one" being half full of coal. There were already about ten other travellers sprawling in various positions amongst the coal.

The first division stop was Wynyard and here my friend turned back. He had a warm bed in Saskatoon, a mother, a father and home — not work. He explained that he was a decent fellow, had never been in jail in his life & didn't like freight riding. What would his mother say if he was arrested? Besides, supposing there was no work in Toronto what would we do? We'd be arrested, vagrants. He had never been in a big city before, our money would not last long, we might even starve to death! In other words, he'd had enough … just chicken hearted.

The sun was warm and I rode on top of a box car all day. Towards evening the train pulled in at the next division stop, Bredenbury. I was hungry & made for the town semi-satisfying my appetite in a "Chinks." Returning to the train I fell in with two of my fellow passengers of the coal car who had been "bumming" the houses. They were lads of 23 also heading for Toronto — happy but broke. Arriving at the tracks we walked boldly towards the freight & walked right into the "bull" who instantly showed his ignorance. "What the hell d'you fellows want here." We put him right as to our wants whilst he accompanied us to the entrance of the yards and the freight steamed out. He informed us that should he see us around again he would put us all in "clink." One of my new-found confederates thanked him very much and suggested that as we had lost the freight and had nowhere to sleep we should very much appreciate his hospitality. But the "bull" was not so hospitable & we slept in the C.P.R. round house beside a boiler. I slept well in spite of the sudden change from feather to concrete mattress. Following morning a pail & water from the boiler brightened our appearance & we made for town agreeing that the inhabitants should pay dearly for their ignorant railway cop. Meeting the oldest resident, I think he must have been, on "Main Street" we enquired as to the whereabouts of the local "town bull," the mayor, the residences of the station agent, the railway cop and the R.C.M.P. local. With this information we commenced our labours for breakfast. Seeing a man working in a garden we wondered whether he would like our aid or company. He was not impressed by either but gave us $1 for "eats." Entering the local hotel we explained our circumstances and gorged for 25 cents per head. During the morning we lay down on some open prairie & slept till roused by a crowd of children who had come to inspect us. One yelled "Hobo, hobo we've got some candy for you," but as I got up hopefully they took to their heals [sic] and ran for town. Our stomaches [sic] informed us dinner time had arrived, one of the boys set out for the mayors house and brought back a fine "hand out" which we consumed. The other set out for another of our addresses, split some wood & received a "sit-down." Then it was my turn to go "bumming." I set out for a large house set back from the town which looked hopeful. I tapped at the door nervously and a large man poked his head cautiously out of the door letting out an equally large dog as he did so. My knees knocked and I stuttered something about work & eat. The man told me he did not feed tramps & would set his dog on me. I moved toward the dog which instantly fled with its tail between its legs and the man slammed the door. As I was walking down the path the man popped his head out of an upstairs window and threatened to inform the police if I did not "get clear" immediately.

Towards evening the Winnipeg freight pulled in and we boarded it as it pulled out of the yards. There were no "empties" but a stock coach on the back, so we sat on the steps of this. As dusk fell we stopped for water at some place & the guard sighted us. He came up & inspected us, then unlocked the coach & told us to get in there for the night, we might go to sleep on the steps & fall off. Next morning we awoke to find our freight standing in the Portage La Prairie yards. Two "bulls" walked up the train, inspected the seals, glanced at the stock coach where we had assumed an attitude of sleep once more, walked off. We left the freight at a street crossing outside Winnipeg, yelled at a passing truck driver and were whirled into the city. The two lads I was with got a free shave at the Barber College and we learnt that the city was handing out meals to transients. After much walking and enquiring we obtained meal tickets and set out for the soup kitchens, which used to be the C.N.R. Immigration Hall where I stopped when first in Canada. The meal was awful! We walked down a counter gradually accumulating our ration which consisted of a piece of bread & square of butter, a small dish containing about a spoonful of sugar, a tin bowl containing a green fluid sometimes called soup, a tin plate on which had been dumped, dirty potatoes, two large hunks of fat, some carrots and thick gravy, and a mug containing hot water the same colour as weak tea. We sat on a bench containing males of all types, nationalities and descriptions and attempted to eat. The gentleman on my right had developed a strange habit of wiping a running nose with the back of his hand between each mouthful which did not increase the flavour of my meal. A large bowl of rice was placed on the table for desert but as I had my plate already filled with leavings I did not try any.

We left the soup kitchens and made enquiries about the times of freight trains. There was one leaving from the C.N.R. Transcona yards at around midnight for Toronto. We commenced the 9 miles walk to Transcona.

On the way we passed over a bridge on the side of which some humorist had written with chalk "I'm fed up; for further information drag the river." Over the bridge is St. Boniface where there is a large catholic church, seminary, school, nuns home etc. etc. Whilst passing the seminary and admiring its size and beauty we espied the kitchen through a basement window. Thoughts concerning the higher arts vanished from our heads, we looked at each other, looked for the nearest door, and entered, coming upon a fat cook. I moved my hand over my chest and wore my most pious expression and one of the boys addressing the cook as "brother" explained that we were extremely undernourished and should be pleased with some bread. The cook prepared some sandwiches containing cold slabs of steak and we departed praising the Lord, the cook and ourselves.

Towards late afternoon we arrived at the yards, parked ourselves on the grass outside the fencing and built a fire of old ties — and commenced a 7 hour wait. We consumed our sandwiches which were delicious — I think I'll become a priest.

As time passed more "travellers" appeared and settled around our fire; soon we had about a dozen fellow "unionists" and grew to discussing "this world of ours" as men often do. In London there are cockney tales, in Scotland, Scotch tales and on the road, hobo tales. Hoboes also have quite a language of their own. The same as farmers but without the large variety of 'swear words' usually associated with the barnyard.

The depression, the railway companies and Bennett were our chief topics. We wisely listened to each others views on depression. Its due to tariffs, to immigration, the price of wheat, the U.S.A., Russia, war, their "big-bugs," religion, the "bohunks." Nothing but war will bring back prosperity; no cancellation of war debts; no socialism; no God; let's have the good old days; scrap machinery, to hell with motor cars, deport the Reds, deport the "bohunks," oust Bennett …

Quite evidently there is no use for a penniless person in this land of opportunity; a person without work and money is considered an outcast, no town or city wants him but he can usually get two meals per day and exist because even Canadians do not usually let dogs starve. When a person has lost all his money and cannot get work he can either take to the road and become a bum or stop in his home town and get a free bed and two meals a day from the city relief for which he has to do as many hours work per week. I estimate that this scheme breaks the spirit of the average man within a year; hence I chose the road. My spirit is by no means broken I just feel angry and the harder Canada kicks me the more I'll retaliate. I do not consider myself an ordinary "bum." If there is any work to be done I'll do it providing I receive what I consider a decent living wage. I will certainly not work for my board and I will not work for the pittance many are receiving today.

Until such time as I get a decent job I intend to live well, dress respectably, eat all thats good for me, keep myself clean and have clean clothes. Canada generally will pay for this. I will obtain what I need by bumming and other comparatively honest methods. If such ways and means should fail I shall resort to thieving and other criminal ways of which I have some knowledge....

FURTHER READINGS

Ballageon, D. "If You Had No Money, You Had No Trouble, Did You? Montreal Working Class Housewives during the Great Depression." In *Canadian Women: A Reader*, ed. W. Mitchinsen *et al.* Toronto: Harcourt and Brace, 1996.

Ballageon, D. *Making Do: Women, Family, and Home in Montreal During the Great Depression*. Waterloo: Wilfrid Laurier University Press, 1999.

Brown, L. *When Freedom Was Lost: The Unemployed, the Agitator and the State*. Montreal: Black Rose, 1987.

Cadigan, S. "Battle Harbour in Transition: Merchants, Fishermen and the State in the Struggle for Relief in a Labrador Community during the 1930s." *Labour* (1990): 125-50.

Christie, N. *Engendering the State: Family, Work, and Welfare in Canada*. Toronto: University of Toronto Press, 2000.

Dumas, E. *The Bitter Thirties in Quebec*, trans. A. Bennett. Montreal: Black Rose, 1975.

Finkel, A. *Business and Social Reform in the Thirties*. Toronto: James Lorimer, 1979.

Francis, R., and H. Ganzevoort, Eds. *The Dirty Thirties in Prairie Canada*. Vancouver: Tantalus, 1980.

Glassford, L. *Reaction and Reform: The Politics of the Conservative Party Under R.B. Bennett*. Toronto: University of Toronto Press, 1992.

Gray, J. *Men Against the Desert*. Saskatoon: Western Producer, 1967.

Gray, J. *The Winter Years: The Depression on the Prairies*. Toronto: Macmillan, 1966.

Healey, T. "Engendering Resistance: Women Respond to Relief in Saskatoon, 1930-33." In *Other Voices: Historical Essays on Saskatchewan Women*, ed. A. Moffat and D. De Brou. Saskatoon: Fifth House, 1995.

Hobbs, M. "Equality and Difference: Feminism and Defence of Women Workers during the Great Depression." *Labour* 32 (Fall 1993): 201-24.

Horn, M., Ed. *The Depression in Canada: Responses to Economic Crisis*. Toronto: Copp Clark Pitman, 1988.

Horn, M., Ed. *The Dirty Thirties: Canadians in the Great Depression*. Toronto: Copp Clark, 1972.

Howard, I. "The Mothers' Council of Vancouver: Holding the Fort of the Unemployed, 1935-1938." *B.C. Studies* 69-70 (1986): 249-87.

MacDowell, L. "Relief Camp Workers in Ontario during the Great Depression of the 1930s." *Canadian Historical Review* 76, 2 (1995): 205-28.

Neatby, H. *The Politics of Chaos: Canada and the Thirties*. Toronto: Macmillan, 1972.

Pierson, R. "Gender and Unemployment Debates in Canada, 1934-1940." *Labour* 25 (Spring 1990): 77-104.

Safarian, A. *The Canadian Economy in the Great Depression*. Toronto: University of Toronto Press, 1959.

Struthers, J. *The Limits of Affluence: Welfare in Ontario, 1920-1970.* Toronto: University of Toronto Press, 1994.

Struthers, J. *No Fault of Their Own: Unemployment and the Canadian Welfare State, 1914-1941.* Toronto: University of Toronto Press, 1983.

Taylor, J. "Relief for Relief: The Cities Response to Depression Dependency." *Journal of Canadian Studies* 14, 1 (May 1979): 1-17.

Thompson, J., and A. Seager. *Canada 1922-1939: Decades of Discord.* Toronto: McClelland and Stewart, 1985.

Wilbur, R., Ed. *The Bennett New Deal: Fraud or Portent?* Toronto: Copp Clark, 1968.

Vigod, B. "The Quebec Government and Social Legislation during the 1930s: A Study in Political Self-Destruction." *Journal of Canadian Studies* 14, 1 (May 1979): 59-67.

CHAPTER 9

"The Question of Loyalty"

JAPANESE CANADIANS AND WORLD WAR II

INTRODUCTION

Vilifying other nations' histories is much easier than attacking one's own. Self-flagellation hurts, after all, and threatens the collective psyche: it upsets national chauvinism and self-righteousness. That is why national histories often exclude, or gloss over, the ugly moments. Modern school curricula in Japan, for example, simply ignore the butchery of hundreds of thousands of Chinese civilians perpetrated by Imperial Japanese forces in World War II. Canada is no exception to this selective interpretation of history, however, and the story of the Japanese Canadians during that same conflict is a stark example. Most Canadians have either not heard about it, or if they have, their knowledge is limited to a vague recollection of benign evacuation.

Even before any official declaration of war against Japan, the federal cabinet formed the Special Committee on Orientals in British Columbia. This occurred immediately after Japan announced its alliance with the Axis powers and amid protests against Asian Canadians serving in Canada's armed forces. All Japanese Canadians were requested to register voluntarily with the RCMP and to be fingerprinted. When war with Japan finally began in December 1941, Order-in-Council PC #1486, issued by the federal government on February 24, 1942, evacuated all people of Japanese extraction to live in a "protected zone" of 100 miles of Canada's West Coast. Ottawa justified the law in two ways: 1) it lessened the chance that *Nisei* (those born in Canada of Japanese ancestry), or *Issei* (naturalized Japanese immigrants) could act as the vanguard for a Japanese surprise attack; and 2) it protected those of Japanese ancestry from abuse in the paranoid aftermath of the bombing of Pearl Harbor. Order-in-Council PC #1486 was not based on nationality since the majority of the 21,000 men, women, and children evacuees were Canadian citizens. Racial background alone decided the internee's fate because it apparently determined patriotism—or lack thereof.

To what degree, if any, was the evacuation based on genuine and legitimate fear, or was it purely an act of racism masquerading as something else? The argument in favour of internment for national security's sake certainly held sway during and immediately after the war. The Japanese military, after all, seemed unstoppable in Southeast Asia and did launch a devastating surprise attack against Pearl Harbor in Hawaii, halfway across the Pacific from British Columbia. Follow the Aleutian Island chain westward from Alaska and where do you end up? Japan. Could the Japanese army not island-hop from Japan to British Columbia via Alaska? And though there was initially no confirmed Japanese naval activity on Canada's coast, unconfirmed sightings abounded, all of which generated very genuine and intense fear.

Other issues heightened suspicion toward the Japanese-Canadian community. Some perceived the Japanese Canadians as unassimilable, as consciously and dangerously isolated from the rest of society by the impenetrable cloak of a radically different culture, language, religion, and appearance. Current historiography posits racism as the primary motivation behind the evacuation. The Canadian government acknowledged this in the 1980s by offering an apology and financial compensation to the Japanese-Canadian community. And Canada did indeed have a long history of racism, nowhere more so than along the West Coast and against "Orientals." Only racism, so the argument goes, can explain why evacuees could not return to British Columbia until four years after the war ended and why children and the aged—hardly security threats—were also evacuated. Further evidence supporting this interpretation comes from the RCMP and military intelligence, which both declared, prior to the evacuation, that Japanese Canadians on the West Coast posed no threat to national security. Neither German nor Italian immigrants, either first or second generation, were interned, though their national origins should logically have made them "enemies" too. On the other hand, neither of those groups lived *en masse* in strategically sensitive areas such as did people of Japanese origin on the West Coast. Prime Minister MacKenzie King stated in 1948 that "no person of Japanese race born in Canada [was] charged with any act of sabotage or disloyalty during the years of the war." This, however, pertained to those who stayed in Canada during the conflict. One Kelowna-born person of Japanese extraction joined the Japanese army and was subsequently tried and executed for heinous crimes against prisoners of war.

Order-in-Council PC #1486 astonished people like Muriel Kitagawa who probably did not believe it until she heard the knock at her door. She should have seen it coming. The Americans, after all, had already passed legislation prohibiting 120,000 Japanese Americans from living within 100 miles of their west coast and simultaneously seized their property. The new Canadian law mimicked American actions by allowing the RCMP to enter homes without warrants and to confiscate property deemed potentially dangerous. This included fishing boats, cameras, radios, and firearms. Vehicles had to be surrendered, and the government imposed a dusk-to-dawn curfew. Japanese-Canadian newspapers and schools closed. After the evacuation, the Custodian of Enemy Alien Property seized all unmoveable goods, such as businesses, homes, and property, and held them in trust until January 1943 when they were auctioned off without the owners' consent. Monies raised alleviated the relocation cost, thereby addressing the demand that Canadian taxpayers not bear the financial burden of incarcerating the country's enemies. Selling their possessions, of course, also ensured that Japanese Canadians could not easily return to their former homes once hostilities ended. The American government released Japanese Americans from detention well before the end of the war and returned their seized possessions.

DISCUSSION POINTS

1. To what extent was Japanese relocation a product of the war or did the war simply provide a convenient means for expressing longstanding racism?

2. Kitagawa implies that Canada's treatment of its Japanese citizens compares to Nazi Germany's anti-Semitic policies and that Canada deluded itself into thinking it fought a war for democracy when, in fact, it was just as guilty of denying civil liberties to its citizens. Was she right?

3. The federal government acknowledged its responsibly for injustices suffered by Japanese Canadians in World War II through a formal apology and compensation for survivors. Are modern Canadians accountable for mistakes in the past?

4. What, if any, lessons should Canadians learn from examining the treatment of Japanese Canadians in World War II?

DOCUMENTS

1. A. Neill, House of Commons, *Debates*, February 19, 1942
(Ottawa: King's Printer, 1942)

Alan Webster Neill (1868–1960) was a farmer and businessman born in Scotland. He became the Progressive Member of Parliament for Comox-Alberni in 1921, switching to an Independent from 1925 onward. He remained an MP until 1945, retiring after some 23 years in office. Throughout, Neill fought to keep British Columbia "white," not only opposing non-white immigration, but railing against inter-racial relationships as well. He declared that "to cross an individual of the white race with an individual of a yellow race, is to produce in nine cases out of ten a mongrel wastrel with the worst qualities of both." A major street and a school in Port Alberni presently bear his name.

Mr. Speaker, I have listened to that appeasement talk for twenty years from the government benches, and I think the time has come to take a different stand. I believe we can best serve the interests of our country, and promote peace, by having plain talk, straightforward discussions and, I hope definite action, with respect to the issues before us....

In September, 1940, Japan signed the deal, agreement or whatever you call it with Italy and Germany. In plain English, they bound themselves to enter into war against us and the United States whenever it suited Germany or either. Pressure was put upon the government by British Columbia, and I suppose some realization of the situation also led the government to take action. They appointed a hand-picked committee to investigate the subject, which ... came back with a number of recommendations, I believe ten in all. There were only two of any importance, Nos. 5 and 7, and I shall deal with them. No. 5 recommended against allowing Japanese to enlist in our volunteer army then being raised. That was a very good idea, otherwise we would have had perhaps 1,500 Japanese training in our army, possibly in key positions, petty officers and the like. They would have been familiar with every detail of our army operations. Protests were made by the mayor of Nanaimo, and I think by other cities and by myself, and the recommendation of the committee carried. That was all right.

Recommendation No. 7 was that there should be a re-registration of the Japanese in Canada. It had been claimed by many people that the registration that had been taken was just a fake as regards the Japanese. Only those who felt like it registered, and there was a demand for a new registration. The recommendation was that they should be photographed at the same time. That was a good idea, but it had one fatal defect, if deception is regarded as a fatal defect. It was clearly understood that this registration was compulsory. We were told how well it was going on, how successful it was, and it was hoped that we malignants would now be satisfied and keep quiet. The whole thing turned on the point that it was compulsory.

If it had been voluntary, what use would it have been?... Was it expected that Japanese who had entered the country illegally would come forward and say, "Yes, I came in illegally, take me." Of course they would not. A Jap is not a fool, any more than we are. The guilty ones did not register and the whole thing was a gigantic failure. It could not be otherwise if it were anything but compulsory.

Our main complaint was that many of them had come into the country illegally and this re-registration would have discovered that. Was it expected that those who had come in illegally would disclose that fact? The thing is ridiculous. When the war came on, after Pearl Harbour, it was discovered that it was not compulsory that it was just a gesture to keep us quiet, just a farce. Then what happened? The war was on and the people know what war means; this government should know what it means. These same people were given two months in which to register; they were given until February 7 to get things fixed up, to get a fake birth certificate or a forged entry card. You can buy them in Vancouver. If they could not get either, they were given two months before they would be subject to the same action as that to which any other enemy alien would be exposed. Why give them two months? We were practically saying to them, "We are at war with you, but we will give you two months in which to get faked papers, or get out of the country." I never heard the like of it before, and I hope I never shall again.

They were given two months in which to fix things up or get out. If that registration had been compulsory, we would have got the best of these Jap agents and the best of their spies. They have now gone home with their charts and plans and with a local knowledge that could not be bought for any money. Perhaps we shall see some of these Japs again peering over the side of the bridge of a German gunboat in Vancouver, Nanaimo or Port Alberni, because we now know that many of them were expert naval men. ...

Paragraph 6 recommends that the government should seize immediately the Japanese fishing boats. That was done. It was done immediately war was declared, and for that action I have nothing but the utmost praise. It was done promptly and thoroughly.... At any rate it was done, and done well. While this is not part of the report, I may as well finish up that matter by saying that after they had 1,200 Japanese boats in their hands, the question arose, what to do with them? It was desirable to get them back into fishing again, so that white men could catch the fish so badly needed for the British market. Therefore they set up a committee to try to sell these boats....: Like all government offices, it is true that they were rather slow in going about their work, but they got started at last. ...

I want to quote recommendation 7 in which it was contained the policy of the cabinet. It reads: For the same period—that is during the war—the sale of gaso-line all explosives to persons of Japanese racial origin will be directly controlled under conditions prescribed by the Royal Canadian Mounted Police.

That is a good idea too, a very good idea, but unfortunately I read in the papers—I have to go to the press for information because I cannot get it any-where else—that these sales are still going on.

Explosives. A man wrote to the "Vancouver Province" the other day and suggested that if this order was in effect, why was the Japanese station at the corner still selling gas the same as usual? That has been going on for two and a half months now, and I rather think; permission may been extended to the 1st of April. The language is doubtful, but if it can be interpreted to the benefit of the Japanese, be sure it will be so interpreted. You are dealing with clever, subtle, unscrupulous enemies—and they are enemies—and when you say that you are not going to stop the sale for two months, that is just an invitation to them to accumulate as much gas and explosives as they can in the meantime. We say to them: "Remember, on the 7th of February or on the 1st of April we are going to shut down on you." Is that not an invitation to them to get explosives and gasoline against a rainy day? That time limit should never have been put in. The order should have been made applicable at once....

There are three classes of Japanese we must deal with. There are the Japanese nationals, those born in Japan and never naturalized in Canada; they are Japanese nationals. Then there is the man born in Japan and naturalized in Canada. He is called a naturalized Japanese or a Canadian. Then there is the Japanese who was born in Canada, who can call himself a Japanese-Canadian if he likes. The gov-ernment orders with regard to seizing the boats and the sale of gas and explosives applied to all three classes. That was all right.

Now I deal with paragraph 8. It says that Japanese nationals will be forbid-den to possess or use short-wave receiving sets or radio transmitters in Canada. A most excellent thing. Hon. members can all understand why it was necessary to do that. That was fine. But it does not come into effect until the 1st of April. Did the Japanese give us four months notice of what they were going to do at Pearl Harbour? Yet we say to them: "Go wandering about with your cameras and take pictures, and use your receiving sets to send word to Japan, and your receivers to get instructions from Japan. You can do this as much as you like until the 1st of April." Even if the order had been withheld, and they had been allowed to continue doing these things without being told of any date when they must stop, it would not have been so bad, because then they would never have known when the order was coming into force. But they were warned—you will not be interfered with until the 1st of April. The order was the equivalent of that. We told them: "Do your dirty work now. Use your radio and your receiving set but, remember, hide or bury them before the 1st of April, and then everything will be lovely." They told the Japanese nationals that they must not use these things in a protected area. But they can use them outside. I have a police order to that effect. It is signed by the police and says:

"No enemy alien shall have in his possession or use while in such protected area any camera, radio transmitter, radio short-wave receiving set, firearm, ammunition or explosive."

… Well, as I said, it is doubtful. There is, however, no question whatever that a man who is not a Japanese national can do these things any time, any place. The order applies only to nationals; that is, to men born in Japan and coming over here, and these are comparatively few in number, something like 1,700 out of 24,000, and only while they are in the area. The remaining 22,000 of naturalized Japanese are free to come and go, as I have said, anywhere. They can photograph what they like, radio what they like. They can do something else which I have not touched upon, and which is not to make a joke—a burning question in British Columbia. Three, two, one of them can do endless damage in British Columbia with a box of matches. The most deadly enemy of the lumber industry in British Columbia is fire. Lumbermen are so afraid of it, it is so dangerous, that they shut their camps down in the middle of summer, as soon as the humidity reaches a certain point. A man can wander out in that bush, ten, fifty, a hundred miles from anywhere, and do more damage with a box of matches than it would take two armies to put out. The large number of forest rangers whom we have could not touch the fringe of the thing if these aliens were determined to commit sabotage. Some of the biggest lumbermen on the coast are much alarmed at this situation. If the Japanese were out of the area, they could not do this damage, because you can't do a thing if you are not there.

I have spoken of the freedom of Japanese to come and go with cameras, radios and matches. That is not restricted to two months or four months; that is for eternity, if the war lasts that long; it is for the duration of the war that the naturalized or Canadian-born Jap can go out and commit sabotage; he is free to do it the whole time, and he is the most dangerous of the lot. The naturalised

Japanese speaks our language fluently, possibly he has been to college. He possesses far greater potentialities of trouble as a spy or an agent than if he had just come from Japan. The fellow dressed up like a white man, speaking our language glibly, is the one who should be interned. It is very hard for me to believe that the government are so remote from what is taking place or may take place as not to understand the situation....

I should now like to make three charges against the government. The first is this, that with the exception of seizing these boats they have been far too slow in handling the Japanese situation. They have let days go by when it should have been hours, and a month when it should have been days. Look at what was done in Mexico. There the government dealt with the whole lot as soon as war was declared, and ordered into the interior every Jap who was on the coast. They did it; they didn't talk about it. Cuba did the same thing. They arrested, I believe eighteen Japanese, all but two of whom were naval officers. Nicaragua took the same course and took it speedily....

I note here that the council of the city of Vancouver has passed a resolution urging the government to get a move on. The report speaks of increasing irritation and criticism at the coast over the apparent failure of the government to implement its announced policy of removing Japanese.

The legislature of British Columbia, before adjourning a few days ago, passed unanimously a resolution urging the dominion government to strengthen Pacific defences. The feeling is very strong at the coast. I wish I could get the government to realize it.

Here is one incident I must quote, reported under a big headline in a leading Vancouver paper, the "Daily Province":

Japanese live undisturbed on dike adjoining airport.

There are 200 Japanese living a mile west of the airport. They are living on a dike. It would be very easy to blow up or open that dike, and the airport would be rendered useless for a long time to come. Yet they are living undisturbed within a mile of the airport; they are on a dike into which a gap could be blown with a few sticks of powder that would make the airport useless for a long time to come. Why does the government not take some action in this case?

The second charge is that even the small restrictions to which I have referred are applicable only to nationals, and I say it is inexcusable that they are not made applicable to all naturalized Japanese aliens in this country. To whom do you suppose they think they owe loyalty? If they were scattered all over Canada, the case might be different, but think what may happen when they are turned loose in a small area, when 25,000 are concentrated in an area where they could so readily combine to take action against Vancouver, or Victoria, as the case may be. It constitutes an unspeakable menace; I cannot understand why it is allowed to continue.

The third charge is that the government have shown indifference to British Columbia defence, also to air raid precautions work and the like of that. I am not blaming the government for preparations which they might have made six years ago. That is not their fault; I know that. We could not get the appropriation through the house.... But I do blame the government for not having taken the situation in hand since war was declared. They are too slack, they appear to adopt the attitude, "Oh, well, we have to take chances; we are doing the best we can; it will be all right." Well, they told us it would be all right about Hong Kong. But people make mistakes—even military men, even high military men. They told us it would be all right at Singapore. Yet we know that mistakes were made there. Here is the government's paper, the "Vancouver Sun," expressing this opinion:

"Canada obviously has not made its plan of defence on the assumption of any real attack on the Pacific coast.... That is the plan which must be reconsidered ... we do expect a well-equipped, mobile striking unit which could pounce upon any Japanese landing attempt from Asia southwards."

No such force exists on our coast. No such force exists in Canada.

I am afraid that is too true. Perhaps in the secret session which is to be held we shall be given more information on this matter. I do not propose to blame the government for things which happened before they had control and knowledge of the situation, or for not having done what at the time was beyond their power. But the government must be ready at that secret session to give us genuine information, not general assurances and smooth-sounding platitudes. There has been too much of this in connection with the management of the war.

There is a certain place—I will not name names, I will call it Y. When the government began to think about building aerodromes I thought that Y would make a good site for one, and I said so. I put it up to the officials, and they said that they were experts and ought to know better than I did. Well, I accepted that decision—but they are building that aerodrome now with frantic haste. I fear we may have to paraphrase the hymn and say:

Too late, too late will be the cry "The Japanese gunboats have gone by."

There was another aerodrome at a place we will call X. I wrote to the government in connection with this one, informing them that there were two things wrong about it. This was a year or two ago. I pointed out to the officials that there was a Jap village 200 yards from the mouth of it where the Japs could take photographs and keep a record of any aeroplanes leaving, with all the details, so that they could have it all recorded for the benefit of the Japanese. I have in my desk a letter in which some official tried to stall me off. I was told that they would expropriate the Japanese, but that they could not do it because there was some hitch. However, they said they would look into the matter. Imagine looking into the question of expropriating this particular property when other nations, as we know, take first what they require and then talk about expropriation. Again, I pointed out to the officials that there was a Jap who had been seen taking photographs from an aeroplane over the harbour, where the aerodrome was being built. It was a civilian aeroplane. I took this matter up with various bodies—I will not mention any names because I do not wish to give them away—and what was the answer? I was informed that the investigation was closed. They had ascertained the name of the man and had found that he had gone to Japan. I suppose he took photographs with him as a momento of us because he loved us so much. Well, he has gone back to Japan with whatever photographs he took—we do not know how many—and God knows how many more may have gone there. But the officials did not seem to think it was important. I was told that it would be difficult to take photographs through the glass of any aeroplane unless you had a particular sort of apparatus with which to do it. Well, would the Japanese not have that type of apparatus? I submitted all these matters to the department, and I have it all on record. One of the officials said to me, "There is nothing to this anyhow because it is not against the laws of the country to take photograph of an aerodrome."

I took it up with some of the higher officials, and they juggled with it and finally explained that they could get the Japs under the Official Secrets Act. The aerodrome is still there; Japs are still staying there under their four months' lease of life, and doubtless they are still taking these photographs, which I have no doubt will be sent to the right place.

These men are not all Canadian nationals. Some of them may be the very best class of spies and foreign agents, and I contend that there has been too much sympathy for the Japanese viewpoint and Japanese interests. We must remember that we are at war with these people. Ottawa is 3,000 miles away from us out there....

We who have taken the position that I am now taking have been called all sorts of names. We have been called agitators. It is said that we are willing to exploit the interests of Canada for our own political advantage; that we are rabble-rousers, Jap-baiters, and that we have a very dangerous influence.... I have heard that sort of thing, and hints of it even in this house, and certainly in the government press. You can get a man to write any letter you want; you can get a white man to make a fool of himself for a Jap if you pay him enough. There was a man who wrote to the papers saying what fine people the Japs are. I laid a trap for him and I discovered that he was a white man all right, but also a paid agent of a Japanese association, but he did not say that when he signed his name.

Yes, we are all bad because we want a white British Columbia and not a place like Hawaii! Fifty years from now, unless something is done to stop it, all west of the Rockies will be yellow. I submit, Mr. Speaker, that we want but little; we simply want to be left alone like New Zealand and Australia, all white. I have no ill-will against the Japanese. Perhaps you may think I have been showing ill-will, but I assure you I have none towards the Japs. No Jap ever "did" me—I never gave him the chance. I wish to be fair to the Japanese, and I think that if we expatriated them, as we ought to do, they should be given full justice in regard to their property, because I am strongly in favour of a Japan controlled by the Japanese, just as I am in favour of a Canada controlled by Canadians. Let us continue to trade with them, let us do business with them across the ocean; but do not force into one nation two peoples separated by something that is wider than the ocean, two peoples who are different in race, in religion, in traditions and in their whole philosophy of life. This difference always has prevented assimilation and always will prevent it, between two nations so utterly divergent in every respect. The greatest path towards assimilation is marriage ... the Japs have been here fifty-eight years and there is no record of a single marriage, although there might be one. I asked a Japanese to produce the record of one marriage and he could not do so. We have heard of second generation Japanese born here going to Japanese schools here to learn Japanese, and that has been regarded as a small matter. We went into their textbooks and had them translated and we found that they were very anti-British. Yet there were people who thought that was a small matter—only the sort of thing that irresponsible people like myself would talk about. But when the war came, it was thought wise to shut down the Jap schools. There were fifty-nine in British Columbia, and leaving out small areas where they could not run a school, the great bulk of those children must have attended some Japanese school.

I have one more word.... We should make an arrangement that when peace time comes, we expatriate all the Japanese left in Canada; do it on fair terms, buy them out, pay them liberally.... It is much easier for us to move 25,000, and it is better to move them while their numbers are so small. Let us settle once and for all this canker in the life of Canada which prevents us from being a united white Canada. And that is what British Columbia wants.

2. Muriel Kitagawa, *This Is My Own: Letters to Wes and Other Writings on Japanese Canadians, 1941–1948* (Vancouver: Talon, 1985)

Muriel Kitagawa (nee Fujiwara) (1912–) came from a family dogged by poverty and disintegration. Her father emigrated from Japan to Victoria in 1890, working in saw

mills before moving to Sidney and New Westminster. Muriel excelled in English lit-
erature, coming second for the Grade 12 Governor General's Award. She attended the
University of British Columbia but could not finish for lack of money. She did, however,
find an outlet for her writing prowess in The New Age *and* The New Canadian. *Like*
many of her compatriots, she found her parents old-fashioned and too Japanese, and she
strove to integrate into mainstream Canadian culture. She was in close touch with her
brother Wes, a medical student in Ontario, and moved there when forced to relocate.

2.1 TO WES, DECEMBER 21, 1941

... So far as the new war affects us, I really haven't much to say. It is too early to estimate the effects. On the whole we are taking it in our stride. We are so used to wars and alarms, and we have been tempered by the anti-feelings these long years. It has only intensified into overt acts of unthinking hoodlumism like throwing flaming torches into rooming houses and bricks through plate glass ... only in the West End so far. What that goes to prove I don't know. We've had blackouts the first few nights but they have been lifted. Bad for the kids, because it frightens them so. Of course we have to be ready just in case and I sure hope there won't be any emergency ... not with the kids around. All three Japanese papers have been closed down. We never needed so many anyway. It is good for the New Canadian though, as it can now go ahead with full responsibility, though at first it is bound to be hard on the inexperienced staff. All Japanese schools have been closed too, and are the kids glad! Of course I have never intended my kids to go anyway so it doesn't affect us in the least. I am glad in a way that they have been closed down. I hope for good. But it is hard on the teachers who depended on them for a living.

There have been the usual anti-letters-to-the-editor in the papers. Some of them are rank nonsense, and some of the writers think like that anyhow, whatever the provocation. The majority of the people are decent and fair-minded and they say so in letters and editorials. The RCMP is our friend too, for they, more than anyone else, know how blameless and helpless we are, and they have already in one instance prevented tragedy when the City Fathers proposed cancelling all business licences, to say that we did not rate such harsh treatment. Now the North Vancouver Board of Trade goes on record to demand that all our autos be confiscated, but I hardly think that could be practical. What then would our doctors and businessmen do? Also, it is hard to take everything away from 22,000 people without the rest of B.C. feeling some of the bad effects. The dog salmon industry is already short-handed because the Japanese cannot fish any more. How they will make up the lack in the next season, I don't know, though the "white" fishermen seem to be confident, if they could use the fishing boats now tied up somewhere in New Westminster.

There was one letter in the "Province" protesting this confiscation of the right to earn a living from 1,880 people ... said it wasn't democracy. Yes sir, when a people get panicky, democracy and humanity and Christian principles go by the board. Rather inconsistent, but human nature I guess. Some silly mothers even go so far as to say, what right have the black-haired kids to go to school with their own precious? One schoolteacher had the courage to say to one of the "white" pupils who wanted all Japs to be kicked out of school— how they reflect their parents' attitude!—that there were no Japs, and in any case they were far better Canadians than the protester. Strange how these protesters are much more vehement against the Canadian-born Japanese than they are against German born Germans, who might have a real loyalty to their land of birth, as we have for Canada. I guess it is just because we look different. Anyway it all boils down to racial antagonism which the democracies are fighting. Who said it was Woman ... or the Moon that was inconstant? Oh well, it is only the occasional one here and there. I personally have had no change in my relationship with my neighbours or my Egg-man, who told me not to worry. Most of the hakujin deplore the war but do not change to their known Japanese friends. It is the small businesses that are most affected ... like the dressmakers, the corner store, etc., because the clientele are rather shy of patronising in public such places, whatever their private thoughts may be. Powell Street is affected too, in that they have a slightly increased volume of sales to people who usually go to Woodwards etc. but so many have been fired from jobs that belts are tightening everywhere. I don't know yet how all this is going to affect Dad. Most of his patients are fishermen or farmers. So far the farmers haven't been touched.

Last Sunday, the national President of the IODE [Imperial Order of the Daughters of the Empire], who must live far from contact from the Nisei because she didn't seem to know the first thing about us, made a deliberate attempt to create fear and ill-will among her dominion-wide members by telling them that we were all spies and saboteurs, and that in 1931 there were 55,000 of us and that number has doubled in the last ten years. Not only a biological absurdity, but the records of the RCMP give the lie to such round numbers. The trouble is that lots of women would like to believe their president rather than actual figures. Seems to me illogical that women who are the conservers and builders of the human race should be the ones to go all out for savagery and destruction and ill-will among fellow-humans. They are the ones who are expected to keep the peace with their neighbours in their particular block, but when it comes to blackballing some unfortunate people, they are the first to cast the stone. In times like this I always think of that line:

If there be any among you that is without sin, let him cast the first stone.

Or words to that effect. And certainly we Nisei are neither harlots nor criminals. We are just people.

But more to the point, how are you getting along, there? Is the feeling worse in Toronto where they don't know the Nisei as B.C. does? How does the war affect you personally? Can you get a loan to get through next year and the year after? After all, you are Canadian born, and the Army needs MDs. ... I guess that when gas rationing starts Dad won't be able to use that darned car so often.... He has to report every month to the RCMP, just because when he first came to B.C., which was over forty years ago, and plenty of time to naturalize, he didn't look far enough ahead to know how it would have helped his children. That for people who live only day to day. Politics never meant a thing to him, and doesn't yet. So long as he can eat and swank in his car he lets important things slide.

We're getting immune to the hitherto unused term "Japs" on the radio and on the headlines of the papers. So long as they designate the enemy, and not us, it doesn't matter much.... Ugh! I hate wars, and I've had one already, though I wasn't old enough to know anything then. Now I'm going through a worse one. War, active war, is easier to bear with courage than this surging up of mass hatred against us simply because we are of Japanese origin. I hope fervently that it will not affect the lives of Shirley and Meiko and the unborn son, as the doctor believes. After all, my kids, as only proper being my kids, are so thoroughly Canadian they would never understand being persecuted by people they regard as one of themselves. Already Meiko came crying home once because some kid on the block whose father is anti, said something. Yet I try to rationalize things for them, so that they won't be inundated by self consciousness. Children are so innocent, but they are savages too, and reflect faithfully their parents' attitudes. That was the one thing my doctor was worried about. Otherwise he, with most of the others, tells us not to worry. We're Canadians and can expect decent treatment from decent people.

2.2 TO WES, FEBRUARY 19, 1942

...Well, I guess you've read in the papers that there isn't a province in Canada that will take the "Japs," and B.C. just has to have us whether she will or no. Ian Mackenzie has again come out with "Volunteer or else—." Vancouver City

Fathers have petitioned Ottawa to put the OK on a ban of trade licences to Japanese here—850 or so. Won't the Relief offices be flooded then! They don't care anyway—under their hypocritical Christian faces. It beats me how they can mouth "Down with Hitler," and at the same time advocate a program against "Japs" (4-letter syllable in place of "Jews"). Now that attack on this coast is becoming more of a concrete threat, feeling is running pretty high—tho' the individuals in most cases are pretty decent. The rabble-rousers and the mob—haven't we learned about "mobs" in Roman days and in Shakespeare's works?—they are the ones to cause all the trouble. Even the Youth Congress has come out with a plea to move us all out someplace, anywhere except on the coast.

    ... Anyway I'm not sure what to believe these days. Dad takes no thought of his eventual transfer to a camp. (They're moving the over-45-year-olds after they get the first batch settled.) In fact, if the war comes any closer we'll all be kicked out. Gosh, but hasn't 1941 been the awfullest year in our life?

2.3 TO WES, MARCH 2, 1942

...Eiko and Fumi were here yesterday, crying, nearly hysterical with hurt and outrage and impotence. All student nurses have been fired from the [Vancouver] General.

    They took our beautiful radio ... what does it matter that some one bought it off us for a song? ... it's the same thing because we had to do that or suffer the ignominy of having it taken forcibly from us by the RCMP. Not a single being of Japanese race in the protected area will escape. Our cameras, even Nobi's toy one, all are confiscated. They can search our homes without warrant.

    As if all this trouble wasn't enough, prepare yourself for a shock. We are forced to move out from our homes, Wes, to where we don't know. Eddie was going to join the Civilian Corps but now will not go near it, as it smells of a daemonic, roundabout way of getting rid of us. There is the very suspicious clause "within and without" Canada that has all the fellows leery.

    The Bank is awfully worried about me and the twins, and the manager has said he will do what he can for us, but as he has to refer to the main office which in turn has to refer to the Head Office, he can't promise a thing, except a hope that surely the Bank won't let us down after all these years of faithful service. Who knows where we will be now tomorrow next week. It isn't as if we Nisei were aliens, technical or not. It breaks my heart to think of leaving this house and the little things around it that we have gathered through the years, all those numerous gadgets that have no material value but are irreplaceable....

"The Question of Loyalty": Japanese Canadians and World War II

Oh Wes, the Nisei are bitter, too bitter for their own good or for Canada. How can cool heads like Tom's prevail when the general feeling is to stand up and fight.

Do you know what curfew means in actual practice? B.C. is falling all over itself in the scramble to be the first to kick us out from jobs and homes. So many night-workers have been fired out of hand. Now they sit at home, which is usually just a bed, or some cramped quarters, since they can't go out at night for even a consoling cup of coffee. Mr. Shimizu is working like mad with the Welfare society to look after the women and children that were left when their men were forced to volunteer to go to the work camps. Now those men are only in unheated bunk-cars, no latrines, no water, snow 15' deep, no work to keep warm with, little food if any. They had been shunted off with such inhuman speed that they got there before any facilities were prepared for them. Now men are afraid to go because they think they will be going to certain disaster ... anyway, too much uncertainty. After all, they have to think of their families. If snow is 15' deep there is no work, and if there is no work there is no pay, and if there is no pay no one eats. The "Province" reports that work on frames with tent-coverings is progressing to house the 2,000 expected. Tent coverings where the snow is so deep! And this is Democracy! You should see the faces here, all pinched, grey, uncertain. If the Bank fails Eddie, do you know what the kids and I have to live on? $39. For everything ... food, clothing, rent, taxes, upkeep, insurance premiums, emergencies. They will allow for only two kids for the Nisei. $6 per., monthly. It has just boiled down to race persecution, and signs have been posted on all highways.... "JAPS ....KEEP OUT." Mind you, you can't compare this sort of thing to anything that happens in Germany. That country is an avowed Jew-baiter, totalitarian. Canada is supposed to be a Democracy out to fight against just the sort of thing she's boosting at home.

And also, I'll get that $39 only if Eddie joins the Chain Gang, you know, forced to volunteer to let the authorities wash their hands of any responsibilities. All Nisei are liable to imprisonment I suppose if they refuse to volunteer ... that is the likeliest interpretation of Ian MacKenzie's "volunteer or else." Prisoners in wartime get short shrift ... and to hell with the wife and kids. Can you wonder that there is a deep bitterness among the Nisei who believe so gullibly in the democratic blah-blah that's been dished out....

There are a lot of decent people who feel for us, but they can't do a thing.

And the horrors that some young girls have already faced ... outraged by men in uniform ... in the hospital ... hysterical. Oh we are fair prey for the wolves in democratic clothing. Can you wonder the men are afraid to leave us behind and won't go unless their women go with them? I won't blame you if you can't believe this. It is incredible Wes, you have to be here right in the middle of it to really know.

How can the hakujin face us without a sense of shame for their treachery to the principles they fight for? One man was so damned sorry, he came up to me, hat off, squirming like mad, stuttering how sorry he was. My butcher said he knew he could trust me with a side of meat even if I had no money.... Yet there are other people who, while they wouldn't go so far as to persecute us, are so ignorant, so indifferent they believe we are being very well treated for what we are. The irony of it all is enough to choke me. And we are tightening our belts for the starvation to come. The diseases ... the crippling ... the twisting of our souls ... death would be the easiest to bear.

The Chinese are forced to wear huge buttons and plates and even placards to tell the hakujin the difference between one yellow peril and another. Or else they would be beaten up. It's really ridiculous....

Can't send you pictures now unless some hakujin takes the snaps ... STRENG VERBOTEN to use even little cameras to snap the twins ... STRENG VERBOTEN is the order of the day.

2.4 TO WES, APRIL 20, 1942

I went to the Pool yesterday to see Eiko who is working there as steno. I saw Sab too who is working in the baggage ... old Horseshow Building. Sab showed me his first paycheque as something he couldn't quite believe ... $11.75. He's been there for an awful long time. Eiko sleeps in a partitioned stall, she being on the staff, so to speak. This stall was the former home of a pair of stallions and boy oh boy, did they leave their odour behind. The whole place is impregnated with the smell of ancient manure and maggots. Every other day it is swept with dichloride of lime or something, but you can't disguise horse smell, cow smell, sheeps and pigs and rabbits and goats. And is it dusty! The toilets are just a sheet metal trough, and up till now they did not have partitions or seats. The women kicked so they put up partitions and a terribly makeshift seat. Twelve year old boys stay with the women too. The auto show building, where there was also the Indian exhibit, houses the new dining room and kitchens. Seats 3000. Looks awfully permanent. Brick stoves, 8 of them, shining new mugs ... very very barrack-y. As for the bunks, they were the most tragic things I saw there. Steel and wooden frames with a thin lumpy straw tick, a bolster, and three army blankets of army quality ... no sheets unless you bring your own. These are the "homes" of the women I saw. They wouldn't let me into the men's building. There are constables at the doors … no propagation of the species … you know … it was in the papers. These bunks were hung with sheets and blankets and clothes of every hue and variety, a regular gipsy tent of colours, age, and cleanliness, all hung with the pathetic attempt at privacy. Here and there I saw a child's doll and teddy bear … I saw babies lying there beside a mother who was too weary to get up … she had just thrown herself across the bed … I felt my throat thicken … an old old lady was crying, saying she would rather have died than have come to such a place … she clung to Eiko and cried and cried. Eiko has taken the woes of the confinees on her thin shoulders and she took so much punishment she went to her former rooms and couldn't stop crying. Fumi was so worried about her. Eiko is really sick. The place has got her down. There are ten showers for 1500 women. Hot and cold water. The men looked so terribly at loose ends, wandering around the grounds, sticking their noses through the fence watching the golfers, lying on the grass. Going through the place I felt so depressed that I wanted to cry. I'm damned well not going there. They are going to move the Vancouver women first now and shove them into the Pool before sending them to the ghost towns.

… The other day at the Pool, someone dropped his key before a stall in the Livestock Building, and he fished for it with a long wire and brought to light rotted manure and maggots!!! He called the nurse and then they moved all the bunks from the stalls and pried up the wooden floors. It was the most stomach-turning nauseating thing. They got fumigators and tried to wash it all away and got most of it into the drains, but maggots still breed and turn up here and there. One woman with more guts than the others told the nurse (white) about it and protested. She replied: "Well, there's worms in the garden aren't there?" This particular nurse was a Jap-hater of the most virulent sort. She called them "filthy Japs" to their faces and Eiko gave her "what-for" and Fumi had a terrible scrap with her, both girls saying: "What do you think we are? Are we cattle? Are we pigs you dirty-so-and-so!" You know how Fumi gets. The night the first bunch of Nisei were supposed to go to Schreiber and they wouldn't, the women and children at the Pool milled around in front of their cage, and one very handsome mountie came with his truncheon and started to hit them, yelling at them, "Get the hell back in there." Eiko's blood boiled over. She strode over to him and shouted at him: "You put that stick down! What do you think you're doing! Do you think these women and children are so many cows that you can beat them back into their place?" Eiko was shaking mad and raked him with fighting words. She has taken it on her to fight for the poor people there, and now she is on the black list and reputed to be a trouble-maker. Just like Tommy and Kunio. I wish I too could go in there and fight and slash around. It's people like us who are the most hurt ... people like us, who have had faith in Canada, and who have been more politically minded than the others, who have a hearty contempt for the whites.

By the way, we got a letter from Uncle ... or rather Auntie got it. He's the gardener, and has to grow vegetables and flowers on the side. Takashima is cook and gets $50 clear. Uncle only nets about $10. All cards and letters are censored, even to the Nisei camps. Not a word about sit-downs, gambaruing or anything makes the papers. It's been hushed. Good thing for us. l wondered why I didn't read about it. I haven't been to meetings so long now that I don't know what's going on. Uncle's camp is 8 miles from the station up into the hills. Men at the first camps all crowd down to the station every time a train passes with the Nationals and hang onto the windows asking for news from home. Uncle said he wept.

But the men are luckier than the women. They are fed, they work, they have no children to look after. Of course the fathers are awfully worried about their families. But it's the women who are burdened with all the responsibility of keeping what's left of the family together. Frances went to Revelstoke, bag and baggage and baby. When I heard that I felt choked with envy, and felt more trapped than ever. Eiko tells me: "Don't you dare bring the kids into the Pool." And Mr. Maikawa says Greenwood is worse. They are propping up the old shacks near the mine shaft. Sab went through there and says it's awful. The United Church parson there says of the Japs "Kick them all out." Sab knows his son who had the room next to him at Union College. Vic and George Saito and family went to the beet fields. Sadas are going tonight. They are going to hell on earth, and will be so contracted that they cannot leave the place or move. Whites will not go there.

I pray that Kath and Mom are safe. Mom's got to live through this. Now that Japan proper has been bombed they will come here.

Sab told me his father has applied to get to Winnipeg or to Toronto. Sab is hoping to get to Queens.

Eiko, Eumi and I, and all of us, have gotten to be so profane that Tom and the rest of them have given up being surprised. Eiko starts out with "what the hell" ... and Eumi comes out with worse. It sure relieves our pent-up feelings. Men are lucky they can swear with impunity.

On account of those fool Nisei who have bucked the gov't, ... our name is mud ... the rest of us who are really conscientious and loyal will never have a chance to become integrated with this country. It's damnable. All we have fought for and won inch by inch has gone down the drain. More than the Nationals, our name is mud. There's over 140 Nisei loose, and many Nationals. The Commission thinks the Nationals are cleared but oh boy there are a lot of them who have greased enough palms and are let alone....

2.5 "WE'LL FIGHT FOR HOME," 1942

The tide of panic, starting from irresponsible agitators, threatens to engulf the good sense of the people of British Columbia. The daily press is flooded with "letters to the editor" demanding the indiscriminate internment of all people of Japanese blood, alien or Canadian-born; demanding the immediate confiscation of our right to work as we like, our right to live like decent human beings. One and all, they add the height of sardonic cynicism: if we are as loyal as we say we are, then we ought to understand why we ought to be treated like poison.

If we were less Canadian, less steeped in the tradition of justice and fair play, perhaps we could understand and bow our heads before this strange, undemocratic baiting of thousands of innocent people.

For the very reason that our Grade School teachers, our High School teachers, and our environment have bred in us a love of country, a loyalty to one's native land, faith in the concepts of traditional British fair play, it is difficult to understand this expression of a mean narrow-mindedness, an unreasoning condemnation of a long suffering people. We cannot understand why our loyalty should be questioned.

After all, this is our only home, where by the sweat of our endeavours we have carved a bit of security for ourselves and our children. Would we sabotage our own home? Would we aid anyone who menaces our home, who would destroy the fruits of our labour and our love? People who talk glibly of moving us wholesale "East of the Rockies," who maintain that it is an easy task, overlook with supreme indifference the complex human character.

They do not think what it would mean to be ruthlessly, needlessly uprooted from a familiar homeground, from friends, and sent to a labour camp where most likely the decencies will be of the scantiest in spite of what is promised. They do not think that we are not cattle to be herded wherever it pleases our ill-wishers. They forget, or else it does not occur to them, that we have the same pride and self-respect as other Canadians, who can be hurt beyond repair. In short, they do not consider us as people, but as a nuisance to be rid of at the first opportunity. What excuse they use is immaterial to them. It just happens to be very opportune that Japan is now an active enemy.

We have often been accused of taking the bread out of "white" folks' mouths. Is there anything against the right to enjoy what one has earned? Our little trades and professions ... what golden loot for our would-be despoilers! No wonder they drool to get at them. These hard-earned, well-deserved small successes ... for out of the total of our enterprises, how many are there that can be classed as wealth? So few!

"Man's inhumanity to man makes countless thousands mourn."

Right here in British Columbia is a God-sent opportunity for the government and the people to practise democracy as it is preached. Not in panicky persecutions that do no one any good but with sensible belief in our very real harmlessness, and consideration for us as a much-maligned people.

Ye gods! Can they not see that we love our home and would fight to protect it from the invader!

3. "And Then Registration"

Author unknown. Journalist and editor Barry Broadfoot collected oral histories from many Japanese Canadians and published them in 1977 as Years of Sorrow, Years of Shame: The Story of Japanese Canadians in World War II *(Toronto: Doubleday, 1977).*

Well, they said that every Japanese or Canadian of Japanese race had to be registered. Now why didn't that tip off our leaders, or if they knew, why didn't they warn us what was going on? It was because they were gutless or just plain stupid. This was in the spring of '41. Pearl Harbor wasn't to come along for months. In December. December 7.

Why did I, and my wife, why did we have to tell the R.C.M.P. all about us, where we were born, our ages, how many children, who they were, where our farm was, what we did? All these things. Why?

Our leaders said, "Okay, go and be registered. That will show the Canadian authorities that you are loyal." What I should have said, although nobody was thinking right in those days, was that I am a Canadian and no other Canadian is being registered this way, so what is this all about? No, we just went and were registered.

I know why it was. Everybody hated us. They hated us for what our fathers had done. My father told me that in the big sockeye run of 1901, when he'd been in Canada just one year, and there were so many fish that all the fishermen in Canada couldn't catch what was running up the Fraser, even then he got bashed on the head because he was catching white man's fish. They hated my old man forty years before Pearl Harbor. Or when we'd go into Woodward's on Hasting Street there, my wife and me, and there'd be three clerks behind a counter, say at the meat counter, and finally—one would come up and serve us and act real snotty as if to say, "Why don't you stay in japtown?"

They hated us for,—well, because we were good—fishermen and farmers and we minded our own business and said to let us alone. A fellow came up to me one day when I was in the yard and said, "Why do you paint your house every two years?" and I said I did because I liked it neat and clean and he said, "You goddamned rotten jap." What can you do with people like that?

So when they registered us, and they didn't register the Germans and the Italians, everybody said it doesn't matter. It is war. Well, you know why they registered us. Because they knew there was war coming with Japan. I'll bet King and Roosevelt knew that. And they wanted to know who we all were and who we were and what we were doing. Then they could jump in with both feet and grab us—and that's just what they did.

You went and you had to produce your Canadian birth certificate or, like my father, his naturalization papers, and they took your picture, your fingerprint, and gave you a serial number. From then on, as it turned out, in relocation, when they dealt with you it was always your name and then your serial number. You were a number to them. They gave you a card and if you didn't carry it, even all the kids under sixteen who were registered by their parents, there could be a fine. I don't know if there ever was. The card was yellow. That must have been old King's joke, eh? Yellow Peril, yellow registration. But pink if you were born in Canada. Just yellow if you were not naturalized. But a joke just the same.

And any time one wanted, a cop could stop you and ask for your registration. I was picked up speeding on my motorcycle once at Hastings and Commercial, and the cop wanted my identification. I gave him my licence and he wanted my registration. I wanted to know why and he told me to button my lip. If I hadn't had that registration I might have been in real trouble and if I had no registration—and I mean none at all—I could have been in the hoosegow.

Why didn't people protest? Because, damn it all, at the time it didn't seem like much. But if you asked yourself why didn't the Germans get the same business, why didn't the Italians? Why—just us? What have we done? Was there one damn thing we did that would make them think we were going to blow up their damned bridges? No, not one thing, and all the investigations they ever had before and since proved that. There was not one thing of sabotage or going to the enemy by one Japanese Canadian or non-Canadian Japanese before that war or during the war. They turned the hose on some stupid guards down at the immigration Hall once, but that was all. A few yelling sessions at the road camps up in the Rockies because of poor food. Hell, I've had guys who were in the army tell me they had real riots over little things. Half the guys would be in jail.

No, there never was anything about the Japanese that would make them feel we were a menace. Just Reid from New Westminster and that other Member of Parliament from the island, those two yelling off. Boy, they must have laughed their fool heads off.

The only time I can remember anybody protesting was when the Japanese Canadian Citizens' League, the JCCL, sent a telegram to Ottawa, to King, saying registration was discrimination. I'll bet the old bastard never even saw it. Somebody else answered it. Anyway, nothing happened about it. By protest, I mean a big rally on Powell Street or in front of the city hall and people protesting. We had newspapers then. Three of them. I don't remember any of them yelling hard enough. Not so I was hearing anyway.

No, everything was kind of mixed up in those days and when our leaders told us to go get our registration cards we went. Mommas and daddies, the old ones, everybody.

Now I ask you, like you take today, if you were Mexican and all of a sudden the government said every Mexican has to be photographed and fingerprinted and given a serial number, wouldn't you think something was very wrong? Damned right you would. You'd call it discrimination and everybody, the NDP, the churches, the universities, everybody, would be yelling for Trudeau's scalp. But just a lot of those dirty Japs. Huh! Nobody cared. Not even us, far as I could see.

4. "Long Before Pearl Harbor"

Author unknown. Journalist and editor Barry Broadfoot collected oral histories from many Canadians and published them as Ten Lost Years 1929-1939: Memoirs of Canadians Who Survived the Depression *(Toronto: McClelland and Stewart, 1973).*

I was born in Vancouver in 1902 so I have the advantage of looking at the problem from three sides—from my parents' side because they were born in Japan, and from my side as a Canadian, and third, also from dealing with Japanese and Canadian people all those years.

People really know nothing of our problem. They only think of the evacuation of the people, the 27,000 people, in 1942. A terrible thing, people say. Too bad. Yes. Yes, but a good thing too. It broke up the ghetto concentration of the

Japanese people around Vancouver, they moved to the Interior, to the prairies, to Toronto and they began new lives. They began new careers. They became successful.

The non-Japanese think that the attack on Pearl Harbor…, the declaration of war, the British and American and Canadian involvement in the Pacific war was the reason for the evacuation of March, 1942, and the internment camps. No, that was not the whole reason. That was the excuse. The decision to move the people out had been made before that. The decision had actually been made in 1940 and the studies to arrive at this conclusion had begun years earlier. In the 1930's, the Japanese government's war on China had been the excuse then and the politicians were just waiting for the right time. The Pearl Harbor attack was the perfect excuse.

If you look underneath it all, back of it all, it was economic. You see, we were Japanese. Canadians, but still Japanese. Look at Our size. Small, aren't we? Our skin. Dark. Not white. We weren't white men. Only about half spoke English, and while there were thousands of German and Italian and Chinese and even French in British Columbia who couldn't read a newspaper in English, we were in the wrong because we were Japanese.

It goes back into the 1880's when we first came. We didn't segregate ourselves. The whites, what you would call the red necks, the politicians, they segregated us. We set up our own schools because how else could our children learn? Our own churches, Christian, but also our own religion, yes. Newspaper. Meeting halls. Restaurants, hotels. Stores. Where else could we get our food, the things our old people wanted, the food that was favorable to our diet? Yes, we became a ghetto.

A Japanese is a good fisherman. There is something about fishing which makes him good or better than anyone. The whites, through laws and pressure, tried to force us out of the fishing through the Twenties and Thirties. Our women could work in the cannery because they were· so fast and efficient, not because they were wanted as Canadians. Even the Chinese were against us. Naturally so, I guess. Old hatreds stretch back through the centuries.

We moved into the woods to work, and laws and brutality forced us out. Farms. The Japanese are excellent farmers. Vegetables. Each little plant is treated with care, with tenderness, fertilized and watered. If we had the land, we could not be forced out. A farm which might support two families would have six, and everybody worked from dawn to dark and there, that was the way vegetable prices were kept so low. The same with stores. Wholesaling, tailoring, laundries. Undercut the white competition. You had to survive. Live in the back of the stores, three or four families in two or three rooms.

It was the whites who forced the Japanese into this position where the white businessman could no longer compete. The Japanese was forced into the worst kind of labor.

Do you know that the 1930's, the period you are asking about, most of the Japanese in British Columbia were Canadian citizens. Born in Canada. Canadian citizens. But we couldn't do this and we couldn't do that. First, we couldn't vote. Yes, we couldn't vote. A Japanese man with a doctor's degree couldn't serve in the provincial legislature, and neither could the market gardener. No Japanese could. Or be an alderman, or a school trustee. You couldn't be a hand logger or a lawyer. Not a druggist. You couldn't work for the government either, even with a shovel on the roads. You couldn't serve on a jury. You don't think this is possible? It is.

I don't say there was all that hatred by all the people but this was the Depression, and things hadn't really been too good in the province for years anyway, and people saw the Japanese-Canadians as a threat. An economic threat. Somebody who just might, just might take a dollar a week out of your pocket by being a sharper businessman, a harder farm worker, a faster stuffer in a cannery. And I don't need to tell you, it doesn't have to go much further than that to translate this economic fear into action. What kind of action? Political action. Kick them out.

A report called the Special Committee on Orientals in British Columbia was published in autumn of 1940, *a year before* Pearl Harbor. This report said there was a great hatred of the Japanese by the whites in British Columbia. The report could not back up its findings with any specific instances, just that there was a great hatred. They said the Japanese were underselling, undercutting their white Canadian competitors. What is competition all about? What we have in the supermarkets now? Do you call that competition? That is monopoly. The report also talked about great smuggling of Japanese nationals in to Canada through B.C., and they talked about spies mapping the coast. This was proved over and over again to be rubbish, so what they came up with was that the Japanese had to be protected from the whites. So they must all be kept in a position of surveillance, watched by the authorities, registered. No military training, because they were not to be trusted. You see what this did, don't you? When the war with the Japanese did come along, the Japanese were all lined up, so to speak, located, numbered, marked, ready to go.

One thing to be said for the committee, its members were not unanimous, but the anti-Japanese obviously were in the majority.

You will have a hard time convincing any Japanese of my generation that all this was not economic, that those whose ox was being gored were not screaming the loudest. A shameful, disgraceful period, and the true story still has to be told. But, shameful as it was, the Japanese accepted it with courage and honor and for that, more credit to them all. For many, as I've said before, it did open up a whole new world, but that was a fortunate end result.

It was never my intention to mean that all the white people were bad, or against us. That definitely was not the case. But that type were there in sufficient number and they made enough noise and the time was ready for them, and there were enough politicians who saw in it a means of getting votes. And this, mind you, at a time when from the docks of New Westminster and Vancouver ship loads of scrap iron were being sent to Japan, and the politicians knew that metal would be used in munitions and that Japan had lined up with Italy and Germany as an ally. That's a politician for you. There are still a few of these men around. I wonder if they have changed. If the faction of West Coast Canadians who were against us in those days had had their way, our children and grandchildren would still be working in coal mines. As slaves.

5. K. Miyazaki, "Memoirs"

Koichiro Miyazaki (1902–78) was a Japanese-born intellectual and teacher living within the 100-mile exclusion zone in British Columbia. He was among the few to become prisoners of war rather than voluntarily be relocated. First incarcerated with other "enemy aliens" at Camp Petawawa, Ontario, he was later transferred with 700 others to Angler Prisoner of War Camp on the north shore of Lake Superior. The camp originally housed German POWs, but became an internment camp for men of Japanese ancestry in 1942. Camp inmates were not released until 1946. No other information is available on Mr. Miyazaki.

My wife remained silent. Soon the radio began to announce the sinking of the battleships Arizona and Utah. Then there was a special announcement telling all off-duty soldiers to get in touch with their regiments immediately. I felt the hustle and bustle of the war. I felt like myself again. Strangely, I felt very light and almost began whistling. Images of the mighty war planes, the bright red rising sun on their flanks as they flew over the Pacific, came to mind. This must be the turning point for the Japanese nation. This thought broke the peaceful silence of Sunday.

For a while I thought about nothing but Japan. I must have forgotten about Canada. It might have been an instinctive reaction nurtured by the many years of discrimination I had suffered here.

That night I could not sleep. All the years I had spent in Canada came flooding back to me. They were all dry, dark and tasteless, like dead leaves. I realized that I had accumulated years without achieving any of the goals that I had set when I left Japan. The faces of my homeland came back to me. The silhouette of Hawaii on the horizon was still fresh in my mind. As a child I had always been told of the inevitability of war and now it was really happening. Fate, I thought. I also remembered those episodes where the Japanese people became angry with Americans prohibiting immigration from Japan and that there were those who swore to take revenge on Americans. The bloody drama between Japan and America which had become popularized among the common people was now to become a reality. Wasn't it an irony of destiny that I was going to experience it in this corner of the American continent?

Accept fate. Yes, that's right. Now that the Japanese nation was gambling with its fate, I too had to throw in my cards. Gambling is a matter of win or lose, I had to win. I would, without fear, bear the name of enemy alien and stand on the Canadian battle front. Yes, this was my fate. As an enemy alien I would be branded and deprived of my freedom. But nobody could take away the freedom and the desire to become a dignified enemy alien. This was my only strategy to fight my war, although highly impractical, I would cling to it for dear life.... I felt terrible that all my thoughts about the war overwhelmed my will power to the point that I couldn't sleep.

I worried about my colleagues being affected by my inevitable arrest, so I resigned from the school, cutting those ties. I sorted through my possessions in preparation for this eventuality. Since I was expecting to be arrested any day, I lived in continual anxiety. I threw the political posters and pamphlets I had obtained in Japan as well as some other useless things I had, into the furnace. I spent half a day watching them turn to ash. I abused my nerves, expecting the worst, as if I was a Japanese spy. I was supposed to be preparing for a house search but the Mounties did not come quickly.

I felt I was in the shadows of normal society. It was March and spring was in full bloom. I felt the forced evacuation getting closer to me, as if I were being slowly suffocated. Japanese men of military age were being slowly rounded up and sent off to the snowy mountains. I was waiting for my turn. In my mind I knew I wouldn't be a pushover who would volunteer to go to a road camp for the sake of a pseudo-democracy. If the real reason for "evacuating" the Japanese had been to protect them from violent mobs, they should have established special camps for the enemy aliens as was stipulated by international law. To me the idea of work camps were a smoke screen. I would prefer to live under the strict conditions imposed on prisoners of war. By living this way I would feel more connected to the war. Thus my mind was leaning toward refusing to go to work in a road camp.

After a while the officer in street clothes came and took me to another room. There he told me once more to go to the camp, but I refused. He took my watch, pen, wallet, gloves, cigarettes, and matches and put them in a big paper bag before bringing me back to the cell.

For the first time I had become reduced to a man devoid of freedom and property. The first forty years of my life came to an end. I didn't feel that I was a victim of the war but rather of my own personality. This is, I thought, a man flirting with his own fate. In my black suit I must look like a bear pacing around the cell. How would my wife and child feel if they saw me? Those men who are departing for the camps tonight must be busy packing. And after all, what is it for, that I am locked up? As my thoughts wandered I felt dizzy, I was hungry and out of cigarettes. I felt a pain in my back and my legs felt numb. The guard looked bored. He peered through a window into the hall and talked with people passing by but he never spoke to me. I thought he might be waiting for me to speak to him but I remained as silent and closed as an oyster. His soft eyes purposefully avoided my hateful, burning eyes.

April 29, 1942

Cloudy. From eight-thirty in the morning we held a worship ceremony of Tencho-setsu [the Emperor's birthday]. We all saluted while watching the sun dance into a new day over the birch forest and we sang Kimigayo [Japan's national anthem]. It was a solemn moment and I felt very refreshed. This was to be one of the most memorable Tenchosetsu for me to have the honour of celebrating.

November 19, 1942

The temperature went up again. I finally received my wife's first letter from Slocan. I can only imagine the very uncomfortable life there. They only have candlelight, so I can picture what the rest of their life is like. Do the authorities still insist that this is to protect Japanese Canadians? Wouldn't it be better under the banner of "persecution." Even in wartime, how can they justify treating civilians and especially women and children, with such cruelty? When the big Japanese victory comes, the people doing this will have to answer for their actions.

Reika's letter was enclosed. I was so surprised to see how good her handwriting is. The way the letters lined up was very impressive. It was also the first time that my wife's letter was cut up by the censors. I am curious to know which words they deemed as dangerous.

December 7, 1942

Clear. This is the anniversary of the beginning of the war between Japan, Britain and the United States. Our new fate began exactly a year ago today, and also that day Japan chose its new destiny. In our proud 2,600 years of history this was the day that changed the face of our nation. It is the day when our great nation asserted itself against the white race. We Japanese who are overseas, have been isolated in enemy countries and our families are scattered. But despite our hardships we believe that everything is for our native country's future. This faith keeps me going. I believe that I am not the only one filled with confidence. I sent a short note to my wife with my feeling on this important day. After morning role call we had one minute of silence and then sang Kimigayo, our national anthem. Our hut leader, Mr. I. made a short speech. I wonder what my eighty-one fellow hut members were thinking and feeling.

January 1, 1943

The New Year began with a mild and fine day. The snow sparkled in the sunshine. I thought, this might be my first New Year's Day spent in such a peaceful and natural environment; then the next moment I realized how unnatural it is for me to be here during the war. I felt like laughing yet I didn't want to laugh. It is a strange New Year with strangely mixed-up feelings. Under the hut leader's orders we worshipped the Emperor before roll call while singing the Japanese national anthem. Images of my country, my family, and my wife and child passed before me. Beer was sold at 10:00. It's so cold that I didn't feel like drinking, yet my legs carried me there. One bottle managed to make me feel warmer and began to put me in a New Year's mood. People greeted one another: *Omedeto*, Happy New Year. I returned to the hut and lay down on the bed. I could not stop thinking about the cheerful and hectic atmosphere of past New Year's and of busily preparing for the occasion. It made me feel nostalgic. Without visitors and with nothing to do the day is meaningless, so I just relaxed without thinking about anything.

December 1, 1943

This is the second December spent in an internment camp. I am watching the white snowflakes dancing outside. Even that makes me feel helpless. I eat, sleep, get up and simply pray for the safety of my wife and child and for Japan's victory. I know that this is my fate and the path that I have chosen. Knowing that I still feel split and dissatisfied. I simply wish to live silently without complaints but sometimes I cannot help complaining. Received a letter from Yoshiko filled with pessimism.

December 31, 1943

A clear sky and the temperature is high. This is the last day of 1943. Many changes occurred in my life this year. Since she has given up hope about going back to Japan by POW exchanges, my wife has become depressed and pessimistic. Her last ray of hope is gone. Since August, most of her letters have been filled with hateful words. She left a ghost town, travelled more than a thousand miles to Montreal to end up as a housemaid. How ironic that she, who grew up spoiled in a good family, became a maid. It is a sad story, yet this too is one phase of our life. I have been trying with all my insight to console her. I am a short-tempered person but I tried hard to control myself to continue writing to her. And I feel that it was the wind of the time that drove me to do so. I have been reading news articles that report how the Allies are winning as demonstrated by Italy's surrender. That only adds to the confusion I feel. Even when I discount the Allied propaganda, it's still very hard to see the light in this war. As the saying goes, the sun is setting and there's still a long way to go along the road. I also have to admit that I could not accomplish my studies as I had planned. I started with lots of energy and determination but it didn't last too long. I know how stupid it is to waste time in such a place and I feel unhappy with myself for not making an effort to change. But another year has come to an end. Time does not wait. A profound truth.

FURTHER READINGS

Adachi, K. *The Enemy That Never Was: A History of the Japanese Canadians*. Toronto: McClelland and Stewart, 1976.

Broadfoot, B. *Years of Sorrow, Years of Shame: The Story of the Japanese Canadians in World War Two*. Toronto: Doubleday, 1977.

Granatstein, J. *A Man of Influence: Norman A. Robertson and Canadian Statecraft, 1929–68*. Ottawa: Deneau, 1981.

Granatstein, J. "The Enemy Within." *Saturday Night* (November 1986). In *Readings in the History of British Columbia*, ed. J. Barman and A. McDonald. Richmond: Open University, 1989.

Hillmer, N., B. Kordan, and L. Luciuk, Eds. *On Guard for Thee: War, Ethnicity, and the Canadian State 1939-1945*. Ottawa: Canadian Committee for the History of the Second World War, 1988.

Miki, R., and C. Kobayashi. *Justice in Our Times: The Japanese Canadian Redress Settlement*. Vancouver: Talon, 1991.

Omatsu, M. *Bittersweet Passage: Redress and the Japanese Canadian Experience*. Toronto: Between the Lines, 1992.

Roy, P. *The Triumph of Citizenship: The Japanese and Chinese in Canada, 1941-1967*. Vancouver: University of British Columbia Press, 2007.

Roy, P., M. Iino, and H. Takamura. *Mutual Hostages: Canadians and Japanese during the Second World War*. Toronto: University of Toronto Press, 1990.

Sunahara, A. *The Politics of Racism: The Uprooting of the Japanese Canadians during the Second World War*. Toronto: James Lorimer, 1981.

Ward, W. "British Columbia and the Japanese Evacuation." *Canadian Historical Review* 57, 3 (September 1976): 289-308.

Ward, W. *White Canada Forever: Popular Attitudes and Public Policy Toward Orientals in British Columbia*. Montreal and Kingston: McGill-Queen's University Press, 1978.

CHAPTER 10

"Cinderella of the Empire"

NEWFOUNDLAND AND CONFEDERATION

INTRODUCTION

To federate or not? That was the question Newfoundlanders faced when they voted in the July 22, 1948 referendum whether to join with Canada. Their answer proved even more ambiguous than expected: 52.34 per cent supported Newfoundland as Canada's tenth province; 47.66 per cent voted against. In a democratic system, the returns were sufficient for Newfoundland to take its place in Confederation, but to suggest that there was much enthusiasm for the marriage would be naïve or willfully blind. Nor has time muted Newfoundland's reticence. Anger toward the rest of Canada periodically explodes on "The Rock." The decision to join Canada in 1949 was a matter of most Newfoundlanders holding their collective noses and accepting what they perceived as inevitable.

The July referendum was the second vote on the same issue. The first, held the previous month, offered Newfoundlanders three choices: regain semi-independent responsible government such as they had for many years in the past; join Canada as a province like any other; or continue the unhappy Commission of Government then ruling Newfoundland directly from Britain. Voters overwhelmingly rejected the last choice, a mere 23,311 supporting it. That was hardly surprising. The Commission of Government was a caretaker administration that took over when the colony slid toward bankruptcy as a result of the Great Depression. People wanted to forget that episode as quickly as possible and to regain both economic self-sufficiency and their former measure of autonomy. Confederationists came out second best in the election, with 64,066 votes to 69,400 for responsible government. Based upon Newfoundlanders' democratic wishes, it looked as though Newfoundland would become an autonomous Dominion in the Gulf of St. Lawrence. In the end, however, most of those who initially voted for the status quo became confederationists on the second ballot—but not without considerable prodding.

Newfoundland's reticence to join Canada was hardly surprising considering its unique historical development outside the experience of the rest of North America. Being part of the British Empire and sharing the same continent, sort of, were arguably the only things uniting Newfoundlanders to Canada, and if we must join somebody, many islanders proclaimed, let it be the United States with whom we have more in common and more ties. Most Newfoundland settlers, with their maritime Gaelic, Irish, and English roots, turned their backs on the North American continent from the moment they arrived and always faced the rolling Atlantic and distant Europe. There lay their prosperity, their sense of history and community, and their futures. Newfoundlanders' Canadian compatriots on the mainland, on the other hand, looked westward or, in the case of French Canadians, inward. Neither looked toward the other.

The problem, however, was that Newfoundland possessed neither the population nor resources to prosper independently. The fishing industry, though healthy, was simply insufficient and there was little else. Britain provided most of the island's funding, and Newfoundland's standard of living languished at poverty levels as the rest of North America flourished. British taxpayers, meanwhile, resented the interminable bills and called for their government to cast The Rock adrift. Newfoundlanders saw the writing on the wall well before World War II, particularly during the calamitous Depression era that cut a bitter swath of social deprivation through the colony. Things had to change. Then, in 1939 and in their moment of despair, Newfoundland miraculously found itself in a strategically critical location. It served as a vital staging post for Atlantic convoys during World War II and acted as the easternmost point jutting into the Atlantic from which Canadian and American patrol aircraft attempted to keep the sea lanes free of U-boats. The United States leased huge military bases for 99-year terms, and thousands of Canadian soldiers and sailors milled about St. John's, preparing to embark for Europe or patrol duty, and spending freely—as did their governments. The Newfoundland economy reignited, and Newfoundlanders concluded that they could indeed support themselves. The problem was, of course, that the boom was artificial and would presumably bust with the armistice. Contingency plans had to be made.

Islanders and island administrators had long wrestled with Newfoundland's future, and the idea of federation with Canada was not new. While one maritime province after the other joined the Canadian federation in the late 1860s and 1870s, Newfoundland hesitated. Newfoundlanders wanted to steer their own course, and Canada's obvious reticence to welcome them into the federation partnership discouraged any courtship between them. Most Canadians knew little about Newfoundland and probably cared less. Newfoundland was, according to the stereotype, a foggy rock in the Atlantic inhabited by vaguely odd fishermen who spoke peculiar English, drank "Screech," and served as the butt of jokes. Not much allure there. Pragmatic Canadians also feared that Newfoundland's precarious financial situation would become a liability to the rest of Canada if it were to federate. Perhaps Canada's sole benefit from a merger was Newfoundland's strategic position as the guardian of the Gulf of St. Lawrence. That, however, was not much of an incentive since The Rock was a brother member of the British Commonwealth and would act as a friendly sentinel regardless. Thus, the average Canadian believed the disadvantages outweighed the advantages of Newfoundland joining Canada.

Newfoundlanders decided to tackle the issue of their future head-on in a National Convention, which was to be convened in September 1946 and which was to issue a final report with recommendations by 1948. Evidence supports the charge that pro-confederationists, led by Joseph Smallwood, quickly hijacked the Convention and split it into two irreconcilable camps. The pro-confederationists headed to Ottawa in 1947 to negotiate Newfoundland's entry into Canada, while anti-confederationists set off the same year for London to try to prevent it. The former succeeded, and the latter felt deeply embittered by the lack of support they received from Westminster. The Colonial Office told the anti-confederationists in no uncertain terms that if they wished to return to their former responsible government, wherein Newfoundland ruled itself, islanders must pay their own way and would not be helped out by the Mother Country. The delegates to London perceived this as blackmail and collusion with Canada.

Was anti-confederationist paranoia legitimate? Newfoundlanders certainly resented Canadian condescension and feared that Canada, patronizing as it was, would absorb Newfoundland and use it as it saw fit with little consideration for islanders' wishes. The very democratic process that finally brought Newfoundland into Confederation also posed a significant threat. Newfoundland's population, tiny in relation to the rest of Canada, could easily be outvoted and ignored in future federal elections. Thus, islanders feared that their distinct and cherished culture could be legislated out of existence once Newfoundland joined Canada. This suspicion deepened during the negotiation process when Newfoundlanders, with good reason, concluded that a conspiracy existed between Britain and Canada to bring the island into Confederation regardless of local opinion.

In 1948 Newfoundlanders voted to join Canada with the slimmest margin after a tumultuous and nasty campaign riddled with dubious campaign tactics and unscrupulous behaviour on all sides. Nor did Canadians have the opportunity to accept or reject Newfoundland's bid to join them. The merger was a *fait accompli* once the "yes" side won on The Rock. Today the Parti Québécois argues that a simple majority of Quebec voters is sufficient to take their province out the Canadian federation, while the federal government argues that all Canadians have a right to decide on the disintegration of Canada and that support for secession must come from a significant majority. Thus Newfoundland's case provides an intriguing contradictory precedent.

DISCUSSION POINTS

1. Was it in the interest of Newfoundland's inhabitants to join Canada in 1949?

2. If the benefits to joining Canada were so obvious, why did such a large percentage of Newfoundlanders oppose federation?

3. Who was more nationalistic: Cashin or Smallwood?

DOCUMENTS

1. Newfoundland National Convention Debates, 1946-48

The Newfoundland National Convention was convened in September 1946. Forty-five representatives were popularly elected from 38 districts of Newfoundland and then subdivided into 10 sub-committees, which compiled reports and recommendations on various aspects of Newfoundland life. The Convention as a whole voted on those ten reports, and its Finance Committee then created a final report based upon the delegates' wishes.

1.1 JOSEPH R. SMALLWOOD

Newfoundlander Joseph "Joey" Roberts Smallwood (1900–91) moved to New York at age 20 to become a journalist, a vocation he continued after returning to The Rock five years later. He established his first newspaper in 1926, entered politics as a Liberal campaign manager in 1928, and ran unsuccessfully for that party in 1932. Through the Depression he worked at various newspapers and in radio, always championing Newfoundland's distinct history. In 1946 Smallwood was elected as a representative to Newfoundland's National Convention, which advised Britain on the colony's future. Smallwood opted for federation with Canada, believing it would bring prosperity. He founded the Confederate Association and in 1947 travelled to Ottawa to negotiate terms for Newfoundland's entry into Canada.

Our people's struggle to live commenced on the day they first landed here, four centuries and more ago, and has continued to this day. The struggle is more uneven now than it was then, and the people view the future now with more dread than they felt a century ago.

The newer conceptions of what life can be, of what life should be, have widened our horizons and deepened our knowledge of the great gulf which separates what we have and are from what we feel we should have and be. We have been taught by newspapers, magazines, motion pictures, radios, and visitors something of the higher standards of well-being of the mainland of North America; we have become uncomfortably aware of the low standards of our country, and we are driven irresistibly to wonder whether our attempt to persist in isolation is the root-cause of our condition. We have often felt in the past, when we learned something of the higher standards of the mainland, that such things belonged to another world, that they were not for us. But today we are not so sure that two yardsticks were designed by the Almighty to measure the standards of well-being: one yardstick for the mainland of the continent; another for this Island which lies beside it. Today we are not so sure, not so ready to take it for granted, that we Newfoundlanders are destined to accept much lower standards of life than our neighbours of Canada and the United States. Today we are more disposed to feel that our manhood, our very creation by God, entitles us to standards of life no lower than those of our brothers on the mainland.

Our Newfoundland is known to possess natural wealth of considerable value and variety. Without at all exaggerating their extent, we know that our fisheries are in the front rank of the world's marine wealth. We have considerable forest, water power, and mineral resources. Our Newfoundland people are industrious, hard-working, frugal, ingenious, and sober. The combination of such natural resources and such people should spell a prosperous country enjoying high standards, Western World standards, of living. This combination should spell fine, modern, well-equipped homes; lots of health-giving food; ample clothing; the amenities of modern New World civilization; good roads, good schools, good hospitals, high levels of public and private health; it should spell a vital, prosperous, progressive country.

It has not spelt any such things. Compared with the mainland of North America, we are fifty years, in some things a hundred years, behind the times. We live more poorly, more shabbily, more meanly. Our life is more a struggle. Our struggle is tougher, more naked, more hopeless. In the North American family, Newfoundland bears the reputation of having the lowest standards of life, of being the least progressive and advanced, of the whole family.

We all love this land. It has a charm that warms our hearts, go where we will; a charm, a magic, a mystical tug on our emotion that never dies. With all her faults, we love her.

But a metamorphosis steals over us the moment we cross the border that separates us from other lands. As we leave Newfoundland, our minds undergo a transformation: we expect, and we take for granted, a higher, a more modern, way of life such as it would have seemed ridiculous or even avaricious to expect at home. And as we return to Newfoundland, we leave that higher standard behind, and our minds undergo a reverse transformation: we have grown so accustomed to our own lower standards and more antiquated methods and old-fashioned conveniences that we readjust ourselves unconsciously to the meaner standards under which we grew up. We are so used to our railway and our coastal boats that we scarcely see them; so used to our settlements, and roads, and homes, and schools, and hospitals and hotels and everything else that we do not even see their inadequacy, their backwardness, their seaminess.

We have grown up in such an atmosphere of struggle, of adversity, of mean times that we are never surprised, never shocked, when we learn that we have one of the highest rates of tuberculosis in the world; one of highest maternity mortality rates in the world; one of the highest rates of beriberi and rickets in the world. We take these shocking facts for granted. We take for granted our lower standards, our poverty. We are not indignant about them. We save our indignation for those who publish such facts, for with all our complacency, with all our readiness to receive, to take for granted, and even to justify these things amongst ourselves, we are, strange to say, angry and hurt when these shocking facts become known to the outside world.

We are all very proud of our Newfoundland people. We all admire their strength, their skill, their adaptability, their resourcefulness, their industry, their frugality, their sobriety, and their warm-hearted, simple generosity. We are proud of them; but are we indignant, does our blood boil, when we see the lack of common justice with which they are treated? When we see how they live? When we witness the long, grinding struggle they have? When we see the standards of their life? Have we compassion in our hearts for them? Or are we so engrossed, so absorbed, in our own struggle to live in this country that our social conscience has become toughened, even case-hardened? Has our own hard struggle to realize a modest competence so blinded us that we have little or no tenderness of conscience left to spare for the fate of the tens of thousands of our brothers so very much worse off than ourselves?

Mr. Chairman, in the present and prospective world chaos, with all its terrible variety of uncertainty, it would be cruel and futile, now that that the choice is ours, to influence the handful of people who inhabit this small Island to attempt independent national existence. The earnings of our 65,000 families may be enough, in the years ahead, to support them half-decently and at the same time support the public services of a fair-sized municipality. But will those earnings support independent national government on an expanding, or even the present, scale? Except for a few years of this war and a few of the last, our people's earnings never supported them on a scale comparable with North American standards, and never maintained a government even on the pre-war scale of service. Our people never enjoyed a good standard of living, and never were able to yield enough taxes to maintain the government. The difference was made up by borrowing or grants-in-aid.

We can indeed reduce our people's standard of living; we can force them to eat and wear and use and have much less than they have; and we can deliberately lower the level of governmental services. Thus we might manage precariously to maintain independent national status. We can resolutely decide to be poor but proud. But if such a decision is made, it must be made by the 60,000 families who would have to do the sacrificing, not the 5,000 families who are confident of getting along pretty well in any case.

We have, I say, a perfect right to decide that we will turn away from North American standards of public services, and condemn ourselves as a people and government deliberately to long years of struggle to maintain even the little that we have. We may, if we wish, turn our backs upon the North American continent beside which God placed us, and resign ourselves to the meaner outlook and shabbier standards of Europe, 2,000 miles across the ocean. We can do this, or we can face the fact that the very logic of our situation on the surface of the globe impels us to draw close to the progressive outlook and dynamic living standards of this continent.

Our danger, so it seems to me, is that of nursing delusions of grandeur. We remember the stories of small states that valiantly preserved their national independence and developed their own proud cultures, but we tend to overlook the fact that comparison of Newfoundland with them is ludicrous. We are not a nation. We are merely a medium-size municipality, a mere miniature borough of a large city. Dr. Carson, Patrick Morris, and John Kent were sound in the first decades of the nineteenth century when they advocated cutting the apron-strings that bound us to the Government of the United Kingdom; but the same love of Newfoundland, the same Newfoundland patriotism, that inspired their agitation then would now, if they lived, drive them to carry the agitation to its logical conclusion of taking the next step of linking Newfoundland closely to the democratic, developing mainland of the New World. There was indeed a time when tiny states lived gloriously. That time is now ancient European history. We are trying to live in the mid-twentieth-century, post-Hitler New World. We are living in a world in which small countries have less chance than ever before of surviving.

We can, of course, persist in isolation, a dot on the shore of North America, ... struggling vainly to support ourselves and our greatly expanded public services. Reminded continually by radio, movie, and visitor of greatly higher standards of living across the Gulf, we can shrug incredulously or dope ourselves into the hopeless belief that such things are not for us. By our isolation from the throbbing vitality and expansion of the continent, we have been left far behind in the march of time, the "sport of historic misfortune" the "Cinderella of the Empire." Our choice now is to continue in blighting isolation or seize the opportunity that may beckon us to the wider horizons and higher standards of unity with the progressive mainland of America.

I am not one of those, if any such there be, who would welcome federal union with Canada at any price. There are prices which I, as a Newfoundlander whose ancestry in this country reaches back for nearly two centuries, am not willing that Newfoundland should pay. I am agreeable to the idea that our country should link itself federally with that great British nation, but I am not agreeable that we should ever be expected to forget that we are Newfoundlanders with a great history and a great tradition of our own. I agree that there may be much to gain from linking our fortunes with that great nation. But I insist that as a self-governing province of the Dominion, we should continue to enjoy the right to our own distinctive culture. I do not deny that once we affiliated with the Canadian federal union, we should in all fairness be expected to extend the scope of our loyalty to embrace the federation as a whole. I do not deny this claim at all, but I insist that as a constituent part of the federation, we should continue to be quite free to hold to our love of our own dear land.

Nor am I one of those, if there be any such, who would welcome union with Canada without regard for the price that the Dominion might be prepared to pay.

I pledge myself to this House and to this country that I will base my ultimate stand in this whole question of Confederation upon the nature of the terms that are laid before the Convention and the country. If the terms are such as clearly to suggest a better Newfoundland for our people, I shall support and maintain them. If they are not of such a nature, I shall oppose them with all the means I can command.

In the price we pay and the price we exact, my only standard of measurement is the welfare of the people. This is my approach to the whole question of federal union with Canada. It is in this spirit that I move this resolution today.

Confederation I will support if it means a lower cost of living for our people. Confederation I will support if it means a higher standard of life for our people. Confederation I will support if it means strength, stability, and security for Newfoundland.

I will support Confederation if it gives us democratic government. I will support Confederation if it rids us of Commission Government. I will support Confederation if it gives us responsible government under conditions that will give responsible government a real chance to succeed. Confederation I will support if it makes us a province enjoying privileges and rights no lower than any other province.

These, then, are the conditions of my support of Confederation: that it must raise our people's standard of living, that it must give Newfoundlanders a better life, that it must give our country stability and security, and that it must give us full, democratic responsible government under circumstances that will ensure its success....

In the name of the people of Bonavista Centre and of thousands of other Newfoundlanders throughout this Island, I move this resolution. I believe that this move will lead to a brighter and happier life for our Newfoundland people. If you adopt this resolution, and Canada offers us generous terms, as I believe she will, and Newfoundland decides to shake off her ancient isolation, I believe with all my heart and mind that the people will bless the day this resolution was moved. With God's grace, let us move forward for a brighter and happier Newfoundland.

I.2 MAJOR P.J. CASHIN

Peter John Cashin (1890-1977) rose to become a major in the British Machine Gun Corps during World War I. Upon returning to Newfoundland, he entered the family fishing supply business, then ran successfully for a seat in the House of Assembly in 1923 and served as Liberal Finance Minister from 1928 to 1932. He hated the Commission of Government and left for Montreal in 1933 when it took over running the colony, not to return until 1942 in order to campaign for the restoration of responsible government. He was elected to the National Convention in 1946 and there, unsurprisingly, championed responsible government. Major Cashin was a passionate and strident anti-confederationist and considered one of the great orators of his day.

... The total federal debt of Canada amounts to over $18 billion, or a per capita debt on every man, woman and child in Canada of $1,492. From information taken from the Report of the Auditor General of Canada, we find that the total interest charge on Canada's national debt is close to $450 million annually, or at the rate of $35 for every Canadian. But just compare this with our own country's finances. Our national debt is roughly $70 million as against Canada's $18 billion. Our per capita debt is $213 as against Canada's $1,492. Our total interest charge, together with sinking fund payments, is $3,375,000 or slightly over $10 per head, as against Canada's $35 per head. Therefore we find that the difference between the national debt of Canada and that of Newfoundland on a per capita basis is approximately $1,200 in excess of ours, which means that if Newfoundland were to become a Canadian province upon the terms offered us, our country would have to become responsible for this extra debt, which would amount to, in all, nearly $400 million as Newfoundland's proportionate share of the entire debt of the Dominion of Canada. It would mean that every man, woman and child in Newfoundland would pay in annual taxes, directly and indirectly, about $230 instead of $120 which is our present per capita tax annually. In all, the people of Newfoundland would have to pay an additional $38-40 million each year in taxation.

But that is not the worst of it. Canada, we are told, in the event of confederation, will be generous enough to take over our sterling debt, which amounts to approximately $64 million. On the face of it, this would look like Canada was giving us something for nothing, but in actuality it is nothing like that. It means that for this $64 million Canada will buy Newfoundland — our railways, public buildings, wharves, lighthouses, telegraph system, docks, steamers and harbours, everything for a paltry $64 million. Why, Mr. Smallwood himself gives the Canadian government the valuation of our railways and its subsidiaries, just one item, as being $72 million. If ever there was a one-sided bargain, this is it. If ever there was a pig-in-a-bag transaction, this is it. ...

This particular feature of the proposals for the union of Newfoundland with Canada is being stressed with every effort by the advocates of confederation. They feel that it is the one bright spot in their annexation platform. They realise that the other terms of union have no basic or solid foundation, and at every opportunity that is afforded them, they try to drill into the minds of our people that once they become a province of Canada all our difficulties will be ended, and the Newfoundland people will at last have entered into a land of milk and honey. They conveniently forget that the taxpayers of the country will be compelled to find these fictitious monies through either direct or indirect taxation. One would imagine to hear some of these people talk, that money is growing on trees. They deliberately try to avoid discussing the present average tax of Canada as compared with the average tax of Newfoundland, which as I have already said, is favourable to Newfoundland in the amount of $110 per head for every man, woman and child in the country. Let me repeat and further emphasize the fact that union with Canada means extra taxation on our people of an additional $35 million annually.

Now let us make a brief review of the Old Age Pension Act as it exists and functions in Canada. A man or woman, to become eligible for this stipend, must be practically a pauper, and then before he or she receives this $30 per month allowance, he or she must assign to the federal government any property or assets they may have; which in the event of death is taken over by the Canadian government and sold in order to repay the federal treasury the amount so paid.

... The people of Canada are raising Cain over the means test. It is wrong to give a man an old age pension if when he dies the government takes his estate, unless he violates a law and has it made over to his successor some years before. It is an inducement to law-breaking. In our Economic Report we outlined a plan whereby we would be in a position to supplement our present old age pension scheme to bring the stipend up to $25 per month. But never in the history of our country, since the old age pension was first instituted some 40 years ago, has the pensioner been compelled to assign or mortgage his properties or assets to the government in order to become eligible for this pension.

Also, with respect to the unemployment insurance scheme now in force in Canada, it is proper that our people should know that those affected or those eligible for recompense under this particular plan, in the event of union with Canada, would not be our primary producers. It does not affect our fishermen, our loggers, our miners, our farmers, our longshoremen or others of the labouring class, and consequently would be of little help to the employed of Newfoundland....

During my recent two weeks in Canada I made enquiries about this whole business, and was invariably told by mining men and other business interests that all Canada wants Newfoundland for is for the iron ore of Labrador, as well as the 50 or 60 million cords of timber which is available there for the manufacture of pulp and paper. Canada today, even though she is in serious financial straits, has great national ambitions for the future. Canada is struggling to be one of the future powers of the world. Canada is sparsely populated. Her per capita population per square mile is less than that of our country. Canada carries a huge national debt, far too great for its present population of something over 12 million people. There is only one redemption for this Dominion to the west of us, and that is increased population. In order that Canada may continue to expand, and equitably place the cost, she must increase her population to not less than 20 million. That is necessary if Canada hopes to survive and develop as a nation. By the inclusion of Newfoundland in the Canadian federation, Canada would be in the position of controlling the steel production of the entire North American continent. This would be her salvation from an economic standpoint. I say that our Labrador possession must be guarded for the future generations of Newfoundland. I realize that strong influences are at work, both governmental and financial, to rob from Newfoundland her God-given rights. We, as a people, owe it to the future generations yet unborn, to guard those interests handed to us by a kindly Providence.

This whole Labrador business looks to me something like the deal made between Russia and the United States ... when Russia sold Alaska for about $7 million. Like Labrador, Alaska was considered a barren wasteland, and the Russians thought they were making a good deal; but hardly was the ink dry on the contract when Russia had the bitter experience of seeing their former territory becoming a land worth billions. Will we, by accepting these proposals made to us by the Canadian government, be guilty of a similar folly? Will we grasp at a few dollars and live to see French Canada take to herself the millions which should be coming to us—and which would have made us one of the richest little countries in the world? What a bitter pill that would be for our children to swallow—what a remorse to carry to our graves—to sacrifice hundreds of millions for a baby bonus!... In addition to paying an annual federal tax of around $230 per annum, every Newfoundlander, will have to find an additional $30 per year in provincial taxation. In all, therefore, the people of the country would have to find over $80 million each year to pay both federal and provincial taxation. In short, the whole thing means that the people of Newfoundland would be taxed to death—that the dole days would be considered luxurious living and opulence in comparison to the manner in which the people of our country would be forced to live in union with Canada....

I am not speaking to hear the sound of my own voice. Nor am I trying to warp the judgement of the delegates to this Convention or the people of the country, or influence their minds with any more airy rhetoric or political spell-binding. My purpose has been, at this time particularly, to give hard, cold facts which cannot be denied or talked away. What I have said emanates from my sincere political belief which is based on the solid and eternal doctrine: first, a country belongs to its people; second, it is the solemn duty of the people of that country to shoulder the responsibility of governing it. Any divergence or avoidance of that doctrine, any excuse for acting contrary to that fundamental truth is cowardly, unethical and immoral. The challenge which faces the people of this country today is the patriotic and moral challenge to do their duty and to face their responsibilities like real men and women. It is a clear-cut issue — as clear and unambiguous as the challenge of right and wrong. But again I say, there are those amongst us who have shown that they are unwilling, or have not the capabilities of facing their responsibilities and accepting obligations of democratic decency. They are prepared instead to assume the garb of mendicants and go begging at the back door of some outside country, asking to be taken in out of the rough world which they fear to face. Like Shakespeare's character, they are prepared to crawl under the huge legs of some foreign colossus and find themselves dishonourable graves. But I know that there are many thousands amongst us who are not prepared to form their opinions on mere moral or ethical grounds. They prefer to deal with matters from a more practical standpoint. They ask for facts. Well, I think I have given them the facts.

In my opinion, Canada is today in a position where she finds she has overreached herself. She reminds me of the frog in the fable who wanted to be as big as a bull and who puffed himself up until he burst. Canada is an ambitious country and in the thirties she got the idea that she wanted to become a big nation. She put on long pants before she became of age. She wanted an army, she wanted a navy and all the trimmings. How she might have gotten on if World War II had not come along we do not know. But like other countries, the blast of war hit her, and today she is left in an exhausted position, struggling for her life, and her financial bloodstream is fast running dry. As I said, she is begging Uncle Sam for dollars and her people are on the rocky road of austerity....

I have lived in Canada and worked there from coast to coast. I like Canada, it is a great country, but after living and working there, I want to give it as an honest opinion, that if confederation were good for Newfoundland there would not be a stronger supporter of it in Newfoundland today, but I am honest in my opinion when I say that confederation will be the worst thing that ever struck Newfoundland.... Canada is in a worse position financially than Newfoundland.... We are not begging for dollars, all we are trying to do is keep people from plundering our treasury. We can sympathize with Canada in her present plight, just as any other allies made prosperous by the war, but nevertheless we must remember that charity begins at home, and our first duty and our first obligation we owe to ourselves, our families, our children and our children's children.... Canada is well aware, as we are, that if she can take over Newfoundland she can richly benefit by our assets. For instance, if she controlled our rich Labrador possession, it would in a few years place her in a position where she could get all these American dollars which she urgently needs....

I would ask you to believe me when I say that I have not said these things merely to make a case for responsible government, or because I am against confederation with Canada. I have made my criticisms against these terms as a Newfoundlander rather than a politician—as a Newfoundlander who sees in them a threat to his people and his country, who sees hidden in their beguiling phrases nothing less than an invitation to national disaster. For I say that I was never as certain of anything in my life, as I am of the worthlessness of these so-called Canadian terms....

To those who, like myself, recognize the fact that the only proper and decent course open to us is to become masters in our own house, no further words of mine are necessary. But to those who may be beguiled to any degree by this confederation mirage, I say do nothing further—make no new steps. Do not consider any negotiations until, as a first step, you have a duly authorized government of your own to consider the whole matter. Any other course is sheer political madness. That is my solemn advice to you. Whether you take it or not rests with yourselves. And if we delegates have failed to carry that one message to the people who sent us here, then I say we have failed dismally in our duty.

In closing I would ask your permission to express a purely personal opinion. I am convinced that although our country and our people are at present enshrouded in a pall of political darkness, they will eventually find their way into the light. This whole matter of bribes and promises will in the end be shown up for what it really is. And I say this not because our people would shrink from the new burden of taxation which confederation with Canada will place on their shoulders, not because of the vision of the thousands of homesteads which may have to be sold to satisfy the Canadian tax gatherers. No. It will not be for these things alone, that our people will spurn this offer for them to sell out the land of their birth. I say our people will win through because of other, greater things. They will triumph, emerge from this ordeal, because there are still in this country such things as pride, courage and faith. Pride in the great traditions which have come down to us through the centuries of independent living. Courage to face up to life and hew out our individual fortunes. And finally faith in our country, and in the great destiny which I am convinced lies ahead of us....

To trifle with a people and a country, to compromise the lives of future generations, are no small things. Yet that is the very thing that is now being attempted, to the end that we shall cease to exist as an independent country, and that Newfoundlanders shall be no longer Newfoundlanders.... Does not all this confederation business come down to a matter of a cold, commercial business deal, whereby we were asked to sell out our country and our future to Canada for a certain sum of money? And speaking of this attitude, I confess it seems to me to be a terribly serious thing for any country or any people to place themselves in the balance against the pull of Canadian dollars. What is the price, or shall I say the bribe, they offer us? The prize bait seems to be that a certain number of our people will get this thing called the baby bonus. But do they tell us that this baby bonus is an unsubstantial thing, that it is something that we cannot depend upon? That it may vanish overnight, and that in the event of a depression in Canada it will die a quick death? Indeed, my own personal opinion is that it will not exist longer than two years. Do they tell us that when our babies reach the age of 16 they will spend the rest of their lives paying back to the Canadian government the amount of their bonus? Do they tell us that when our babies reach military age they will almost certainly be conscripted into the Canadian military forces? Do they tell us that in the event of confederation a big percentage of these young people will have to emigrate from this country to seek employment which cannot be found at home? Of course they do not tell us those things, because they know, and know well, that if we saw the truth of these things this baby bonus would be no longer able to bluff and deceive us....

Soon I trust, Mr. Chairman, our people will be called upon to once again mark their cross upon a national ballot paper.... That "X" will be written by every real Newfoundlander on a day not too far distant. It too will indicate, if correctly placed, our love and our affection for the land of our birth. I ask you gentlemen to ponder and hesitate before you make that little mark by which you, your children, and your children's children can be blessed or blasted. That cross must be the kiss of love given by every loyal citizen to our own mother—Newfoundland. Take care, I say, that it is placed with zeal and loyalty just where it belongs, just where she wishes it, and tremble like Iscariot ere you place it on your own shame and future despair, in the place that means your traitorous denial of your mother country's best interests ... once done it cannot be undone. It is final, irrevocable and unchangeable....

1.3 G.F. HIGGINS

Gordon Francis Higgins (1905-57) joined his father's St. John's law firm in 1931 and became active in a wide number of charitable and community organizations such as the St. John's Housing Society and the Benevolent Irish Society. He won a seat for the 1946 National Convention as a champion of responsible government but seems to have felt ambivalent about Newfoundland's future. On the one hand he supported and joined the delegation Joey Smallwood sent to Ottawa to negotiate entry into Confederation, while on the other he actively campaigned for the responsible government side during the ensuing Newfoundland referenda.

With respect to union with the States. As we are aware, there does exist a very definite wish amongst a number of our countrymen that the ballot at the referendum should include union with the United States. It is too late now for this Convention to explore the possibility of union with that great country, and consequently the Convention will be unable to recommend that this form of government be placed on the ballot. Whilst it is quite definite that the future economic security of Newfoundland makes it essential that we have a definite arrangement with the United States, this now must be left for an elected government to handle. If this country were to federate with Canada, the opportunity to negotiate with the United States for trade concessions would be impossible, and any wish to join in union with the United States would be lost forever. Most thinking people agree that at some time in the future the North American continent will be in union. That is, the United States will assimilate Canada. The time when such union takes place may be greatly accelerated by world events. What a position to bargain Newfoundland would be in, if she was independent when such union takes place!

In mentioning the United States, another most important matter in considering confederation with Canada arises. We have listened for many, many months to the advantages of joining with this land of heart's desire—Canada. Would Mr. Smallwood in his reply care to state why so many Canadians are leaving Canada to reside in the United States? In the 90 years between 1851 and 1941, 6,700,000 people immigrated to Canada. With all the hard work put in by the Canadian government, and all the money spent in 90 years to encourage immigration, the net gain was 400,000 people. In the last boom period from 1920 to 1930, Canada lost some 500,000 of her citizens to the United States, an average of 50,000 a year. Since the end of the war in Europe in 1945, it is stated that about 40,000 Canadians per year have made applications to emigrate to the United States.

How many Canadians go across the border without being granted permission is impossible to estimate. It is stated that two-thirds of all those emigrating to the United States from Canada are under 37 years of age. Due to United States immigration requirements, those granted permission are usually a picked group, and the result is Canada is losing her best type of citizens, the thrifty and better-trained people. The chief reason for the immigration appears to be the better wages paid in the United States. The earnings in manufacturing in the United States averaged $1.20 per hour to the Canadian 78 cents per hour. The statement that the increased wages in the United States is equalized by the higher cost of living does not appear to be correct. It would appear that for the same standard of living of a middle-income group, the weekly expenditure for cost of living is $5 higher in the States but wages are $20 higher per week there than in Canada. The reasons given for the difference in the wage scale is that business firms in Canada cannot afford to pay the same wages as paid in the United States. This argument, however, should not apply to the pulp and paper industry in which the Canadians believe they lead the world. In this industry, the average hourly earnings of pulp and paper workers in Canada is 85 cents and in the United States $1.43. The real reason however, for this difference in wages is not in industry, but in the Canadian people themselves, because of what they pay their citizens in Canadian schools, colleges and the civil service ...

1.4 M.F. HARRINGTON

Michael Francis Harrington (1916–) was a Newfoundland writer and broadcaster born in St. John's. He worked for the Newfoundland Broadcasting Corporation and in 1943 succeeded Joey Smallwood as host of the radio show "The Barrelman," a popular daily radio program celebrating Newfoundland's heritage. Harrington was a strong supporter of the return to responsible government, both at the National Convention of 1946 and during the ensuing referenda.

... I have said that confederation would mean a fundamental change in our national life. That need not be a bad thing necessarily. But it can be a bad thing, and will be if the people of this country are stampeded into such a union against what would be, under other circumstances, their better judgment.

What seems to be overlooked in this whole affair is that to be a success and a good thing for Newfoundland, confederation must work, and work a whole lot more smoothly than it does in the Maritime Provinces, for example. For these provinces are part and parcel of confederation, they grew up with it and within it. We have remained aloof until now, and in the meantime we have labouriously built up a country, a culture, traditions, faiths, hopes and, indeed, a certain kind of charity and a hospitableness that is unique. We are as separate a race of people, with ideas and standards of our own, as different from the Canadians as the Canadians are from the Americans. The adjustment of our whole lives, and our outlook on life, government, religion, everything would be a tremendous and shaking process. We might easily never become emotionally, psychologically or mentally adjusted to living under confederation at this stage in our development as a separate people, and might end up as the last and most neurotic and hard-to-live-with member of the confederation family. For a period now of 14 years, over three ordinary parliamentary government administrations, we have been without a vote or a voice in the control of our own affairs. To rush into confederation at this time would be to wake up tomorrow to find we had a vote and a voice—but that the control of our affairs, at a time when that control could be used to immense advantage to ourselves, is gone forever to a capital 2,000 miles away where our faint protests would fail to reach; or if they did, would fall on deaf ears....

1.5 W.J. KEOUGH

William Joseph Keough (1913–71) was one of the editors of the left-leaning Labour Herald, *which was published in St. John's during the 1930s and 1940s. He later left journalism to organize the West Coast Co-Operative Association and became a staunch ally of Joey Smallwood and the pro-Confederation team. Keough served as one of the elected delegates on the 1947 visit to London to negotiate terms of federation with Canada.*

... There is one further matter that should give us cause for concern in considering this whole matter of union, and that is whether union would prejudice the survival of a distinctive national culture and civilization that we should seek to maintain. There are people in this island to whom the whole confederation issue is like a red rag to a bull, and for about much the same reason they just don't like it no how. Mention confederation, and they'll rant and they'll roar in the approved grand manner about 30 pieces of silver, and niggers in the woodpile, and selling our sacred heritage up the St. Lawrence. Indeed, there has been so much of that sort of thing going on both within and without this Convention that one has to pause to enquire if perhaps there might be a modicum of truth in it all. I must confess that I am not too clear as to just exactly what the poets and the politicians have in mind when they take to being sentimental over our sacred heritage. I remember that I did one time see a fisherman's wife shovel fish guts into a brin bag and spell it on her back to her gardens a mile away. I feel certain that that is not what they have in mind by our sacred heritage. I remember that I did one time spend February in a most picturesque little cottage nailed to a cliff beside the sea. I didn't get warm for a month, and I feel certain that the people living there didn't get warm for the winter. I feel that that is not the sacred heritage over which our poets work themselves up into ecstasies, and over which our politicians work themselves into a lather. Indeed, it must be something altogether different than the most of what one comes across in making the rounds of this country. But if by our sacred heritage the poets and the politicians mean that we know in this island a culture and civilization so different, and so much more advanced than the culture and civilization of the North American mainland that they are worth any sacrifice to preserve them, they had better stop wool-gathering on Mount Olympus, and come down and walk among the people and learn how the people live. You know, it could be that the best authority on the desirability of baby bonuses would be the people who have the babies.

I have come to conclude that there would not be involved in confederation any issue of the preservation of a distinct national culture and civilization. Now that is not to say, mind you, that we have not evolved our own customs, our own institutions, our own peculiar way of life. We have. It so happens that we are the inheritors of what I have sometimes called a fish and brewis culture, ... Of that fish and brewis culture I am as proud as any Newfoundlander. It is true that we are the inheritors of a great national tradition of bravery against the seas, of hero-ism defying the sea to do its worst—bravery and heroism exemplified for all time on a bleak October day on the bleak Labrador coast when a man named Jackman did 27 times head into the storm and 27 times come ashore with a human life on his back. It is true that in this land we are the inheritors of a great Christian tradition; that at the end of every week, after we have braved the sea and dug the land and cut the pulpwood, we do still after the manner of our fathers land gather in a thousand churches to pray as our fathers prayed.... All these things are true. It is true too that all these things can remain to be so in the event of confederation. The things dearest to our hearts in this land will not in the event of union be at issue. I give it to you as my considered opinion, for what it is worth, that if the confederation alternate shall come to confront us in the referendum, that there shall be involved therein no issue involving our distinct character as Newfoundlanders, no issue involving our national honour, no issue involving our distinct culture and way of life ...

1.6 E.L. ROBERTS

Edgar Leslie Roberts (1901–71) was a successful businessman dealing with general merchandise, tourism, and farming. Born and educated at Woody Point, Newfoundland, Roberts also served as a Justice of the Peace. He was a pro-Confederationist during the National Convention.

… Dozens of my relatives and friends, after vainly trying to make a living, have gathered together a bit of money with the help of their relatives abroad and travelled to Canada. Ask these people if they wish to come back to the living conditions they left, and they would surely think it quite a joke. My own mother, widowed in the early years of her marriage, left with three small children and little means of support, struggled for three or four years to keep her family together and maintain them; she had to give it up, give away her children, and on the advice of a relative in Canada went there and made a comfortable living. So I have a warm spot in my heart for the country which befriended my mother, above all other people on this earth.

We people on the west and northwest coasts have been in close contact with Canadians, both fishermen and financiers, for years and years, and have not found them the big bad wolves that the people in the interior and on the east coast seem to think they are. Surely, so many of our people would not stay in Canada if they were so tax-ridden as some people try to make us believe they are. As I said before, the people of the west coast who have been in close contact with Canadians all their lives, must certainly regard the ravings that have been going on here about all thing Canadian as pure and simple stuff and nonsense.

I wish to touch briefly on two very much ridiculed subjects, namely family allowances and old age pensions. I have in mind a family not far from my home; a man with ten children and a sick wife. You can imagine, or can you, the awful struggle that man is having to make a living. I wonder would he scoff at a family allowance of $60 a month, would he worry about the dozens of taxes on a loaf of bread, if under confederation, he would get his flour for $12 a barrel, when he is paying $22 for it in Bonne Bay today? Would he worry about the hundreds of taxes on a pair of shoes, when under confederation he would be able to buy three pairs in the place of the two pairs he buys today? Boots and bread, sir, take a very large slice out of his budget. His fish he can get a scant half mile from his door, and his vegetables can be grown around his home. If he does pay property taxes, which he knows he is likely to pay, they will be small on his acre of land and his small unfinished, unfurnished home. He is paying plenty now, far more than his pocket can stand. He is not worrying either about the man who can afford to drive a motor car, own a fine house, he figures the man can well afford under confederation to pay his taxes and help pay some for him as well.

Old age pensions. I have in mind an old couple nearly 80 years of age each, living alone, getting very little help from relatives, trying to live on their old age pension. That man still has to go in the fishing boat to try and earn a few dollars to augment his pension. What a help it would be to receive $60 a month instead of the $10 they receive today. His property would not exceed $1,500, and even if it did exceed $2,000 and under Canadian rule the government did take it, would not they be entitled to it after his family had forsaken them and let the government look after them? I think they would have a perfect right to it, and I feel sure the old couple would think so too. The old age pensioners of Newfoundland need not worry about the government taking their property. Very few of them whom I have seen in the outports have property over $2,000, and if they have, they would not receive old age pensions. I have made out quite a number of applications the past 20 years. I have a good idea of their property value. I am not going to touch on other taxations, this has been ably and thoroughly gone into by other speakers.

There will, no doubt, be many changes and adjustments in the event of union, especially in the business world. But my thought about all that is, if our business men cannot adjust themselves to competition, they are not the men I take them to be. The proper thing to happen to them is to fold up. But don't worry, Water Street of St. John's, and all the little Water Streets of the outports, will be carrying on under confederation when I am drawing my old age pension.

And please don't let some people make you believe the only reason Canada wants Newfoundland is to make a fortune out of us, and for the inhumane purpose of starving to death our 300,000 people. That has not been the history of the democratic government of Canada. In my opinion Newfoundland has nothing to lose and very much to gain by closer contact with our neighbour, Canada, which fact will strengthen our bargaining power which members like to talk so much about. In union is strength. So let's hope Newfoundlanders will remember that at the referendum. I will, by voting for confederation.

FURTHER READINGS

Blake, R. *Canadians at Last: Canada Integrates Newfoundland as a Province.* Toronto: University of Toronto Press, 1994.

Bannister, J. "The Campaign for Representative Government in Newfoundland." *Journal Canadian Historical Association* 5 (1994): 19-40.

Chadwick, S. *Island into Province*. Cambridge: Cambridge University Press, 1967.

English, C. "The Judges go to Court: The Cashin Libel Trial of 1947." In *Essays in the History of Canadian Law: Vol IX Two Islands Newfoundland and Prince Edward Island*, ed. C. English. Toronto: Osgoode Society, 2005.

Fitzgerald, J. "Newfoundland Politics and Confederation Revisited." *Newfoundland Studies* 9, 1 (1993): 103-24.

Fitzgerald, J. "The Newfoundland Referenda Campaigns of 1948." *Beaver* (February-March, 1998): 2-3.

Gilmore, W. "Law, Constitutional Convention, and the Union of Newfoundland and Canada." *Acadiensis* (Spring 1989): 111-26.

Gwyn, R. *Smallwood: The Unlikely Revolutionary*. Rev. ed. Toronto: McClelland and Stewart, 1972.

Hiller, J. *Confederation. Deciding Newfoundland's Future, 1943-1949*. St. John's: Newfoundland Historical Society, 1998.

Hiller, J. "Newfoundland Confronts Canada, 1867-1949." In *The Atlantic Provinces in Confederation*, ed. E. Forbes and D. Muise. Toronto: University of Toronto Press, 1993.

Hiller, J. "Robert Bond and the Pink, White, and Green: Newfoundland Nationalism in Perspective." *Acadiensis* 36, 2 (Spring 2007): 113-33.

Hiller, J., and P. Neary, Eds. *Newfoundland in the Nineteenth and Twentieth Centuries: Essays in Interpretation*. Toronto: University of Toronto Press, 1980.

Horwood, H. *Joey: The Life and Political Times of Joey Smallwood*. Toronto: Stoddart, 1969.

Long, G. *Suspended State: Newfoundland Before Confederation*. St. John's: Breakwater Press, 1999.

Mackenzie, D. *Inside the Atlantic Triangle: Canada and the Entrance of Newfoundland into Confederation, 1939–1949*. Toronto: University of Toronto Press, 1986.

MacLeod, M. *Peace of the Continent: The Impact of Second World War Canadian and American Bases in Newfoundland*. St. John's: H. Cuff, 1986.

McCann, P. "British Policy and Confederation." *Newfoundland Studies* 14, 2 (1998): 154-68.

Neary, P. *Newfoundland and the North Atlantic World 1929–1949*. Montreal and Kingston: McGill-Queen's University Press, 1988.

Neary, P. "Newfoundland's Union with Canada: Conspiracy or Choice." *Acadiensis* 12, 2 (Spring 1983): 110-19.

Neary, P., Ed. *The Political Economy of Newfoundland 1929–1972*. Toronto: Copp Clark, 1973.

Noel, S. *Politics in Newfoundland*. Toronto: University of Toronto Press, 1971.

Walsh, B. *More Than a Poor Majority: The Story of Newfoundland's Confederation with Canada*. St. John's: Breakwater, 1985.

Webb, J. "Confederation, Conspiracy, and Choice: A Discussion." *Newfoundland Studies* 14, 2 (1998): 169-84.

Webb, J. "Responsible Government League and the Confederation Campaigns of 1948." *Newfoundland Studies* 5, 2 (1989): 203-20.

CHAPTER II

"A Glow of Fulfilled Femininity"

WOMEN IN THE 1950S AND 1960S

INTRODUCTION

Second wave feminism burst onto the Canadian scene with such unexpected vehemence and vigour that the federal government, in 1967, called a Royal Commission on the Status of Women to examine the issue. Since tectonic shifts of this type do not occur in a vacuum, historians have subsequently wondered why Women's Liberation occurred at that specific point in time and with such force. The 1960s was a time of considerable social upheaval, and some pundits suggested that the new wave of feminism simply rode that tidal wave of discontent. That explanation, however, proved insufficient. The apparent disjunction between the feminist anger of the 1960s and the maternal bliss of the 1950s was particularly puzzling. How, people asked, could the happy cookie-making June Cleaver of the 1950s suddenly metamorphose into the raging feminist of the 1960s? That question led historians to re-evaluate the 1950s. Research now suggests that, despite appearances to the contrary, Canadian women actually found considerable fault in both the mythology and reality of that decade but felt their voices censored until the climate became more conducive to revolt—which it did in the 1960s.

The 1950s were, at least superficially, very good for Canada. World War II had partially receded into memory, and Canadian industry worked at full capacity to fill orders from a rebuilding world. Jobs were plentiful and well-paid, standards of living rose dramatically, taxes and mortgages remained low, and a pervasive sense of optimism suffused the country. The size of the middle class consequently grew enormously, and hundreds of thousands of formerly marginalized Canadians reached for the Canadian dream. That dream, similar to the United States, revolved around owning a detached house, purchasing the plethora of new consumer goods, keeping children in school past Grade 8, taking annual vacations, and having mom stay at home. A married woman's place, according to the ideal social conventions of the day, was not in the paid workforce, but instead in one of the many new suburbs built for freshly minted middle-class Canadians and their desire for respectable inclusion. There, she was to create her familial nest while dad worked downtown and the kids attended school. This image pervaded the North American psyche, promoted by the popular new mass medium, television. American shows beamed into Canada—such as "Leave it to Beaver" and "Father Knows Best"—became icons of the decade, their stereotypical descriptions of middle-class suburban life further strengthened by the messages in the frequent commercial breaks.

Despite the seductive promise of suburban coziness, however, there was a dark side to the 1950s, one that society subconsciously and consciously hid because it threatened the apple pie image. Life for women in particular was not all it was cracked up to be. Suburbia, with its much-lauded benefits, suffered a number of very serious and unforeseen shortcomings, the brunt of which women bore. A key issue was the housewife's loneliness. Women now had their own homes and gardens, true, but they were separated from their neighbours, both emotionally and physically. The kids were in school during the day, and husbands commuted to work. Thus, the only daytime company came from radio and television, with its increasingly hollow middle-class boosterism, or from other housewives in the same boat. No one, of course, admitted to being lonely because that suggested a fundamental personal failing.

Suburban planning ironically bears responsibility for much of this loneliness. Planners with noble intentions created suburbs like Scarborough, Ontario (now derisively known as "Scarberia") to be spacious and private. The new subdivisions gave each family its own "castle" with a private fenced garden instead of the former crowded inner-city tenements where streets served as communal living rooms and where everyone knew each other. The very roominess of the new suburbs created spatial and psychological distance between families, which modern architecture further exacerbated. Gone was the front porch or stoop from which neighbours formerly interacted with their community, replaced by the insular living room where families focused on the television, not the community. Gone was the communal corner store, replaced by the mall—a Canadian invention.

Canadian women experienced other unexpected problems in the 1950s. Modern appliances, for example, turned out to be double-edged swords. They supposedly did away with the drudgery of housework and, indeed, helped enormously. Compare an electric wringer-washer to heating water on the stove and using a washboard. How can a vacuum cleaner compare to the broom, the electric refrigerator to the icebox, and the electric range to the wood stove? The problem was, however, that the new technology facilitated heretofore impossible standards of cleanliness, and a consequent diminution of what was formerly acceptable. Housewives' work actually increased in some areas as they now strove to match June Cleaver's spotless home or to conform to standards set by cleaning product advertisements in popular women's magazines. Appliances did indeed liberate time, but not nearly as much as expected, and they created their own relentless tyranny.

Social conformity also became an unexpected problem for the new suburban house-wife. Suburbia, with its homogenous physical layout, narrow demographic background, and lack of history, helped generate a sub-current of uniformity that stifled individualism and creativity. The sad irony was that housewives now had the time to nurture their individuality but found doing so unacceptable.

Other issues plagued Canadian women in the 1950s. The law remained paternalistic, calculated to side with men in cases of divorce, property or custodial rights, rights over children, and employment and pension eligibility. A woman's body remained controlled by a male-dominated state that refused her access to abortion and tried to manage birth control as well. Equality in the workforce, either in pay or opportunity, was nonexistent, and many institutions, such as the federal government, refused to hire married women.

Enormously popular during this period, the Canadian women's magazine *Chatelaine* was, in fact, years ahead of its American counterparts in discussing issues such as suburban boredom, women's sexuality, abortion, birth control, women's legal rights, lesbianism, and issues of gender equality. These were unheard-of topics in a mass circulation magazine, if for no other reason than some of the advice went counter to the message the maga-zine's advertisers promoted. Nor was it merely middle-class suburban housewives who subscribed. Records show that some 70 per cent of the readership was lower middle class and 30 per cent was rural, and that women from all ethnic backgrounds and all regions of the country bought it and made it part of their community. Impassioned letters to the editor plus the significant circulation clearly indicate that *Chatelaine* was an important magazine for a segment of the population. Editor Doris Anderson's feminist campaign did not receive universal support from her readers. What most women appreciated, however, was that Anderson's regular lead editorial columns asked them to think for themselves. Canadian women became used to her scabrous pen, often directed at what she perceived as the complacency of women themselves, and a decade of such thought-provoking material helped build the foundation for Canadian second wave feminism of the 1960s and 1970s.

1. How significant were the differences between women who stayed at home and those who worked? Would this remain a problem in uniting women into a single coherent movement?

2. Were the problems of the suburban housewife significant or merely so many tempests in teapots?

3. Who were more likely to become feminists—frustrated housewives or ambitious businesswomen?

DOCUMENTS

1. Beverly Gray, "Housewives Are a Sorry Lot," *Chatelaine*, March 1950

Beverly Gray (dates unknown) remains unknown. It is possible that she was an editorial invention, possibly taking her name from the American mystery novels popular from 1934 to 1955 in which the heroine, Beverley Gray, is a feisty journalist and travel writer.

> *Get mad if you like. But somewhere in this article there's a truth for every one of us.*

Beverly Gray, a business girl, looks over her married friends, shudders, takes a reef in her girdle and strikes out with these observations:

Marriage brings almost a full stop in mental development.

As soon as the wedding is over a woman drops phoney interests in such things as sports, politics and world events.

Her life channels into a narrow domestic little tunnel.

A girl expects her husband to be a combination of Ronald Colman, Gregory Peck and Humphrey Bogart.

Chat with any housewife and she's sure to bring the conversation round to how terribly frustrated she is.

If the individual housewife is a saddening sight, housewives in the mass are appalling.

YOU CAN'T SAY: "She is a housewife, so she is blond." You can't say: "She is a housewife, so she is fat." You can't even say: "She is a housewife, so she is a good cook." But nine times out of 10 you can say: "She is a housewife, so she is unhappy."

Young or old, fat or thin, pretty or homely, a housewife is not a happy person. She is miserable, frustrated, underprivileged, abused and oppressed. Nobody loves her and she hasn't any money. Chat with any housewife for five minutes, and she will tell you how she suffers.

She has three main complaints: poverty, loneliness and drudgery. Of these, poverty is the most deadly, not because she actually goes around naked and undernourished, but because poverty is a weapon with which she can beat her husband literally into the grave. A housewife, like a baby, is quick to learn: she soon finds that if she talks long enough and loud enough and often enough about what other husbands give their wives, she can goad hers into anything from borrowing money at the bank to embezzling it at the office.

No woman believes for an instant that any other woman is as poor as she is. She is convinced that all husbands but hers ladle out clothes and caviar and cleaning women in a never-ending stream; they give their wives a generous allowance and money besides (as well as paying the rent and the utilities and the grocery bill); they take their wives out to dinner when it's too hot to cook, and on carefully casual occasions they land home with their arms full of roses.

SOAP OPERA DIET

No wonder she feels badly, this bedraggled drudge, scrubbing the floor on her hands and knees, chained between the kitchen stove and the washing machine, with her current account overdrawn and without a rag to her name. The worst of it is, her poverty is genuine, although she is mistaken in its nature. It's not coin of the realm she lacks, it's currency of the spirit, and a bucketful of ten-dollar bills won't cure it.

Marriage seems to bring about a full stop in mental development. How many wives have any interest outside the home—or inside it? As soon as the wedding ring is safely on her finger, a woman drops the phoney interest in sports, politics, the stock market, or whatever it was that made her seem too remarkable to the bemused bachelor. She lets her mind crystalize into a narrow, dark, domestic little tunnel, with no surprises, no clear, cool streams of thought, and no pleasant sunny places. Almost any married woman can have a baby, but it takes an unusual matron to have a new idea.

Notice what the housewife reads: movie periodicals, love stories, murder mysteries. Or what she listens to on the radio—and don't let her tell you she doesn't. Walk down a middle-class residential street on a hot afternoon when the doors are open, and hear the soap operas.

OTHER WOMEN BORE HER

As for the housewife's second complaint, her loneliness, since the invention of the telephone there probably isn't an hour in the day when she isn't talking to somebody. The trouble is, it's women she talks to, and women bore her to death. Society has hounded her husband out to provide her with gadgets (and she has nothing to say to him anyway) and she doesn't dare have any men friends. So she is reduced to stultifying, niggling gossip that leaves her unsatisfied and lonely.

Looking at her drudgery from a vantage point behind a hot typewriter, it seems that it must take years of patience and persistence to develop work habits to keep her busy in a modern home from eight in the morning until 10 at night. Even if she has children, in these days of sitters and playsuits (and nursery schools that take babies at three) children shouldn't be too much of a drag on her.

It seems, however, that this idea is wrong, as she will tell you at length. This modern feeling that children are an unmitigated nuisance would have fascinated Freud, with his theories on the scarring of childish minds. "The doctor thinks Mary's little boy is going to be all right. Poor Mary—she's been tied in the house all week."

"Tied" in the house by a sick child.

Obviously, women feel that they are wasting their time looking after a home and family, and that they ought to be out in the world. Yet surely the snappiest adding machine lacks the lure of flesh of your flesh and bone of your bone, all done up in satiny skin and dimples.

Any married man will tell you that a wife is a lovable, warmly affectionate creature—closely resembling a halibut. She is too busy to go to the hockey game, too tired to iron a clean shirt, too bored to be amorous and silly. She is suspicious of every move her husband makes, and automatically jealous of any friend, man or woman—how many masculine friendships ever survive a marriage? A wife's normal attitude seems to be that she doesn't much want her husband herself, but she's going to see to it that nobody else gets him.

As for her suspicions, usually when her husband lies to her, she deserves it. The instinct for self-preservation is strong in husbands, and after one or two unfortunate brushes with the truth, they find it easier to lie. Sooner or later they get caught, and from then on their wives (silently, loudly or tearfully, depending on type) doubt every remark.

HER WASTED LIFE

This, of course, is the obvious result of expecting too much. When she marries, a girl expects her husband to be a combination of Ronald Colman, Gregory Peck and Humphrey Bogart: a man at once tender, gorgeous and brutal: a man who will praise every shining floor, every fried egg. When he turns out to be a heel who snorts and gurgles in his sleep, who takes all her sacrifices for granted, and who yawns when she tells him about the shooting pains in her heart, she suddenly realizes that she has wasted her life on an insignificant individual who is all running to belly and baldness.

If he's not an outstanding success in business, she never forgets how successful she might have been, if she had not married. There are many, many wives in this world who never forgive their husbands for marrying them, for burying their abilities under a heap of dirty dishes, for cutting short a glamorous career as salesclerk or stenographer. They would be furious if anyone suggested that real talent won't be smothered by circumstances, and that they are merely making marriage a handy excuse for their own shortcomings.

The truth is, most housewives are lazy. They are too lazy to put down their magazine and write the story they think they could; too lazy to walk a block to do their shopping in person; too lazy to learn to sew if they can't afford new underwear. They cover up for their laziness with monologues on their backaches and the cost of meat and how hard it is to get anything for a change when He doesn't like asparagus. As they have nothing to wear, there is no point in combing their hair or mending the lining in their old coat, or in scrounging 40 cents out of the canned goods money to get new heel lifts on their shoes.

And if the individual housewife is saddening, housewives in the mass are appalling.

Look at what comes out from behind the woodwork the morning of a sale, each specimen mistress of some man's castle and queen of his heart. Their transportation manners are atrocious. They elbow their way to the front of a queue waiting for a streetcar, and then make everybody wait while they search for their fare. They forget to ask for transfers as they get on, and then plow their way back through the maimed and dismembered for them later. If they must stand, they look fixedly at a seated man or make pointed remarks to a friend. They discuss personal problems (their own and other people's), complete with names, ages, vices and vital statistics, at the pitch of their voices.

THE MILITANT MATRON

Then there is the way they look. One might think, charitably, that they can't possibly be held responsible for that: that God in His infinite wisdom must have created a special type of costume and facial expression for housewives. But when she considers that they must have been, at some time, reasonably attractive, the business girl shudders and takes another reef in her girdle.

The militant matron, shopping bag under her arm and a wild light in her eye, is an object to behold with awe. And where there is one there are usually two or three. Listen to them in restaurants, watch them at bargain counters, hear them on buses and street corners. Discontent rises from them in waves. They have no sense of humor and no sense of honor; they would stone any man who talked about his wife as they talk about their husbands. Ply a housewife with tea and kindness, and she will tell you anything from her husband's weight to what his boss said to him in confidence.

They have one other subject of conversation besides their husbands, and a popular one it is. Any housewife can tell you (and will, unless stopped by force) every lugubrious, gory detail of every childbirth in her acquaintance, even unto the third and fourth generation back. She herself is never without an ailment, whether she is sickening for it, actually in its throes, or convalescing and waiting morbidly for the next.

This illness seems to go with marriage. Perhaps it is because when she is ill a woman can get masculine attention, even if she (or her husband) has to pay for it. All doctors know that half of the illnesses afflicting married women are the result of too much spare time and too little to think about. Judging from the great and growing number of widows, the married state can't be too unhealthy for women, but if you ask any housewife how she feels, any place, any time, in front of any company, she will tell you, ache by ache, retch by retch, flux by flux.

Housewives are a race apart, a separate division of the human species, bearing little relation to ordinary unmarried females. Their complaints fill the air and their horrid plight is obvious. Housewives are a sorry lot.

2. "Housewives Blast Business Girl," *Chatelaine*, June 1950

"Housewives are a sorry lot," said Beverly Gray in March Chatelaine. "They have three main complaints—their poverty, loneliness and drudgery. Marriage seems to bring about a full stop in mental development. The average woman lets her mind crystalize into a narrow, domestic tunnel."

Developing these ideas, Miss Gray criticized housewives for their appearance and manners.

Over five hundred women protested in letters and articles. Through all of them ran a vein of tolerance and good humor. But the three things which most of them resented were the attacks on their happiness, their mental status, and their laziness.

Since no reply was, in itself, a completely satisfactory answer to Miss Gray, we have selected excerpts—typical of the point of view of Canadian housewives.—The Editors.

MISS GRAY is guilty of the most sweeping generalizations. She has taken a few of the most unattractive human emotions—frustration, envy, suspicion, discontent and laziness, and she has landed them squarely in the housewife's lap. She has allowed for no individual talents or virtues, condemning in one sweep every woman who dares possess husband, hearth and home.... Granted nearly every housewife in her off moments is guilty of one or even all these undesirable traits. She is, however, playing her role, not merely as a housewife but as an individual, or—as any man would maintain—a woman. The editorial comment that there is a truth for every one of us is just. The article mirrors the darker side of all of us, whatever may be our *chosen* profession and should not be directed specifically at the housewife.

IN MY OPINION the term housewife is outmoded. The next time the census man comes to the house and asks, "Occupation?" I am going to reply "Homemaker," or "Nation Builder," or "The most important job in the world," instead of answering meekly, Housewife.

OUR MENTAL development hasn't stopped dead—it's simply changed its direction. From baseball to babies, politics to pastry, stock markets to supermarkets. We still have our old interests plus innumerable new ones. And, lady, try just once, baking, marketing or caring for your baby without putting a bit of mental effort into it.

THE BUSINESS GIRL claims that the housewife drops "phony" interests when the wedding ring encircles her third finger, left hand. If these interests were not genuine, but developed merely to please the "bemused bachelor" I'd say it's a good thing matrimony made an honest woman of her.

. . . You think the "bemused bachelor" who was inveigled into matrimony talked to his girl about politics and stock markets! Well, guess again. And to quote you, "Almost any married woman can have a baby but it takes an unusual matron to have a new idea!" Most married women who get a new idea mention it to their husbands so tactfully that they soon think it was theirs in the first place.

. . . Any girl who expects that a man is going to marry her because she knows how the Grand Llama of Tibet is elected, or can swim the English Channel in November had better stay with her desk job. Somewhere along the line she has been sadly misinformed. It takes a different kind of brainwork to be a reasonably efficient combination of cleaning woman, dietitian, nurse, teacher, dressmaker, economist, psychologist, sweetheart and mother. While I'm not a grey-haired grandmother, I've been a housewife long enough to see the rewards that come from an established home and family.

B.G. COMPLAINS how voluble a woman is on the subject of her husband's shortcomings. Golly, what a fascinating, tell-all bunch of gals she hobnobs with! I, unfortunately, seem to have gone through life tuned to the wrong wave lengths. I have known women whose husbands were alcoholics, niggardly misers or just plain skunks and I have always believed them to be just too stupid to see the flaws. But obviously they have been deliberately secretive during their visits with me, waiting only until they got into a public restaurant to let down their hair and give with the dirt. Even my best friends have never shown any inclination to let me in on the excitement of their marital tribulations, so you can imagine how furious it makes me to find how unnaturally they have been behaving toward me.

IT REALLY must be terrible for the housewives who are the unfortunate possessors of caddish husbands such as Miss Gray talks of so understandingly. You'd think even smart business girls could recognize the type of character who'd refer to his wife as a "halibut." Of course, such a husband probably has for his motto — "There's lots of good fish in the sea — and if those lucky business girls want to be suckers, that's entirely their business."

WHEN WE'RE poking about the kitchen with runs in our nylons, hair in wisps, we don't look like your Marie Holmes illustrating how to make marmalade (who does?), but give us any day the crowded nursery, the round of ups and downs — of joy and laughter, of heartache and anxiety — for of threads such as these the fabric of life is woven.

You say our lives channel into a "narrow domestic little tunnel." Well, I'll tell you a secret — you don't know it, but you are in a straight and narrow ditch.

Same old office hours, same old desk, same old people around you every day, same old letters, same old boss, same old routine, same old restaurant, same old bus—my, but what a variety of exciting things your day contains! Beverly, is that really what you prefer to running a house to suit yourself by day—and having evenings to share with your children and your guy? Reef your girdle and stay at that desk if you will. I'll reef my clothesline and thank my silver polish I'm not there!

... Just now, for us young house wives, life "may channel into a narrow domestic little tunnel," dark in spots, but it's a tunnel with light at the end of it—a family decently reared, our own home and a husband who has helped in the hard work and good planning; and certain sacrifices do come out right at the end of the tunnel. And sister, didn't you hear of "kissing tunnels?" They're fun!

I DENY that as a group housewives are unhappy. We're happy because we know we are loved and appreciated in spite of our curlers and last year's coat. We're happy because we're released from the tension of office competition and the competition for affection and because we can put all our heart into the home and community service.

LAZY? Who are those two million women I meet at the supermarket, those lazy creatures with two armfuls of groceries, pushing a carriage with one or two occupants, holding the harness of a third between their teeth? Housewives trying to fill their empty days?

... If all housewives were as moronic, lazy and lacking in imagination as pictured, how could they raise their daughters to grow into such smart, intelligent and very self-assured young business girls?

NOW WHAT's all this hullabaloo about us listening to soap operas? Some of us do and some of us don't. So what? They are merely a form of entertainment to occupy part of the mind while, say, washing dishes. Don't tell me we should have a waterproof copy of "The Rise and Fall of the Roman Empire" to reach for instead.

... Suppose we do listen to soap operas—don't we get the news every hour on the hour sandwiched in between? And what husband will take your latest theories on why Russia will wait three years before declaring war, in place of lemon pie for supper?

WE ARE accused of lack of outside interests. How then does B.G. account for the number of women's organizations? In my town every year without exception it has been a married woman who collected for the Community Chest. In our choir are housewives. I see them donating afternoons to all sorts of charitable work. Who bakes the pies and cakes at the fairs, prepares the church suppers? Who makes up the Parent-Teacher groups?

"A Glow of Fulfilled Femininity": Women in the 1950s and 1960s

DISCOURTESY is not a disease specifically attributable to the housewife. I have often waited patiently to be served in department stores while giggling clerks stood in a huddle discussing last night's date, until I was finally forced to leave without making a purchase.

UNTIL READING Miss Gray's article, I had always been under the impression that women as such might be grouped en bloc, but that beyond this it became necessary to recognize a vast variation in ability and character. But according to her there are only two classifications—single girls and housewives. Housewives, all having been cut from the same shoddy piece, must be classified under the same generalized accusations. How simple! I should very much like to know whether she keeps her office correspondence in the same type of all-inclusive folders.

This new type of reasoning requires neither consistency nor veracity—how easy it becomes to state a case. For instance, the movie magazines, it seems, are read only by housewives; but it has been my observation that they are to be found in greatest profusion at the beauty parlors where, we are led to infer, no housewife ever sets foot!

SO THE writer thinks housewives are the only females addicted to long telephone calls. I might remark that I know a good dozen firms in one city who have had to deny employees use of the phones for personal use, the reason being that female employees have carried on such interminable gossip sessions with their cronies that incoming business calls were badly delayed.

THE MOVIES have made you "career girls" a very glamorous lot. But from where I stand on my corner waiting for a homeward bus, dinner under my arm, I see a swarm of tired, bedraggled and irritable young business girls who elbow their way just as fast, if not faster, than I to the only available seats.

SO YOU consider our children a nuisance. Well, you're dead right! And who has a better right to say so than we? They haven't invented a toddler yet with a push-button mechanism and if we talk about what we went through producing the little dears, why not? They don't do that with mirrors either. Evidently you have missed the note of living pride usually wrapped up in our complaints about our offspring.

AND WHO ARE "all" the doctors who know that half the illnesses of married women are imaginary? For every wife who fakes illness there are at least 10 who do their day's work, and I mean work with aches and pains that would keep you home from the office for a month, Miss Gray. And since you mentioned widows, statistics prove that married men live longer than bachelors and I'll bet you're just the one who'll come back with "It only seems longer!"

YOU SAY women talk too much about childbirth. One session of pregnancy would put some of the critics out of business completely. Yet the so-called "spineless" housewife, lacking all the determination, strength of character and other virtues of her unmarried sister is supposed to recover and rebound from the ordeal with the elasticity of a rubber band. The amazing thing about her is she does!

BEVERLY, I can't help but wonder who your married friends are. If it is from them you have gleaned your rather wild ideas about us, you had better look up from polishing your nails, open your eyes, and really see. If we had so ghastly an existence—why weren't women frightened away from it generations ago?

WHATEVER IS the matter with you, Beverly Gray—I hope its curable. Stop being a sour-puss and you will find that married women are people too, and very nice. Often they are tense with worries that are not as controllable as a typewriter or adding machine.

In our village the women are clever and kind, some more efficient than others. Our children are healthy and usually very happy. We like our husbands. We give service to our community. We understand municipal affairs and work to improve them. We have political opinions and we don't fight over disagreements. When we are in trouble we help one another. Our women are smart-looking and well-groomed—and I expect they are where you live too.

ONE CAN'T blame these spotless specimens of business girls shuddering at the sight of a housewife going about her business. I shudder myself when I think of it. But that fly-away look in our eyes and hair seems unavoidable when trying to shop in a limited time and keep small fingers from creating too much damage in the store. When those smooth b.gs. approach with their unruffled hair, unblemished make-up and in up-to-the-minute tailoring, my inferior complex reaches a new low. And if the need to speak arises, their cool husky tones are a positive delight—but I've often wondered would their voice pitch rise as high as mine if in an emergency a child tried crossing the street in front of a moving car!

IT SEEMS to me from Beverly Gray's article that her position at the console of her typewriter encompasses a much smaller horizon than the narrow domestic circle in which, according to her, we housewives are groveling. But her ideas will doubtless cause more smiles than scowls—for we realize how very young she must be, at least in experience. Perhaps Chatelaine should sponsor a Womanhood Week—so that one half may learn how the other half lives. But don't let Beverly scare you, girls. Countless thousands of us in Canada are homemaking—and loving it! And it only takes one hug and goodnight kiss from sleepy cherubs to bring back all the love and energy which has been given so freely during the day.

"A Glow of Fulfilled Femininity": Women in the 1950s and 1960s

WE ARE SORRY to see one member of the female sex allowing her sublime ignorance and noticeably narrow-minded opinions to carry her away. We can only suppose that Miss Gray's vitriolic tongue has reduced her circle of friends to such an extent that she has been forced to retaliate in a verbal barrage against her own kind.

ALL HOUSEWIVES will no doubt agree it's a smart business girl who, knowing her own limitations, decides to sidestep the idea of becoming one of us. But don't think for a moment that we, "a race apart, a separate division of the human species," would change places—oh, no, we're housewives, and darned proud of it!

3. Dr. Marion Hilliard, "Stop Being Just a Housewife," *Chatelaine*, September 1956

Anna Marion Hilliard (1902–58) studied medicine at the University of Toronto and did post-graduate work in Britain before joining the staff of Women's College Hospital in Toronto in 1928. She headed the Department of Gynecology and Obstetrics from 1947 to 1957. During that time she helped devise the simplified pap test that became standard procedure. By 1956 she convinced the provincial authorities to make Women's College Hospital a teaching institution. Hilliard took a commonsense view on women's health issues, demystifying events like childbirth, which made her popular among Canadian women. She published many magazine articles on women's health and eventually compiled them into her 1957 book A Woman Doctor Looks at Love and Life, *which was ghostwritten by the feminist journalist June Callwood.*

When I was an adolescent in Morrisburg, Ont., I used to sing a song that contained the line, "Men must work but women must weep." The rest of the song is gone from my memory but that one line has been haunting me ever since. I believe that the most important thing I know about women, after twenty-five years as an obstetrician and gynecologist, is that women need not weep, *but they must work*.

I know exactly how most men and a lot of women will feel about my attitude. There is a prevailing image of womanhood, slightly plump in a cotton print dress, surrounded by adoring, golden-haired children as she bends over an oven door to take out a pan of biscuits. In this pink picture, the woman's face is brimming with contentment, tears of tender joy stand in her eyes and she is bathed in a glow of fulfilled femininity. She's wonderful all right, but she's no more real than the fantasy image millions of men have of themselves, exultant and virile, stripped to the waist in the sunshine, splitting rocks with Gargantuan strength.

People in our culture are too complicated to have more than fleeting moments of such acute sensation. Splitting rocks is unprofitable, making it impossible for a man to raise his family in a spacious neighborhood, and it also is incapable of satisfying his intelligence. The desire to be half naked and muscular must give way to the reality of a pallid face and a grey-flannel figure crouched over a desk.

Similarly, women cannot perpetually achieve the ideal state of enriched motherhood. Motherhood, in reality, turns out to be a state with well-spaced-out rewards—the thrill of nursing a baby, the look on a small child's face when he is comforted after a fall, a remark of a school-going child that shows understanding and warmth, a shared laugh with an adolescent, a first date, a graduation, a wedding, a grandchild. In between are periods of monotony and a feeling of stagnation.

Much of the fault for the current mood of nameless longing that is sweeping modern housewives is to be found in their so-called blessings. Women no longer weave their own cloth, make their own soap, put down a cellarful of preserves. Consider the mid-twentieth-century woman: she is alone in her house, miles from her family and the friends of her childhood; her work has been simplified to the glorious point where she can keep her house glittering in two hours a day; she stares into her own thoughts while the refrigerator clicks on, the oven bakes the prepared cake mix and her children play in denims that need no ironing. She has married young, earlier every year in Canada according to the statistics. She's strong, intelligent and responsible. She sits with a cigarette in her fingers and feels futile. I say she needs to work.

I'd like to emphasize immediately that I have several convictions about *why* women should work, and none of them include money. To take a job merely for the sake of a pay cheque is a spiritless and degrading business. It's the blight of our times—men and women working at grey, loathed occupations purely for the sake of income. It flies in the face of the human necessity to take pride in a job, and the repetitious agony of an occupation that gives no satisfaction can lead to mental or physical breakdown. I am shocked by the number of our adolescents who take light, aimless jobs when they leave school, putting in time until marriage. College girls wait on tables at summer resorts in order to purchase cashmere sweaters. Young married women stand behind counters in department stores so they can pay the next installment on the refrigerator—and when that is paid off they'll make a down payment on a clothes dryer. These women have settled on a materialistic standard, filling their closets with clothes and their kitchens with electric appliances. They don't realize that their vitality is turning to cold ashes and their spirit is impoverished.

Women must work, all women must work. There is no place in our society for an indolent woman. But as a doctor I am certain that it is good health therapy to work and that women must work for values other than purely economic. Women need to work to gain confidence in themselves. Women need to work in order to know achievement. Women need to work to escape loneliness. Women need to work to avoid feeling like demihumans, half woman and half sloth.

Work, as I mean it, includes any activity that fulfills these needs. It includes hospitality, a complicated and rewarding occupation. It includes active membership in an organization that is performing a vital function in the community. It includes part-time work in a dress shop, if the woman is stimulated by handling new clothes and meeting a variety of people. It includes full-time work at a job that challenges and delights her, providing she has some enthusiasm and glow left over afterward for her home.

I am not speaking of the unmarried woman, who will work all her adult life. She too needs to choose an occupation in which she can find some expression of her personality, whether it be chatting with people over a bakeshop counter or peering through a microscope in search of a cure for cancer. But she is not fooled, as the married woman is fooled, into believing she can spend her whole life without acquiring a single skill.

This is the deep dark water under the thin ice of a married woman's composure. Frittering away the scant years before she marries, she learns no trade. She comes to marriage with little ability beyond a certain flair for looking attractive in strong sunlight. On this house of cards, she builds her self-assurance. She rises in the morning full of the delight of greeting her young loveliness in a mirror. But time won't hold still and this butterfly reaches her mid-thirties, when her children are almost independent and her one small talent is beginning to weather. The change in her appearance, which had counted for so much, makes her unsure. She is now ready, with her family nearly grown, to take part in the bustle outside her home, but she is newly timid and has no training. Unskilled occupations look wearying, unworthy and dull; so she sits at home and becomes more despondent with each empty, wasted day.

One such woman came to me a few years ago. She was expensively dressed, given to tapping her fingers sharply on the arm of her chair and full of vague symptoms of irritability, sleeplessness and pains that changed location with each medical article she read. Both sons were in high school and her husband was absorbed in a business boom.

"You need to work," I told her.

"My husband is quite successful," she said coldly.

I shifted patiently. "I mean for your own sake," I explained. "What can you do?"

She butted her cigarette viciously. "Dr. Hilliard, I am thirty-six years old. I have two years of university education, sixteen years of marriage and a pretty good IQ. I believe I am qualified to be a baby sitter."

I met an older version of the same woman not long ago. Her husband had died, in his mid-fifties, and she was devastated.

"I know that self-pity isn't helping me," she commented sadly, "but I just sit in our pretty little home and cry."

"You'd better get a job," I said.

"A job!" she exclaimed. "I've never had a job in my life. What could I do?"

"Start down the street of the shopping district nearest you," I advised her, "and go into every store and ask for work until you find a job."

She took my suggestion and landed a job the next day in a dime store. Wrestling with the problems of learning to ring up sales and make change for the purchase of 59-cent wallets, she found new strength to accept her loneliness and an awakened interest in people. She left that job for a better one and I haven't heard from her since. I suspect she is just fine.

It is time women took a good long look at their lives and realized that they will spend most of the years working. Most women realize that they will work before their marriage, but they don't know that this is only the beginning. If their husbands need to finish their educations or become ill for a long period of time, the wives will have to work. If the marriage suffers either separation or divorce, both of which are increasingly common, the women go back to work. When the children are entering their teens, the women can easily fit a job into the home schedule. They'll be grandmothers in their forties, eagerly looking for something to fill their time. Women live longer than men, so it is likely that they'll spend the end of their lives, if they're lucky, working at a job that interests and delights them. In the long view, marriage and childbearing, although a desperate need, may be only an interlude in a woman's life.

Young people today approaching adulthood are betrayed by the ease with which they can make money. They need no skill at all and life is a lark. A teen-age girl with indifferent ability to type can make fifty dollars a week in an office and conserve all her animation for the coffee breaks and after-five dates. A boy I know made eighty dollars a week on a road-construction gang, guiding traffic with a red flag. He had the wit to be ashamed of himself, but his savings paid his first-year medical-school fees.

With jobs so easy to come by, many adolescent girls are fooled into believing that only the salary is an important factor in choosing an occupation. The jobs that require training and education, such as nursing and teaching, have little charm. They'll be marrying soon, they figure, so why bother?

Once a generation becomes adjusted to the notion that happiness varies in a direct ratio with dollars, desperate aberrations appear in its behavior. Last winter I had three mothers in three months come to me in their early pregnancies and tell me that they wanted their babies placed for adoption. These mothers were married, giving birth to legitimate babies. "Why give up your baby?" I asked.

"We can't afford to give this new baby the advantages it should have," the first mother told me. "We have two children now and we can't manage another."

"Do you think dancing lessons and brand-new snowsuits are more important to a child than being with his own parents?" I enquired.

The mother was surprised. "Certainly," she answered.

I discovered to my sorrow that the adoption department of at least one children's aid society had to hire a special case worker to deal with the growing number of married couples who place their children for adoption. What has happened to our values if we can give up our babies because they strain the family budget? We pride ourselves on our Western way of life. "What shall it profit a man, if he shall gain the whole world, and lose his own soul?"

This trend is evident in the mothers of teenage girls who chat with pride about their daughters. "She's so pretty," they tell me gaily. "We belong to the country club because we want her to meet a nice crowd of people and we try to keep her well dressed. She studied at the conservatory for years but now she's more interested in badminton. She's having such a wonderful time!"

I wonder. Does she know what life is about, I think to myself. Does she have a core of serenity, derived from the knowledge that she is a capable, coherent human being? Is she prepared to live a long time and be able to respect herself most of those years? Or will she be bored for twenty or thirty years, turning her bitter venom on her children, her husband, her friendships that show signs of waning? Don't tell me your daughter can figure-skate like Barbara Ann Scott. Tell me instead that she is generous and kind and that she has forethought enough to prepare herself for a creative vocation.

Men preparing themselves for a profession usually continue with their education after marriage, but a woman almost invariably stops her education at the first clang of the wedding bell. She believes, and she is dead wrong, that her training is of no importance. Many women tell themselves that they can always finish the course later, but later never happens. A middle-aged housewife is so rare in a university that she's newspaper copy. No woman should ever be concerned that her training as a teacher, a business-machine operator or a dietician will ever be wasted when she marries. She will be using it, all right, and probably a lot sooner than she expects.

This brings us to the mothers of preschool children. Society agrees that babies and little children need their mother, an absolutely steady and reliable, loving woman. The mother who rushes her children through a dawn breakfast, nags them to hurry with their clothes so she can deposit them somewhere on her way to work and then returns, exhausted, in the early evening to prepare an ugly meal and send her children testily to bed is suffering a defeat on all fronts. She isn't a mother, wife or woman. She's a wage-earner and the $42.97 she gets every week, after deductions, cannot possibly justify what she is doing to herself.

It isn't the time she's away from the children, it's what happens in the hours she has them with her. I have known many mothers of preschool children who stayed home stubbornly to raise their small ones and managed to do as much harm as the working mother I have just described. These are the mothers who can never accept the estrangement of being a housewife. They remember the conviviality of the office they left for motherhood; lunching in laughter-filled restaurants; the lullaby relaxation of routine. They survey their present existence: an adult, spending an entire day in the company of a two-year-old, subject to the whims and demands of the child at erratic intervals, including the middle of the night; a highly skilled office worker, reduced to removing dust from the coffee table. She screams at her child, who is the cause of her plight, and afterward is wracked by guilt. She soaks herself in radio and television to distract her mind, ordering her child to be quiet and go away. When she can't stand it any longer she goes out, leaving the child with some makeshift supervision. She prides herself on being a "good" mother because she isn't working; in her heart she must know she is a terrible mother.

This woman needs to work at something she can be proud of, in order to increase her importance to herself. It doesn't need to be a major occupation, lasting several hours a day, but it must be regular so she can look forward to it and plan the supervision of her child. I know of one woman in a northern Ontario city who discovered there was no kindergarten in the local schools. She campaigned, became a school-board trustee and led a movement to establish kindergartens. Another woman spends an afternoon a week teaching a cerebral-palsy victim of thirty-three how to read. I know another who became an expert gardener, growing hybrid roses, and another who, in a rebellion against depression one grey winter day, started to scrape the finish off the dining-room table and eventually refinished with professional technique all the furniture in her house. All of these fulfill my requirements for working women, since they have the heavy remuneration of self-esteem and worth.

As the children grow older, I believe that they will gain by having a working mother. They can learn responsibility in no better way. There are, of course, two different ways of performing any assigned task. The twelve-year-old who is supposed to do the dinner dishes can feel abused—and be loquacious on the subject—and will try to avoid the chore at every opportunity. But if he understands that this is his contribution to his family and that he is an active participant in the machinery that makes the family work efficiently, there is rarely much difficulty.

Children have a great capacity for responsibility. Without any exception, mothers who have teenage children and become pregnant tell me that their older children showed a solicitude and thoughtfulness that astounded their parents. "I didn't know they were capable of such understanding," the mother tells me. Those children are capable all right and they and their parents both gain enormously in the discovery.

Although few mothers go back to university to finish courses, a surprising number are taking night-school training in accounting or business machines, or refresher courses in some type of nursing or teaching. A woman social worker I know kept her hand in all through the years her three children were small by intensive reading. She bought a small filing cabinet and kept all useful information in well-organized files. She went back to work, when her youngest child was ten, as knowledgeable as any fresh graduate.

Work is a wonderful antidote to the blues of menopause. This is a period when a woman's sense of uselessness is so acute that she can, literally, be driven to drink, dope or mental illness. Her family is grown, her childbearing years are ending, her husband often could do just as well with a hired housekeeper. If she has some consuming occupation, whether it is a study of fourteenth-century Chinese art or an office to manage, she isn't in much danger of being shattered by what is happening to her physiology.

Work is a great healer, for a woman. A woman who discovered her husband, much adored by their children, was chronically unfaithful, soothed her ravaged emotions by going back to work. Another woman, who was languishing in misery because she was sterile, pulled herself out of her own private pit by spending a morning a week bathing babies at an infants' home. The babies responded instantly to her loving gentleness in the midst of their institutional life; babies and woman helped one another through a bad time.

I'd like to add a special word for a woman trained in some profession such as medicine or law before her marriage. In our busy new country, it is a tragic loss to have such a person disappear into the suburbs, and agonizingly difficult for such a woman to be content with peeling potatoes. Three quarters of the staff of Women's College Hospital where I work are married and many of them have children. Quite a few women dentists and architects continue to work after their marriages. These women cannot possibly be motivated by money, I am delighted to say. The cost of housekeepers, the increased needs of their wardrobes, the whopping income tax they pay, at single-woman rates, all combine to reduce the possibility that a fondness for a bank account is a main factor. I know a woman doctor who last year, after paying her office upkeep, her secretary, her housekeeper and her income tax, made six hundred dollars. She works, as happy, well-adjusted women everywhere work, because it satisfies her need to work, gives her joy in a job she loves.

Every Thursday night for twenty years I have been met by a gentle radiance in my living room. It uplifts my heart and dispels my fatigue. My staunch Scots friend has been there all day "bringing up" the shine, even of the window sills. That room is full of enduring integrity and devotion of one who loves to clean, and loves me too. She did not go to work to meet any deep psychological need, she went to work to feed her children—now they are financially successful but she still works. It is the centre of her life, for we are all dependent on her faithfulness. I pay this special tribute to all those cheerful women who do hard rough work, so that the mother, the business and professional woman can be refreshed and do a better job. I hope they see their reward and we justify their devotion.

Some women have no struggle as to whether they will continue to work outside their home when they marry. No indecision or longing for activity will wrack them. They marry a farmer, a minister or a country doctor and it becomes a two-way partnership. Who will carry the heavier load? Who will sustain and support the community? I'll bet on the wife every time.

Next year I reach retirement age at my hospital. Many friends have asked if this will mean that I will quit work. Quit work! Not until I quit breathing. I'll work wherever I can; somewhere, I'll always work. Work is medicine, good medicine. I wholeheartedly prescribe it for every woman.

4. Cynthia Steers, "How Much Are You Worth to Your Husband?," *Chatelaine*, April 1959

How much is a housewife worth? Even leaving aside the incalculables—for instance, your blue eyes and smiling face, your role as family comforter and psychologist—it's an impressive amount.

Suppose, as we did, that yours is a city family in a middle-income bracket ($5,000 to $8,000), three children, living in a moderate-priced home. Now, you take the month off.

Here's what your husband would have to pay out in cold hard cash—and, if anything, our figures veer to the conservative. The housewives we questioned sometimes also pickled, jammed and canned out of their own gardens, sewed *all* the children's clothes, papered and painted, helped their husbands with office work at home—but the average wife's work added up like this:

HOUSEKEEPER AND CLEANING WOMAN: For better or worse the wife does all the cleaning, light dusting, heavy scrubbing and floor cleaning. She takes care of the three children all of the time, naturally—a job that lasts usually from at least seven in the morning till eight at night (on a good day).

A paid housekeeper who sleeps in charges $125 to $140 a month, with at least a day off a week. She does the light cleaning but not the heavy work. So a cleaning woman to take care of the onerous duties costs $7 a week plus carfare and lunch—or $30 a month.

LAUNDRESS: All a part of the day's work, the housewife takes care of the household, children's, her husband's and her own personal laundry, washing, ironing, spot-cleaning, pressing.

A paid housekeeper keeps the children's clothes and household linen in order. She doesn't take care of the husband's attire. Laundry bills for shirts alone total $1.75 to $2 a week for five to six white shirts and a couple of sports shirts—adding up to $8 a month. Turning collars costs 50 cents a shirt, pressing pants, 50 cents, pressing suits, $1.25.

An average $1 a month for valeting would keep the husband fairly neat, making the total for his personal appearance $9 a month.

HOME ECONOMIST AND SHOPPER: Chicken wings, sausages, beef Strogonoff—the housewife plans economical family meals and shops on her own, usually one big trip a week to the supermarket with a gaggle of children trailing her.

The housekeeper plans the meals but orders supplies from the corner grocery which delivers. This adds dollars to the grocery bill in extra delivery costs and higher charges on most grocery items in the smaller stores which deliver. Add about $5 a month to the food budget.

CHAUFFEUR: The housewife squires her children about in the family car for visits to the doctor and dentist, for shopping trips for children's shoes and clothes, to parties and extra lessons of one kind or another.

The housekeeper must use a taxi for these expeditions. At three outings a month, taxi fares amount to approximately $5.

BABY SITTER: Whoever thinks of a mother being a baby sitter? She's baby sitting all the time! However, without her, her husband must still be away from home for business meetings, club meetings, extra working days, on weekends, and days off for golf or skiing. And the paid housekeeper must also have her time off. Thus babysitting fees must be added to the account.

The going rate for baby sitters is 60 cents an hour. Since a baby sitter will probably be needed twice a week, for an average four-hour period each time, the minimum total is $20.

HANDYMAN: Almost without thinking about it, the housewife will pick up a screwdriver or hammer to right some small wrong about the house. Such small extras as the odd painting job (shelves or chairs in the children's rooms), fixing the front-door number plaque that fell off, or putting up the magnetic knife holder, or hammering a few nails into the back steps, or putting a washer into a leaky faucet, are part and parcel of a housewife's day.

Upkeep for a house on this level, considering handyman's charges of $1 an hour, would amount to at least $3 a month.

CLEANER: Spot-cleaning or cleaning rugs, chesterfields and chairs is another wifely task—especially with grubby small fingers leaving imprints on everything they touch.

Professional cleaners charge $7.50 for a chesterfield and $2.50 for large chairs. Rugs, depending on size, could be cleaned from about $10. Considering once-a-year cleaning, the break-down amounts to about $2 a month, for chesterfield, two chairs, and one rug.

SEAMSTRESS: Quite aside from the darning, button sewing and sheet mending a wife often acts as professional seamstress—even if only for the children's curtains and bedspreads, or school-play costumes, or cushions for the living room. The cost of making them at home is just half what it costs to have them made outside.

And clothes sewed for the children save fifty percent on their clothing budget. Children's party dresses, velvet or smocked, cost $12 to $15 to buy and can be made at home for $3 to $5. Overalls, smocks, pyjamas can be made for half price. Estimating an average six articles a year for the ordinary, not-mad-about sewing mother, the saving is approximately $5 a month.

GARDENER AND GROUNDSKEEPER: Into shorts for gardening in summer or on with the toque and mitts in the winter for snow-shoveling duties—it's all part of the working day for a housewife. With gardeners and snow shovelers charging $1 an hour, and working an average hour and a bit a week over the changing seasons, the monthly cost would be around $5.

HOSTESS: Clean the floor, vacuum, whip up a divine dinner after feeding the children, jump into something glamorous and the housewife is ready to play hostess to her husband's business associates and clients as well as to family friends.

Without his wife, a husband would probably have to entertain (other than personal friends) at a dinner in a restaurant, at a cost of $20 for three, rather than the $5 it might cost at home. And he would probably give one cocktail party a year at home to entertain all his friends. Catering for food for this for thirty people would cost $25 rather than the $10 a wife could manage on. With one dinner a month and a cocktail party a year, entertainment would cost him about $17 a month extra.

TAX DEDUCTION: And not to be forgotten, the one figure everyone can pinpoint is the $1,000-a-year tax deduction stay-at-home wives are worth to their husbands—which is a pretty $16.65 a month.

Grand total—$257.65 a month at least.

5. Anna Davies, "I Hate Housekeeping," *Chatelaine*, March 1961

Nothing in my early education prepared me for housekeeping, and I'm not sorry. On the contrary, I'm thankful now for all the hours I spent reading and studying, instead of learning time-honored methods of making short pastry and starching frills.

I was trained for what I fondly hoped would be the life of a modern woman. My educators, assuming this would require an ability to think, taught me to think. And the thinking I have done during fourteen years of marriage, over dishwashing, bedmaking and vacuuming, has led me to the conclusion that our methods of housekeeping in this age of industrial organization and scientific accomplishment are obsolete.

It's time to revolt!

My dissatisfaction, which I share with many others, arises not out of an immature disinclination to do necessary work, but out of the recognition that I spend my days in completely futile and unnecessary toil. And for that reason alone, I hate housekeeping.

Moreover, I am no longer interested in learning how to do housework quickly, painlessly, efficiently or well. I'm only interested in abolishing it. Should this necessitate a social revolution, so much the better. Societies thrive on them.

If a bowling alley can provide mothers with a fully equipped and supervised nursery to care for their children while they bowl, then surely we could make provision for those who want to spend time more constructively—on an afternoon's work which they enjoy and are trained for.

And if an afternoon—why not two or three? Why not a short working week for both men and women? We're always talking about it.

As an enthusiastic proponent of marriage and motherhood, I attack only the outworn image of a backdrop against which the family phase of human existence should be enacted. I'm intolerant of the old routines, increasingly impossible for women to play with conviction.

I realize I was led up the educational garden path, as thousands of girls were and still are, but I do not reproach those responsible, I wish them luck and success with the next generation. As a mother of girls, I'll help from my end.

Some say education is "wasted" on girls who will ultimately be "only housewives." Therefore, we are urged to put the clock back and train them all in the homemaker arts. But the days of the housewife are numbered, and in the meantime we're not wasting education on women, we're wasting educated women!

Women did "men's jobs."

After the Industrial Revolution the home and the women in it lost their former economic and educational function. Until then, the family's livelihood' and the children's training largely centred in the home. Now the men went off to factories to earn a living, and much of the training of the children was taken over by schools.

Girls, also integrated into this public-school system, tagged along with a curriculum designed to equip male children to earn a living in industry.

Thus women stumbled upon a means to develop individual talents and achieve economic independence of men. World War I, by drawing large numbers of them into factories and offices, helped prove they could do "men's jobs" efficiently and well.

The girls born in the years between the two world wars, who are now wives and mothers, were the first to receive, as a matter of public policy, higher education on a par with their brothers'. They entered business, industry and the professions in the hundreds of thousands, leaving home, mother and domestic service in droves.

So far, so good. That was progress. Now comes the rub.

Although public policy demands equal effort and standards of excellence from all students regardless of sex, the boy who despairs of surpassing the high grades of a female fellow student needn't worry. The competition and challenge she presents in the schoolroom will not be carried into later life. Her abilities will be withdrawn from the world through marriage: her so-called "true" womanly talents better employed within the confines of house and family.

In forty years we have reached a halfway mark. We have created an elaborate, expensive and unnecessary ritual whereby the modern girl prepares to be an old-fashioned wife. Property, dowries, the domestic arts are no longer factors influencing the planning of a marriage. Mutual attraction in looks, common interests, ideas, and other intangibles, are.

Not a word before marriage of cooking, cleaning, washing, polishing, ironing, mothproofing, putting out garbage, cleaning basements, weeding, raking leaves, baby sitters, staying in for cleaner, breadman, deliveryman, picking up clothes, toys, papers, and so on and on. That's conversation for a courting couple? Horrifying thought.

Funny thing though—it's conversational material for many married couples these days. Even we women like to talk about our work occasionally.

With what kind of work do I justify my existence? After the family's clothes have been washed and dried automatically, I am required to fold them and put them away. I see no future in this job, the play-learning potential of which I long ago exhausted. But such jobs are all mine now....

In other words, while women who would have been domestic workers in the past now go into industry, we try to fill the gap they leave in homes with all our married women—the intelligent, the average and the dumb—regardless of talent, ability or inclination.

No wonder there is frustration and dissatisfaction among women who, brought up in the confident expectation of ultimately achieving satisfaction from the work of their choice, find that merely through marriage they are demoted, left to cope with the disorganized remnants of what was work of purpose and worth—well over a century ago. Even their duties as citizens are subordinated to the traditional housewifely tasks (and as a result, we probably get the world we deserve).

This study was of four countries with older cultures and less initial educational opportunity for girls than we have in North America. The education and training of our girls should lead them to expect more than that "natural order of things"; the tragedy is that it doesn't.

A vote but no real voice

Whatever we women may think about our situation soon goes up in the steam of our electric kettles, down the drain with the water from our washing machines, is lost in the ceaseless daily round from small child to appliance, from telephone to family station wagon. In our secure little nests alone and unaided, we haven't much time for thought about or for contact with the outside world.

Regressing willy-nilly to our former childish and dependent state, we leave the affairs of the world to our husbands, to the men of the world everywhere. We have a vote, for what it is worth, but no real voice.

The values of a vote seem remote from daily concern with leaky taps, dribbly noses and meal-planning.

Again Professor Duverger: "Under a democratic system, political activity is essentially adult. It presupposes that anyone engaged in it takes full responsibility for his fate and does not leave it to another to decide for him."

This is interesting, considering that girls, officially encouraged to the dizzy heights of adult freedoms and responsibilities, are as women precipitated back into a world of children, childish tasks and contained horizons. We proclaim the supreme importance of this little world to all women. Then we complain of their inertia and reluctance to taken on civic responsibilities.

This is drudgery in every job, in every profession; but in most, early stints of drudgery well done are rewarded by promotion, by more responsibility and less drudgery. Not so for the "career" of homemaker. More responsibility invariably is accompanied by more drudgery. The best, the most interesting part of educating a child is siphoned off by better-organized institutions such as schools and youth groups.

It might be argued that the intelligent woman could find challenge enough in her older children, in guiding and teaching the nascent minds. But when the baby needs changing, the phone answering ("It's for you, Ma!"), the dinner putting in the oven and tears of a toddler drying, it is useless to discuss political parties or the aims of World Refugee Year with an inquiring nine-year-old—this being the time he is likely to ask for such information. And as the years slip by mother's mental development stagnates for want of exercise.

Husbands are expected to fill this void in their wives' mental requirements and be good fathers, lovers, breadwinners, and do odd jobs around the house besides. Frankly, I think it is too much to expect of any man.

Since we are making no effort to curtail our girls' educational opportunities (on the contrary, the trend being to seek improvements in our co-educational system), the New Class will just keep on growing.

Marriage is not *a career.*

More women will embark on careers and professions they enjoy; more mental skills will be developed in the female half of the population; more vocational opportunities will open to them.

Let's face the fact that domestic work is only one job—for someone; not everyone, not every woman. Let's admit that marriage, motherhood and homemaking are not careers, but human conditions. With a little reorganization of contemporary society they need not interfere with a woman's chosen work any more than marriage and fatherhood does with a man's.

We can encourage girls to attain and stay in the adult world. Let them have marriage, home and all the babies they want — but not necessarily in our way, on our terms.

Women who go out to work seeking a personal satisfaction missing in the home are reproached by public opinion for neglecting their duties, and so feel guilt. They worry about their children in "empty houses," "running wild in the streets," and so on — all the bogeys conjured up by their critics.

They also worry, with justification, because adequate community care and facilities for children are lamentably lacking.

All we can provide instead of these is one private slave — mother! ...

Our standard of material living may be as high as modern technology permits, but our scale of culture is low because the exploitation of our productive capacity is inefficient. It does not help fulfil the individual's human potential — especially woman's.

The answer lies not in bigger and better and more elaborate mechanical gadgets. It lies in reorganizing our roster of life's priorities; in extending some of our social and commercial services and initiating others.

We need crèches, nursery schools, day nurseries, cafeterias, laundries, home help, more and better public transportation, parks, libraries, and recreation centres. We can do with more and better varieties of precooked, prepackaged family-size meals, with less variety and simpler styles in clothing. There is a limit to the need for Things: in our "affluent society" the need for services is greater.

I am not advocating abolition of the home. I am for abolishing our present understanding of home as a private box; repository of the family's worldly goods. "Home is where the heart is" runs a saying, but for us it seems to be "where the things are kept."

Upkeep of property is deemed more important than development of mind and senses; mom's baking more treasured than her mental health; the monotony of daily life broken only by purchasing yet another luxury.

And every new, private thing requires its routines of care and upkeep.

We haven't begun to use our vast industrial potential and scientific know-how for real, free living. We are still devoted to making, selling and buying merely newer versions of what was made in the past to suit another way of life.

Our industries could provide us with more disposable objects of living than it does. If we can have disposable handkerchiefs and prefabricated kitchens, we can go on up the scale to prefabricated housing assembled and dismantled at will; buildings such as schools that could be added to or subtracted from as the need arises.

Let's throw things away.

Plastics haven't begun to come into their own. We make useless toys and copies of conventional articles with a material that, if imaginatively applied, has thousands of original uses. Furniture, utensils, clothes, toys could be cheaply made to last only as long as they are useful, then be discarded without a qualm.

We could have all these things, objects of superb design, utility and variety, but we're so convinced of the enduring values of possessions that when we are told we would not want things any different we believe it.

What is worse, we are never given the opportunity to test our opinions. Extended social services and industry satisfying real consumer needs, instead of catering to obsolescent and artificially stimulated wants, could combine to bring women into the twentieth century before it is over.

Could we not in future divide breadwinning and child care equally between husband and wife? We would then have completed the cycle set in motion by the Industrial Revolution and regained the adult, human partnership which men and women in the home enjoyed before that time.

Nor is my seeking to free women from domestic toil tantamount to advocating the breakup of family life. If we had real faith in ourselves and the future and suffered less nostalgia for a vanished age, we might come up with a fresh and more applicable conception of family life for our day.

Women can be equal.

We know we face a challenge from the East, behind and in front of the Iron Curtain. There, people are much less concerned with annihilating us (and themselves in the process) than they are with achieving our standards of education, technology and living — in that order — and eventually surpassing us in all three.

Therefore, if we are truly concerned about the perpetuation of our democratic way of life, we should match their effort with ours. A first step would be to ensure equality of opportunity to be human to our own women, thus doubling the human achievement potential on our side.

If it means that we thereby draw women away from a conventional family-home structure as we long ago drew their husbands out of the home and into the factory, then let's make up for lost time and progress right away. . . .

In exercising my critical faculties on hateful housekeeping I am vindicating my early training. I ask others to join me in a battle against futility; in inventing ways to circumvent the accepted and abolish the unnecessary. Let us at last demand unashamedly the means to realize our full potential as women.

A rebellion is justified, for, far from being detractors of our civilization, we are the pioneers of inevitable changes for the better. What was bad for our mothers is no longer good enough for us.

FURTHER READINGS

Adamson, N. "Feminists, Libbers, Lefties, and Radicals: The Emergence of the Women's Liberation Movement." In *A Diversity of Women; Ontario 1945-1980*, ed. J. Parr. Toronto: University of Toronto Press, 1995.

Adamson, N. *et al. Feminist Organizing for Change: The Contemporary Women's Movement in Canada*. Toronto: Oxford University Press, 1988.

Backhouse, C., and D. Flaherty, Eds. *Challenging Times: The Women's Movements in Canada and the United States*. Montreal and Kingston: McGill-Queen's University Press, 1992.

Bashevkin, S. *Toeing the Lines: Women and Party Politics in English Canada*. Don Mills: Oxford University Press, 1993.

Bashevkin, S. *Women of the Defensive: Living through Conservative Times*. Toronto: University of Toronto Press, 1998.

Brodie, J. *Politics on the Margins: Restructuring and the Canadian Women's Movement*. Halifax: Fernwood, 1995.

Boyd, M. *Canadian Attitudes Toward Women: Thirty Years of Change*. Ottawa: Government of Canada, 1984.

Gleason, M. "Psychology and the Construction of the 'Normal Family' in Postwar Canada, 1945-1960." *Canadian Historical Review* 78, 3 (1997): 442-77.

Iacovetta, F., and M. Valverde, Eds. *Gender Conflicts: New Essays in Women's History*. Toronto: University of Toronto Press, 1992.

Korinek, V. *Roughing It in the Suburbs: Reading Chatelaine Magazine in the Fifties and Sixties*. Toronto: University of Toronto Press, 2000.

Kostash, M. *Long Way From Home: The Story of the Sixties Generation in Canada*. Toronto: James Lorimer, 1980.

Owram, D. *Born at the Right Time: A History of the Baby Boom Generation*. Toronto: University of Toronto Press, 1996.

Pierson, R. *et al.*, Eds. *Canadian Women's Issues: Twenty-Five Years of Women's Activism in English Canada*. Toronto: James Lorimer, 1993.

Rebick, J. *Ten Thousand Roses: The Making of a Feminist Revolution*. Toronto: Penguin, 2005.

Sangster, J. "Doing Two Jobs: The Wage-Earning Mother, 1945-1970." In *A Diversity of Women: Ontario 1945-1980*, ed. J. Parr. Toronto: University of Toronto Press, 1995.

Strong-Boag, V. "Canada's Wage-Earning Wives and the Construction of the Middle Class, 1945-1960." *Journal of Canadian Studies* 29 (Fall 1994): 5-25.

Strong-Boag, V. "Home Dreams: Women and the Suburban Experiment in Canada." *Canadian Historical Review* 72, 4 (1991): 471-504.

Strong-Boag, V. "Their Side of the Story: Women's Voices from Ontario Suburbs, 1945-1960." In *A Diversity of Women: Ontario 1945-1980*, ed. J. Parr. Toronto: University of Toronto Press, 1995.

Vickers, J. "The Intellectual Origins of the Women's Movement in Canada." In *Challenging Ties: The Women's Movement in Canada and the United States*, ed. C. Backhouse and D. Flaherty. Montreal and Kingston: McGill-Queen's University Press, 1992.

Vickers, J. *et al. Politics as if Women Mattered: A Political Analysis of the National Action Committee on the Status of Women*. Toronto: University of Toronto Press, 1993.

Wine J., and J.L. Ristock, Eds. *Women and Social Change: Feminist Activism in Canada*. Toronto: Lorimer, 1991.

CHAPTER 12

"Hippies, Bikers, and Greasers"

YOUTH IN THE 1960S

INTRODUCTION

Has adolescent behaviour always irritated the older generation? Did Neanderthal mothers wring hairy hands in despair at sons and daughters who challenged their authority and wouldn't keep the cave clean? Doubtful. Modern mass youth culture and the teenager were products of the post-World War II era. The 1950s were boom times in the United States and Canada, the first period in North American history when most adolescents no longer had to contribute to the family's economic welfare and could instead remain in school until graduation from high school and possibly even enter university. Perhaps the single biggest contributor to the creation of the teenager was the affluent society's ability to grant youth time and money — time they could call their own and money with which to enjoy it. This, for the majority of working-class North Americans, was indeed entirely new. The economy generated sufficient wealth for teenagers to hold jobs done by adults in previous generations, such as waitressing, gardening, errands, babysitting, gas jockeys, and the like. Thus, the teenager was an artificial construct by a society enjoying two critical attributes, one material, and the other philosophical: sufficient wealth to sustain a cohort between childhood and adulthood, and a basis of individualism and liberal democracy. That is why teenagers first appeared in North America, not elsewhere.

With money and time to spare, these new "teens" created a culture distinctly their own—one based upon a rejection of what they perceived as their parents' stuffy conservatism. It did not take long for Madison Avenue to discover this untapped market and to create, by the late 1950s, a whole industry from fan magazines to records, clothing, and films focused directly at teenagers' hearts and wallets. Heartthrobs like Pat Boone, though marketed to teens as their own creation, were, in fact, generated in boardrooms by the old capitalist establishment. The 1950s teenager was a consumer *par excellence*, just like his parents.

The problem for this new generation, however, was its lack of rules of engagement. Previously, and in less affluent societies, average people abruptly shifted from childhood at home to being adults at work typically at age 14. Even "childhood" was not a particularly distinct period in a person's life. Young children had very real responsibilities within the family unit and to the wider society. British common law, for example, did not distinguish between juvenile and adult delinquency until well into the nineteenth century. Thus, if definitions of childhood were awkward, a new sub-genre straddling childhood and the adult world proved even more problematic. There were no previous teenagers to tell the participants how to behave or to offer them codes of behaviour. That being the case, behaviour outside "the norm" could, and was, logically construed as "rebellious," whether it really was or not. It is hardly surprising that James Dean rebelled "without a cause" in the 1950s. He knew something was amiss and that he was adrift in an un-codified period of his life, but he couldn't put a finger on it and consequently expended much energy on melancholy pouting. No wonder the poor boy was riddled with *angst*. He didn't know where he fitted in and therefore gravitated to kindred souls drifting through the same process. Nor is it surprising that his father ranted against what he perceived as his son's disrespectful attitude—young men weren't that way when he was young! And he was right. They weren't. Just the same, and despite this emerging generation gap, 1950's teenagers were decidedly apolitical, quite naïve, and quite unthreatening to the social fabric.

That changed by the late 1960s. Youth culture entered a new phase where it was indeed perceived by its members, and by the opposing "establishment," as menacing. New personae, dubbed hippies, threatened to tear down the old order by tuning in, turning on, and dropping out, thus rejecting everything their parents represented. Their musicians sang about revolutions and class solidarity, not sock-hops or going to the drive-in on a Saturday night. The image of the parental generation transformed into something very different from James Dean's stodgy and vaguely stupid father who wouldn't let the kids stay out past ten o'clock. Youth now saw the older generation as the political enemy that created the Vietnam War, environmental degradation, repression of women and minority

"Hippies, Bikers, and Greasers": Youth in the 1960s

290

groups, and an unfeeling capitalist economy based upon unbridled consumerism. The new generation hated sprawling suburbia with its hollow boosterism, pretentiousness, and conformity. No wonder the flower children cried: "Don't trust anyone over 30!"

The hippies rejected their parents' culture, but what did they take as their own? Logically experimentation was required to discover what fitted their needs. If Western European religion, for example, formed part of their parents' rotten world, then they would reject it in favour of something else—or no religion at all. Hinduism from India and Buddhism became essential parts of the new creed. Youth leaders such as The Beatles, The Who, and even the bad boys, The Rolling Stones, departed for ashrams in India and took to heart messages from Hindu gurus. Religious practices of Indigenous people, such as those of the southwest United States, became popular—especially when they legitimized use of hallucinogens. That is not to say that youth became expert in Hindu philosophy. They posed with their copies of the *Bhagavad Gita* for acceptance and conformity among their peers and to confront their parents. Gopala Alampur, whose study follows, used his middle name "Krishna," a very common Indian name, while he went underground to study Yorkville's youth culture. The consequence, he says, was that many thought him to be a guru because he was Indian and shared a name with the Hare Krishnas.

Those youth leaders who went off to India brought back more than new religious convictions from their forays. The superficial trappings of Indian culture, from incense to colourful cotton print cloth, became their badges. George Harrison, one of The Beatles, brought back a sitar and incorporated it into his music, soon followed by anyone with pretensions to the *avant garde*. Outrageous clothing, based on a mix-and-match premise, became the visible hippie style, perhaps because it was so completely at odds with their parents' clean-cut conformity. Nor was eclecticism limited to a geographical potpourri of clothing. Historical dress made appearances too, leading to marvelous mixtures of top hats, Indian prints, old military uniforms, "granny glasses," miniskirts, jeans, long flowing skirts, and lots of beads.

Youth turned to mystical literature, too, in rejection of the supposed conformist views of their parents. Unsurprisingly, the most popular novels were about quests, about searching for place and meaning. The Beat writer and Catholic mystic Jack Kerouac saw sales of his *On the Road* explode. The German writer Hermann Hesse's 1929 novel *Steppenwolf* became a youth Bible, and a major rock band took its name; their song "Born to be Wild" became an anthem. American urban poets like Allen Ginsberg grew in stature, partly from their romanticized bohemian lifestyles and partly because the obscurity of their writing could mean anything to anyone. No parent read Ginsberg! Youth championed freedom, individualism, idealism, and Youth itself. Perhaps The Who's Pete Townshend best encapsulated the creed: "I hope to die before I get old." It was very romantic, enormously egocentric, and remarkably self-indulgent—despite its practitioners' protests to the contrary.

Drugs became fundamental to the new youth generation because their mind-altering properties supposedly facilitated the quest for new horizons. That, at least, was the initial rationale for experimentation before addiction reared its head. The very act of experimenting with drugs, too, was part of the process. Not only did it flout Canadian law, there was also the seduction of the implicit danger of taking powerful pharmaceuticals. Older experimenters like Aldous Huxley were rediscovered, and his 1954 book on his experiments with hallucinogenic drugs, *The Doors of Perception*, again gave its name to one of the most influential bands of the day, The Doors. Influential teachers like Timothy Leary extolled the virtues of LSD as mind-expanding and encouraged its use. Everyone rejected heroin, but too many followed the trajectory toward stronger and stronger drugs until they fell prey to its allure; Canadian rocker Neil Young sang of "[seeing] the needle and the damage done."

Sexual liberation also formed a cornerstone to youth culture in the 1960s, and though practitioners may have argued that promiscuity was philosophically based, it is more likely that it was based upon the development and popularization of the birth control pill. Traditional conceptions of marriage and fidelity were dismissed as outmoded and repressive. Instead, everyone should be able to "do their own thing" with whomever they wished. That included members of the same sex after the decriminalization of homosexuality in Canada under Liberal Justice Minister Pierre Trudeau in 1969. Women asserted their sexual independence to a degree heretofore unseen, with decidedly mixed reactions from men. This was perhaps best symbolized by women's campaigns to "burn the bra" as a garment of repression. There were indeed experiments with "free love," but they were never normalized. Serial monogamy and sexual satisfaction, however, became ends unto themselves, and virginity at marriage disappeared in practice, if not in concept.

That is not to suggest that all Canadian youth became hippies in the late 1960s. Far from it. It is safe to say that most young people accepted some attributes of what they perceived as hippie culture, be it music, clothing, or dabbling in left-wing politics, but most of them remained deeply and safely entrenched in Canadian suburbia. Statistics categorically show that the majority of Canadian teenagers of the 1960s did not smoke marijuana, let alone indulge in harder drugs. Most of their rebellion was intermittent posturing. Nonetheless, the high visibility of the serious hippie made waves throughout the social fabric and did lead many members of the older generation to believe that Canadian society was on the brink of anarchy.

Protest was, after all, a manifestation of the age. Students in Paris almost overthrew the French government in 1968, goaded on by major philosophers like Jean-Paul Sartre. Franz Fanon's *The Wretched of the Earth* espoused the popular uprising by imperialized people in the Third World. Che Guevara died fighting for the liberty of Bolivian peasants, the Red Brigade sought revolution in Italy, and the Front de libération du Québec bombed anything it perceived as symbolic of Anglo-domination in that province. It was a restive time when controversy raged over the Vietnam War and American imperialism, and when women marched for equal rights and control over their bodies. In the United States, African Americans took to the streets for justice and in sheer frustration at a society that categorized them as second class. Highly politicized music, like Winnipeg band The Guess Who's "American Woman," blasted across the airwaves. And for the willfully blind and naïve there was the seduction of communism as practiced under Mao in China, the Soviet Union, and increasingly in newly liberated African nations like Zimbabwe under Robert Mugabe. It was all heady stuff and distressing to the traditional movers and shakers of the Western world.

It was motorcycle gangs—the bikers—who posed a greater menace to society, both then and certainly now. Ironically of all the subcultures from the late 1960s, only they still exert an influence. The bike gang, a distinctly North American phenomenon, has its roots in the immediate post-World War II period. Demobilized American soldiers—with their back pay and an inability to settle down as "normal" citizens after the carnage they witnessed—grouped together, bought surplus American army Harley Davidson motorcycles, and hit the road. They created an odd contradiction. Despite considering themselves beyond the law and making their living illicitly, they were, in fact, fiercely conformist—but to their own laws. Any biker who transgressed the code of the group could expect ferocious retribution. This was not "doing your own thing." Gangs set themselves up as "nations" and fought each other and the wider citizenry as a way of proving their lawlessness and independence. Where the hippie preached love and peace, the biker ruled by might and was not averse to regular "rumbles." No wonder hippies and bikers did not see eye to eye. Bikers were also deeply conservative. One look at their treatment of women, both then and now, says it all.

Why did youth culture die to be replaced by vacuous disco and "Stayin' Alive" in the 1970s? Perhaps because it was a house largely built on sand. It could also be that young people came to recognize that the comforts of suburbia weren't really all that bad and, conversely, that living rough wasn't all it was cracked up to be. Perhaps youth came to realize that Indian mysticism really did not change the world, especially when one didn't really understand it, and that "dropping out" was at odds with political and environmental activism. Perhaps it was the demise of so many champions of youth culture—Janis Joplin, Jimi Hendrix, Brian Jones, Marc Bolan, and so many others—who died sordid deaths of substance abuse. So many more squandered their lives and creativity by becoming junkies. That was not romantic.

DISCUSSION POINTS

1. What factors explain the emergence of 1960s counterculture?

2. Which aspects of the counterculture have had the longest impact?

3. The counterculture's call for social awareness, responsibility, and action failed to coincide with its emphasis on personal freedom, individuality, and "dropping out." Was the philosophy of the counterculture more consistent or inconsistent?

DOCUMENTS

1. "Turn On, Tune In, Take Over," *Georgia Straight*, September 8, 1967

The Georgia Straight *weekly news magazine exploded onto the Vancouver scene in May 1967, the "Summer of Love," as a 12-page radical alternative to mainstream news media and specifically as a voice of youth. It was unremittingly left-wing, tackling what it perceived as the hypocrisy in modern society and offering in-depth analysis of topics such as homosexuality, environmentalism, feminism, modern imperialism, drugs, and the Vietnam War. What it lacked in objective journalism it made up for with irreverence and enthusiasm, and it became a chronic irritant to "the establishment"—which was exactly what it sought to be. Harassment by police and Vancouver city politicians and bureaucrats only increased its circulation.*

If you drop out of school, you'll probably have to get a job. You'll hate that, too. The pay will be low, and it'll be even more boring than school was. If you don't get a job, your parents will do all they can to make life rough for you. You could leave home, but what happens then? It's getting too cold for sleeping outside, or hitch-hiking around the country. Staying with friends can be fun—for a while. But you'll find it impossible to do anything. You'll soon grow tired of "making the scene," and living on somebody else's terms.

ACTION is the answer. When you close yourself up in your own little world, you're just avoiding questions that will have to be answered, sooner or later. If school is a drag, it's up to you to make it better. If you're thinking of leaving school anyway, what's wrong with getting "KICKED OUT"? Nobody has the right

"Hippies, Bikers, and Greasers": Youth in the 1960s

to tell you how to run your life. You know more than the "elders" do, about the things that are really important today. Make school interesting by taking it over. How can [you] begin? Here are some ideas:

**Organize a union, to put pressure on the teachers and principals, so they'll give you what you want.

**Petitions can be circulated, to get rid of bad teachers and principals.

**A delegation can be sent to every PTA meeting, to present student demands. Don't ask for permission; tell them what you intend to do.

**Fight against all age restrictions. If you want to do something, go ahead. If you get caught, call the GEORGIA STRAIGHT Defense Fund. The "laws" are so bad that, nowadays, it is dishonorable not to have a criminal record. Just forget about building a future in their society. You can do better.

**Organize love-ins in schoolyards, perhaps every noon-hour.

**During fire drills, act as if there were a real fire. Once you get outside, keep going.

***If you don't like a textbook, lose it.

TAKE OVER!

****Stamp out corporal punishment. If any teacher or principal hits you, charge him with assault. One student actually hit back, when a teacher attacked him. This is not recommended, however, except in extreme emergencies.

****Insist that schools be left open at night, so you can have a place to sleep, in case conditions at home become unbearable.

****Plan out your own courses, and teach them yourselves. Ask sympathetic teachers to help you.

****Start up school newspapers…

****Let your imagination run wild. Each day should bring new ideas. Once you get started, nothing can stop you.

2. "Grass in Class," *Georgia Straight*, February 17-24, 1971

Lucky students in King George and several other Vancouver high schools yesterday (Tuesday) received a free marijuana cigarette, says the Vancouver High School Underground, an organization of revolutionary high school students.

One was even mailed to the *Vancouver Sun*, taped to a copy of their program and plans for future actions. Their statement reads as follows:

Taped to this sheet of paper is a joint of Marijuana. The Vancouver High School Underground is placing ten letters, containing ten joints, in this prison today.

"The jailers who run this school (prison) say that grass is dangerous and heads to heroin, etc. They are lying. Grass is a harmless herb. It is not habit forming, it's less dangerous than aspirin, and it makes you feel good. Try it. You'll like it.

We are revolutionary High School students (prisoners) who believe that the time has come for a jail break. We are going to break FREE. We're going to toke up in the halls, we're going to dance in the classrooms, we're going to neck or make love wherever we please.

We're going to start turning our schools, which parents and principals and pigs make us go to, into OUR SCHOOLS. Places where we can laugh.

Places where we can live. Places where we can learn. Places where we have a SAY in what goes on.

We are giving you this joint to turn you on to yourself, to conditions in this prison, and to a revolutionary five point program for making this school a place where we decide what happens to us—instead of being herded into classes every day and having stuff crammed down our throats whether we like it or not. Here is the five point program of the Vancouver High School Underground.

1. Freedom to smoke grass in school. No narks in the schools. No lies about grass being bad for you.

2. Freedom of appearance. Whatever clothes we want. Whatever hair length we want. Whatever make up or face paint we want.

3. Freedom to plan our own courses. We demand the right for each class to decide what it will do, how it will learn, and what teachers it will work with. We are forced to attend this school whether we like it or not. We have every right and more to decide what we will do here. You can't learn very much in a prison.

4. Freedom to skip classes, for any reason, at any time if all you're getting out of a class is boredom, why the hell should you go there? There are some pretty boring classes in this school. Maybe some of the teachers would smarten up and maybe we'd learn a bit more if we didn't have to be there.

5. Freedom from grades. The whole idea of grades is sick. It makes us compete against each other. It makes us go after grades instead of knowledge. Down with grades, up with learning.

Giving away grass is the first action of the Vancouver High School Underground. It won't be the last!!!"

3. B. Cummings, "Obscenity: Who Really Cares, All Is Phoney,"
Georgia Straight, January 12-25, 1968

Robert "Bob" Howard Cummings (dates unknown) was a convicted juvenile delinquent mentored by journalist Ben Metcalf who got him a job at the Vancouver Province *newspaper. He soon quit, finding it too "bourgeois," and began writing regularly for the* Georgia Straight *under the pen name Wanis Kouri. Cummings was arrested and charged with criminal libel in 1968, making him a celebrity and anti-establishment hero. He also participated in a major anti-Vietnam War protest at the University of British Columbia during which he, American activist Jerry Rubin, and several hundred others occupied the Faculty Club for several days. Cummings joined Greenpeace in 1969 and was on the organization's 1971 maiden voyage against American nuclear testing at Amchitka, Alaska.*

The way they manage to stir people up, they should be packaged and sold as "pep" pills. They are usually short and of simple construction, but the way they affect some people makes them a potent force. Users most often render their intended purpose meaningless through improper usage, but even then they are so powerful as to render the non-immunized to a state of shock. Science can find no cure, theology tried and failed to crush them, and society long ago gave up the fight to eliminate them. They are, of course, those infamous four letter words. They are of the sub specie obscenity and can also be called "dirty words" and "bad language." At times they contain more than four letter[s] and longshoremen, taxi-drivers and editors of the *GEORGIA STRAIGHT* have been known to string them in almost poetic chains to emphasize a point where mere words fail.

The mere presence of them have gotten books, plays and magazines banned, thus insuring a fortune for the author. ... They live best on toilet walls, daily conversation and in great literature where the hero, who has just lost his wife, his job and his sexual capacity, needs a word stronger than "drat" to express his feelings....

What? Some idiot just asked "What is a dirty word?" Why, that's simple. A dirty word is a......... It's a collection of letters that......... It's a damn good question?

Let's start at the basics. A word is made of letters. Letters in themselves can't be dirty. Soooo, it must be the combination of letters that is dirty. Fine! Let's take an "F", a "U," a "C", and a "K," and put them together in a pronounceable order. Then we have "CUFK" ... Sounds Armenian?...

If the obscenity has nothing to do with the letters, or combination, it must be the meaning that is dirty. So, here they are, obscene words with their approximate meanings:

FUCK: sexual intercourse—usually warm and most often accompanied by another four letter word, "Love." What's obscene about love?

FART: heavenly release—only obscene in a closed room when done by somebody else. The only available single word for the act.

SHIT: people droppings—not overly pleasant, but hardly a secret to anyone over the age of toilet training. Dirty only when the toilet seat is faulty or broken.

CUNT: female sex organ—a giver and receiver of enjoyment, a gift of love to husbands or lovers. The only non-Latin word available....

Something is wrong. Every word there concerns a natural function or an act of love or both. Only a pervert could consider them obscene. Either that or the P.T.A. Ladies who defined them for us were putting us on.

We seem to have flopped in finding four-letter words, so lets try three-letter four-letter words. Ready?

SEX: male, female, or act of —?????? bit loose in the interpretation but hardly obscene....

WAR: organized murder usually for political gain—AaaaaaaHaanaaaa, now we've got one. Definitely obscene. Must crush it before it gets out and begins to multiply. What's that? You say it's too late? It already dominates the press, radio and TV. Lives in the minds of all decent establishment type people who want to educate other peoples to our way of purity even if it kills them? Oh come on … You must be joking? It's only a little three letter word. Here. I'll open the dictionary for a better look … Oh my God, it's getting out … There's a whole cesspool of dirty words in there … here they come … Forget me, save yourself … "INJUSTICE … HATRED … INTOLERANCE … BOMBS … PREJUDICE … NAPALM … TORTURE … GUNS … KILLING … INFANTICIDE …" They're all over … They're reaching for me … I'm going … fast! Make up some new censorship laws before it's too late. Wipe them out start a new society where they will die of malnutrition. Make them a part of the past. Destroy them, for the sake of humanity.

4. Dr. Murray Ross, "Why Students Rebel,"
Speech to the Empire Club of Canada, February 8, 1968

Murray Gordon Ross (1912–2000) received a B.A. from Acadia University, an M.A. in sociology from the University of Toronto, and a Ph.D. in education and psychology from Columbia. UNESCO sent him to study in Britain, France, and Israel in 1953, and he was Canada's delegate to the Conference on the North Atlantic Community in 1957. He then studied education in the Soviet Union and China. Ross taught at the University of Toronto, rose to become its vice-president from 1957 to 1960, and was the first president of York University in 1960. His many books and articles explored

education and community development and the idea of an inclusive, non-elitist, and
relevant university environment.

These are hard times for university administrators. They are apt to spend their
days in ceaseless debate with angry student leaders, reviewing contingency plans
for riot control, or desperately attempting to extricate some hapless recruiter from
the basement of the university employment service. They may share the experience of one of my colleagues whose office was literally invaded or, which has
become quite a common practice in North American universities, simply be prevented from using their offices at all. Returning home in the evening they could
find their front lawns covered with students protesting the dismissal of a faculty
member or the raising of residence fees. Not for them the gentle pleasures of quietly perusing Euripides nor even, which is more serious, do they have sufficient
time for the exhilarating and vitally significant work of academic planning, and
budget preparation, and consideration of senior appointments. In another sense
than the physical, the student has forced his way into the university president's
office, and he will not be dislodged.

The current wave of student protest has provoked many differing public
reactions. Radicals of another age, who may have been inflamed by Sacco and
Vanzetti or inspired by the Regina Manifesto, but who have long since ceased to
feel the fire in their bellies, have experienced a vicarious thrill at what they have
perceived to be the long-awaited movement for the final reconstruction of society. In this delusion they have been assisted by the apostles of student activism.
Paul Goodman, for one, has called today's undergraduates "The New Aristocrats,
America's emerging power elite." And the news media have further exaggerated
both the numbers of student protesters, the coherency of their programmes and
the potency of their leaders. The availability of television cameras and newspaper
reporters to cover every outbreak of student dissent has caused many student
leaders to stress exhibitionism in their style and strategy, and extremism in their
programmes. In consequence of this intensive coverage by the media the general
public has been badly misled about the quality and quantity of student protest.
In fact, Clark Kerr of the University of California, with some justification, calls
this the "exaggerated generation."

The most common reaction to student rebellion is the conservative one, typical of most of the older generation. It is a reaction of disapproval compounded by
bewilderment. The public seem to hold an image of the student activist, or even
of the average student, which is generally a sort of mental mélange of leather
jackets, waving placards, long greasy hair, LSD and flaming sex, and to which the

wholly inappropriate terms of "beatnik" or "hippy" are indiscriminately applied. This distorted image is also, to an extent, the fault of radio, television and the newspapers. Its distortion is the greater because the older generation has failed to grasp the tremendous cultural transformation which the campus has undergone in the last decade and a half. Rebellion and causes of rebellion aside, our present students are far more conscious than their predecessors of the importance of education for themselves and their society. They are also far more likely to be concerned about events beyond the campus, for they have known the television set almost all their lives and it has indelibly impressed them with the immediacy and significance of a bombing raid on Hanoi, a march on Selma in Alabama, or the squalor of a Métis community in Saskatchewan. And norms of student behaviour have changed too. The campus of football heroes, debating teams and Saturday night dances has been transformed into the campus of self-examination, teach-ins, and community projects....

All the varieties of student rebel—political activists, Bohemians, volunteer social workers—do not together amount to even close to a majority of our undergraduate population. You may then ask why so much attention is paid to them by university presidents like myself. Are they indeed representative of the mainstream of students and can they ever claim to have the whole campus behind them?

Certainly the majority of students do not share all the views of the radicals, or even know and understand them. On several Ontario campuses lately the vanguard of student protest has been stopped in its tracks by open and organized opposition from within the student body. But neither are the student radicals entirely unrepresentative. Most of the time they articulate some of the suppressed and unarticulated notions of the majority of students who may not themselves join in protest activity, either because the social skein holds them a little more tightly than their radical fellows, or because they are antagonized by some of the more blatantly childish tactics of the radicals, or because they think that there are more important things to do at college than wave placards, man picket lines, or enter student politics. But it would be an error of great proportion to assume that the "silent majority" is a collection of deadwood. Generalizations about this particular group of students are difficult but I would guess that it exhibits a greater degree of consciousness about self and about society than has been witnessed before on the campus. In the event of a major crisis, like one of academic freedom, it could be marshalled behind the radicals. What is important is to recognize that there has been a deep and pervasive change in student attitudes. The activists are merely the most obvious manifestation of this change.

"Hippies, Bikers, and Greasers": Youth in the 1960s

There are two reasons why radical activists are taken seriously on the campus. One is their strategy, borrowed from the civil rights movement, of sit-ins and demonstrations which has caught many administrators, accustomed to quieter times, completely off guard. We have suddenly found we have to reconsider our role and responsibilities with respect to students and sort out our priorities; one such priority we are now intent upon establishing is that law and order will be preserved on campus. The other, and hopefully more significant, reason for whatever success the activists have enjoyed is that we in the faculty and administration of the universities have had to admit the considerable force of many of their arguments. Revolutions are always made by minorities and are usually initiated by small groups of intellectuals. The mere fact that our student activists have constituted a minority is no reason for treating them lightly.

What is it that periodically raises the temperature of a campus to the boiling point in the 1960s? What are the underlying causes of student rebellion — the noisy rebellion of the placard carrier, the sullen rebellion of the alienated, or the silent rebellion of the many who have not yet committed themselves to open conflict?

My first point must be a paradox. Contrary to some of our common notions of revolt, it is the affluent society which is the breeding ground for student dissent. For the protesters are not themselves the disadvantaged, they are the advantaged, as are most of those who are in the process of gaining a higher education. They are chief beneficiaries of two decades of economic progress since the War [World War II] and yet if anything their well-being appears to have sharpened the critical gaze they turn on society.

It is not to disparage the quality of their criticism to say that they are the first generation that can afford to be critical. The pressure to earn a living which often served to resolve their parents' problems of conscience, and made it easier to compromise one's principles in the name of survival is not a pressure which they feel. Eric Hoffer, the celebrated San Francisco longshoreman, has said of the student generation: "They haven't raised a blade of grass. They haven't laid a brick." But he neglected to add that, as far as youth are concerned, they haven't missed anything by not doing so. The competitive struggle for affluence holds no challenge for them when they have already achieved a measure of affluence without struggling for it; the customary ways of earning a living are likely to appear rather drab to them in such circumstances. Nor does the enjoyment of affluence excite them for they have known this enjoyment most of their lives; some of them will have travelled farther than their parents before they even get to university. They may actually begin to romanticize poverty because they react negatively to the way their parents have handled their new wealth. In short then, our society has lost its grip on them.

Thus no practical or material concerns stand in the way of face-to-face confrontation with the anomalies, the inconsistencies and the hypocrisies with which past generations have borne. Today's students measure our society's practices by its principles; and they find the practices to be woefully wanting. We profess, in our classrooms, our churches and our parliaments and, I confess, in convocation addresses, certain notions of equality and justice and freedom and dignity of the individual and we drum these notions into the heads of our younger generation. Could we not expect they would throw them back at us? The unlikelihood of children from poorer homes going on to university offends their notion of equality. The depraved condition of the Canadian Indian offends their notion of justice. The quality of life in the Spadina slums or in the negro quarter of Halifax offends their notion of the dignity of the individual. They can't muster the enthusiasm and energy of American student reformers because they don't have the impetus provided by Vietnam and widespread and glaring social injustices. Yet, among a certain segment, the reforming instinct is strong. Their complaint is an angry one for the old values, it appears, are being given mere lip service. The older generation talk about love and brotherhood and peace but accept a way of life that seems to repudiate these values. The radical voice is an impatient one which argues that those who warn of complications and see the need for restraint and compromise, simply seek to excuse inaction. It echoes Dante when he said: "the hottest places in Hell are reserved for those who, in times of moral crisis, preserve their neutrality."

Apart from the glaring gap between aspiration and actuality it is the general quality and direction of our society which most disturbs and antagonizes the student generation. Under the impetus of an increasingly sophisticated technology every branch and institution of this society is becoming more rationalized, more specialized, more bureaucratized. The large corporation, the computerized government department, the vast multiversity, are indicative of this trend and the consequence of it is a considerable increase in shared attitudes among those who run our major institutions. In the students' eyes, they inhabit the great grey world of a homogeneous bureaucracy where their highly trained minds are focused on highly specialized areas. They are prevented from taking an overview of society by the narrowness of their orientation. Professors, lawyers, businessmen or civil servants, all branches of the meritocracy are driving themselves to become more and more proficient in their specific fields and there is no one left to rescue the human values and ideals which may be going under.

The student is not a primitive Luddite; he is not trying to turn back the clock. But to him the trend to a hyperorganized, highly skilled, technologically based society seems to imply the abandonment of human individuality. It is the narrowness and sterility of this new order which accounts for the old values being lost from view. Its first priorities are efficiency and organization which are not necessarily the first human priorities. Furthermore, it seems to be all-pervasive, which not only makes dissent from it practically and psychologically difficult but also militates against variety and individuality which are essential if we are to continue to live as persons and not as white-coated creatures of the machine. The student agrees with Archibald MacLeish's belief that "slavery begins when men give up the human need to know with the whole heart—to know for themselves." The student is particularly concerned to be recognized as an individual because he has only recently become aware of all his personal and intellectual faculties and has no desire to have them crippled by a sterile conformity. Yet all institutions, all power elites seem to acquiesce in the new and stultifying order. Old radicals thought politics provided a chance to accomplish real social change. Though more students from the mainstream take part in politics than before, the young radicals and activists generally regard orthodox politics with some suspicion. Perhaps their last link with the old politics was with President Kennedy or in Canadian terms with two middle-aged intellectual swingers—Pierre Trudeau and Dalton Camp.

For today's student then, society is definitely out of joint. Furthermore, the traditional avenues of change appear to be clogged by the new all-pervasive bureaucratic culture. There is no one to shake up society if he doesn't do it himself. In the old days students rebelled in order to gain a change of policy or attitude on the part of their elders. Now they rebel in order to win a place in the decision-making process for themselves. They don't want to be excluded or ordered because they think they have a clearer insight and a more lively conscience than their seniors. They want to be able to translate their social ideals into practical positive actions, and they want to do it now, before they themselves are "taken in" by the organized society.

The student's impatience with the role of an anonymous subject, his desire to be treated like an autonomous individual, are reflected in his objections to prefabricated norms of behaviour. When confronted by rules in a university residence he wants to know the reasons behind the rules, or, more likely, why he himself is not considered capable of governing his own moral life. He is reinforced in this stand by what he quite accurately diagnoses as the insecurity of the older generation. When his elders appear to advocate one code of personal conduct but to live by a rather different one, it becomes clear to the student that he need not consider himself bound by approved standards and that there is probably something seriously wrong with them. The traditional props of social life have crumbled; in particular, the family no longer exerts its former influence on the upbringing and attitudes of its members. If, as suggested earlier, the student shares the values of his parents, he sees his parents and his teachers no longer deeply concerned about translating these values into concrete prescriptions or standards of behaviour. That is another thing which sets apart the current wave of student protest from past incidents of youthful revolt. The old guidelines of behaviour are gone and, in a way quite different from his predecessors, the student stands alone.

Though politicians and parents have certainly felt the force of student activism, it is the universities which have borne its brunt. The student feels particularly at home in, and identifies with, the university not just because of formal affiliation but because it is one institution which has traditionally shared his rebellion against materialism and conformity. Yet now it appears to be becoming just the handmaiden of the new technology. Its methods, its organization, its curriculum, all seem to be tailored to the requirements of the outside world. When a computerized grade report is the only means the student has of measuring his intellectual progress, when professors cannot be found in their offices because they are away on "task forces" and consulting missions, the student may conclude that the university has abjectly surrendered the job of stirring up and challenging its students and its society and is instead trying to enfold itself in it. As he sees it, the university nowadays is bent solely on producing grist for the economic mill, turning out generation upon generation of dull unimaginative and highly skilled recruits for computerized careers in the lifeless world of the machine and efficiency expert. He views the university as Professor Henry Aiken of Brandeis saw it in a recent lecture which he gave at York University: "an educational monster which devours its young, processing them into a kind of all-purpose compost for refertilizing the great briar patch of the national society."

The university, nevertheless, remains capable of spawning its own rebels. It awakens them to social injustice, develops their sensibilities and emotions, heightens their sense of their own individuality, and when they come to want to exercise these new faculties it is the university which confronts them in all its imperfections. For the student rebel the campus is not a training ground; it is a battleground. It is the first opportunity to put his theories of social action into practice but it is more than that for it has, potentially, a primary role to play in shaping the values and attitudes of society. They demand the right of participation in the government of the university because they believe that only by the involvement of all its members can the university regain its humane values and provide constant witness of those values to the outside world. But they also want this right so that the university can be at very least the scene of serious social experiments and at best a real engine for social change.

One of the reasons we are instantly repelled by the picture of students on picket lines and in mass rallies is that our idea of education is simply not consistent with these activities. We are offended by the notion, which many students enthusiastically support, that the university is a political community, and we find it hard to understand the passions that go into student revolt and the energy devoted to making seemingly niggling points. We have accustomed ourselves to the idea that universities exist for the preservation, propagation and increase of knowledge and for us the technological age, with its sophisticated systems of information retrieval and data processing appears to hold fantastic promise for the carrying out of this role. "That is your biggest mistake," the students are telling us. "Knowledge isn't a community and the university isn't, or shouldn't be, a factory for its production. The real educational experience is the awakening of one's own sense of personality and of one's relations with other people and this comes by participating in the conduct of our moral and political lives and not by the simple absorption of knowledge. The only kind of knowledge that really matters is knowing how to live and our university years should be a preparation for living."

What should be our response to the unease and disquiet that pervade the campuses of North America? In the current language of the student generation we must "keep our cool." I think we can open the most fruitful sort of interchange with the younger generation by taking an attitude that is at once sophisticated, tolerant and critical. We should be challenging the naivety of some of their notions of decentralized decision-making. We should be pointing out to them that eccentricity in dress and behaviour does not really amount to independence. We should remind them that the frequent use of four-letter words does not necessarily reveal creativity nor maturity. At the same time we should admit that they are one of the few segments of society interested in the great religious values of the ages and in genuine social experiment, and that they have held in front of us principles which we have only preached and too often have forgotten how to practise. For this, they deserve our genuine respect. But we are not all wrong any more than they are always in the right. We each have something to say to each other. We can each benefit from each other's views. We must start the long and demanding dialogue that is essential if we are not to succumb to angry extremisms. But let us not be too concerned with neutralizing student rebellion. Its better side is a worthy attempt to build a more human environment for us, and to compensate for the deadening influence of an over-organized society. That is an aspiration and an endeavour in which we should all want to participate.

5. R. Smart and David Jackson, "Yorkville Subculture," in W. Mann,
The Underside of Toronto (Toronto: McClelland and Stewart, 1970)

Dr. Reginald George Smart (1936–) was a psychologist and associate research direc-tor for the Addiction Research Foundation of Toronto. Dr. David Jackson's identity remains unknown. They recruited Gopala "Krishna" Alampur (1941–), an Indian anthropology graduate student, to don sandals and beads and go undercover into Yorkville from October 27, 1967, to May 1, 1968 to study youth culture. They rented him an apartment that served as a "crash pad" for all comers and afforded him subjects for observation. According to Alampur, the Toronto police supported his activities and protected his alibi. They regularly arrested him for appearance's sake before releasing him out the back door of the station. Smart and Jackson synthesized Alampur's find-ings into the 1969 report titled The Yorkville Subculture: A Study of Lifestyles and Interactions Between Hippies and Non-Hippies.

... Very few people in Yorkville like the labels usually applied to them. During the interviews for this study, no one was willing to say that he was a hippie. Even those considered hippies by others in the village answered the question, "Are you a hippie?" with, "I am I" or "I am a person." However, people we interviewed were less reluctant to apply labels to other groups. But it is essential to divide the major groups into some "ideal types" if we are to describe the people in the village and the ways in which they relate to each other.

The Hippies

"Hippies" are typically between the ages of sixteen and twenty four years with an average of about nineteen or twenty. About 60 per cent are males. One of the most distinctive features of the hippie in Yorkville is his appearance. There is no uniform, but there is a costume—a style characterized by comfort, freedom, and eccentricity. Hippies are set apart by their shabbiness; torn and dirty clothes, worn shoes. During the winter, some wrap rags around their shoes to keep their feet warm; in the summer, many pad along the pavements barefoot.

The costume aspect in the hippie dress is designed to reflect individuality; hippies may look alike in characteristics such as long hair, dirty clothes, and beads, but each is dressed to portray a unity. To add to the element of self-expression, some hippies decorate their bodies, especially the face and hands, with paintings of flowers and other designs. They also write inscriptions, such as "love," "flower power," or "lsd," on their clothes. Badges with inscriptions are commonly worn.

There are child-like, carefree features to their dress, expressed in beads, bells, and the flowers which some carry in their hands. The poncho is a popular costume, often worn with high boots to which bells are attached. There are no limits to the number of necklaces and beads that are worn.

In many instances, hair is worn long and usually uncombed, yet there is a certain charm and style in its appearance. Beards of every dimension bristle, flow, and sprout from the young men's chins. The general impression is that, "I am unique, I am relaxed and having fun, and I don't care what the conventional world thinks of it."

Hippies generally do not work. Actually, the hippies resent work because they see it as forcing conformity to an oppressive system. They resent giving up eight hours of their day to a boss. Their goal is to simplify the complex systems of society, and this leads them to decry bureaucracy, the search for status, and the power games which are so evident in most organizations. Thus, they repudiate the Protestant Ethic and do as little work as possible. Most hippies are not conventionally acquisitive, and they totally reject materialistic goals. In discussing their attitude towards work, there is an element of asceticism; they strive for freedom from the oppression created by possessions. Thus, the shabby dress and lack of permanent quarters make sense in ethical terms.

With this asceticism is a curious mixture of hedonism. One hippie explained his philosophy in these words, "To hell with it. I don't care. I want to live life the easiest, fastest way." If hippies do want to work, their appearance bars them from most jobs. Generally, they work at menial tasks like dishwashing. Because they have little money, they often are without a place to live. "Crashing," or staying with someone else who has a room, is common. In the summer, they often sleep outside. Some, in desperation, sleep in garages or hallways of apartments, but they usually stay within a twenty-block radius of the village. The most common ways of obtaining money are begging and bumming, selling drugs, working part-time (at such jobs as selling the local village newspaper), and committing petty crimes such as theft or prostitution.

"Doing your own thing" is the term the Yorkville hippies use to express their desire for independence. This implies that one should act independently of the opinion of others and submit to no group control. Whether this is a conscious wish on their part or a result of "abnormal" personalities is open to question. The hippies have no chosen leaders, and they form no governing structures. Perhaps it is the resistance to conformity to any norms—even those described as typical of hippies—which sets them apart from society and from other Yorkville groups.

Their disregard for convention extends into such basic concepts as time. Hippies, as well as other groups in Yorkville, usually stay up most of the night and sleep until the afternoon. Their time sense is present-oriented. Plans for tomorrow or for life in the future are either vague or grossly unrealistic.

Crucial to the definition of a Yorkville hippie is his use of drugs. Again, this is not exclusive to the hippie in the village. As one villager put it, "Hippies won't accept anyone who dresses well or doesn't take drugs." This drug-taking is a necessary but not sufficient requirement for being a hippie. Drug-taking is an extremely important part of the hippie's life.

Among hippies, knowledge of philosophy, religion, and psychology carries prestige. They are particularly attracted to Oriental and Indian religions as well as to mysticism and spiritualism. In Ruth Benedict's terms, they put greater value on activities which allow them to escape from reality than those which allow them to deal with reality. Yet their knowledge of these subjects is superficial. Religious and philosophical terms are used more to make a good impression than to communicate substantial meaning. Philosophical books are carried but infrequently read; religions such as Zen Buddhism are often talked of but rarely understood.

Hippies are the most intelligent and intellectual of the groups in Yorkville. They enjoy parties and music—especially rhythmic, hypnotic types. Their commitment to peaceful pursuits is paralleled by passive behaviour on the streets. It is *not* normal for a hippie to be beaten up by more aggressive members of the village. With this non-violent image goes a reputation for being quiet.

Accepting and amicable relationships with others is a part of the hippie life style which has diffused throughout the entire Yorkville community. All groups recognize this as a valuable feature of the village. For the hippie, communal living is appealing; he may subscribe to an unstructured socialism which could be simply characterized as "helping others." Relationships with others—or, to use their term, "to love or groove on others"—are important to the hippies. Perhaps this is so because they have had difficulty relating to others in a satisfying way. Many describe themselves as having been shy and lonely before coming to the village. When they discuss their pasts or their plans for the future, there is a strong interest in dealing with people.

To this concern with human relationships has been grafted the concept of free love. Relationships, while important, are generally transitory. Sexual relations are seen as an aspect of human relationships, and hippies enter into them freely, without the concern for lasting fidelity of people in the "straight" world. If you like the person, a relationship is formed, and sexual relations follow naturally. The important factor is that a binding relationship need not exist before sexual relations can occur. In the jargon of the street, there are many "one-night stands." Sometimes couples live together for several months. The rituals of courting and institutions of legal marriage are merely another restriction of the hated "system." For this reason, children are not desired by couples. Conception is usually seen as an unfortunate mistake which the girl must deal with alone.

Most Yorkville hippies come from middle-class homes; their fathers are salesmen, clerks, executives, and professionals. It is notable that the hippie and the weekender seem to be uninvolved in status struggles, common topics among greasers and motorcycle gang members. In the words of one hippie, "Status is not our hang-up."

Hippies have made at least a temporary break with their families. In most cases, the family is remembered as an unhappy environment from which the hippie felt he must escape. Some hippies are products of broken marriages, while others describe a family where children did not fit in. Whatever the cause, the hippie recalls he wanted out.

Thus, the emphasis on "freedom" heard so often in Yorkville in part reflects the hippie's escape from an unsatisfying family life.

The Weekenders

"Weekenders" range from twelve to twenty years with an average age around seventeen. About 60 per cent are males, as in the hippies' group.

Weekenders are substantially different from hippies. They have various social and ethnic backgrounds. They do not come to Yorkville only to look at the residents, as do the "tourists," but to participate in the village life for the weekend. Consciously or unconsciously, they identify with the different groups in the village and take pride in building associations with the natives according to their group identifications.

The "teeny-boppers" are the youngest segment of the group. They are shunned by the residents because association with them could lead to arrest on charges of contributing to juvenile delinquency. Some of these are "runaways," children who have impulsively left home and now look for refuge in Yorkville.

Most weekenders are students in high school or university, but some are permanently employed. Some are fond of the party atmosphere of Yorkville, while others are searching for drugs or sex.

An employed weekender will occasionally live in Yorkville, but usually he lives with his parents or in an apartment in another part of Toronto. Many weekenders travel to Yorkville regularly from communities within 100 miles of the city.

Weekenders bring charm, colour, and money to Yorkville. They wear more expensive and more colourful clothing than the other groups. Bell-bottom pants, brightly coloured shirts, and psychedelic miniskirts are common. Unlike hippies, they are clean and well-groomed. Whether the costume is designed to resemble that of the motorcycle gang, the hippie, or the greaser, it is always more expensive and more conservative than is typical of those groups.

The weekenders' visits are not always restricted to the weekends. On a sunny day in early spring the village is peopled mostly by weekenders who are truant from school. Some can be seen sitting on the sidewalk trying to do their homework.

When the weekenders come, they bring money. They can frequent the shops and coffee houses, and they can buy drugs. A weekender generally buys drugs from a friend who is a hippie, who in turn buys from a pusher. A weekender is part of both worlds, he enjoys "pot" parties and other activities at the village, and he often carries "stuff" back for parties at home or at a friend's house. Some are pushers in their own schools or offices.

People from Toronto who enter the village as permanent residents generally begin as weekenders. As one hippie describes it, "They start off listening to the Beatles and hearing their friends talk about Yorkville." He attributes their entrance into village life to the realization that, "What is happening is not a social renaissance. People are smoking pot."

The weekenders—or "plastic hippies," as many of the village residents call them—are not committed to a group in Yorkville. They are in a state of transition; eventually they will either become committed to a village group or they will leave, having satisfied their curiosity.

Motorcycle Gangs

The weekenders may be faint carbon copies of the other groups in Yorkville, but the motorcycle gangs stand distinctly apart in dress, values, and behaviour. They are the oldest of the groups, ranging in age from eighteen to twenty-eight years. All official motorcyclists are males, but women are associated with them in roles carrying lesser status.

There are several gangs—Hell's Angels, Paradise Riders, Satan's Choice, Vagabonds, and Thunderbolts. These all-male organizations are composed of sixteen- to twenty-five-year-olds who are generally bigger and more sturdily built than the other inhabitants of Yorkville. The gangs are distinguished from hippies and from other gangs by their distinctive uniforms. They wear leather or levi jackets with the sleeves cut out, with jeans and cowboy boots. On their backs they wear their "colours"—mass produced emblems giving the name of their club. They wear long hair and beards. They seem to take pride in being dirty, but their chrome-plated motorcycles are always polished to gleaming perfection. The swastika and iron cross are commonly worn in military fashion on the chest or around the neck.

Each motorcycle gang has a formal organizational structure with a president, secretary-treasurer, lieutenant-at-arms, road captain, and assistant road captains. Each has specific duties, responsibilities, and privileges. Meetings are held weekly; while attendance is not compulsory, long periods of absence without an adequate excuse are frowned upon. At these meetings members are asked what they have done for the club that week. Also, grievances between members can be aired and suggestions for changes or for new activities can be made at meetings. Girls are not allowed to attend these meetings.

It can be seen that, in contrast to the hippies, the motorcycle gangs are well-organized along military lines. Members pay $10 for their colours and a dollar a week for dues which are used as bail money and to finance club parties. This banding together creates the important advantages of protection and prestige for members.

In the ethos of the motorcycle gangs, powerful elements of the romanticized cowboy are combined with aspects of the street gang. "Bike boys" generally prefer western movies. They talk of fights between motorcycle gangs as "range wars." One gang member described his activities in terms which could have come from a cowboy picture sound track. "We'd rather ride than fight. When there is a range war, you don't have to wear your colours." In other respects, the motorcycle gangs seem to be nothing more than street gangs with wheels. The members are quick to point out that the street gangs of Toronto are younger and poorer. But iron discipline, the wish to identify, and the emphasis on masculine bravery are predominant in both types of gangs.

The aggressiveness of the motorcycle gangs, together with their distinctive dress, gives them prominence when they enter the village. Some villagers see the bike boys as protectors, but most fear them and stay out of their way. The gang members often see themselves as defenders of the village, but they are always the enemies of the police. This is primarily due to their occasional criminal activities. Petty theft and vandalism are not uncommon among the motorcyclists. While members have been involved in some criminal activities at one time or another, it would be incorrect to imply that their major interest is delinquent activity.

The gang members' emphasis on sexual gratification and their relationships with women are direct and unambiguous. Females are property, but males are not. A motorcycle gang member may be married or go steady with his "old lady," but she is completely dependent on him for her status and protection. As his old lady, she will not be molested by other members of his gang or other gangs. The girls are conscious of their lower status and conscious that it gives them less autonomy than in either Yorkville or regular Canadian society.

The motorcycle girl is vulnerable if she is abandoned by her "old man"; she then faces the prospect of ending her association with the gang or possibly being "gang-splashed." There are kudos associated with unusual sexual practices such as oral-genital stimulation and intercourse in groups of three to fifteen people.

Most motorcycle gang members come from working-class families. Generally, their early experiences include violent or delinquent behaviour on the part of their parents. Unlike hippies, most live at home or with their wives outside of Yorkville. While a large number work regularly as drivers or mechanics, another subgroup works only sporadically to maintain themselves and their bikes. Some of the members of the gang have no obvious means of support, and one can only suspect that they get money from their families, other gang members, or illegal activities. Most members have done poorly in school, read few books, and appear to be primarily interested in machinery, sex, and alcohol.

Non-alcoholic drugs are not so important to this group as to the others in the village. They prefer alcohol, which is used at parties in much the same way as it is used by straight adolescents. However, motorcyclists drink far more heavily. Marijuana has been used by many gang members recently, but it is still not the preferred drug. A small number of motorcycle gang members push drugs for profit in the village, but the majority prefer to get their kicks from "booze, broads, and bikes," as one member put it.

Yorkville is one of the places most frequently visited by the bike boys. Like weekenders, they live most of their lives in other parts of the city. Yorkville is attractive to the gangs because of its tolerance for all types of people and because of the girls who can be picked up there.

The Greasers

"Greasers" are between sixteen and twenty-five years of age, and about 70 per cent are males. The term "greaser" is used because, "They put grease on their hair and grease in their food," to use the words of one villager. This statement implies that many come from eastern and southeastern European backgrounds. Greasers also have a large representation of people from countries such as the United States and the West Indies, although there are many Canadian-born members of the group. Greasers are more aggressive and more delinquent than the other groups. Usually they do not live in the village, but they go there frequently. With the greasers, there are basically two subgroups—the young criminal on his way to becoming a "rounder" and the drug addict whose habit has caused him to be completely alienated from straight society.

In terms of dress, they reflect the two extremes of the Yorkville spectrum. Those involved in drugs are attired in a dirty, unkempt way, much like the hippie. For greasers, this appearance is dictated by necessity rather than philosophical principle. The young professional criminal may be arrayed in a leather jacket and jeans or stovepipe pants, with ear-rings, chains around the neck, and other accoutrements which make him look hard-boiled. At other times, he may appear in continental suits, double-breasted jackets, and fancy shirts. The latter type of greaser generally wears short, well-manicured hair with the "grease" which gives him his name. In general, the greasers' group is fastidious in dress.

The greasers are distinguished from the motorcycle gang members by their lack of close group attachments. They do not have an organization. In fact, they are called the "paranoid people" because they fear that intimate relations may cause them to divulge evidence of criminal activity to informers.

Because of their suspiciousness, greasers rarely work with a partner. There are many more male greasers than females. Many of the girls are lesbians who work with a male greaser as a prostitute but have no sexual interest in men. The male greasers are very interested in "hustling broads" from the hippie and weekender groups. When a greaser forms a permanent liaison with a greaser girl, their attitudes are similar to that of the motorcycle gangs—women are property and are afraid to be unfaithful. They are only allowed to choose other men after they have been given up by their boy-friends. To the male greaser who is not a junkie, sex is more important than drugs.

Most greasers are highly motivated to achieve in material and economic terms. Often they take legitimate jobs as a cover against police surveillance. Their economic aspirations are middle-class, but their methods come from the underworld. A motorcycle gang member who looks down on greasers said they were "gonna" people: they are always going to do big things. As this description implies, their plans are often unrealistic. Many are entrepreneurs who become involved in the drug trade because of the lucrative profits it offers. As they talk about their criminal activities, it becomes apparent that they take craftsman-like pride in such activities as stealing or peddling. They rise early, by Yorkville standards, and this adds to the image of the energetic greaser businessman. Greaser girls take short taxi rides and hand out cigarettes to impress their village associates with their wealth. The general topics of discussion among the greasers are their recent exploits, fights they have had, and success or failure with women.

Among the village residents, the greasers have a reputation for starting trouble. For example, a hippie said that, "They want to take everyone on." Greasers find the more passive hippies easy prey. Not only do they steal from them and cheat them in drug sales, but they sometimes force hippies to steal for them, through fear of physical punishment. Sadism is sometimes mixed with aggression.

Greasers generally appear less intelligent than hippies and weekenders. They tend to be grandiose and loud when in Yorkville and to dominate the discussion with their tales of exploitation and big schemes. For these reasons, it is not difficult to see why they are often feared and despised in the village. Motorcycle gangs enjoy the opportunity to beat them up because other villagers condone this activity as justified.

Usually the greaser lives outside the village, at home, with relatives, or in an apartment. They come to Yorkville for the same reasons the motorcycle gangs do—"To get some action."

Most greasers come from lower-class families and many have suffered severe deprivation in semi-criminal environments. This deprivation has caused them to seek relief in drugs or to fight aggressively for material symbols of the sort of life denied them. They resent the hippies as drop-outs and lazy ne'er-do-wells. As one greaser said, "Rich people can afford to be bums. Poor people have no choice."

Greasers display various patterns of drug use. Some indulge in very frequent, indiscriminate drug-taking. The term "speed freak," which is applied to some greasers, denotes the distaste with which the average villager views greasers addicted to amphetamines. Other greasers have a pattern of heavy alcohol and light marijuana usage more typical of the motorcycle gang member. In general, greasers are not devoted to the psychedelic drugs in the true hippie manner.

YORKVILLE AND THE LARGER SOCIETY

Some hard things have been said about the meaning of Yorkville. It should be pointed out that Yorkville could not have developed or continue to develop without the open or tacit acceptance of the larger society. All adolescent rebellions point to difficulties in the larger society, and it is interesting to speculate about what these difficulties could be.

In the past, the period of adolescence was short, but our society gives youth an extended period of adolescence. It is hoped that during this extended period a greater education can be obtained which will help the young adult to cope with the demands of our changing technology. The paradox of the extended adolescence is that there is a greater demand on educational institutions to keep pace with technological change. When these institutions do not keep up, the youth is made to feel that what he is learning is not relevant to the demands on him. He is made to feel that he has no real skills to help him in the working world. His feeling of inadequacy leaves him with no occupational identity. He may feel that it is necessary to rebel in some way against his situation and against the existing educational institutions.

In itself, the failure of the educational institutions has not created the dilemmas which cause migration to Yorkville. The church has also failed to maintain relevance in its dealings with some young people. Adult society has shown an increasing disillusionment with the religious institutions, and adolescents have also turned elsewhere for a spiritual identity. While many of the Yorkville inhabitants claim to be atheists, they try to find a spiritual identity in less institutionalized religions, such as the eastern paths to "liberation." There is a pressing concern for the development of a life philosophy in the village and for spiritual identity.

Many villagers emphasize poor communication with parents as a reason for going to Yorkville. The family is supposed to help the adolescent to find his personal identity as an autonomous individual. The pressures of the family have increased in a technological society which exhibits a large degree of de-personalization. Yet the increased educational standards of the youth have widened the intellectual gulf between parent and child. Much of what the parent has to say is not relevant to the broader interests of today's youth. Lack of communication in the home, referred to time and time again by the villagers, left the adolescent with no one with whom to identify. We saw that the Yorkville cult exhibited tendencies which verged on hero-worship. Villagers often decorate their apartments with posters of personalities, most of whom are from a time long past. The regression to the fantasies and hero-worship of childhood may be seen as a futile attempt to find the identity models which were lacking in the home life. The existing institutions, family, church, and schools, have failed to communicate with the adolescent in a way which he finds meaningful or relevant.

While many in the adult world look at the Yorkville experiment with despair, they still do not try to put an end to it. Perhaps Yorkville is allowed to exist because, to the majority of straight people, the hippie movement offers no real threat to society. The passive nature of this movement and its emphasis

on love and peace stand as a direct contrast to the militancy of the racial violence, minority dissent, and student protests in North American society. The very
introspection and passivity of the hippie movement may be seen as a welcome
change from the violence of social movements which threaten the stability of
the community.

It could be surmised that the Yorkville experiment is encouraged because the
hippie ethos has a special appeal for the straight world. The adult society may be
changing slightly because of its association with a viable alternative to the present way of life. The concept of work in the Protestant Ethic is being challenged
as leisure time becomes more important. The straight world, while not accepting
a doctrine of non-work, is redefining the position of work in the technological
age. Also, the highly idealistic religious view of the hippies may appeal to an
adult world disillusioned by the present lack of faith in institutionalized religion.
The humanistic approach in the hippie philosophy may help the straight person
to re-define his position in the system. Also, the use of psychoactive and mood-
modifying drugs is increasing in the larger society, and many may feel that their
drug use does not fully differentiate them from Yorkville inhabitants.

6. J. Callwood, "Digger House," in W. Mann, *The Underside of Toronto* (Toronto: McClelland and Stewart, 1970)

*June Rose Callwood (1924–2007) was a journalist for magazines, newspapers, and
TV, including* Maclean's, *and the* Globe and Mail. *She wrote some 30 books and ghost-
wrote autobiographies (such as that by Dr. Marion Hilliard, excerpted in Chapter 11).
Callwood was also a social activist who fought for justice, especially for women and
children. Her radicalization stemmed from visiting Yorkville and becoming entranced
by the hippie movement and its dark side. After middle-class hippies returned home,
she found a core of "[hippies] whose teeth were rooting out of their heads and they were
shooting speed." In response, Callwood created "Digger House" in 1968, a hostel for
homeless youth named after the seventeenth-century English communitarians. That
same year she was arrested for protesting police conduct in Yorkville.*

The Toronto street sign that reads Yorkville marks the tomb of the hippie movement, which died of success after flowering for only a year or two.

The Movement represented, however, the implacable force of a good idea
whose time had come—humanism without humbug—and it helped to change
the world. The 1966 hippies were the gentlest and earliest embodiments of what
Marcuse has called "the great refusal," the beginning of *Hell No, We Won't Go!*

which retired God, Doris Day movies, - - - -, basic black, final examinations, brassieres, and charity.

The hippies came out of the middle class because no source but affluence and liberalism could have produced them. The bound beyond abundance is scarcely possible for those unfamiliar with it, and few can live for extended periods in a state of risk without having safety in their bones.

Because they were at first so few, and needed the confirmation of mutuality, the hippies clumped together in a downtown commune with a geographical hub: Yorkville. There they jubilantly and conspicuously proclaimed that they were in the brotherhood business: acceptance, sharing, peace, love, freedom, *happiness!* They fretted about inter-personal truth and talked until dawn; they discarded their last names as unnecessary luggage—some of them had famous fathers; they experimented with pot and acid, with sex based on Camaraderie, and with costume clothing superimposed on practical, durable jeans. But the most reckless adventure of all was poverty; they found they could learn from it.

Fortunately, they had health to squander. Their childhood legacy of warm beds, orange juice, pediatricians, regular dental checkups, and summers at the lake paid off in adult durability as they thumbed rides beside frozen highways, slept in the rain, went without food for a day, two days, three.

They were deliberate bums, a breed not rare in human history but always significant. It has included founders of religions, philosophers, poets, explorers, inventors, revolutionaries. The hippies of the mid-'60's were gifting the Industrial Age's declining years with a new life-style, the first alternative in a hundred years to the work-or-school choices offered youth. Their donation earned them the usual welcome which society accords divergence: they were feared by most because they represented tempting anarchy—and, as always, fear fled from knowledge and emerged as anger; they were adored and romanticized by a few.

In the spring of 1967, their destruction began. Camera crews were making movies of them; love-ins made front pages; clergymen, sociology professors, and writers were weaving garlands for their brows; policemen were vigorously filling jails with them; parents and high-school principals were stamping on the most visible and vulnerable symptom of the movement: long hair.

It was a superlative aid to recruitment. The hippies found themselves smothered with tourists who glared at them, tourists of their own age who imitated their dress, motorcycle gangsters who plundered their girls, toughs fresh from training schools who stole their possessions, narcotics police who infiltrated them ...

The population who came to Yorkville to stay was even more disturbing. A few were hippies, but the newcomers were much younger than their predecessors;

the seasoned hippies, university drop-outs themselves, were slightly shocked to find their community invaded by high-school drop-outs. But hundreds upon hundreds of the new migration were not hippies at all, though their rags made them indistinguishable from the others. These were young people the hippies had never imagined: the brokenhearted and nearly destroyed victims of multiple foster homes, parents who were drunks, or insane, or hotly hostile; homes that were bleak and dangerous because of bitter, angry poverty. They were not school drop-outs, but school throw-outs. They had come to Yorkville in search of love.

For a heroic long while, the Yorkville hippies struggled to make good their promise of brotherhood and shared bread. They housed, fed, and nursed the desolate newcomers through suicidal nights and were aghast at their guests' greed for dope—any dope at all, but preferably the chemicals with destruction in them. Eventually, resources and human warmth were exhausted, and the hippies, imperceptibly at first, began to move away from Yorkville.

By the autumn of 1967, only a dogged band remained, hanging on in the hope of opening a hostel which would provide emergency food and shelter and a referral service for desperately-needed medical attention. It was shatteringly obvious that the newcomers, the products of malnutrition and neglected teeth and illnesses undiagnosed and untreated, crumbled readily under exposure and hunger. They had no money for medicine and, with the exception of Dr. Anne Keyl and Women's College Hospital, doctors and hospitals turned them away.

The remnants of the hippie movement who remained called themselves Yorkville Diggers Inc. Their tenacity almost cost them their sanity; by the end of 1967, they resembled men in shock.

The Yorkville Digger House opened in January, 1968, after a year's delay spent in trying to find a landlord who would rent for such a purpose. Very reluctantly, Metro Toronto made an old house available for $250 a month. It was supposed to accommodate no more than twenty residents at a time; a week after Digger House unlocked the front door, someone counted 115 young people sleeping there. There were appeals for food, to which the poor responded most generously: "they understand hunger," a resident explained. But many times there was no food at all in the Digger House, and one week the entire diet was rice. Another time, the residents dined exclusively on artichokes from a slightly spoiled bushel basket thrown out by St. Lawrence market.

A curious Board of Advisors was born, comprised of representatives from most of the community's social agencies, from the police, from the religious denominations who had donated the initial rent money, from elegant women's organizations. Three patrician ladies split the cost of putting twenty beds in the House, plus mattresses, pillows, blankets, and sheets.

There were miracles. One day a woman, a stranger, put $500 in the mail for Digger House. Holy Blossom Temple all but adopted the project, and the Jewish Family and Child Service sent staff help. One afternoon, when more than twenty young people were facing a day without food, Dr. Ernest Howse of the United Church sent a cheque for $100. Another time, when there was no money left for the rent, the Presbyterian Congress of Concern donated the required $250.

The Digger House staggered along, and gave social workers, employment services, doctors, and educators an opportunity to adjust themselves to a problem they had never faced: the waste products of the baby boom of the 1950's, cast aside mindlessly because the hurdles had been too high, accident victims of a collision between increased education requirements and decreased job opportunities for youth. The agencies and scientists were appalled at the extent and depth of the damage. A doctor who made a house call to Digger House every Thursday after-noon, free of charge, said he had never seen people so sick; a psychologist said that the diagnosis "agitated depression" would cover every resident; a social worker reported on their lack of "self-image," a school principal on their history of early school failure; Manpower noted that only a small percentage was employable.

Home-damaged and school-damaged, they had become a part of what the Durants term "unmoored youth"; they belong nowhere, no one knows them, they have nowhere to go.

Some of the professionals who visited Digger House found the kids infu-riating—they were too apathetic and unsure to keep appointments or follow instructions; others, who sat among them and listened, came to love them for their decency and candour and dignity....

Digger House, meanwhile, had evolved into what its director called a "group-living situation." Twelve homeless young people at a time live there, sorting them-selves out with the aid of a relaxed staff. Some attend school, some find jobs, some make jewelry and leather goods to sell in Yorkville boutiques. When they leave, Digger House keeps in touch ...

Yorkville today is a curiosity where geologists may find evidence of all the life forms that once existed there. Occasionally, but rarely, a genuine hippie saunters through; he has all he owns on his back, but he also owns himself—it shows. His visit is brief, for most hippies now are in universities, or living quietly on communal farms or in well-kept houses; a great many are artisans and merchants.

The hippies, they say, turned the Vagabonds on to marijuana with a resultant improvement in that gang's violent tendencies; Satan's Choice, however, prefers beer, and there are dark stories of the gang-rapes in neighbourhood basements.

In the summer, migrant youths stop by to stare; in the winter, suburban teenagers inspect Yorkville boldly. These leave no trace; they are risking nothing, and there is Vulgarity in their health and new shoes and lack of cavities.

The regulars now are those too tired to move. Plugged into drugs that are killing them slowly, they languish. They came to find love, but it's gone, and what can you do? As they decay, the police pick them over; so do the dealers who cut the product with poisons and the thugs who take the girls and sell them....

FURTHER READINGS

Adams, M. *The Trouble with Normal: Postwar Youth and the Making of Heterosexuality*. Toronto: University of Toronto Press, 1997.

Coacchio, C. *The Dominion of Youth: Adolescence and the Making of Modern Canada, 1920-1950*. Waterloo: Wilfrid Laurier University Press, 2006.

Daly, M. *The Revolution Game: The Unhappy Life of the Company of Young Canadians*. Toronto: New Press, 1970.

Fetherling, D. *Travels by Night: A Memoir of the Sixties*. Toronto: Lester, 1994.

Gleason, M. *Normalizing the Ideal: Psychology, Schooling, and Family in Postwar Canada*. Toronto: University of Toronto Press, 1999.

Hamilton, I. *The Children's Crusade: The Story of the Company of Young Canadians*. Toronto: Peter Martin, 1970.

Henderson, S. "Toronto's Hippie Disease: End Days in the Yorkville Scene, August 1968." *Journal of the Canadian Historical Association* 17, 1 (2006): 205-34.

Jasen, P. "In Pursuit of Human Values: The Student Critique of the Arts Curriculum in the 1960s." In *Youth, University, and Canadian Society: Essays on the Social History of Higher Education*, ed. P. Axelrod and J. Reid. Montreal and Kingston; McGill-Queen's University Press, 1989.

Kinsman, G. *The Regulation of Desire: Sexuality in Canada*. Montreal: Black Rose Books, 1987.

Kostash, M. *Long Way From Home: Toronto: The Story of the Sixties Generation in Canada*. Toronto: James Lorimer, 1980.

Levitt, C. *Children of Privilege: Student Revolt in the Sixties*. Toronto: University of Toronto Press, 1984.

Martel, M. *Not This Time: Canadians, Public Policy, and the Marijuana Question, 1961–1975*. Toronto: University of Toronto Press, 2006.

Mietkiewica, H., and B. Mackowycz. *Dream Tower: The Life and Legacy of Rochdale College*. Toronto: McGraw Hill Ryerson, 1988.

Owram, D. *Born at the Right Time: A History of the Baby Boom Generation*. Toronto: University of Toronto Press, 1996.

Pauls, N., and C. Campbell, Eds. *The Georgia Straight: What the Hell Happened*. Vancouver: Douglas and McIntyre, 1997.

Ricard, F. *The Lyric Generation: The Life and Times of the Baby Boomers*. Toronto: Stoddart, 1994.

Sharpe, D. *Rochdale: The Runaway College*. Toronto: Anansi, 1987.

Tillotson, S. *The Public at Play: Gender and the Politics of Recreation in Post-War Ontario*. Toronto: University of Toronto Press, 2000.

Westhues, K. "Intergenerational Conflict in the Sixties." In *Prophecy and Protest: Social Movements in Twentieth Century Canada*, ed. S. Clark, J. Grayson, and L. Grayson. Toronto: Gage, 1975.

CHAPTER 13

" *The Very Essence of Canadian Identity* "

MULTICULTURALISM

INTRODUCTION

Canadians often define themselves through comparisons between Canada and the United States. Of these, perhaps the most common is contrasting the Canadian multicultural "mosaic" to the American monocultural "melting pot," lauding the former and condemning the latter. According to this theory, immigrants to Canada maintain and celebrate their heritage, creating a national mosaic of cultures, while newcomers to the United States must abandon all cultural baggage and melt into homogenous Americans. Fond of this image as Canadians are, it is grossly simplistic. Ask an Uzbek-Canadian how Uzbecky he and his children can remain while functioning in Canadian society.

Government-supported multiculturalism in Canada is, in fact, a recent phenomenon. Until it became official national policy in 1971, many Canadians had an expectation that other cultures, including those already present such as Native and French-Canadian, should assimilate into the dominant Anglo-Protestant society. As a result, the Department of Immigration usually sought immigrants from the British Isles while discouraging most others. Immigration remained very selective before 1945, and restrictions, such as head taxes and official discouragement, kept immigration virtually exclusive of visible minorities. This was particularly true of the 1920s and 1930s when Eastern Europeans and Jews, who earlier came in large numbers, lost access. Canada was, in fact, among the least welcoming democracies to Jews fleeing Nazi persecution. The overriding justification for this precise selectivity was to preserve and promote the "Britishness" of the nation.

Things changed after World War II. The Canadian economy soared from the ashes of war and required significantly more workers than were available—these jobs were filled by waves of "DPS" (Displaced Persons) escaping the post-war chaos of Europe. Visible minority immigrants from "exotic" homelands also became more common after the war, partly from the collapsing British Empire, but also because of the removal of overtly discriminatory barriers from the Immigration Act of 1967. This encouraged a large influx of immigrants from Africa, South and Central America, the Caribbean, and Asia. The process accelerated in 1978 with the creation of Canada's refugee program. Consequently, by the end of the twentieth century, 40 per cent of Canada's population was neither of French nor English ancestry. This reality was particularly graphic in Canada's urban environments. Toronto's population, for example, is 38 per cent foreign-*born* (not just of foreign ancestry). Vancouver is similar. In a recent survey of first-year students at the University of Toronto, more than half considered themselves non-white and only about one-third spoke English as a first language. In contrast, the clear majority remains French, English, or Native in rural regions, particularly in Quebec and Atlantic Canada.

The huge increase in immigration after the war, both in volume and countries of origin, begged a central question: should Canada expect its newcomers to assimilate into one of the two traditionally dominant cultures? Canadian Prime Minister John Diefenbaker, for example, railed against the "hyphenated Canadian": the "German-Canadian," "Italian-Canadian," et cetera. In 1963 the federal government appointed the Royal Commission on Bilingualism and Biculturalism to examine French-English relations, but the Commission's mandate also encompassed recommendations on the new multicultural reality of Canada. The result was a profound shift in cultural policy. The Commission advised that the best solution for Canada, both to heal the rift between French and English and to acknowledge the multicultural reality of the country, was to promote no single culture—except in the area of language where both French and English would share official status. The Commission argued that a nation of multiple ethnicities is the basis of the Canadian identity. Prime Minister Pierre Trudeau accepted the recommendations and made them official on October 8, 1971.

Multiculturalism as a policy came under intense scrutiny. The arguments against it were primarily threefold: 1) that the motivation for multiculturalism was a cynical attempt to grab ethnic votes for the Liberals; 2) that it attempted to diffuse Quebec separatism rather than address the needs of immigrants; and 3) that it was more divisive than constructive. Writers such as Neil Bissoondath, for example, argued that it meant little else than encouraging ethnic ghettoization that perpetuated values from the "Old Country." To him, ethnic parades and festivals also demonstrated superficial patronizing—all at taxpayers' expense—and rarely translated into anything beyond recreation. If language is the key to cultural retention, some questioned whether multiculturalism can exist within a bilingual framework. Other critics also maintained that multiculturalism promotes ethnic divisions, therefore reinforcing differences rather than promoting Canadian unity. Some argued that multiculturalism encourages racism.

Supporters of multiculturalism stated that the policy simply recognizes the Canadian reality and thereby affords protection to those who might be discriminated against by virtue of their ethnicity. They also insisted that multiculturalism is anything but divisive, that it generates a sense of harmony by encouraging Canadians to share their heritage, thereby promoting understanding and tolerance. The world is increasingly homogenous, they argued, and official multiculturalism will create significant benefits for the country by creating a vibrant and open cultural climate that invites the best and brightest from across the world.

According to its supporters, Canada is simply the vanguard of a general trend, and progressive nations like Australia now borrow from the Canadian legislation. Supporters also point to an increase in mixed marriages since Canada became officially multicultural, suggesting that the policy has successfully engineered the social fabric in a more inclusive direction. There is also the philosophical question: why should everyone conform to traditional British or French culture when the clear majority of Canadians now no longer traces its heritage to either the British Isles or France? Finally, they claim that racism cannot be eradicated without officially sanctioning cultural background as a badge of honour, not an impediment to inclusion.

The late 1980s saw the debate on Canada's multiculturalism hijacked by the Political Correctness movement, and reasoned discussion gave way to semi-hysteria. Accusations of "white privilege" and cultural imperialism suddenly tyrannized the discourse. White novelists could no longer have characters speak with Black voices because it amounted to "cultural appropriation." Discussing problems specific to certain cultural groups became taboo across the nation, and Canadians clammed up for fear of the racist label. One British Columbia MP stated that white supremacists burned Ku Klux Klan-type crosses on lawns in Prince George, a nonsensical accusation without foundation. That unfortunate situation has improved. The South Asian community in Vancouver, for example, does take responsibly for problems of gang violence among its young men and does not accuse the wider society of racism for pointing out the problem.

The issue, however, still causes considerable controversy. Consider a recent child custody case that occurred in Vancouver and that questioned the ethnicity of a child conceived between an African-American basketball player and a white Vancouver woman. Is that child Black or White, or does it even matter in a multicultural environment? According to the estranged father and his lawyers it matters very much. A single drop of Black blood, they argued, made the child Black and required it to be brought up in a Black household. Canadian courts demurred.

Some Canadians expect judges to consider lighter sentences for Natives because the Native population is over-represented in Canadian prisons. Equally, Native Canadians can access Sentencing Circles where their community decides punishment after a guilty verdict; non-Native Canadians do not have that right. Should a Canadian woman be permitted to wear a full burka at a polling station when all other Canadians must show their faces? Some Ontario Muslims fought to have Islamic Sharia law introduced into the courts in cases of Muslim family disputes. Others fought against it, arguing that Sharia discriminates against women. Should a Sikh student be able to wear the symbolic dagger, the Kirpan, to school when a non-Sikh would be in deep trouble for doing the same thing? Some cultures practice female genital mutilation on young girls. Should that be permitted in a multicultural Canada that encourages all to celebrate their cultural heritage? Multiculturalism and its definition remains a contentious and divisive minefield.

DISCUSSION POINTS

1. In practical terms does multiculturalism exist in Canada?

2. Has multiculturalism gone too far or not far enough?

3. Does multiculturalism produce a sense of national identity and unity?

4. Was Bissoondath right about multiculturalism promoting racism?

DOCUMENTS

1. Government of Canada, Appendix to *Hansard*, October 8, 1971

The government accepts and endorses the recommendations and spirit of Book IV of the Royal Commission on Bilingualism and Biculturalism. It believes the time is overdue for the people of Canada to become more aware of the rich tradition of the many cultures we have in Canada. Canada's citizens come from almost every country in the world, and bring with them every major world religion and language. This cultural diversity endows all Canadians with a great variety of human experience. The government regards this as a heritage to treasure and believes that Canada would be the poorer if we adopted assimilation programs forcing our citizens to forsake and forget the cultures they have brought to us.

The federal government hopes that the provinces will also respond positively to those recommendations which the commissioners addressed to them. The Prime Minister has written to each of the provincial premiers outlining the policies and programs which the Federal Government is initiating and asking for their co-operation. Some provinces have already taken the initiative and are responding to the recommendations directed to them.

The government while responding positively to the commission's recommendations, wishes to go beyond them to the spirit of Book IV to ensure that Canada's cultural diversity continues.

Cultural diversity throughout the world is being eroded by the impact of industrial technology, mass communications and urbanization. Many writers have discussed this as the creation of a mass society—in which mass produced culture and entertainment and large impersonal institutions threaten to denature and depersonalize man. One of man's basic needs is a sense of belonging, and a good deal of contemporary social unrest—in all age groups—exists because this need has not been met. Ethnic groups are certainly not the only way in which this need for belonging can be met, but they have been an important one in Canadian society. Ethnic pluralism can help us overcome or prevent the homogenization and depersonalization of mass society. Vibrant ethnic groups can give Canadians of the second, third, and subsequent generations a feeling that they are connected with tradition and with human experience in various parts of the world and different periods of time.

Two misconceptions often arise when cultural diversity is discussed.

(A) CULTURAL IDENTITY AND NATIONAL ALLEGIANCE

The sense of identity developed by each citizen as a unique individual is distinct from his national allegiance. There is no reason to suppose that a citizen who identifies himself with pride as a Chinese-Canadian, who is deeply involved in the cultural activities of the Chinese community in Canada, will be less loyal or concerned with Canadian matters than a citizen of Scottish origin who takes part in a bagpipe band or highland dancing group. Cultural identity is not the same thing as allegiance to a country. Each of us is born into a particular family with a distinct heritage: that is, everyone—French, English, Italian and Slav included—has an "ethnic" background. The more secure we feel in one particular social context the more we are free to explore our identity beyond it. Ethnic groups often provide people with a sense of belonging which can make them better able to cope with the rest of society than they would as isolated individuals. Ethnic loyalties need not, and usually do not, detract from wider loyalties to community and country.

Canadian identity will not be undermined by multiculturalism. Indeed, we believe that cultural pluralism is the very essence of Canadian identity. Every ethnic group has the right to preserve and develop its own culture and values within the Canadian context. To say we have two official languages is not to say we have two official cultures, and no particular culture is more "official" than another. A policy of multiculturalism must be a policy for all Canadians.

(B) LANGUAGE AND CULTURE

The distinction between language and culture has never been clearly defined. The very name of the royal commission whose recommendations we now seek to implement tends to indicate that bilingualism and biculturalism are indivisible. But, biculturalism does not properly describe our society; multiculturalism is more accurate. The Official Languages Act designated two languages, English and French, as the official languages of Canada for the purposes of all the institutions of the Parliament and government of Canada; no reference was made to cultures, and this act does not impinge on the role of all languages as instruments of the various Canadian cultures. Nor, on the other hand, should the recognition of the cultural value of many languages weaken the position of Canada's two official languages. Their use by all of the citizens of Canada will continue to be promoted and encouraged.

The government is concerned with preserving human rights, developing Canadian identity, strengthening citizenship participation, reinforcing Canadian unity and encouraging cultural diversification within a bilingual framework. These objectives can best be served through a policy of multiculturalism composed of four main elements.

1. The government of Canada will support all of Canada's cultures and will seek to assist, resources permitting the development of those cultural groups which have demonstrated a desire and effort to continue to develop, a capacity to grow and contribute to Canada, as well as a clear need for assistance.

The special role of the government will be to support and encourage those cultures and cultural groups which Canadians wish to preserve.

The stronger and more populous cultural groups generally have the resources to be self-supporting and general cultural activities tend to be supportive of them. The two largest cultures, in areas where they exist in a minority situation, are already supported under the aegis of the government's official languages programs. New programs are proposed to give support to minority cultural groups in keeping with their needs and particular situations.

However, the government cannot and should not take upon itself the responsibility for the continued viability of all ethnic groups. The objective of our policy is the cultural survival and development of ethnic groups to the degree that a given group exhibits a desire for this. Government aid to cultural groups must proceed on the basis of aid to self-effort. And in our concern for the preservation of ethnic group identity, we should not forget that individuals in a democracy may choose not to be concerned about maintaining a strong sense of their ethnic identity.

2. The Government will assist members of all cultural groups to overcome cultural barriers to full participation in Canadian society.

The law can and will protect individuals from overt discrimination but there are more subtle barriers to entry into our society. A sense of not belonging, or a feeling of inferiority, whatever its cause, cannot be legislated out of existence. Programs outlined in this document have been designed to foster confidence in one's individual cultural identity and in one's rightful place in Canadian life. Histories, films and museum exhibits showing the great contributions of Canada's various cultural groups will help achieve this objective. But, we must emphasize that every Canadian must help eliminate discrimination. Every Canadian must help contribute to the sense of national acceptance and belonging.

3. The Government will promote creative encounters and interchange among all Canadian cultural groups in the interest of national unity. As Canadians become more sensitive to their own ethnic identity and to the richness of our country, we will become more involved with one another and develop a greater acceptance of differences and a greater pride in our heritage. Cultural and intellectual creativity in almost all societies has been fostered by the interaction and creative relationship of different ethnic groups within that society. Government aid to multicultural centres, to specific projects of ethnic groups, and to displays of the performing and visual arts as well as the programs already mentioned, will promote cultural exchange. The Government has made it very clear that it does

not plan on aiding individual groups to cut themselves off from the rest of society. The programs are designed to encourage cultural groups to share their heritage with all other Canadians and with other countries, and to make us all aware of our cultural diversity.

4. The Government will continue to assist immigrants to acquire at least one of Canada's official languages in order to become full participants in Canadian society. The federal government, through the Manpower and Immigration Department and the Citizenship Branch of the Department of the Secretary of State, already assists the provinces in language training for adults, but new arrivals in Canada require additional help to adjust to Canadian life, and to participate fully in the economic and social life of Canada.

2. Neil Bissoondath, *Selling Illusions, the Cult of Multiculturalism*, 1994

Neil Devindra Bissoondath (1955-) is a novelist, short story writer, and essayist. He was born of Indian ancestry in the Caribbean nation of Trinidad and Tobago. After immigrating to Canada in 1973, Bissoondath completed his B.A. at the University of Toronto in 1977 and became a teacher of English as a second language and of French. The success of his 1985 book of short stories, Digging up the Mountains, *allowed him to devote himself to full-time writing. Most of his fiction deals with the immigrant experience: issues of alienation, cultural clashes, returns to home countries, and the collision between inter-generational immigrants. Bissoondath believes the policy of multiculturalism is well-intentioned but wrong.*

... Their voices were almost aggressive in dismissing any discomfort that they might have experienced by flaunting the only government policy that seemed to cause no resentment: Canada as a multicultural land. Officially. Legally. Here, they insisted, you did not have to change. Here you could—indeed, it was your obligation to—remain what you were. None of this American melting-pot nonsense, none of this remaking yourself to fit your new circumstances: you did not have to adjust to the society, the society was obliged to accommodate itself to you.

An attractive proposal, then, a policy that excused much and required little effort. It was a picture of immigration at its most comfortable.

And yet I found myself not easily seduced.

The problem was that I had come in search of a new life and a new way of looking at the world. I had no desire simply to transport here life as I had known it: this seemed to me particularly onerous baggage with which to burden one's shoulders. Beyond this, though, the very act of emigration had already changed me. I was no longer the person I had been when I boarded the flight in Trinidad bound for Toronto: I had brought to the aircraft not the attitudes of the tourist but those of someone embarking on an adventure that would forever change his life. This alone was a kind of psychological revolution.

Multiculturalism, as perceived by those at whom it was most explicitly aimed, left me with a certain measure of discomfort....

Many have long suspected that multiculturalism, proclaimed official policy in 1971, was initially boosted into the limelight not as a progressive social policy but as an opportunistic political one, not so much an answer to necessary social accommodation as a response to pressing political concerns. If the emphasis on federal bilingualism had seemed to favour francophone Quebec at the expense of the rest of the country, enhanced multiculturalism could be served up as a way of equalizing the political balance sheet. As René Lévesque once commented, "Multiculturalism, really, is folklore. It is a 'red herring.' The notion was devised to obscure 'the Quebec business,' to give an impression that we are *all* ethnics and do not have to worry about special status for Quebec."

But even a program born of manipulative cynicism does not necessarily have to be bereft of a certain amount of heart and sincerity. The Act for the Preservation and Enhancement of Multiculturalism in Canada, better known by its short title, the Canadian Multiculturalism Act, offers up—as do all such documents—gentle and well-meaning generalizations.

The act recognizes "the existence of communities whose members share a common origin and their historic contribution to Canadian society" and promises to "enhance their development"; it aims to "promote the understanding and creativity that arise from the interaction between individuals and communities of different origins" and commits the federal government to the promotion of "policies and practices that enhance the understanding of and respect for the diversity of the members of Canadian society." It talks about being "sensitive and responsive to the multicultural reality of Canada."

Recognition, appreciation, understanding; sensitive, responsive, respectful; promote, foster, preserve: these words and others like them occur time and again in the Multiculturalism Act, repeated in the thicket of legalistic phrasing like a mantra of good faith.

Beyond this, the act goes from the general to the concrete by authorizing the minister responsible to "take such measures as the Minister considers appropriate to ... (a) encourage and assist individuals, organizations and institutions to project the multicultural reality of Canada in their activities in Canada and abroad; ... (c) encourage and promote exchanges and cooperation among the diverse communities of Canada; … (e) encourage the preservation, enhancement, sharing and evolving expression of the multicultural heritage of Canada; … (h) provide support to individuals, groups or organizations for the purpose of preserving, enhancing and promoting multiculturalism in Canada."

The Multiculturalism Act is in many ways a statement of activism. It is a vision of government, not content to let things be, determined to play a direct role in shaping not only the evolution of Canadian—mainly *English*-Canadian—society but the evolution of individuals within that society. As a political statement it is disarming, as a philosophical statement almost naive with generosity. Attractive sentiments liberally dispensed—but where in the end do they lead?

The act, activist in spirit, magnanimous in accommodation, curiously excludes any ultimate vision of the kind of society that it wishes to create. It never addresses the question of the nature of a multicultural society, what such a society is and what it means. Definitions and implications are conspicuously absent, and this may be indicative of the political sentiments that prompted adoption of the act in the first place. Even years later, the act—a cornerstone of federal social policy—shows signs of a certain haste. In its lack of long-term consideration, in its delineation of action with no discussion of consequence, one can discern the opportunism that underlay it all. One senses the political hand, eager for an instrument to attract ethnic votes, urging along the drafting—and damn the consequences.

In its rush the act appears to indulge in several unexamined assumptions: that people, coming here from elsewhere, wish to remain what they have been; that personalities and ways of doing things, ways of looking at the world, can be frozen in time; that Canadian cultural influences pale before the exoticism of the foreign. It treats newcomers as exotics and pretends that this is both proper and sufficient.

Nor does the act address the question of limits: how far do we go as a country in encouraging and promoting cultural difference? How far is far enough, how far too far? Is there a point at which diversity begins to threaten social cohesion? The document is striking in its lack of any mention of unity or oneness of vision. Its provisions seem aimed instead at encouraging division, at ensuring that the various ethnic groups have no interest in blurring the distinctions among them.

A cynic might be justified in saying that this is nothing more than a cleverly disguised blueprint for a policy of "keep divided and therefore conquered," a policy that seeks merely to keep a diverse populace amenable to political manipulation.

The Canadian Multiculturalism Act is in many senses an ill-considered document, focused so squarely on today that it forgets about tomorrow. And it is this short-sightedness that may account for the consequences that it has brought about for individuals, for communities, for the country and people's loyalty to it.

CONSEQUENCES

The Simplification of Culture

The consequences of multiculturalism policy are many and varied, but none is as ironic — or as unintended — as what I would call the simplification of culture.

The public face of Canadian multiculturalism is flashy and attractive, emerging with verve and gaiety from the bland stereotype of traditional Canada at festivals around the country. At Toronto's "Caravan," for instance, various ethnic groups rent halls in churches or community centres to create "pavilions" to which access is gained through an ersatz passport. Once admitted — passport duly stamped with a "visa" — you consume a plate of Old World food at distinctly New World prices, take a quick tour of the "craft" and "historical" displays, then find a seat for the "cultural" show, traditional songs (often about wheat) and traditional dances (often about harvesting wheat) performed by youths resplendent in their traditional costumes.

After the show, positively glowing with your exposure to yet another slice of our multicultural heritage, you make your way to the next pavilion, to the next line up for food, the next display, the next bout of cultural edification. At the end of the day, you may be forgiven if you feel you have just spent several long hours at a folksy Disneyland with multicultural versions of Mickey, Minnie, and Goofy.

This in fact is all you have really done. Your exposure has been not to culture but to theatre, not to history but to fantasy: enjoyable, no doubt, but of questionable significance. You come away knowing nothing of the language and literature of these places, little of their past and their present — and what you have seen is usually shaped with blatantly political ends in mind. You have acquired no sense of the everyday lives — the culture — of the people in these places, but there is no doubt that they are each and every one open, sincere, and fun-loving.

Such displays are uniquely suited to seeking out the lowest common denominator. Comfortable only with superficialities, they reduce cultures hundreds, sometimes thousands, of years old to easily digested stereotypes. One's sense of Ukrainian culture is restricted to perogies and Cossack dancing: Greeks, we learn, are all jolly Zorbas, and Spaniards dance flamenco between bouts of "Viva España"; Germans gulp beer, sauerkraut, and sausages while belting out Bavarian drinking songs; Italians make good ice-cream, great coffee, and all have connections to shady godfathers. And the Chinese continue to be a people who form conga lines under dragon costumes and serve good, cheap food in slightly dingy restaurants.

Our approach to multiculturalism thus encourages the devaluation of that which it claims to wish to protect and promote. Culture becomes an object for display rather than the heart and soul of the individuals formed by it. Culture, manipulated into social and political usefulness, becomes folklore—as Lévesque said—lightened and simplified, stripped of the weight of the past. None of the cultures that make up our "mosaic" seems to have produced history worthy of exploration or philosophy worthy of consideration.

I am reminded of the man who once said to me that he would never move into an apartment building that housed any East Indian families because the building was sure to be infested with roaches: East Indians, he explained, view cockroaches as creatures of good luck, and they give live ones as gifts to each other. I had known the man for some time, was certain that he was in no way racist—a perception confirmed by the fact that he was admitting this to me, someone clearly of East Indian descent. His hesitation was not racial but cultural. I was not of India: he would not hesitate in having me for a neighbour. So searching for an apartment, he perceived the neighbours not as fellow Canadians old or new but as cockroach-lovers, a "cultural truth" that he had accepted without question. But what would he have done, I wondered later with some discomfort, had he seen me emerging from a building that he was about to visit?

The vision that many of us have of each other is one of division. It is informed by misunderstanding and misconception: what we know of each other is often at best superficial, at worst malicious. And multiculturalism, with all of its festivals and its celebrations, has done nothing to foster a factual and clear-headed vision of the other. Depending on stereotype, ensuring that ethnic groups will preserve their distinctiveness in a gentle form of cultural apartheid, multiculturalism has done little but lead an already divided country down the path to further social divisiveness....

It has become a commonplace that we who share this land—we who think of Canada as home—suffer an identity crisis stemming from a fragile self-perception.

Certain segments of the population profess a dogged loyalty to the monarchy, a manifestation of mental colonialism hardly in evidence in other parts of the former British empire. Other groups, in contrast, have evolved a sense of self independent of their colonial origins, one that, coalescing around language and distinctive culture, at times hints at a kind of besieged tribalism. There are even some, emerging from both groups, who quietly yearn for a kind of wider continentalism, the self as simply North American: the anglophone who professes to see no difference between Canadians and Americans; the francophone who holds that his rights would be more respected under the American constitutional umbrella.

To such fracturing must now be added a host of new divisions actively encouraged by our multiculturalism policy and aided and abetted by politicians (a cheque here, a cheque there) of every ideological stripe.

When, a few months ago, Yugoslavia was beginning its inexorable slide into horror, a CBC news report stated that an estimated two hundred and fifty sons of Croatian immigrants, young men of able body and (presumably) sound mind, had left this country to take up arms in defence of Croatia. The report prompted a question: how did these young men define themselves? As Canadians of Croatian descent? As Croatian Canadians? Or as Croatians of Canadian birth? And I wondered which country they would choose if one day obliged to: the land of their parents, for which they had chosen to fight, or the land of their birth, from which they had chosen to depart?

It seems an unfair question. Not only does federal law accept the concept of dual citizenship—which implies dual loyalties—but Canadians have a long and honourable history of inserting themselves into foreign wars. Norman Bethune is just one among hundreds of Canadians, for instance, who enlisted in battle on the republican side of the Spanish civil war....

To leave one's country, to commit oneself to conflict in the land of one's forbears for ideals not intellectual but racial, is at best to reveal loyalties divided between country and ethnicity. The right to decide on the distribution of one's commitments is of course fundamental: freedom of belief, freedom of conviction, freedom of choice. It says much about the new country, however, that its command of its citizens' loyalties is frequently so tenuous.

Divided loyalties reveal a divided psyche, and a divided psyche, a divided country. For these young Canadians of Croatian descent are not alone in their adulterated loyalty to Canada. Others, too, find it impossible to make a whole-hearted commitment to the new land, the new ideals, the new way of looking at life.

Imported Old World feuds—ethnic, religious, and political hatreds—frequently override loyalties to the new country. If the aiming of a gun at one's Old World enemies breaks the laws of Canada, so be it: the laws of Canada mean little against the older hatreds. And multiculturalism, in encouraging the wholesale retention of the past, has done nothing to address what is a serious—and has at times been a violent—problem. In stressing the differences between groups, in failing to emphasize that this is a country with its own ideals and attitudes that demand adherence, the policy has instead aided in a hardening of hatreds. Canada, for groups with resentments, is just another battleground....

And this insistent vision, passed down to the next generation, has already led—and will continue to lead—to suspicion, estrangement, vandalism, physical attack, and death threats; it is yet another aspect of the multicultural heritage that we seek to preserve, promote, and share.

Marginalization

One never really gets used to the conversation. It will typically go something like this:

"What nationality are you?"

"Canadian."

"No, I mean what nationality are you *really*?"

To be simply Canadian untinged by the exoticism of elsewhere seems insufficient, even unacceptable, to many other Canadians. This fact clearly stems, in part, from the simple human attraction to the exotic. But it seems to me that it also has much to do with a wider issue: the uncertainty that we feel as a people.

We reveal this uncertainty by that other quintessential (and quite possibly eternal) Canadian question: who are we? The frequent answer—Well, we're not like the Americans ... —is insufficient; a self-perception cast in the negative can never satisfy. Lacking a full and vigorous response, we search for distinctiveness—exoticism—wherever we can find it. And we find it most readily in our compatriots more recently arrived.

For professional ethnics—they who enjoy the role of the exotic and who depend on their exoticism for a sense of self—this is a not unpleasant state of affairs. For those who would rather be accepted for their individuality, who resent having their differences continually pointed out, it can prove a matter of some irritation, even discomfort. The game of exoticism can cut two ways: it can prevent you from being ordinary, and it can prevent you from being accepted.

The finest example of this remains the sprinter Ben Johnson. Within a shattering twenty-four-hour period, Mr. Johnson went in media reports from being the "Canadian" who had won Olympic gold through effort to the "Jamaican immigrant" who had lost it through use of drugs. The only thing swifter than Johnson's drug-enhanced achievement was his public demotion from "one of us" to "one of them." The exotic multicultural concept of the ever-lasting immigrant has come to function as an institutional system for the marginalization of the individual: Ben Johnson was, in other words, a Canadian when convenient, an immigrant when not. Had he, success or failure, been accepted as being simply

Canadian, it would have been difficult for anyone to distance him in this way. Thus the weight of the multicultural hyphen, the pressure of the link to exoticism, can become onerous — and instead of its being an anchoring definition, it can easily become a handy form of estrangement.

There is also evidence of this in the infamous Sikh turban issue that keeps bubbling up on the placid surface of our cultural mosaic. The two well-known controversies — turbans in the RCMP and turbans in Canadian Legion Halls — are in themselves indications of the failure of multiculturalism to go beyond superficiality in explaining us to each other. To view the turban as just another kind of hat, with no significance beyond sheltering the head, is to say that a cross worn on a chain is of no significance beyond a decoration for the neck: it is to reveal a deep ignorance of the ways and religious beliefs of others. To ban either is to revel in that ignorance and to alienate the other by rejecting a fundamental part of his or her self.

Of greater interest, however, is what these controversies reveal about our idea of ourselves and our traditions. We are not a country of ancient customs, and multiculturalism seems to have taught us that tradition does not admit change: that traditions, in Canada, turn precious and immutable. This helps explain why, although RCMP headgear has changed throughout the years, there are those passionate in their opposition when faced with the possibility of seeing a turban among the stetsons. It also explains, in part, why a Legion Hall's desire to honour Canadian military men by banning headgear cannot make room for turbans. (In Britain, which is often seen as a tradition-bound society, turbans have long been accepted as part of the military and London police uniforms.)

But if, in our cultural insecurity, we have decided that tradition is immutable, what happens when two contradictory traditions come together? Only conflict can result, the natural outcome of our inflexible view of tradition and multicultural heritage: so that protests with distinctly racist overtones are raised against turbans in the RCMP; so that a Sikh wishing to enter an Alberta Legion Hall is told to use the back door.

A final consequence of the marginalization to which we can so easily subject one another comes frequently in times of economic hardship. The stresses of unemployment — the difficulty of the present and the invisibility of a future — create a need for scapegoats: we need something or someone to blame. We can rail against politicians, taxes, corporations — but these are all distant, untouchable in their isolation. But no one is more easily blamed for the lack of opportunity than the obvious "foreigner" who is cleaning tables in the local doughnut shop. Maybe he has brown skin, maybe he speaks with an accent: clearly he is out of place here, filling a paid position that should by rights have gone to a "real" Canadian. All differences always so close to the surface, are seized upon; are turned into objects of ridicule and resentment, the psychology of exoticism once more cutting both ways.

Encouraging people to view each other as simply Canadian would not solve this problem—humans, in times of pain and anger, have unique ability for seeking out bull's-eyes in each other—but it may help redirect the resentment, so that in expressing the hurt we do not also alienate our fellow citizens. Differences between people are already obvious enough without their being emphasized through multiculturalism policy.

The Multiculturalism Act suggests no limits to the accommodation offered to different ethnic practices, so that a Muslim group in Toronto recently demanded, in the name of respect for its culture, the right to opt out of the Canadian judicial system in favour of Islamic law, a body of thought fundamental to the life and cultural outlook of its practising members. In the opinion of its spokesmen, this right should be a given in a truly multicultural society.

More recently, the Ontario College of Physicians and Surgeons expressed concern over a rise, unexplained and unexpected, in the number of requests for female circumcision. According to a report in the *Toronto Star* on 6 January 1992, the procedure, long viewed in Western culture as a kind of mutilation, involves "cutting off a young girl's external genital parts, including the clitoris. In some countries, it includes stitching closed the vulva until marriage, leaving a small opening for urination and menstrual flow.... Various health risks have been linked to it, including immediate serious bleeding, recurring infections, pain during intercourse, hemorrhaging during childbirth and infertility.... Charles Kayzze, head of Ottawa's African Resource Centre, believes it is being performed here by members of the community. In some cases, he says, families are sending their children to Africa to have it done." The result is the reduction of the woman to the status of machine, capable of production but mechanically, with no pleasure in the process.

It is curious that such ideas can be brought to this land, survive, and then present a problem to doctors for whom policy guidelines, never before necessary, are now being established. ("The policy," the report states, "is likely to say Ontario doctors should not perform the operation.") Yet one awaits with bated breath calls for public performance of the ancient Hindu rite of suttee in which widows are cremated alive on their husband's funeral pyres.

There is a certain logic to all of this, but a logic that indicates a certain disdain for the legal and ethical values that shape, and are shaped by, Canadian society—and therefore for Canadian society itself.

And why not, given that the picture that the country transmits of itself is one that appears to diminish a unified whole in favour of an ever-fraying mosaic? If Canada, as a historical, social, legal, and cultural concept, does not demand respect, why should respect be expected?...

Canada has long prided itself on being a tolerant society, but tolerance is clearly insufficient in the building of a cohesive society. A far greater goal to strive for would be an *accepting* society. Multiculturalism seems to offer at best provisional acceptance, and it is with some difficulty that one insists on being a full—and not just an associate—member. Just as the newcomer must decide who best to accommodate himself or herself to the society, so the society must in turn decide how it will accommodate itself to the newcomer. Multiculturalism has served neither interest; it has highlighted our differences rather than diminished them, has heightened division rather than encouraged union. More than anything else, the policy has led to the institutionalization and enhancement of a ghetto mentality. And it is here that lies the multicultural problem as we experience it in Canada: a divisiveness so entrenched that we face a future of multiple solitudes with no central notion to bind us ...

3. Dick Field, "Multiculturalism Undermines Values Held by Canadians," *Toronto Star*, December 23, 1994

Richard "Dick" Field (1924–) was born in Toronto, served with the Royal Artillery during World War II, and then graduated with degrees from the University of Toronto and Queen's. A businessman with a varied career, he became chairman of the Voice of Canadians Committee. This group later merged into the Ontario provincial Freedom Party, created in 1984, an organization that defines itself as right-wing and capitalist, and whose creed states that "the purpose of government is to protect every individual's fundamental freedoms, not to restrict them." He believes that multicultural policies have compromised Canadian and British traditions; he also opposes bilingualism.

Thirty-five years ago, the majority of Canadians accepted the concept of multiculturalism because we felt that it would help newcomers integrate into Canadian society.

Unfortunately, no sooner had the concept been proclaimed by the federal government than the added concept of a "mosaic of cultures" was pushed on an unsuspecting public. This concept put forth the very damaging idea that newcomers could come to Canada and keep their own culture and that we, the taxpayers, would pay them to do so.

This concept was diametrically opposed to the strongly held Canadian tradition that newcomers should come to Canada, leave their problems and ancient hatreds in the old country, join the majority culture here, and work together to build Canada.

The concept of separate cultures, each of equal value, maintained at the majority taxpayers' expense, has spawned a nightmare of destructive self-interest. Minority spokespeople have built personal political fiefdoms as have an army of bureaucrats, politicians, educators and other people who manipulate the system for their own advantage.

All this at the expense of undermining Canadian values and traditions. Even worse, at the expense of the good will which the vast majority of Canadians have, in the past, extended to all newcomers.

Canadians are not opposed to having other cultures join us in Canada. We are not opposed to other cultures preserving those parts of their culture that they wish to preserve, provided it is at their own expense and provided those cultural values are not in fundamental conflict with Canadian values and traditions (for example, female circumcision and polygamy).

In a positive sense there is much to learn from all cultures, especially in the area of the arts, foods and perspective.

What we are now experiencing, unfortunately, is a growing sense of being strangers in our own country. Our values and traditions as a free and independent people are under assault.

We do not blame the minorities themselves, when we are thoughtful. We know it is the crassness of our political leaders and the wrongness of the many laws, policies and programs they institute that are causing the upset.

We know it is not the majority within the minorities causing these problems. Unfortunately minorities must bear the brunt of the backlash, when we are pushed beyond thoughtfulness.

There are, however, too many minority members who do not speak out when they know their spokespeople are wrong. There are also too many Canadians willing to accept this chipping away at our values because they fear that if they do speak out they will be labelled as racists or bigots.

The employment equity law of Ontario is but one manifestation of the appeasement policies of insensitive governments reacting to the loud and insistent voices of the taxpayer-funded minorities. This horrendous concept, now law, fractures an unwritten principle of our society, which is that all of us must be equals under and before the law.

This is a law of inequality. This law judges us by skin colour, sex, or whatever other "disadvantaged" designation bureaucrats or politicians may decide is appropriate.

For the last 35 years, Canadian and British history, which embody the fundamental traditions and values of this free society, have been dishonoured. Among other things, they have even been excluded from our school curriculums.

As a consequence, young Canadians of all backgrounds are confused as to their heritage. In an attempt to be fair, the values of all cultures have been taught as being the equivalent of the values of this country.

This is a dangerous and divisive concept, as well as being untrue. Take an honest look at the countries where most recent ethnic and visible minority refugees and immigrants come from. Ask yourselves if those countries operate on the fundamental principles of a free and democratic country such as Canada. That is why it is the duty of all citizens to understand the principles and values underlying our country and to uphold them.

The vast majority of Canadians expect newcomers to do just that. The majority of new immigrants expected to do so when they came here but they are now being taught that Canadians have no values.

We now have many new immigrants who after three years in Canada obtain a piece of paper that says they are citizens, but they have no concept of Canadian values. Such people may be legal Canadians but they are not and never will be Canadians in mind or spirit.

Yes, "official taxpayer-funded" multiculturalism is dead. It is dead because the majority of Canadians no longer accept such a divisive and destructive policy and increasingly, they resent paying for it. All of us must make sure the beast lies down by withdrawing all funding designed to appease the spokespeople of ethnic and racial minority groups.

The answer lies in all of us joining together as Canadians, as unhyphenated human beings, and subscribing to the traditional values of Canada. Until we do, racial and ethnic upset will only get worse.

FURTHER READINGS

Abu-Laban, Y., and D. Stasiulis. "Ethnic Pluralism under Siege: Popular and Partisan Opposition to Multiculturalism." *Canadian Public Policy* 18, 4 (1992): 365-86.

Abu-Laban, Y., and C. Gabriel. *Selling Diversity: Immigration, Multiculturalism in Canada*. Peterborough: Broadview Press, 2002.

Angus, I. *A Border Within: National Identity, Cultural Plurality, and Wilderness*. Montreal and Kingston: McGill-Queen's University Press, 1997.

Banting, K., T. Courchene, and F. Seidle, Eds. *Belonging? Diversity, Recognition, and Shared Citizenship in Canada*. Montreal: Institute for Research on Public Policy, 2007.

Berry, J., and J. Laponce, Eds. *Ethnicity and Culture in Canada: The Research Landscape*. Toronto: University of Toronto Press, 1994.

Bibby, R. *Mosaic Madness*. Toronto: Stoddart, 1990.

Breton, R. *et al. Ethnic Identity and Equality*. Toronto: University of Toronto Press, 1990.

Cairns, A., and C. Williams. *The Politics of Gender, Ethnicity and Language*. Toronto: University of Toronto Press, 1986.

Cardozo A., and L. Musto, Eds. *The Battle over Multiculturalism*. Ottawa: Pearson-Shoyama Institute, 1997.

Day, R. *Multiculturalism and the History of Canadian Diversity*. Toronto: University of Toronto Press, 2001.

Dahlie, J., and T. Fernando, Eds. *Ethnicity, Power, and Politics in Canada*. Toronto: Methuen, 1981.

Driedger, L., Ed. *Ethnic Mosaic: A Quest for Identity*. Toronto: McClelland and Stewart, 1978.

Dodge, W., Ed. *The Boundaries of Identity: A Quebec Reader*. Toronto: Lester, 1992.

Fieras, A. *Engaging Diversity: Multiculturalism in Canada*. Scarborough: Nelson Thomson Learning, 2001.

Foster, L. *Turnstile Immigration, Multiculturalism, Social Order, and Social Justice in Canada*. Toronto: Thompson Educational Publishing, 1998.

Gairdner, W. *The Trouble with Canada*. Toronto: General, 1991.

Gwyn, R. *Nationalism Without Walls: The Unbearable Lightness of Being Canadian.* Toronto: McClelland and Stewart, 1995.

Hutcheon, L., and M. Richmond, Eds. *Other Solitudes: Canadian Multicultural Fictions.* Toronto: Oxford University Press, 1990.

Hryniuk, S., Ed. *20 Years of Multiculturalism: Successes and Failures.* Winnipeg: St. John's College, 1992.

Kallen, E. "Multiculturalism: Ideology, Policy and Reality." *Journal of Canadian Studies* 17, 1 (1982): 51-63.

Kaplan, W., Ed. *Belonging: The Meaning and Future of Canadian Citizenship.* Montreal and Kingston: McGill-Queen's University Press, 1993.

Kymlicka, W. *Multicultural Citizenship.* Oxford: University of Oxford Press, 1995.

McRoberts, K. *Misconceiving Canada: The Struggle for National Unity.* Oxford: Oxford University Press, 1997.

Padolsky, E. "Multiculturalism at the Millennium." *Journal of Canadian Studies* 35, 1 (Spring 2000): 138-60.

Pal, L. *Interests of State: The Politics of Language, Multiculturalism, and Feminism in Canada.* Montreal and Kingston: McGill-Queen's University Press, 1993.

Palmer, H. *Immigration and the Rise of Multiculturalism.* Toronto: Copp Clark, 1975.

Reitz, J., and R. Breton. *The Illusion of Difference.* Toronto: C.D. Howe Institute, 1994.

Satzewich, V., Ed. *Deconstructing a Nation: Immigration, Multiculturalism, and Racism in '90s Canada.* Halifax: Fernwood, 1992.

Taylor, C. *Multiculturalism and the Politics of Recognition.* Princeton: Princeton University Press, 1992.

CHAPTER 14

"A People in Bondage"

QUEBEC AND INDEPENDENCE

INTRODUCTION

S mall numbers of separatists have fought for their independence ever since Quebec came under British rule in 1760. Formation of the separatist Parti Québécois in 1968 forced the issue to the front of the political agenda, both within Quebec and in Canada as a whole. There it remains. Thus, though separatism may appear new, the present iteration is actually the latest and most successful manifestation in a long tradition of separatist thought and organizations emanating from *La Belle Province*.

French Canada had, by 1763 when the British Conquest became official, developed a unique and distinct culture, one its people cherished and wished to preserve. This, of course, was awkward with Quebec under British tutelage and its official policy of Anglo-assimilation. Though assimilationist efforts largely failed and led to some acceptance of French Canada's uniqueness within British North America, as enshrined in the 1774 Quebec Act, the latent expectation of assimilation remained. Many French-Canadian nationalists concluded that the only way to preserve and nurture Quebec's culture was to create an independent nation beyond Britain's grasp. That was what the rebels of 1837 sought, and what nationalists like the conservative Abbé Lionel Groulx promoted in the 1920s and 1930s. It was not before the late 1950s, however, that French-Canadian separatism emerged in its modern version and became a formidable and popular force.

Economic conditions in Quebec not only played a major part in fomenting modern separatism, they still contribute to the waxing and waning of separatist support. French Canadians discovered by the late 1950s that most things worth owning in their province—the wood, minerals, electrical generation potential, commerce, banking—belonged to *les étrangers*, "foreigners," most either Montreal Anglophones or American corporations. Meanwhile, disproportionately high unemployment and narrow job prospects haunted the French-Canadian majority.

If, argued separatists in the 1950s and 1960s, the Québécois wished to improve their lot, they must create a new and independent nation in which French Canadians could truly rule their own house. Conversely, they argued, tinkering with the federal system, no matter how noble the intentions, would leave Quebec unable to manage its own affairs because it would remain "colonized" by the federal government. There was no shortage of enthusiasm for independence in the heady social flux of the 1960s, especially on Quebec's campuses; the question was how to achieve it. Some argued that the Anglo "bosses" would never voluntarily relinquish control because it suited their ends. Marxists contended that independence could logically only come through revolution—and the militant underground organization, the *Front de libération du Québec* (FLQ) was born. Though the FLQ's campaign of bombing and kidnapping symbols of Anglo-domination through the 1960s cost it mass support, the organization's eloquent fury and ultimate goals struck a responsive chord within Quebec. Most Québécois separatists, however, preferred to follow legal channels, and a number of political organizations dedicated to separatism emerged, the major one being the *Rassemblement pour l'indépendance nationale* (RIN). When René Lévesque quit the provincial Liberal party in 1967, he fused the RIN with his own converts to independence, and created the dynamic Parti Québécois (PQ) in 1968.

Pundits across Canada who prophesized Lévesque's political suicide soon were proved wrong. Separatism gained popularity among many progressive Quebec urbanites, and the party's support rose to the point where it won a quarter of the popular vote in the 1970 provincial election. This astonishing victory, however, translated into only seven seats in the National Assembly, a situation which separatists held up as proof that the system was stacked against French Canadians and their aspirations. The 1973 provincial election increased the PQ's popular vote to almost one-third—but they lost a seat. The tide turned in the 1976 provincial election, and Lévesque's party swept to power with three-quarters of the seats and 41 per cent of the popular vote, largely on the promise to hold a referendum on the right to begin negotiating separation with the federal government within its first term in office.

Terry Mosher, drawing as cartoonist "Aislin," captured Canada's mood the day after the PQ gained power. His predictably scabrous editorial cartoon depicted a disheveled Lévesque, ubiquitous cigarette in hand, against a black background. The caption was: "Okay, everybody take a Valium." Canada awakened from its complacent slumber to discover that one of the country's provincial governments and some 30 per cent of the nation's population apparently wished to leave what was supposedly the finest country on earth.

The PQ kept its promise to hold a referendum on the right to negotiate sovereignty-association, doing so in 1980 after postponing it for as long as politically feasible. Polls proved that separatist support was, in fact, dangerously soft. The PQ knew, however, that a large percentage of Québécois were unhappy with the federal-provincial *status quo*. Thus, Lévesque and his team spent four years carefully cultivating the idea of separatism, casting it as a logical, safe, and advantageous route for the province — or at least as implied leverage in federal-provincial negotiations. Gentle persuasion was the order of the day. Lévesque de-emphasized the PQ's avowed independence agenda in favour of simple good government, thereby hoping to gain credibility and support among "soft separatists" and undecided voters. Claude Morin, one of the separatist referendum architects, logically pointed out that "you don't make a flower grow by pulling at it."

Prime Minster Pierre Trudeau responded to the PQ's 1976 electoral victory and to the 1980 referendum by promising to work toward creating a sense of inclusion for the Québécois within Canada. A made-in-Canada Constitution, he argued, would begin the process by removing the symbolic thorn of English domination. Vote "no," he promised, and Canada will ensure that Quebec gains its deserved sense of equality.

The 1980 referendum results became official on May 20. The vote in favour of a mandate to negotiate sovereignty-association was 40.4 per cent; opposed, 59.6 per cent. While separatists wept over their seemingly catastrophic defeat, federalists collectively sighed with relief. Closer examination of the referendum results, however, allowed sovereignists to dry their tears and draw comfort from a result that was far more ambiguous than simple numbers initially suggested. Federalists certainly had no cause for smugness. The sizable non-Francophone community in Quebec, for example, predictably voted overwhelming *non* to sovereignty-association. Francophones, however, voted almost 50-50 *oui*, and young secular urbanites, the next generation of Quebec leaders, supported independence by a reasonably wide margin. The 1981 provincial election saw the PQ, still dedicated to a sovereign Quebec, swept back into power, winning 80 out of the 122 seats—a two-thirds majority—and this despite losing the referendum. The dream of an independent Quebec certainly did not die in 1980.

Trudeau was as good as his word and set out to create a new constitution immediately after the referendum. Reaching consensus with the other provinces, however, proved all but impossible. The new Canada Act of 1982 became law without Quebec's support and with grudging acceptance from the rest of the country. Quebec separatists saw this development as just the latest incarnation of colonialism—a constitution that Quebec did not support but had to obey. Subsequent federal governments, particularly Brian Mulroney's Progressive Conservatives, sought to placate Quebec. Negotiations such as the Meech Lake and Charlottetown Accords offered glimmers of hope of achieving this by calling for a significantly decentralized federation and special status for Quebec within Canada. The rest of Canada, however, found this unacceptable, and all negotiations ultimately failed—just as the separatists had predicted.

The most contentious part of the Canada Act, the new Constitution of 1982, was its "notwithstanding clause," which provinces insisted upon including and which Trudeau railed against but ultimately had to accept in order to have the new act pass with provincial support. The clause seriously eroded federal powers by allowing provinces to override the new Charter of Rights and Freedoms. If, for example, a province passed legislation that went against the Charter, such as language legislation in Quebec that forbade English signage, an individual could challenge that legislation in the Supreme Court. If the Court agreed, the federal government should intercede based upon its right to uphold the "peace, order, and good government" of the country. The offending legislation would thus be annulled by federal command. At that point, however, the province now had the right to override the federal government and the Charter by declaring that "in spite of the fact that (notwithstanding) the Charter says the law is unconstitutional, we are going to have it anyway." This is what Quebec did to retain its French-only language legislation despite it having been declared against the Charter, which guarantees freedom of expression. Ironically, Quebec did not accept the new Constitution, but it is the only province to have employed the notwithstanding clause in a pervasive way.

As promised, the PQ held a second referendum on separatism in 1995. This time the *non* side won by less than 1 per cent after a calamitous campaign that saw thousands of Canadians from across the country reach out to Quebec. Bitter PQ Premier Jacques Parizeau blamed Quebec's ethnic minorities and "big money" for the referendum's failure, and the party vowed to hold yet another when conditions appeared ripe for victory, which did not occur by the time the PQ lost power to the provincial Liberals under Jean Charest in 2003. Meanwhile, separatists shifted their focus by creating the separatist Bloc Québécois (Bloc) in 1990. Operating on the *federal* level, it was initially led by Lucien Bouchard, a long-time veteran of the separatist wars. The Bloc shares the ideals of sovereignty and social democracy with the PQ, and the two act in unison. The current period of minority federal governments in Ottawa assures the Bloc a considerable voice in federal politics and guarantees that no federal government can ignore Quebec.

Other issues, particularly economic struggles, have pushed separatism to the back burner, but the stove remains lit and there is no reason why the pot may not boil again.

In the interim, the federal government passed the Clarity Act in 2000. It sets rules of engagement for hypothetical Quebec separation, though it also applies to other provinces. It stipulates that the referendum to separate must be clearly worded for the voters, with no ambiguity or obfuscation in its language. It further states that for independence to occur a clear majority of the province's voters must support it; 50 per cent plus one, the traditional method for deciding elections and the one used for allowing Newfoundland *into* Confederation, is insufficient. This, say the separatists, is yet another example of Canada's imperialistic domination over Quebec, since by it Ottawa is dictating how French Canadians are to decide their own fate. Though relegated to second-party status behind the Liberals in the December 2008 provincial election, the PQ is rebuilding and may, like the phoenix, rise from the ashes to again hover over the national agenda. The political journalist who dubbed the process the "neverendum" was indeed correct.

DISCUSSION POINTS

1. Do the aims, ambitions, and grievances of the separatists justify the creation of an independent state?

2. Would Canada be better off without Quebec?

3. Is sovereignty-association a contradiction in terms? Utopian? Realistic? Does it fit into the movement toward larger units of economic and political co-operation such as the European Union and the North American Free Trade Association, or not?

4. Is the Quebec situation simply the most severe version of regional forces that threaten to de-confederate Canada? Do any other regions of Canada have a similar basis for claiming a separate identity?

5. During his tenure as premier of Quebec, Lucien Bouchard stated that Canada is not a country. Was he right?

DOCUMENTS

1. Marcel Chaput, *Why I Am a Separatist*, 1961

Marcel Chaput (1918-91) was a French-Canadian chemist working as a civil servant for the federal government's Department of National Defence. He gained attention in 1960 with a series of articles published by Le Devoir *newspaper in which he complained about the lack of French in the federal civil service, particularly in the* DND. *From there he helped found the sovereignist organization the* Rassamblement pour l'indépendance nationale *(RIN), becoming first its vice-president, then president in late 1961. Chaput's book* Why I Am a Separatist *appeared that same year. His political activism led to his suspension without pay from the federal civil service, which forbids civil servants from holding political office. Chaput quit the* DND *in 1961 to devote himself to Quebec independence.*

The world is made up of Separatists. The man who is master of his home is a Separatist. Each of the hundred nations striving to maintain its national identity is Separatist. France and England are mutually Separatist, even in relation to the Common Market. And you who long for a real Canadian Constitution, you are a Separatist. The only difference between you and me is that you want Canada to be free in relation to England and the United States, and I want Quebec to be free in relation to Canada. In mathematical terms, Quebec's independence is to Canada as Canada's independence is to the United States and England. But Quebec is far more justified than English Canada in asserting its individuality, since of the four territories, Quebec alone has a distinct culture, whereas English Canada, the United States and England tend to be very similar.

In spite of this, Separatism has always received a poor press in Quebec. The very term Separatism is certainly responsible in part. It is negative and doesn't seem to encourage a constructive approach.

And yet, for anyone who pauses to reflect on it, Separatism leads on to great things: to Independence, Liberty, Fulfillment of the Nation, French Dignity in the New World.

It has become fashionable in some quarters to treat Separatists as dreamers. Thank heaven that there are still men and women in French Canada capable of dreaming! But to grasp the distinction between a practical dream and a utopia, you must at least be able to put aside the sort of subjective dogmatism which immediately rejects the idea of independence for Quebec without a thought.

It is true that independence is a matter of character rather than of logic. Everyone is not capable of being independent. A feeling of pride is even more essential than having a reasonable claim.

If you possess this pride of which free men are made, if you can shake off all preconceived notions about the subject and bring a sincere, discerning attitude to the discussion, then, and only then, should we sit down and talk. ...

Most of all, you would be wrong to think that I consider independence the solution to all of Quebec's problems; on the contrary, I believe that it would create many more new ones.

Why independence then?

Because it is highly desirable that a normal man or nation be free.

I just don't believe, as do certain M.P.'s, that the bilingualism of French-Canadians is an indication of their superiority, but rather a proof of their enslavement. I cannot stand by silently, as others seemingly can, and watch the day-by-day extermination of my people, even if by our own foolishness we are more to blame than the "damned English."

The six million French-Canadians are no longer obliged to accept this minority position, which makes of us a people without a future, shut up in the vicious circle of destructive bilingualism.

Since I naturally owe my first allegiance to French Canada, before the Dominion, I must ask myself the question: which of two choices will permit French-Canadians to attain the fullest development—Confederation, in which they will forever be a shrinking minority, doomed to subjection?—or the independence of Quebec, their true native land, which will make them masters of their own destiny?

But judging by the reaction of some of my compatriots to this basic question, it seems to me that truly free French-Canadians are even harder to find than you would think, which is after all normal for a people in bondage.

Faced with Separatism, some smile ironically, others hide their eyes, the established well-to-do have proved to themselves that independence isn't necessary to the Good Life, the bourgeois have other things on their minds, and the petty workers are afraid of losing their jobs.

And then, after all, we aren't so badly off. Actually, we are quite well off. Who do these Separatist people think they are, coming along to disturb our serenity? Do they want to shut themselves up in the "Quebec reservation"?

And so on through the whole list of current objections.

But let's not get ahead of ourselves. Let us start at the beginning....

THE HISTORICAL DIMENSION

A World-Wide Trend to Independence

We of the mid-twentieth century are living historic years. Since World War II more than thirty former colonies have liberated themselves from foreign domination to attain national and international sovereignty. In 1960 alone, seventeen African colonies, fourteen of them French-speaking, have obtained their independence. And now it is the turn of the French-Canadian people to arise and claim their rightful place among free nations.

Why Independence? We Are Free

Why independence? you may ask. What is this Separatism that is making so much fuss? We French-Canadians are free. We are free to speak our language, to practise our religion. We have the right to vote, even the right to be elected. Is not the very presence of a French-Canadian as Governor-General an outright refutation of Separatist claims? And what of the two French-Canadian Prime Ministers? And the head of the Supreme Court? And the generals? Are the Separatists trying to compare the French-Canadians to the African tribes who have recently won their independence? These Negroes, often illiterate, sometimes deprived of the most basic rights, exploited, living in under-developed countries, had a right to claim the independence they lacked. But as for us French-Canadians, the situation is quite different.

Similarity and Difference

It is true that our situation in French Canada is not identical with that of the African Negroes. It is true that we have enjoyed rights for a long time which these people have only recently acquired. But we are not assured of total independence by the mere fact that we have certain rights which give us a partial control of our national affairs, even if this control be much greater in practice than that held by the newly decolonized countries. You may be closer to your goal than a neighbour is, without having reached the goal.

In the rise of people toward independence, no two cases are identical. But French Canada *is* like all these new sovereign nations in that she too has been taken by force, occupied, dominated, exploited, and in that even today, here destiny rests to a great extent in the hands of a nation which is foreign to her....

Confederation: The Lesser of Two Evils

To affirm, as some do, that Confederation was freely accepted by the French-Canadians of the time, is to play with words, to distort the meaning of liberty. First of all, the B.N.A. Act was never put to the vote. It was imposed by a decree of parliament at Westminster, and by a majority vote of twenty-six to twenty-two among the Canadian representatives.

For Confederation to have been labeled the free choice of the French-Canadians, it would have been necessary to have given them the freedom of choice between Confederation or total sovereignty. And this freedom was not granted, either by the London parliament or by the English-speaking colonies of America.

In 1867, French Canada, Lower Canada, old Canada in short, was a British colony, and the alternatives offered her did not include independence. She was a colony and was to remain so, inside or outside Confederation. If there was any freedom of choice, it was that of the convicted man who is allowed to choose between a fine and prison. Just as the prisoner chooses the fine, if he can afford it, French Canada entered Confederation. It was, in her opinion, the lesser of two evils....

What About the Canadian Nation?

There is no Canadian nation. We cannot have a Canadian nation and a French-Canadian nation at the same time. There is a Canadian State.

Certain groups, invariably English, would like to see a genuine Canadian nation. But this would involve the negation of the French-Canadian group as such.

The Canadian State is a purely political and artificial entity formed originally by armed force and maintained by a submission of the French-Canadians to the federal government.

On the contrary, the French-Canadian nation is a natural entity whose bonds are those of culture, flesh and blood.

If the American army were to invade Mexico and force its amalgamation with the United States, there would still be a Mexican nation. In the same way there is still a French-Canadian nation.

The Confrontation of Two Nationalisms

The Separatists also urge French-Canadians to make their presence felt everywhere in Canada, in America, in the world. But we feel just as strongly that French-Canadians must be *in control* somewhere, in a country of their own, specifically in Quebec.

That is why modern Separatism constitutes an irreconcilable opposition to traditional nationalism. Whereas the latter is employed to uphold rights in a vast Canada in which French-Canada is a minority group, Separatists, the Freedom Fighters of Quebec, are aspiring to set up the French-Canadians as masters of their own destiny.

It has nothing whatsoever to do with Anglophobia, chronic discontent, or vengefulness. The removal of each individual injustice suffered by the French-Canadians will not cause the idea of an independent Quebec to disappear.

We want independence for a totally different reason. It is because dignity requires it. It is because of the idea that minorities, like absentees, are always wrong...

A Pact between Two Great Races

French Canada is unfortunately populated with people who, for want of reality, like to tell themselves stories. One of the dangerous ones is that Confederation is a sacred pact between two great races, French and English. It is a poetic idea. It inspires you. But the fact remains that it is an illusion. For you can search in vain, in the texts and especially in the facts, without finding a single word or action to justify it.

All political decisions of importance in Canada are made by the Parliament or the Cabinet, where the French-Canadians are in a minority. Proof? Newfoundland's entrance to Confederation, Canada's membership in the UN, in NATO or in NORAD, had no need of French-Canada's approval. Even if we had been consulted, we couldn't have done anything because of our minority position.

You may retort that French is still an official language, but you would be wrong—or at least you would be only partly right. French is, along with English, official in Quebec—this makes us the *only* bilingual province in our dealings with the Ottawa Parliament and the Federal Courts of Justice. This limitation puts French on an unequal footing with the English from the outset.

In Parliament, nine per cent of the speeches have been given in French since the installation of simultaneous interpretation. Are the members from Quebec less talkative than their English colleagues? Or perhaps they simply want to show off their "bilingual superiority"? Nonsense! It is nothing but a minority reflex, conditioned by two hundred years of subjection.

The final result is that, internally, Canada is a predominantly English country and, from the outside, Canada is also an English country, a country in which, they say, English and French live in perfect harmony for the edification of humanity.

THE ECONOMIC DIMENSION

After All, We're Not So Badly Off

For many people, not only French-Canadians, the economic aspect of a problem is always the most important. Faced with the prospect of Quebec's independence, they invariably say that they will support the idea as soon as they see proof that Quebec would gain economically.

This subsection was not written to prove that an independent Quebec would be an economically sound proposition. We shall discuss this later. My only purpose for the moment is to remind you that the French-Canadians have gained nothing from Confederation; on the contrary, they are losing continuously.

Perhaps the relative comfort you enjoy makes you fear a lowering of your standard of living, a serious change in your habits, a prolonged economic recession. After all, the French-Canadians aren't so badly off, no matter what they say.

Let me hasten to remind you that individual liberty is not under discussion here. Certainly there are rich men, even millionaires, among the French-Canadians, which seems to show that a French-Canadian can make a lot of money, even under Confederation. But we are discussing French-Canadians as a people, as a nation, in their province of Quebec. The French-Canadian nation is economically weak and economically under-developed, living in economic bondage ...

A People in Bondage

There is no need to be an economist, statistician or informed industrialist to realize that the French-Canadians are not the masters, are not the proprietors of their own province or cities. You have only to take a stroll through any city in Quebec with your eyes open, to seize at a glance our economic insignificance. Our contribution is limited to furnishing cheap raw materials, cheap manpower and five million docile consumers. All this for the sake of a few crumbs.

We French-Canadians made up twenty-nine per cent of Canada's population in 1951, but our participation in the economy was limited to five or ten per cent, closer to five than to ten. In Quebec we are eighty-three per cent of the population, but less than twenty per cent of the economy is in our hands. At the Montreal Stock Exchange (you rarely hear it called *la Bourse de Montréal*), it is said that one per cent of the business is based on French-Canadian capital—in a city containing at least a million French-Canadians! Scarcely a month goes by that you don't learn in the papers or by word of mouth that another French-Canadian enterprise has sold out to a big American or Anglo-Canadian firm. It is a well-known fact, appearing in the papers every year, that Quebec has the greatest number of bankruptcies in Canada. The corner grocery, which used to be our own, has been supplanted, or rather, strangled, by the supermarkets, all of which are under foreign control. And the small grocer who has managed to survive has done so only by joining some *chain*, and the main link of this chain is invariably in the hands of foreign control as well.

The Labour Market

On the labour market, the French-Canadians are at the bottom of the ladder. You may insist that it is their own fault, that all they have to do is get more education to prepare themselves for better positions. But I insist that I am not attempting an assessment of commendation and rebuke—I am establishing facts.

For equal labour, workers in Quebec are paid less than in Ontario. If there is an economic recession or unemployment, Quebec always has the longest list of unemployed. If anyone receives a good salary, he is almost certain to be in the employ of a foreign company. But at the higher levels of these foreign companies, at directorship-level, French-Canadians are no longer found. Even in the Federal corporations our compatriots are significantly rare. Out of the seventeen directors of the Bank of Canada, one is a French-Canadian; out of the seventeen vice-presidents of the C.N.R., none is French-Canadian. Out of the seven top officials in the new Federal ministry of forests, none is French-Canadian, although Quebec has twenty-five per cent of Canada's commercial forest area. In public office, the higher you go, the fewer French-Canadians you meet. The situation is the same in the armed forces. We are good enough when it comes to paying taxes, or playing the role of consumer and soldier, but we are not good enough to take our rightful place on the well-paid levels of Canadian life.

Quebec — Ottawa's Private Treasure Chest

If only Quebec got back in service what it gave to Ottawa. But far from it—it pays to have itself Anglicized and to maintain its state of bondage.

Quebec pays two billion dollars a year to Ottawa in taxes. It gets back only five hundred million dollars per year, twenty-five per cent of its contribution. . . .

English, Language of Labour and Thought

Any country in the world must have its bilinguals. Interpreters and translators are required in diplomatic service, transport, communications, hotels, the army, even in the civil service. But in what proportion? That is the problem. Let us be generous and say five per cent. But in French-Canada, at least half the workers must know English to earn their living. Of these, at least half must, like me, throw off their native language with their overcoats at the office or factory entrance each morning—their native language, French, an international language, used by one hundred and fifty million people.

For the majority of French-Canadian workers, even in Quebec, English is the language of labour and thought. French? It is used in translations, in the family, in folklore. In his own language, the French-Canadian leads a fairytale existence. Active life, the life of earning enough to keep bread on the table, the life of entertainment, the life of the mind, is carried on in English as often as not....

You think you are going to a French show—if you can find one at all. Two times out of three you will see the French version of a Hollywood hit. You open your French newspaper and read the French translation of an English translation of a speech given in French by General de Gaulle. The Canadian Press (there is no such thing as *la Presse Canadienne*) has not even passed on the original, and this in a country where they say French is an official language. You subscribe to a Canadian magazine of genuinely French content, only to find that it has recently been bought out by Anglo-American capital. You pass by a large building, even in Montreal—you will find three words of French on a bronze plaque and a bilingual elevator-boy. Seek no further. That is the extent of the French. "Patrons are requested to leave their tongue in the umbrella rack."

What About the Schools?

Why should our schools teach French, real French, if the language is of so little use here? It is English that we need, and more and more of it. Really, can you imagine a more absurd situation than the one in which you and I have found ourselves? Six, eight, ten, twelve years of French studies, when this language, which is supposedly so beautiful, is of no use in earning your daily bread. So many long years spent learning a language when English is what you really need when you leave school. As a result, parents demand more English, and those parents are right. Far be it from me to criticize them, for their logic is impeccable. Parents see things in their true light, and children too. They realize quite well that without English you might not be able to earn your keep in Canada, that without English you run the risk of swelling the ranks of Quebec's unemployed.

But what is the result of these repeated demands, which are heard today more than yesterday, and tomorrow more than today? The more bilingual our children become, the more they will use English; the more they use English, the less use they will get from French; and the less use they get from French, the more they will use English. *It is a paradox of French-Canadian life: the more bilingual we become, the less need there is to be bilingual.* This is a path which can lead us only to Anglification. Moreover, we have already come such a long way in this direction that we would be better off to know only English—so let's get on with the process and speak no more about it.…

Bilingualism—a Sign of Bondage or Superiority?

It may seem strange to some people that a French-Canadian like me, who earns his living in English, should not appreciate the benefits of bilingualism.

Well, I do; I am very happy that I know English, and if I didn't know it yet, I would learn it. I derive satisfaction from knowing English, just as I should like to do with several more languages, English even more than other languages because it is the most widespread in North America. But it is not a question of deciding whether it is useful or not for French-Canadians to know English, but of discovering what this knowledge and its constant use is costing them.

They learn English to the detriment of their native language which is deteriorating, their French culture which is wilting away, their dignity which is being insulted.

I didn't learn English out of intellectual curiosity. I learned it because it was the language of the stronger side, because I needed it to earn my living. Perhaps a man who knows two languages is worth two men, but a man who is forced to speak the Other Fellow's language in order to eat is worth only half a man. The misfortune of the French-Canadian people is to mistake the fetters of its bilingualism for a sign of superiority. Just as a little boy afraid of the dark will whistle to bolster his courage, the brow-beaten French-Canadian prides himself on his bilingualism to hide his inferiority complex.…

THE SOCIAL DIMENSION

We Are Inferior to Ourselves

As in other spheres, or perhaps even more here than elsewhere, French-Canadians are inferior to themselves. You often hear it said: What have we to complain about? We have accomplished a great deal. Haven't we produced two prime ministers, a governor-general, a chief justice? Don't we have our artists, our scientists, our writers?

It is true that, in spite of serious difficulties, French-Canadians have nevertheless produced a lot. But, for nations, just as for men, it isn't enough to know whether they have produced; we must ask whether they have produced enough—whether they have produced as much as their capabilities permit. This is the parable of the talents.

Far be it from me to excuse my compatriots by blaming the "damned English" for our inferiority. But all the same we must recognize the fact that the French-Canadians have not had the same history as the English-speaking Canadians during the past two hundred years, not even in the ninety-four years of Confederation. Armed with abundant capital, political authority and numerical superiority, the English Canadians had an easier time of it than we. We had the talents—and we still have—but we lacked the financial boost and political favour, so that, socially, we are second-rate citizens.

In the Workaday World

In the workaday world of industry and commerce, we are on the bottom rung of the ladder. Quebec is the place to go for cheap labour; in times of crisis or economic recession, Quebec always has the greatest number of unemployed. This was obvious in the winter of 1960-1961. Across the country, eleven per cent of the working force was idle in March, according to the papers; in Quebec, the figure was fourteen per cent....

All you have to do is open your eyes: all the large industries in Quebec make excessive use of the English to the detriment of the French. In so doing, they are merely following the example of those around them, but this marked predominance of English places the French-Canadian worker in an inferior position from the start. That is obvious. There is a dividing line between the management and the labour force. The first is English, the second French....

But in the face of the imminent dangers confronting the French-Canadian nation, I fear that the outgrown methods of this noble society are no longer sufficient. Confederation, pan-Canadianism, bilingualism and the whole Canadian way of life have depersonalized the French-Canadian, have even robbed him, over the years, of his capacity for indignation. At his most brash, he is no more than a beggar. The schools have forgotten about nationalist education, and life in Quebec doesn't even teach us our language. Something better than the repetition of the same old reports must be found if we are going to change things....

INDEPENDENCE OF QUEBEC

The Rejection of Liberty

You have just read, a few pages back, that a minority which wishes to live cannot hand over the control of its affairs to a foreign majority. That is the simple reason why the Separatists want Quebec to be independent. As long as the French-Canadians form a linguistic and cultural minority, they will be doomed to subjection and mediocrity. It is not because of hostility or a desire for revenge against the English; it is not a way of finding an alibi for all our stupidities and cowardly acts; it is not a way of excusing men by blaming the institutions. On the contrary, it is based on a purely mathematical truth of democracy—the majority prevails over the minority. Either we must bow to the decisions of the majority and stop complaining, or withdraw from Confederation. The desire to stick with Confederation at all costs is a search for excuses to justify the rejection of liberty.

Commonwealth and Crown

Why should we kid ourselves any longer? For two hundred years the French-Canadians have been trying to free themselves from the British Crown, the symbol of foreign domination. All the French-Canadian nationalist movements of the past have embodied this subconscious or avowed refusal to submit. It is high time that English Canada realized the fact that, outside of a few rare politicians, the French-Canadians have *never* accepted subjection to British Royalty. They simply endured it. We had to submit to it under force of arms; you can't reproach us all the same if we want to free ourselves from it now.

The formation of a new confederation with English Canada can only mean continued domination for the French. It is normal that English Canada should be attached to the British Crown and all its symbols—the Union Jack, the Red Ensign, protocol, etc., and they cannot be reproached for it, but nothing holds the French Canadians to these things.

In the year 1961, the British Crown can mean only one thing: the free, voluntary and intentional acceptance of a tie, on the part of a people which has the right to turn down this tie. If the British Crown is imposed where it is not wanted, then it becomes imperialistic ...

Well, we French-Canadians *do* form a nation, simply by possessing all necessary attributes. We are certainly large enough—five or six million is more than necessary for the foundation of an independent nation. Half of the members of the U.N. are smaller.

But the population figure alone does not make us a nation. We have numerous institutions—we have a territory which we have occupied for almost four centuries, Quebec, which belongs to us by virtue of Article 109 of the B.N.A. Act, we speak the same language, French; above all, we have maintained a collective will to live unbroken even by the events of the past two centuries.

A nation we certainly are, all the more since our ties are those of flesh and blood and spirit, whereas our membership in what some people call the Canadian nation is a merely political one imposed by circumstances....

In practice, this situation is at our throats every day. Every day we have to choose between being French-Canadian or Canadian because there is no longer any equivalence or conciliation possible between the two. Nowadays, if you want to be *Canadian*, you must be English....

Nevertheless, the theory of Quebec's independence has other claims to desirability than that of being normal. As surely as Confederation has kept us in an unfavourable position by making us into a minority group, Quebec's independence will ensure our advancement by handing over to us the control of our own destiny.

Quebec's independence is therefore desirable for the same reasons that Confederation, in which we are the minority, is not.

Historically, Quebec's independence would allow the French-Canadians to enjoy liberty. History intended that there should be a free French people on American soil. By claiming independence for Quebec, we are merely leading our people back to its historic destiny. After being conquered by armed might, dominated by a foreign nation, after having fought the hard battle for survival, French Canada, by leaving Confederation, will be doing nothing more than leaving behind it one further stage in its long march toward full sovereignty.

Politically, Quebec's independence is desirable because it would take the French-Canadians out of their position of numerical helplessness. In politics as in everything else, for the French-Canadians as for all people, numerical balance is essential to the smooth running of affairs. Starting with our Independence Day, Quebec will negotiate on equal terms with other countries, including the rest of Canada. Once it has become the recognized master of its destiny, a sovereign Quebec can then approve any unions, sign any treaties, practise any amount of friendly relations, set up any plans for helping under-developed countries or Canadian provinces, that are dictated by its own responsibilities and interests.

Independence is politically desirable because it is always good for people to be free, and because no nation has ever become great by leaving the political control of its destiny in the hands of another.

Economically, political independence is desirable for Quebec because, without control over political power, economic independence remains a sweet daydream....

There will always be some who assert that the economy has nothing to do with nationalistic spirit, but this is only true for the man without a country. It is also true, however, that nationalistic spirit is not something you can acquire at will. It is something permanent which penetrates into all realms of activity and which springs from a deeper feeling—that of a nation that is well-defined, and quite capable of conducting its own affairs.

Culturally, independence would be the nation's salvation. Do you realize what life would be like in a unilingual country? Morning to night you would hear the same language, the national language.

It would mean the end of the absurd and deadly situation, economically and culturally, for the majority of French-Canadians, the situation of working in English after having gone to French schools.

It would mean the end of this noxious co-existence of two languages and two systems of thought which makes French-Canadian bilingualism into the *doubtful art of speaking two languages at once.*

Do not misunderstand me; I consider English to be a beautiful language, when spoken properly. It is the mutual penetration of two languages, of two thought-patterns, which is harmful. And Quebec's independence would separate them—not by raising a cultural wall around Quebec, which would be impossible and undesirable. Since it is geographically part of America, a totally French Quebec will obviously have to open its doors to Anglo-American culture.

But as in everything, it is a question of balance. A French Quebec can make no cultural progress unless it feeds principally on French cultural traditions, in lesser proportions on traditions from English Canada, America and elsewhere.

At present, under Confederation, Anglo-American language and culture are weighing down too heavily on the French consciousness....

Basing our case on the United Nations Charter which stipulates—Article 1, paragraph 2—that all peoples have the right of self-determination, we will then begin negotiations with Ottawa. And Ottawa, which has also signed this Charter, cannot do other than agree.

2. Peter Nesbitt Thomson, "Separatism a Dangerous Philosophy," Speech to the Empire Club of Canada, February 6, 1964

Peter Nesbitt Thomson (1927–) was the son of P.A. Thomson who, with his partner A.J. Nesbitt, created Power Corporation in 1925 as a holding company in the burgeoning hydroelectric power industry. P.N. Thomson attended Lower Canada College and received a doctorate of law from St. Thomas University, Fredericton. He began his professional career at his father's other major company, the investment firm Nesbitt Thomson. Power Corporation prospered, and P.N. Thomson took over jointly with Nesbitt's son in 1956 at his father's death, assuming the mantle of president and CEO in 1962. He was active in community affairs and served as governor of Montreal General Hospital and director of the Canadian Welfare Council. He married a French Canadian.

... As an English-speaking Canadian I am greatly concerned over this situation. As an English-speaking Quebecer identified with business I cannot help wondering if emotions have not superseded hard facts....

No one who has ever lived in Montreal can say that Quebec is like the rest of Canada—it isn't. It is this very difference which makes Montreal one of the greatest cities in the world, and makes Quebec the most fascinating province in this country of ours. I, for one, cannot conceive of a Canada without Quebec, nor can I conceive of a Quebec without a Canada. For it is this very intermingling of races which has created the aura that surrounds Quebec.

That there is bigotry in Quebec between the two main races and religions cannot be denied, no more than we can deny that bigotry exists across the whole of this country. It has been intensified, and divided the races by identifying the English as Protestant and the French as Catholic. There is exaggeration here, but unfortunately it is too close to the truth to be completely dismissed. That this is an offshoot of the divergences too often voiced by religious leaders in the past is unfortunately true, as it is throughout the world....

The separatist movement in Quebec has been likened to the movements for freedom in Africa which has seen the emergence of many new nations. Of the control of industry in Quebec we had a prominent French-Canadian member of parliament, speaking in Toronto, assaying the new attitude in Quebec, saying that it makes no difference to Quebecers whether their industry is controlled by American or by English-speaking Canadians—"They both speak English: it is all the same to us," he said.

In this kind of language and reasoning lies the crux of much of the problem of Quebec today. There is a growing sentiment among the separatists and their supporters that anything that is wrong with Quebec must be the fault of the English, and it is this very attitude that makes the separatist philosophy dangerous.

I suggest to you that the separatists are wrong: that the fault lies as much in themselves as in anything the English have done or have not done with respect to French-Canadians. I feel that they are developing a philosophy based upon a fallacy....

The classical traditions of French-Canadian colleges prevented its students from playing a full part in the scientific, engineering and business development of their province. This is something the separatist overlooks when he comes to apportion blame. To realize how much blame attaches to the educational system, with which the English had nothing to do, he need only look at the intense efforts now being made to reform the educational system, to fit it better to the times in which we live. The government's determination to reform the system, made manifest only a while ago in the much discussed Bill 60, is a tacit admission that the educational system has been the most inhibiting factor in French-Canadian life. It left him unfit for commerce or industry, and by that token left the greater part of commerce and industry to the English with their vastly different educational background.

This leads me to think the time has come for an honest appraisal. How much of the present problem is due to the French-Canadian himself? Certainly more than he cares to admit. French-Canadians who liken the attitude of Quebec to that of the new nations seeking freedom are using spurious analogies to lessen the burden of their own responsibility. They belong to the colonial school of thought. They believe that all Quebec has to do to regain its feet is to free itself from the "colonialism" of the English regime. However honestly held, this view is fallacious for French-Canadian colonialism is a state of mind, and not a reality.

One would think, from the expression of separatist sentiment, that French-Canadians were in a minority role in Quebec, whereas the reverse is true....

Economic opportunities have always been present in Quebec for both races. That the French-Canadian prepared himself for politics, the professions and the priesthood in preference to commerce and industry was of his own choosing. If he entered the business arena later than his English speaking contemporaries, no one is to blame but those who perpetuated the parochial educational system that failed to prepare him for a role in business. The French-Canadian is a product of his own system—of a system which he himself has controlled from the beginning, and in which the English speaking Quebecer has had little, if any, voice whatever.

To say, as some separatists argue, that business opportunity was denied to him is to close the eyes to the facts. To base the separatist argument wholly on economic difficulties is to insult the myriad French-Canadians who have contributed to the grandeur of this country and of their province in the judiciary, in politics, in the legal profession, in the arts and in medicine. It discredits the many French-Canadians who, despite a late start as compared with the English, still managed to build industries and business complexes that compare favourably in size to any in the whole country. Since when is accomplishment based on the language one speaks?

Yet we see today the spectacle of English businessmen surreptitiously taking lessons in French to hide their ignorance of the language, to appease the French-Canadian hunger for equality of language. If more French-Canadians are bilingual than are English-Canadians it is to their credit, as it is to any nationality that encourages the growth of knowledge.

But to speak French to satisfy the nationalistic feelings of some French-Canadians is merely to cover up the hard, cold facts of life. Even if all the English-Canadians in Canada learned to speak French, what of the 180,000,000 English-speaking Americans who are our closest neighbours and with whom we have to do business? In this respect the French-Canadian separatist is far from realistic—if he wants to do business outside Quebec—and, mind you, he does—he must learn to speak English, and since our biggest market is to the south of us, and probably always will be, realism will not take a back seat to nationalism.

It is the very opportunity and, if you will, insistence, to do as he chooses that, ironically, has harmed French-Canadian aspirations. Guarantees of the right to their own language in all French-Canadian institutions of learning, government and law have, in fact, contributed to the very economic dependency they are now bemoaning, for it is through their language that they separated themselves from the main stream of progress and development in North America. I am not arguing that it should have been otherwise. I merely point out that exclusive development in French has been a greater inhibiting factor than any other. There is a great fear among French-Canadians that their cultural identity will someday be submerged by the English. . . . Some voices are now being raised, however, and in places where they will do the most good. More and more French-Canadians are coming to believe that their future lies, not in separatism, but in a revised Canadianism within a revised constitution that will give the French-Canadian the realization that he has the right to stand equally beside the millions of other Canadians of many origins who accept Canada as their own country. . . .

We need to get the dialogue on a basis of facts, and not of nationalistic ideologies. We have a lesson to learn from the Common Market. While no barriers have separated Canadians as a nation, in Quebec the language and a way of life have. We, as English-Canadians, must take a share of the blame if the French-Canadian feels that he has been treated like an inferior citizen. Whether by accident or design many of us have made no effort to speak French in centres where French was the predominant language, thereby imparting an attitude of English superiority. The lesson we have to learn is one of trade—trade among ourselves, with ourselves, and share among ourselves. It is only in this domain that both French and English-speaking Canadians can be made to realize that they are part of the same scheme of things. The lack of affinity has not been one-sided. One hears of few French-Canadians on the boards of English companies, but what about the lack of English-Canadians on French-Canadian boards?

Let me say in closing that though I make no pretence at speaking French well, I feel, at least, that I can show my impartiality in that I am married to a

French-Canadian and have two children who are perfectly bilingual, and while I am not proposing that all of you duplicate this feat, I do honestly feel that we, as English-Canadian businessmen, could accomplish much more in French-Canadian understanding, if we opened our offices to French-Canadian students to let them see and learn the inner workings of industry and business, than we would by taking furtive, and not always too successful, lessons in speaking French....

3. René Lévesque, "Quebec Independence," 1978

The bilingual René Lévesque (1922–87) grew up in Quebec's Gaspé region and studied law at Laval, quitting in 1943 to became a liaison officer for American forces in Europe during World War II. He later worked for the French section of the CBC and reported on the Korean War. Personable and engaging, he became a household name in Quebec in the 1950s, hosting a weekly television news program. Lévesque won a seat for the provincial Liberals in the 1960 election that ushered in the "Quiet Revolution" and was instrumental in creating the provincially owned Hydro Quebec. He veered toward socialism and separatism and quit the party in 1967. Lévesque amalgamated several separatist organizations into the Parti Québécois in 1968 and became Quebec's premier when the PQ took office in 1976.

The picture of our society is not one of misery or persecution comparable to many parts of the world. But everyone is familiar with the perception of unfairness, or inequality, or injustice, which is tied to one's environment. You compare yourself with others, with people in your neighbourhood, and with your peers. That is where the feeling grows.

The results of over 110 years of Canadian federal institutions, with their consistent preferences in economic and development policies, have led Quebec to build a strong feeling of being too often overlooked and neglected and even the object of discrimination. The feeling is essentially one of a colonial people (although no doubt a well-fed colonial people). As in other countries where an important segment, though smaller than the majority, feels more or less cooped up, depending on circumstances, in institutions that are controlled outside themselves, we in Quebec are an inner colony. The feeling of being cooped up inside the Canadian structure, inhibited, basically dependent, has been growing in Quebec over many years, and it is based primarily on the following statistic.

More than 80% of Quebec's people are French, and that is not folklore or museum French. It is a language with its own accent, its own quirks, its North American flavor (we are old North Americans). It is not only a living language; it is also vibrantly alive because it is the essential tool of communication, of cultural expression. It is the tool of everything: work, play, love, for practically each and every one of five million people.

The central fact of language makes Quebec the one Canadian province out of ten which is radically (in the root sense of the word) different from the rest of Canada. It makes Quebec the home base, the homeland, of a compact, very deeply rooted, and rapidly evolving cultural group; a cultural group—there should be no mistake—which sees itself as a national group. Democratic control of provincial institutions in Quebec supplies the Quebec people with a powerful springboard for self-affirmation and self-determination. And self-determination is rooted in the tradition of democracy, in bills of rights internationally recognized, in the rights of different peoples to choose their own institutions.

Since the French people in Quebec are surrounded by a continental ocean of English-speaking people both in Canada and in the United States, the question is often asked: "Why don't you just give up the ghost? What is the use of holding on and going on, more and more insistently in recent years, having all that noise and that confrontation and tension about your century-old and eminently respectable political structure? After all, all of us in North America—the United States, Canada, even Mexico—we are all under federal systems, federal institutions and structures. Nobody has been complaining all that much until now; why not go on? If it has been good for the United States, and not so bad for Canada, apparently, why are you guys in Quebec raising such a ruckus, such a lot of sound and fury about the whole thing—even talking about opting out of such a good deal?"

... In Canada, when our federal system developed, some 40% of the population was French. More than 25% still is, with a language, tradition, cultural outlook, and aspirations different from those of the English-speaking majority. I believe that the most essential ingredient determining whether a political structure works, whether it has staying power, does not depend on it being federal or unitary. It depends, rather, on cultural and national homogeneity.

And that is the story of Quebec. Not only are we a different cultural body, a different society in many ways, but among all European settlers we were the first on this continent (excluding Mexico). We were the first discoverers, the first pioneers, the first settlers and now our roots go back ... 370 years. We have worked the same land. We were born on it in the Valley of the St. Lawrence; all our forefathers are buried there. The tradition is tied also to a language which made us different; it is not our fault, but we keep going on. It is tied to the fact that there is this will, with the ups and downs we shared throughout the generations, of staying together. And now it is also tied to something which ties up with the central misunderstanding of our federal institutions.

A nation is made in 370 years. Nationalism often has a bad connotation, but it can be either positive or negative. Quebec nationalism, the tie to home, and the driving aspirations, the urge for development, is not anti-anyone; it is pro-us. I think it is positive, a national feeling of a national group deeply rooted, durable for the future. There lies the central misunderstanding of the whole Canadian structure.

TWO SOLITUDES

From the very start, Canadian federalism has been a dialogue of the deaf. To the English majority in Canada, we are nothing. The feeling has not been hidden very well through history. We are little more than a conquered and dependent minority. The English hoped this relatively small group would dwindle and eventually fade away like old soldiers.

When Canada was devised structurally, the main effort on the English-Canadian side was to develop federal institutions as central and powerful as possible. The French view was exactly the opposite. The federal system was looked upon as decentralization, enhancing, in American parlance, a state power, state rights, and a better chance for the future. And the French dreamt a normal dream for any cultural, national group—that somewhere, sometime, the nation would achieve self-government.

This competing vision of the founding explains, in a nutshell, the century of two solitudes. More recently, since World War II and especially since the "Quiet Revolution" of the 60s, Quebec at a dizzying speed has come of age; what used to be called "cheap-labor Quebec," "priest-ridden," a folkloric society, is growing by leaps and bounds.

We are entitled, like all societies, to this growth, but the structures have become a constraint on our development. Quebec and Ottawa have been at loggerheads practically on a permanent basis for the last 35 years. Quebec citizens have been caught up in a schizophrenic tug-of-war between the two levels of government for which they pay, with an incredible waste of energy, of time, of resources and, more worrisome, with an evergrowing danger of bad blood between the two communities.

THE GROWTH OF THE PARTI QUÉBÉCOIS

It is in the context of two solitudes and federal-provincial discord that the *Parti Québécois* (PQ) grew from a few hundred members in 1967 to 23% of the voters in the first election three years later, in 1970. We polled 31% in 1973 and we emerged as the official opposition. In 1976 we became the government with a 41% plurality.

The *Parti Québécois* is the first political party in the Western world, as far as I know, to rise from nothing to become the government while refusing, year after year, any money from any group—either corporate on the right or union on the left—because groups do not vote. We made it a basic principle to keep them at arm's length. No slush funds. With thousands of canvassers all over the place, door to door, we solicited citizens' money, which is not supposed to be, of course, a serious factor in politics. It was serious enough to build a party into the government of a society of six million people. And our government has passed Bill No. 2, the legislation of which I am proudest, requiring all parties to open their books.

When people start, subtly or otherwise, to give us lessons in basic democracy, they should come to see how democracy now works in Quebec. We are in a very imperfect world where democracy has never quite been a reality, but we are the most staunchly dedicated to democracy of all parties anywhere in the Western world. We were elected promising good government, and over the last 16 months we have tried to do the job. We intend to keep government clean.

SOVEREIGNTY-ASSOCIATION AND THE REFERENDUM

We were elected for good government. We were also elected on a platform of sovereignty with association. Those are two key words, "sovereignty" and "association," and we are committed to a democratic referendum about them before the next election. The enabling legislation is passing laboriously, for the wheels of parliament turn slowly, but the referendum will be held as promised.

Many people say the referendum creates uncertainty in Canada and in Quebec. In fact, uncertainty has been with us because of the many misconceptions and misunderstandings, grown in like barnacles, around our federal structures. Uncertainty has been with us for 35 years. It has shaken Canada's structures and the relationship between Quebec and Canada. For the first time, we are offering a chance to get rid of uncertainty, to get rid of it democratically, when people have had a chance to make up their minds, to be consulted, to get information. It is up to Quebecers to decide what they want. It will be the first chance ever for our people to decide for themselves about their institutions and about the whole future of their community.

If Quebecers vote as we hope, then soon afterwards we will acquire sovereignty, self-government. To use a good phrase of basic democracy, there would be no more representation of Quebec in Ottawa because no more taxation would go to Ottawa from Quebec.

The trend is universal. There were 50 recognized sovereign countries when World War II ended. Now there are 155, and many are comparable to Quebec. Denmark and Norway each has 4 million people; there are 6 million in Switzerland and 8 million in Sweden. These countries are leaders, not just in standard of living, but also in many other accomplishments. No fraternal counsels, no propaganda, will convince us that 6 million should give up the ghost and not pursue democratically normal accomplishments. It is the trend of the last half century.

In addition to sovereignty, we have been proposing from the beginning what we call "association." It is inspired by another universal trend; it is not contradictory. We are convinced that it is just as inevitable as sovereignty. Whatever its eventual shape—whether as a customs union or a common market—it will require still further research and study. The most open-minded people in the rest of Canada, however, are now giving it serious consideration, even though the present climate is hostile. Those courageous enough to look are becoming convinced that some form of association is common sense, responding to the real, hard facts of the situation.

CONSEQUENCES OF SOVEREIGNTY-ASSOCIATION

Politically, Canada without Quebec, a lot of people say, would disintegrate. It is the old domino theory, and after all the pieces go, the huge maw next door (that's you) will just gobble it up. I think Canada has a lot of staying power. I know Canada well, both because I have lived there and because I am a former newspaperman. Without the foreign body, which more and more we are, Canada would have more coherence and a chance to reorganize according to its own views and its own preferences. Quebec is a roadblock now because Canadians fear that any change must pose the question, "What the hell is going to happen to Quebec?"

We propose association, first, in order not to "pakistanize" Canada between the Maritimes to the east of Quebec and Ontario and the rest to the west. It is not to build walls of hostility that would take years to break down again. We care about Canada. We do not care about the structures, but we care about the people. We care about the common things we have, many of them, with the Maritimes, with practically as long a tradition as ours and the same kind of outlook in many ways. We care for the fruitful relationships, very mutually profitable, between Quebec and Ontario mostly, and growing with the rest of Canada. But we also care about our own identity. There is no reason why there should be any contradiction, except for people who think that institutions become sacred because they are old. You do not change them like you change your shirt, but not because they are old do you hang on to them when they have passed their day and become obsolete, when they have become like straitjackets.

For political reasons, then, we have proposed a new association, if and when Quebec democratically decides to opt out. There is no reason why it should not be arranged on a free-flow basis. When Alaska became a state of the Union, with some 1100-1200 miles between the state of Alaska and the continental United States, I did not hear any voices of doom. Two civilized countries made arrangements about the free flow of communications and goods. In our case, it would be good for Canada, and so we should do it.

There are also economic reasons for association, ... 105,000 jobs next door in Ontario are tied directly to the Quebec market, and there is more or less the equivalent in Quebec facing Ontario. Western beef, with some protection, finds its major market in Quebec. The existence of the Maritimes is tied to a new rapport with Quebec. Newfoundland needs Quebec as a buyer or transmitter of its enormous undeveloped energy resources. We are initiating negotiations with Newfoundland on that subject. Prince Edward Island needs to sell potatoes to the voracious Montreal market.

The Western European Union is our inspiration. It finally gave the French and the Germans the first chance, for centuries, to bridge a chasm of blood and of world war. Adapted to our own needs, sovereignty-association will give our two societies what we think is terribly needed leeway—breathing space—to protect us from the dangerous risk of growing too far apart.

THE CHALLENGE OF MAJOR CHANGE

Almost everybody, even staunch federalists, even Mr. Trudeau, are at long last admitting publicly the need for a rethinking and a revamping of our political and constitutional arrangements. The temptation is always present, and I can see it in Mr. Trudeau's eyes when we meet occasionally, for the true believers of the *status quo*, for the hangers-on and the careerists, to try to sell or con people into accepting superficial arrangements, mere plastic surgery. But we are convinced that it would not work. There are too many generations of more solitudes facing each other. There is a danger of bad blood. And all the cosmetic constitutional operations over the last 25 or 50 years have failed to give Canada a truly new face.

The only true solution, from our point of view, for our two peoples, has to lie somewhere in the direction we are indicating. And there, also, lies the first chance for real understanding, the only base for mutual respect and equality and cooperation. Maybe, at long last, there is a promise of real friendship between our peoples which up until now we have not really found....

4. Maurice King, "Betrayal of Basic Rights in Futile Appeasement of Quebec Nationalism," *Canadian Speeches, Issues of the Day*, February, 1995

Maurice Joseph King (1927-) was born in Quebec, is past president of the Chateau-guay Valley English-Speaking Peoples' Association, and served as mayor of Green-field Park, a former town in what is now Longueuil, Quebec, from 1967 to 1978. In 1993 he and Gordon McIntyre took the Quebec government's Bill 178 on English language signage to the United Nations Human Rights Committee where they won a decision that declared it in contravention of their freedom of expression. A long time advocate for the rights of freedom of expression, King in 1993 published the book The First Step: A Study of Quebec Nationalism and Its Effects on Canadian Values, *and in 1987 jointly with Janet K. Hicks he created the bi-monthly non-profit magazine* Dialogue, *which is devoted to freedom of speech.*

Fundamental rights of English-speaking Canadians living in Quebec have been betrayed by politicians who have sought to appease the demands of Quebec nationalists. But appeasement has backfired. Instead of satisfying the demands of the nationalists, it has whetted their appetite for ever greater special privi-leges. Instead of enhancing national unity and increasing Quebec's attachment to Canada, it has promoted discord and increased the danger of Quebec's separa-tion. Those who want to keep Canada intact must make clear to Quebecers what the province would lose by separating. They must be told that an independent Quebec would lose much of the present territory of the province, including vast lands belonging to Aboriginal peoples, those areas of the province that vote to remain in Canada, and a transportation corridor across the new state between Ontario and New Brunswick, and that it stands to lose much more than just land.

I am not anti-Quebec nor am I anti-French. I have lived all my life in the prov-ince of Quebec. My family arrived in this province in 1823 and my great-grandfa-ther, grandfather and father are all buried in Shannon, Quebec. Sometime—in the far distant future, I hope—I will be with them, and still in Canada. I have spent my whole life working with the people of Quebec, first in the trade union movement, then the co-operative movement, and in municipal politics where I was mayor of my community for some 15 years. I was elected to all of these positions by both French and English voters in Quebec. I have brought up five daughters in the province of Quebec. I believe my credentials are in order, so that what I am about to say—which is not politically correct—will be understood to be coming from a Canadian who lives in the province of Quebec and loves La Belle Province.

The message I am going to deliver to you today is one that says: let's build a strong and united Canada; let us include in our Canada all those who share the Canadian values of freedom, justice and equality that we fought for and many died to defend. The bad news I have to bring you is that Quebec nationalism is an ideology that denies Canadian values and is built on the superiority of an ethnic majority that is entitled to rights and privileges denied to other citizens in Quebec society. Let me make it clear: there is a difference between Quebec nationalists and the majority of French-speaking people in Quebec. When I speak of the threat of Quebec nationalism to Canadian values I am also speaking about the threat of nationalism to the future of the people of Quebec as well as to other Canadians.

In 1988, Gordon McIntyre, a funeral director in Huntington, Quebec, a small town located in the southwest corner of the province, received a notice from the Office de langue Français ordering him to remove the words "funeral home" from his sign outside his business. The sign with English words on it was a violation of Bill 101, the Quebec French Language Charter.

If Gordon did not comply with the notice, he would receive a court summons and, if found guilty of using English on a commercial sign, would be fined. If the fine were not paid, he would be sentenced to a jail term. Gordon came to see me in my capacity as president of the Chateauguay Valley English-Speaking Peoples Association (CVESPA), an English-rights organization in southwest Quebec. My advice to him was to await the decision of the Supreme Court of Canada, which was studying the bill at that time. In December 1988, the court ruled that it was a violation of the Canadian Charter of Rights and Freedoms to deny the use of a language on commercial signs.

The great "trickster," Premier Robert Bourassa made use of section 33 of the Canadian Charter which allows a "notwithstanding" clause and permits a government to ignore the Canadian Charter of Rights. The passage of Bill 178 by the Quebec government, in December 1988, effectively denied any further recourse to the courts by Canadians. Our association made representation and demonstrated on Parliament Hill, requesting that Prime Minister Mulroney use section 90, the "Override clause" of the Canadian Constitution which empowers the federal government to rescind provincial legislation. The federal government refused.

There was no alternative but to appeal to the United Nations.... After three years, the UN committee ruled that Canada was in violation of Article 19 of the International Covenant on Civil and Political Rights, which guarantees freedom of expression....

... Quebec nationalism is based on ethnicity: it was created not to define a territory but rather an ethnic group—their language, religion and values....

One may understand this nationalism in the 18th and even 19th century, as a survival strategy of the Church. What becomes more difficult to appreciate is that it continued into the 20th century, with Cannon Lionel Groulx, who claimed that all Canadian history can be summed up, since 1763, as the struggle for the French to survive. He viewed the English conquerors, their descendants and all the other newcomers as the source of all discord in Quebec. Groulx inspired thousands of young Quebecois with a pride in their French roots and a confidence in their ability to manage Quebec's future. But, at the same time, he also laid the modern day foundations of Quebec nationalism by claiming the supremacy of the pure Quebecois and he planted the seeds of racism and xenophobia by claiming that les autres were a danger to the Quebecois.

The election of Mike Pearson as prime minister of Canada, at the time in the 60s when there was open violence in the province of Quebec, led to the beginning of an attack on Canadian values from within the very federal government entrusted with the responsibility of protecting them. Mr. Pearson viewed the actions of (at that time) a very few radicals as the beginning of an attack on the unity of Canada. His view, and that of the prime ministers who followed him, was that only by appeasement and compliance with the demands of Quebec nationalists would Quebec remain a part of Canada. Prime Minister Pearson created a commission on Bilingualism and Biculturalism....

At the same time as French was being given equal status to English in Canada, in Quebec English was being denounced as a threat to the future of the province and being erased from the face of Quebec. Robert Bourassa led his Quebec Liberal Party in the implementation of Bill 22 in 1974. This legislation made French the official language in the province of Quebec and created apartheid amongst the school children of that province. In 1977, the Parti Quebecois passed the Quebec French Language Charter, which further entrenched Quebec's denial of basic Canadian values of freedom of speech and freedom of choice.

The outcome of the B & B commission was Canada's Official Languages Act, which started Canada officially down a road that has led, not to harmony, equality and constitutional peace, but to national disunity, mistrust, fragmentation and to the erosion of Canadian values.

The policies of the federal parties in attempting to buy the loyalty of the citizens of Quebec for Canada is a complete failure. The Official Languages Act, as a means of keeping Quebec within Canada, is also a failure. The Act has never been applied with the same vigor in Quebec, for the English-speaking minority, has it as in the other provinces of Canada, for the French-speaking minority. The concept of a French Canada from coast to coast has not succeeded in increasing the attachment of the Quebecois to Canada. Today, Canada is more divided than ever, separation with Quebec is stronger than ever before.

Meanwhile, we have none of the federal parties that will tell the people of Quebec the consequences of voting for separation. They continue their bankrupt policies of bribery and appeasement. Every time that the federal government appeases a nationalist demand, the credibility of the nationalists in Quebec increases. What do you expect? Lucien Bouchard and his Bloc Quebecois are elected only in the province of Quebec and with the clear understanding that they are committed to separation of Quebec from Canada. How does Canada react? Bouchard is made "the Leader of Her Majesty's Loyal Opposition." He is hosted by the Canadian ambassador in Washington, while he tells Americans that the destiny of Quebec is as a separate nation. What do the people of Quebec think? The idea of separation can't be too bad! Look how Bouchard is treated.

Our prime minister and the leaders of the other political parties refuse to say openly and clearly that Quebec cannot unilaterally declare its independence. International constitutional experts called before a Quebec government commission on the constitutional future of the province said, several years ago, that a unilateral declaration of independence would not be accepted internationally. Meanwhile, the people of Quebec are being told that they can do it, simply by agreeing to separate in a provincial referendum. Quebecers are told they can keep their Canadian citizenship, the Canadian dollar, the Canadian passport, the Canadian post office service, an agreement to jointly manage the $80 billion space agency in St. Hubert, Quebec, along with other federal and international institutions that have been built in the province.

Quebecers are also told there will be an economic association with Canada, Quebec will be part of the North American Free Trade Agreement, Quebec will not be required to pay off its share of the national debt (maybe some interest payments only). In other words, the only difference in an independent Quebec will be that the French-speaking people of Quebec will no longer be hindered by the Supreme Court of Canada in their treatment of minorities. They will have their own constitution containing their own values, values that include the dominance of the collectivity and the protection of the French language by denying equal rights to other languages in a new state. Sounds pretty good if you are a French-speaking Quebecer who has no strong loyalty to Canada.

The federal political parties are counting on winning the referendum. I say that they are closer to losing than winning. Federal politicians must let Quebecers know what they are voting for in the referendum. The people of Quebec have a right to know what are the consequences of voting Yes. They must be told that a "yes" vote means that Canadians will hold a referendum to decide if they are agreed to allow Quebec to separate and, if so, the terms to be negotiated. Those terms will include the definition of the new Quebec territory, which must exclude: the capital region of Canada (created in Hull, Quebec, at a cost of billions of dollars); the lands of the Aboriginal peoples in the province; the regions throughout the province that vote to remain Canadian; a corridor across the southern section of the province, required to maintain the geographical integrity of Canada, connecting Ontario and New Brunswick.

If we want to keep Canada united then we must speak directly to Quebecers over the head of the Quebec nationalists who control the economic and political systems in Quebec. We must put an end to the nationalist infiltration of the Canadian political system and their compliance with Quebec nationalism....

We must not be frightened by the politicians with their threats of gloom and doom if Quebec separates. Canada is a strong country with a national pride that is shared by all Canadians and with established Canadian values of freedom, justice and equality. Yes, we all wanted a united Canada. But not by eroding our values and diminishing our economic strength in favor of one province. Canadians must decide to put the values and needs of Canada first.

FURTHER READINGS

Behiels, M., Ed. *Quebec Since 1945: Selected Readings*. Toronto: Copp Clark Pitman, 1987.

Bercuson, D., and B. Copper. *Deconfederation: Canada without Quebec*. Toronto: Key Porter, 1991.

Bothwell, R. *Canada and Quebec: One Country, Two Histories*. Vancouver: University of British Columbia Press, 1995.

Bourgault, P. *Now or Never: Manifesto for an Independent Quebec.* Toronto: Key Porter, 1991.

Carens, J., Ed. *Is Quebec Nationalism Just?: Perspectives from Anglophone Canada.* Montreal and Kingston: McGill-Queen's University Press, 1995.

Clift, D. *The Decline of Nationalism in Quebec.* Montreal and Kingston: McGill-Queen's University Press, 1982.

Coleman, W. *The Independence Movement in Quebec, 1945-1980.* Toronto: University of Toronto Press, 1984.

Covell, M. *Thinking About the Rest of Canada: Options for Canada Without Quebec.* North York: York University Centre for Public Law and Public Policy, 1992.

Dion, S. *Straight Talk: On Canadian Unity.* Montreal and Kingston: McGill-Queen's University Press, 1999.

Fraser, G. *The PQ: René Lévesque and the Parti Québécois in Power.* Toronto: Macmillan, 1984.

Fournier, L. *F.L.Q. The Anatomy of an Underground Movement.* Toronto: NC Press, 1984.

Gairdner, W. *Constitutional Crack-Up: Canada and the Coming Showdown with Quebec.* Toronto: Stoddart, 1994.

Griffen, A. *Quebec: The Challenge of Independence.* Rutherford: Fairleigh Dickinson University Press, 1984.

Guindon, H. *Quebec Society: Tradition, Modernity, and Nationhood.* Toronto: University of Toronto Press, 1988.

Jacobs, J. *The Question of Separatism: Quebec and the Struggle over Sovereignty.* New York: Random House, 1980.

Jones, R. *Community in Crisis: French Canadian Nationalism in Perspective.* Toronto: McClelland and Stewart, 1972.

Lemco, J. *The Quebec Sovereignty Movement and Its Implications for Canada and the United States*. Toronto: University of Toronto Press, 1994.

McRoberts, K. *Quebec: Social Change and Political Crisis*. 3rd ed. Toronto: McClelland and Stewart, 1988.

Moniere, D. *L'Indépendence: Essai*. Montreal: Quebec/Amerique, 1992.

Saywell, J. *The Rise of the Parti Québécois*. Toronto: University of Toronto Press, 1977.

Weaver, R., Ed. *The Collapse of Canada*. Washington: Brookings Institution, 1992.

Young, R. *The Secession of Quebec and the Future of Canada*. Montreal and Kingston: McGill-Queen's University Press, 1995.

CHAPTER 15

"The Whites Were Terrorists"

RESIDENTIAL SCHOOLS

INTRODUCTION

I n January 1998 the Minister of Indian Affairs, Jane Stewart, apologized to Canada's Aboriginal community on behalf of the federal government for its complicity in the treatment of Natives in government-sponsored residential schools. She said she was "deeply sorry" and established a "healing fund" of $350 million to help Aboriginal communities and individuals to overcome traumas resulting from their residential school experiences. This came on the heels of similar confessions of guilt and apologies from the Catholic and United Churches of Canada—though the Catholic Church was far more circumspect about admitting any culpability. On June 11, 2008, Stephen Harper, flanked by Native leaders including Assembly of First Nations Chief Phil Fontaine, again apologized to Native people, the first prime minister to do so. This occasion, in the House of Commons and to a packed public gallery, was far more formal and ceremonial than Minister Stewart's *mea culpa* and was marked by official and spontaneous celebrations across Canada. The Prime Minister said: "The treatment of children in Indian residential schools is a sad chapter in our history.... Today, we recognize that this policy of assimilation was wrong, has caused great harm, and has no place in our country.... The government now recognizes that the consequences of the Indian residential schools policy were profoundly negative and that this policy has had a lasting and damaging impact on Aboriginal culture, heritage and language." As part of the apology, the federal government mandated a Truth and Reconciliation Commission, modelled after the post-apartheid version in South Africa, to tour Canada, hear survivors' stories, and affect reconciliation between Native and non-Native people. The process was to take five years. The three-person commission quickly derailed when, in October 2008, its chair, Justice Harry LaForme, resigned, citing irreconcilable differences with the other two. Few could fail to see the irony of this as the legacy of the residential school policy continues to mar relations between Canada's First Nations and non-Natives.

The government's apologies came years after former residents of the schools began coming forward *en masse* with a litany of horrors about life in those institutions. Natives sued both the federal government and religious organizations that ran the schools, and prosecutors successfully convicted a number of former staff members. Some churches presently face potential bankruptcy as a result of court-imposed settlements against them. Native communities, meanwhile, still languish with suicide and substance abuse rates significantly higher than the national average, and the percentage of Native peoples in Canadian jails is way out of proportion to their absolute numbers. Native leaders put much of the blame for this tragedy squarely on the impact of residential schooling.

The most common accusations against the system concern sexual and physical abuse, including neglect, of the children in the institutions' care. There are, however, philosophical and ideologically issues too. Perhaps the most far-reaching and comprehensive is the accusation that successive federal governments and their partners perpetrated "cultural genocide" against Canada's Aboriginal population by, among other things, forbidding Native languages from being spoken in the schools and forcibly removing Native children from their homes and cultural roots.

Apart from the philosophical and ideological issues of assimilation and "cultural genocide," a major day-to-day problem with the policy, and one never rectified, was its chronic underfunding at all levels. This often resulted in school buildings that were, at best, mediocre and, at worst, unfit for habitation. It meant inadequate food and medical care for some children in some areas. Low wages and extreme isolation frequently led to unqualified or poor teachers being hired and to insufficient general staffing levels. Poor funding meant inadequate government supervision of the schools and of background checks on staff hired to work in them. Abusers and abuses, even when reported—and they rarely were—tended to continue unchecked, sometimes for decades. The Catholic Church, in particular, quietly transferred known problem staff to new locations, still within the system, when complaints arose. Thus, some priests left trails of devastation across the country.

The list of complaints against the residential school system is long and the evidence damning, but the story has another side—one far less frequently and stridently voiced. Many Native parents supported residential schools and regularly requested more be built. They argued that their children stood a better chance of integrating into mainstream society if they received a European-based education and training, something they could not get from their own people in the traditional villages. This belief became increasingly common as traditional modes of life, like the buffalo hunt, disappeared or became untenable. A number of Natives, such as Reverend Peter Jones, devoted their lives to bringing European education to their people, and there was never a shortage of residential school students who wished to become nuns and priests.

The story of what happened at residential schools is particularly problematic because the evidence may be skewed, unreliable, or insufficient. Some former residential school residents reminisce fondly over their years as students, maintaining that the education they received from devoted and friendly staff served them well in later years. These people, however, often complain of finding themselves ostracized by their own kind for speaking up in favour of their residential school experiences because it threatens the "industry of victimhood." As well, many staff who offered love and care and years of dedicated service to their Native charges are now shamed into silence and unwilling to admit they ever worked in the system because all former staff bear the stigma of abuse by association. Thus, another voice is silenced. There is also the problematic issue of evidence in sexual abuse cases. Typically, a trial amounts to the word of one individual against another, based upon memory and usually without material evidence because the event occurred unwitnessed by a third party. According to Canadian law an accused is presumed innocent as long as there is "reasonable doubt" that the event transpired, and the veracity of an accuser's word against the accused can logically be doubted because one essentially nullifies the other. Many victims refuse to testify because the experiences were too humiliating to parade in public. Some sublimated the experiences so deeply in their subconscious that it is unknown even to them—though it festers for the rest of their lives. Tragically, some victims of sexual abuse even blame themselves for the incidents, thus making them less willing to charge a perpetrator who, of course, swears his innocence. All told, the issue is an evidentiary minefield.

No single date marks the beginning of the residential school system, but one of the most significant early milestones was the 1842 Bagot Commission Report. It advised the government of Upper Canada that Natives should acquire "European industry and knowledge" unattainable, so the report stated, within the confines of Native communities where author Charles Bagot believed "primitive" culture stultified its citizens. His overriding philosophical bent was to assimilate Native children into mainstream culture by removing them from their homes and placing them into Eurocentric environments where they would learn to become "white." His recommendations, by chance, coincided with a period of intense missionary effort on the part of major Christian denominations seeking to save souls and fill pews throughout the New World. Egerton Ryerson, a Methodist minister prominent in Canada West's (Ontario) political circles, consolidated the emerging philosophical direction in his 1847 report, which recommended that "the education of Indians consist not merely of training of the mind but of weaning from the habits and feelings of their ancestors and the acquirements of the language, arts and customs of a civilized life." A symbiotic partnership between church and state therefore, not surprisingly, emerged whereby Christian missionaries ran government-funded schools for Native children.

Early efforts to create a residential school system remained haphazard, however, until Confederation in 1867. At that time the federal government made Natives wards of the state in a paternalistic move that facilitated further legislation, such as the 1876 Indian Act that consolidated the assimilationist underpinnings of Native education policy. The 1879 Davin Report did much the same, recommending the establishment of a comprehensive residential school system modelled after the ones in the United States. An Order-in-Council in 1892 finally instituted regulations for operating residential schools, and a more formal contractual agreement between religious groups and the federal government detailed the administrative partnership between church and state.

In 1920 Duncan Campbell Scott, federal Superintendent of Indian Affairs, made school attendance for Natives mandatory for seven to 15-year-olds after discovering how few Native children attended school. This, of course, required most Native students to board away from their families since facilities rarely existed in remote villages. Despite subsequent concerted efforts to implement the letter of the law, including accusations of kidnapping, only a small percentage of Native children ever attended residential schools.

There were, at their maximum extent, some 80 residential schools, with a total population of approximately 10,000 students, in all provinces and territories except New Brunswick, Prince Edward Island, and Newfoundland and Labrador. Serious criticism along several fronts mounted until bureaucrats in the Department of Indian Affairs conceded by the end of World War II that residential schools did not, in fact, achieve their goals and also suffered from a number of grave problems that jeopardized the health and well-being of Native children.

The solution was to phase out the schools and integrate Indian youth into regular provincial schools. It took two more decades, however, for the system to wind down. The federal government took direct control of school management and subsequently relinquished control of many to Native communities themselves. The last government-run residential school closed in 1983.

DISCUSSION POINTS

1. Sexual abuse is, by its nature, difficult to prove. Is the evidence and conclusion of sexual and physical abuse from the first document sufficiently convincing? Why or why not?

2. When the anti-Potlatch laws were passed Natives protested and found various ways to avoid the law. Why did they keep sending one generation after another of their children to residential schools?

3. Is the residential school experience the primary source of Native social problems today or are there other critical factors?

4. Many similarities exist between the abuse Natives suffered in residential schools and what occurred in places like Mt. Cashel, a Catholic residential school for boys in Newfoundland. Is the basic problem the nature of custodial care, rather than racism?

5. One political scientist argues that the "Aboriginal movement depends on the cultivation of grievances" and that the "apology reinforces segregation." Is he right?

DOCUMENTS

1. Rev. K. Annett, "Hidden from History: The Canadian Holocaust,"
Nexus, March-April 2002

Rev. Kevin Annett (1956–) received a B.A. in anthropology and an M.A. in political science from the University of British Columbia and a Masters degree in Divinity from the Vancouver School of Theology in 1990. The Minister of Port Alberni's St. Andrew's United Church in 1992, he resigned in 1995 in advance of expulsion from the church ministry in 1997 when he unearthed evidence alleging that Native children were killed by the staff at the United Church Residential School in Port Alberni, BC. Under the auspices of the International Human Rights Association of American Minorities, Annett organized the first independent tribunal into Canadian residential schools in June 1998. He has written two books: Hidden from History: The Canadian Holocaust *(2001, updated 2005) and* Love and Death in the Valley *(2002).*

FOREWORD

Jasper Joseph is a sixty-four-year-old native man from Port Hardy, British Columbia. His eyes still fill with tears when he remembers his cousins who were killed with lethal injections by staff at the Nanaimo Indian Hospital in 1944.

I was just eight, and they'd shipped us down from the Anglican residential school in Alert Bay to the Nanaimo Indian Hospital, the one run by the United Church. They kept me isolated in a tiny room there for more than three years, like I was a lab rat, feeding me these pills, giving me shots that made me sick. Two of my cousins made a big fuss, screaming and fighting back all the time, so the nurses gave them shots, and they both died right away. It was done to silence them. (November 10, 2000)

Unlike post-war Germans, Canadians have yet to acknowledge, let alone repent from, the genocide that we inflicted on millions of conquered people: the aboriginal men, women and children who were deliberately exterminated by our racially supremacist churches and state.

As early as November 1907, the Canadian press was acknowledging that the death rate within Indian residential schools exceeded 50%. And yet the reality of such a massacre has been wiped clean from the public record and consciousness in Canada over the past decades. Small wonder; for that hidden history reveals a system whose aim was to destroy most native people by disease, relocation and outright murder, while "assimilating" a minority of collaborators who were trained to serve the genocidal system.

This history of purposeful genocide implicates every level of government in Canada, the Royal Canadian Mounted Police (RCMP), every mainstream church, large corporations and local police, doctors and judges. The web of complicity in this killing machine was, and remains, so vast that its concealment has required an equally elaborate campaign to cover-up that has been engineered at the highest levels of power in our country; a cover-up that is continuing, especially now that eyewitnesses to murders and atrocities at the church-run native residential "schools" have come forward for the first time.

For it was the residential "schools" that constituted the death camps of the Canadian Holocaust, and within their walls nearly one-half of all aboriginal children sent there by law died, or disappeared, according to the government's own statistics.

These 50,000 victims have vanished, as have their corpses—"like they never existed," according to one survivor. But they did exist. They were innocent children, and they were killed by beatings and torture and after being deliberately exposed to tuberculosis and other diseases by paid employees of the churches and government, according to a "Final Solution" master plan devised by the Department of Indian Affairs and the Catholic and Protestant churches.

With such official consent for manslaughter emanating from Ottawa, the churches responsible for annihilating natives on the ground felt emboldened and protected enough to declare full-scale war on non-Christian native peoples through the 20th century.

The casualties of that war were not only the 50,000 dead children of the residential schools, but the survivors, whose social condition today has been described by United Nations human rights groups as that of "a colonized people barely on the edge of survival, with all the trappings of a third-world society." (November 12, 1999)

The Holocaust is continuing.

This report is the child of a six-year independent investigation into the hidden history of genocide against aboriginal peoples in Canada. It summarises the testimonies, documents and other evidence proving that Canadian churches, corporations and the government are guilty of intentional genocide, in violation of the United Nations Convention on Genocide, which Canada ratified in 1952 and under which it is bound by international law.

The report is a collaborative effort of nearly 30 people. And yet some of its authors must remain anonymous, particularly its aboriginal contributors, whose lives have been threatened and who have been assaulted, denied jobs and evicted from their homes on Indian reserves because of their involvement in this investigation.

As a former minister in one of the guilty institutions named in our inquiry—the United Church of Canada—I have been fired, black-listed, threatened and publicly maligned by its officers for my attempts to uncover the story of the deaths of children at that church's Alberni residential school.

Many people have made sacrifices to produce this report, so that the world can learn of the Canadian Holocaust, and to ensure that those responsible for it are brought to justice before the International Criminal Court.

Beginning among native and low-income activists in Port Alberni, British Columbia, in the fall of 1994, this inquiry into crimes against humanity has continued in the face of death threats, assaults and the resources of church and state in Canada.

It is within the power of the reader to honour our sacrifice by sharing this story with others and refusing to participate in the institutions which deliberately killed many thousands of children.

This history of official endorsement of, and collusion in, a century or more of crimes against Canada's first peoples must not discourage us from uncovering the truth and bringing the perpetrators to justice.

It is for this reason that we invite you to remember not only the 50,000 children who died in the residential school death camps, but the silent victims today who suffer in our midst for bread and justice.

SUMMARY OF EVIDENCE OF INTENTIONAL GENOCIDE IN CANADIAN RESIDENTIAL SCHOOLS

Article II: The intent to destroy, in whole or in part, national ethnic, racial or religious group; namely, non-Christian aboriginal peoples in Canada

The foundational purpose behind the more than one hundred Indian residential schools established in Canada by government legislation and administered by Protestant and Catholic churches was the deliberate and persistent eradication of aboriginal people and their culture, and the conversion of any surviving native people to Christianity.

This intent was enunciated in the Gradual Civilization Act of 1857 in Upper Canada, and earlier, church-inspired legislation which defined aboriginal culture as inferior, stripped native people of citizenship and subordinated them in a separate legal category from non-Indians. This Act served as the basis for the federal Indian Act of 1874, which recapitulated the legal and moral inferiority of aboriginals and established the residential school system. The legal definition of an Indian as "an uncivilized person, destitute of the knowledge of God and of any fixed and clear belief in religion" (Revised Statutes of British Columbia, 1960) was established by these Acts and continues to the present day.

Then, as now, aboriginals were considered legal and practical non-entities in their own land and, hence, inherently expendable.

This genocidal intent was restated time and again in government legislation, church statements and the correspondence and records of missionaries, Indian agents and residential school officials . Indeed, it was the very *raison d'être* of the state-sanctioned Christian invasion of traditional native territories and of the residential school system itself, which was established at the height of European expansionism in the 1880s and persisted until 1984.

By definition, this aim was genocidal, for it planned and carried out the destruction of a religious and ethnic group: all those aboriginal people who would not convert to Christianity and be culturally extinguished. Non-Christian natives were the declared target of the residential schools, which practised wholesale ethnic cleansing under the guise of education.

As well, such "pagans" were the subject of government-funded sterilisation programs administered at church-run hospitals and tuberculosis sanatoriums on Canada's west coast.

According to an eyewitness, Ethel Wilson of Bella Bella, BC, a United Church missionary doctor, George Darby, deliberately sterilised non-Christian Indians between 1928 and 1962 at the R.W. Large Memorial Hospital in Bella Bella. Ms Wilson, who is now deceased, stated in 1998:

"Doctor Darby told me in 1952 that Indian Affairs in Ottawa was paying him for every Indian he sterilised, especially if they weren't churchgoers. Hundreds of our women were sterilised by Doctor Darby, just for not going to church." (Testimony of Ethel Wilson to International Human Rights Association of American Minorities [IHRAAM] Tribunal, Vancouver, BC, June 13, 1998)

According to Christy White, a resident of Bella Bella, records of these government-funded sterilisations at the R.W. Large Hospital were deliberately destroyed in 1995, soon after a much-publicised police investigation was to open into residential school atrocities in British Columbia. Ms White stated in 1998:

"I worked at the Bella Bella hospital, and I know that Barb Brown, one of the administrators there, dumped sterilisation records at sea on two occasions. Some of the records were found washed up on the beach south of town. That was just after the cops opened their investigation into the schools, in the spring of 1995. They were covering their tracks. We all knew Ottawa was funding sterilisations, but we were told to keep quiet about it." (Testimony of Christy White to Kevin Annett, August 12, 1998)

Legislation permitting the sterilisation of any residential school inmate was passed in BC in 1933 and in Alberta in 1928 (see "Sterilization Victims Urged to Come Forward" by Sabrina Whyatt, *Windspeaker*, August 1998). The Sexual Sterilization Act of BC allowed a school principal to permit the sterilisation of any native person under his charge. As their legal guardian, the principal could thus have any native child sterilised. Frequently, these sterilisations occurred to whole groups of native children when they reached puberty, in institutions like the Provincial Training School in Red Deer, Alberta, and the Ponoka Mental Hospital. (Former nurse Pat Taylor to Kevin Annett, January 13, 2000)

Of equal historical significance is the fact that the Canadian federal government passed legislation in 1920, making it mandatory for all native children in British Columbia—the west coast of which was the least Christianised area among aboriginals in Canada—to attend residential schools, despite the fact that the same government had already acknowledged that the death rate due to communicable diseases was much higher in these schools and that, while there, the native children's "constitution is so weakened that they have no vitality to withstand disease." (A.W. Neill, West Coast Indian Agent, to Secretary of Indian Affairs, April 25, 1910)

That is, the Canadian government legally compelled the attendance of the most "pagan" and least assimilated of the native peoples in residential schools at precisely the time when the death rate in these schools had reached their pinnacle—about 40%, according to Indian Affairs officers like Dr Peter Bryce. This fact alone suggests a genocidal intent towards non-Christian aboriginals.

Article II (a): Killing members of the group intended to be destroyed

That aboriginal people were deliberately killed in the residential schools is confirmed by eyewitness testimonies, government records and statements of Indian agents and tribal elders. It is also strongly suggested by the bare fact that the mortality level in residential schools averaged 40%, with the deaths of more than 50,000 native children across Canada (see Bibliography, inc. the report of Dr Peter Bryce to Department of Indian Affairs Superintendent Duncan Campbell Scott, April 1909).

The fact, as well, that this death rate stayed constant across the years, and within the schools and facilities of every denomination which ran them—Roman Catholic, United, Presbyterian or Anglican—suggests that common conditions and policies were behind these deaths. For every second child to die in the residential school system eliminates the possibility that these deaths were merely accidental or the actions of a few depraved individuals acting alone without protection.

Yet not only was this system inherently murderous, but it operated under the legal and structural conditions which encouraged, aided and abetted murder and which were designed to conceal these crimes.

The residential schools were structured like concentration camps, on a hierarchical military basis under the absolute control of a principal appointed jointly by church and state, and who was usually a clergyman. This principal was even given legal guardianship rights over all students during the early 1930s by the federal government, at least in west coast residential schools. This action by the government was highly unusual, considering that native people were by law the legal wards of the state, and had been so since the commencement of the Indian Act. And yet such absolute power of the school principal over the lives of aboriginal students was a requirement of any system whose killing of aboriginals had to be disguised and later denied.

The residential schools were constructed behind this deception in such a way that the deaths and atrocities that constitute genocide could be hidden and eventually explained. In the Canadian context, this meant a policy of gradual but deliberate extermination under a protective legal umbrella, administered by "legitimate and trusted" institutions: the mainline churches.

It should be clarified from the outset that the decisions concerning the residential schools, including those which caused the deaths of children and resulting cover-ups, were officially sanctioned by every level of the churches that ran them and the government which created them. Only such sanction could have allowed the deaths to continue as they did—and the perpetrators to feel protected enough to operate with impunity for many years within the system, which they universally did.

EXPOSURE TO DISEASES

In 1909, Dr Peter Bryce of the Ontario Health Department was hired by the Indian Affairs Department in Ottawa to tour the Indian residential schools in western Canada and British Columbia and report on the health conditions there. Bryce's report so scandalised the government and the churches that it was officially buried and only surfaced in 1922 when Bryce—who was forced out of the civil service for the honesty of his report—wrote a book about it, entitled *The Story of a National Crime* (Ottawa, 1922).

In his report, Dr Bryce claimed that Indian children were being systematically and deliberately killed in the residential schools. He cited an average mortality rate of between 35% and 60%, and alleged that staff and church officials were regularly withholding or falsifying records and other evidence of children's deaths.

Further, Dr Bryce claimed that a primary means of killing native children was to deliberately expose them to communicable diseases such as tuberculosis and then deny them any medical care or treatment—a practice actually referred to by top Anglican Church leaders in the *Globe and Mail* on May 29, 1953.

In March 1998, two native eyewitnesses who attended west coast residential schools, William and Mabel Sport of Nanaimo, BC, confirmed Dr Bryce's allegation. Both of them claim to have been deliberately exposed to tuberculosis by staff at both a Catholic and a United Church residential school during the 1940s.

"*I was forced to sleep in the same bed with kids who were dying of tuberculosis. That was at the Catholic Christie residential school around 1942. They were trying to kill us off, and it nearly worked. They did the same thing at Protestant Indian schools, three kids to a bed, healthy ones with the dying.*" (Testimony of Mabel Sport to IHRAAM officers, Port Alberni, BC, March 31, 1998)

"*Reverend Pitts, the Alberni school principal, he forced me and eight other boys to eat this special food out of a different sort of can. It tasted really strange. And then all of us came down with tuberculosis. I was the only one to survive, 'cause my Dad broke into the school one night and got me out of there. All of the rest died from tuberculosis and they were never treated. Just left there to die. And their families were all told they had died of pneumonia. The plan was to kill us off in secret, you know. We all just began dying after eating that food. Two of my best friends were in that group that was poisoned. We were never allowed to speak of it or go into the basement, where other murders happened. It was a death sentence to be sent to the Alberni school.*" (Testimony of William Sport to IHRAAM officers, Port Alberni, BC, March 31, 1998)

HOMICIDES

More overt killings of children were a common occurrence in residential schools, according to eyewitnesses. The latter have described children being beaten and starved to death, thrown from windows, strangled and being kicked or thrown down stairs to their deaths. Such killings occurred in at least eight residential schools in British Columbia alone, run by all three mainline denominations.

Bill Seward of Nanaimo, BC, age 78, states:

"*My sister Maggie was thrown from a three-storey window by a nun at the Kuper Island school, and she died. Everything was swept under the rug. No investigation was ever done. We couldn't hire a lawyer at the time, being Indians. So nothing was ever done.*" (Testimony of Bill Seward, Duncan, BC, August 13, 1998)

Diane Harris, Community Health Worker for the Chemainus Band Council on Vancouver Island, confirms accounts of the murders.

"*We always hear stories of all the kids who were killed at Kuper Island. A grave-yard for the babies of the priests and girls was right south of the school until it was dug up by the priests when the school closed in 1973. The nuns would abort babies and some-times end up killing the mothers. There were a lot of disappearances. My mother, who is 83 now, saw a priest drag a girl down a flight of stairs by her hair and the girl died as a result. Girls were raped and killed, and buried under the floorboards. We asked the local* RCMP *to exhume that place and search for remains but they've always refused, as recently as 1996. Corporal Sampson even threatened us. That kind of cover-up is the norm. Children were put together with kids sick with* TB *in the infirmary. That was standard procedure. We've documented thirty-five outright murders in a seven-year period."* (Testimony of Diane Harris to the IHRAAM Tribunal, June 13, 1998)

Evidence exists that active collusion from police, hospital officials, coroners, Indian Agents and even native leaders helped to conceal such murders. Local hospitals, particularly tuberculosis sanatoriums connected to the United and Roman Catholic churches, served as "dumping grounds" for children's bodies and routinely provided false death certificates for murdered students.

In the case of the United Church's Alberni residential school, students who discovered dead bodies of other children faced serious retribution. One such witness, Harry Wilson of Bella Bella, BC, claims that he was expelled from the school, then hospitalised and drugged against his will, after finding the body of a dead girl in May 1967.

Sadly, the two-tiered system of collaborators and victims created among native students at the schools continues to the present, as some of the state-funded band council officials — themselves former collaborators — appear to have an interest in helping to suppress evidence and silence witnesses who would incriminate not only the murderers but themselves as agents of the white administration.

A majority of the witnesses who have shared their story with the authors and at public tribunals on the west coast have described either seeing a murder or discovering a body at the residential school he or she attended. The body count, even according to the government's own figures, was enormously high. Where, then, are all these bodies? The deaths of thousands of students are not recorded in any of the school records, Indian Affairs files or other documentation submitted thus far in court cases or academic publications on the residential schools. Some 50,000 corpses have literally and officially gone missing.

The residential school system had to hide not only the evidence of murder but the bodies as well. The presence of secret gravesites of children killed at Catholic and Protestant schools in Sardis, Port Alberni, Kuper Island and Alert Bay has been attested to by numerous witnesses. These secret burial yards also contained the aborted foetuses and even small babies who were the offspring of priests and staff at the schools, according to the same witnesses. One of them, Ethel Wilson of Bella Bella, claims to have seen "rows and rows of tiny skeletons" in the foundations of the former Anglican residential school of St Michael's in Alert Bay when a new school was built there in the 1960s.

"There were several rows of them, all lined up neatly like it was a big cemetery. The skeletons had been found within one of the old walls of St. Mike's school. None of them could have been very old, from their size. Now why would so many kids have been buried like that inside a wall, unless someone was trying to hide something?" (Testimony of Ethel Wilson to Kevin Annett, Vancouver, BC, August 8, 1998)

Arnold Sylvester, who, like Dennis Charlie, attended Kuper Island school between 1939 and 1945, corroborates this account.

"The priests dug up the secret gravesite in a real hurry around 1972 when the school closed. No one was allowed to watch them dig up those remains. I think it's because that was a specially secret graveyard where the bodies of the pregnant girls were buried. Some of the girls who got pregnant from the priests were actually killed because they threatened to talk. They were sometimes shipped out and sometimes just disappeared. We weren't allowed to talk about this." (Testimony of Arnold Sylvester to Kevin Annett, Duncan, BC, August 13, 1998)

Local hospitals were also used as a dumping ground for children's bodies, as in the case of the Edmonds boy and his "processing" at St Paul's Hospital after his murder at the Catholic school in North Vancouver. Certain hospitals, however, seem to have been particularly favourite spots for storing corpses.

The Nanaimo Tuberculosis Hospital (called The Indian Hospital) was one such facility. Under the guise of tuberculosis treatment, generations of native children and adults were subjected to medical experiments and sexual sterilizations at the Nanaimo Hospital, according to women who experienced these tortures. But the facility was also a cold storage area for native corpses.

The West Coast General Hospital in Port Alberni not only stored children's bodies from the local United Church residential school; it was also the place where abortions were performed on native girls who were made pregnant at the school by staff and clergy, and where newborn babies were disposed of and possibly killed, according to witnesses like Amy Tallio, who attended the Alberni school during the early 1950s.

Irene Starr of the Hesquait Nation, who attended the Alberni school between 1952 and 1961, confirms this.

"Many girls got pregnant at the Alberni school. The fathers were the staff, teachers, the ones who raped them. We never knew what happened to the babies, but they were always disappearing. The pregnant girls were taken to the Alberni hospital and then came back without their babies. Always. The staff killed those babies to cover their tracks. They were paid by the church and government to be rapists and murderers." (Testimony of Irene Starr to Kevin Annett, Vancouver, BC, August 23, 1998)

"The Whites Were Terrorists": Residential Schools

Article II (b): Causing serious bodily or mental harm

Early in the residential schools era, the Indian Affairs Superintendent, Duncan Campbell Scott, outlined the purpose of the schools thus: "to kill the Indian within the Indian."

Clearly, the genocidal assault on aboriginals was not only physical but spiritual: European culture wished to own the minds and the souls of the native nations, to turn the Indians it hadn't killed into third-class replicas of white people.

Expressing the "virtues" of genocide, Alfred Caldwell, principal of the United Church school in Ahousat on Vancouver Island's west coast, wrote in 1938:

"The problem with the Indians is one of morality and religion. They lack the basic fundamentals of civilised thought and spirit, which explains their child-like nature and behaviour. At our school we strive to turn them into mature Christians who will learn how to behave in the world and surrender their barbaric way of life and their treaty rights which keep them trapped on their land and in a primitive existence. Only then will the Indian problem in our country be solved." (Rev. A.E. Caldwell to Indian Agent P.D. Ashbridge, Ahousat, BC, Nov 12, 1938)

The fact that this same principal is named by eyewitnesses as the murderer of at least two children—one of them in the same month that he wrote this letter—is no accident, for cultural genocide spills effortlessly over into killing, as the Nazis proved so visibly to the world.

Nevertheless, Caldwell's letter illuminates two vital points for the purpose of this discussion of mental and bodily harm inflicted on native students: (a) the residential schools were a vast project in mind control, and (b) the underlying aim of this "reprogramming" of native children was to force aboriginals off their ancestral lands in order to allow whites access to them.

To quote Alberni survivor Harriett Nahanee:

"They were always pitting us against each other, getting us to fight and molest one another. It was all designed to split us up and brainwash us so that we would forget that we were Keepers of the Land. The Creator gave our people the job of protecting the land, the fish, the forests. That was our purpose for being alive. But the whites wanted it all, and the residential schools were the way they got it. And it worked.

We've forgotten our sacred task, and now the whites have most of the land and have taken all the fish and the trees. Most of us are in poverty, addictions, family violence. And it all started in the schools, where we were brainwashed to hate our own culture and to hate ourselves so that we would lose everything. That's why I say that the genocide is still going on." (Testimony of Harriett Nahanee to Kevin Annett, North Vancouver, BC, December 11, 1995)

It was only after the assumption of guardianship powers by the west coast school principals, between 1933 and 1941, that the first evidence of organised pedophile networks in those residential schools emerges. For such a regime was legally and morally free to do whatever it wanted to its captive native students.

The residential schools became a safe haven—one survivor calls it a "free fire zone"—for pedophiles, murderers and brutal doctors needing live test subjects for drug testing or genetic and cancer research.

Particular schools, such as the Catholic one at Kuper Island and the United Church's Alberni school, became special centres where extermination techniques were practised with impunity on native children from all over the province, alongside the usual routine of beatings, rapes and farming out of children to influential pedophiles.

Much of the overt mental and bodily harm done to native students was designed to break down traditional tribal loyalties along kinship lines by pitting children against each other and cutting them off from their natural bonds. Boys and girls were strictly segregated in separate dormitories and could never meet.

One survivor describes never seeing her little brother for years, even though he was in the same building at the Alert Bay Anglican school. And when children at the schools broke into each other's dormitories and older boys and girls were caught exchanging intimacies, the most severe punishments were universally applied. According to a female survivor who attended the Alberni school in 1959:

"They used the gauntlet on a boy and girl who were caught together kissing. The two of them had to crawl naked down a line of other students, and we beat them with sticks and whips provided by the principal. The girl was beaten so badly she died from kidney failure. That gave us all a good lesson: if you tried having normal feelings for someone, you'd get killed for it. So we quickly learned never to love or trust anyone, just do what we were told to do." (Testimony of anonymous woman from the Pacheedat Nation, Port Renfrew, BC, October 12, 1996)

According to Harriett Nahanee:

"The residential schools created two kinds of Indians: slaves and sell-outs. And the sellouts are still in charge. The rest of us do what we're told. The band council chiefs have been telling everyone on our reserve not to talk to the Tribunal and have been threatening to cut our benefits if we do." (Harriett Nahanee to Kevin Annett, June 12, 1998)

The nature of that system of torture was not haphazard. For example, the regular use of electric shocks on children who spoke their language or were "disobedient" was a widespread phenomenon in residential schools of every denomination across Canada. This was not a random but an institutionalised device.

Specially constructed torture chambers with permanent electric chairs, often operated by medical personnel, existed at the Alberni and Kuper Island schools in British Columbia, at the Spanish Catholic school in Ontario, and in isolated hospital facilities run by the churches and Department of Indian Affairs in northern Quebec, Vancouver Island and rural Alberta, according to eyewitnesses.

Mary Anne Nakogee-Davis of Thunder Bay, Ontario, was tortured in an electric chair by nuns at the Catholic Spanish residential school in 1963 when she was eight years old. She states:

"The nuns used it as a weapon. It was done on me on more than one occasion. They would strap your arms to the metal arm rests, and it would jolt you and go through your system. I don't know what I did that was bad enough to have that done to me." (From *The London Free Press*, London, Ontario, October 22, 1996)

Such torture also occurred at facilities operated by the churches with Department of Indian Affairs money, similar to the sterilisation programs identified at the W.R. Large Memorial Hospital in Bella Bella and the Nanaimo Indian Hospital.

Frank Martin, a Carrier native from northern BC, describes his forcible confinement and use in experiments at the Brannen Lake Reform School near Nanaimo in 1963 and 1964:

"I was kidnapped from my village when I was nine and sent off to the Brannen Lake school in Nanaimo. A local doctor gave me a shot and I woke up in a small cell, maybe ten feet by twelve. I was kept in there like an animal for fourteen months. They brought me out every morning and gave me electric shocks to my head until I passed out. Then in the afternoon I'd go for these X-rays and they'd expose me to them for minutes on end. They never told me why they were doing it. But I got lung cancer when I was eighteen and I've never smoked." (Videotaped testimony of Frank Martin to Eva Lyman and Kevin Annett, Vancouver, July 16, 1998)

Such quack experimentation combined with brutal sadism characterised these publicly funded facilities, especially the notorious Nanaimo Indian Hospital. David Martin of Powell River, BC, was taken to this hospital in 1958 at the age of five and used in experiments attested to by Joan Morris, Harry Wilson and other witnesses quoted in this report. According to David:

"I was told I had tuberculosis, but I was completely healthy; no symptoms of TB at all. So they sent me to Nanaimo Indian Hospital and strapped me down in a bed there for more than six months. The doctors gave me shots every day that made me feel really sick, and made my skin all red and itchy. I heard the screams of other Indian kids who were

locked away in isolation rooms. We were never allowed in there to see them. Nobody ever told me what they were doing to all of us in there." (David Martin to Kevin Annett, Vancouver, November 12, 2000)

A recurring and regular torture at the residential schools themselves was operating on children's teeth without using any form of anaesthesia or painkiller. Two separate victims of this torture at the Alberni school describe being subjected to it by different dentists, decades apart. Harriett Nahanee was brutalised in that manner in 1946, while Dennis Tallio was "worked on by a sick old guy who never gave me painkillers" at the same school in 1965....

Former employees of the federal government have confirmed that the use of "inmates" of residential schools was authorised for government-run medical experiments through a joint agreement with the churches which ran the schools.

According to a former Indian Affairs official:

"A sort of gentlemen's agreement was in place for many years: the church provided the kids from their residential schools to us, and we got the Mounties to deliver them to whoever needed a fresh batch of test subjects: usually doctors, sometimes Department of Defense people. The Catholics did it big time in Quebec when they transferred kids wholesale from orphanages into mental asylums. It was for the same purpose: experimentation. There was lots of grant money in those days to be had from the military and intelligence sectors: all you had to do was provide the bodies."

"*The church officials were more than happy to comply. It wasn't just the residential school principals who were getting kickbacks from this: everyone was profiting. That's why it's gone on for so long. It implicates a hell of a lot of top people.*" (From the Closed Files of the IHRAAM Tribunal, containing the statements of confidential sources, June 12-14, 1998)

Such experiments and the sheer brutality of the harm regularly inflicted on children in the schools attest to the institutional view of aboriginals as "expendable" and "diseased" beings. Scores of survivors of 10 different residential schools in BC and Ontario have described under oath the following tortures inflicted on them and other children as young as five years old between the years 1922 and 1984:

* tightening fish twine and wire around boys' penises;
* sticking needles into their hands, cheeks, tongues, ears and penises;
* holding them over open graves and threatening to bury them alive;
* forcing them to eat maggot-filled and regurgitated food;
* telling them their parents were dead and that they were about to be killed;

* stripping them naked in front of the assembled school and verbally and sexually degrading them;
* forcing them to stand upright for more than 12 hours at a time until they collapsed;
* immersing them in ice water;
* forcing them to sleep outside in winter;
* ripping the hair from their heads;
* repeatedly smashing their heads against concrete or wooden surfaces;
* daily beating without warning, using whips, sticks, horse harnesses, studded metal straps, pool cues and iron pipes;
* extracting gold teeth from their mouths without painkillers;
* confining them in unventilated closets without food or water for days;
* regularly applying electric shocks to their heads, genitals and limbs.

Perhaps the clearest summary of the nature and purpose of such sadism are the words of Bill Seward of Nanaimo, a survivor of the Kuper Island school:

"The church people were worshipping the devil, not us. They wanted the gold, the coal, the land we occupied. So they terrorised us into giving it to them. How does a man who was raped every day when he was seven make anything out of his life? The residential schools were set up to destroy our lives, and they succeeded. The whites were terrorists, pure and simple." (Testimony of Bill Seward to Kevin Annett and IHRAAM observers, Duncan, BC, August 13, 1998)

2. Ted Byfield, "Weren't We All Physically Abused in Schools? So When Do We Get Our Money for Healing," *Alberta Report*, January 19, 1998

Edward Bartlett "Ted" Byfield (1929–) was born in Toronto but moved to the United States as a teenager and became a copy boy at the Washington Post. *He returned to Canada in 1948 and worked for leading Canadian newspapers including the* Ottawa Journal *and the* Winnipeg Free Press. *Byfield converted to Anglicanism in the 1950s and left journalism to help found two private Anglican boys' schools in which he taught history and where the staff lived communally and received $1 per day. A journalist again by 1973, he amalgamated two small publications in 1979 into the conservative news magazine* Alberta Report. *It tapped into growing western disaffection and alienation. Its anti-abortion and anti-gay messages, and its attacks on public education, were popular with social conservatives.*

That the government of Canada should apologize and compensate for any sexual abuse of native children at government-supervised residential schools between the 1930s and 1980s seems altogether appropriate. What we consider sexual abuse of children has not changed at all from the 1930s until today, although we are under increasing pressure to do so.

But the government apology and compensation for physical abuse of children raises a fundamental question. What's considered physical abuse has changed radically since the 1950s. So the question is: Did the commission whose report led to this apology and accompanying half-billion-dollar compensation package judge those schools by today's standards or by yesterday's? The former, one suspects—in which case Ottawa, to be consistent, had better apologize to several million other Canadians as well.

Suppose, that is, that some investigator, thoroughly imbued with the current theories of raising children, was asked to peer into the typical urban elementary school back in the '30s, '40s or even '50s. At the public school I attended in suburban Toronto between about 1936 and 1940 here is what she would have seen:

When the school bell rang, children from kindergarten to Grade 8 marched in to martial music played on a gramophone, while the principal kept time like a drum major. Standing rigidly by their desks, they sang "God Save the King" and recited the Lord's Prayer. In the younger grades, they chorused to the teacher, "Good morning, Miss Smith" before seating themselves. To ask a question, you raised your hand, rising when acknowledged. Teachers were addressed as "Mr. Jones," "Miss Smith" (or "Sir" or "Ma'am").

Discipline came in three levels—a sharp verbal reprimand, a detention to stay after class, or "the strap." The latter was a flat, stiff 14-inch leather instrument, administered sharply across the outstretched palm, anywhere from three to maybe eight strokes per occasion. How often this happened depended on the teacher: in some classes almost daily, in others perhaps once a month. The recipient was almost invariably male—I can't actually remember a girl ever "getting it." From what I've heard, country schools were much the same, perhaps even more prone to corporal punishment.

Such was emphatically the case at a private boys' residential school I attended for two years at great expense to my parents and grandparents. Known as Lakefield, near Peterborough, Ont., it is still very much operative today. Here the instrument was not a strap but a stick about two feet long, often a hockey stick handle, administered across the hind end while the accused bent over. Three to maybe 10 swats was the usual quota, which could be delivered not only by teachers (whom we called "masters") but also by "prefects," senior students who shared in the school's administration. These "beatings" occurred routinely in classes, dormitories, wherever and whenever misconduct occurred, which was everywhere and often.

Now the point, of course, is this: Any educator or social worker schooled since the '60s would regard these institutions as houses of horror. She would see rigid "authoritarianism" in their methodology, individual spontaneity being endlessly stifled, and repugnant brutality in their methods of discipline. Her report would denounce and deplore them, and if compensation for the "victims" of such appalling institutions were available, she would surely recommend it.

Without doubt, the inquiry into native residential schools found instances of physical injury that exceeded what I've described here. But I'm equally sure that an exhaustive examination of public schools of that era would have produced much the same. I heard of a teacher once breaking a youngster's arm, for example, and another in high school who punched a kid in the face. My Grade 1 teacher at a Toronto school suffered a nervous breakdown and was eventually carted off the premises after doing heaven knows what. (I alone cannot claim credit for this, but I likely contributed.) With such incidents incorporated in the investigator's report the case for compensation would grow accordingly.

So one suspects that by the reasoning of the native residential school inquiry, most Canadian-born citizens over the age of, say, 55 were "abused" in like manner. Are we all to receive an apology from the government? What will be our compensation? Will there be a provision for counselling us? How much will we get for "healing initiatives"?

Two points need to be added to my portrayal of education in the '30s and '40s. In the elementary school I have described, Courcellette Road in Toronto, I received a grounding in English language and grammar out of which I have made a living all my life. However "authoritarian," the teachers were competent, dedicated, in no rational sense whatever "abusive," and probably ill-paid. As for Lakefield, the two years I spent there were among the happiest in my life, and I became acquainted for the first time with two realities. One was history and the other was God. And while I can easily believe some of the native residential schools were far from idyllic, I have read a woman's published memory of one of them that is both fond and thankful, and categorically denies that either sexual or physical abuse occurred in it.

All this casts real doubt on what the government is now doing, but it accords with everything else we see in Ottawa's approach to the aboriginal peoples. What Ottawa does today at great expense it will no doubt be apologizing for tomorrow at even greater expense. You can look back at an unbroken record of muddle-headedness.

Consider this, for instance. We have enshrined in our Charter of Rights and Freedoms an absolute prohibition against racism, which is regarded as anathema—something to be abhorred and outlawed. Yet at the same time we are zealously establishing and segregating with the full thrust of the law an entire category of citizenship, founded rigorously and exclusively on racism. The definitions of who is, and who is not, a native read like Hitler's racial purity laws. The government has abandoned its past policies of "assimilation," says a news story, explaining the official "apology." It is now intent on preserving the cultural and communal identity of the native peoples, and this "reconciliation statement" is "the centrepiece" of the new policy.

How will they square this bold new venture into legislated racism, you wonder, with the charter's condemnation of it? How is Canada to ride two horses at the same time when they're galloping in opposite directions? Nobody in the Ottawa hierarchy ever seems to raise this question, let alone answer it.

You get the impression that our native policy is directed, not by moral principle nor even by common sense, but by whatever is currently fashionable. That's how we got the residential schools, and that's why we're now apologizing for them. Soon no doubt some other liberal fad will take hold and Ottawa will be apologizing for the apology. How luckless for the natives that they were left under federal jurisdiction.

3. P. Donnelly, "Scapegoating the Indian Residential Schools: The Noble Legacy of Hundreds of Christian Missionaries Is Sacrificed to Political Correctness," *Alberta Report*, January 26, 1998

Patrick Donnelly (dates unknown) is an Alberta journalist. His article "Scapegoating the Indian Residential Schools...," which appeared in Alberta Report *in 1998, caused immediate controversy. Assembly of First Nations leader Phil Fontaine had University of Calgary law professor Kathleen Mahoney levy a complaint against the article and* Alberta Report *with the Alberta Human Rights and Citizenship Commission, alleging that the magazine "expose[d] First Nations people to hatred or contempt on the basis of their race or ancestry." Professor Mahoney asked for remedies including "an apology, damages, and an order that the respondents attend education sessions about human rights in Alberta." The Commission ruled that there were insufficient grounds to proceed with the complaint.*

In the week following the Chrétien government's apology to natives for residential schools, news media characterized the historic institutions as "brutal," "miserable," "genocidal" and "horrendous." They were repeating vaguely recounted and unchallenged testimony to a royal commission which concluded that the poorly funded and allegedly abusive schools bear large responsibility for the woeful present plight of many Indians. In none of the media coverage was the possibility raised that the schools were on the whole beneficial and widely supported by the Indians who attended them and voluntarily sent their children to them. Nor was the possibility admitted that the Indian leaders who now revile the schools might be motivated by the prospect of federal compensation.

On January 7 the Chrétien government said it was "deeply sorry" for the treatment of natives in residential schools. The apology, part of the government's official response to recommendations of a Royal Commission on Aboriginal Peoples, carried with it a "healing" fund of $350 million, or $500,000 on average per reserve.

Initiated in 1991 by then-prime minister Brian Mulroney, the commission's mandate was to examine all aspects of the federal government's relationship with aboriginal people. There were seven commissioners, four native and three white, balanced also for gender and region. By the time they had wrapped up their cross-country hearings in 1996, the aboriginal commission had become the most expensive in Canada's history, with a final cost of $58 million and 445 recommendations, the cost of which were estimated in total at $20 billion. While it dealt with a broad range of issues including treaty rights, self-government, social programs, education and land claims, the commission's most damning indictment was reserved for residential schools.

Travelling in threes, the commissioners held meetings in communities all across Canada, from cities to Inuit villages and Indian reserves. At the height of its undertaking, the commission employed over 100 staff in Ottawa and countless others in local communities who encouraged people to come forward and make submissions. Paul Chartrand, a Metis commissioner from Manitoba, explains that witness testimonies were not tested for accuracy or truthfulness. "We were a body of inquiry and were not there to cross-examine people appearing before us. We were not a judicial process. We listened to submissions, applied our understanding of the issues, and came up with policy recommendations."

Mr. Chartrand concedes that not all the testimony was critical of residential schools. "The report acknowledges that attendance for many people was not an unhappy experience," he says carefully. "[And] the report doesn't contain a blanket condemnation of the schools."

Fellow commissioner Mary Sillett, an Inuit from Ottawa representing Labrador, agrees that there were positive stories. However, she believes that the negative testimony far outweighed the positive. "Residential schools hurt a lot of people very deeply. Little kids were forcibly removed from their homes, beaten, and taught to despise their families. The stories were absolutely horrifying. How can you ever apologize adequately for the abuse those children suffered?" she says. "However, it's significant that the decision-makers have shown the courage to recognize the hurt and damage that was caused by residential schools."

The commission concluded, "Tragically, the future that was created [by the schools] is now a lamentable heritage for those children and generations who came after.... The school system's concerted campaign to obliterate Aboriginal languages, traditions, and beliefs was compounded by mismanagement and the woeful mistreatment, neglect, and abuse of many children.... The memory has persisted, festered and become a sorrowful monument, still casting a deep shadow over the lives of many Aboriginal people and over the possibility of a new relationship between Aboriginal and non-Aboriginal Canadians."

Since the commission's report was published in November 1996, the federal government has been preparing its response. Amid sweetgrass smoke and the beating of drums, on January 7 Indian Affairs Minister Jane Stewart expressed "profound regret" for the residential schools. The apology was hailed by aboriginal leaders as a first step in recognizing the suffering of the aboriginal people over the 300 years of Canada's history. Phil Fontaine, grand chief of the Assembly of First Nations, told the *Calgary Herald*, "Let this moment mark the end of paternalism in our relations and the beginning of the empowerment of First Nations, the end of the official victimization of First Nations." Chief Fontaine, from Pine Falls, Man., has said in the past he was sexually molested at one of the schools, but was travelling last week and could not be reached for an interview.

However, it remains a question, in many Indian minds as well as white, whether the general legacy of the Indian schools may actually have been quite good. While there have been some documented cases of sexual abuse over the 120-year history of the schools, a handful of which still operate, the available evidence is vague and almost entirely anecdotal.

Far-removed from Ottawa's corridors of power, many native people say they are bewildered by the vilification of residential schools. For example, Dora and Donald Cardinal of Onion Lake, Sask. near Lloydminster attended St. Anthony's Residential School on the reserve in the 1950s.

"It was a great, big white-frame building," recalls Mrs. Cardinal of the structure which was demolished in 1972. "I was sad to see it go; I have a lot of fond memories from that school, I really liked it there." One of her most vivid memories is of the kitchen, with big wood-burning stoves all along one wall. "There was a lot of food, we were practically forced to eat," she recalls wistfully. "Every day there was delicious fresh bread, porridge, peanut butter and lots of stew. I was a picky eater back then, and the food was always very good." Mrs. Cardinal explains that children from the reserve attended one of several area boarding schools, depending on their religious affiliation. As Roman Catholics, she and her older brother and sister were sent to St. Anthony's, operated by the Oblates of Mary Immaculate and the Grey Nuns.

Donald Cardinal adds that although speaking their native Cree was against the rules, he can not remember ever being punished for it. "It was the boys' job to look after the garden," he explains. "We chopped wood, worked on the farm, and looked after the cows while the girls learned to sew, mend, crochet." Dora Cardinal recounts that the Onion Lake reserve was very poor, and so was her family with six children. "We lived in a cabin, my dad did a little trapping; we had to survive somehow. I remember nights at home that were so cold, and we never had enough blankets. Sometimes my mother's bread wouldn't rise because it was so cold. I also remember that if we got some secondhand, old clothes, mother would cut off the sleeves and we used them for socks. Many parents at the time thought the school was a blessing."

The Blood Reserve near Lethbridge had two residential schools; Catholic St. Mary's and the Anglican St. Paul's Residential School. Rufus Goodstriker, a retired pro rodeo rider and boxer, and now a rancher and herbalist, attended St. Paul's for eight years in the 1940s. A three-storey, steam-heated brick building, St. Paul's at one time had over 500 students. "We were supposed to speak English, but I spoke Blackfoot all the time anyway," Mr. Goodstriker remembers. "It was good teaching for survival in society. We learned reading, writing, history, science, as well as how to operate machinery and farm chores. I really appreciated being able to learn all that. I'm a rancher now, and I use a lot of what I learned at the school."

A typical day began at 6:45, with breakfast and chapel before morning classes. After a half-day in the classroom, boys worked on the farm or in the shop. The children often went on hikes and camping trips through the surrounding countryside, and the older students were allowed to visit nearby Cardston on Saturdays. Each Friday night there was a co-education social event, usually a dance.

Although the children often visited their parents on weekends, school was a lonely experience at first. Mr. Goodstriker recalls that once his older brother ran away. "But my father immediately loaded him up in the wagon and brought him right back and said 'you don't run away from school' although, looking back, it probably would have been better to keep the children with their parents."

For Mr. Goodstriker, the sports program was the real highlight of school. Although St. Paul's lacked an indoor gym, the students were coached in soccer and softball. In the winter they flooded a rink for hockey, and numerous social events were organized by staff and students. Notwithstanding all these pleasant recollections, indeed almost as an afterthought, Mr. Goodstriker remarks that the schools were practising "cultural genocide." Asked to elaborate, he declines.

Another former resident at St. Paul's remembers that each week began with a chore work-list, which the students worked through in groups. "We worked together on everything; repairing equipment, cleaning washrooms, sweeping dormitories. I really enjoyed my time at the school; not only did I learn to work with other people, I also learned to respect them and respect myself."

The informant, who did not wish his name to be used because he says it could cause trouble, attended the school for eight years in the late 1940s. "I was never lonely there," he says. "When I went home on holidays, I was always lonesome for the school. The staff was very supportive of the students, and there were always lots of activities organized. Besides sports there was choir, piano, even a first-aid course. I even remember the staff reading stories to the younger children."

In the 1940s, the schools were already two generations old. Following the decimation of the buffalo and the movement of the nomadic plains Indians to reserves, the first residential schools in the West were started in 1884 by Catholic Father Albert Lacombe and Bishop Vital Grandin. With the plains steadily filling up with settlers, and game scarce, the schools were envisioned as a means of endowing native children with the skills necessary to survive in their changed world.

Initially termed "industrial schools," the facilities were established by the churches and staffed by religious workers, in an era when few white people had much sympathy for Indians. Besides core academics, various schools taught blacksmithing, woodworking, carpentry, cobbling, tailoring and farming. By the 1890s the federal government had established control over the schools, and provided enrolment grants while the churches continued running them. The number of schools peaked in 1946 when there were 76 scattered across Canada, most of them in the West.

Of those schools, 45 were affiliated with the Roman Catholic Church, 19 with the Anglican Church, 10 with the Presbyterians and two with the United Church. By most estimates, over 150,000 native children were educated in residential schools between 1867 and the late 1960s.

Some schools, located on reserves, operated as day schools and the students went home to their parents at night. Others had day populations and boarders from farther afield. Some served very scattered populations and were entirely residential; prohibitions against speaking Indian were more common at these, especially where the students came from different tribes historically at war with each other. Some of the early industrial schools, for example the Dunbow School near Calgary, were established in white communities so that the students could apprentice with local tradesmen.

According to Gerry Kelly, coordinator for the National Catholic Working Group on Native Residential Schools, the Indian people themselves recognized the need for education. "In several cases, Indian bands asked the government to establish schools," he explains. "In the 1930s, the Sechelt band near Vancouver lobbied the Oblates for such a school; some aboriginal communities wanted the schools so badly that they built them themselves. It's disrespectful to the natives' history to suggest that they played no part in the system, that they were herded mindlessly along by the government. Natives exercised some authority."

Mr. Kelly points out that, often, problems resulted after the native students left the industrial schools and attempted to find work in white communities. "For instance, a boy would train as a blacksmith, but then no one would hire him, however good he was at blacksmithing." Mr. Kelly is disappointed that the residential schools have been made scapegoats for all the suffering of the Indian people. "In some cases," he argues, "the very existence of these schools saved communities, for example in the North. In times of epidemics, the institutions were there to care for people. Also, the irony is that the only [white] people who were concerned about the Indians worked in the schools."

Mr. Kelly explains that, after World War II, there was a growing movement to shut down the residential schools and transfer the responsibility of educating native children first to the provinces, and then to the natives themselves. "The viability of the provincial systems was growing, and there was a growing movement to integrate native children with non-native." In 1946 a joint committee of the House of Commons and Senate recommended that Indian children be schooled with non-native children wherever possible. According to the compilation of essays entitled Indian Education in Canada, by 1960 nearly 25% of Indian children in Canada were being schooled in provincial institutions.

However, there was also a growing desire among Indian people to control their children's education directly. In 1971, the federal government handed control of the Blue Quills Residential School near St. Paul, Alta., to local bands, making it the first federal Indian school to be run by natives. The process of turning over the schools, both residential and day facilities, to local bands accelerated during the 1970s and 1980s. By 1993, there were only seven residential schools left in Canada and these were administered solely by native bands.

By the late 1980s many natives, especially politicians, were pointing accusing fingers at the residential schools. Highly-publicized incidents of sexual abuse, coupled with white liberal guilt about cultural assimilation, transformed the old residential schools into symbols of "degradation" and "cultural genocide" where the native children were systematically stripped of their culture, forced to adopt non-native ways, and undergo physical torture and sexual abuse by the school staff.

Chief Greg Smith of the Peigan reserve told the *Calgary Herald* that the legacy of the residential schools was terrible. "It was appalling, I see the effects of those schools everywhere. For me to lose my language, being part of the residential school system hurt me later on. I've had to go back and learn my language because it was taken away by someone else." However, he conceded that he suffered no abuse worse than having his hair cut. Warner Scout attended St. Paul's on the Blood Reserve after his mother froze to death while drinking and his alcoholic father was unable to care for him. He also told the *Herald*, "A lot of us graduated from there to jails. We knew nothing else to do except get drunk."

Flora Northwest of Hobbema, Alta., attended the Ermineskin Residential School in the 1950s. She told the *Edmonton Journal* that the loneliness at the school was terrible. "Because of what happened, I became the alcoholic that I never wanted to be," she said. "I became a woman with no values."

Though it is true that many Indians feel this way, many others are appalled at the demonization of residential schools. Rod Lorenz, a Metis Catholic lay missionary at Lloydminster, is sceptical of the government's apology for imposing residential schools on the native people. "If you look at it historically, the priests were very well-travelled and intelligent. They realized that the natives' food supply was diminishing, and they realized that the schools were one way the natives would learn the new tools they needed to survive—and a lot of those kids did learn.

"My own mother attended the residential school in Lebret from 1909 to 1916 in Saskatchewan and she loved it. The nuns taught her everything; how to sew, cook, read and write. How would she have learned otherwise? Certainly, the European style of discipline was different than native culture, but what could you do? If you let the children leave, a lot of them would have starved. You needed discipline." Mr. Lorenz points out that, in some cases, the separation of children from their parents was difficult. "Sure, mistakes were made but there are two sides to this story and you have to look at the positive side."

Rev. Stanley Cuthand, a Cree Indian and retired Anglican priest, grew up on Saskatchewan's Little Pine Reserve, boarded at the La Ronge Residential School in 1944, and was chaplain of Saskatchewan's La Ronge and Gordon Residential Schools, and of St. Paul's School at the Blood Reserve in the 1960s. "The schools weren't terrible places at all," he recalls. "They were certainly not prisons, although the principals were a little strict."

Rev. Mr. Cuthand recalls only one incident of sexual abuse of a student, at the Gordon Reserve, where one of the staff members was later convicted and sent to prison for several years. "Most of the kids had no complaints about sexual abuse; if they did, they would have told me. However, they did get homesick and some tried to run away. There was also plenty of food; raisins, fish, potatoes, bread with lard, stew. In those days everyone lived on fish."

As for the oft-alleged conscription of unwilling students, Rev. Mr. Cuthand recalls that the only children who were "forced" to attend a residential school were orphans or children from destitute families. "The idea that all children were forced into the schools is an exaggeration," he explains. "The idea of the separation of students [from parents] came from England. Practically all the [upper class] English were brought up in residential schools. In Canada, the main idea at the time was to civilize and educate the children; and that couldn't be done if the kids were at home on the trapline."

Mr. Cuthand also scoffs at the accusation that Indians had no influence in their children's education. "The Little Pine reserve wanted its own day school, and in 1910 after petitioning Ottawa, we got our own day school. Our parents had never had schools before, but they wanted us to learn English. When the school was built, there was so much cooperation between everyone that everyone on the reserve sent their kids there." He explains that the reason the children were forbidden to speak their language was because they used to swear in Cree, and had nicknames for their supervisors. "Of course they would be punished for swearing," he says. "The kids were not saints. But generally, language was not an issue. The La Ronge school also allowed fiddle dances every Saturday night; that was the students' culture. By then, most of them had already forgotten the traditional Cree dances."

Rev. Mr. Cuthand enjoyed his time on the Blood Reserve in southwest Alberta. "It was an exciting place to live," he recalls. "The Bloods were rich and very traditional. The school was a fine place with some very good teachers." The parents were involved in the school, with some parents living there as staff members. "[Blood] Senator Gladstone sent his kids there, and many of the students from St. Paul's went on to university." Mr. Cuthand remembers that his school was particularly committed to recognizing the native culture. "One principal had tepees set up on the front lawn," he remembers with a laugh.

That principal, Archdeacon Samuel H. Middleton, with the support of the tribal leadership, was a resourceful school promoter starting in the 1920s. "He started the honorary Kainai chieftainships," explains Mr. Cuthand, whereby prominent people were named as honorary chiefs to support the school. It was an exclusive club: the Prince of Wales, later King Edward VIII, and John Diefenbaker, to name only two. It also came to include three former principals and three former superintendents. Mr. Cuthand remembers the archdeacon, who spoke Blackfoot, changing the Sunday School curriculum to make it more relevant to native culture. "The school was well respected by the Bloods," Mr. Cuthand says. "We used to take students climbing up Chief Mountain because the Indians there believed it was a sacred place." Though not universal, respect for native culture was fostered elsewhere: for example, at the Blue Quills Residential School near St. Paul, religion classes were often conducted in Cree and Chipewyan.

Father Antonio Duhaime of the Oblates was principal at the Duck Lake Residential School from 1962 to 1968, and then principal at St. Mary's Residential School on the Blood reserve from 1968 to 1980. Given the name Black Eagle, Fr. Duhaime speaks some Blackfoot and in 1988 was made an honourary chief of the Blood. "The parents brought us their kids in September, and said 'Father, I want my children to learn English' and now they're accusing us of forbidding them to speak their native languages," he says, shaking his head. "If some of the natives are successful today, they can thank the residential schools. No one else was interested in the Indian people back then."

Fr. Duhaime remembers the schools as a defence against assimilation, not a promoter of it. "At the time, there was a low budget for each school. The federal government was insisting on assimilating the natives, and they were pressuring the children to attend non-native schools off the reserve." However, the sports program at St. Mary's remained an attraction. "We had two provincial high-school basketball championships," he says proudly. "Our teams travelled all over the world; Ireland, Mexico City, Europe. The kids loved to play because on the basketball courts, they were equal or superior to whites."

Dora Cardinal can recall only one instance of physical punishment at St. Anthony's School at Onion Lake. "One time one of the older girls was strapped because she had run away. But the nuns were generally very caring, and a lot of fun," she says. "My Grade 1 teacher in particular was always trying to cheer me up, and she never yelled at us. The way I see it, kids were better off then than today," she says firmly. "Kids today get away with everything; they have no respect for anyone. When I was at the school, I learned a lot about patience and self-discipline, and I learned to persevere."

That Indian reserves today are rife with social problems is everywhere admitted. According to Statistics Canada, the suicide rate among natives is five to eight times the national average, infant mortality is almost double the Canadian average, poverty is three to five times more common, and 60% of reserve residents depend on welfare. In Saskatchewan, the mortality rate on Indian reserves is an annual 5.0 per 1,000, compared to a provincial rate of 3.5. In 1995-96, 22% of all inmates sentenced to prison in Canada were aboriginal, about five times their share of the Canadian population.

But can the residential schools be blamed for this horrific misery? Rita Galloway grew up on the Pelican Lake Cree reserve in Saskatchewan. Today she is a teacher and president of the Saskatchewan-based First Nations Accountability Coalition. "I had many friends and relatives who attended residential schools," she comments. "Of course there were good and bad elements, but overall their experiences were positive. Today those people are now productive citizens; professionals, consultants, and business people. They learned the ethic of hard work."

Mrs. Galloway believes that it is unfair to blame residential schools for the conditions found on many reserves. "The suicide rates are very high, there is a lot of sexual abuse on the reserve; some of my siblings were sexually abused by band members. But my parents never attended a residential school, and they still had problems; my father lost his logging business because of drinking. A lot of these problems were present before the schools. When you put a group of people together in a small area like a reserve there will be problems. But it's always easier to blame others.

"The real problem is lack of financial accountability," insists Mrs. Galloway. "Each year, Indian Affairs doles out $13 billion to 680 reserves across Canada; and we don't know where a lot of it goes. And now, with this apology, the government is handing out another $350 million. When that money is gone, we'll be having the same discussion in 10 years, and there will be the same excuses for more money. But more money doesn't solve anything. Someone has to have the guts to say we need accountability; only then will you see real changes and growth."

Mrs. Galloway taught at the Prince Albert Indian Residential School from 1988 to 1990, when the school was operated by the Prince Albert tribal office. "Within the last five years, there was a police investigation for sexual abuse," she reports. "They didn't run a clean school themselves, and they're pointing the finger at others. As aboriginal people we have to be aware that other aboriginal people are abusers, and it's an oversimplification to blame the residential schools."

Mrs. Galloway also believes that residential schools still have a vital role to play. "Nowadays, there's lots of children who don't even attend school," she points out. "There is a very high drop-out rate among native children who attend school off-reserve. It's attributed to racism, but the deeper problem is that these kids don't get the support at home that they need. There are too many distractions, and many reserve homes are overcrowded. The morning after welfare day, children come to school tired because their parents were partying all night. We have to give these children some normalcy in their lives. When I taught at the Prince Albert school, I was able to give the students the academics they needed, and they were able to focus on their studies."

One of two residential schools still operating in Saskatchewan is the Whitecalf Collegiate in Lebret. Formerly the Oblate-run Qu'Appelle Industrial School, in a 1983 land claims deal the school and 55 acres of surrounding land were ceded to the nearby Star Blanket Cree Reserve. Verne Bellegarde, today executive director of the collegiate, attended the school for Grades 1 to 12, from 1947 to 1959. Mr. Bellegarde says that the band now operates the school with a great deal of success. "For only 200 positions, we have over 500 applicants from Indian reserves all across western Canada." The school's attraction, he believes, is its solid academic record plus its strong emphasis on sports. "Nearly 90% of our graduates go on to some form of post secondary education; with 50% of our grads attending university."

Mr. Bellegarde believes that most parents feel their children would be better-educated at the collegiate than in reserve-based schools. "I would definitely say that we don't have an absentee list," he points out, "and we can isolate them from home to some extent." Mr. Bellegarde points out that, while he was a victim of sexual abuse himself, he doesn't believe that such abuse was widespread through the residential school system. "You can't dwell on that," he reflects. "I've put it behind me, because I can forgive." He prefers to remember his positive experiences. "I learned discipline, and the 3 Rs. Through my experience with sports I realized that I could compete against non-Indians."

Rod Lorenz agrees. "There can be a lot of distractions on the reserve," he says. "I think boarding school can be a great way to study and apply yourself. My own son is attending a residential school; but it's a Ukrainian residential school in Manitoba. Residential schools—or boarding schools—have a lot of resources and can be a real advantage to young people. They're a good idea for the advanced grades, but not the younger children. They need mom and dad."

Mr. Lorenz believes that it is convenient for the native political leadership to overlook the positive side of residential schools. "Victimhood gets money," he says simply, "and there are certain vested political interests who have no reason to say anything good about residential schools. If you're trying to get money, balance is not what you want." Mr. Lorenz also believes that adherents to native religions like to discredit Christianity by smearing the residential schools. "There are definitely some people who see Christianity as a rival religion. Those who spearhead the native spirituality revival are very hostile. If they can use the schools as a stick to beat the Catholics, they're going to use it. If someone says that the schools weren't so bad, they become pariahs; they sold out to the whites."

The churches have been brow-beaten into line. In 1992, the Oblate order issued an apology for "certain aspects of their ministry" including "recent criticisms of Indian residential schools." The wordy document, delivered by Father Doug Crosby, then president of the Oblate Conference of Canada and now Bishop of Labrador, apologized for imposing "cultural, linguistic and religious imperialism over the native people."

Retired Oblate priest Duhaime believes that the smear of residential schools cheapens the sacrifices of many lay workers and missionary priests over the years who gave their lives in the service of Indian children. "It's very disappointing," he remarks. "All the years we worked in these schools, trying to make a difference, and all you hear today is negative. It's very hard to take."

FURTHER READINGS

Assembly of the First Nations. *Breaking the Silence: An Interpretive Study of Residential School Impact and Healing as Illustrated by the Stories of First Nations Individuals.* Ottawa: Assembly of First Nations, 1994.

Barmen, J. "Aboriginal Education at the Crossroads: The Legacy of Residential Schools and the Way Ahead." In *Visions of the Heart: Canadian Aboriginal Issues*, ed. D. Long *et al.* Toronto: Harcourt Brace, 1996.

Barman, J. *et al.*, Eds. *Indian Education in Canada.* Vancouver: University of British Columbia Press, 1986.

Bull, L. "Indian Residential Schooling: The Native Perspective." *Canadian Journal of Native Education* 18 (1991): 1-64.

Canada. *Looking Forward, Looking Back: Report of the Royal Commission on Aboriginal People.* Ottawa: Canada Communication Group, 1996.

Chrisjohn, R., S. Young, and M. Maraun. *The Circle Game: Shadows and Substance in the Indian Residential School Experience in Canada*. Penticton: Theytus Books, 1997.

Coates, K. "'Betwixt and Between': The Anglican Church and the Children of Carcross (Chooutla) Residential School." *BC Studies* 64 (Winter 1984-85): 27-47.

Deiter, C. *From Our Mothers' Arms: The Intergenerational Impact of Residential Schools in Saskatchewan*. Etobicoke: United Church, 1999.

Dyck, N. *Differing Visions: Administering Indian Residential Schooling in Prince Albert 1867-1995*. Halifax: Fernwood, 1997.

Fiske, J. "Gender and the Paradox of Residential Education in Carrier Society." In *Women and Education: A Canadian Perspective*, 2nd ed., ed. J. Gaskell and A. McLaren. Edmonton: Detsileg Enterprises, 1991.

Fournier, S., and E. Crey. *Stolen From Our Embrace: The Abduction of First Nations Children and the Restoration of Aboriginal Communities*. Vancouver: Douglas and McIntyre, 1997.

Furniss, E. *Victims of Benevolence: Discipline and Death at Williams Lake Indian Residential School, 1891-1920*. Williams Lake: Cariboo Tribal Council, 1992.

Graham, E. *The Mush Hole: Life in Two Residential Schools*. Waterloo: Heffle Publications, 1997.

Grant, A. *No End of Grief: Indian Residential Schools in Canada*. Winnipeg: Pemmican Publications, 1996.

Grant, W. *Residential Schools: An Historical Overview*. Ottawa: Assembly of First Nations, 1993.

Haig-Brown, C. *Resistance and Renewal: Surviving the Indian Residential School*. Vancouver: Tillacum Library, 1988.

Indian Residential Schools: The Nuu-chah-nulth Experience. Port Alberni: Nuu-chah-nulth Tribal Council, 1996.

Ing, R. "The Effects of Residential Schooling on Native Child-Rearing Practices." *Canadian Journal of Native Education* 18 (1991): 65-118.

Jack, A. *Behind Closed Doors: Stories from the Kamloops Indian Residential School.* Penticton: Secwepemc Cultural Education Society, 2001.

Jaine, L., Ed. *Residential School: The Stolen Years.* Saskatoon: University of Saskatchewan Press, 1993.

Knockwood, I. *Out of the Depths: The Experiences of Mi'kmaw Children at the Indian Residential School at Shubenacadie, Nova Scotia.* Lockeport: Roseway Publishing, 1992.

Miller, J. *Shingwauk's Vision: A History of Native Residential Schools.* Toronto: University of Toronto Press, 1996.

Million, D. "Telling Secrets: Sex, Power, and Narrative in Residential School Histories." *Canadian Women Studies* 20, 2 (Summer 2000): 92-107.

Milloy, J. *National Crime: The Canadian Government and the Residential School System, 1879 to 1986.* Winnipeg: University of Manitoba Press, 1999.

Raibmon, P. "A New Understanding of Things Indian: George H. Raley's Negotiation of the Residential School Experience." *BC Studies* 110 (Summer 1996): 69-96.

Titley, B. "Red Deer Indian Industrial School: A Case Study in the History of Native Education." In *Exploring Our Educational Past: Schooling in the Northwest Territories and Alberta*, ed. N. Kach and K. Mazurek. Calgary: Detselig Enterprises, 1992.

Titley, B. *A Narrow Vision: Duncan Campbell Scott and the Administration of Indian Affairs in Canada.* Vancouver: University of British Columbia Press, 1986.

CHAPTER 16

"A Cherished Reputation"

PEACEKEEPING

INTRODUCTION

Few images warm the collective Canadian heart more than the image of our blue-helmeted soldiers with Canadian flags on their sleeves leaping into the world's hot-spots, politely separating warriors and shepherding women and children to safety. Though much divides the country, "Canada-as-peacekeeper" rallies Canadians in a bond of justified pride that statistically transcends political, regional, or ethnic affiliation. The idea makes us feel whole. Maybe we can't fix our own national problems, but the world's we can cure! Nor is this mere delusion. The 100,000 Canadian men and women soldiers who have served in virtually every United Nations (UN) peacekeeping operation since 1949, some 30 in total and more than any other nation, have brought comfort to thousands of innocent victims caught in the jaws of war. Though some operations failed in their objectives, and though over 100 Canadian peacekeepers have died for their efforts in UN peacekeeping missions (not counting the 516 Canadians who died in the Korean War, which some refer to as a "police action," nor the Afghanistan mission that is fought under NATO auspices), polls consistently show popular support for peacekeeping. It now enjoys a mythology that may transcend reality or close scrutiny of the evidence—and may mask less noble, or at least more troublesome, aspects of Canada's international military role.

Peacekeeping did not officially emerge until after the creation of the UN in which Canada played a significant role. Nor was Canada's first peacekeeping role well planned or executed. A handful of Canadian soldiers under UN auspices acted as observers mediating the rift over Kashmir between India and Pakistan in 1949. That conflict simmers on today, occasionally bubbling over, and now does so between two nations who both have the dubious distinction of having nuclear weapons. No, it was Suez in 1956 that inextricably linked Canada to peacekeeping, both in its own eyes and to the world. The Suez operation also began inauspiciously, when Minister of External Affairs Lester "Mike" Pearson proposed that British and French troops, who had just invaded Egypt, be converted into international policemen. Egypt's President Nasser naturally refused. From that emerged Pearson's alternative plan—for which he later won the Nobel Peace Prize—to create an international force made up of soldiers from uninvolved nations, who would serve under a United Nations command wedged between the combatants while politicians brokered a resolution. Nasser agreed to the plan but not to the use of Canadian troops, since their "neutrality" was compromised by the Union Jack on Canada's flag and by the British uniforms its soldiers wore. Nasser eventually, and grudgingly, acceded to Canada playing a minor communications role in the operation.

Despite initial political reservation in Canada, something about the role fired the public imagination, and just three years later, when Prime Minister John Diefenbaker refused to send Canadian peacekeepers to the Congo, public outrage forced him to reconsider. Next it was off to Cyprus in 1964, a mission that lasted 30 years. Although the federal government elevated peacekeeping to top priority for the Department of Defence in 1964, the scope of the missions it undertook was not particularly ambitious in these first three decades. There was little talk of humanitarianism, international justice, or even of maintaining peace after violence ceased. Instead, Canada and other peacekeepers simply encouraged the pre-conflict *status quo*. Disputes such as civil wars were also off limits to peacekeepers because the UN mandate did not allow meddling in a nation's internal affairs. Thus, the two key reasons for the relative success of the earlier missions were not necessarily anything Canada did *per se* but was due to the limited mandates of the peacekeeping forces and the fact that most conflicts erupted along clearly delineated borders between sovereign nations. This kept missions straightforward and mandates unambiguous.

Peacekeeping, however, did create a strong sense of national unity and identity within Canada. Canadians found comfort in their heroic peacekeepers when domestically they struggled with mundane problems such as inflation, unemployment, and national discord. A high peacekeeping profile also let Canada believe that it upheld its international obligations, despite simultaneously cutting defence spending and reneging on obligations to organizations like the North Atlantic Treaty Organization (NATO). Furthermore, peace-keeping generated enormous international prestige, partly because the operations occurred under UN mandate, thereby creating distance between Canada and the United States, a situation which suited the Canadian public, especially during the Vietnam War. Finally, peacekeeping diverted attention from the fact that Canada was, and remains, one of the world's leading producers and exporters of sophisticated military equipment.

Canadian peacekeeping efforts changed in the late 1980s. Reasonably clear-cut UN missions suddenly became murky and deadly in Yugoslavia, Somalia, Rwanda, and parts of the Middle East and Southeast Asia. To make matters worse, the new flashpoints ignored recognized national borders, often involved far more than two combatants, and erupted with unimaginable savagery. Civilians, too, became more involved, often with unprecedented levels of barbarism. Finally, the combatants frequently no longer wanted or respected the peacekeepers' presence—or worse, used them as leverage for their own ends. All this, of course, made peacekeeping very difficult and dangerous.

Canada's policy on peacekeeping had to adapt to those changing world circum-stances. In 1991 Minister of External Affairs Barbara McDougall stated that "the concept of sovereignty must respect higher principles, including the need to preserve human life from wanton destruction." This called for a dramatic shift from traditionally passive peace-keeping to aggressive peacemaking—and it could involve interfering in the internal affairs of a sovereign state. Canada suggested a peacemaking force for Yugoslavia, the first nation to do so, fully aware that Canadian forces would have to create peace against the will of zealous and nihilistic combatants. Some 1,200 Canadians arrived in the former Yugoslavia in March 1992, their mandate to make peace as members of the UN force (UNPROFOR). The mission indeed proved as deadly as feared, and a number of international peacekeepers lost their lives. There were other problems, the major one being the lack of a clear man-date in a fluid war zone where rules of engagement and conduct simply ceased to exist. Despite enormous adversity, peril, frustration, and some tragic failures—particularly in Bosnia—UN peacekeepers undoubtedly saved countless innocent lives, but at a cost.

The Canadian public initially reacted positively to this new shift. Strange bed-fellows like the NDP and Reform (later the Alliance Party, and now the Conservative Party of Canada) abandoned their traditional reticence and, if anything, called for greater peacekeeping action with even stronger force. Slowly, however, Canadians perceived how aggressive and dangerous peacekeeping really was, and the public became increasingly skittish about the whole thing. The UN created 14 new peacekeeping missions between 1988 and 1993, as many in five years as over the previous four decades, and Canada participated in them all. Not only that, Canadian peacekeepers now often died, or were injured, or captured and abused. And peacekeeping was terribly expensive at a time when Canadian governments teetered on insolvency.

Liberal Prime Minister Jean Chrétien's Minister of Finance, Paul Martin, gutted defence spending from $12.83 billion in 1992 to $10.5 billion by 1995 while the government simultaneously increased the country's peacekeeping obligations from $12 million in 1992 to $130 by 1994. Canadian forces became so stretched by cutbacks and mounting international obligations that some doubted their ability to contend with potential domestic problems.

Two further events forced Canada to again rethink its international role. On March 16, 1993 a group of Canada's elite Airborne soldiers, sent to Somalia, caught and tortured to death Somali teenager Shidane Arone. At least a dozen other Canadian soldiers witnessed the event and did nothing as the young thief died, repeating the only English words he knew: "Canada," "Canada," "Canada." The trophy photograph of grinning trooper Kyle Brown holding Arone's bloody body rocked the country and burst the myth of the noble Canadian peacekeeper. The incident led to the ignominious dismantling of the once-proud Canadian Airborne Regiment, and some commentators mused on the apparent contradiction of sending trained killers, which soldiers are, to make peace.

Then, in 1994, came the UN's darkest hour: Rwanda. There, the international community proved itself to be willfully blind to incomprehensible savagery. Canadian Major-General Romeo Dallaire arrived early in the conflict with his peacekeepers but quickly realized that he could not fulfill his mandate with the very limited resources the UN sent him. Meanwhile, the situation in the tiny African country spiralled out of control. Rampaging mobs butchered ten Belgian UN peacekeepers, and the UN, rather than reinforce its forces, panicked and evacuated 2,050 of Dallaire's 2,500 soldiers. Dallaire, in fury, warned the UN and Canada in January 1994 that he needed at least 5,000 peacekeepers to avert the brewing genocide. His bosses demurred, and Dallaire witnessed approximately 800,000 men, women, and children hacked to death, mostly by Hutu tribesmen. A humiliated world looked away and muttered darkly about the impossibility of peacekeeping in the new reality.

The destruction by Islamic militants of the Twin Trade Towers in New York on September 11, 2001 again changed the face of peacekeeping and further muddied the waters of Canada's position in the twenty-first century. The United States unilaterally sought to destroy elements threatening its security, virtually sidelining the UN. President George W. Bush invited Canada to participate when the United States and Britain invaded Afghanistan on October 7, 2001. With Canada's acquiescence, 100 Canadian soldiers who happened to be on an exchange in the United States at the time, became part of an invading force outside the auspices of any international body. Those first few Canadians received further support from 40 members of Canada's elite commando unit, Joint Task Force Two (JTF2). Regular Canadian ground forces arrived in Afghanistan in January 2002.

The fact that the Afghanistan effort is not one but two distinctly different missions causes particular confusion about Canada's role. There was the initial American-British assault, called Operation Enduring Freedom, to topple Afghanistan's reprehensible Taliban government and neutralize al-Qaeda terrorist camps. Then the international community created a second force, known as the International Security Assistance Force (ISAF), over which NATO took command in 2003. Canada is now a senior partner of that NATO coalition, and as of November 2008, ISAF had some 50,000 troops from 40 countries operating in Afghanistan. Meanwhile, the Americans and British maintain about 28,000 non-ISAF personnel there. Both forces work in conjunction with the Afghan National Army and police as they struggle to gain control of a nation deeply steeped in tribalism, warlordism, corruption, and instability. Despite optimistic assurances to the contrary, evidence suggests that the elected Afghan government controls only the capital, Kabul.

Apart from the military mission, which has cost Canada $7.7-$10.5 billion and will eventually cost an estimated $22 billion, Canada actively engages in reconstruction and aid efforts in Afghanistan. The money devoted to these tasks is approximately one-tenth of the cost of the military operation. Opposing forces work hard to undermine all Canada's aid efforts. So far, Canada has lost over 100 soldiers and more than 300 have been seriously injured. The security situation in Afghanistan, meanwhile, appears no better than it was early in the operation, and Canadians are increasingly concerned about the country's presence in an operation outside UN auspices and in a hostile terrain where gains appear minimal. Canada has committed to remain in Afghanistan until 2011 but only if other NATO members agree to share the dangers by offering at least 1,000 more troops and stationing them in the deadly southern province of Kandahar where Canada has taken so many casualties. So far its NATO partners have demurred.

Canada's traditional participation in multilateral operations through the UN has become increasingly untenable. The cumulative effect of increasingly difficult and ambiguous peacekeeping missions, economic constraints in Canada, tarnished peacekeepers, and a realization that Canada's are stretched beyond endurance has led to profound soul searching by Canadians on the nature of peacekeeping and Canada's role in it. Should Canada stick to its original agenda of working solely within multilateral organizations such as the UN? What if that body seems militarily moribund, such as it was in Rwanda? Is it acceptable to join a single nation such as the United States in a military operation that could alienate Canada from the rest of the world and that makes a mockery of multilateralism? Is it acceptable to become involved in a purely internal national affair, such as in Yugoslavia, when doing so ostensibly goes beyond the UN's scope but may save thousands of lives? Is doing something better than doing nothing? Is peacekeeping worth the cost in dollars, lives, and failures when it fosters a Canadian sense of identity that we so sorely lack? Peacekeeping, initially such a simple concept, has become a national conundrum.

DISCUSSION POINTS

1. Does Canada deserve the title "international boy scout"?

2. Have we followed a consistent international policy with respect to international conflicts?

3. American military commanders have rejected using regular soldiers as peacekeepers. Should Canada continue with peacekeeping operations or do these assignments actually work to weaken the military?

4. In an era of fiscal restraint when we can't defend our own soil or even airlift our heavy military equipment, should we continue to act as peacekeepers elsewhere? Is peacekeeping still something "we can't afford not to become involved with"?

DOCUMENTS

1. Barbara McDougall, "Peacekeeping, Peacemaking, and Peacebuilding":
Statement to the House of Commons Standing Committee on External Affairs
and International Trade, Ottawa, February 17, 1993

Barbara Jean McDougall (1937–) received a B.A. in political science and economics from the University of Toronto and became an investment analyst, rising to the position of vice president of A.E. Ames and Co. of Toronto by 1976. Throughout this period she regularly commented on political affairs through radio and television, and in magazine and newspaper articles. She also worked for the Progressive Conservative Party and entered politics in 1984 when she won a seat as an MP for Toronto. Serving under Progressive Conservative Prime Minister Brian Mulroney, McDougall held several portfolios and had wide-ranging responsibilities. She replaced Joe Clark in 1991 as Minister of External Affairs but did not seek re-election and returned to the business world in 1993.

Canadians are the most experienced peacekeepers in the world. Since the first United Nations peacekeeping forces were sent out 45 years ago, our forces have always been in demand. Ten percent of all peacekeepers now on duty in the world are Canadian. Canadians have always seen peacekeeping as a reflection of

Canadian values, as a way of promoting our international objectives—peace and security, respect for human rights and democratic freedoms, and a say in decisions that shape the world.

The specific challenges that face us, however, have changed dramatically in the last five years. The end of the global Cold War has been followed by outbreaks of conflicts in many parts of the world. These conflicts are very different one from the other—just compare the situations in Somalia and the former Yugoslavia, for example—and the range of diplomatic and military tools needed to deal with them has correspondingly expanded.

At the same time, the sheer volume of demand for international crisis management is now overwhelming. More such UN operations have been authorized in the last five years than in the previous forty. Partially as a way of sharing the burden, more and more regional organizations have also become involved such as the Organization of American States (OAS) in Haiti, the Commonwealth in South Africa, or the Conference on Security and Cooperation in Europe (CSCE), the European Community (EC), and the North Atlantic Treaty Organization (NATO) in former Yugoslavia. There are many situations where traditional peacekeeping, based on the consent of all parties, will not lead to a resolution of the conflict. We are faced with situations where the consent of all parties cannot be obtained, or where effective authority does not in fact exist. The use of force has had to be considered more often, as other measures have failed.

If you work closely with the UN, you cannot fail to observe the extreme pressure on the crisis management system, which has built up since its creation.

This system threatens to become seriously overloaded, not just in terms of the management of all these crises, but also in terms of the personnel and financial resources needed to deal with them on the ground. The UN budget for peacekeeping operations jumped from $700 million in 1991 to $2.8 billion in 1992. Associated financial and personnel costs have begun to stretch the resources of even major powers.

It is against this background that I would like to focus on six instruments for crisis management. These derive from the Agenda for Peace issued last summer by UN Secretary General Boutros-Ghali. Taken together, they reflect a spectrum of ways to handle potential or actual conflict situations.

At one end of the spectrum, we find preventive diplomacy: the attempt to head off the outbreak of hostilities by dealing with the underlying problems. It includes such measures as early-warning mechanisms to ensure that potential conflicts can be anticipated, perhaps in time to head them off; fact-finding missions and monitoring; confidence-building measures, such as mutual military inspections; warnings to potential combatants; sponsorship of consultations; and offers to mediate.

Canada is already active in this area. In the former Yugoslavia, Canadians have taken part in a wide range of initiatives, including the EC-led CSCE monitoring mission, the Canadian-led CSCE fact-finding mission last June on the military situation in Kosovo and subsequent CSCE conflict-prevention missions in other parts of the former Yugoslavia. Canada also provided logistical and expert support to the fact-finding mission of the CSCE chairman-in-office to Nagorno-Karabakh, and will shortly be participating in the CSCE mission to Estonia. This is intended to stabilize relations between the Estonian majority and the large Russian minority in Estonia.

A related option in the crisis management spectrum is preventive deployment or preventive peacekeeping. This involves the deployment of peacekeeping forces before hostilities break out for purposes such as the separation of forces, the observation of frontiers and the creation of demilitarized zones.

A recent example is the UN decision to send such a force to the former Yugoslav republic of Macedonia. Canadians in the UN Protection Force II (UNPROFOR) were asked to establish this operation pending the arrival of a Scandinavian force.

Next is peacemaking following the outbreak of conflict. This can include, for example, large-scale international peace negotiations like the ones in Cambodia, which resulted in the Paris accords of 1991. In this process, Canada chaired the key First Committee on Peacekeeping. Another example would be the International Conference on Former Yugoslavia, co-chaired by the UN and the EC, in which Canada participated.

Also included under peacemaking are indirect means of exerting pressure on recalcitrant parties, without actually engaging in military action. One well-known method is, of course, sanctions and embargoes. Canada has participated in the naval embargo on Iraq and supplied a ship last year to the Adriatic sanctions monitoring fleet organized by NATO. A Revenue Canada customs officer leads the mission in the former Yugoslav republic of Macedonia, which is helping to implement sanctions on Serbia. Let me draw your attention to another such form of pressure: the establishment of an international court or tribunal for the consideration of criminal charges under international humanitarian law. Canada urged that this be set up to hear charges arising out of the situation in the former Yugoslavia. A team of war crimes investigators and a leading legal expert have been provided to the UN Commission of Experts that is compiling and analysing the evidence of atrocities.

Peacekeeping, as generally understood, occurs in an environment where the parties to a dispute agree to a cessation of hostilities. This has been the case in Cyprus, the Golan Heights, and the first UNPROFOR operation in Croatia. Peacekeeping has evolved to incorporate objectives over and above supervising a ceasefire. In the case of Somalia, for instance, the initial goal was the protection of humanitarian assistance under conditions of on-going conflict. In El Salvador, in Central America, the peacekeeping mission was essentially political and human-rights related. There were at times more civilians and police officers in place than military. In Namibia, from 1989 to 1990, operations involved overseeing the creation of a new state and, in Cambodia, essentially managing the country while competing factions shift from military to political competition.

We currently have 4,700 men and women with UN operations, plus RCMP and civilian personnel.

Should peacemaking or peacekeeping fail, the fifth option is peace enforcement. Enforcement has been sanctioned by the UN under Chapter VII of the Charter only as a last resort—Korea, the Congo, the Gulf War, and Somalia being the main examples so far. Canada has taken part in these UN enforcement actions; our largest current contingent is in Somalia, where we have 1,300 military personnel. The main emphasis in Somalia, as in many enforcement actions, has been to establish a secure environment in which civil peace can be restored and humanitarian relief operations carried out. Enforcement has also been discussed in the case of former Yugoslavia. However, the situation there is radically different from that in Somalia and it is widely recognized (most recently by the new U.S. Administration) that imposing a political settlement by military force is unlikely to achieve a viable long-term solution.

Finally, the UN Agenda for Peace raises the concept of peacebuilding. It is not always enough simply to end a conflict, whether by peacemaking, peacekeeping, or peace enforcement. The society in question must often be assisted to heal itself and rebuild, whether in political, social, or economic terms. Some aspects are military, such as helping local armed forces to reshape for democratic conditions or clearing mines, which Canada is doing in Cambodia and the Iraq-Kuwait border area.

More dramatic examples of peacebuilding involve long-term nation building as envisaged by the UN in Namibia and Cambodia, or in its original plan for Somalia. I am speaking here of measures that run the gamut from refugee relief to resettlement operations and from free elections to restoration of civil administration. Peace does not automatically continue once the troops leave, but it can be maintained if there is an opportunity for a better life. The idea that international security has roots in development and democracy has, of course, long been part of Canadian policy.

Each of these options involves a different basic approach, different strengths and constraints, and different types and levels of resource commitment. Clarity of objective is fundamental. When we are contemplating action to handle a current or potential conflict, it is important to know whether we are sending troops for preventive deployment, peacekeeping, or peace enforcement. Each involves different risks and costs, training, equipment, and rules of engagement.

This being said, real life is not political science. Realities on the ground rarely lend themselves to definitions as clear as the six foregoing options. Conditions in Bosnia, for example, have never been those of a classic peacekeeping operation and yet Canada is participating because the reality of human suffering is so compelling. As well, situations evolve. Somalia (like the Congo) began as a peacekeeping operation and moved to enforcement when that was judged necessary by the UN Security Council.

Experience has made it clear that one kind of action used in isolation may well lead to partial, short-term, or ineffective conclusions. Canada has been peacekeeping in Cyprus for almost 30 years, without a political solution coming noticeably closer: peacekeeping has become a permanent fixture there rather than the means to an end. This is one reason for Canada's announcement that it would no longer contribute forces to this operation. Peacekeeping is not an end in itself.

The international community is seeking new approaches to crisis management. We have at our disposal a full range of potential actions, but we need to apply them more coherently. Better early-warning mechanisms, triggering earlier international responses, should be a priority. In this context, we are addressing how Canada can best support and contribute to international efforts to prevent or resolve conflicts. For example: Are there ways in which we can help the international community to improve its early-warning capabilities? What are the most effective Canadian contributions? Should we be concentrating, for example, on military tasks or on civilian activities? Can we better assist the UN in efforts to strengthen its own crisis management capabilities?

These are not theoretical questions. Our answers will affect the futures of men, women, and children around the world. Also, we must ensure that Canada's limited resources — political, diplomatic, civilian, and military — are used in the most effective way possible.

2. Unnamed Canadian Soldier, "To Jane Snailham," Sirac, Croatia, April 29, 1992

Jane Snailham (1941–) grew up in Liverpool, Nova Scotia, in a family with a strong military tradition. In 1992 she wrote a letter of encouragement to a young Nova Scotian soldier after watching a CTV television story about his training in Germany in preparation for a tour with the UN in Yugoslavia. This connection unexpectedly expanded, and she soon regularly corresponded with service personnel who appreciated the support of a voice from "back home." With editorial assistance she compiled the letters into a 1998 book entitled Eyewitness to Peace: Letters from Canadian Peacekeepers. *Mrs. Snailham continues to write to Canadian troops stationed overseas.*

Dear Jane,

First of all, thank you very much for sending the card and letter of support, you have no idea what it means to a solider whose mind is being tested every moment. I guess it is only polite to tell you who I am and a little of my background. I was born in a small town in Nova Scotia and finished high school with no future to look forward to. I spent six years in the Militia [in the infantry] then joined the regular force in 1985. My first posting was Winnipeg for three years, then off to Germany in 1988 for a five-year tour. I have obtained the rank of master-corporal and have been on many courses dealing with the infantry. I have seen every province in Canada and been in many countries around the world. And I can assure you that Canada comes out on top. I am married to a wife who goes through everything I do and supports me in whatever I do. I also have been blessed with two boys who were born in Germany [and] who I would die for at the blink of an eye.

As I write, the sun is going down in Croatia and I have no idea of what tomorrow brings. I have never in my life seen or witnessed the death and destruction as I have in this past month. Our company is positioned in a small town [called] Sirac, which is 10 kilometres southeast from Daruvar, which is 20 kilometres south from Zagreb. If you have a good enough map you can probably locate it. The fighting continues seven kilometres from our position. Every night the silence is broken with gunfire and artillery which lights up the sky. The people here are very grateful for the UN being here, but are sometimes confused with our purpose. Everyone from the age of 16 and up carries a gun and whatever else he or she likes to carry.

Our first night here, 232 soldiers from my company were welcomed with 14 rounds of artillery from Serbia into our position. I still have no idea how or why no one was killed. It was the first time since Korea that Canadian soldiers were shelled.

My job consists of policing the area. I have an armoured personnel carrier with one driver and radioman. Every day we go out and patrol the front lines to observe what is going on. At the present time all the UN soldiers in our area have not arrived, only the Canadians, until the remaining soldiers arrive we cannot start working towards peace. I have no idea what the news programmes are saying as I have not heard or saw any news since I left Germany. But I believe in about four months, this is only my opinion, that [the] fighting will stop in Croatia. For the rest of the remaining country, your guess is as good as mine. The men I work with are pretty well much like my brothers. The morale is very high among the soldiers and we enjoy and believe in what we are doing. My stay will only be six months but long enough to miss out on my children's progress.

We are being looked after very well, being fed and equipped with the proper weapons and protective clothing. I find it very difficult to write as I hope you understand. The land here is much like Nova Scotia with mountains only slightly higher. Every town has been destroyed and burnt. Dead animals and the remaining livestock roam the streets; the old money is blowing in the wind. It is really hard to enter a house to check for life when everything is destroyed, usually the family picture is hanging on the wall and it's hard to understand how something like this can happen. Please be very thankful that you live in a safe place. I know [Canada] is being harassed by the language issue and unemployment, but this does not even compare to a lot of places here....

3. Unnamed Canadian Soldier, "To Jane Snailham," Daruvar, Croatia, July 28, 1993

Our situation here is deteriorating, that's why most of our battalion has deployed south. Sometimes we have Croatians that do get restless and tend to get a little violent by throwing grenades at the camp or fire their weapons and there have been gang beatings when entering the town. Most of this violence comes from the young Croatians probably with nothing else to do. They no doubt see us UN soldiers as a threat. I just assume leave this country and let the Croatians and Serbs continue with what they want most and get it over with, genocide. After all, it seems that they have their heart set on it. We're just in their way. Sorry for being so negative, but I think you'd understand if you've had to live around these people. These people just don't comprehend that their little war has taken me away from my family and home.

I don't mean to be so pessimistic, but this place is starting to get to me. Not much longer before I head home so I keep reminding myself.

My UN tour here is a little hectic. Twice a week, I have a duty called a roving patrol. At all hours of night, two of us on duty have to patrol Camp Polom's three gates and also the interior of the camp. This certain duty was started due to threats and gun and mortar fire around the camp.

I live in a small trailer with another girl, and our shower and bathroom facilities are across the camp. There are approximately 30 military girls and over 1,000 guys camped here with me. Mind you, the guys are spread out around the camp in different areas. Some of the trades that the girls are in are medical assistants, pay clerks, administrative clerks (like myself), vehicle mechanic, truck drivers, military police and cooks. There are still a lot of men here that don't believe that women should be allowed in a combat zone or wear a uniform, but if women can do the job just as good as the men, why not. The camp's kitchen and drinking mess are located in tents, like a MASH [mobile army surgical hospital] unit, and my office is in a building riddled with bullet holes. The Croatian army had control of this camp before the Canadian UN troops moved in, so most of the buildings have either been blown up or shot up. Our construction engineer teams are still making repairs around the camp. The odd time our vehicles hit anti-tank mines that have been planted in the road, there were no serious injuries....

4. Unnamed Canadian Warrant Officer Serving with Canadian Contingent to UNAMIR, "To Jane Snailham," Somewhere in Rwanda, December 21, 1995

Dear Jane,

Letters and cards from all across Canada, addressed to Canadian peacekeepers in Rwanda have been flooding into our contingent mail room for the past couple of weeks. When we can find the time, soldiers have been happily responding to any which included a return address. Since I am from the Halifax area, I would like to say hello from Rwanda and take this opportunity to tell you about some of the things we do here.

I am a warrant officer and I have been in Rwanda since July. It is a very small country, being only half the size of Nova Scotia. There are a little more than 100CE personnel serving with the UN in Rwanda. UNAMIR was established in October 1993 to police a ceasefire between the Hutu and Tutsi tribes who were fighting for control of the country. UNAMIR is helping the Rwandan people rebuild their nation by assisting in national reconciliation and providing for the voluntary and safe return of refugees to their homes. The job of Canadian peacekeepers is firstly, to provide logistical support to UNAMIR, and secondly, to support humanitarian activities throughout the country, in general....

Last year, fighting erupted once again. This time it was genocidal in nature, and hundreds of thousands of people died over a period of a few months. It has to rank among the most socially destructive and tragic events of this generation. Men, women and children killed and were killed. Even now, a year later, the evidence of this horrific event still lingers. From the despair of genocide, UNAMIR has assisted the Rwandan people in many ways to alleviate their grim predicament. We have rebuilt and supported schools and orphanages for tens of thousands of children, helping them to deal with the trauma of war. UNAMIR has contributed to the building of extensions to prisons to ease the appallingly overcrowded conditions for those incarcerated. In Rwanda today, over 55,000 prisoners are housed in facilities designed for a maximum of 13,000. Other assistance includes training of police, provision of more advanced medical care and the restoration of national medical services, repairing of roads and bridges, restoration of telephone services and the building of refugee transit camps. These contributions have helped bring back some normalcy to a country severely disrupted by war. Not that long ago, the capital city of Kigali was dead in every sense of the word. Bodies still lay in the street, packs of dogs fattened from the corpses ruled the city, houses were destroyed and there was no electricity, water, nothing. All that seemed to remain was the stench of genocide and children abandoned by war, pathetically wandering the streets, traumatized by the death and destruction they had witnessed. Today, with UNAMIR's assistance, Kigali is essentially, a fully functioning city. You won't see any dogs, though, since many had to be shot to prevent the spread of disease.

There are over 12,000 orphans in Rwanda. The Canadian Contingent sponsors a number of orphanages and visits them regularly, providing medical care, water supplies, repairs to electrical and plumbing problems, building playgrounds and donating medical supplies, blankets and shoes. It is important to let these children know that someone cares about them and that they have a reason to hope and believe in the future. I helped deliver some food to an orphanage, recently. The children seemed rather amused at my white skin, but were very happy to see us. Before we left, they gathered outside the orphanage and sang and danced for us. On a separate occasion, I viewed some drawings made by children from another orphanage. Sadly, many of the drawing depicted the terrible experiences endured by the littlest victims.

As we carry out our duties, we travel all around the country. There are only a few good roads, and it can take a long time to travel a short distance. When it rains, the dirt roads become very muddy and slippery, as if covered with a layer of snow and ice. There are few trees, because they have been cut down to clear land for farming and for heating. In many areas, there are buried mines, so we are careful to exercise mine awareness, wherever we go. Everybody has so far stayed safe, but some of us have been very, very lucky. Unfortunately, many Rwandans are still being hurt by these mines. These weapons do not discriminate. Men, women and children are being killed or maimed almost everyday. There is still an ongoing low-level insurgency war which can make traveling through some parts of the country somewhat entertaining on occasion. Certainly, we try to avoid moving by night wherever we are and have adopted measures to enhance our security when we do....

Outside of Rwanda and adjacent to its borders, there are still close to two million Rwandan refugees. The vast majority refuse to accept assurances from the international community and the Rwandan government that it is safe for them to return. They continue to fear being arrested as suspected genocidaries and thrown into one of Rwanda's notoriously appalling prisons, where they could languish for months until their case is brought to trial. Another reason many will not return, is that they enjoy a better quality of life in the refugee camps than do their counterparts living in Rwanda. However, the presence of these refugees, concentrated as they are into camps close to the country's border, is causing significant environmental damage.

The UN is not well liked by some Rwandans. It is important for us to remember though, that the UN was slow to intervene when so many people were being killed here last year. Rwandans are still distrustful of us, and only grudgingly accept our presence. However, despite the frustrations and the dangers, we must now allow ourselves to turn away from the challenges we face. I become concerned when I hear some Canadians complaining about our participating in UN missions because it is too expensive, too risky, or because they don't understand why we should care about problems in Rwanda or other places like Haiti and the former Yugoslavia. I can only respond that based on my personal experiences in Rwanda and other UN missions, we can't afford not to become involved. The Blue Beret with UN badge, and the distinctive red and white Canadian flag we wear on our shoulders, symbolizes Canada's long-standing and consistently demonstrative commitment to promoting peace and stability in the world's trouble spots and to safeguarding human rights. It is what we are known for the world over, and it is what helps to define us as Canadians. Peacekeeping is among the noblest of any nation's undertakings. I hope it is something that we will never allow ourselves to forget, nor cease to find reasons to keep doing.

I would like to think that we can stop the fighting here or anyplace where the UN has its troops, but conflict can only really end when the warring sides agree to resolve their problems, peacefully. Meanwhile, we try to deter the use of deadly force by any of the sides, and work to encourage a dialogue between them that will foster peace and stability. Sometimes it can be very exasperating work. The importance of any success is often measured against the efforts applied to achieve it. Consequently, in peacekeeping, even a little progress can be perceived as monumental and tantamount to having scaled Mount Everest to reach it.

We were able to follow the great referendum debate, but our circumstances here lead many of us to wonder why we can't accommodate each other in a country as rich in resources and stable as Canada is. We are a mixed group here: men, women, French and English speaking. We work with a unity of spirit and purpose. We have to. Because failure to do so would undermine the job that we have been sent here to do, and could jeopardize the safety and well being of each other. We recently had an occasion to sing Canada's national anthem as a group. It was spontaneous, and we sang it in French (those of us who didn't know all the words just hummed along). When we finished, there were not afterthoughts, save one. Whatever language we sang in, it was no less the national anthem of our country. I'm not sure what one can infer from this, but from my perspective in this reality, our Canadian-made problems at home quickly lose that precipitous aspect that we tend to award them, especially when one starts to make the inevitable comparisons ...

5. Richard Sanders, "Canada's Peacekeeping Myth," The Canadian Centre for Teaching Peace, 1998

Richard Sanders (1957-) studied cultural anthropology as an undergraduate at Trent University and received an MA from the University of Western Ontario. Since graduating in 1984, he has worked as a researcher, writer, editor, and organizer in the peace/anti-war movement. In 1989 he founded the Ottawa-based "Coalition to Oppose the Arms Trade," a network of individuals and nongovernment organizations across Canada and around the world dedicated to stopping, or at least to exposing, the international arms trade and Canada's role in it. He is COAT's coordinator, the editor of its magazine Press for Conversion!, *and its webmaster. Sanders remains a regular contributor to peace and environmental publications, as well as to more mainstream magazines and newspapers.*

The belief that Canada is a major force for global peace forms the basis of a powerful myth that is integral to our culture. This myth shapes the image that we have constructed of ourselves and moulds the way that others see us. Like all myths, it has very little basis in reality.

The symbolic gestures and diplomatic postures that our government parades in public, compose a carefully calculated mask to hide their behind-the-scenes actions. Our government makes proud statements about its restrictive arms trade guidelines while encouraging and assisting military producers to make deals that undermine international peace and security. During this, the UN Year for a Culture of Peace, Canadian peace activists will continue to challenge our national "peacemaker" myth by helping people face the truth about this country's real role as a "war maker." To do this, it is important to expose Canada's active participation in:

* the international arms trade,
* undeclared wars against Iraq, Somalia and Yugoslavia, in the 1990s,
* the provision of weapons testing ranges (air, land and sea) for use by foreign militaries,
* a military alliance that threatens to use nuclear weapons, i.e., NATO,
* the proliferation of uranium and nuclear power plants.

INTERNATIONAL ARMS TRADE

Canada was the world's ninth largest arms exporter in 1997. We ranked even higher, however, in terms of our military exports to the "Third World." In that category, we ranked seventh. Data on Canada's military exports are contained in reports published by the Department of Foreign Affairs and International Trade (DFAIT), called Export of Military Goods from Canada. These reports are significantly flawed. They omit all data on military exports to the U.S., which is by far, our largest buyer. The magnitude of this flaw is evidenced by DFAIT's estimate that 80% of Canadian military exports in 1997 went to the U.S.

Toothless Guidelines

As anyone who has written to protest Canada's military exports will know, DFAIT is proud of its "guidelines" governing military exports. These guidelines state, in part, that: "Canada closely controls the export of military goods and technology to countries that are involved in or under imminent threat of hostilities ... and whose governments have a persistent record of serious violations of the human rights of their citizens, unless it can be demonstrated that there is no reasonable risk that the goods might be used against the civilian population."

These guidelines are worse than toothless, they are essentially meaningless. They do not state that Canadian companies cannot sell military equipment to governments engaged in war, or that might be used against civilians. They merely state that such sales will be "closely controlled." In the bureaucratic, through-the-looking-glass world of government bureaucracies, "closely controlled" can actually refer to concerted efforts to assist corporations in their relentless drive to increase military exports (as long as that increase is "closely controlled"). DFAIT's most recently published policy document on aerospace and defence sector exports states that: "China, Japan, India, South Korea, Taiwan and the Philippines offer potential for Canadian defence products ... Australia offers important opportunities for defence ... in addition to good prospects for the development of strategic alliances aimed at penetrating markets in Southeast Asia.... Countries such as Chile, Argentina, Mexico and Peru represent emerging markets that require strategic positioning by Canada and Canadian A&D [i.e., "aerospace and defence"] firms, especially in terms of follow-up to the success of Canadian participation at FIDAE '96 [Latin America's largest arms bazaar!]. The Middle East remains an important market, particularly for defence-security firms.... The region accounts for more than 40% of all defence-product transfers and is expected to absorb over $150 billion by the year 2000. Saudi Arabia is expected to purchase $32 billion worth of military equipment and other targets include the United Arab Emirates and Kuwait."

Aiding and Abetting Wars

During the 1990s, Canada exported military equipment to several governments engaged in war. Chief among these was, of course, the U.S. that has always been Canada's largest purchaser of military equipment. Even during the worst excesses of the 1960s—during the Vietnam War, when three million people were killed in Southeast Asia—Canadian industries were assisted by our government in ensuring a steady supply of military hardware to fuel the U.S. war machine.

The fact that the U.S. has engaged in more interventions and invasions than any other country this century has never stopped the Canadian government from actively promoting military exports to our friendly neighbour to the south. Neither have Canada's military exports been stopped because the U.S. has armed, financed, trained and equipped dozens of covert wars, organized death squads, backed military coups against elected governments, undermined and rigged elections, assassinated foreign leaders and propped up ruthless dictators who offer bargain basement, union-free factories and all-round cheap access to natural resources.

In 1991, the U.S. led the devastating war against Iraq, and with the support of Canada and the UN, has lead the economic blockade which has killed almost two million people! Canada also supplied military hardware to many of the other "coalition forces" which participated in that war. In 1998, the U.S. overtly bombed Afghanistan, Iraq and Sudan.

One might reasonably expect that the U.S. government's standing as the world's rogue superpower and its unbridled thirst for starting wars and backing military dictatorships should mean that it would be subject to more arms export restrictions than other, less violent governments. Unfortunately, as usual, the opposite is true. Our government has never placed any restrictions on military exports to the U.S. In fact, there is only one country for which Canadian companies have never been required to obtain military export permits from our government. That country is, of course, the U.S.

In the 1990s, DFAIT permitted military exports to at least 17 governments that engaged in wars during the late 1990s. These mostly internal wars, which SIPRI and the Center for Defense Information called "major armed conflicts," were in: Algeria, Bangladesh, Cambodia, Ethiopia, India, Indonesia, Israel, Kenya, Pakistan, Peru, Philippines, Russia, Sri Lanka, Turkey, the United Kingdom, Yugoslavia and Zaire. Canada's declared military exports to these warring nations, during the 1990s, totalled just over $300 million.

Supporting Repression

One need only examine the evidence amassed here to see that Canadian corporations and the government are still very much complicit in crimes against peace, crimes against humanity and war crimes. Some of the governments purchasing Canadian military hardware are notorious for violating human rights. Many so-called "security" forces armed by Canada are well known to routinely engage in torture and extrajudicial executions. In 1998, the following countries purchased Canadian military hardware, even though torture by their military and/or police was reported that year by Amnesty International to be "widespread," "endemic," "systematic," "officially sanctioned," "frequent" or "commonplace": Argentina, Brazil, China, Egypt, Israel, Mexico, Peru, Philippines, Turkey and Venezuela. Between 1990 and 1998, the Canadian government permitted the military exports to numerous undemocratic and repressive regimes. For instance, Canada has sold arms to:

* Brunei, Qatar, Saudi Arabia and Oman: Countries which have never had any elections;
* Bahrain: Its only legislature has been dissolved by decree since 1975;
* Kuwait: Women still do not have the right to vote or stand for election;
* Algeria, Egypt, Jordan, Kenya, Mauritania, Morocco, Lebanon, Pakistan, Singapore, St. Vincent, Togo and Turkey: Women held less than 5% of the seats in parliament in 1999;

* Bahrain, China, Oman, Qatar, Saudi Arabia and the UAE: Unions, strikes and collective bargaining are strictly outlawed; and
* India, Kuwait, Lebanon, Mozambique, Oman, Pakistan, Russia, Saudi Arabia, Singapore, Sri Lanka, Tanzania and UAE: Central governments spent more on their militaries than on health and education combined.

Canada is selling military hardware to foreign police and military institutions that are well known to be regularly and systematically abusing human rights. The regimes that our government continues to prop up are guilty of the most extreme forms of civil rights violations: secret arrests, unfair trials, cruel treatment of prisoners, torture, disappearances and extrajudicial executions. Economic and social rights to education, health, housing and employment are ignored or undermined by many recipients of Canadian military exports. Canada is selling tools of war and repression to many regimes spending vast amounts on security structures to quell demonstrations and strikes by those striving for a better life. For several years, the UN has declared Canada to be the best place in the world to live. Does this privileged rank depend upon exploiting our position in an unjust global economic order? When purchasing inexpensive products from farms, mines and factories around the world, we might ask ourselves: Why are these products so cheap? Do the workers receive fair wages? Are their living and working conditions safe and healthy? Dismantling the myth of "Canada the Peacemaker," is one step toward building a culture of peace in which citizens refuse to support corporations and governments that are profiting from war and repression.

6. Peter Topolewski, "Canadian Soldiers Die for the UN,"
Laissez Faire City Times 3, 33 (August 23, 1999)

Peter Topolewski (1972–) is a professed libertarian who ran a corporate communications business in Vancouver, BC. He wrote for Laissez-Faire City Times, *the successful on-line newspaper representing the cyberspace "country" of Laissez-Faire City, which was set up by a group of libertarians who in 1994 tried, and failed, to create a new nation on the model of Hong Kong.* Laissez Faire City Times *ceased publication in 2002.*

Lethal contaminants. Shredded files. Unwitting victims. Mysterious illnesses. Is it beginning to smell like a Clinton scandal around here or are these the ingredients for the latest episode of the X-Files?

Neither. These are keys in another case of the hierarchy in the Canadian Armed Forces abandoning its soldiers. And in the recent history of giving short shrift to the men and women who volunteer their lives to the whim of the Prime Minister and the minister of defense, this shrift is the shortest of them all. The lack of respect for human life that has become institutionalized in the military has evolved from years of neglect—neglect that has let the condition of the military sink to new depths . . .

While the quality of Canadian troops has never slipped, and the military to this day meets Canada's NATO and UN obligations shiningly, Canada's forces offer little protection from an attack against the home turf. Canadians and interested observers openly acknowledge that the military is wholly inadequate to protect the country's people and land. It is reasonable to argue that no army in the world could capably protect Canada's huge landmass, nor any navy properly patrol the largest coastline in the world; nevertheless, since the end of the Second World War, Canada has come to maintain a force of about 60,000 regulars with less than 200 CF-18s. Upgrading a thirty-year old fleet of rescue helicopters has become a shameful embarrassment to the government—bickering over dollar signs has sent several crewmen to their deaths in antique aircraft and rendered the rescue forces virtually useless.

The penny pinching has understandably hurt morale. No wonder. Perennially low wages trap many soldiers below poverty level. In the last year national television newscasts have run stories on soldiers who are forced to visit food banks to feed their families. Two soldiers in Winnipeg, Manitoba garnered some much needed media attention for their food-drive—they promised to camp out atop a few stories high scaffold for food donations for their base. Well-wishers and supporters stopped at the foot of the scaffold and gave what they could.

That the Canadian military could come to this is hard to conceive. Yet the wonder grows greater when we see the politicians so willing to send this military on UN missions. In the early 90s Canada shipped troops to Somalia, a hell on earth so volatile and confused that a Somali prisoner sadly, but not surprisingly, was beaten and killed while held in custody by Canadian soldiers. To the hate war in Bosnia, Canadians went as unarmed gatekeepers and to stuff body bags. Their role was much the same in Croatia, enforcing peace in a place where nothing was what it seemed—even the dirt.

THE UN, DEALER OF DEATH

Six years after Canadian troops went to work in Croatia on behalf of the UN, they are learning that they made their bunkers out of earth contaminated with PCBS and bauxite. These days scores of those who served in Croatia are sick. Some are going blind, other deteriorating at the joints. Who has stepped forward to treat them, to provide them with a pension? Not the organization (the UN) that sent them to Croatia. Actually, since the story has hit the media, the military is grudgingly offering some assistance, but this story gets much worse. In 1993 a doctor had a memo placed in the files of all soldiers who served in Croatia that year, stating that they might have been exposed to harmful substances and faced a risk of illness. Those memos were systematically removed and shredded.

With overwhelming predictability, the Ministry of Defense has convened an inquiry to determine the source and nature of possible illnesses caused by materials or events in Croatia. A separate criminal investigation into the memo shredding has also commenced. Meanwhile, Matt Stopford, a former Canadian soldier who served in Croatia, is leading the charge for compensation. Already blind in one eye and swallowing handfuls of medication a day, he's lived through six years of zero progress with his onetime employer. He claims that he's been contacted by more than 30 people just like him, and 70 others have spoken with veterans groups and another soldier who is compiling a list of sick former service-men. Not surprisingly, Stopford says that none of the affected are contacting the military, not only because the Forces are downplaying complaints, but the soldiers don't trust the military leadership.

Maintaining the armed forces is one of the few duties the federal govern-ment should consider an obligation. Somehow the best fighting force Canada can produce in the 1990s is a bunch of soldiers who do not believe their leaders will look out for them. A defense budget that has armed soldiers with outdated equip-ment and left them in the poorhouse might reflect the priorities of peace-loving Canadians. Other ventures and adventures and programs are more important to the voters, you can almost hear the politicians saying. And so the obligation to maintain a national defense has instead become very much more like a luxury.

This might be how it is, but it is totally wrong. The "luxury" spending on the military comes at cost to the men and women who volunteer to offer their lives for Canada's protection. If the government cannot properly pay and supply its soldiers it cannot justify sending them on peacekeeping missions. In these circumstances the Canadian contributions to UN and NATO missions look more and more like efforts to maintain a cherished reputation in the international community. I find it hard to believe that any human could send others into such danger easily, or without the decision weighing heavy in the heart. And yet the evidence shows, at the home base and on the peacekeeping mission, that the Canadian leadership treats Canadian soldiers as if their lives have no value. This cannot be tolerated.

They must have proper supplies, whether that means more money or fewer soldiers. Though treated like it, these soldiers are not toys.

FURTHER READINGS

Arbuckle, J. *The Level Killing Fields of Yugoslavia: An Observer Returns*. Clementsport: Canadian Peacekeeping Press, 1998.

Bercuson, D. *Significant Incident: Canadian Army, the Airborne, and the Murder in Somalia*. Toronto: McClelland and Stewart, 1996.

Bercuson, D., and J. Granatstein. *War and Peacekeeping: From South Africa to the Gulf— Canada's Limited Wars*. Toronto: Key Porter, 1991.

Brodeur, J-P. *Violence and Racial Prejudice in the Context of Peacekeeping*. Ottawa: Queen's Printer, 1997.

Canada. *The Dilemmas of a Committed Peacekeeper: Canada and the Renewal of Peacekeeping*. Ottawa: Queen's Printer, 1993.

Commission of Inquiry into the Deployment of Canadian Forces to Somalia. *Dishonoured Legacy: The Lessons of the Somalia Affair*. Ottawa: Queen's Printer, 1997.

Dallaire, R. *Shake Hands with the Devil*. Toronto: Random House, 2003.

English, J., and N. Hillmer, Eds. *Making a Difference: Canada's Foreign Policy in a Changing World*. Toronto: Lester, 1992.

Gaffen, F. *In the Eye of the Storm: A History of Canadian Peacekeeping*. Toronto: Deneau and Wayne, 1987.

Gammer, N. *From Peacekeeping to Peacemaking: Canada's Response to the Yugoslav Crisis*. Montreal and Kingston: McGill-Queen's University Press, 2001.

Gizewski, P. *The Burgeoning Cost of UN Peace-keeping: Who Pays and Who Benefits?* Ottawa: Canadian Centre for Global Security, 1993.

Granatstein, J. "Peacekeeping: Did Canada Make a Difference? And What Difference Did Peacekeeping Make to Canada?" In *Making a Difference: Canada's Foreign Policy in a Changing World*, ed. J. English and N. Hillmer. Toronto: Lester, 1992.

Granatstein, J. *Shadows of War, Faces of Peace: Canada's Peacekeepers*. Toronto: Key Porter, 1992.

Grant, T. "The History of Training for Peacekeeping in the Canadian Forces, 1956-1998." In *Canadian Military History Since the 17th Century*, ed. Y. Tremblay. Ottawa: Department of National Defence, 2001.

Hewitt, D. *From Ottawa to Sarajevo: Canadian Peacekeepers in the Balkans*. Kingston: Centre for International Relations, 1998.

Jockel, J. *Canada and International Peacekeeping*. Toronto: Canadian Institute of Strategic Studies, 1994.

LeBeuf, M-E. *Participation of Members of the Royal Canadian Mounted Police as Civilian Police Monitors in United Nations Peace-keeping Missions: Assessment and Perspectives*. Ottawa: RCMP, 1994.

Legault, A. *Canada and Peacekeeping: Three Major Debates*. Clementsport: Canadian Peacekeeping Press, 1999.

Loomis, D. *The Somalia Affair: Reflections of Peacemaking and Peacekeeping*. Ottawa: DGL, 1997.

Mackenzie, L. *Peacekeeper: The Road to Sarajevo*. Vancouver: Douglas and McIntyre, 1993.

Maloney, S. *Canada and UN Peacekeeping: Cold War by Other Means*. St. Catherines: Vanwell, 2002.

Morrison, A. "Canada and Peacekeeping: A Time for Reanalysis?" In *Canada's International Security Policy*, ed. D. Dewitt and D. Leyton-Brown. Toronto: Prentice Hall, 1994.

Morrison, A., Ed. *The Changing Face of Peacekeeping.* Toronto: Canadian Institute of Strategic Studies, 1993.

Morrison, A., Ed. *Peacekeeping and International Relations.* Clementsport: Canadian Peacekeeping Press, 1995.

Razack, S. *Dark Threats and White Knights: The Somalia Affair, Peacekeeping, and the New Imperialism.* Toronto: University of Toronto Press, 2004.

Ross, D. *In the Interests of Peace: Canada and Vietnam 1954–73.* Toronto: University of Toronto Press, 1984.

Savard, C. *Journal Intime d'un Beret Bleu Canadien en ex-Yugoslavie.* Outremont: Quebecor, 1994.

Sens, A. *Somalia and the Changing Nature of Peacekeeping: The Implications for Canada.* Ottawa: Queen's Printer, 1997.

Sigler, J., Ed. *International Peacekeeping in the Eighties: Global Outlook and Canadian Priorities.* Ottawa: Carleton University Press, 1982.

Sokolsky, J. *The Americanization of Peacekeeping: Implications for Canada.* Kingston: Centre for International Relations, 1997.

Taylor, A., *et al. Peacekeeping: International Challenge and Canadian Response.* Toronto: Canadian Institute of International Affairs, 1968.

Taylor, S., and B. Nolan. *Tested Mettle: Canadian Peacekeepers at War.* Ottawa: Esprit de Corps, 1998.

Wagner, E. "The Peaceable Kingdom? The National Myth of Canadian Peacekeeping and the Cold War." *Canadian Military Journal* (Winter 2006-07): 45-54.

Worthington, P., and K. Brown. *Scapegoat: How the Army Betrayed Kyle Brown.* Toronto: Seal, 1977.

Wirick, G., and R. Miller. *Canada and Missions for Peace: Lessons from Nicaragua, Cambodia, and Somalia.* Ottawa: International Development Research Centre, 1998.

CHAPTER 17

"Stand Up and Be Counted"

ENVIRONMENTALISM

INTRODUCTION

Consideration for the Canadian environment is no longer the parvenu of granola-eating hippies, as it was in the 1960s. It has become part of mainstream culture. Nobody at the beginning of this new millennium bats an eye at a "blue box," and we all agree we should ride the bus—though we don't. This may offer a cushion of comfort, a feeling that Canadians have seen the error of our ways and now strive for a healthy national ecosystem. The federal election in 2008 brought the environment to the forefront of the political agenda, for example, and though voters rejected both the Liberals' Green Shift plan and the Green Party itself, environmental realities such as greenhouse gas emissions and global warming are now issues of debate among all but a few willfully blind ostriches. Have we reached the point where we are willing to abbreviate our standards of living for the sake of the earth's survival? Results from the 2008 election suggest not, but at least Canadians now talk the talk, even if we have yet to walk the walk.

While there is room for at least a hint of optimism we do, however, remain deeply mired in the problem. The federal government estimates that 5,500 Canadians die of smog-related causes per year. Canadians are per capita the world's highest energy consumers—large four-wheel-drive SUVs that will never see anything rougher than a mall parking lot, for example, remain popular despite their antisocial gas guzzling. Corpses of beluga whales turning up in the St. Lawrence are sufficiently full of chemicals to be declared toxic waste. Meanwhile, only 8 per cent of the world's population lives in North America, but we produce 50 per cent of the world's garbage, and, despite a successful recycling program that lowered by 60 per cent the amount of paper reaching Canadian landfills, Toronto alone produces enough garbage to fill the Sky Dome stadium every four months. The amount of Canadian garbage washing up on Scottish beaches has increased by 1,000 per cent since 1988. If that is not enough, flying over British Columbia, in particular, reveals a leprous carpet of devastation from clear-cut logging. The list goes on. If it isn't Atlantic cod in danger of disappearing, then it's grizzly bears, and if not them, any one of the myriad of plants and animals teetering on extinction from human insensitivity. This sorry situation, of course, begs two central questions: how did Canada find itself in this state; and what wrought the change that now offers a glimmer of optimism?

That the Canadian landscape appeared as an inexhaustible storehouse of natural resources ripe for harvesting forms a major explanation for the ongoing environmental predation that began off the coast of Newfoundland in the sixteenth century. Explorers, trappers, settlers, administrators—all were mere specks on the vast continent. Surely, they believed, no amount of beaver hunting, whaling, tree cutting, fishing, mining, or other extraction could possibly empty the larder, and any incidental civilizing of the landscape that might occur *en route* was, of course, a good thing.

Capitalism and *laissez-faire* liberalism also contributed to Canada's present sorry environmental state. They are, after all, economic and political systems that put private shareholder profits and individualism above public social needs, particularly if the latter costs money or impedes economic activity—as it often does. An investor in a fishing boat, for example, wants a rapid and hefty return on his investment. A trawl net dragging along the ocean bottom efficiently scoops up anything saleable and does so much more cheaply than a line and hook. Which of the two offers the biggest bang for the buck? The former, of course. That the seabed may suffer irreparably damage in the long term is inconsequential because of the investor's need for instant financial gratification. Nor is it the state's place to legislate how a fisherman makes his catch because that interferes with individual freedom.

A number of women activists, called ecofeminists, charge that environmental degradation results from men dominating world political and economic systems. Men, they assert, are biologically aggressive and predatory conquerors who cannot naturally nurture—as women can. Put women in positions of economic and political power, they say, and the environment has a chance. Women would collaboratively create legislation that would curb the smash-and-grab, competitive, anti-environmental tactics men have used since time immemorial.

Regardless of the causes of environmental depredation, many Canadians now labour under a superficial and false interpretation of Canadian men engaged in an unrelenting orgy of environmental rape from the early 1500s until the 1960s when Greenpeace saved the day and all was well. Environmentalists, in fact, championed their cause throughout the twentieth century, and we have certainly not fixed the environmental ills that plague us.

The kernels of an attitudinal sea change toward the environment emerged in Western industrialized nations around the beginning of the twentieth century. Progressive social theorists concluded that rubbing shoulders with nature was highly beneficial for humankind, as was a more symbiotic relationship between ourselves and our environment. This new mindset, for example, led to the creation of inner city parks where fresh air and greenery supposedly cured working people's social and physical ills. It also facilitated the creation of the first five national parks in Canada, between 1885-97, and to the federal government enacting the world's first dedicated parks service in 1911. The idea was to protect and preserve specific chunks of national splendour for future generations of Canadian tourists. Thus, parks did not emerge from any recognition that we should be less polluting, less consuming, and more nurturing to the environment. On the contrary, plundering the rest of Canada's natural environment continued unabated and with ever-increasing ferocity as technology streamlined the process. Inventions like the chainsaw, for example, allowed relatively few individuals to harvest hitherto unimaginable quantities of timber with amazing rapidity, and this has been true throughout the extraction industries. Nevertheless, the environmentalist seed was sewn.

There were a few voices in the wilderness warning of unconscionable and irreparable damage to the Canadian ecosystem without major attitudinal modifications toward the environment. Lone souls, such as the popular novelist Grey Owl, worked, wrote, and lectured tirelessly on environmental issues in the 1930s and were largely responsible for Canadians reconsidering, or at least considering, their relationship to nature. Though he alleged partial half-Apache heritage, Grey Owl was actually an Englishman named Archie Belaney, nobody discovered that until after his death, and his eloquent pleas and personal example did much to encourage the nascent environmental movement. Roderick Haig-Brown, among others, took up the cause in the post-World War II era, railing against what he referred to as our "romance with the bulldozer," and helped set the foundation for the Canadian environmental movement that burst on the scene in the 1960s.

Environmental degradation was worse in the United States, largely because of greater population pressures and very aggressive industrialization. There, in the 1950s and 1960s, seminal books such as *Silent Spring* and *River of Grass* led directly to creating populist movements that saved areas like the Florida everglades from the ravages of civilization. The American socio-political situation was also far more tense than the Canadian. Opposition to the Vietnam War and the struggle for civil rights, in particular, focused popular protest and inspired activism among the normally disengaged. Impending environmental calamity, not surprisingly, became one of the key issues of the day—a motherhood concern anyone could support. Similar to most protest of the era, the environmental movement claimed the moral high ground by employing Gandhian non-violent and consciously public tactics. Some Canadians looked across their border and recognized that American activists had a point.

The threat of nuclear catastrophe, whether by war, testing, or accident, fused peace movements with environmentalism and internationalized both. Nuclear fallout, after all, respects no borders. American and French nuclear testing, for example, contributed to the creation of Greenpeace in Vancouver. Greenpeace's success, from the beginning, derived partly from empowering ordinary citizens, initially by attempting to sail an old halibut boat into a nuclear blast zone and daring the Americans to risk the fallout from frying the Canadian crew. From protesting nuclear testing in Amchitka and French Polynesia, Greenpeace activists set their sights on the whaling industry, this time putting themselves between the whales and the harpoons on the high seas—and on camera. This very dramatic television footage brought a formerly invisible carnage into the world's living rooms and led to international outrage and condemnation. The impact on whaling was swift and stark. Next Greenpeace tackled the sealing industry, cruise missile testing, pollution, and other environmental threats, both at home and abroad. In the 1980s, clear-cut logging in British Columbia, particularly on Vancouver Island, became one of the critical battlegrounds between the now sophisticated environmental movement and a forest industry increasingly on the defensive. Environmental activists were by then very successful at shutting down markets for environmentally dubious practices. Convincing European women that sealskin coats were morally reprehensible, for example, essentially killed the Canadian sealing industry and saved the Harp seal. Convincing Home Depot in the United States not to sell lumber from old-growth forests meant that Canadian lumber producers could not simply carry on as before and dismiss environmental activists as dope-smoking tree huggers and social misfits.

The 1980s saw two shifts in the Canadian environmental movement, one small and possibly short-lived, the other major. The first came when a number of activists abandoned pacifism for direct action, arguing that peaceful protests took too long—so long that success came too late. There is no point, they argued, in eventually having whaling banned if there are no whales left. Greenpeace veterans such as Paul Watson, for example, became unrepentant "ecoterrorists"; in his case, he outfit a ship to hunt, ram, and sink rogue whalers, which he did with great effect. Much of Iceland's whaling fleet went to the bottom thanks to the Sea Shepherd Society's direct action. Others spray-painted fur coats as their wearers sashayed down the street; smashed logging equipment; spiked trees to make them deadly for the faller; or engaged in other forms of illegal, and sometimes very dangerous, activity. Ecoterrorism, however, remains marginal to an overall movement that perceives non-violence and legal protest as a key philosophical tenant.

The second shift will, in the long run, likely be more significant. Women now lead much of the environmental movement, both in Canada and internationally. Seeking inspiration from the peace camps in Britain, such as the one outside the airbase at Greenham Common, Canadian women joined together, found strength in their community, and became a formidable force throughout the environmental movement. Two-thirds of the 856 people arrested at Clayoquot Sound on Vancouver Island in 1993, where they were protesting clear-cut logging of a stand of old-growth forest, were this new breed of eco-feminists. By the beginning of the new millennium, Canadian women played key roles in Greenpeace, the Sierra Club, the Green Party, and most other environmental groups.

The protest at Clayoquot Sound in 1993 remains Canada's largest peaceful act of civil disobedience, with some 12,000 participants visiting the roadblocks and "peace camp," of whom almost 1,000 were arrested. They were charged with criminal contempt for violating a court injunction to stop blockading loggers' access to the woods. Sentences ranged from probation and fines to six months in jail. What started as a grass-roots local effort to save the 2,650 square kilometres of virgin West Coast wilderness gained international attention and the direct support of such major environmental organizations as Greenpeace and the Sierra Club. The origin of the protest was the British Columbia government's 1993 "Clayoquot Land Use Decision" to protect a minority of the area as parkland while allowing forestry company MacMillan Bloedel to cut the rest of the old-growth forest, home to some of Canada's oldest and largest trees and to a multiplicity of flora and fauna, plus the marine environment off its coast. Logging in the Sound was not new, and the previous year MacMillan Bloedel had logged 460,000 cubic metres of old-growth timber there (equivalent to about 460,000 telephone poles). The 1992 logging volume was, in fact, small compared to some previous years. In 1988, for example, the company cut just under one million cubic metres. Large and enthusiastic as the protest was, it could not change the land use plan, and logging continues in the Sound to this day. UNESCO declared Clayoquot Sound a world biosphere reserve in 2000, which in no way protects the area, but does draw international attention to it. When MacMillan Bloedel wound down its logging operations in the area in 1997, environmentalists perceived a victory for their side although the company asserted it was part of its long-term business strategy. Presently, logging occurs at a much reduced level and by a local First Nations consortium rather than by a multinational logging company. Interestingly, though cutting between 1993 and 2006 remained relatively low, mostly below 100,000 cubic metres annually, the 2007 figure jumped to 150,000 cubic metres.

All told, the Canadian environmental movement has enjoyed considerable success, both in elevating environmental issues into the mainstream national debate and in achieving significant environmental protection. However, environmental degradation continues in Canada, and Canadians still live with the legacy of four centuries of environmental damage.

DISCUSSION POINTS

1. Internationally Canada's reputation for strip mining, clear-cutting, seal bludgeoning, acid rain, over-fishing, and refusal to sign the Kyoto Accord has overshadowed local environmental movements. Greenpeace has moved its international headquarters to Amsterdam, and Canada's Green Party lacks significant popularity. Why haven't Canadians been able to advance the environmentalist cause further?

2. Are environmentalists chiefly urban dwellers with romantic notions of nature, unfamiliar with the reality of wilderness life? In other words, is it easy to talk about saving nature when you actually don't live and work in rural areas?

3. Is ecoterrorism justified?

4. Early environmentalist leaders tended to be men. Now they are women. Why?

DOCUMENTS

1. Nicole Parton, "Let Preppies in Preservationist Clothes Pay Cost," *Vancouver Sun*, August 14, 1991

Nicole Parton (1946–) was a journalist for the Vancouver Sun *and* Vancouver Province *newspapers for over 25 years. During that time she wrote investigative pieces, became an advice columnist, and simultaneously co-wrote a number of well-received self-help books. Parton courted controversy and never shied away from taking unpopular stances in her columns, but was known for her common sense attitude. She ran unsuccessfully for the British Columbia Social Credit Party in the 1990 provincial election.*

The sloganeers and buccaneers are at it again; something about "saving" rather than "shaving" trees. Cute.

I personally think they're petty tin-pot dictators who want to hold B.C. to ransom, while the platoons they command include a whole lot of spoiled kids. I also think the public's catching on.

This time they're bound to save the Walbran and hey, why not? Save every forested valley! Call for boycotts! Rouse the troops!

But quell those inconsistencies; they're embarrassing, to say the least.

Environmentalists gave new meaning to the term "tough love" a while ago. Besotted with the Carmanah's Sitka spruce, so many nature lovers wanted to touch and caress (aw, let's say it — hug) the big trees, the disturbed soil and ground cover exposed their shallow roots.

Had hundreds and possibly thousands of tree worshippers continued this hands-on approach, the giants would have been killed by kindness, toppling prematurely.

As it is, the biggest trees are now chained off to keep their "protectors" away.

Likewise, ardent get-close-to-nature types have pointed and yelled from Robson Bight's shores, not to mention buss-bombing the area's killer whales in their boats. When the number of whales in the Bight diminished, the preservationists blamed the bogey man: clearcut logging.

A recent Greenpeace newsletter arguing against logging states: "Just think, the cure for cancer or heart disease from some unknown organism could right now be living on the forest floor, just waiting to be discovered!"

Right. So what happens when it is discovered? Can anyone spell "taxol"?

As the Greenpeace newsletter continues: "But we might never know about it, because it may soon be gone, destroyed either by the incredible greed and short-sightedness of big business or the callousness and inactivity of our elected officials OR BOTH!"

Now which will it be? Do we find the cancer cure, then just let it sit there because we mustn't molest the flora? Or do we succumb to the "incredible greed and short-sightedness of big business or the callousness and inactivity of our elected officials OR BOTH!" and actually try to cure people?

Some of these pinkos are so far left, they're infra-red.

Well, let me tell you, I don't mind their antics one bit but it's time for a social readjustment. Let the banshees place their bodies before the blade when the woodsman swings his axe. Suits me fine. I'm easy. No problem.

But just don't make me pay for it.

I don't want my tax dollars subsidizing their whiny selfishness and their stay in the pokey.

You see, I'm just a little fed up shelling out money for their deliberate irresponsibility. When the preservationists win their battle and the valley-of-the-month gets saved, I pay: My taxes go up to replace the lost forest revenue.

But when the preservationists lose, I also pay: It's my money that supports the legal system to which their actions are ultimately accountable.

I don't want to pay any more. Let them pay, for a change. Let them foot the salaries of the RCMP squads they like to taunt. Let them make up the lost wages of the idled industry workers. Let them compensate for the damage to our tourist and business profile through the European boycott they're urging of our forest products.

Tell them to buy the groceries for unemployed loggers' families. Not me. Not you. We've paid quite enough. Our welfare dollars are already stretched to the limit.

So when the preppies in preservationists' clothing declare the Clayoquot or Walbran or Carmanah theirs and theirs alone, present them with the bill.

They'll say it's too much, but no sweat. They'll be sharing it with future generations, for years and years to come....

2. Tzeporah Berman, *Clayoquot and Dissent*, 1994

Tzeporah Berman (circa 1970-) grew up in a Jewish home and connects her faith to her activism. She received a B.A. from the University of Toronto and an M.A. in Environmental Studies from York University. Her Clayoquot Sound fieldwork made her an activist; the nesting area for the Marbled Murelets she had studied for years had disappeared when she returned there in 1992, the area entirely clear-cut. This galvanized her, and she spent the next year mustering volunteers to protect the Sound. British Columbia's Premier Glen Clark called her an "enemy of the state." After the 1993 protest she worked for Greenpeace in Europe and in the United States in the organization's "Market Campaign," which forced major forestry companies to amend some practices or face losing major customers such as Home Depot.

TAKIN' IT BACK

The protests in Clayoquot Sound represent one of the largest civil disobedience actions in Canada's history. In the summer of 1993 over 800 people were arrested for standing on a logging road in one of the largest areas of temperate rainforest left in the world. Many were there for less than ten minutes. Hundreds have gone to jail. The people who protested in Clayoquot Sound have been referred to as "spoilt children," "welfare bums," "hippies" and most recently by Patrick Moore of the industry-funded "B.C. Forest Alliance" as "wacked out nature worshippers who pray to the moon." They have also been called heroes. In reality they were courageous grandmothers, children, students, seniors and others from all walks of life who found freedom in incarceration and strength in the ability to stand together and make change.

In 1969 the Canadian Council of Christians and Jews wrote that, "Law and order, though vital for society, can often be used to cover injustice. It is no longer sufficient merely to advocate obedience to law. The attainment of justice is first; without it, law is merely a facade." Law is the product of an evolving process and as such it should reflect issues important to society. As values and perceptions change, the law must be recast to reflect new realities. Throughout history, social conflict has proven necessary to attain dramatic social change. At one time blacks were treated as slaves and women were considered their husband's property. For many people who stood on the road in Clayoquot Sound, viewing "nature" as a commodity which humans have the right to exploit seems equally as absurd. Before thousands of black people were given their freedom or women were given the right to vote, there were the lunch counters and buses in the South and thousands of women jailed for picketing polling stations and chaining themselves to legislatures. Any attempt to reevaluate our basic perceptions of worth and value will not be easy and will not come without a dramatic struggle. For many, the catalyst necessary to begin to see the forests for the trees and to reevaluate our relationship with "nature" was the summer of 1993 in Clayoquot Sound.

Located on the west coast of Vancouver Island, Clayoquot (pronounced Klak'wat) Sound is one of very few areas of coastal lowland temperate rainforest left on the planet. It is a unique and beautiful region of white sand beaches, deep green valleys with rich salmon spawning streams, fjords, fresh water lakes, and snow-capped alpine mountains. Clayoquot Sound is home to ancient western red cedars over a thousand years old and Douglas firs that tower 250 feet above the ground. Because of its diverse geography, the area provides habitat for the black bear, cougar, wolves, bald eagles, the elusive marbled murrelet, orca and grey whales and some of the rarest sharks in the world.

Given its intense beauty and high "resource" value, it is not surprising that Clayoquot Sound has become the scene of a showdown of epic proportions. The protests in Clayoquot Sound began over a decade ago on Meares Island. After a two-year planning process, timber giant MacMillan Bloedel pulled out and refused all three options presented by the negotiators. When the logging boats headed out to the island, they were met with a blockade of Nuu-chah-nulth

First Nations people and local environmentalists. Eventually the Nuu-chah-nulth obtained an injunction to prevent the company from logging the island, but the issue is still before the courts and has already cost the native community over a million dollars in legal fees.

The first protests were the beginning of a growing relationship between First Nations and the environmental community, a relationship that has matured considerably over the last year. Non-native environmentalists are gradually coming to realize what had been obvious from the First Nations' perspective all along: people don't live in parks and an ancient burial ground is not a recreational site. While the environmental community has still much to learn, Clayoquot Sound has sparked a deeper understanding of the links between social and environmental issues. We are at a point of consensus between the environmental and native communities—that clearcutting irreparably damages our ecological, social and cultural landscapes.

The committees, government processes and subsequent blockades and protests continued intermittently over the years, but didn't reach a fever pitch until 1993, after the provincial government's announcement of the Clayoquot Land Use Decision. After much time and fanfare, Premier Harcourt announced that 62% of Clayoquot Sound would be open to clearcut logging; 33% of Clayoquot Sound would be "protected." What the Premier didn't say is that almost half of the protected area was previously protected and the 62% of Clayoquot Sound open to clearcut logging translates into 74% of the rainforest. Adding insult to injury, the government designated some areas of forests as "scenic corridors" and others as "special management zones." In reality, scenic corridors have proven to be thin strips of trees left along the water while the mountains above are stripped clean. For all intensive purposes "special management zones" appear to be another term for what was previously "modified landscape"—clearcuts.

Almost 70% of Vancouver Island's ancient forests have been clearcut. Where there were once 170 intact watersheds on the island, now there are only eleven. Five are in Clayoquot Sound. Under the new decision, two intact watersheds would be protected. The decision was touted far and wide as a "responsible compromise." Before the decision, the industry was clearcutting 540,000 cubic metres of rainforest a year in Clayoquot Sound; after the decision they were allowed to log 600,000 cubic metres.

The Clayoquot Land Use Decision sparked cries of protest around the province which quickly spread around the globe. On July 1, the Clayoquot Sound Peace Camp opened and protests were held at Canadian consulates in Austria, Germany, England, Australia and the United States.

The Peace Camp was set up by the Friends of Clayoquot Sound to provide a meaningful forum for grassroots protests. It was a ramshackle village of tents and trailers symbolically situated in an old clearcut known as "the Black Hole." In the four months that it was operating, over 12,000 people visited the camp and joined the protests. In the Peace Camp we created a fluctuating, chaotic and warm community that functioned somewhat as a large extended family, through intense stress and upheaval. In this community, business people rolled up their sleeves beside students, musicians and doctors to wash dishes, help with twenty-four-hour security, or plan the protests to come. Functioning solely on donations, the camp managed to feed at least 200 people a day with healthy vegetarian meals.

In many respects the Peace Camp was a vehicle for and an embodiment of social change. Everyone who entered the camp agreed to abide by a basic set of principles that formed the foundations upon which the community functioned and the context within which we protested. The Peaceful Direct Action Code, as it was called, was developed through an analysis of the philosophies of nonviolent civil disobedience. It was built upon Gandhian principles and the lessons learned from civil rights and environmental protests around the globe. It is as follows:

Peaceful Direct Action Code
1.   Our attitude is one of openness, friendliness and respect toward all beings we encounter.
2.   We will not use violence either verbal or physical towards any being.
3.   We will not damage any property and we will discourage others from doing so.
4.   We will strive for an atmosphere of calm and dignity.
5.   We will carry no weapons.
6.   We will not bring or use alcohol or drugs.

Each day at the Camp, workshops were held which explored the philosophy of nonviolence and civil disobedience, consensus decision-making and legal issues, as well as the history and ecology of Clayoquot Sound. The workshops and "Peaceful Direct Action Code" helped to ensure that the massive protests and the camp community remained peaceful at all times. People learned how to work together, diffuse anger, to refocus fear and anxiety constructively, and most of all, to listen to and respect one another. The philosophy of nonviolence has a great deal to do with abolishing power as we know it and redefining it as something common to all. *Power over* is to be replaced by *shared power*, by the power to do things, by the discovery of our own strength as opposed to a passive receiving of power exercised by others, often in our name. Individuals feel, and in many ways are, powerless against the state, but when we are more than individuals we can find strength, confidence and real power in working together. The success of the Peace Camp was not only in the peaceful daily blockades at the Kennedy River Bridge but the skills, knowledge and experience that thousands of individuals took back to their communities. What grew out of the "Black Hole" was a common understanding that we have a right, indeed a responsibility, to stand up for what we believe in—and together we have the ability to do it effectively.

The government and industry have responded to the protests with fear and aggression. They have called environmentalists "hysterical," and worse. We've heard this before. They took a similar line up to the day the Atlantic cod stocks collapsed. For years Dupont called environmentalists "hysterical" for claiming that CFC's eat away at the ozone layer. Our challenge is to reverse the burden of proof. It is the corporations and governments who now must prove that their practices are ecologically and culturally responsible.

Government and industry have characterized the present debate as a choice between liking trees or liking workers. But the thousands of people who came to Clayoquot realized that we simply cannot negate our dependence on natural systems; scientists call it biodiversity. "Biodiversity is no frill. It is life and all that sustains life." Biodiversity resembles a hammock: as destructive industrial practices like clearcutting dramatically alter existing ecosystems, species go extinct, the hammock unravels. Eventually the hammock can no longer hold anything. We need to begin to understand our dependence on natural systems and to develop mechanisms to have this understanding translate into socio-economic and political realities.

Ultimately, the struggle for Clayoquot Sound is not only a struggle for "wilderness" or sound forest practices but fundamentally a struggle with how we interact with the natural world; and whether we have a right to irreversibly change, and in some cases irreversibly damage the environment. It is a struggle to value the future over monetary gain and, in so doing, to recognize that short-term economic gain will not benefit human or non-human communities. It is a struggle for justice. And may be no more complicated than simply recognizing that we all need to breathe air and drink water.... The message rings clear: When we stand, we stand for our lives.

3. Dr. M. Gibbons, "The Clayoquot Papers," *Clayoquot and Dissent*, 1994

Dr. Maurice Gibbons (1931–) grew up on Canada's West Coast, receiving his B.A. from the University of British Columbia, an M.A. in English from the University of

Washington, and his Ph.D. from Harvard where he served on the editorial board of the Harvard Education Review. *He taught in both elementary and secondary schools before becoming a professor of education at the University of British Columbia and in 1969 at Simon Fraser University. His main academic focus is self-directed learning, global education, and sustainable development. Professor Gibbons was never an activist before participating in the Clayoquot Sound demonstrations.*

After our arrest, the Clayoquot experience shifted location from the woods to the courtroom. What began as a confrontation with a logging company removing old-growth rainforest ended up as a confrontation with the Supreme Court of British Columbia over our violation of its injunction. That confrontation became critical when we were informed that the charge against us had been raised from civil to criminal contempt. If we were found guilty we faced fines, jail, community service and the possibility of a criminal record. With a criminal record we would be unable to travel to most countries, and that meant that Margot and I would be unable to visit our office in the United States or to keep business engagements abroad, including several already arranged for the coming year. Discussions with other protesters at our arraignment in court and with lawyers who were volunteering their services increased our concern. No promising line of defense was emerging. When Judge Bouck's horrendous sentences for the first group of protesters were announced — 45 days in jail and fines up to $1500.00 — our concern turned to panic. We began looking for a lawyer.

When we explained our situation and our reasons, the first lawyer we consulted said, "You don't seem to understand; the business of the court is law, not justice. There is only one issue here; whether or not you disobeyed a court injunction — a law — against interfering with MacMillan Bloedel's logging operations in Clayoquot Sound. The police and the company both have you on videotape, and you were both on the evening news. If you were there — and you were — you are guilty of civil contempt; if you flagrantly attracted public attention to your acts — and you did — it's criminal contempt."

We were beginning to feel hopeless. "What can we do?" we asked. "Your defence," he replied, "is either to attack the law itself, or plead guilty and get off with the lightest sentence possible. Challenging the law would cost a great deal of money, and the result would still be in doubt. I think we should argue for a light sentence, take as little of the court's time as possible and get this over with." What would that mean? "First we will plead guilty and present as many character references as possible to show that you are otherwise upstanding citizens. Then we will claim that you were confused and didn't realize what you were doing, that you never intended to show contempt for the law. You will take the stand and apologize to the court for your contemptuous acts and promise that you will never do such a thing again. It is really the only plea that will help you."

But what about the reason we were there, the preservation of the old-growth forests in Clayoquot Sound? "That is your motive," the lawyer told us; "the reason you went to Kennedy River Bridge. The court is only interested in your intent, what your acts were implicitly intended to accomplish. Because you flagrantly attracted attention to your contempt for the law, you must be punished to preserve order and prevent chaos. The trees, the environment, the rights of native people, logging practices like clearcutting, shipping unworked logs abroad may all be important issues, but the court will say that they have nothing to do with these charges and this case." Although our consultant did not end up defending us, he proved to be absolutely right about the court's point of view.

Margot and I pleaded guilty—we were according to the court—and although we neither apologized nor assured the court we would not do such things again, we could say truthfully that we did not act to show contempt for the court. I must admit, however, that, as we experienced the court in action against us, our contempt for its proceedings steadily deepened. We are not lawyers, we cannot argue the law; but as thoughtful citizen, we can argue whether or not we felt unjustly treated.

My first concern was that the court seemed grimly determined to make criminals out of people who were not criminals at all, for deeds that are difficult to characterize as crimes. These people—mostly young people representing many walks of life, most if not all, without any previous record of trouble with the law—went to Clayoquot at their own expense and endured considerable discomfort living on the land, some of them for several summers, for the single purpose of drawing public attention to the massive logging of old-growth rain-forests in Clayoquot Sound. Their camp was run in an orderly way and their protest was conducted according to rigorous rules. No intimidation or attack was ever conducted against any person associated with the logging operations, no property was ever damaged or destroyed as part of the protest; no damage to the environment was allowed or any mess or litter left behind. We stayed overnight at the bridge and the next morning where 1000 people had been milling the day before, we could find no trace, not even a cigarette butt. While logging was delayed on a number of occasions, it was never halted, and when anyone was arrested they went with the police without resisting. Above all, not one protester was there for personal gain; no one stood to profit from his or her actions in any way. The outcome they sought was a benefit for the province at large and for future generations.

These are the strangest criminals I have ever met, committing a crime so strange it is difficult to distinguish from an act of citizenship or public service. The government's subsequent attention to Clayoquot and logging proves that the protesters had an important point to make. Why did the authorities not establish a dialogue rather than criminalize worthy young people for attempting to contribute?

Faced with criminalizing non-criminals, the court understandably practiced law in a cave, focused on its own arcane ground without any reference to the world outside or to the critical issues involved. The legal options open to the defendants were severely limited. Applications for a jury trial and requests to call expert witnesses were routinely denied. All arguments based on the peoples' rights protected by the Canadian constitution, all arguments based on precedents in law and in protest, and all arguments based on local and global forest and environmental issues were denied, along with all appeals lodged in a higher B.C. court. It is difficult to feel justice at work in a court of such foregone conclusions. The only issue the court would consider was the insult to its injunction, proven with an interesting update on the Star Chamber, namely, "We turn on the VCR: if your face appears, you are guilty; if it doesn't you are innocent." The protest was about forestry issues of vital concern to the people of this province, but the charge was interpreted so that no forestry issue was ever considered. By restricting all debate to injunction law, the court effectively disarmed the protesters of their strongest and most appropriate defense, eliminated all the significant issues and trivialized proceedings that continued for nearly a year. As a result, the courts spent hundreds of hours and millions of dollars without clarifying a single issue in the debate, except, "Don't infuriate a Supreme Court judge who has signed an injunction." Law in a cave, far from the world.

What made our situation worse was the feeling that the RCMP, MacMillan Bloedel and the Supreme Court considered it their case against us. Of course, it was the Supreme Court's injunction granted to M&B to be enacted by the RCMP, so they were the front-line triumvirate. Despite their protests to the contrary, the government and the Attorney General's office also appeared to be on the team determined to silence us. I have always believed that the law is scrupulously even-handed and dedicated to protecting the rights of the people in action against those with power and in positions of privilege. It seems that we are the people, but we were on a very steep playing field against very powerful and privileged opponents. There was never a single opportunity for us to prevail; none of us did; and we saw no effort by the courts to ensure that we ever had a glimmer of hope. There is an obscenity in so much power massed to crush citizens with so little. Democracy shudders.

Even if we grant the court its focus on injunction law, we can still argue that we were driven to act by a situation of imminent peril. It seems to me that there are situations where it is essential to violate an injunction, or at least where one can act without obedience to the law as one's first consideration. The following are extreme examples but, as analogies, show the possibility of exception. If the court issued an injunction to keep us at least 200 yards away from a sex offender living in our community, and we violated it to stop him from forcing a young girl into his van, we would, I assume, be praised, not punished by the court. Similarly, if the public were forbidden by injunction from entering a property, but ignored it to save the children inside the house when a fire broke out, they would at least be pardoned on the grounds of imminent peril. This is exactly our case. We did not go to Clayoquot Sound with any thought about violating a court injunction, but rather because of our perception that irreplaceable old-growth is in imminent peril of destruction. Studies conducted before and since the protest confirm that the peril is real. If we wait for police, the young girl will be gone; if we wait for firemen, the children will be burned alive; and if we wait for legislation or an election, the old-growth in Clayoquot will be cut and shipped. Surely the issue is not, can the court prove we were naughty, but can we prove that we responded to a situation of imminent peril: the loss of threatened, irreplaceable, very valuable old-growth rainforests.

I am also convinced that these judges had no right to try us, that all decisions against us should be reversed and that the court should issue a public apology, on the grounds that accusers cannot fairly judge those they accuse because they have a predisposition to find them guilty. It is not justice when the accuser—the supreme court—sits in judgement of those they have accused—the Clayoquot protesters. The fair judge is not predisposed to find a defendant guilty, but weighs, like Justice herself, innocence or guilt evenly in the balance and is blind to any circumstance or condition that might unfairly tip the scales. The accuser has already declared his prejudice, making him fit to prosecute guilt, but clearly unfit to fairly judge it. But that is only the beginning. These men were not accusing us of violating just any law; they were accusing us of violating a law they created themselves. They had not only a predisposition but a necessity to find the protesters guilty. They had to find us guilty to preserve their power by injunction. Think of it. Someone makes a rule, accused you of breaking it and then is appointed to judge whether you are innocent or guilty of breaking the rule he has made and accused you of breaking. Not only that, but only by finding you guilty can your judge maintain the authority of the rules he makes. And he is angry at what you have done. If that makes you think of kangaroos, too, you won't be surprised by the final score: Supreme Court judges—630 (at last count); Clayoquot protesters—0.

Even the injunction law we were tried under seems shaky to me. Judge J.A. Middleton of Ontario said that, "Government by injunction is a thing abhorrent to the Law of England and of this Province." He was referring to the fact that by issuing an injunction, a judge is making law where none existed before. Laws normally emanate from legislation passed by elected representatives of the people, not by individual, politically-appointed judges. But there was no law regulating logging, only a forestry code, and no officers of the law to enforce these regulations or laws, if any existed, since foresters can hardly be expected both to work with loggers and to police them. Despite the evidence that logging companies exceeded allowable cuts, for instance, no charges were laid by foresters. Surely, "exceeding allowable cuts" is a technical way of saying stealing our trees. If anyone gets caught exceeding the allowable shopping they have paid for, they get arrested, and they don't get to keep the goods. Logging companies seriously exceed the allowable cut—apparently they are on a self-monitoring honour system—are caught, but never charged, and get to keep the stolen trees. So technically, the only law of the forests was made by the judge who signed an injunction against the protests. That judge, apparently, made no effort to study the forestry situation or to seek arguments from the protesters, but simply heard the complaint from the company and signed.

Surely it is time to take this power to make temporary legislation away from judges in cases of public dispute. They do not represent the people or follow a democratic decision-making process. Let us instead assign legislation by injunction to a legislative committee responsible to the province and its citizens. This shabby, so-called law that had to be defended at all costs is an outrage to any thoughtful person and should be an embarrassment to the judiciary. Only royalty and tyrants have the power to make arbitrary law and then stomp on the people who will not obey it....

After we had been sentenced, we returned to court in support of two colleagues from the University of British Columbia whose cases were to be heard. During the proceedings, Jessica Michalofsky's name was called. She rose and said something close to the following: "My Lord, I cannot afford a lawyer so I will defend myself." She was tall, self-assured, simply dressed and had her hair cut short. "I plead guilty to criminal contempt. I went to Clayoquot to preserve the old-growth forest. I did not go to show contempt for the law, but I'm not sorry I went either, and I cannot promise that I will never do such a thing again." The judge asked how he should sentence her. She replied, "I am a student at college and cannot afford a fine; I live in too remote a place for electronic monitoring so I will have to take a jail sentence. I would like to begin it right away because I have a

of working within the democratic system, and despite relatively modest sentences, disobedience of court orders continues. Many people do not seem to get the message.... The only way the law can deal with continuous breaches of court orders is to increase the penalty in the hope it will dissuade others from committing the same kinds of acts.

FURTHER READINGS

Barnes, T., and R. Hayter, Eds. *Troubles in the Rainforest: British Columbia's Forest Economy in Transition.* Victoria: Western Geographical Press, 1997.

Bohlen, J. *Making Waves: The Origin and Future of Greenpeace.* Montreal: Black Rose, 2001.

Carroll, J. *Acid Rain: An Issue in Canadian-American Relations.* Toronto: C.D. Howe Institute, 1982.

Cashore, B., G. Hoberg, M. Howlett, J. Rayner, and J. Wilson. *In Search of Sustainability: British Columbia Forest Policy in the 1990s.* Vancouver: University of British Columbia Press, 2001.

Gaffield, C., and P. Gaffield. *Consuming Canada: Readings in Environmental History.* Toronto: Copp Clark, 1995.

Gillis, P., and T. Roach. *Lost Initiatives: Canada's Forest Industries, Forest Policy, and Forest Conservation.* Westport: Greenwood, 1986.

Hessing, M. "The Fall of the Wild? Feminist Perspectives of Canadian Wilderness Protection." In *This Elusive Land: Women and the Canadian Environment,* ed. M. Hessing, R. Ragon, and C. Sandilands. Vancouver: University of British Columbia Press, 2004.

Hunter, R. *Warriors of the Rainbow: A Chronicle of the Greenpeace Movement.* New York: Holt, Rinehart and Winston, 1979.

Kline, M. *Beyond the Land Itself: Views of Nature in Canada and the United States.* Cambridge, MA: Harvard University Press, 1970.

Lorimer, R. *et al.*, Eds. *To See Ourselves/To Save Ourselves: Ecology and Culture in Canada*. Montreal: Association of Canadian Studies, 1991.

Marchal, P. *Green Gold: The Forest Industry in British Columbia*. Vancouver: University of British Columbia Press, 1983.

Marchak, M., S. Aycock, and D. Herbert. *Falldown: Forest Policy in British Columbia*. Vancouver: David Suzuki Foundation, 1999.

MacIssac, R., and A. Champagne, Eds. *Clayoquot Mass Trials: Defending the Rainforest*. Philadelphia: New Society, 1994.

McKenzie, J. *Environmental Politics in Canada: Managing the Commons into the Twenty-First Century*. Toronto: Oxford, 2002.

Mies, M., and V. Shiva. *Ecofeminism*. Halifax: Fernwood, 1993.

Nelson, J., Ed. *Canadian Parks in Perspective*. Montreal: Harvest House, 1970.

Rajala, R. *Clearcutting the Pacific Rim Forest: Production, Science, and Regulation*. Vancouver: University of British Columbia Press, 1998.

Rogers, R. *Solving History: The Challenge of Environmental Activism*. Montreal: Black Rose, 1998.

Sandberg, L., Ed. *Trouble in the Woods: Forest Policy and Social Conflict in Nova Scotia and New Brunswick*. Fredericton: Acadiensis Press, 1992.

Stefanick, L. "Baby Stump and the War in the Woods: Competing Frames of British Columbia Forests." *BC Studies* 130 (Summer 2001): 41-68.

Tollefson, C. *The Wealth of Forests: Markets, Regulation, and Sustainable Forestry*. Vancouver: University of British Columbia Press, 1998.

Warecki, G. *Protecting Ontario's Wilderness: A History of Changing Ideas and Preservation Politics, 1927-1973*. New York: Peter Lang, 2000.

Wilson, J. *Talk and Log: Wilderness Politics in British Columbia*. Vancouver: University of British Columbia Press, 1998.

Sources

Introduction

Excerpt from Al Purdy, "A Walk on Wellington Street," 1968. Reprinted with permission.

Chapter 1: "A Fate Worse Than Death": Sexual Advice in Victorian Canada

B. Jefferis and J. Nichols, *Searchlights on Health, Light on Dark Corners: A Complete Sexual Science and A Guide to Purity and Physical Manhood, Advice to Maiden, Wife and Mother, Love, Courtship and Marriage* (Toronto: J.L. Nichols, 1894); "Female Cyclists," *Dominion Medical Monthly and Ontario Medical Journal* VII, 3 (September 1896); *The Ladies Book of Useful Information Compiled from Many Sources* (London, ON : 1896); J.E. Hett, *The Sexual Organs, Their Use and Abuse the Subject upon Which Men and Women Know Least, Yet Ought to Know the Most: Guide to Man* (Kitchener, ON: J.E.H. Hett, 1899).

Chapter 2: "Two Distinct Personalities": The Question of Riel's Sanity

Documents by Roy, Fitzpatrick, Robinson, and Riel can be found reprinted in D. Morton (ed.), *The Queen v. Louis Riel* (Toronto: University of Toronto Press, 1974); a copy of Valade's document is included in T. Flanagan, "The Riel 'Lunacy Commission': The Report of Dr. Valade," *Revue de l'Universite d'Ottawa* 46 (1976); Dr. Daniel Clark, "A Psycho-Medical History of Louis Riel," *Journal of Insanity* (July 1887).

Chapter 3: "Broken Promises": Treaties in the Far North

Charles Mair, *Through the Mackenzie Basin* (Toronto: William Briggs, 1908); All of the other documents can be found in R. Fumoleau, *As Long as the Land Shall Last: A History of Treaty 8 and Treaty 11, 1870-1939* (Toronto: McClelland and Stewart, 1975), reprinted by permission of McClelland and Stewart, Ltd.

Chapter 4: "The Unfriendly Reception": Immigration

W.D. Scott, "The Immigration by Races," in A. Short and A. Doughty (eds.), *Canada and Its Provinces, Volume 7* (Toronto: Glasgow, 1914); W.A. Cum Yow, Testimony before the *Royal Commission on Chinese and Japanese Immigration, Canada Sessional Papers* No. 54 (1903); Dr. Sundar Singh in Empire Club of Canada, *Addresses Delivered to the Members during the Session of 1911-12* (Toronto, 1913); Maria Adamowska, "Beginnings in Canada," reprinted in H. Piniuta (ed. and trans.), *Land of Pain, Land of Promise* (Saskatoon: Western Prairie Books, 1978).

Chapter 5: "Perfect Justice and Harmony": Votes for Women

Hon. John Dryden, Minister of Agriculture, "Womanhood Suffrage" (Toronto: Warwick, 1893); the James L. Hughes document was reproduced in R. Cook and W. Mitchenson (eds.), *The Proper Sphere: Women's Place in Canadian Society* (Toronto: Oxford University Press, 1976); the Bate article was reproduced in B. Kelcey and A. Davis (eds.), *A Great Movement Underway: Women and the Grain Growers' Guide, 1908-1928* (Winnipeg: Manitoba Record Society, 1997); Nellie McClung, *In Times Like These* (Toronto: McLeod and Allen, 1915); Stephen Leacock, "The Woman Question," in *Essays and Literary Studies* (New York: John Lane, 1916); H.D.P., "The Failure of the Suffrage Movement to Bring Freedom to Women," *The Woman Worker* (December 1928) recently reproduced in J. Sangster and M. Hobbs (eds.), *The Woman Worker, 1926-1929* (St. John's: Canadian Committee on Labour History, 1999).

Chapter 6: "What Is Our Duty?": Military Service in World War I

Peter McArthur, "Country Recruits," *Globe*, January 30, 1915; Talbot M. Papineau, "An Open Letter from Capt. Talbot Papineau to Mr. Henri Bourassa" (March 21, 1916), and Henri Bourassa, "Mr. Bourassa's Reply to Capt. Talbot Papineau's Letter" (August 2, 1916) in *Canadian Nationalism and the War* (Montreal, 1916); Robert Borden's speech on conscription is found in R. Borden (ed.), *Robert Laird Borden: His Memoirs, Volume 2* (Toronto: Macmillan, 1938); Francis Marion Beynon, "Women's View of Conscription," *Grain Growers' Guide* (May 30, 1917).

Chapter 7: "Ruthless Butchers of Men and Morals": The Drug Traffic

Emily Murphy, *The Black Candle* (Toronto: Thomas Allen, 1922); Tom MacInnes, "The Futile Fight against Dope," *Saturday Night*, October 3, 1925.

Chapter 8: "This Is My Last Chance": Depression and Despair

With the exception of the last document, "Experiences of a Depression Hobo," *Saskatchewan History* 22 (Spring 1969), reprinted by permission of Saskatchewan Archives Board, all of the other accounts were reproduced in L. Grayson and M. Bliss (eds.), *The Wretched of Canada: Letters to R.B. Bennett, 1930–1935* (Toronto: University of Toronto Press, 1971), reprinted by permission of University of Toronto Press.

Chapter 9: "The Question of Loyalty": Japanese Canadians and World War II

A. Neill, House of Commons, *Debates* (February 19, 1942); Muriel Kitagawa, "To Wes, December 21, 1941," "To Wes, February 19, 1942," "To Wes, March 2, 1942," "To Wes, April 20, 1942" and "We'll Fight for Home, 1942," in *This Is My Own: Letters to Wes and Other Writings on Japanese Canadians, 1941–1948* (Vancouver: Talon, 1985), copyright © 1985 Talon Books, reprinted by permission of Talon Books Limited, Vancouver, BC, Canada, all rights reserved; "And Then Registration," in B. Broadfoot, *Years of Sorrow, Years of Shame: The Story of Japanese Canadians in World War II* (Toronto: Doubleday, 1977) and "Long Before Pearl Harbour," in B. Broadfoot, *Ten Lost Years 1929–1939: Memoirs of Canadians Who Survived the Depression* (Toronto: Doubleday, 1973), reprinted by permission of Doubleday Canada, a division of Random House of Canada Ltd.; K. Miyazaki, "Memoirs," in K. Oiwa (ed.), *Stone Voices: Wartime Writings of Japanese Canadian Issei* (Montreal: Véhicule Press, 1991), reprinted by permission of Véhicule Press.

Chapter 10: "Cinderella of the Empire": Newfoundland and Confederation

Smallwood's speech is reproduced in *I Chose Canada* (Toronto: Macmillan, 1973), reprinted by permission of the Smallwood family; all other speeches are reprinted in J. Hiller and M. Harrington (eds.), *The Newfoundland National Convention 1946-1948* (Montreal and Kingston: McGill-Queen's University Press, 1995), reprinted by permission of McGill-Queen's University Press.

Chapter 11: "A Glow of Fulfilled Femininity": Women in the 1950s and 1960s

Beverly Gray, "Housewives Are a Sorry Lot," *Chatelaine*, March 1950; "Housewives Blast Business Girl," *Chatelaine*, June 1950; Dr. Marion Hilliard, "Stop Being Just a Housewife," *Chatelaine*, September 1956, reprinted by permission of June Callwood; Cynthia Steers, "How Much Are You Worth to Your Husband?," *Chatelaine*, April 1959; Anna Davies, "I Hate Housekeeping," *Chatelaine*, March 1961.

Chapter 12: "Hippies, Bikers, and Greasers": Youth in the 1960s

"Turn On, Tune In, Take Over," *Georgia Straight*, September 8, 1967; "Grass in Class," *Georgia Straight*, February 17-24, 1971, reprinted by permission; Bob Cummings, "Obscenity: Who Really Cares, All Is Phoney," *Georgia Straight*, January 12-25, 1968; Dr. Murray Ross, "Why Students Rebel," Speech to the Empire Club of Canada, February 8, 1968; R. Smart and David Jackson, "Yorkville Subculture," and June Callwood, "Digger House," in W. Mann (ed.), *The Underside of Toronto* (Toronto: McClelland and Stewart, 1970), reprinted by permission of McClelland and Stewart Ltd.

Chapter 13: "The Very Essence of Canadian Identity": Multiculturalism

Government of Canada, Appendix to *Hansard*, October 8, 1971, reprinted by permission; Neil Bissoondath, *Selling Illusions, the Cult of Multiculturalism* (Toronto: Penguin, 1994), copyright © 1994 by Neil Bissoondath, reprinted by permission of Penguin Group (Canada), a division of Pearson Canada, Inc.; Dick Field, "Multiculturalism Undermines Values Held by Canadians," *Toronto Star*, December 23, 1994, reprinted by permission of Dick Field.

Chapter 14: "A People in Bondage": Quebec and Independence

Marcel Chaput, *Why I Am a Separatist* (Toronto: Ryerson, 1961), reprinted by permission of McGraw-Hill Book Company, Inc.; Peter Nesbitt Thomson, "Separatism—a Dangerous Philosophy," Speech to the Empire Club of Canada, February 6, 1964, reprinted by permission of the Empire Club of Canada; Lévesque's Harvard speech is found in C. Cassidy et al. (eds.), *Authority and Influence* (New York: Mosaic Press, 1985), reprinted by permission of the Weatherhead Center for International Affairs, President and Fellows of Harvard College; Maurice King, "Betrayal of Basic Rights in Futile Appeasement of Quebec Nationalism," *Canadian Speeches, Issues of the Day* (February 1995), reprinted by permission of Maurice King.

Chapter 15: "The Whites Were Terrorists": Residential Schools

Rev. Kevin Annett, author's note from "Hidden from History: The Canadian Holocaust," *Nexus* (March-April 2002), copyright © 2001 The Truth Commission into Genocide in Canada, reprinted by permission; Ted Byfield, "Weren't We All Physically Abused in Schools? So When Do We Get Our Money for Healing," *Alberta Report*, January 19, 1998, reprinted by permission of Ted Byfield; Patrick Donnelly, "Scapegoating the Indian Residential Schools: The Noble Legacy of Hundreds of Christian Missionaries Is Sacrificed to Political Correctness," *Alberta Report*, January 26, 1998, reprinted by permission.

Chapter 16: "A Cherished Reputation": Peacekeeping

Barbara McDougall, "Peacekeeping, Peacemaking and Peacebuilding": Statement to the House of Commons Standing Committee on External Affairs and International Trade, Ottawa, February 17, 1993, reprinted by permission of Barbara McDougall; documents by unnamed authors were located in Jane Snailham, *Eyewitness to Peace: Letters from Canadian Peacekeepers*, ed. A. Morrison and S. Torrisi (Clementsport: Canadian Peacekeeping Press, 1998), copyright © 1998 Canadian Peacekeeping Press; Richard Sanders, "Canada's Peacekeeping Myth," The Canadian Centre for Teaching Peace, 1998, reprinted by permission of Richard Sanders, Coordinator, Coalition to Oppose the Arms Trade, Editor, *Press for Conversion!*; Peter Topolewski, "Canadian Soldiers Die for the UN," *Laissez Faire City Times* 3, 33 (August 23, 1999), reprinted by permission.

Chapter 17: "Stand Up and Be Counted": Environmentalism

job tree planting that begins in three weeks." My wife and I were impressed by her quiet strength and clarity. The judge was in a quandary; this was no criminal, and he, like us, would be proud to have her as a daughter. "Can't you suggest any alternatives?" he asked with concern, but she couldn't and was sentenced to six days in jail with nine months probation added to deter her from further "criminal" activity.

When the country begins to devour its strong and dedicated young people, it is in great need of deep reflection, a rededication of purpose and some dramatic changes in process. Fortunately, young people like Jessica can take great pride in the significant changes their protest has already wrought in forestry practice in this province since August, 1993: a new and tougher forestry code, much stiffer fines against companies that violate logging regulations, a prohibition against exporting whole logs, increased payments from companies for logging our trees and the Vancouver Island Core Report extending the amount of protected old-growth forest. It is easy to see these developments as admissions that the protesters were right all along, and that their action drew attention to an outrage in our forests. Outrage happens and we should be both reassured and grateful that Jessica Michalofsky, and many people like her, are ready to stand up and be counted whenever it does. Jessica's trial for C-Day was on the fiftieth anniversary of D-Day....

4. Mr. Justice J. Bouck, "The Price of Throwing an Illegal Public Tantrum," *Globe and Mail*, October 18, 1993

Mr. Justice John. C. Bouck (1931–) was born in Calgary and graduated from the University of British Columbia Law School in 1955. He practiced law in Vancouver until appointed to British Columbia's Supreme Court in 1974. He remained a trial judge until his retirement in 2006. Justice Bouck also served with the Royal Canadian Air Force (RCAF) as a fighter pilot during the 1950s. He has written extensively on Canadian jurisprudence, both in monographs and articles, including co-authoring the definitive book on instructions for juries.

Testimony and arguments presented by the defendants indicate they became involved in this dispute because they honestly believed the decision of the elected representatives of the people allowing the logging was wrong. They see themselves as guardians of the environment. They want to preserve the trees for all of us and for future generations. They consider themselves morally right in defying the injunction order. Some refer to their actions as "civil disobedience."

The democratic process is frustrating and time-consuming. It rarely brings instant gratification. Few people ever get their own way entirely. There are just too many reasonable arguments on both sides of almost every issue. Sometimes even the best arguments fail to persuade. At other times, democratic governments pursue long-term policies that do much harm. Years later they are found to be misguided. But these faults are the price we must pay for democracy, because the alternatives are worse. Democracy will never be perfect, since it is run by human beings.

In saying this, I do not wish to suggest in any way that the decision of the government to allow the logging was wrong. That is a judgment for the elected representatives of the people and not one for unelected judges to decide.

Some contend the democratic process did not work because the defendants were unable to persuade others as to the rightness of their cause. They say that disobedience to the law was their last and only resort. However, democracy does not fail just because a minority is unable to persuade the majority. It is the arguments of the minority that fail. When that happens, democracy expects the minority to refine their proposals and try again. Democracy does not accept their right to commit a public display of ill temper by defying a court order.

Unwilling to take rejection of their point of view, the defendants took the easy way out. They were not interested in the legal rights of MacMillan Bloedel Ltd. They were not interested in pursuing their goals throughout the democratic process. Instead, they decided to express their disagreement by acts of obstruction. They were looking for instant results. They dramatized their concerns by throwing an illegal public tantrum.

On the basis of the defence evidence and submissions presented during the whole of the trial, the following theme seems to arise. The defendants say they are kind and gentle people. They are full of love for the trees, wild animals, insects and other of nature's creatures. Because of their high-mindedness, their intellect, their good character and their superior knowledge of the environment, only they know what is the best forestry policy for the citizens of this province.

Standing on the sidelines and complaining about government policy is no test of character. Neither does it take much to go and sit on a road, block traffic and ask to be carried away by the police. What really shows a commitment to this country and to an idea is persistent involvement in the political process, listening to opposing points of view, fashioning reasonable replies and persuading others. That is difficult and time-consuming work. But this is what democracy is all about.

Throughout this trial, many defendants seemed to lack any understanding about the duties of a judge. They seemed to think that judges could make any order that suited their fancy; that they were only bound by what they considered to be fair; and that they should determine what is fair by listening to the political views of litigants and examining the media to see what people really think. In other words, judges should try and make themselves popular.

As I said throughout the trial, the defendants are entitled to justice under the law, not what a judge many personally think is justice.... If legislators enact a law that allows anybody to infringe upon the rights of others without penalty, then that will be the law the judges must try and administer. Until that happens, judges will follow the law that says people who infringe upon the legal rights of others and disobey an injunction protecting those rights must pay a penalty....

Some contend the defendants are following a time-honoured path of so-called civil disobedience. They use the non-violent behaviour of Mahatma Gandhi as one of their models. It is not an apt comparison. In the first place, Mr. Gandhi lived in a colonial state. He had no opportunity to change the laws democratically. British rulers controlled the levers of power. Disobedience of colonial-made laws was the last and only resort for Mr. Gandhi and his followers....

There is another distinction.... At the time of his first trial on March 18, 1922, he admitted disobeying the law. He asked the court to impose upon him the highest penalty. In his statement to the British judge he said in part: "I do not ask for mercy. I do not plead any extenuating act. I am here therefore to invite and cheerfully submit to the highest penalty that can be inflicted upon me...."

In these proceedings 42 defendants pleaded not guilty, They advanced a variety of excuses for their behaviour. If they have to pay for their illegal behaviour, all but one seeks the lowest possible penalty. They are mistaken if they believe they are following in the footsteps of Mr. Gandhi.

Others compare the defendants to Martin Luther King and his admirable struggle to obtain the vote for black people in the southern United States. Again, there is little similarity. Black Americans in many southern states did not have the right to vote. Thus, they were unable to influence change. Mr. King and his followers did not try to take away the rights of other citizens in order to get a right for themselves. They simply wanted equal rights to those possessed by the white population. It is true that Mr. King dramatized his plight by defying various segregation laws, but that was for the purpose of getting the right to vote so the laws could be changed.

Similar protests occurred in this century when women were denied the right to vote. They took to the streets. Yet they did not infringe upon the rights of others. Nor did they ask that society deny men the vote. They simply wanted that right extended to themselves.

Had Mr. Gandhi, Mr. King and the suffragettes been given the right to vote in the first place, their protests would never have occurred.

Except for the out-of-province defendants, the others have the right to vote. They were simply unable to persuade the elected representative of the people to adopt their point of view.... Their behaviour in no way follows the noble ideals of Mr. Gandhi, Mr. King or the suffragette movement....

The words "civil disobedience" are tossed around by the defendants and others as if they amount to some sort of a legal right. No one is sure what they mean. They are certainly not part of any legal principle or legal rule. Disobedience of the law invites a penalty no matter how it is performed.

The word civil means polite. In the context of the phrase civil disobedience, it may mean polite or non-violent behaviour. The word disobey means to defy or resist. Hence, civil disobedience may mean polite or non-violent defiance of the law. Usually, polite or non-violent disobedience of the law will lead to a lesser penalty than if the disobedience were violent.

Nonetheless, those who break the law and try to classify their actions as civil disobedience will suffer penalties and the distinct possibility of acquiring a criminal record....

I turn now to fix the sentence for each of the defendants found guilty of contempt of the court orders made July 20, 1992, and July 16, 1993. It is not a pleasant duty. I take no joy in the task.

Many of these defendants are intentionally or carelessly indifferent to the reason why they should obey court orders. Many seemed proud of the fact that they did not read newspapers or watch the news on television. While allegedly educated in environmental matters, many choose to remain uninformed about the world at large, except where they believed a particular concept fitted within their set of beliefs. While choosing to remain ignorant of the system they so despise, they insisted on receiving all the benefits that it has to offer.

When they decided to blockade the road, they seemed to feel that they only needed to sign an undertaking after their arrest and they would be released. Later on, they might appear in a courtroom, make a speech about their cause, receive a lecture from a judge, get a suspended sentence and go on their way. They appeared to think that they could try the issue of provincial-government forestry policies if they wished. They were astounded when this did not happen and found they were being tried for their illegal actions....

Over the last four to five years, an increasing number of criminal contempt-of-court cases has come before this court relating to logging and forestry practices on Vancouver Island. I have been referred to one of my earlier judgments and 10 judgments of my colleagues on the same subject. They cover a period from 1988 to 1993. Despite repeated comments by various judges concerning the necessity